# GOD'S WORD

**DAILY
REFLECTIONS** *2021*

ST PAULS

**Editors:** Fr Michael Goonan SSP & Fr Joshy Joseph SSP

**Associate Editor:** Julie Whiteford

**Contributors:**

| | | | |
|---|---|---|---|
| January: | Rt Rev Bishop John Arnold | July: | Fr Joe Eruppakkatt, SSP |
| February: | Sr Elizabeth Gilroy LCM | August: | Teresa Pirola |
| March: | Fr Innocent Ezeonyeasi | September: | Sr Elaine Penrice FSP |
| April: | Fr Daniel Weatherley | October: | Rev. Jose Jereus Bangcaya |
| May: | Fr Francis J Moloney SDB | November: | Sr Judy McLeod RSM |
| June: | Fr Matthew Pittam | December: | Fr John O'Connor |

## GOD'S WORD 2021

ISBN: 978-1-910365-87-8

Copyright © ST PAULS Publishing 2021

Scripture readings from the Jerusalem Bible, published and © 1966, by Darton, Longman and Todd Ltd and Doubleday & Co. Inc. are used by permission of the publishers

Cover design and internal layout by Domenika Fairy

Illustrations by Sr Dorothy Woodward RSJ

Cover painting: *Christ and the Rich Young Ruler* (1889) by Heinrich Hofmann

Artwork: January 1, *Our Lady of Vladimir*, 12th century; February 2, *Presentation of Christ in the Temple*, German, 15th century; March 19, *Saint Joseph with the Infant Jesus* by Guido Reni, c. 1635; March 25, *The Annunciation*, Fra Angelico, c. 1440–1445; March 28, *Entry into Jerusalem*, Nativity of the Theotokos Church, Bitola, Macedonia; April 2, *Christ on the Cross*, by Carl Heinrich Bloch, c. 1871; May 31, *The Visitation* by Giotto 1311; June 29, *Sts Peter and Paul* by El Greco, c. 1590; July 22, *Noli Me Tangere* by Fra Angelico, c. 1440-1442; August, 6 *Transfiguration* by Cristofano Gherardi, 1555; September 8, *Nativity of Mary*, Spain, 17th century; October 2, *Guardian Angel* by Pietro da Cortona, 1656; November 1, *All Saints* by Fra Angelico, c. 1420; December 25, *Nativity of Jesus*, c. 1473-1475, by Sandro Botticelli; December 27: *Peter and John running to the tomb* by Eugène Burnand, 1898. All artwork in the public domain (source Wikimedia Commons).

| | |
|---|---|
| ST PAULS by Westminster Cathedral | ST PAULS PUBLISHING |
| Morpeth Terrace, Victoria | Moyglare Road, Maynooth |
| London, SW1P 1EP | Co. Kildare, Ireland |
| Ph: +44 (0) 207 828 5582 | Ph: +353 (1) 628 5933 |
| www.stpauls.org.uk | www.stpauls.ie |

Printed by Melita Press, Malta.

ST PAULS is an activity of the priests and brothers of the Society of St Paul who proclaim the Gospel through the media of social communication.

## MESSAGE

*The passage of time marks our journey in this life. Indeed, each day is another step on our pilgrimage to our heavenly home. It is fitting, then, that as we mark the passing of the days, at each step we reflect again on the deepest dimension of our life: it is our journey to God. This* **God's Word 2021** *helps us to do this: chosen words of Scripture, God's living Word to us, guiding us each day, making sure that the day is more than duty and responsibility, turning our hearts to the great gift of faith! I pray that this* **God's Word 2021** *will help each of us to be rooted in the presence of God, always sure of God's compassion and mercy, and so able to reach out to everyone we meet with these same gifts.*

+ HE Cardinal Vincent Nichols
Archbishop of Westminster

## MESSAGE

It gives me great pleasure to write a brief introduction to the **God's Word 2021**. I suspect that many of you, like myself, greet each new year with the traditional new year's resolutions. Your **God's Word 2021** will be a constant reminder that time, given to us day by day, is one of God's greatest gifts.

Theologians, and indeed the scriptures themselves, frequently emphasise the gulf that lies between the Creator and the creature. Our days are like the grass that withers, no more than watch in the night. The Word of God alone endures forever. His thoughts are not our thoughts. As the heavens are beyond the earth, so are the thoughts of God beyond our imagining. (*Cf. Isaiah 55:6-9*)

All the more reason, therefore, at the beginning of the New Year, to rejoice in the birth of our Saviour, the living Word who speaks to our hearts. Here is the God who has entered our days, who has redeemed our history, whose presence gives meaning and direction to each unfolding moment of our lives.

'The Word was made flesh, and dwelt amongst us, and we have seen his glory, the glory of the Son of the Father, full of grace and truth.'

For all who use this book, I paraphrase St Paul's prayer from the *Letter to the Ephesians*. Day by day, may 'your hidden selves grow strong, so that planted in love and built on love, and knowing the love of Christ, which is beyond all knowledge, you might be filled with the utter fullness of God.' (*Cf. Ephesians 3:14-21*)

+ Bishop David McGough
Auxiliary Bishop of Birmingham

**Mary, The Holy Mother of God**
Solemnity
White

### Numbers 6:22-27

The Lord spoke to Moses and said, 'Say this to Aaron and his sons: "This is how you are to bless the sons of Israel. You shall say to them: May the Lord bless you and keep you. May the Lord let his face shine on you and be gracious to you. May the Lord uncover his face and bring you peace." This is how they are to call down my name on the sons of Israel, and I will bless them.'

### Psalm 66:2-3.5.6.8. R. v.2

*O God, be gracious and bless us.*

### Galatians 4:4-7

When the appointed time came, God sent his Son, born of a woman, born a subject of the Law, to redeem the subjects of the Law and to enable us to be adopted as sons. The proof that you are sons is that God has sent the Spirit of his Son into our hearts: the Spirit that cries, 'Abba, Father', and it is this that makes you a son, you are not a slave anymore; and if God has made you son, then he has made you heir.

### Luke 2:16-21

The shepherds hurried away to Bethlehem and found Mary and Joseph, and the baby lying in the manger. When they saw the child they repeated what they had been told about him, and everyone who heard it was astonished at what the shepherds had to say. As for Mary, she treasured all these things and pondered them in her heart. And the shepherds went back glorifying and praising God for all they had heard and seen; it was exactly as they had been told.

When the eighth day came and the child was to be circumcised, they gave him the name Jesus, the name the angel had given him before his conception.

### Reflection

What were the thoughts in Mary's mind as she saw her new-born son being honoured by shepherds and wise men? What could happen? What was he to become? The Gospel says, "She treasured all these things and pondered them in her heart." The future was so uncertain. As we begin a New Year, let us ask for God's blessing on all that is to come and that our Faith may guide us on our way.

## 1 John 2:22-28

The man who denies that Jesus is the Christ – he is the liar, he is Antichrist; and he is denying the Father as well as the Son, because no one who has the Father can deny the Son, and to acknowledge the Son is to have the Father as well. Keep alive in yourselves what you were taught in the beginning: as long as what you were taught in the beginning is alive in you, you will live in the Son and in the Father; and what is promised to you by his own promise is eternal life. This is all that I am writing to you about the people who are trying to lead you astray. But you have not lost the anointing that he gave you, and you do not need anyone to teach you; the anointing he gave teaches you everything; you are anointed with truth, not with a lie, and as it has taught you, so you must stay in him. Live in Christ, then, my children, so that if he appears, we may have full confidence, and not turn from him in shame at his coming.

## Psalm 97:1-4. R. v.3

*All the ends of the earth have seen the salvation of our God.*

## John 1:19-25

This is how John appeared as a witness. When the Jews sent priests and Levites from Jerusalem to ask him, 'Who are you?' he not only declared, but he declared quite openly, 'I am not the Christ.' 'Well then, ' they asked 'are you Elijah?' 'I am not' he said. 'Are you the Prophet?' He answered, 'No.' So they said to him, 'Who are you? We must take back an answer to those who sent us. What have you to say about yourself?' So John said, 'I am, as Isaiah prophesied: a voice that cries in the wilderness: Make a straight way for the Lord.'

Now these men had been sent by the Pharisees, and they put this further question to him, 'Why are you baptising if you are not the Christ, and not Elijah, and not the prophet?' John replied 'I baptise with water; but there stands among you – unknown to you – the one who is coming after me; and I am not fit to undo his sandal-strap.' This happened at Bethany, on the far side of the Jordan, where John was baptising.

**Saturday before Epiphany**
**Sts Basil the Great and Gregory Nazianzen,**
*bishops, doctors*
**Memorial**
**White**

## Reflection

The writer of the Letter to the Hebrews reminds us that our Faith is not just some words that we believe, it is something that changes our whole state of being and should influence everything that we do and say. Jesus lives within us and believing in Him changes who we are and what we are about as we live our lives day by day.

**Second Sunday of Christmas**
Psalter Week 2
White

### Ecclesiasticus 24:1-2.8-12

Wisdom speaks her own praises, in the midst of her people she glories in herself. She opens her mouth in the assembly of the Most High, she glories in herself in the presence of the Mighty One; 'Then the creator of all things instructed me, and he who created me fixed a place for my tent. He said, "Pitch your tent in Jacob, make Israel your inheritance." From eternity, in the beginning, he created me, and for eternity I shall remain. I ministered before him in the holy tabernacle, and thus was I established on Zion. In the beloved city he has given me rest, and in Jerusalem I wield my authority. I have taken root in a privileged people, in the Lord's property, in his inheritance.'

### Psalm 147:12-15.19-20

*The Word was made flesh, and lived among us.*

### Ephesians 1:3-6.15-18

Blessed be God the Father of our Lord Jesus Christ, who has blessed us with all the spiritual blessings of heaven in Christ. Before the world was made, he chose us, chose us in Christ, to be holy and spotless, and to live through love in his presence, determining that we should become his adopted sons, through Jesus Christ for his own kind

purposes, to make us praise the glory of his grace, his free gift to us in the Beloved.

That will explain why I, having once heard about your faith in the Lord Jesus, and the love that you show towards all the saints, have never failed to remember you in my prayers and to thank God for you. May the God of our Lord Jesus Christ, the Father of glory, give you a spirit of wisdom and perception of what is revealed, to bring you to full knowledge of him. May he enlighten the eyes of your mind so that you can see what hope his call holds for you, what rich glories he has promised the saints will inherit.

## John 1:1-18

In the beginning was the Word, and the Word was with God and the Word was God. He was with God in the beginning. Through him all things came to be, not one thing had its being but through him. All that came to be had life in him and that life was the light of men, a light that shines in the dark, a light that darkness could not overpower. A man came, sent by God. His name was John. He came as a witness, as a witness to speak for the light, so that everyone might believe through him. He was not the light, only a witness to speak for the light. The Word was the true light that enlightens all men; and he was coming into the world. He was in the world that had its being through him, and the world did not know him. He came to his own domain and his own people did not accept him. But to all who did accept him he gave power to become children of God, to all who believe in the name of him who was born not out of human stock or urge of the flesh or will of man but of God himself. The Word was made flesh, he lived among us, and we saw his glory, the glory that is his as the only Son of the Father, full of grace and truth. John appears as his witness. He proclaims: 'This is the one of whom I said: He who comes after me ranks before me because he existed before me.' Indeed, from his fullness we have, all of us, received – yes, grace in return for grace, since, though the Law was given through Moses, grace and truth have come through Jesus Christ. No one has ever seen God; it is the only Son, who is nearest to the Father's heart, who has made him known.

## Reflection

All the readings this Sunday speak of the presence of Christ in our lives and the love of God who has always planned to be close to us, guiding us through wisdom and helping us to change our lives so that we can live what we believe in our every thought and action. God is not a long way away – he is closer to us than our very breath.

# JANUARY

# 4

MONDAY

**Monday before
Epiphany
White**

## 1 John 3:7-10

My children, do not let anyone lead you astray: to live a holy life is to be holy just as he is holy; to lead a sinful life is to belong to the devil, since the devil was a sinner from the beginning. It was to undo all that the devil has done that the Son of God appeared. No one who has been begotten by God sins; because God's seed remains inside him, he cannot sin when he has been begotten by God. In this way we distinguish the children of God from the children of the devil: anybody not living a holy life and not loving his brother is no child of God's.

## Psalm 97:1.7-9. R. v.3

*All the ends of the earth have seen the salvation of our God.*

## John 1:35-42

As John stood with two of his disciples, Jesus passed, and John stared hard at him and said, 'Look, there is the lamb of God.' Hearing this, the two disciples followed Jesus. Jesus turned round, saw them following and said, 'What do you want?' They answered, 'Rabbi,' – which means Teacher – 'where do you live?' 'Come and see' he replied; so they went and saw where he lived, and stayed with him the rest of that day. It was about the tenth hour.

One of these two who became followers of Jesus after hearing what John had said was Andrew, the brother of Simon Peter. Early next morning, Andrew met his brother and said to him, 'We have found the Messiah' – which means the Christ – and he took Simon to Jesus. Jesus looked hard at him and said, 'You are Simon son of John; you are to be called Cephas' – meaning Rock.

## Reflection

Our Faith is never something that simply stands still. It is something 'alive and active' and it needs to grow with us and help us to mature in our lives. We nourish the Faith within us by prayer and by learning about Jesus in the Scriptures. The two disciples in today's Gospel are at the beginning of their journey of Faith and they will learn and be changed as they follow the Lord.

## 1 John 3:11-21

This is the message as you heard it from the beginning: that we are to love one another; not to be like Cain, who belonged to the Evil One and cut his brother's throat; cut his brother's throat simply for this reason, that his own life was evil and his brother lived a good life. You must not be surprised, brothers, when the world hates you; we have passed out of death and into life, and of this we can be sure because we love our brothers. If you refuse to love, you must remain dead; to hate your brother is to be a murderer, and murderers, as you know, do not have eternal life in them. This has taught us love – that he gave up his life for us; and we, too, ought to give up our lives for our brothers. If a man who was rich enough in this world's goods saw that one of his brothers was in need, but closed his heart to him, how could the love of God be living in him? My children, our love is not to be just words or mere talk, but something real and active; only by this can we be certain that we are children of the truth and be able to quieten our conscience in his presence, whatever accusations it may raise against us, because God is greater than our conscience and he knows everything.

My dear people, if we cannot be condemned by our own conscience, we need not be afraid in God's presence.

## Psalm 99:1-5. R. v.1

*Cry out with joy to the Lord, all the earth.*

## John 1:43-51

After Jesus had decided to leave for Galilee, he met Philip and said, 'Follow me.' Philip came from the same town, Bethsaida, as Andrew and Peter. Philip found Nathanael and said to him, 'We have found the one Moses wrote about in the Law, the one about whom the prophets wrote: he is Jesus son of Joseph, from Nazareth.' 'From Nazareth?' said Nathanael 'Can anything good come from that place?' 'Come and see' replied Philip. When Jesus saw Nathanael coming he said of him, 'There is an Israelite who deserves the name, incapable of deceit.' 'How do you know me?' said Nathanael. 'Before Philip came to call you,' said Jesus 'I saw you under the fig tree.' Nathanael answered, 'Rabbi, you are the Son of God, you are the King of Israel.' Jesus replied, 'You believe that just becaus`e I said: I saw you under the fig tree. You will see greater things than that.' And then he added 'I tell you most solemnly, you will see heaven laid open and, above the Son of Man, the angels of God ascending and descending.'

## Reflection

"Our love is not to be just words or mere talk, but something real and active." Our love for God will show itself best in the opportunities we take each day to show love for our neighbour. Faith is very practical, and every action, choice and decision has an impact on our brothers and sisters throughout the world. We must be sure that our actions show care for our common home.

**Tuesday before
Epiphany
White**

**Epiphany of the Lord**
**Solemnity**
**White**

### Isaiah 60:1-6

Arise, shine out Jerusalem, for your light has come, the glory of the Lord is rising on you, though night still covers the earth and darkness the peoples. Above you the Lord now rises and above you his glory appears. The nations come to your light and kings to your dawning brightness. Lift up your eyes and look round: all are assembling and coming towards you, your sons from far away and daughters being tenderly carried. At this sight you will grow radiant, your heart throbbing and full; since the riches of the sea will flow to you; the wealth of the nations come to you; camels in throngs will cover you, and dromedaries of Midian and Ephah; everyone in Sheba will come, bringing gold and incense and singing the praise of the Lord.

### Psalm 71:1-2.7-8.10-13. R. v.11

*All nations shall fall prostrate before you, O Lord.*

### Ephesians 3:2-3.5-6

You have probably heard how I have been entrusted by God with the grace he meant for you, and that it was by a revelation that I was given the knowledge of the mystery. This mystery that has now been revealed through the Spirit to his holy apostles and prophets was unknown to any men in past generations; it means that pagans now share the same inheritance, that they are parts of the same body, and that the same promise has been made to them, in Christ Jesus, through the gospel.

### Matthew 2:1-12

After Jesus had been born at Bethlehem in Judaea during the reign of King Herod, some wise men came to Jerusalem from the east. 'Where is the infant king of the Jews?' they asked. 'We saw his star as it rose and have come to do him homage.' When King Herod heard this he was perturbed, and so was the whole of Jerusalem. He called together all the chief priests and the scribes of the people, and enquired of them where the Christ was to be born. 'At Bethlehem in Judaea, ' they told him 'for this is what the prophet wrote: And you, Bethlehem, in the land of Judah, you are by no means least among the leaders of Judah, for out of you will come a leader who will shepherd my people Israel.'

Then Herod summoned the wise men to see him privately. He asked them the exact date on which the star had appeared, and sent them on to Bethlehem. 'Go and find out all about the child', he said 'and when you have found him, let me know, so that I too may go and do him homage.' Having listened to what the king had to say, they set out. And there in front of them was the star they had seen rising; it went forward and halted over the place where the child was. The sight of the star filled them with delight, and going into the house they saw the child with his mother Mary, and falling to their knees they did him homage. Then, opening their treasures, they offered him gifts of gold and frankincense and myrrh. But they were warned in a dream not to go back to Herod, and returned to their own country by a different way.

### Reflection

Jesus is shown to the world. He does not come in majesty, as a mighty judge and ruler. He comes as a helpless child, needing to be loved. He comes in poverty and in his infancy he will be a refugee. He has come to show us the way of love and truth and he begins with nothing. His invitation is always new for each one of us: "Follow me."

## 1 John 3:22-4:6

Whatever we ask God, we shall receive, because we keep his commandments and live the kind of life that he wants. His commandments are these: that we believe in the name of his Son Jesus Christ and that we love one another as he told us to. Whoever keeps his commandments lives in God and God lives in him. We know that he lives in us by the Spirit that he has given us. It is not every spirit, my dear people, that you can trust; test them, to see if they come from God, there are many false prophets, now, in the world. You can tell the spirits that come from God by this: every spirit which acknowledges that Jesus the Christ has come in the flesh is from God; but any spirit which will not say this of Jesus is not from God, but is the spirit of Antichrist, whose coming you were warned about. Well, now he is here, in the world.

Children, you have already overcome these false prophets, because you are from God and you have in you one who is greater than anyone in this world; as for them, they are of the world, and so they speak the language of the world and the world listens to them. But we are children of God, and those who know God listen to us; those who are not of God refuse to listen to us. This is how we can tell the spirit of truth from the spirit of falsehood.

## Psalm 2:7-8.10-11. R. v.8

*I will give you the nations for your heritage.*

## Matthew 4:12-17.23-25

Hearing that John had been arrested, Jesus went back to Galilee, and leaving Nazareth he went and settled in Capernaum, a lakeside town on the borders of Zebulun and Naphtali. In this way the prophecy of Isaiah was to be fulfilled:

'Land of Zebulun! Land of Naphtali! Way of the sea on the far side of Jordan, Galilee of the nations! The people that lived in darkness has seen a great light; on those who dwell in the land and shadow of death a light has dawned.' From that moment Jesus began his preaching with the message, 'Repent, for the kingdom of heaven is close at hand.'

He went round the whole of Galilee teaching in their synagogues, proclaiming the Good News of the kingdom and curing all kinds of diseases and sickness among the people. His fame spread throughout Syria, and those who were suffering from diseases and painful complaints of one kind or another, the possessed, epileptics, the paralysed, were all brought to him, and he cured them. Large crowds followed him, coming from Galilee, the Decapolis, Jerusalem, Judaea and Transjordania.

**Thursday after Epiphany**
**White**
or
**St Raymond of**
**Penyafort,** *priest*
**(Optional, White)**

## Reflection

St John reminds us that we must use our judgement because there are always the possibilities of being tempted away from what is good and right and true. We have intelligence and we need to use it in deciding how we act. We also have the gift of the power and grace of God and we must ask for it to be active in our lives and to show us the right path.

**Friday after Epiphany**
**White**

## 1 John 4:7-10

My dear people, let us love one another since love comes from God and everyone who loves is begotten by God and knows God. Anyone who fails to love can never have known God, because God is love. God's love for us was revealed when God sent into the world his only Son so that we could have life through him; this is the love I mean: not our love for God, but God's love for us when he sent his Son to be the sacrifice that takes our sins away.

## Psalm 71:1-4.7-8 R. Cf.v.11

*All nations shall fall prostrate before you, O Lord.*

## Mark 6:34-44

As Jesus stepped ashore he saw a large crowd; and he took pity on them because they were like sheep without a shepherd, and he set himself to teach them at some length. By now it was getting very late, and his disciples came up to him and said, 'This is a lonely place and it is getting very late. So send them away, and they can go to the farms and villages round about, to buy themselves something to eat.' He replied, 'Give them something to eat yourselves.' They answered, 'Are we to go and spend two hundred denarii on bread for them to eat?' 'How many loaves have you?' he asked. 'Go and see.' And when they had found out they said, 'Five, and two fish.' Then he ordered them to get all the people together in groups on the green grass, and they sat down on the ground in squares of hundreds and fifties. Then he took the five loaves and the two fish, raised his eyes to heaven and said the blessing; then he broke the loaves and handed them to his disciples to distribute among the people. He also shared out the two fish among them all. They all ate as much as they wanted. They collected twelve basketfuls of scraps of bread and pieces of fish. Those who had eaten the loaves numbered five thousand men.

## Reflection

The miracle of the multiplication of the loaves and fish is a clear sign that Jesus not only wants to provide for us, but he is ready to give us much more than we actually need, more than enough. Jesus was teaching the crowds but he was also willing to provide for their needs, and to feed them. We are invited to ask in Faith for our practical needs as well.

**1 John 4:11-18**

My dear people, since God has loved us so much, we too should love one another. No one has ever seen God; but as long as we love one another God will live in us and his love will be complete in us. We can know that we are living in him and he is living in us because he lets us share his Spirit. We ourselves saw and we testify that the Father sent his Son as saviour of the world. If anyone acknowledges that Jesus is the Son of God, God lives in him, and he in God. We ourselves have known and put our faith in God's love towards ourselves. God is love and anyone who lives in love lives in God, and God lives in him. Love will come to its perfection in us when we can face the day of Judgement without fear; because even in this world we have become as he is. In love there can be no fear, but fear is driven out by perfect love: because to fear is to expect punishment, and anyone who is afraid is still imperfect in love.

**Psalm 71:1-2.10-13 R. Cf.v.11**

*All nations shall fall prostrate before you, O Lord.*

**Mark 6:45-52**

After the five thousand had eaten and were filled, Jesus made his disciples get into the boat and go on ahead to Bethsaida, while he himself sent the crowd away. After saying goodbye to them he went off into the hills to pray. When evening came, the boat was far out on the lake, and he was alone on the land. He could see they were worn out with rowing, for the wind was against them; and about the fourth watch of the night he came towards them, walking on the lake. He was going to pass them by, but when they saw him walking on the lake they thought it was a ghost and cried out; for they had all seen him and were terrified. But he at once spoke to them, and said, 'Courage! It is I! Do not be afraid.' Then he got into the boat with them, and the wind dropped. They were utterly and completely dumbfounded, because they had not seen what the miracle of the loaves meant; their minds were closed.

**Saturday after Epiphany**
**White**

**Reflection**

In the Gospel, Jesus is having to emphasise, time and again, that His love for us means more than His teaching. He wants to show that He wants to be present in every part of our lives. He had provided food for the crowd and now safety for his disciples in the storm. He wants to be present to each of us, wherever we are and whatever is happening.

**The Baptism of the Lord**
Feast
Psalter Week 1
White

### Isaiah 55:1-11
Thus says the Lord:

Oh, come to the water all you who are thirsty; though you have no money, come! Buy corn without money, and eat, and, at no cost, wine and milk. Why spend money on what is not bread, your wages on what fails to satisfy? Listen, listen to me, and you will have good things to eat and rich food to enjoy. Pay attention, come to me; listen, and your soul will live. With you I will make an everlasting covenant out of the favours promised to David. See, I have made of you a witness to the peoples, a leader and a master of the nations. See, you will summon a nation you never knew, those unknown will come hurrying to you, for the sake of the Lord your God, of the Holy One of Israel who will glorify you. Seek the Lord while he is still to be found, call to him while he is still near. Let the wicked man abandon his way, the evil man his thoughts. Let him turn back to the Lord who will take pity on him, to our God who is rich in forgiving; for my thoughts are not your thoughts, my ways not your ways – it is the Lord who speaks. Yes, the heavens are as high above earth as my ways are above your ways, my thoughts above your thoughts.

Yes, as the rain and the snow come down from the heavens and do not return without watering the earth, making it yield and giving growth to provide seed for the sower and bread for the eating, so the word that goes from my mouth does not return to me empty, without carrying out my will and succeeding in what it was sent to do.

### Isaiah 12:2-6. R. v.6
*With joy you will draw water from the wells of salvation.*

### 1 John 5:1-9
Whoever believes that Jesus is the Christ has been begotten by God; and whoever loves the Father that begot him loves the child whom he begets. We can be sure that we love God's children if we love God himself and do what he has commanded us; this is what loving God is – keeping his commandments; and his commandments are not difficult, because anyone who has been begotten by God has already overcome the world; this is the victory over the world – our faith. Who can overcome the world? Only the man who believes that Jesus is the Son of God: Jesus Christ who came by water and blood, not with water only, but with water and blood; with the Spirit as another witness – since the Spirit is the truth – so that there are three witnesses, the

Spirit, the water and the blood, and all three of them agree. We accept the testimony of human witnesses, but God's testimony is much greater, and this is God's testimony, given as evidence for his Son.

## Mark 1:7-11

In the course of his preaching John the Baptist said, 'Someone is following me, someone who is more powerful than I am, and I am not fit to kneel down and undo the strap of his sandals. I have baptised you with water, but he will baptise you with the Holy Spirit.'

It was at this time that Jesus came from Nazareth in Galilee and was baptised in the Jordan by John. No sooner had he come up out of the water than he saw the heavens torn apart and the Spirit, like a dove, descending on him. And a voice came from heaven, 'You are my Son, the Beloved; my favour rests on you.'

## Reflection

St Peter recognises that Jesus welcomes everyone who might want to come to him. By being baptised by John the Baptist in the Jordan, Jesus shows that he does not wish to be different from us in any way. He has come to live within our human nature and he wants to walk with us every day and be close to us whenever we need him.

**1st Week
in Ordinary Time
Green**

**Hebrews 1:1-6**

At various times in the past and in various different ways, God spoke to our ancestors through the prophets; but in our own time, the last days, he has spoken to us through his Son, the Son that he has appointed to inherit everything and through whom he made everything there is. He is the radiant light of God's glory and the perfect copy of his nature, sustaining the universe by his powerful command; and now that he has destroyed the defilement of sin, he has gone to take his place in heaven at the right hand of divine Majesty. So he is now as far above the angels as the title which he has inherited is higher than their own name.

God has never said to any angel: You are my Son, today I have become your father; or: I will be a father to him and he a son to me. Again, when he brings the First-born into the world, he says: Let all the angels of God worship him.

**Psalm 96:1-2.6-7.9. R. cf. v.7**
*All you angels, worship the Lord.*

**Mark 1:14-20**

After John had been arrested, Jesus went into Galilee. There he proclaimed the Good News from God. 'The time has come' he said 'and the kingdom of God is close at hand. Repent, and believe the Good News.'

As he was walking along by the Sea of Galilee he saw Simon and his brother Andrew casting a net in the lake – for they were fishermen. And Jesus said to them, 'Follow me and I will make you into fishers of men.' And at once they left their nets and followed him.

Going on a little further, he saw James son of Zebedee and his brother John; they too were in their boat, mending their nets. He called them at once and, leaving their father Zebedee in the boat with the men he employed, they went after him.

**Reflection**

As Jesus begins his ministry, he calls four strangers to follow him. They begin their journey in Faith. It is a journey that will be full of extraordinary experiences. They will see miracles and hear the teaching of Jesus. There will be difficult and challenging times as well as misunderstandings and setbacks. But they will stay close to Jesus and he will stay close to them – just as he stays close to each of us.

**Hebrews 2:5-12**

God did not appoint angels to be rulers of the world to come, and that world is what we are talking about. Somewhere there is a passage that shows us this. It runs: What is man that you should spare a thought for him, the son of man that you should care for him? For a short while you made him lower than the angels; you crowned him with glory and splendour. You have put him in command of everything. Well then, if he has put him in command of everything, he has left nothing which is not under his command. At present, it is true, we are not able to see that everything has been put under his command, but we do see in Jesus one who was for a short while made lower than the angels and is now crowned with glory and splendour because he submitted to death; by God's grace he had to experience death for all mankind.

As it was his purpose to bring a great many of his sons into glory, it was appropriate that God, for whom everything exists and through whom everything exists, should make perfect, through suffering, the leader who would take them to their salvation. For the one who sanctifies, and the ones who are sanctified, are of the same stock; that is why he openly calls them brothers in the text: I shall announce your name to my brothers, praise you in full assembly.

**Psalm 8:2.5-9. R. v.7**

*You gave your Son power over the works of your hand.*

**Mark 1:21-28**

Jesus and his disciples went as far as Capernaum, and as soon as the sabbath came he went to the synagogue and began to teach. And his teaching made a deep impression on them because, unlike the scribes, he taught them with authority.

In their synagogue just then there was a man possessed by an unclean spirit, and it shouted, 'What do you want with us, Jesus of Nazareth? Have you come to destroy us? I know who you are: the Holy One of God.' But Jesus said sharply, 'Be quiet! Come out of him!' And the unclean spirit threw the man into convulsions and with a loud cry went out of him. The people were so astonished that they started asking each other what it all meant. 'Here is a teaching that is new' they said 'and with authority behind it: he gives orders even to unclean spirits and they obey him.' And his reputation rapidly spread everywhere, through all the surrounding Galilean countryside.

**Reflection**

The ministry of Jesus combines both his teaching and his actions. He lived a life of service, being sure to help anyone who came to him in need. Our discipleship means learning about the Lord and being sure to use that knowledge to come to the help of those whom God places in our lives who are in need. That must be the way that we live our faith, with integrity.

# JANUARY
# 13
## WEDNESDAY

**1st Week
in Ordinary Time
Green
or
St Hilary, *bishop, doctor*
(Optional, White)
or
Saint Kentigern (Mungo),
Bishop (Scotland – Feast)**
*(See Appendix A-1)*

**Hebrews 2:14-18**
Since all the children share the same blood and flesh, Jesus too shared equally in it, so that by his death he could take away all the power of the devil, who had power over death, and set free all those who had been held in slavery all their lives by the fear of death. For it was not the angels that he took to himself; he took to himself descent from Abraham. It was essential that he should in this way become completely like his brothers so that he could be a compassionate and trustworthy high priest of God's religion, able to atone for human sins. That is, because he has himself been through temptation he is able to help others who are tempted.

**Psalm 104:1-4.6-9. R. v.8**
*The Lord remembers his covenant for ever.* (or *Alleluia!*)

**Mark 1:29-39**
On leaving the synagogue, Jesus went with James and John straight to the house of Simon and Andrew. Now Simon's mother-in-law had gone to bed with fever, and they told him about her straightaway. He went to her, took her by the hand and helped her up. And the fever left her and she began to wait on them.

That evening, after sunset, they brought to him all who were sick and those who were possessed by devils. The whole town came crowding round the door, and he cured many who were suffering from diseases of one kind or another; he also cast out many devils, but he would not allow them to speak, because they knew who he was.

In the morning, long before dawn, he got up and left the house, and went off to a lonely place and prayed there. Simon and his companions set out in search of him, and when they found him they said, 'Everybody is looking for you.' He answered, 'Let us go elsewhere, to the neighbouring country towns, so that I can preach there too, because that is why I came.' And he went all through Galilee, preaching in their synagogues and casting out devils.

## Reflection
Jesus was very busy in his exhausting and demanding ministry as people crowded around him with their questions and needs. But he always found time and silence for prayer. In our busy lives it is so important that we make sure to carve out times of quiet when we can speak to God in prayer, reflecting on the events of each day and learning from our experiences, and even learning from our mistakes.

## Hebrews 3:7-14

The Holy Spirit says: If only you would listen to him today; do not harden your hearts, as happened in the Rebellion, on the Day of Temptation in the wilderness, when your ancestors challenged me and tested me, though they had seen what I could do for forty years. That was why I was angry with that generation and said: How unreliable these people who refuse to grasp my ways! And so, in anger, I swore that not one would reach the place of rest I had for them. Take care, brothers, that there is not in any one of your community a wicked mind, so unbelieving as to turn away from the living God. Every day, as long as this 'today' lasts, keep encouraging one another so that none of you is hardened by the lure of sin, because we shall remain co-heirs with Christ only if we keep a grasp on our first confidence right to the end.

## Psalm 94:6-11. R. v.8

*O that today you would listen to his voice! 'Harden not your hearts.'*

## Mark 1:40-45

A leper came to Jesus and pleaded on his knees: 'If you want to' he said 'you can cure me.' Feeling sorry for him, Jesus stretched out his hand and touched him. 'Of course I want to!' he said. 'Be cured!' And the leprosy left him at once and he was cured. Jesus immediately sent him away and sternly ordered him, 'Mind you say nothing to anyone, but go and show yourself to the priest, and make the offering for your healing prescribed by Moses as evidence of your recovery.' The man went away, but then started talking about it freely and telling the story everywhere, so that Jesus could no longer go openly into any town, but had to stay outside in places where nobody lived. Even so, people from all around would come to him.

**JANUARY**

# 14

**THURSDAY**

**1st Week
in Ordinary Time
Green**

## Reflection

We must be careful not to underestimate the generosity and determination of Jesus to help us. "Of course, I want to cure you", he says to the leper. We remember that he tells us that he has not come for the healthy, but for the sick – because, in his love for us, he wants to help and to provide us all with what we need, and to heal and encourage us even when we fail.

**1st Week
in Ordinary Time
Green**

## Hebrews 4:1-5.11

Be careful: the promise of reaching the place of rest God had for the Israelites still holds good, and none of you must think that he has come too late for it. We received the Good News exactly as they did; but hearing the message did them no good because they did not share the faith of those who listened. We, however, who have faith, shall reach a place of rest, as in the text: And so, in anger, I swore that not one would reach the place of rest I had for them. God's work was undoubtedly all finished at the beginning of the world; as one text says, referring to the seventh day: After all his work God rested on the seventh day. The text we are considering says: they shall not reach the place of rest I had for them.

We must therefore do everything we can to reach this place of rest, or some of you might copy this example of disobedience and be lost.

## Psalm 77:3-4.6-8 R. cf. v.7

*Never forget the deeds of the Lord.*

## Mark 2:1-12

When Jesus returned to Capernaum, word went round that he was back; and so many people collected that there was no room left, even in front of the door. He was preaching the word to them when some people came bringing him a paralytic carried by four men, but as the crowd made it impossible to get the man to him, they stripped the roof over the place where Jesus was; and when they had made an opening, they lowered the stretcher on which the paralytic lay. Seeing their faith, Jesus said to the paralytic, 'My child, your sins are forgiven.' Now some scribes were sitting there, and they thought to themselves, 'How can this man talk like that? He is blaspheming. Who can forgive sins but God?' Jesus, inwardly aware that this was what they were thinking, said to them, 'Why do you have these thoughts in your hearts? Which of these is easier: to say to the paralytic, "Your sins are forgiven" or to say, "Get up, pick up your stretcher and walk"? But to prove to you that the Son of Man has authority on earth to forgive sins, ' – he said to the paralytic – 'I order you: get up, pick up your stretcher, and go off home.' And the man got up, picked up his stretcher at once and walked out in front of everyone, so that they were all astounded and praised God saying, 'We have never seen anything like this.'

## Reflection

We do not know who those stretcher bearers were. By their generous actions, they brought the paralytic to Jesus and made it possible for Jesus to forgive and cure him. We can bring people to Jesus in our prayers so that he can act in their lives in ways that we cannot even begin to imagine. We are privileged to pray for others. What a difference we may be able to make in their lives.

## Hebrews 4:12-16

The word of God is something alive and active: it cuts like any double-edged sword but more finely: it can slip through the place where the soul is divided from the spirit, or joints from the marrow; it can judge the secret emotions and thoughts. No created thing can hide from him; everything is uncovered and open to the eyes of the one to whom we must give account of ourselves.

Since in Jesus, the Son of God, we have the supreme high priest who has gone through to the highest heaven, we must never let go of the faith that we have professed. For it is not as if we had a high priest who was incapable of feeling our weaknesses with us; but we have one who has been tempted in every way that we are, though he is without sin. Let us be confident, then, in approaching the throne of grace, that we shall have mercy from him and find grace when we are in need of help.

## Psalm 18:8-10.15. R. cf. John 6:63

*Your words are spirit, Lord, and they are life.*

## Mark 2:13-17

Jesus went out to the shore of the lake; and all the people came to him, and he taught them. As he was walking on he saw Levi the son of Alphaeus, sitting by the customs house, and he said to him, 'Follow me.' And he got up and followed him.

When Jesus was at dinner in his house, a number of tax collectors and sinners were also sitting at the table with Jesus and his disciples; for there were many of them among his followers. When the scribes of the Pharisee party saw him eating with sinners and tax collectors, they said to his disciples, 'Why does he eat with tax collectors and sinners?' When Jesus heard this he said to them, 'It is not the healthy who need the doctor, but the sick. I did not come to call the virtuous, but sinners.'

## JANUARY
# 16
### SATURDAY

**1st Week
in Ordinary Time
Green**

## Reflection

The Gospel reading reminds us that we must never dismiss or abandon those around us who have problems and difficulties and broken lives. These are the very people for whom we should show concern and seek to help. Jesus came for the sick. He came for sinners and those who were lost or confused and forgotten. In fact, he came for us all because none of us is perfect. We all need his love.

**2nd Sunday
in Ordinary Time
Psalter Week 2
Green**

### 1 Samuel 3:3-10.19

Samuel was lying in the sanctuary of the Lord where the ark of God was, when the Lord called, 'Samuel! Samuel!' He answered, 'Here I am.' Then he ran to Eli and said, 'Here I am, since you called me.' Eli said, 'I did not call. Go back and lie down.' So he went and lay down. Once again the Lord called, 'Samuel! Samuel!' Samuel got up and went to Eli and said, 'Here I am, since you called me.' He replied, 'I did not call you, my son; go back and lie down.' Samuel had as yet no knowledge of the Lord and the word of the Lord had not yet been revealed to him. Once again the Lord called, the third time. He got up and went to Eli and said, 'Here I am, since you called me.' Eli then understood that it was the Lord who was calling the boy, and he said to Samuel, 'Go and lie down, and if someone calls say, "Speak, Lord, your servant is listening."' So Samuel went and lay down in his place.

The Lord then came and stood by, calling as he had done before, 'Samuel! Samuel!' Samuel answered, 'Speak, Lord, your servant is listening.'

Samuel grew up and the Lord was with him and let no word of his fall to the ground.

### Psalm 39:2.4.7-10. R. vv. 8.9

*Here I am, Lord! I come to do your will.*

### 1 Corinthians 6:13-15.17-20

The body is not meant for fornication; it is for the Lord, and the Lord for the body. God who raised the Lord from the dead, will by his power raise us up too.

You know, surely, that your bodies are members making up the body of Christ; anyone who is joined to the Lord is one spirit with him.

Keep away from fornication. All the other sins are committed outside the body; but to fornicate is to sin against your own body. Your body, you know, is the temple of the Holy Spirit, who is in you since you received him from God. You are not your own property; you have been bought and paid for. That is why you should use your body for the glory of God.

### John 1:35-42

As John stood with two of his disciples, Jesus passed, and John stared hard at him and said, 'Look, there is the lamb of God.' Hearing this, the two disciples followed Jesus. Jesus turned round, saw them following and said, 'What do you want?' They answered, 'Rabbi' – which means Teacher – 'where do you live?' 'Come and see' he replied; so they went and saw where he lived, and stayed with him the rest of that day. It was about the tenth hour.

One of these two who became followers of Jesus after hearing what John had said was Andrew, the brother of Simon Peter. Early next morning, Andrew met his brother and said to him, 'We have found the Messiah' – which means the Christ – and he took Simon to Jesus. Jesus looked hard at him and said, 'You are Simon son of John; you are to be called Cephas' – meaning Rock.

### Reflection

Samuel is called by God. He must listen to all that the Lord asks of him. St John Henry Newman wrote "God created me to do Him some definite purpose. He has committed some work to me that he has not committed to another...". We all have a God-given purpose. We need to listen to all that God wants to say to us, as He shows us the way He wants us to go.

**2nd Week
in Ordinary Time
Green**

### Hebrews 5:1-10

Every high priest has been taken out of mankind and is appointed to act for men in their relations with God, to offer gifts and sacrifices for sins; and so he can sympathise with those who are ignorant or uncertain because he too lives in the limitations of weakness. That is why he has to make sin offerings for himself as well as for the people. No one takes this honour on himself, but each one is called by God, as Aaron was. Nor did Christ give himself the glory of becoming high priest, but he had it from the one who said to him: You are my son, today I have become your father, and in another text: You are a priest of the order of Melchizedek, and for ever. During his life on earth, he offered up prayer and entreaty, aloud and in silent tears, to the one who had the power to save him out of death, and he submitted so humbly that his prayer was heard. Although he was Son, he learnt to obey through suffering; but having been made perfect, he became for all who obey him the source of eternal salvation and was acclaimed by God with the title of high priest of the order of Melchizedek.

### Psalm 109:1-4. R. v.4

*You are a priest for ever, a priest like Melchizedek of old.*

### Mark 2:18-22

One day when John's disciples and the Pharisees were fasting, some people came and said to Jesus, 'Why is it that John's disciples and the disciples of the Pharisees fast, but your disciples do not?' Jesus replied, 'Surely the bridegroom's attendants would never think of fasting while the bridegroom is still with them? As long as they have the bridegroom with them, they could not think of fasting. But the time will come for the bridegroom to be taken away from them, and then, on that day, they will fast. No one sews a piece of unshrunken cloth on an old cloak; if he does, the patch pulls away from it, the new from the old, and the tear gets worse. And nobody puts new wine into old wineskins; if he does, the wine will burst the skins, and the wine is lost and the skins too. No! New wine, fresh skins!'

### Reflection

Sometimes we cannot just make small adjustments and changes and repairs to things. When we embrace Faith we need to be open to questioning our whole lives and the way that we live. Our Faith cannot be something that we simply add to established routines and set ideas. When Faith takes root in our lives, we make it the foundation of all that we believe and do. We build our lives on Faith in Christ.

**2nd Week
in Ordinary Time
Green**

## Hebrews 6:10-20

God would not be so unjust as to forget all you have done, the love that you have for his name or the services you have done, and are still doing, for the saints. Our one desire is that every one of you should go on showing the same earnestness to the end, to the perfect fulfilment of our hopes, never growing careless, but imitating those who have the faith and the perseverance to inherit the promises.

When God made the promise to Abraham, he swore by his own self, since it was impossible for him to swear by anyone greater: I will shower blessings on you and give you many descendants. Because of that, Abraham persevered and saw the promise fulfilled. Men, of course, swear an oath by something greater than themselves, and between men, confirmation by an oath puts an end to all dispute. In the same way, when God wanted to make the heirs to the promise thoroughly realise that his purpose was unalterable, he conveyed this by an oath; so that there would be two unalterable things in which it was impossible for God to be lying, and so that we, now we have found safety, should have a strong encouragement to take a firm grip on the hope that is held out to us. Here we have an anchor for our soul, as sure as it is firm, and reaching right through beyond the veil where Jesus has entered before us and on our behalf, to become a high priest of the order of Melchizedek, and for ever.

## Psalm 110:1-2.4-5.9.10. R. v.5

*The Lord keeps his covenant ever in mind.*

## Mark 2:23-28

One sabbath day Jesus happened to be taking a walk through the cornfields, and his disciples began to pick ears of corn as they went along. And the Pharisees said to him, 'Look, why are they doing something on the sabbath day that is forbidden?' And he replied, 'Did you never read what David did in his time of need when he and his followers were hungry – how he went into the house of God when Abiathar was high priest, and ate the loaves of offering which only the priests are allowed to eat, and how he also gave some to the men with him?'

And he said to them, 'The sabbath was made for man, not man for the sabbath; so the Son of Man is master even of the sabbath.'

## Reflection

The author of the Letter to the Hebrews reminds us that our pursuit of Faith is a continuing journey. Our lives in Faith will include times of progress and purpose but there may well be times of dryness and even frustration. Jesus experienced his own trials throughout his ministry, ending in his death on the cross. But his perseverance brought him to the Resurrection and the gift of new life for all.

# JANUARY
# 20
## WEDNESDAY

**2nd Week
in Ordinary Time
Green
or
St Fabian,** *pope, martyr*
**(Optional, Red)
St Sebastian,** *martyr*
**(Optional, Red)**

## Hebrews 7:1-3.15-17

You remember that Melchizedek, king of Salem, a priest of God Most High, went to meet Abraham, who was on his way back after defeating the kings, and blessed him; and also that it was to him that Abraham gave a tenth of all that he had. By the interpretation of his name, he is, first, 'king of righteousness' and also king of Salem, that is, 'king of peace'; he has no father, mother or ancestry, and his life has no beginning or ending; he is like the Son of God. He remains a priest for ever.

This becomes even more clearly evident when there appears a second Melchizedek, who is a priest not by virtue of a law about physical descent, but by the power of an indestructible life. For it was about him that the prophecy was made: You are a priest of the order of Melchizedek, and for ever.

## Psalm 109:1-4. R. v.4

*You are a priest for ever, a priest like Melchizedek of old.*

## Mark 3:1-6

Jesus went into a synagogue, and there was a man there who had a withered hand. And they were watching him to see if he would cure him on the sabbath day, hoping for something to use against him. He said to the man with the withered hand, 'Stand up out in the middle!' Then he said to them, 'Is it against the law on the sabbath day to do good, or to do evil; to save life, or to kill?' But they said nothing. Then, grieved to find them so obstinate, he looked angrily round at them, and said to the man, 'Stretch out your hand.' He stretched it out and his hand was better. The Pharisees went out and at once began to plot with the Herodians against him, discussing how to destroy him.

## Reflection

Rules and regulations are important as they give us guidelines and direct our behaviour for a particular purpose. But rules are not an end in themselves. Sometimes rules can even become obstacles in the way of doing the right thing. The test must always be that what we do is always done in love for our neighbour. Loving God and our neighbour as ourselves is the most important rule of all.

## Hebrews 7:25–8:6

The power of Jesus to save is utterly certain, since he is living for ever to intercede for all who come to God through him.

To suit us, the ideal high priest would have to be holy, innocent and uncontaminated, beyond the influence of sinners, and raised up above the heavens; one who would not need to offer sacrifices every day, as the other high priests do for their own sins and then for those of the people, because he has done this once and for all by offering himself. The Law appoints high priests who are men subject to weakness; but the promise on oath, which came after the Law, appointed the Son who is made perfect for ever.

The great point of all that we have said is that we have a high priest of exactly this kind. He has his place at the right of the throne of divine Majesty in the heavens, and he is the minister of the sanctuary and of the true Tent of Meeting which the Lord, and not any man, set up. It is the duty of every high priest to offer gifts and sacrifices, and so this one too must have something to offer. In fact, if he were on earth, he would not be a priest at all, since there are others who make the offerings laid down by the Law and these only maintain the service of a model or a reflection of the heavenly realities. For Moses, when he had the Tent to build, was warned by God who said: See that you make everything according to the pattern shown you on the mountain.

We have seen that he has been given a ministry of a far higher order, and to the same degree it is a better covenant of which he is the mediator, founded on better promises.

## Psalm 39:7-10.17. R. cf. vv. 8.9

*Here I am, Lord! I come to do your will.*

## Mark 3:7-12

Jesus withdrew with his disciples to the lakeside, and great crowds from Galilee followed him. From Judaea, Jerusalem, Idumaea, Transjordania and the region of Tyre and Sidon, great numbers who had heard of all he was doing came to him. And he asked his disciples to have a boat ready for him because of the crowd, to keep him from being crushed. For he had cured so many that all who were afflicted in any way were crowding forward to touch him. And the unclean spirits, whenever they saw him, would fall down before him and shout, 'You are the Son of God!' But he warned them strongly not to make him known.

## Reflection

The crowds that are gathering to listen to Jesus are coming from many different places, some from a distance. Jesus never turns anyone away. Even those who criticise him and argue with him are not sent away. In his welcome and acceptance of all, many people are changed. Can we welcome people who differ from us in their views and traditions? We may build harmony and understanding and even help others to change.

**2nd Week
in Ordinary Time**
St Agnes, *virgin, martyr*
**Memorial
Red**

# JANUARY

# 22

## FRIDAY

**2nd Week
in Ordinary Time
Green
or
St Vincent, *deacon,
martyr*
(Optional, Red)**

### Hebrews 8:6-13

We have seen that Jesus has been given a ministry of a far higher order, and to the same degree it is a better covenant of which he is the mediator, founded on better promises. If that first covenant had been without a fault, there would have been no need for a second one to replace it. And in fact God does find fault with them; he says:

See, the days are coming – it is the Lord who speaks – when I will establish a new covenant with the House of Israel and the House of Judah, but not a covenant like the one I made with their ancestors on the day I took them by the hand to bring them out of the land of Egypt. They abandoned that covenant of mine, and so I on my side deserted them. It is the Lord who speaks. No, this is the covenant I will make with the House of Israel when those days arrive – it is the Lord who speaks I will put my laws into their minds and write them on their hearts. Then I will be their God and they shall be my people.

There will be no further need for neighbour to try to teach neighbour, or brother to say to brother, 'Learn to know the Lord.' No, they will all know me, the least no less than the greatest, since I will forgive their iniquities and never call their sins to mind.

By speaking of a new covenant, he implies that the first one is already old. Now anything old only gets more antiquated until in the end it disappears.

### Psalm 84:8.10-14. R. v.11

*Mercy and faithfulness have met.*

### Mark 3:13-19

Jesus went up into the hills and summoned those he wanted. So they came to him and he appointed twelve; they were to be his companions and to be sent out to preach, with power to cast out devils. And so he appointed the Twelve: Simon to whom he gave the name Peter, James the son of Zebedee and John the brother of James, to whom he gave the name Boanerges or 'Sons of Thunder'; then Andrew, Philip, Bartholomew, Matthew, Thomas, James the son of Alphaeus, Thaddaeus, Simon the Zealot and Judas Iscariot, the man who was to betray him.

## Reflection

Early in his ministry, Jesus chooses his companions. He knows nothing about them. They will have a lot to learn. Jesus does not choose scholars or the best candidates; sometimes the chosen ones do not understand or make the right decisions. But, having chosen them, Jesus remains utterly faithful to them. We can say he has chosen "me", and we can be sure that he will always be faithful and never leave us without his help

## Hebrews 9:2-3.11-14

There was a tent which comprised two compartments: the first, in which the lamp-stand, the table and the presentation loaves were kept, was called the Holy Place; then beyond the second veil, an innermost part which was called the Holy of Holies.

But now Christ has come, as the high priest of all the blessings which were to come. He has passed through the greater, the more perfect tent, which is better than the one made by men's hands because it is not of this created order; and he has entered the sanctuary once and for all, taking with him not the blood of goats and bull calves, but his own blood, having won an eternal redemption for us. The blood of goats and bulls and the ashes of a heifer are sprinkled on those who have incurred defilement and they restore the holiness of their outward lives; how much more effectively the blood of Christ, who offered himself as the perfect sacrifice to God through the eternal Spirit, can purify our inner self from dead actions so that we do our service to the living God.

## Psalm 46:2-3.6-9. R. v.6

*God goes up with shouts of joy; the Lord goes up with trumpet blast.*

## Mark 3:20-21

Jesus went home, and such a crowd collected that they could not even have a meal. When his relatives heard of this, they set out to take charge of him, convinced he was out of his mind.

## Reflection

Even those closest to Jesus could not always understand what he was saying and doing. At times he must have felt very alone and frustrated but he was determined to carry out the ministry that had been given to him. When we try to do the right thing, we may sometimes be misunderstood by others and draw criticism and opposition, but we can be sure of God's helping hand.

**3rd Sunday
in Ordinary Time
Psalter Week 3
Green**

## Jonah 3:1-5.10

The word of the Lord was addressed to Jonah: 'Up!' he said 'Go to Nineveh, the great city, and preach to them as I told you to.' Jonah set out and went to Nineveh in obedience to the word of the Lord. Now Nineveh was a city great beyond compare: it took three days to cross it. Jonah went on into the city, making a day's journey. He preached in these words, 'Only forty days more and Nineveh is going to be destroyed.' And the people of Nineveh believed in God; they proclaimed a fast and put on sackcloth, from the greatest to the least.

God saw their efforts to renounce their evil behaviour. And God relented: he did not inflict on them the disaster which he had threatened.

## Psalm 24:4-9. R. v.4

*Lord, make me know your ways.*

## 1 Corinthians 7:29-31

Brothers, our time is growing short. Those who have wives should live as though they had none, and those who mourn should live as though they had nothing to mourn for; those who are enjoying life should live as though there were nothing to laugh about; those whose life is buying things should live as though they had nothing of their own; and those who have to deal with the world should not become engrossed in it. I say this because the world as we know it is passing away.

## Mark 1:14-20

After John had been arrested, Jesus went into Galilee. There he proclaimed the Good News from God. 'The time has come' he said 'and the kingdom of God is close at hand. Repent, and believe the Good News.'

As he was walking along by the Sea of Galilee he saw Simon and his brother Andrew casting a net in the lake – for they were fishermen. And Jesus said to them, 'Follow me and I will make you into fishers of men.' And at once they left their nets and followed him.

Going on a little further, he saw James son of Zebedee and his brother John; they too were in their boat, mending their nets. He called them at once and, leaving their father Zebedee in the boat with the men he employed, they went after him.

## Reflection

Discipleship has two dimensions. As disciples, we are learning to follow the Lord and to understand what he taught us by his word and example. We grow in our knowledge and understanding of him. But just as important is that sense of discipleship that sends us out to show to others, by our own word and example, what we believe and so we bring Jesus to our world. These two dimensions work and grow together.

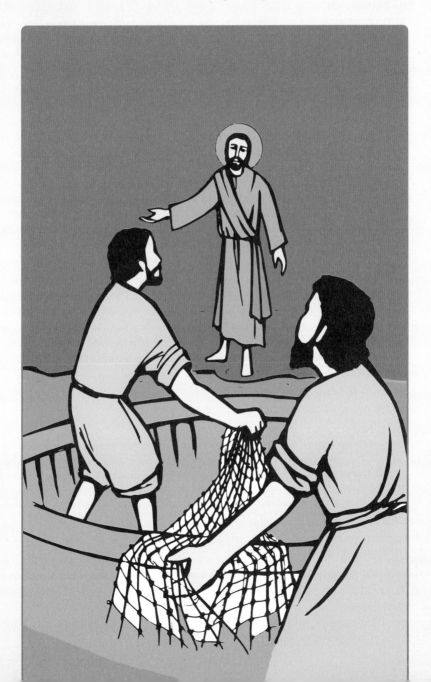

**The Conversion
of St Paul,** *apostle*
**Feast**
**White**

**Acts 22:3-16** *(Alternative First Reading Acts 9:1-22)*
Paul said to the people, 'I am a Jew and was born at Tarsus in Cilicia. I was brought up here in this city. I studied under Gamaliel and was taught the exact observance of the Law of our ancestors. In fact, I was as full of duty towards God as you are today. I even persecuted this Way to the death, and sent women as well as men to prison in chains as the high priest and the whole council of elders can testify, since they even sent me with letters to their brothers in Damascus. When I set off it was with the intention of bringing prisoners back from there to Jerusalem for punishment.

'I was on that journey and nearly at Damascus when about midday a bright light from heaven suddenly shone round me. I fell to the ground and heard a voice saying, "Saul, Saul, why are you persecuting me?" I answered: who are you, Lord? and he said to me, "I am Jesus the Nazarene, and you are persecuting me." The people with me saw the light but did not hear his voice as he spoke to me. I said: What am I to do, Lord? The Lord answered, "Stand up and go into Damascus, and there you will be told what you have been appointed to do." The light had been so dazzling that I was blind and my companions had to take me by the hand; and so I came to Damascus.

'Someone called Ananias, a devout follower of the Law and highly thought of by all the Jews living there, came to see me; he stood beside me and said, "Brother Saul, receive your sight." Instantly my sight came back and I was able to see him. Then he said, "The God of our ancestors has chosen you to know his will, to see that Just One and hear his own voice speaking, because you are to be his witness before all mankind, testifying to what you have seen and heard. And now why delay? It is time you were baptised and had your sins washed away while invoking his name."'

**Psalm 116:1-2. R. Mark 16:15**
*Go out to the whole world; proclaim the Good News.* (or *Alleluia!*)

**Mark 16:15-18**
Jesus showed himself to the Eleven and said to them, 'Go out to the whole world; proclaim the Good News to all creation. He who believes and is baptised will be saved; he who does not believe will be condemned. These are the signs that will be associated with believers: in my name they will cast out devils; they will have the gift of tongues; they will pick up snakes in their hands, and be unharmed should they drink deadly poison; they will lay their hands on the sick, who will recover.'

**Reflection**
St Paul's life was completely changed by his conversion on the Damascus Road. Everything he had believed as a Pharisee was challenged and he had to begin again to build his faith and understanding of what it meant to believe in Jesus. He began a journey which is a model for all Christians. If we are to believe in Christ, how may that effect the way that we live and the priorities that we have?

## 2 Timothy 1:1-8

From Paul, appointed by God to be an apostle of Christ Jesus in his design to promise life in Christ Jesus; to Timothy, dear child of mine, wishing you grace, mercy and peace from God the Father and from Christ Jesus our Lord.

Night and day I thank God, keeping my conscience clear and remembering my duty to him as my ancestors did, and always I remember you in my prayers; I remember your tears and long to see you again to complete my happiness. Then I am reminded of the sincere faith which you have; it came first to live in your grandmother Lois, and your mother Eunice, and I have no doubt that it is the same faith in you as well.

That is why I am reminding you now to fan into a flame the gift that God gave you when I laid my hands on you. God's gift was not a spirit of timidity, but the Spirit of power, and love, and self-control. So you are never to be ashamed of witnessing to the Lord, or ashamed of me for being his prisoner; but with me, bear the hardships for the sake of the Good News, relying on the power of God who has saved us and called us to be holy.

## Psalm 95:1-3.7-8.10

*Proclaim the wonders of the Lord among all the peoples.*

## Mark 3:31-35

The mother and brothers of Jesus arrived and, standing outside, sent in a message asking for him. A crowd was sitting round him at the time the message was passed to him, 'Your mother and brothers and sisters are outside asking for you.' He replied, 'Who are my mother and my brothers?' And looking round at those sitting in a circle about him, he said, 'Here are my mother and my brothers. Anyone who does the will of God, that person is my brother and sister and mother.'

**3rd Week
in Ordinary Time
or
Sts Timothy and Titus,
*bishops*
Memorial, White**

## Reflection

How close does Jesus want to be to each one of us? This Gospel may surprise and even shock us. It reassures us that Jesus welcomes every believer not just as a disciple but as a member of his closest family. As our brother, he is always there to help and encourage us. There is no need ever to be afraid of him. We can trust him and love him just as he loves us.

**3rd Week
in Ordinary Time
Green**
or
**St Angela Merici,** *virgin*
**(Optional, White)**

**Hebrews 10:11-18**
*(See Appendix B-1)*

**Psalm 109:1-4. R. v.4**
*You are a priest for ever, a priest like Melchizedek of old.*

**Mark 4:1-20**
Jesus began to teach by the lakeside, but such a huge crowd gathered round him that he got into a boat on the lake and sat there. The people were all along the shore, at the water's edge. He taught them many things in parables, and in the course of his teaching he said to them, 'Listen! Imagine a sower going out to sow. Now it happened that, as he sowed, some of the seed fell on the edge of the path, and the birds came and ate it up. Some seed fell on rocky ground where it found little soil and sprang up straightaway, because there was no depth of earth; and when the sun came up it was scorched and, not having any roots, it withered away. Some seed fell into thorns, and the thorns grew up and choked it, and it produced no crop. And some seed fell into rich soil and, growing tall and strong, produced crop; and yielded thirty, sixty, even a hundredfold.' And he said, 'Listen, anyone who has ears to hear!'

When he was alone, the Twelve, together with the others who formed his company, asked what the parables meant. He told them, 'The secret of the kingdom of God is given to you, but to those who are outside everything comes in parables, so that they may see and see again, but not perceive; may hear and hear again, but not understand; otherwise they might be converted and be forgiven.'

He said to them, 'Do you not understand this parable? Then how will you understand any of the parables? What the sower is sowing is the word. Those on the edge of the path where the word is sown are people who have no sooner heard it than Satan comes and carries away the word that was sown in them. Similarly, those who receive the seed on patches of rock are people who, when first they hear the word, welcome it at once with joy. But they have no root in them, they do not last; should some trial come, or some persecution on account of the word, they fall away at once. Then there are others who receive the seed in thorns. These have heard the word, but the worries of this world, the lure of riches and all the other passions come in to choke the word, and so it produces nothing. And there are those who have received the seed in rich soil: they hear the word and accept it and yield a harvest, thirty and sixty and a hundredfold.'

**Reflection**
The disciples were having difficulty in understanding all Jesus was teaching, particularly at the beginning of his ministry. But Jesus is patient with them, explaining everything to them. Understanding God's presence and plan in our lives takes time and develops through the years. We need to be the good soil, accepting the words of Scripture and allowing them to grow within us, bringing new and deeper understanding and guiding our actions and decisions.

## Hebrews 10:19-25

Through the blood of Jesus we have the right to enter the sanctuary, by a new way which he has opened for us, a living opening through the curtain, that is to say, his body. And we have the supreme high priest over all the house of God. So as we go in, let us be sincere in heart and filled with faith, our minds sprinkled and free from any trace of bad conscience and our bodies washed with pure water. Let us keep firm in the hope we profess, because the one who made the promise is faithful. Let us be concerned for each other, to stir a response in love and good works. Do not stay away from the meetings of the community, as some do, but encourage each other to go; the more so as you see the Day drawing near.

## Psalm 23:1-6. R. cf. v.6

*Such are the men who seek your face, O Lord.*

## Mark 4:21-25

Jesus said to the crowd: 'Would you bring in a lamp to put it under a tub or under the bed? Surely you will put it on the lamp-stand? For there is nothing hidden but it must be disclosed, nothing kept secret except to be brought to light. If anyone has ears to hear, let him listen to this.'

He also said to them, 'Take notice of what you are hearing. The amount you measure out is the amount you will be given – and more besides; for the man who has will be given more; from the man who has not, even what he has will be taken away.'

**3rd Week
in Ordinary Time
St Thomas Aquinas,
priest, doctor
Memorial
White**

## Reflection

Jesus reminds us that our Faith is something that we show to others by our actions in our lives. We cannot believe in Jesus without wanting to show that belief in the way that we live. What a privilege we have in continuing the mission that Jesus began: a mission of love for all people, as our brothers and sisters, and our care for them. Caring for others will bring us fulfilment and happiness.

**3rd Week
in Ordinary Time
Green**

### Hebrews 10:32-39

Remember all the sufferings that you had to meet after you received the light, in earlier days; sometimes by being yourselves publicly exposed to insults and violence, and sometimes as associates of others who were treated in the same way. For you not only shared in the sufferings of those who were in prison, but you happily accepted being stripped of your belongings, knowing that you owned something that was better and lasting. Be as confident now, then, since the reward is so great. You will need endurance to do God's will and gain what he has promised.

Only a little while now, a very little while, and the one that is coming will have come; he will not delay. The righteous man will live by faith but if he draws back, my soul will take no pleasure in him.

You and I are not the sort of people who draw back, and are lost by it; we are the sort who keep faithful until our souls are saved.

### Psalm 36:3-6.23-24.39-40. R. v.39
*The salvation of the just comes from the Lord.*

### Mark 4:26-34

Jesus said to the crowd: 'This is what the kingdom of God is like. A man throws seed on the land. Night and day, while he sleeps, when he is awake, the seed is sprouting and growing; how, he does not know. Of its own accord the land produces first the shoot, then the ear, then the full grain in the ear. And when the crop is ready, he loses no time: he starts to reap because the harvest has come.'

He also said, 'What can we say the kingdom of God is like? What parable can we find for it? It is like a mustard seed which at the time of its sowing in the soil is the smallest of all the seeds on earth; yet once it is sown it grows into the biggest shrub of them all and puts out big branches so that the birds of the air can shelter in its shade.'

Using many parables like these, he spoke the word to them, so far as they were capable of understanding it. He would not speak to them except in parables, but he explained everything to his disciples when they were alone.

### Reflection

If we are intent on doing what is right, caring for our brothers and sisters in their need, even in the detailed actions of our daily lives, God will be building His Kingdom in our world. Every good action, every gift of kindness, will be a building block in God's design. We must never underestimate the value of even our smallest actions when we undertake them in Faith and do them in love.

**3rd Week
in Ordinary Time
Green**

**Hebrews 11:1-2.8-19**

Only faith can guarantee the blessings that we hope for, or prove the existence of the realities that at present remain unseen. It was for faith that our ancestors were commended.

It was by faith that Abraham obeyed the call to set out for a country that was the inheritance given to him and his descendants, and that he set out without knowing where he was going. By faith he arrived, as a foreigner, in the Promised Land, and lived there as if in a strange country, with Isaac and Jacob, who were heirs with him of the same promise. They lived there in tents while he looked forward to a city founded, designed and built by God.

It was equally by faith that Sarah, in spite of being past the age, was made able to conceive, because she believed that he who had made the promise would be faithful to it. Because of this, there came from one man, and one who was already as good as dead himself, more descendants than could be counted, as many as the stars of heaven or the grains of sand on the seashore.

*(See Appendix B-1)*

**Psalm Luke 1:69-75. R. cf. v.68**

*Blessed be the Lord, the God of Israel! He has visited his people and redeemed them.*

**Mark 4:35-41**

With the coming of evening, Jesus said to his disciples, 'Let us cross over to the other side.' And leaving the crowd behind they took him, just as he was, in the boat; and there were other boats with him. Then it began to blow a gale and the waves were breaking into the boat so that it was almost swamped. But he was in the stern, his head on the cushion, asleep. They woke him and said to him, 'Master, do you not care? We are going down!' And he woke up and rebuked the wind and said to the sea, 'Quiet now! Be calm!' And the wind dropped, and all was calm again. Then he said to them, 'Why are you so frightened? How is it that you have no faith?' They were filled with awe and said to one another, 'Who can this be? Even the wind and the sea obey him.'

**Reflection**

We would be naïve to think that our lives will ever be without challenges and problems. We need to remember that, when we face difficulties, Jesus is still there with us and we need to call on him. He may not solve all the problems in the way that we might wish but we can be sure that we will never be overwhelmed and there is a way ahead and a guiding hand.

## JANUARY

# 31

**4th Sunday
in Ordinary Time**
Psalter Week 4
Green

### Deuteronomy 18:15-20

Moses said to the people: 'Your God will raise up for you a prophet like myself, from among yourselves, from your own brothers; to him you must listen. This is what you yourselves asked of the Lord your God at Horeb on the day of the Assembly. "Do not let me hear again" you said "the voice of the Lord my God, nor look any longer on this great fire, or I shall die"; and the Lord said to me, "All they have spoken is well said. I will raise up a prophet like yourself for them from their own brothers; I will put my words into his mouth and he shall tell them all I command him. The man who does not listen to my words that he speaks in my name, shall be held answerable to me for it. But the prophet who presumes to say in my name a thing I have not commanded him to say, or who speaks in the name of other gods, that prophet shall die."'

### Psalm 94:1-2.6-9. R. v.9

*O that today you would listen to his voice! Harden not your hearts.*

### 1 Corinthians 7:32-35

I would like to see you free from all worry. An unmarried man can devote himself to the Lord's affairs, all he need worry about is pleasing the Lord; but a married man has to bother about the world's affairs and devote himself to pleasing his wife: he is torn two ways. In the same way an unmarried woman, like a young girl, can devote herself to the Lord's affairs; all she need worry about is being holy in body and spirit. The married woman, on the other hand, has to worry about the world's affairs and devote herself to pleasing her husband. I say this only to help you, not to put a halter round your necks, but simply to make sure that everything is as it should be, and that you give your undivided attention to the Lord.

### Mark 1:21-28

Jesus and his followers went as far as Capernaum, and as soon as the sabbath came Jesus went to the synagogue and began to teach. And his teaching made a deep impression on them because, unlike the scribes, he taught them with authority.

In their synagogue just then there was a man possessed by an unclean spirit, and it shouted, 'What do you want with us, Jesus of Nazareth? Have you come to destroy us? I know who you are: the Holy One of God.' But Jesus said sharply, 'Be quiet! Come out of him!' And the unclean spirit threw the man into convulsions and with a loud cry went out of him. The people were so astonished that they started asking each other what it all meant. 'Here is a teaching that is new' they said 'and with authority behind it: he gives orders even to unclean spirits and they obey him.' And his reputation rapidly spread everywhere, through all the surrounding Galilean countryside.

## Reflection

We have seen Jesus beginning his ministry as recorded by St Mark. He is challenged by some who are disturbed by his radical teaching but he turns no one away and he teaches and heals all who come to him, because that is his purpose. We have that same purpose to bring love to every encounter that we have with people. The challenge is new each day, but Jesus is always there to help us.

**4th Week
in Ordinary Time
Green
or
Saint Brigid, Abbess,
Secondary Patron of
Ireland – Feast**
*(See Appendix A-2)*

**Hebrews 11:32-40**
*(See Appendix B-1)*

**Psalm 30:20-24. R. v.25**
*Let your hearts take comfort, all who hope in the Lord.*

**Mark 5:1-20**
Jesus and his disciples reached the country of the Gerasenes on the other side of the lake, and no sooner had he left the boat than a man with an unclean spirit came out from the tombs towards him. The man lived in the tombs and no one could secure him any more, even with a chain, because he had often been secured with fetters and chains but had snapped the chains and broken the fetters, and no one had the strength to control him. All night and all day, among the tombs and in the mountains, he would howl and gash himself with stones. Catching sight of Jesus from a distance, he ran up and fell at his feet and shouted at the top of his voice, 'What do you want with me, Jesus, son of the Most High God? Swear by God you will not torture me!' – For Jesus had been saying to him, 'Come out of the man, unclean spirit.' 'What is your name?' Jesus asked. 'My name is legion, ' he answered 'for there are many of us.' And he begged him earnestly not to send them out of the district. Now there was there on the mountainside a great herd of pigs feeding, and the unclean spirits begged him, 'Send us to the pigs, let us go into them.' So he gave them leave. With that, the unclean spirits came out and went into the pigs, and the herd of about two thousand pigs charged down the cliff into the lake, and there they were drowned. The swineherds ran off and told their story in the town and in the country round about; and the people came to see what had really happened. They came to Jesus and saw the demoniac sitting there, clothed and in his full senses – the very man who had had the legion in him before – and they were afraid. And those who had witnessed it reported what had happened to the demoniac and what had become of the pigs. Then they began to implore Jesus to leave the neighbourhood. As he was getting into the boat, the man who had been possessed begged to be allowed to stay with him. Jesus would not let him but said to him, 'Go home to your people and tell them all that the Lord in his mercy has done for you.' So the man went off and proceeded to spread throughout the Decapolis all that Jesus had done for him. And everyone was amazed.

## Reflection
The reading from Hebrews and the message of the Responsorial Psalm speak strongly of courage, hope and faith in God – the faith of people in the existence of a personal God and their belief that this personal God loves them and will care for them. This example gives us hope and courage when so often during the day we face contradiction and suffering from others, and from ourselves.

**Malachi 3:1-4**
*(See Appendix B-2)*

**Psalm 23:7-10. R. v.10**
*Who is the king of glory? It is the Lord.*

**The Presentation
of the Lord
Feast
White**

**Hebrews 2:14-18**
Since all the children share the same blood and flesh, Jesus too shared equally in it, so that by his death he could take away all the power of the devil, who had power over death, and set free all those who had been held in slavery all their lives by the fear of death. For it was not the angels that he took to himself; he took to himself descent from Abraham. It was essential that he should in this way become completely like his brothers so that he could be a compassionate and trustworthy high priest of God's religion, able to atone for human sins. That is, because he has himself been through temptation he is able to help others who are tempted.

**Luke 2:22-32** *(Longer form: Luke 2:22-40)*
When the day came for them to be purified as laid down by the Law of Moses, the parents of Jesus took him up to Jerusalem to present him to the Lord – observing what stands written in the Law of the Lord: Every first-born male must be consecrated to the Lord – and also to offer in sacrifice, in accordance with what is said in the Law of the Lord, a pair of turtledoves or two young pigeons. Now in Jerusalem there was a man named Simeon. He was an upright and devout man; he looked forward to Israel's comforting and the Holy Spirit rested on him. It had been revealed to him by the Holy Spirit that he would not see death until he had set eyes on the Christ of the Lord. Prompted by the Spirit he came to the Temple; and when the parents brought in the child Jesus to do for him what the law required, he took him into his arms and blessed God, and he said: 'Now, Master, you can let your servant go in peace, just as you promised; because my eyes have seen the salvation which you have prepared for all the nations to see, a light to enlighten the pagans and the glory of your people Israel.'

**Reflection**
Mary and Joseph must have really wondered what this child will become. First, they had to take flight into Egypt, to be refugees because of threats to the child. Now as they were fulfilling the Law in Jerusalem, they listened to the wise Simeon as he held the child Jesus with such tenderness, looking into the future of this child. Let us pray that we remain alert and listen to the messages given to us by the Holy Spirit as Mary and Joseph were. Let us imagine ourselves holding the child Jesus in our arms. What would we feel?

# FEBRUARY
# 3
## WEDNESDAY

**4th Week
in Ordinary Time**
Green
or
St Blaise, *bishop, martyr*
(Optional, Red)
St Ansgar, *bishop*
(Optional, White)

## Hebrews 12:4-7.11-15

In the fight against sin, you have not yet had to keep fighting to the point of death.

Have you forgotten that encouraging text in which you are addressed as sons? My son, when the Lord corrects you, do not treat it lightly; but do not get discouraged when he reprimands you. For the Lord trains the ones that he loves and he punishes all those that he acknowledges as his son. Suffering is part of your training; God is treating you as his sons. Has there ever been any son whose father did not train him?

Of course, any punishment is most painful at the time, and far from pleasant; but later, in those on whom it has been used, it bears fruit in peace and goodness. So hold up your limp arms and steady your trembling knees and smooth out the path you tread; then the injured limb will not be wrenched, it will grow strong again.

Always be wanting peace with all people, and the holiness without which no one can ever see the Lord. Be careful that no one is deprived of the grace of God and that no root of bitterness should begin to grow and make trouble; this can poison a whole community.

## Psalm 102:1-2.13-14.17-18. R. cf. v.17

*The love of the Lord is everlasting upon those who hold him in fear.*

## Mark 6:1-6

Jesus went to his home town and his disciples accompanied him. With the coming of the sabbath he began teaching in the synagogue and most of them were astonished when they heard him. They said, 'Where did the man get all this? What is this wisdom that has been granted him, and these miracles that are worked through him? This is the carpenter, surely, the son of Mary, the brother of James and Joset and Jude and Simon? His sisters, too, are they not here with us?' And they would not accept him. And Jesus said to them, 'A prophet is only despised in his own country, among his own relations and in his own house'; and he could work no miracle there, though he cured a few sick people by laying his hands on them.

## Reflection

"And they would not accept him." As soon as Jesus stepped out of the role of an ordinary carpenter and showed great wisdom when speaking, he was rejected and not listened to. How often do we reject people we think do not have knowledge or wisdom? Let us pray for a listening and open heart.

**Hebrews 12:18-19.21-24**

What you have come to is nothing known to the senses: not a blazing fire, or a gloom turning to total darkness, or a storm; or trumpeting thunder or the great voice speaking which made everyone that heard it beg that no more should be said to them. The whole scene was so terrible that Moses said: I am afraid, and was trembling with fright. But what you have come to is Mount Zion and the city of the living God, the heavenly Jerusalem where the millions of angels have gathered for the festival, with the whole Church in which everyone is a 'first-born son' and a citizen of heaven. You have come to God himself, the supreme Judge, and been placed with spirits of the saints who have been made perfect; and to Jesus, the mediator who brings a new covenant and a blood for purification which pleads more insistently than Abel's.

**Psalm 47:2-4.9-11. R. cf. v.10**

*O God, we ponder your love within your temple.*

**Mark 6:7-13**

Jesus made a tour round the villages, teaching. Then he summoned the Twelve and began to send them out in pairs giving them authority over the unclean spirits. And he instructed them to take nothing for the journey except a staff – no bread, no haversack, no coppers for their purses. They were to wear sandals but, he added, 'Do not take a spare tunic.' And he said to them, 'If you enter a house anywhere, stay there until you leave the district. And if any place does not welcome you and people refuse to listen to you, as you walk away shake off the dust from under your feet as a sign to them.' So they set off to preach repentance; and they cast out many devils, and anointed many sick people with oil and cured them.

**Reflection**

Jesus was organised! He had a message and he checked around the villages to see who needed help. Then in his thoughtfulness Jesus sent the Twelve out into the villages, giving them authority to speak, to heal, taking no extra worldly goods that would hold them back from being effective. If we are rejected, do not take it personally, just move on.

**4th Week
in Ordinary Time**
St Agatha *virgin, martyr*
Memorial
Red

**Hebrews 13:1-8**
*(See Appendix B-2)*

**Psalm 26:1.3.5.8-9. R. v.1**
*The Lord is my light and my help.*

**Mark 6:14-29**
King Herod had heard about Jesus, since by now his name was well-known. Some were saying, 'John the Baptist has risen from the dead, and that is why miraculous powers are at work in him.' Others said, 'He is Elijah'; others again, 'He is a prophet, like the prophets we used to have.' But when Herod heard this he said, 'It is John whose head I cut off; he has risen from the dead.'

Now it was this same Herod who had sent to have John arrested, and had him chained up in prison because of Herodias, his brother Philip's wife whom he had married. For John had told Herod, 'It is against the law for you to have your brother's wife.' As for Herodias, she was furious with him and wanted to kill him; but she was not able to, because Herod was afraid of John, knowing him to be a good and holy man, and gave him his protection. When he had heard him speak he was greatly perplexed, and yet he liked to listen to him.

An opportunity came on Herod's birthday when he gave a banquet for the nobles of his court, for his army officers and for the leading figures in Galilee. When the daughter of this same Herodias came in and danced, she delighted Herod and his guests; so the king said to the girl, 'Ask me anything you like and I will give it to you.' And he swore her an oath, 'I will give you anything you ask, even half my kingdom.' She went out and said to her mother, 'What shall I ask for?' She replied, 'The head of John the Baptist.' The girl hurried straight back to the king and made her request. 'I want you to give me John the Baptist's head, here and now, on a dish.'

The king was deeply distressed but, thinking of the oaths he had sworn and of his guests, was reluctant to break his word to her. So the king at once sent one of the bodyguard with orders to bring John's head. The man went off and beheaded him in prison; then he brought the head on a dish and gave it to the girl, and the girl gave it to her mother. When John's disciples heard about this, they came and took his body and laid it in a tomb.

## Reflection
Today we are remembering a young martyr who saw God as her 'Light and help' as reflected in the Responsorial Psalm. Then in the letter to the Hebrews we are encouraged strongly to love and to be thoughtful of others. It is easy to forget their suffering; to forget to be kind and thoughtful, yet when we reflect and practise kindness in welcoming the stranger, or thinking of the poor and the suffering, we become a 'Light' and we encourage others even without knowing it.

### Hebrews 13:15-17.20-21

Through Jesus, let us offer God an unending sacrifice of praise, a verbal sacrifice that is offered every time we acknowledge his name. Keep doing good works and sharing your resources, for these are sacrifices that please God.

Obey your leaders and do as they tell you, because they must give an account of the way they look after your souls; make this a joy for them to do, and not a grief – you yourselves would be the losers.

I pray that the God of peace, who brought our Lord Jesus back from the dead to become the great Shepherd of the sheep by the blood that sealed an eternal covenant, may make you ready to do his will in any kind of good action, and turn us all into whatever is acceptable to himself through Jesus Christ, to whom be glory for ever and ever, Amen.

### Psalm 22. R. v.1
*The Lord is my shepherd: there is nothing I shall want.*

### Mark 6:30-34

The apostles rejoined Jesus and told him all they had done and taught. Then he said to them, 'You must come away to some lonely place all by yourselves and rest for a while'; for there were so many coming and going that the apostles had no time even to eat. So they went off in a boat to a lonely place where they could be by themselves. But people saw them going, and many could guess where; and from every town they all hurried to the place on foot and reached it before them. So as he stepped ashore he saw a large crowd; and he took pity on them because they were like sheep without a shepherd, and he set himself to teach them at some length.

**4th Week
in Ordinary Time**
St Paul Miki, *priest*, and
his Companions, *martyrs*
Memorial
Red

### Reflection
So often we feel the need to be alone, away from the noise of people and machines. Jesus also had this need to be alone with the people who knew and understood him. Together they escaped, but they could not escape for long. People followed Jesus, they saw the Light in him, and Jesus did not disappoint them. He understood and spoke to them and listened to them with love.

## FEBRUARY
# 7
### SUNDAY

**5th Sunday
in Ordinary Time
Psalter Week 1
Green**

### Job 7:1-4.6-7

Job began to speak: Is not man's life on earth nothing more than pressed service, his time no better than hired drudgery? Like the slave, sighing for the shade, or the workman with no thought but his wages, months of delusion I have assigned to me, nothing for my own but nights of grief. Lying in bed I wonder, 'When will it be day?' Risen I think, 'How slowly evening comes!' Restlessly I fret till twilight falls. Swifter than a weaver's shuttle my days have passed, and vanished, leaving no hope behind. Remember that my life is but a breath, and that my eyes will never again see joy.

### Psalm 146:1-6. R. v.3

*Praise the Lord who heals the broken-hearted.* (or *Alleluia!*)

### 1 Corinthians 9:16-19.22-23

I do not boast of preaching the gospel, since it is a duty which has been laid on me; I should be punished if I did not preach it! If I had chosen this work myself, I might have been paid for it, but as I have not, it is a responsibility which has been put into my hands. Do you know what my reward is? It is this: in my preaching, to be able to offer the Good News free, and not insist on the rights which the gospel gives me.

So though I am not a slave of any man I have made myself the slave of everyone so as to win as many as I could. For the weak I made myself weak. I made myself all things to all men in order to save some at any cost; and I still do this, for the sake of the gospel, to have a share in its blessing.

### Mark 1:29-39

On leaving the synagogue, Jesus went with James and John straight to the house of Simon and Andrew. Now Simon's mother-in-law had gone to bed with fever, and they told him about her straightaway. He went to her, took her by the hand and helped her up. And the fever left her and she began to wait on them.

That evening, after sunset, they brought to him all who were sick and those who were possessed by devils. The whole town came crowding round the door, and he cured many who were suffering from diseases of one kind or another; he also cast out many devils, but he would not allow them to speak, because they knew who he was.

In the morning, long before dawn, he got up and left the house, and went off to a lonely place and prayed there. Simon and his companions set out in search of him, and when they found him they said, 'Everybody is looking for you.' He answered, 'Let us go elsewhere, to the neighbouring country towns, so that I can preach there too, because that is why I came.' And he went all through Galilee, preaching in their synagogues and casting out devils.

## Reflection

How quickly word spreads when a miracle happens. That is what happened in this account of Mark. Everyone wanted Jesus' attention and to be cured. Why did Jesus ask them not to speak about this? Jesus knew he had to be very careful about his "Messianic Secret". Jesus did not want people to get a false impression of his mission. So, Jesus went into the country towns to preach and tell the Good News, healing and casting out devils. Jesus did not restrict his miracles to only a few, but to all; his miracles were a manifestation of his 'Messiahship'.

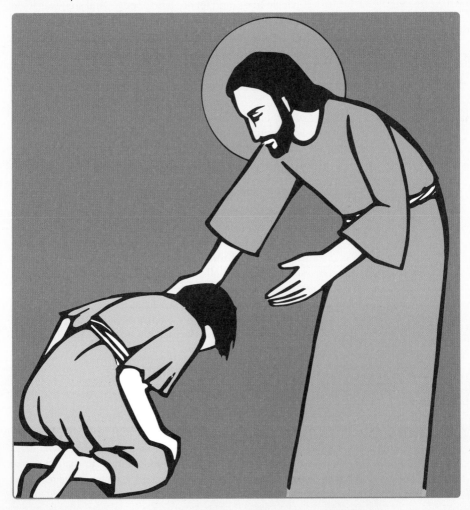

**5th Week
in Ordinary Time
Green
or
St Jerome Emiliani
(Optional, White)
St Josephine Bakhita,
*virgin*
(Optional, White)**

### Genesis 1:1-19

In the beginning God created the heavens and the earth. Now the earth was a formless void, there was darkness over the deep, and God's spirit hovered over the water.

God said, 'Let there be light, ' and there was light. God saw that light was good, and God divided light from darkness. God called light 'day', and darkness he called 'night'. Evening came and morning came: the first day.

God said, 'Let there be a vault in the waters to divide the waters in two.' And so it was. God made the vault, and it divided the waters above the vault from the waters under the vault. God called the vault 'heaven'. Evening came and morning came: the second day.

God said, 'Let the waters under heaven come together into a single mass, and let dry land appear.' And so it was. God called the dry land 'earth' and the mass of waters 'seas', and God saw that it was good.

God said, 'Let the earth produce vegetation: seed-bearing plants, and trees bearing fruit with their seed inside, on the earth.' And so it was. The earth produced vegetation: plants bearing seed in their several kinds, and trees bearing fruit with their seed inside in their several kinds. God saw that it was good. Evening came and morning came: the third day. *(See Appendix B-2)*

### Psalm 103:1-2.5-6.10.12.24.35. R. v.31

*May the Lord rejoice in his works!*

### Mark 6:53-56

Having made the crossing, Jesus and his disciples came to land at Gennesaret and tied up. No sooner had they stepped out of the boat than people recognised him, and started hurrying all through the countryside and brought the sick on stretchers to wherever they heard he was. And wherever he went, to village, or town, or farm, they laid down the sick in the open spaces, begging him to let them touch even the fringe of his cloak. And all those who touched him were cured.

### Reflection

The verses prior to this have Jesus walking on the water and telling his disciples not to be afraid. Then as they crossed the sea and landed at Gennesaret it was as if a loudspeaker was announcing that Jesus had landed. At no time did Jesus lose patience and say, 'I need space'. Jesus was very much available to attend to the sick and the hurt, to share the love of his Father to all. What an example for us all to go out to others even when we feel tired and overwhelmed by work and there are requests for help.

**Genesis 1:20–2:4**
*(See Appendix B-2)*

**Psalm 8:4-9. R. v.2**
*How great is your name, O Lord our God, through all the earth!*

**Mark 7:1-13**
The Pharisees and some of the scribes who had come from Jerusalem gathered round Jesus, and they noticed that some of his disciples were eating with unclean hands, that is, without washing them. For the Pharisees, and the Jews in general, follow the tradition of the elders and never eat without washing their arms as far as the elbow; and on returning from the market place they never eat without first sprinkling themselves. There are also many other observances which have been handed down to them concerning the washing of cups and pots and bronze dishes. So these Pharisees and scribes asked him, 'Why do your disciples not respect the tradition of the elders but eat their food with unclean hands?' He answered, 'It was of you hypocrites that Isaiah so rightly prophesied in this passage of scripture:

This people honours me only with lip-service, while their hearts are far from me. The worship they offer me is worthless, the doctrines they teach are only human regulations.

You put aside the commandment of God to cling to human traditions.' And he said to them, 'How ingeniously you get round the commandment of God in order to preserve your own tradition! For Moses said: Do your duty to your father and your mother, and, Anyone who curses father or mother must be put to death. But you say, "If a man says to his father or mother: Anything I have that I might have used to help you is Corban (that is, dedicated to God), then he is forbidden from that moment to do anything for his father or mother." In this way you make God's word null and void for the sake of your tradition which you have handed down. And you do many other things like this.'

## Reflection
The readings today flow with emphasis on the environment and care for the environment. Waters teem, earth produces. All are blessed by God. The Psalm praises God's name through all the earth. The earth and its environment also need care and the Gospel speaks of care of ourselves too, by washing our hands and arms, as far as the elbow; but it is not just washing the outside of the body, we are asked to be good within. Jesus is speaking about a 'clean heart', a heart that loves.

**5th Week
in Ordinary Time
St Scholastica,** *virgin*
**Memorial
White**

### Genesis 2:4-9.15-17

At the time when the Lord God made earth and heaven there was as yet no wild bush on the earth nor had any wild plant yet sprung up, for the Lord God had not sent rain on the earth, nor was there any man to till the soil. However, a flood was rising from the earth and watering all the surface of the soil. The Lord God fashioned man of dust from the soil. Then he breathed into his nostrils a breath of life, and thus man became a living being.

The Lord God planted a garden in Eden which is in the east, and there he put the man he had fashioned. The Lord God caused to spring up from the soil every kind of tree, enticing to look at and good to eat, with the tree of life and the tree of the knowledge of good and evil in the middle of the garden. The Lord God took the man and settled him in the garden of Eden to cultivate and take care of it. Then the Lord God gave the man this admonition, 'You may eat indeed of all the trees in the garden. Nevertheless of the tree of the knowledge of good and evil you are not to eat, for on the day you eat of it you shall most surely die.'

### Psalm 103:1-2.27-30. R. v.1

*Bless the Lord, my soul!*

### Mark 7:14-23

Jesus called the people to him again and said, 'Listen to me, all of you, and understand. Nothing that goes into a man from outside can make him unclean; it is the things that come out of a man that make him unclean. If anyone has ears to hear, let him listen to this.'

When he had gone back into the house, away from the crowd, his disciples questioned him about the parable. He said to them, 'Do you not understand either? Can you not see that whatever goes into a man from outside cannot make him unclean, because it does not go into his heart but through his stomach and passes out into the sewer?' (Thus he pronounced all foods clean.) And he went on, 'It is what comes out of a man that makes him unclean. For it is from within, from men's hearts, that evil intentions emerge: fornication, theft, murder, adultery, avarice, malice, deceit, indecency, envy, slander, pride, folly. All these evil things come from within and make a man unclean.'

### Reflection

Jesus' constant theme is love from the HEART. He even got frustrated when the people could not understand the depth of his message. The rules and regulations in Israel taught that one must wash, and in particular wash their hands and arms before eating. Jesus was speaking about what the heart is about, what is within a person. Is it a loving heart? Or is it a heart that does not care about love or loving others, a heart that is evil and cares only about what is seen and the 'good' impression they make.

## Genesis 2:18-25

The Lord God said, 'It is not good that the man should be alone. I will make him a helpmate.' So from the soil the Lord God fashioned all the wild beasts and all the birds of heaven. These he brought to the man to see what he would call them; each one was to bear the name the man would give it. The man gave names to all the cattle, all the birds of heaven, and all the wild beasts. But no helpmate suitable for man was found for him. So the Lord God made the man fall into a deep sleep. And while he slept, he took one of his ribs and enclosed it in flesh. The Lord God built the rib he had taken from the man into a woman, and brought her to the man. The man exclaimed:

'This at last is bone from my bones, and flesh from my flesh! This is to be called woman, for this was taken from man.' This is why a man leaves his father and mother and joins himself to his wife, and they become one body. Now both of them were naked, the man and his wife, but they felt no shame in front of each other.

## Psalm 127:1-5. R. cf. v.1

*O blessed are those who fear the Lord.*

## Mark 7:24-30

Jesus left Gennesaret and set out for the territory of Tyre. There he went into a house and did not want anyone to know he was there, but he could not pass unrecognised. A woman whose little daughter had an unclean spirit heard about him straightaway and came and fell at his feet. Now the woman was a pagan, by birth a Syrophoenician, and she begged him to cast the devil out of her daughter. And he said to her, 'The children should be fed first, because it is not fair to take the children's food and throw it to the house-dogs.' But she spoke up: 'Ah yes, sir, ' she replied 'but the house-dogs under the table can eat the children's scraps.' And he said to her, 'For saying this, you may go home happy: the devil has gone out of your daughter.' So she went off to her home and found the child lying on the bed and the devil gone.

## Reflection

The story of a Gentile woman of Syrophoenician origin is wonderful. She was a mother, and what do mothers do well? They love and protect their children, and that is their focus. Jesus certainly heard what she had to say. Sometimes when we pray, we can be direct as this mother was. Jesus does recognise her strength and love, and Jesus recognises also our love and faith. Of course, Jesus healed her daughter. Jesus cares for all of us, does not matter what faith we have. We are loved.

**5th Week
in Ordinary Time
Green**

### Genesis 3:1-8

The serpent was the most subtle of all the wild beasts that the Lord God had made. It asked the woman, 'Did God really say you were not to eat from any of the trees in the garden?' The woman answered the serpent, 'We may eat the fruit of the trees in the garden. But of the fruit of the tree in the middle of the garden God said, "You must not eat it, nor touch it, under pain of death."' Then the serpent said to the woman, 'No! You will not die! God knows in fact that on the day you eat it your eyes will be opened and you will be like gods, knowing good and evil.' The woman saw that the tree was good to eat and pleasing to the eye, and that it was desirable for the knowledge that it could give. So she took some of its fruit and ate it. She gave some also to her husband who was with her, and he ate it. Then the eyes of both of them were opened and they realised that they were naked. So they sewed fig-leaves together to make themselves loin-cloths.

The man and his wife heard the sound of the Lord God walking in the garden in the cool of the day, and they hid from the Lord God among the trees of the garden.

### Psalm 31:1-2.5-7. R. v.1

*Happy the man whose offence is forgiven.*

### Mark 7:31-37

Returning from the district of Tyre, Jesus went by way of Sidon towards the Sea of Galilee, right through the Decapolis region. And they brought him a deaf man who had an impediment in his speech; and they asked him to lay his hand on him. He took him aside in private, away from the crowd, put his fingers into the man's ears and touched his tongue with spittle. Then looking up to heaven he sighed; and he said to him, 'Ephphatha,' that is, 'Be opened.' And his ears were opened, and the ligament of his tongue was loosened and he spoke clearly. And Jesus ordered them to tell no one about it, but the more he insisted, the more widely they published it. Their admiration was unbounded. 'He has done all things well,' they said 'he makes the deaf hear and the dumb speak.'

### Reflection

In this Gospel, Jesus is seen to be 'earthy', not afraid to touch another, and through that 'touching' he brought about healing. Jesus also understands that the man was held back because of his speech. Today, in the 21stCentury, tongue-tie can be treated with a surgical cut to release the frenulum, (usually in babies who are born with tongue-tie). This man had not been treated and Jesus immediately knew what the problem was. Jesus was so lovingly practical.

## Genesis 3:9-24

The Lord God called to the man. 'Where are you?' he asked. 'I heard the sound of you in the garden, ' he replied 'I was afraid because I was naked, so I hid.' 'Who told you that you were naked?' he asked. 'Have you been eating of the tree I forbade you to eat?' The man replied, 'It was the woman you put with me; she gave me the fruit, and I ate it.' Then the Lord God asked the woman, 'What is this you have done?' The woman replied, 'The serpent tempted me and I ate.'

Then the Lord God said to the serpent, 'Because you have done this, 'Be accursed beyond all cattle, all wild beasts. You shall crawl on your belly and eat dust every day of your life. I will make you enemies of each other: you and the woman, your offspring and her offspring. It will crush your head and you will strike its heel.'
*(See Appendix B-3)*

## Psalm 89:2-6.12-13. R. v.1

*O Lord, you have been our refuge from one generation to the next.*

## Mark 8:1-10

A great crowd had gathered, and they had nothing to eat. So Jesus called his disciples to him and said to them, 'I feel sorry for all these people; they have been with me for three days now and have nothing to eat. If I send them off home hungry they will collapse on the way; some have come a great distance.' His disciples replied, 'Where could anyone get bread to feed these people in a deserted place like this?' He asked them, 'How many loaves have you?' 'Seven,' they said. Then he instructed the crowd to sit down on the ground, and he took the seven loaves, and after giving thanks he broke them and handed them to his disciples to distribute; and they distributed them among the crowd. They had a few small fish as well, and over these he said a blessing and ordered them to be distributed also. They ate as much as they wanted and they collected seven basketfuls of the scraps left over. Now there had been about four thousand people. He sent them away and immediately, getting into the boat with his disciples, went to the region of Dalmanutha.

## Reflection

Each day we are experiencing another story of Jesus' miracles and his practicality. How do we feed a large crowd with no food or shops to buy some? Not only is Jesus practical, he is organised. His questions to his Disciples and to the people are clear. How much food do we have? Sit down. Share what we have! Common sense and care. Miracles do happen even today when there is such care and common sense. There is always a way.

**6th Sunday
in Ordinary Time
Psalter Week 2
Green**

### Leviticus 13:1-2.44-46

The Lord said to Moses and Aaron, 'If a swelling or scab or shiny spot appears on a man's skin, a case of leprosy of the skin is to be suspected. The man must be taken to Aaron, the priest, or to one of the priests who are his sons.

'The man is leprous: he is unclean. The priest must declare him unclean; he is suffering from leprosy of the head. A man infected with leprosy must wear his clothing torn and his hair disordered; he must shield his upper lip and cry, "Unclean, unclean." As long as the disease lasts he must be unclean; and therefore he must live apart; he must live outside the camp.'

### Psalm 31:1-2.5.11. R. v.5

*You are my refuge, O Lord; you fill me with the joy of salvation.*

### 1 Corinthians 10:31–11:1

Whatever you eat, whatever you drink, whatever you do at all, do it for the glory of God. Never do anything offensive to anyone – to Jews or Greeks or to the Church of God; just as I try to be helpful to everyone at all times, not anxious for my own advantage but for the advantage of everybody else, so that they may be saved.

Take me for your model, as I take Christ.

### Mark 1:40-45

A leper came to Jesus and pleaded on his knees: 'If you want to' he said 'you can cure me.' Feeling sorry for him, Jesus stretched out his hand and touched him. 'Of course I want to!' he said. 'Be cured!' And the leprosy left him at once and he was cured. Jesus immediately sent him away and sternly ordered him, 'Mind you say nothing to anyone, but go and show yourself to the priest, and make the offering for your healing prescribed by Moses as evidence of your recovery.' The man went away, but then started talking about it freely and telling the story everywhere, so that Jesus could no longer go openly into any town, but had to stay outside in places where nobody lived. Even so, people from all around would come to him.

## Reflection

Both Leviticus and the Gospel of Mark tell us about illnesses. In Leviticus we read about the prevention of Infectious Diseases, in particular, 'Hansen's disease, then called Leprosy, which was a bacterial disease. In the Gospel we read of Jesus' great compassion and his healing of this dreaded disease. In Jesus' day it was very infectious and because there was no understanding of the disease, or of infection control, there was great fear. Jesus is teaching us not to fear, to be practical and be compassionate.

### Genesis 4:1-15.25

The man had intercourse with his wife Eve, and she conceived and gave birth to Cain. 'I have acquired a man with the help of the Lord' she said. She gave birth to a second child, Abel, the brother of Cain. Now Abel became a shepherd and kept flocks, while Cain tilled the soil. Time passed and Cain brought some of the produce of the soil as an offering for the Lord, while Abel for his part brought the first-born of his flock and some of their fat as well. The Lord looked with favour on Abel and his offering. But he did not look with favour on Cain and his offering, and Cain was very angry and downcast. The Lord asked Cain, 'Why are you angry and downcast? If you are well disposed, ought you not to lift up your head? But if you are ill disposed, is not sin at the door like a crouching beast hungering for you, which you must master?' Cain said to his brother Abel, 'Let us go out'; and while they were in the open country, Cain set on his brother Abel and killed him.

The Lord asked Cain, 'Where is your brother Abel?' 'I do not know' he replied. 'Am I my brother's guardian?' 'What have you done?' the Lord asked. 'Listen to the sound of your brother's blood, crying out to me from the ground. Now be accursed and driven from the ground that has opened its mouth to receive your brother's blood at your hands. When you till the ground it shall no longer yield you any of its produce. ... *(See Appendix B-3)*

### Psalm 49:1.8.16-17.20-21. R. v.14

*Pay your sacrifice of thanksgiving to God.*

### Mark 8:11-13

The Pharisees came up and started a discussion with Jesus; they demanded of him a sign from heaven, to test him. And with a sigh that came straight from the heart he said, 'Why does this generation demand a sign? I tell you solemnly, no sign shall be given to this generation.' And leaving them again and re-embarking he went away to the opposite shore.

### Reflection

"A sigh that came straight from the heart". Oh! Jesus, the depth of that sigh. What is happening? Why are they demanding a sign? Is there any faith in this generation? We well may ask that today. Where is our Faith? If there are problems and we cannot solve them, do we lose hope? Speak to Jesus and tell Him. But, do listen to what Jesus has to say to you. Can we hear him? Are we listening to Jesus?

## Genesis 6:5-8; 7:1-5.10

The Lord saw that the wickedness of man was great on the earth, and that the thoughts in his heart fashioned nothing but wickedness all day long. The Lord regretted having made man on the earth, and his heart grieved. 'I will rid the earth's face of man, my own creation, ' the Lord said 'and of animals also, reptiles too, and the birds of heaven; for I regret having made them.' But Noah had found favour with the Lord.

The Lord said to Noah, 'Go aboard the ark, you and all your household, for you alone among this generation do I see as a good man in my judgement. Of all the clean animals you must take seven of each kind, both male and female; of the unclean animals you must take two, a male and its female (and of the birds of heaven also, seven of each kind, both male and female), to propagate their kind over the whole earth. For in seven days' time I mean to make it rain on the earth for forty days and nights, and I will rid the earth of every living thing that I made.' Noah did all that the Lord ordered.

Seven days later the waters of the flood appeared on the earth.

## Psalm 28:1-4.9-10. R. v.11
*The Lord will bless his people with peace.*

## Mark 8:14-21

The disciples had forgotten to take any food and they had only one loaf with them in the boat. Then Jesus gave them this warning, 'Keep your eyes open; be on your guard against the yeast of the Pharisees and the yeast of Herod.' And they said to one another, 'It is because we have no bread.' And Jesus knew it, and he said to them, 'Why are you talking about having no bread? Do you not yet understand? Have you no perception? Are your minds closed? Have you eyes that do not see, ears that do not hear? Or do you not remember? When I broke the five loaves among the five thousand, how many baskets full of scraps did you collect?' They answered, 'Twelve.' 'And when I broke the seven loaves for the four thousand, how many baskets full of scraps did you collect?' And they answered, 'Seven'. Then he said to them, 'Are you still without perception?'

## Reflection

Just a few verses back Mark described the feeding of the four thousand. Did the disciples not only forget their food, but also the lesson they learnt from then? Jesus burst out in frustration, "Do you not yet understand? Have you no perception?" Sometimes we feel today that we have problems. What can Jesus do to help the disciples? He teaches them, he shares food with them. What more can he do? "Jesus, teach us to listen, to hear your message, to be thoughtful of others."

**Ash Wednesday**
**Violet**

**Joel 2:12-18**
*(See Appendix B-4)*

**Psalm 50:3-6.12-14.17. R. v.3**
*Have mercy on us, O Lord, for we have sinned.*

**2 Corinthians 5:20–6:2**
We are ambassadors for Christ; it is as though God were appealing through us, and the appeal that we make in Christ's name is: be reconciled to God. For our sake God made the sinless one into sin, so that in him we might become the goodness of God. As his fellow workers, we beg you once again not to neglect the grace of God that you have received. For he says: At the favourable time, I have listened to you; on the day of salvation I came to your help. Well, now is the favourable time; this is the day of salvation.

**Matthew 6:1-6.16-18**
Jesus said to his disciples:

'Be careful not to parade your good deeds before men to attract their notice; by doing this you will lose all reward from your Father in heaven. So when you give alms, do not have it trumpeted before you; this is what the hypocrites do in the synagogues and in the streets to win men's admiration. I tell you solemnly, they have had their reward. But when you give alms, your left hand must not know what your right is doing; your almsgiving must be secret, and your Father who sees all that is done in secret will reward you.

'And when you pray, do not imitate the hypocrites: they love to say their prayers standing up in the synagogues and at the street corners for people to see them. I tell you solemnly, they have had their reward. But when you pray go to your private room and, when you have shut your door, pray to your Father who is in that secret place, and your Father who sees all that is done in secret will reward you.

'When you fast do not put on a gloomy look as the hypocrites do: they pull long faces to let men know they are fasting. I tell you solemnly, they have had their reward. But when you fast, put oil on your head and wash your face, so that no one will know you are fasting except your Father who sees all that is done in secret; and your Father who sees all that is done in secret will reward you.'

### Reflection
'Your Father who sees all that is done in secret will reward you.' This Gospel is so full of basic commonsense messages for living only for God. Certainly, do good works, help others, but do it with a graciousness that is quiet, unobtrusive, and generous. Even in Jesus' day, the disciples wanted to show others how good they were in helping others. Jesus is telling us to give naturally. Venerable Mary Potter wrote, "All we do is for God, and if no one sees what we do but God, so much the better." (*Mary's Conferences – Little Company of Mary*).

## Deuteronomy 30:15-20

Moses said to the people: 'See, today I set before you life and prosperity, death and disaster. If you obey the commandments of the Lord your God that I enjoin on you today, if you love the Lord your God and follow his ways, if you keep his commandments, his laws, his customs, you will live and increase, and the Lord your God will bless you in the land which you are entering to make your own. But if your heart strays, if you refuse to listen, if you let yourself be drawn into worshipping other gods and serving them, I tell you today, you will most certainly perish; you will not live long in the land you are crossing the Jordan to enter and possess. I call heaven and earth to witness against you today: I set before you life or death, blessing or curse. Choose life, then, so that you and your descendants may live in the love of the Lord your God, obeying his voice, clinging to him; for in this your life consists, and on this depends your long stay in the land which the Lord swore to your fathers Abraham, Isaac and Jacob he would give them.

## Psalm 1:1-4.6. R. Psalm 39:5

*Happy the man who has placed his trust in the Lord.*

## Luke 9:22-25

Jesus said to his disciples: 'The Son of Man is destined to suffer grievously, to be rejected by the elders and chief priests and scribes and to be put to death, and to be raised up on the third day.'

Then to all he said, 'If anyone wants to be a follower of mine, let him renounce himself and take up his cross every day and follow me. For anyone who wants to save his life will lose it; but anyone who loses his life for my sake, that man will save it. What gain, then, is it for a man to have won the whole world and to have lost or ruined his very self?'

**Thursday after Ash Wednesday**
**Violet**

## Reflection

We are constantly offered choices in life. What do we do, how do we choose? Very clearly, in Deuteronomy we are called to CHOOSE LIFE. Choose God, to follow the voice of God, being constantly aware of the message we have been given. We know that it is not always easy to do this, especially when we are tempted to take the 'easy way out.' We have choices and God is offering us the choice of life. We know that when we choose life, we choose God.

**Friday after
Ash Wednesday
Violet**

### Isaiah 58:1-9
Thus says the Lord:

Shout for all you are worth, raise your voice like a trumpet. Proclaim their faults to my people, their sins to the House of Jacob. They seek me day after day, they long to know my ways, like a nation that wants to act with integrity and not ignore the law of its God. They ask me for laws that are just, they long for God to draw near: 'Why should we fast if you never see it, why do penance if you never notice?' Look, you do business on your fastdays, you oppress all your workmen; look, you quarrel and squabble when you fast and strike the poor man with your fist. Fasting like yours today will never make your voice heard on high. Is that the sort of fast that pleases me, a truly penitential day for men? Hanging your head like a reed, lying down on sackcloth and ashes? Is that what you call fasting, a day acceptable to the Lord? Is not this the sort of fast that pleases me – it is the Lord who speaks – to break unjust fetters and undo the thongs of the yoke, to let the oppressed go free, and break every yoke, to share your bread with the hungry, and shelter the homeless poor, to clothe the man you see to be naked and not turn from your own kin? Then will your light shine like the dawn and your wound be quickly healed over. Your integrity will go before you and the glory of the Lord behind you. Cry, and the Lord will answer; call, and he will say, 'I am here.'

### Psalm 50:3-6.18-19. R. v.19
*A humbled, contrite heart, O God, you will not spurn.*

### Matthew 9:14-15
John's disciples came to Jesus and said, 'Why is it that we and the Pharisees fast, but your disciples do not?' Jesus replied, 'Surely the bridegroom's attendants would never think of mourning as long as the bridegroom is still with them? But the time will come for the bridegroom to be taken away from them, and then they will fast.'

### Reflection
There are many ways to fast. Just reflect on the fasting of the homeless, the hungry. They need feeding, company and love. Their fasting may not be by choice, that is their life. Then there is the fasting of our behaviour towards our neighbour. Are we just? Is fasting making you irritable? We are called to act with integrity, to show love and understanding, even when we fast. As Jesus said, there is a time to fast, and when we do fast do it with love.

## Isaiah 58:9-14

The Lord says this:

If you do away with the yoke, the clenched fist, the wicked word, if you give your bread to the hungry, and relief to the oppressed, your light will rise in the darkness, and your shadows become like noon. The Lord will always guide you, giving you relief in desert places. He will give strength to your bones and you shall be like a watered garden, like a spring of water whose waters never run dry. You will rebuild the ancient ruins, build up on the old foundations. You will be called 'Breach-mender', 'Restorer of ruined houses'. If you refrain from trampling the sabbath, and doing business on the holy day, if you call the sabbath 'Delightful' and the day sacred to the Lord 'Honourable', if you honour it by abstaining from travel, from doing business and from gossip, then you shall find happiness in the Lord and I will lead you triumphant over the heights of the land. I will feed you on the heritage of Jacob your father. For the mouth of the Lord has spoken.

## Psalm 85:1-6. R. v.11

*Show me, Lord, your way so that I may walk in your truth.*

## Luke 5:27-32

Jesus noticed a tax collector, Levi by name, sitting by the customs house, and said to him, 'Follow me.' And leaving everything he got up and followed him.

In his honour Levi held a great reception in his house, and with them at table was a large gathering of tax collectors and others. The Pharisees and their scribes complained to his disciples and said, 'Why do you eat and drink with tax collectors and sinners?' Jesus said to them in reply, 'It is not those who are well who need the doctor, but the sick. I have not come to call the virtuous, but sinners to repentance.'

**Saturday after
Ash Wednesday
Violet**

## Reflection

How comforting it is to know that Jesus did not judge others. He only showed love and acceptance. Levi was obviously so taken up with Jesus that he held a reception in his house to honour him. All the tax collectors and his friends were there. Then the judgement of others came! Jesus did not worry; he knew the inner goodness of Levi and Levi felt accepted and was able to follow Jesus. Forgiveness and love bring out the best in all of us.

**1st Sunday of Lent**
**Psalter Week 1**
**Violet**

### Genesis 9:8-15

God spoke to Noah and his sons, 'See, I establish my Covenant with you, and with your descendants after you; also with every living creature to be found with you, birds, cattle and every wild beast with you: everything that came out of the ark, everything that lives on the earth. I establish my Covenant with you: no thing of flesh shall be swept away again by the waters of the flood. There shall be no flood to destroy the earth again.'

God said, 'Here is the sign of the Covenant I make between myself and you and every living creature with you for all generations: I set my bow in the clouds and it shall be a sign of the Covenant between me and the earth. When I gather the clouds over the earth and the bow appears in the clouds, I will recall the Covenant between myself and you and every living creature of every kind. And so the waters shall never again become a flood to destroy all things of flesh.'

### Psalm 24:4-9. R. cf. v.10

*Your ways, Lord, are faithfulness and love for those who keep your covenant.*

### 1 Peter 3:18-22

Christ himself, innocent though he was, died once for sins, died for the guilty, to lead us to God. In the body he was put to death, in the spirit he was raised to life, and, in the spirit, he went to preach to the spirits in prison. Now it was long ago, when Noah was still building that ark which saved only a small group of eight people 'by water', and when God was still waiting patiently, that these spirits refused to believe. That water is a type of the baptism which saves you now, and which is not the washing off of physical dirt but a pledge made to God from a good conscience, through the resurrection of Jesus Christ, who has entered heaven and is at God's right hand, now that he has made the angels and Dominations and Powers his subjects.

### Mark 1:12-15

The Spirit drove Jesus out into the wilderness and he remained there for forty days, and was tempted by Satan. He was with the wild beasts, and the angels looked after him.

After John had been arrested, Jesus went into Galilee. There he proclaimed the Good News from God. 'The time has come' he said 'and the kingdom of God is close at hand. Repent, and believe the Good News.'

## Reflection

"Jesus was tempted, and the angels looked after him." How often have we been out in the wilderness feeling all alone? Danger all around and no escape. This is the time for us to call out and ask for help. This demands trust and courage. Yes, Jesus is there to help, Jesus has always said He will be with us to help us. Let us reflect on the times this has happened, and then pray that we will be alert in the future to ask for help. It will not be refused.

## FEBRUARY

# 22

**MONDAY**

**Chair of St Peter,**
*apostle*
**Feast**
**White**

**1 Peter 5:1-4**

I have something to tell your elders: I am an elder myself, and a witness to the sufferings of Christ, and with you I have a share in the glory that is to be revealed. Be the shepherds of the flock of God that is entrusted to you: watch over it, not simply as a duty but gladly, because God wants it; not for sordid money, but because you are eager to do it. Never be a dictator over any group that is put in your charge, but be an example that the whole flock can follow. When the chief shepherd appears, you will be given the crown of unfading glory.

**Psalm 22. R. v.1**

*The Lord is my shepherd; there is nothing I shall want.*

**Matthew 16:13-19**

When Jesus came to the region of Caesarea Philippi he put this question to his disciples, 'Who do people say the Son of Man is?' And they said, 'Some say he is John the Baptist, some Elijah, and others Jeremiah or one of the prophets.' 'But you, ' he said, 'who do you say I am?' Then Simon Peter spoke up, 'You are the Christ, ' he said, 'the Son of the Living God.' Jesus replied, 'Simon son of Jonah, you are a happy man! Because it was not flesh and blood that revealed this to you but my Father in heaven. So I now say to you: You are Peter and on this rock I will build my Church. And the gates of the underworld can never hold out against it. I will give you the keys of the kingdom of heaven: whatever you bind on earth shall be considered bound in heaven; whatever you loose on earth shall be considered loosed in heaven.'

**Reflection**

Clearly the readings for this feast of St Peter's Chair are giving instructions on how to lead. Good leadership comes not from personal power, but the right attitude, not looking for money, not being a dictator, but from the right intentions of leading people like the One who leads us always in the right direction. Jesus was teaching the disciples how to lead, not by money or power, but by the love of God. What a good teacher. When I am in leadership situations, how do I deal with people? Do I listen, do I respect the other?

Isaiah 55:10-11
Thus says the Lord:

As the rain and the snow come down from the heavens and do not return without watering the earth, making it yield and giving growth to provide seed for the sower and bread for the eating, so the word that goes from my mouth does not return to me empty, without carrying out my will and succeeding in what it was sent to do.

Psalm 33:4-7.16-19. R. v.18
*The Lord rescues the just in all their distress.*

Matthew 6:7-15
Jesus said to his disciples: 'In your prayers do not babble as the pagans do, for they think that by using many words they will make themselves heard. Do not be like them; your Father knows what you need before you ask him. So you should pray like this: 'Our Father in heaven, may your name be held holy, your kingdom come, your will be done, on earth as in heaven. Give us today our daily bread. And forgive us our debts, as we have forgiven those who are in debt to us. And do not put us to the test, but save us from the evil one.

'Yes, if you forgive others their failings, your heavenly Father will forgive you yours; but if you do not forgive others, your Father will not forgive your failings either.'

**1st Week of Lent**
Violet
or
**St Polycarp,** *bishop,*
*martyr*
**(Commemoration)**

### Reflection
The 'Our Father' is a prayer that if said slowly with thought can cause us to be vulnerable and open to change. This is a prayer to 'Our Father', it is a prayer for all people, not just Christians. Yes, this is challenging when we reflect on how Jesus prayed to his Father in Heaven; he prayed with trust, with love and he prayed for all. We have been invited to call God 'Our Father' 'Abba', what a gift. This prayer then leads us to giving praise, honour and respect to God, while at the same time, asking for help in our lives.

**1st Week of Lent**
**Violet**

### Jonah 3:1-10

The word of the Lord was addressed to Jonah: 'Up!' he said, 'Go to Nineveh, the great city, and preach to them as I told you to.' Jonah set out and went to Nineveh in obedience to the word of the Lord. Now Nineveh was a city great beyond compare: it took three days to cross it. Jonah went on into the city, making a day's journey. He preached in these words, 'Only forty days more and Nineveh is going to be destroyed.' And the people of Nineveh believed in God; they proclaimed a fast and put on sackcloth, from the greatest to the least. The news reached the king of Nineveh, who rose from his throne, took off his robe, put on sackcloth and sat down in ashes. A proclamation was then promulgated throughout Nineveh, by decree of the king and his ministers, as follows: 'Men and beasts, herds and flocks, are to taste nothing; they must not eat, they must not drink water. All are to put on sackcloth and call on God with all their might; and let everyone renounce his evil behaviour and the wicked things he has done. Who knows if God will not change his mind and relent, if he will not renounce his burning wrath, so that we do not perish?' God saw their efforts to renounce their evil behaviour. And God relented: he did not inflict on them the disaster which he had threatened.

### Psalm 50:3-4.12-13.18-19. R. v.19

*A humbled, contrite heart, O God, you will not spurn.*

### Luke 11:29-32

The crowds got even bigger and Jesus addressed them. 'This is a wicked generation; it is asking for a sign. The only sign it will be given is the sign of Jonah. For just as Jonah became a sign to the Ninevites, so will the Son of Man be to this generation. On Judgement day the Queen of the South will rise up with the men of this generation and condemn them, because she came from the ends of the earth to hear the wisdom of Solomon; and there is something greater than Solomon here. On Judgement day the men of Nineveh will stand up with this generation and condemn it, because when Jonah preached they repented; and there is something greater than Jonah here.'

### Reflection

Do we believe because we see signs? Jesus is speaking about a depth of faith, a faith that does not look for signs. The Gospels speak of love, love of God and of neighbour. How can we show love if all we see and call for are signs? Sometimes in our insecurity we do ask for signs, it helps our 'certainty' of God. Yet, we are called to let go of looking for proof of God's existence and to just believe. Jesus tells us that the real sign is himself. In him God has become a human being, and one who sees him, sees the Father.

## Esther 4:17

Queen Esther took refuge with the Lord in the mortal peril which had overtaken her. She besought the Lord God of Israel in these words: 'My Lord, our King, the only one, come to my help, for I am alone and have no helper but you and am about to take my life in my hands. 'I have been taught from my earliest years, in the bosom of my family, that you, Lord, chose Israel out of all the nations and our ancestors out of all the people of old times to be your heritage for ever; and that you have treated them as you promised. Remember, Lord; reveal yourself in the time of our distress. 'As for me, give me courage, King of gods and master of all power. Put persuasive words into my mouth when I face the lion; change his feeling into hatred for our enemy, that the latter and all like him may be brought to their end. 'As for ourselves, save us by your hand, and come to my help, for I am alone and have no one but you, Lord.'

## Psalm 137:1-3.7-8. R. v.3

*On the day I called, you answered me, O Lord.*

## Matthew 7:7-12

Jesus said to his disciples; 'Ask, and it will be given to you; search, and you will find; knock, and the door will be opened to you. For the one who asks always receives; the one who searches always finds; the one who knocks will always have the door opened to him. Is there a man among you who would hand his son a stone when he asked for bread? Or would hand him a snake when he asked for a fish? If you, then, who are evil, know how to give your children what is good, how much more will your Father in heaven give good things to those who ask him!

'So always treat others as you would like them to treat you; that is the meaning of the Law and the Prophets.'

## Reflection

"I am alone, Lord, and have no one but you" (Esther 4). "Ask, and it will be given to you" (Matthew 7). Such a real prayer, so often spoken by each one of us. Crying out for help. The response so warm. Jesus just tells us to ask. This asking does leave us vulnerable, because we must acknowledge our need. Do we believe that the door will be opened? This asking does require humility, I cannot do it on my own. How will God answer my prayer? Leave that to God. It does not help to treat God as 'magic', this is not the message. God knows what we need before we ask. We need to ask God, that is part of our humanity. When we ask, leave it with God in trust.

**Ezekiel 18:21-28**

Thus says the Lord God: 'If the wicked man renounces all the sins he has committed, respects my laws and is law-abiding and honest, he will certainly live; he will not die. All the sins he committed will be forgotten from then on; he shall live because of the integrity he has practised. What! Am I likely to take pleasure in the death of a wicked man – it is the Lord who speaks – and not prefer to see him renounce his wickedness and live?

'But if the upright man renounces his integrity, commits sin, copies the wicked man and practises every kind of filth, is he to live? All the integrity he has practised shall be forgotten from then on; but this is because he himself has broken faith and committed sin, and for this he shall die. But you object, "What the Lord does is unjust." Listen, you House of Israel: is what I do unjust? Is it not what you do that is unjust? When the upright man renounces his integrity to commit sin and dies because of this, he dies because of the evil that he himself has committed. When the sinner renounces sin to become law-abiding and honest, he deserves to live. He has chosen to renounce all his previous sins, he shall certainly live; he shall not die.'

**Psalm 129. R. v.3**

*If you, O Lord, should mark our guilt, Lord, who would survive?*

**Matthew 5:20-26**

Jesus said to his disciples: 'If your virtue goes no deeper than that of the scribes and Pharisees, you will never get into the kingdom of heaven.

'You have learnt how it was said to our ancestors: You must not kill, and if anyone does kill he must answer for it before the court. But I say this to you: anyone who is angry with his brother will answer for it before the court; if a man calls his brother "Fool" he will answer for it before the Sanhedrin, and if a man calls him "Renegade" he will answer for it in hell fire. So then, if you are bringing your offering to the altar and there remember that your brother has something against you, leave your offering there before the altar, go and be reconciled with your brother first, and then come back and present your offering. Come to terms with your opponent in good time while you are still on the way to the court with him, or he may hand you over to the judge and the judge to the officer, and you will be thrown into prison. I tell you solemnly, you will not get out till you have paid the last penny.'

**Reflection**

These readings are very clearly about integrity. We all must make choices, and some choices we make can be less than responsible. Jesus gives us examples of how to make good choices and be people of integrity and people of life. Even giving us words of wisdom about coming to terms in forgiving in good time so we do not regret our actions and cause further stress. Today, this example is so relevant and such a good example of common sense and forgiveness.

## FEBRUARY
# 27
**SATURDAY**

**1st Week of Lent**
**Violet**

### Deuteronomy 26:16-19
Moses said to the people: 'The Lord your God today commands you to observe these laws and customs; you must keep and observe them with all your heart and with all your soul.

'You have today made this declaration about the Lord; that he will be your God, but only if you follow his ways, keep his statutes, his commandments, his ordinances, and listen to his voice. And the Lord has today made this declaration about you: that you will be his very own people as he promised you, but only if you keep all his commandments; then for praise and renown and honour he will set you high above all the nations he has made, and you will be a people consecrated to the Lord, as he promised.'

### Psalm 118:1-2.4-5.7-8. R. v.1
*They are happy who follow God's law!*

### Matthew 5:43-48
Jesus said to his disciples: 'You have learnt how it was said: You must love your neighbour and hate your enemy. But I say this to you: love your enemies and pray for those who persecute you; in this way you will be sons of your Father in heaven, for he causes his sun to rise on bad men as well as good, and his rain to fall on honest and dishonest men alike. For if you love those who love you, what right have you to claim any credit? Even the tax collectors do as much, do they not? And if you save your greetings for your brothers, are you doing anything exceptional? Even the pagans do as much, do they not? You must therefore be perfect just as your heavenly Father is perfect.'

### Reflection
Jesus was asking his disciples to go one step further in showing kindness. Go further than the standards of the day, go deeper than today's standards. We, too, are asked to go deeper in loving our neighbour especially those who do not like us. It is so easy to love those who love us. What about those people who irritate us, or disregard us? How do I let go the hurt and the sense of being disliked? This is hard, but this is the message of Jesus, 'Love one another'.

**2nd Sunday of Lent**
Psalter Week 2
Violet

**Genesis 22:1-2.9-13.15-18**

God put Abraham to the test. 'Abraham, Abraham' he called. 'Here I am' he replied. 'Take your son', God said 'your only child Isaac, whom you love, and go to the land of Moriah. There you shall offer him as a burnt offering, on a mountain I will point out to you.'

When they arrived at the place God had pointed out to him, Abraham built an altar there and arranged the wood. Then he stretched out his hand and seized the knife to kill his son.

But the angel of the Lord called to him from heaven. 'Abraham, Abraham' he said. 'I am here' he replied. 'Do not raise your hand against the boy' the angel said. 'Do not harm him, for now I know you fear God. You have not refused me your son, your only son.' Then looking up, Abraham saw a ram caught by its horns in a bush. Abraham took the ram and offered it as a burnt-offering in place of his son.

The angel of the Lord called Abraham a second time from heaven. 'I swear by my own self – it is the Lord who speaks – because you have done this, because you have not refused me your son, your only son, I will shower blessings on you, I will make your descendants as many as the stars of heaven and the grains of sand on the seashore. Your descendants shall gain possession of the gates of their enemies. All the nations of the earth shall bless themselves by your descendants, as a reward for your obedience.'

**Psalm 115:10.15-19 R. Psalm 114:9**
*I will walk in the presence of the Lord in the land of the living.*

**Romans 8:31-34**
With God on our side who can be against us? Since God did not spare his own Son, but gave him up to benefit us all, we may be certain, after such a gift, that he will not refuse anything he can give. Could anyone accuse those that God has chosen? When God acquits, could anyone condemn? Could Christ Jesus? No! He not only died for us – he rose from the dead, and there at God's right hand he stands and pleads for us.

**Mark 9:2-10**
Jesus took with him Peter and James and John and led them up a high mountain where they could be alone by themselves. There in their presence he was transfigured: his clothes became dazzlingly white, whiter than any earthly bleacher could make them. Elijah appeared to them with Moses; and they were talking with Jesus. Then Peter spoke to Jesus. 'Rabbi', he said 'it is wonderful for us to be here; so let us make three tents, one for you, one for Moses and one for Elijah'. He did not know what to say; they were so frightened. And a cloud came, covering them in shadow; and there came a voice from the cloud, 'This is my Son, the Beloved. Listen to him'. Then suddenly, when they looked round, they saw no one with them any more but only Jesus.

As they came down the mountain he warned them to tell no one what they had seen, until after the Son of Man had risen from the dead. They observed the warning faithfully, though among themselves they discussed what 'rising from the dead' could mean.

**Reflection**
Imagine the height of the mountain, the silence, being with Jesus. What happened? The apostles saw Jesus absorbed in prayer to his Father. His face radiant. Peter was so moved to be there especially as he saw Jesus' face, that he started to talk too much, probably from fright and nervousness. Jesus was in prayer in complete communion with his Father. For the apostles to see their friend Jesus in such radiance moved them deeply. Sometimes in prayer, there is no need for words, just silence. 'This is my Son, the Beloved, Listen to him.'

## MARCH

# 1

## MONDAY

**2nd Week of Lent**
Violet
or
**Saint David, Bishop**
**Wales – Solemnity**
*(See Appendix A-3)*
**England - Feast**
*(See Appendix A-4)*

**Daniel 9:4-10**

O Lord, God great and to be feared, you keep the covenant and have kindness for those who love you and keep your commandments: we have sinned, we have done wrong, we have acted wickedly, we have betrayed your commandments and your ordinances and turned away from them. We have not listened to your servants the prophets, who spoke in your name to our kings, our princes, our ancestors, and to all the people of the land. Integrity, Lord, is yours; ours the look of shame we wear today, we, the people of Judah, the citizens of Jerusalem, the whole of Israel, near and far away, in every country to which you have dispersed us because of the treason we have committed against you. To us, Lord, the look of shame belongs, to our kings, our princes, our ancestors, because we have sinned against you. To the Lord our God mercy and pardon belong, because we have betrayed him, and have not listened to the voice of the Lord our God nor followed the laws he has given us through his servants the prophets.

**Psalm 78:8-9.11.13. R. Psalm 102:10**
*Lord, do not deal with us as our sins deserve.*

**Luke 6:36-38**

Jesus said to his disciples: 'Be compassionate as your Father is compassionate. Do not judge, and you will not be judged yourselves; do not condemn, and you will not be condemned yourselves; grant pardon, and you will be pardoned. Give, and there will be gifts for you: a full measure, pressed down, shaken together, and running over, will be poured into your lap; because the amount you measure out is the amount you will be given back.'

## Reflection

'Ours is the look of shame we wear today.' As a church community we have much to feel ashamed about, especially the abuse of the most vulnerable in our midst – the young, the elderly, the mentally ill, people with disabilities. Sadly, there are people who carry the shame of circumstances over which they were never responsible. There is the shame of the sinner and the shame of the victim. Psychologists tell us that shame can be transforming if we engage with it in a constructive way, and we see this happening in today's first reading from Daniel. Acknowledging the shame can make possible a greater understanding of our self and others, greater empathy and compassion, and a heightened awareness of injustice. The season of Lent is a good time to acknowledge any feelings of shame we may be experiencing; to seek forgiveness if sin is at the base of our shame; and to reach out in compassion to anyone we know who may be weighed down by a personal shame.

### Isaiah 1:10.16-20

Hear the word of the Lord, you rulers of Sodom; listen to the command of our God, you people of Gomorrah. 'Wash, make yourselves clean. Take your wrong-doing out of my sight. Cease to do evil. Learn to do good, search for justice, help the oppressed, be just to the orphan, plead for the widow. Come now, let us talk this over, says the Lord. Though your sins are like scarlet, they shall be as white as snow; though they are red as crimson, they shall be like wool. If you are willing to obey, you shall eat the good things of the earth. But if you persist in rebellion, the sword shall eat you instead.' The mouth of the Lord has spoken.

### Psalm 49:8-9.16-17.21.23. R. v.23

*I will show God's salvation to the upright.*

### Matthew 23:1-12

Addressing the people and his disciples Jesus said, 'The scribes and the Pharisees occupy the chair of Moses. You must therefore do what they tell you and listen to what they say; but do not be guided by what they do, since they do not practise what they preach. They tie up heavy burdens and lay them on men's shoulders, but will they lift a finger to move them? Not they! Everything they do is done to attract attention, like wearing broader phylacteries and longer tassels, like wanting to take the place of honour at banquets and the front seats in the synagogues, being greeted obsequiously in the market squares and having people call them Rabbi.

'You, however, must not allow yourselves to be called Rabbi, since you have only one Master, and you are all brothers. You must call no one on earth your father, since you have only one Father, and he is in heaven. Nor must you allow yourselves to be called teachers, for you have only one Teacher, the Christ. The greatest among you must be your servant. Anyone who exalts himself will be humbled, and anyone who humbles himself will be exalted.'

### Reflection

Holiness of life as demanded of us this Lenten season and always does not happen by mistake. Holiness is driven by a conscious decision backed up with prayers and good works. One needs God's grace in order to cleanse oneself of past offences and keep the struggle for sanctity of life. A deep reflection on what life is all about and a humble image of oneself would be of great benefit in one's spiritual renewal and growth.

### Jeremiah 18:18-20

'Come on, ' they said 'let us concoct a plot against Jeremiah; the priest will not run short of instruction without him, nor the sage of advice, nor the prophet of the word. Come on, let us hit at him with his own tongue; let us listen carefully to every word he says.'

Listen to me, Lord, hear what my adversaries are saying. Should evil be returned for good? For they are digging a pit for me. Remember how I stood in your presence to plead on their behalf, to turn your wrath away from them.

### Psalm 30:5-6.14-16. R. v.17
*Save me in your love, O Lord.*

### Matthew 20:17-28

Jesus was going up to Jerusalem, and on the way he took the Twelve to one side and said to them, 'Now we are going up to Jerusalem, and the Son of Man is about to be handed over to the chief priests and scribes. They will condemn him to death and will hand him over to the pagans to be mocked and scourged and crucified; and on the third day he will rise again.'

Then the mother of Zebedee's sons came with her sons to make a request of him, and bowed low; and he said to her, 'What is it you want?' She said to him, 'Promise that these two sons of mine may one sit at your right hand and the other at your left in your kingdom.' 'You do not know what you are asking, Jesus answered. 'Can you drink the cup that I am going to drink?' They replied, 'We can.' 'Very well, ' he said 'you shall drink my cup, but as for seats at my right hand and my left, these are not mine to grant; they belong to those to whom they have been allotted by my Father.'

When the other ten heard this they were indignant with the two brothers. But Jesus called them to him and said, 'You know that among the pagans the rulers lord it over them, and their great men make their authority felt. This is not to happen among you. No; anyone who wants to be great among you must be your servant, and anyone who wants to be first among you must be your slave, just as the Son of Man came not to be served but to serve, and to give his life as a ransom for many.'

### Reflection

Lent is a time to connect to the inner desires of the heart. One should never allow what people might think discourage one from attaining greater heights in spirituality. Let every believer invest his/her time in getting closer to Jesus with a pure intention of gaining eternal salvation. If Jesus were to ask you to make one request; what would that be? For James and John, being close to Jesus was their greatest desire. May our daily desires be in accordance with the divine will.

## Jeremiah 17:5-10

The Lord says this: 'A curse on the man who puts his trust in man, who relies on things of flesh, whose heart turns from the Lord. He is like dry scrub in the wastelands: if good comes, he has no eyes for it, he settles in the parched places of the wilderness, a salt land, uninhabited. 'A blessing on the man who puts his trust in the Lord, with the Lord for his hope. … *(See Appendix B-4)*

## Psalm 1:1-4.6. R. Psalm 39:5

*Happy the man who has placed his trust in the Lord.*

## Luke 16:19-31

Jesus said to the Pharisees: 'There was a rich man who used to dress in purple and fine linen and feast magnificently every day. And at his gate there lay a poor man called Lazarus, covered with sores, who longed to fill himself with the scraps that fell from the rich man's table. Dogs even came and licked his sores. Now the poor man died and was carried away by the angels to the bosom of Abraham. The rich man also died and was buried.

'In his torment in Hades he looked up and saw Abraham a long way off with Lazarus in his bosom. So he cried out, "Father Abraham, pity me and send Lazarus to dip the tip of his finger in water and cool my tongue, for I am in agony in these flames." "My son, " Abraham replied "remember that during your life good things came your way, just as bad things came the way of Lazarus. Now he is being comforted here while you are in agony. But that is not all: between us and you a great gulf has been fixed, to stop anyone, if he wanted to, crossing from our side to yours, and to stop any crossing from your side to ours."

'The rich man replied, "Father, I beg you then to send Lazarus to my father's house, since I have five brothers, to give them warning so that they do not come to this place of torment too." "They have Moses and the prophets, " said Abraham "let them listen to them." "Ah no, father Abraham, " said the rich man "but if someone comes to them from the dead, they will repent." Then Abraham said to him, "If they will not listen either to Moses or to the prophets, they will not be convinced even if someone should rise from the dead."'

## MARCH

# 4

### THURSDAY

**2nd Week of Lent**
Violet
or
**St Casimir**
**(Commemoration)**

## Reflection

One of the factors that discourages people from pursuing holiness is people's behaviour. The rich man disappointed Lazarus by not offering him the needed help. If you have the grace to detect a similar neglect around you, do not allow it to discourage you. On your part, use every opportunity to help others in need. It could be that the rich man had a plan for Lazarus, but no one is sure. So, never postpone for the next day any kindness you can do today.

**2nd Week of Lent**
Violet

### Genesis 37:3-4.12-13.17-28

Israel loved Joseph more than all his other sons, for he was the son of his old age, and he had a coat with long sleeves made for him. But his brothers, seeing how his father loved him more than all his other sons, came to hate him so much that they could not say a civil word to him.

His brothers went to pasture their father's flock at Shechem. Then Israel said to Joseph, 'Are not your brothers with the flock at Shechem? Come, I am going to send you to them.' So Joseph went after his brothers and found them at Dothan. *(See Appendix B-4)*

### Psalm 104:16-21. R. v.5

*Remember the wonders the Lord has done.*

### Matthew 21:33-43.45-46

Jesus said to the chief priests and the elders of the people: 'Listen to another parable. There was a man, a landowner, who planted a vineyard; he fenced it round, dug a winepress in it and built a tower; then he leased it to tenants and went abroad. When vintage time drew near he sent his servants to the tenants to collect his produce. But the tenants seized his servants, thrashed one, killed another and stoned a third. Next he sent some more servants, this time a larger number, and they dealt with them in the same way. Finally he sent his son to them. "They will respect my son, " he said. But when the tenants saw the son, they said to each other, "This is the heir. Come on, let us kill him and take over his inheritance." So they seized him and threw him out of the vineyard and killed him. Now when the owner of the vineyard comes, what will he do to those tenants?'

They answered, 'He will bring those wretches to a wretched end and lease the vineyard to other tenants who will deliver the produce to him when the season arrives.' Jesus said to them, 'Have you never read in the scriptures: It was the stone rejected by the builders that became the keystone. This was the Lord's doing and it is wonderful to see?

'I tell you, then, that the kingdom of God will be taken from you and given to a people who will produce its fruit.'

When they heard his parables, the chief priests and the scribes realised he was speaking about them, but though they would have liked to arrest him they were afraid of the crowds, who looked on him as a prophet.

### Reflection

Talents attract admiration or jealousy. Joseph was sold because his father loved him. Jesus was hated because he was a light in the midst of a darkened world. Has your talent become an invitation to jealousy and hatred? Be aware that there is nothing you can do about it except to remain humble and make yourself endearing in the midst of success. Talk more about what God has done for you and with you. Let your talents glorify God.

Micah 7:14-15.18-20
*(See Appendix B-5)*

Psalm 102:1-4.9-12. R. v.8
*The Lord is compassion and love.*

Luke 15:1-3.11-32
The tax collectors and the sinners were all seeking the company of Jesus to hear what he had to say, and the Pharisees and the scribes complained. 'This man' they said 'welcomes sinners and eats with them.' So he spoke this parable to them:

'A man had two sons. The younger said to his father, "Father, let me have the share of the estate that would come to me." So the father divided the property between them. A few days later, the younger son got together everything he had and left for a distant country where he squandered his money on a life of debauchery.

'When he had spent it all, that country experienced a severe famine, and now he began to feel the pinch, so he hired himself out to one of the local inhabitants who put him on his farm to feed the pigs. And he would willingly have filled his belly with the husks the pigs were eating but no one offered him anything. Then he came to his senses and said, "How many of my father's paid servants have more food than they want, and here am I dying of hunger! I will leave this place and go to my father and say: Father, I have sinned against heaven and against you; I no longer deserve to be called your son; treat me as one of your paid servants." So he left the place and went back to his father.

'While he was still a long way off, his father saw him and was moved with pity. He ran to the boy, clasped him in his arms and kissed him tenderly. Then his son said, "Father, I have sinned against heaven and against you. I no longer deserve to be called your son." But the father said to his servants, "Quick! Bring out the best robe and put it on him; put a ring on his finger and sandals on his feet. Bring the calf we have been fattening, and kill it; we are going to have a feast, a celebration, because this son of mine was dead and has come back to life; he was lost and is found." And they began to celebrate.

'Now the elder son was out in the fields, and on his way back, as he drew near the house, he could hear music and dancing. Calling one of the servants he asked what it was all about. … *(See Appendix B-5)*

## Reflection

We all need God's mercy for we all have sinned. The only road back to God's house passes through the mercy field. Mercy is God's unmerited favour, of which we are "qualified" to receive because no qualification is needed. Both those who have gone far away from the Father's house like the prodigal son, and those who are in the house like the first son, need God's mercy and grace to understand deeply what it means to truly belong to God's household.

2nd Week of Lent
Violet

**3rd Sunday of Lent**
**Psalter Week 3**
**Violet**

### Exodus 20:1-3.7-8.12-17
*(Longer form Exodus 20:1-17)*

God spoke all these words. He said, 'I am the Lord your God who brought you out of the land of Egypt, out of the house of slavery.

'You shall have no gods except me.

You shall not utter the name of the Lord your God to misuse it, for the Lord will not leave unpunished the man who utters his name to misuse it.

'Remember the sabbath day and keep it holy.

'Honour your father and your mother so that you may have a long life in the land that the Lord your God has given to you.

'You shall not kill. 'You shall not commit adultery. 'You shall not steal. 'You shall not bear false witness against your neighbour. 'You shall not covet your neighbour's house. You shall not covet your neighbour's wife, or his servant, man or woman, or his ox, or his donkey, or anything that is his.'

### Psalm 18:8-11. R. John 6:68
*You, Lord, have the message of eternal life.*

### 1 Corinthians 1:22-25
While the Jews demand miracles and the Greeks look for wisdom, here are we preaching a crucified Christ; to the Jews an obstacle that they cannot get over, to the pagans madness, but to those who have been called, whether they are Jews or Greeks, a Christ who is the power and the wisdom of God. For God's foolishness is wiser than human wisdom, and God's weakness is stronger than human strength.

### John 2:13-25
Just before the Jewish Passover Jesus went up to Jerusalem, and in the Temple he found people selling cattle and sheep and pigeons, and the money changers sitting at their counters there. Making a whip out of some cord, he drove them all out of the Temple, cattle and sheep as well, scattered the money changers' coins, knocked their tables over and said to the pigeon-sellers, 'Take all this out of here and stop turning my Father's house into a market.' Then his disciples remembered the words of scripture: Zeal for your house will devour me. The Jews intervened and said, 'What sign can you show us to justify what you have done?' Jesus answered, 'Destroy this sanctuary, and in three days I will raise it up'. The Jews replied, 'It has taken forty-six years to build this sanctuary: are you going to raise it up in three

days?' But he was speaking of the sanctuary that was his body, and when Jesus rose from the dead, his disciples remembered that he had said this, and they believed the scripture and the words he had said.

During his stay in Jerusalem for the Passover many believed in his name when they saw the signs that he gave, but Jesus knew them all and did not trust himself to them; he never needed evidence about any man; he could tell what a man had in him.

## Reflection

No true believer should remain indifferent in the midst of desacralization of holy places, persons or things. Jesus stood his ground and resisted the desacralization of the Temple. Sometimes, God seems silent because believers are yet to allow Him to act through them in such circumstances. If you have a singing faith, then let the angels dance along with it. If you are not passionate about your faith, then you need to upgrade your faith. Always give due reverence to consecrated places, persons and things.

**3rd Week of Lent**
**Violet**
*or*
**St John of God,** *religious*
**(Commemoration)**

### 2 Kings 5:1-15

Naaman, army commander to the king of Aram, was a man who enjoyed his master's respect and favour, since through him the Lord had granted victory to the Aramaeans. But the man was a leper. Now on one of their raids, the Aramaeans had carried off from the land of Israel a little girl who had become a servant of Naaman's wife. She said to her mistress, 'If only my master would approach the prophet of Samaria. He would cure him of his leprosy.' Naaman went and told his master. 'This and this' he reported 'is what the girl from the land of Israel said.' 'Go by all means, ' said the king of Aram 'I will send a letter to the king of Israel.' So Naaman left, taking with him ten talents of silver, six thousand shekels of gold and ten festal robes. He presented the letter to the king of Israel. It read: 'With this letter, I am sending my servant Naaman to you for you to cure him of his leprosy.' When the king of Israel read the letter, he tore his garments. 'Am I a god to give death and life, ' he said 'that he sends a man to me and asks me to cure him of his leprosy? Listen to this, and take note of it and see how he intends to pick a quarrel with me.' *(See Appendix B-5)*

### Psalm 41:2-3; 42:3-4. R. Psalm 41:3

*My soul is thirsting for God, the God of my life; when can I enter and see the face of God?*

### Luke 4:24-30

Jesus came to Nazara and spoke to the people in the synagogue: 'I tell you solemnly, no prophet is ever accepted in his own country.

'There were many widows in Israel, I can assure you, in Elijah's day, when heaven remained shut for three years and six months and a great famine raged throughout the land, but Elijah was not sent to any one of these: he was sent to a widow at Zarephath, a Sidonian town. And in the prophet Elisha's time there were many lepers in Israel, but none of these was cured, except the Syrian, Naaman.'

When they heard this everyone in the synagogue was enraged. They sprang to their feet and hustled him out of the town; and they took him up to the brow of the hill their town was built on, intending to throw him down the cliff, but he slipped through the crowd and walked away.

### Reflection

It is commendable to recognise God in others, for God uses whomever He wishes to minister to us. The slave girl ministered to Naaman, and a poor widow of Zarephath saved Elijah. Appreciating and loving human beings irrespective of colour, race, profile, amongst others, is a sure sign of someone on the road to success and eternal salvation. Someone in your household or someone unexpected could also minster to you; so, never ignore anyone in life.

Daniel 3:25.34-43
*(See Appendix B-6)*

Psalm 24:4-9. R. v.6
*Remember your mercy, Lord.*

Matthew 18:21-35

Peter went up to Jesus and said, 'Lord, how often must I forgive my brother if he wrongs me? As often as seven times?' Jesus answered, 'Not seven, I tell you, but seventy-seven times.

'And so the kingdom of heaven may be compared to a king who decided to settle his accounts with his servants. When the reckoning began, they brought him a man who owed ten thousand talents; but he had no means of paying, so his master gave orders that he should be sold, together with his wife and children and all his possessions, to meet the debt. At this, the servant threw himself down at his master's feet. "Give me time, " he said "and I will pay the whole sum." And the servant's master felt so sorry for him that he let him go and cancelled the debt. Now as this servant went out, he happened to meet a fellow servant who owed him one hundred denarii; and he seized him by the throat and began to throttle him. "Pay what you owe me, " he said. His fellow servant fell at his feet and implored him, saying, "Give me time and I will pay you." But the other would not agree; on the contrary, he had him thrown into prison till he should pay the debt. His fellow servants were deeply distressed when they saw what had happened, and they went to their master and reported the whole affair to him. Then the master sent for him. "You wicked servant, " he said "I cancelled all that debt of yours when you appealed to me. Were you not bound, then, to have pity on your fellow servant just as I had pity on you?" And in his anger the master handed him over to the torturers till he should pay all his debt. And that is how my heavenly Father will deal with you unless you each forgive your brother from your heart.'

## Reflection

One wonders how it is possible to pray in the heart of the fire. In the Gospel, Jesus gives us a basic disposition for handling suffering especially when inflicted by others – forgiveness. Without forgiveness of others' faults, no one can truly pray according to the mind of Christ. Let go, forgive and then it is time to commune with your Father – God in a single-minded and undisrupted link. With forgiveness, it is possible to pray authentically in the heart of the fire.

**3rd Week of Lent**
**Violet**
or
**Saint John Ogilvie,**
**Priest, Martyr**
**(Scotland – Feast)**
*(See Appendix A-5)*

### Deuteronomy 4:1.5-9

Moses said to the people: 'And now, Israel, take notice of the laws and customs that I teach you today, and observe them, that you may have life and may enter and take possession of the land that the Lord the God of your fathers is giving you. See, as the Lord my God has commanded me, I teach you the laws and customs that you are to observe in the land you are to enter and make your own. Keep them, observe them, and they will demonstrate to the peoples your wisdom and understanding. When they come to know of all these laws they will exclaim, "No other people is as wise and prudent as this great nation." And indeed, what great nation is there that has its gods so near as the Lord our God is to us whenever we call to him? And what great nation is there that has laws and customs to match this whole Law that I put before you today?

'But take care what you do and be on your guard. Do not forget the things your eyes have seen, nor let them slip from your heart all the days of your life; rather, tell them to your children and to your children's children.'

### Psalm 147:12-13.15-16.19-20. R. v.12

*O praise the Lord, Jerusalem!*

### Matthew 5:17-19

Jesus said to his disciples: 'Do not imagine that I have come to abolish the Law or the Prophets. I have come not to abolish but to complete them. I tell you solemnly, till heaven and earth disappear, not one dot, not one little stroke, shall disappear from the Law until its purpose is achieved. Therefore, the man who infringes even one of the least of these commandments and teaches others to do the same will be considered the least in the kingdom of heaven; but the man who keeps them and teaches them will be considered great in the kingdom of heaven.'

### Reflection

Jesus in the Gospel makes it clear that he has not come to abolish the Law but to fulfil it. Whenever one is placed in a position of authority, one should remember that all authority comes from God. No leader or believer should promote or practise any law that cannot promote the values of the Gospel of Jesus Christ. Never be tired of promoting the values of the Gospel everywhere and always; let the struggle continue.

## Jeremiah 7:23-28

These were my orders: Listen to my voice, then I will be your God and you shall be my people. Follow right to the end the way that I mark out for you, and you will prosper. But they did not listen, they did not pay attention; they followed the dictates of their own evil hearts, refused to face me, and turned their backs on me. From the day your ancestors came out of the land of Egypt until today, day after day I have persistently sent you all my servants the prophets. But they have not listened to me, have not paid attention; they have grown stubborn and behaved worse than their ancestors. You may say all these words to them: they will not listen to you; you may call them: they will not answer. So tell them this, 'Here is the nation that will not listen to the voice of the Lord its God nor take correction. Sincerity is no more, it has vanished from their mouths.'

## Psalm 94:1-2.6-9. R. v.8

*O that today you would listen to his voice! 'Harden not your hearts.'*

## Luke 11:14-23

Jesus was casting out a devil and it was dumb; but when the devil had gone out the dumb man spoke, and the people were amazed. But some of them said, 'It is through Beelzebul, the prince of devils, that he casts out devils.' Others asked him, as a test, for a sign from heaven; but, knowing what they were thinking, he said to them, 'Every kingdom divided against itself is heading for ruin, and a household divided against itself collapses. So too with Satan: if he is divided against himself, how can his kingdom stand? – since you assert that it is through Beelzebul that I cast out devils. Now if it is through Beelzebul that I cast out devils, through whom do your own experts cast them out? Let them be your judges, then. But if it is through the finger of God that I cast out devils, then know that the kingdom of God has overtaken you. So long as a strong man fully armed guards his own palace, his goods are undisturbed; but when someone stronger than he is attacks and defeats him, the stronger man takes away all the weapons he relied on and shares out his spoil.

'He who is not with me is against me; and he who does not gather with me scatters.'

## Reflection

I believe it is difficult to remain peaceful when someone we love is upset for the right reasons. The Israelites disobeyed God. Consequently, the tone of the message from the prophet Jeremiah shows that God is not happy with them. When we refuse to take correction and obey God's commandments, God is upset, and no true believer can withstand making God upset. So, let everyone remain obedient and single-minded in his/her service to our ever-loving God.

**3rd Week of Lent**
Violet

**3rd Week of Lent**
**Violet**

### Hosea 14:2-10

The Lord says this: Israel, come back to the Lord your God; your iniquity was the cause of your downfall. Provide yourself with words and come back to the Lord. Say to him, 'Take all iniquity away so that we may have happiness again and offer you our words of praise. Assyria cannot save us, we will not ride horses any more, or say, "Our God!" to what our own hands have made, for you are the one in whom orphans find compassion.' – I will heal their disloyalty, I will love them with all my heart, for my anger has turned from them. I will fall like dew on Israel. He shall bloom like the lily, and thrust out roots like the poplar, his shoots will spread far; he will have the beauty of the olive and the fragrance of Lebanon. They will come back to live in my shade; they will grow corn that flourishes, they will cultivate vines as renowned as the wine of Helbon. What has Ephraim to do with idols any more when it is I who hear his prayer and care for him? I am like a cypress ever green, all your fruitfulness comes from me. Let the wise man understand these words. Let the intelligent man grasp their meaning. For the ways of the Lord are straight, and virtuous men walk in them, but sinners stumble.

### Psalm 80:6.8-11.14.17. R. vv. 9.11

*I am the Lord, your God; listen to my warning.*

### Mark 12:28-34

One of the scribes came up to Jesus and put a question to him, 'Which is the first of all the commandments?' Jesus replied, 'This is the first: Listen, Israel, the Lord our God is the one Lord, and you must love the Lord your God with all your heart, with all your soul, with all your mind and with all your strength. The second is this: You must love your neighbour as yourself. There is no commandment greater than these.' The scribe said to him, 'Well spoken, Master; what you have said is true: that he is one and there is no other. To love him with all your heart, with all your understanding and strength, and to love your neighbour as yourself, this is far more important than any holocaust or sacrifice.' Jesus, seeing how wisely he had spoken, said, 'You are not far from the kingdom of God.' And after that no one dared to question him any more.

### Reflection

The invitation to conversion from our loving God is irresistible. The unholy fear of conversion cripples the desire to become better. Unholy fear of conversion is a compound fear, caused by the fear of leaving a seeming comfort zone of sin and the fear of starting afresh in the struggle to live a holy life. One should draw strength from all who love us for they show us a glimpse of God's love. May God give every soul the grace to love Him more dearly.

## Hosea 5:15–6:6

The Lord says this: They will search for me in their misery: 'Come, let us return to the Lord. He has torn us to pieces, but he will heal us; he has struck us down, but he will bandage our wounds; after a day or two he will bring us back to life, on the third day he will raise us and we shall live in his presence. Let us set ourselves to know the Lord; that he will come is as certain as the dawn, he will come to us as showers come, like spring rains watering the earth.' What am I to do with you, Ephraim? What am I to do with you, Judah? This love of yours is like a morning cloud, like the dew that quickly disappears. This is why I have torn them to pieces by the prophets, why I slaughtered them with the words from my mouth, his judgement will rise like the light, since what I want is love, not sacrifice; knowledge of God, not holocausts.

## Psalm 50:3-4.18-21. R. cf. Hosea 6:6

*What I want is love, not sacrifice.*

## Luke 18:9-14

Jesus spoke the following parable to some people who prided themselves on being virtuous and despised everyone else: 'Two men went up to the Temple to pray, one a Pharisee, the other a tax collector. The Pharisee stood there and said this prayer to himself, "I thank you, God, that I am not grasping, unjust, adulterous like the rest of mankind, and particularly that I am not like this tax collector here. I fast twice a week; I pay tithes on all I get." The tax collector stood some distance away, not daring even to raise his eyes to heaven; but he beat his breast and said, "God, be merciful to me, a sinner." This man, I tell you, went home again at rights with God; the other did not. For everyone who exalts himself will be humbled, but the man who humbles himself will be exalted.'

## MARCH

# 13

## SATURDAY

**3rd Week of Lent**
Violet

## Reflection

The Gospel presents the parable of two men that went up to the Temple to pray. One could quickly evaluate the episode by comparing the two men. What of the other person who has never been to church, or the one who used to go to church but has stopped going to church, or visits the church only occasionally? Let everyone practise the faith in humility of heart, look out for one another, and populate the house of God.

# MARCH
# 14
## SUNDAY

**4th Sunday of Lent**
**Psalter Week 4**
**Violet**

**2 Chronicles 36:14-16.19-23**

All the heads of the priesthood, and the people too, added infidelity to infidelity, copying all the shameful practices of the nations and defiling the Temple that the Lord had consecrated for himself in Jerusalem. The Lord, the God of their ancestors, tirelessly sent them messenger after messenger, since he wished to spare his people and his house. But they ridiculed the messengers of God, they despised his words, they laughed at his prophets, until at last the wrath of the Lord rose so high against his people that there was no further remedy.

Their enemies burned down the Temple of God, demolished the walls of Jerusalem, set fire to all its palaces, and destroyed everything of value in it. The survivors were deported by Nebuchadnezzar to Babylon; they were to serve him and his sons until the kingdom of Persia came to power. This is how the word of the Lord was fulfilled that he spoke through Jeremiah, 'Until this land has enjoyed its sabbath rest, until seventy years have gone by, it will keep sabbath throughout the days of its desolation.'

And in the first year of Cyrus king of Persia, to fulfil the word of the Lord that was spoken through Jeremiah, the Lord roused the spirit of Cyrus king of Persia to issue a proclamation and to have it publicly displayed throughout his kingdom: 'Thus speaks Cyrus king of Persia, "The Lord, the God of heaven, has given me all the kingdoms of the

earth; he has ordered me to build him a Temple in Jerusalem, in Judah. Whoever there is among you of all his people, may his God be with him! Let him go up."'

**Psalm 136. R. v.6**
*O let my tongue cleave to my mouth if I remember you not!*

**Ephesians 2:4-10**
God loved us with so much love that he was generous with his mercy: when we were dead through our sins, he brought us to life with Christ – it is through grace that you have been saved – and raised us up with him and gave us a place with him in heaven, in Christ Jesus.

This was to show for all ages to come, through his goodness towards us in Christ Jesus, how infinitely rich he is in grace. Because it is by grace that you have been saved, through faith; not by anything of your own, but by a gift from God; not by anything that you have done, so that nobody can claim the credit. We are God's work of art, created in Christ Jesus to live the good life as from the beginning he has meant us to live it.

**John 3:14-21**
Jesus said to Nicodemus: 'The Son of Man must be lifted up as Moses lifted up the serpent in the desert, so that everyone who believes may have eternal life in him. Yes, God loved the world so much that he gave his only Son, so that everyone who believes in him may not be lost but may have eternal life. For God sent his Son into the world not to condemn the world, but so that through him the world might be saved. No one who believes in him will be condemned; but whoever refuses to believe is condemned already, because he has refused to believe in the name of God's only Son. On these grounds is sentence pronounced: that though the light has come into the world men have shown they prefer darkness to the light because their deeds were evil. And indeed, everybody who does wrong hates the light and avoids it, for fear his actions should be exposed; but the man who lives by the truth comes out into the light, so that it may be plainly seen that what he does is done in God.'

**Reflection**
In today's Gospel, Jesus replies Nicodemus, a Pharisee who secretly visited him by night. Jesus had earlier told him that one "must be born again from above" in order to be saved (John 3:7). This revelation must have made a great impact on Nicodemus as he alone stood by Jesus when the Jews threatened to condemn him without a hearing (John 7:51).  May every divine encounter impart to us pastoral courage to uphold Gospel values in our world.

## MARCH
# 15
## MONDAY

**4th Weekday of Lent**
Violet

### Isaiah 65:17-21

Thus says the Lord: Now I create new heavens and a new earth, and the past will not be remembered, and will come no more to men's minds. Be glad and rejoice for ever and ever for what I am creating, because I now create Jerusalem 'Joy' and her people 'Gladness'. I shall rejoice over Jerusalem and exult in my people. No more will the sound of weeping or the sound of cries be heard in her; in her, no more will be found the infant living a few days only, or the old man not living to the end of his days. To die at the age of a hundred will be dying young; not to live to be a hundred will be the sign of a curse. They will build houses and inhabit them, plant vineyards and eat their fruit.

### Psalm 29:2.4-6.11-13. R. v.2

*I will praise you, Lord, you have rescued me.*

### John 4:43-54

Jesus left Samaria for Galilee. He himself had declared that there is no respect for a prophet in his own country, but on his arrival the Galileans received him well, having seen all that he had done at Jerusalem during the festival which they too had attended.

He went again to Cana in Galilee, where he had changed the water into wine. Now there was a court official there whose son was ill at Capernaum and, hearing that Jesus had arrived in Galilee from Judaea, he went and asked him to come and cure his son as he was at the point of death. Jesus said, 'So you will not believe unless you see signs and portents!' 'Sir,' answered the official 'come down before my child dies.' 'Go home,' said Jesus 'your son will live.' The man believed what Jesus had said and started on his way; and while he was still on the journey back his servants met him with the news that his boy was alive. He asked them when the boy had begun to recover. 'The fever left him yesterday' they said 'at the seventh hour.' The father realised that this was exactly the time when Jesus had said, 'Your son will live'; and he and all his household believed.

This was the second sign given by Jesus, on his return from Judaea to Galilee.

### Reflection

God is always doing something new and noble for his children. He promises "new heavens and a new earth" and those who have faith are already in that new world. The gift of faith is important in our relationship with God. One should have a singled-minded and total dependence on God in every situation and trust that whatever God offers is the best. The faith of the court official uplifted the faith of his household, giving rise to a new world of believers.

### Ezekiel 47:1-9.12

The angel brought me to the entrance of the Temple, where a stream came out from under the Temple threshold and flowed eastwards, since the Temple faced east. The water flowed from under the right side of the Temple, south of the altar. He took me out by the north gate and led me right round outside as far as the outer east gate where the water flowed out on the right-hand side. ... *(See Appendix B-6)*

### Psalm 45:2-3.5-6.8-9. R. v.8

*The Lord of hosts is with us; the God of Jacob is our stronghold.*

### John 5:1-3.5-16

There was a Jewish festival, and Jesus went up to Jerusalem. Now at the Sheep Pool in Jerusalem there is a building, called Bethzatha in Hebrew, consisting of five porticos; and under these were crowds of sick people – blind, lame, paralysed. One man there had an illness which had lasted thirty-eight years, and when Jesus saw him lying there and knew he had been in this condition for a long time, he said, 'Do you want to be well again?' 'Sir, ' replied the sick man 'I have no one to put me into the pool when the water is disturbed; and while I am still on the way, someone else gets there before me.' Jesus said, 'Get up, pick up your sleeping-mat and walk.' The man was cured at once, and he picked up his mat and walked away.

Now that day happened to be the sabbath, so the Jews said to the man who had been cured, 'It is the sabbath; you are not allowed to carry your sleeping-mat.' He replied, 'But the man who cured me told me, "Pick up your mat and walk."' They asked, 'Who is the man who said to you, "Pick up your mat and walk"?' The man had no idea who it was since Jesus had disappeared into the crowd that filled the place. After a while Jesus met him in the Temple and said, 'Now you are well again, be sure not to sin any more, or something worse may happen to you.' The man went back and told the Jews that it was Jesus who had cured him. It was because he did things like this on the sabbath that the Jews began to persecute Jesus.

### Reflection

The man at the Sheep Pool at Bethzatha has an illness and waited for thirty-eight years to be healed but was not successful. Thirty-eight years is a very long time and one wonders how this man coped. Sometimes in life, when one has challenges, it becomes more difficult to have faithful friends. If you have felt "abandoned" at difficult moments, never give up! May everyone be more aware of people who are in need and give them every possible support.

**St Patrick,** *bishop*
**(England, Wales &
Scotland – Feast,
Ireland – Solemnity)
White**
*(See Appendix A-6)*

## 1 Peter 4:7-11

Everything will soon come to an end, so, to pray better, keep a calm and sober mind. Above all, never let your love for each other grow insincere, since love covers over many a sin. Welcome each other into your houses without grumbling. Each one of you has received a special grace, so, like good stewards responsible for all these different graces of God, put yourselves at the service of others. If you are a speaker, speak in words which seem to come from God; if you are a helper, help as though every action was done at God's orders; so that in everything God may receive the glory, through Jesus Christ, since to him alone belong all glory and power for ever and ever. Amen.

## Psalm 95:1-3.7-8.10

*Proclaim the wonders of the Lord among all the peoples.*

## Luke 5:1-11

Jesus was standing one day by the Lake of Gennesaret, with the crowd pressing round him listening to the word of God, when he caught sight of two boats close to the bank. The fishermen had gone out of them and were washing their nets. He got into one of the boats – it was Simon's – and asked him to put out a little from the shore. Then he sat down and taught the crowds from the boat.

When he had finished speaking he said to Simon, 'Put out into deep water and pay out your nets for a catch.' 'Master,' Simon replied, 'we worked hard all night long and caught nothing, but if you say so, I will pay out the nets.' And when they had done this they netted such a huge number of fish that their nets began to tear, so they signalled to their companions in the other boat to come and help them; when these came, they filled the two boats to sinking point.

When Simon Peter saw this he fell at the knees of Jesus saying, 'Leave me, Lord; I am a sinful man.' For he and all his companions were completely overcome by the catch they had made; so also were James and John, sons of Zebedee, who were Simon's partners. But Jesus said to Simon, 'Do not be afraid; from now on it is men you will catch.' Then, bringing their boats back to land, they left everything and followed him.

## Reflection

Today is St Patrick's Day. When St Patrick was born, no one ever thought he would be a great evangelizer. He was kidnapped by Irish raiders at the age of sixteen and was able to escape. Adversity has the possibility of bringing out the best in people or the worst. He did not allow his past to affect him adversely. St Patrick is a blessing beyond the boundaries of Ireland. Never underestimate what you can contribute to the whole human family, give your talents a trial.

**4th Week of Lent**
**Violet**
*or*
**St Cyril of Jerusalem,**
*doctor*

## Exodus 32:7-14

The Lord spoke to Moses, 'Go down now, because your people whom you brought out of Egypt have apostasised. They have been quick to leave the way I marked out for them; they have made themselves a calf of molten metal and have worshipped it and offered it sacrifice. "Here is your God, Israel, " they have cried, "who brought you up from the land of Egypt!" I can see how headstrong these people are! Leave me now, my wrath shall blaze out against them and devour them; of you, however, I will make a great nation.' *(See Appendix B-6)*

## Psalm 105:19-23. R. v.4

*O Lord, remember me, out of the love you have for your people.*

## John 5:31-47

Jesus said to the Jews: 'Were I to testify on my own behalf, my testimony would not be valid; but there is another witness who can speak on my behalf, and I know that his testimony is valid. You sent messengers to John, and he gave his testimony to the truth: not that I depend on human testimony; no, it is for your salvation that I speak of this. John was a lamp alight and shining and for a time you were content to enjoy the light that he gave. But my testimony is greater than John's: the works my Father has given me to carry out, these same works of mine testify that the Father has sent me. Besides, the Father who sent me bears witness to me himself. You have never heard his voice, you have never seen his shape, and his word finds no home in you because you do not believe in the one he has sent. 'You study the scriptures, believing that in them you have eternal life; now these same scriptures testify to me, and yet you refuse to come to me for life! As for human approval this means nothing to me. Besides, I know you too well: you have no love of God in you. I have come in the name of my Father and you refuse to accept me; if someone else comes in his own name you will accept him. 'How can you believe, since you look to one another for approval and are not concerned with the approval that comes from the one God? Do not imagine that I am going to accuse you before the Father; you place your hopes on Moses, and Moses will be your accuser. If you really believed him you would believe me too, since it was I that he was writing about; but if you refuse to believe what he wrote, how can you believe what I say?'

## Reflection

The Israelites apostasised by worshipping a molten calf. God's complaint always echoes in the hearts of those who are near him. You are close to God's heart. If you were Moses, how would you respond to God's complaint? Moses responded with a persuasive prayer and by reproaching the Israelites. It is the grace of God that makes one discover or become aware of where things are not moving well and it could be an invitation from God to make things better.

**St Joseph, Spouse of the Blessed Virgin Mary**
Solemnity
White

2 Samuel 7:4-5.12-14.16
*(See Appendix B-7)*

Psalm 88:2-5.27.29. R. v.37
*His dynasty shall last for ever.*

Romans 4:13.16-18.22

The promise of inheriting the world was not made to Abraham and his descendants on account of any law but on account of the righteousness which consists in faith. That is why what fulfils the promise depends on faith, so that it may be a free gift and be available to all of Abraham's descendants, not only those who belong to the Law but also those who belong to the faith of Abraham who is the Father of all of us. As scripture says: I have made you the ancestor of many nations – Abraham is our father in the eyes of God, in whom he put his faith, and who brings the dead to life and calls into being what does not exist.

Though it seemed Abraham's hope could not be fulfilled, he hoped and he believed, and through doing so he did become the father of many nations exactly as he had been promised: Your descendants will be as many as the stars. This is the faith that was 'considered as justifying him'.

Matthew 1:16.18-21.24
*(Alternative Gospel: Luke 2: 41-51)*

Jacob was the father of Joseph the husband of Mary; of her was born Jesus who is called Christ.

This is how Jesus Christ came to be born. His mother Mary was betrothed to Joseph; but before they came to live together she was found to be with child through the Holy Spirit. Her husband Joseph, being a man of honour and wanting to spare her publicity, decided to divorce her informally. He had made up his mind to do this when the angel of the Lord appeared to him in a dream and said, 'Joseph son of David, do not be afraid to take Mary home as your wife, because she has conceived what is in her by the Holy Spirit. She will give birth to a son and you must name him Jesus, because he is the one who is to save his people from their sins.' When Joseph woke up he did what the angel of the Lord had told him to do.

### Reflection

Today we celebrate the feast of St Joseph. This holy man lived all his life playing his role wholeheartedly in ensuring that the will of God comes to fulfilment. Aligning one's will with the will of God should be everyone's continuous goal. When God comes into any circumstance, it is enough reason to humbly obey and allow the will of God to be carried out. St Joseph's understanding of God is amazing and profound. Life lived for God is always meaningful. St Joseph lived a meaningful life.

**4th Week of Lent**
**Violet**

### Jeremiah 11:18-20

The Lord revealed it to me; I was warned. Lord, that was when you opened my eyes to their scheming. I for my part was like a trustful lamb being led to the slaughter-house, not knowing the schemes they were plotting against me, 'Let us destroy the tree in its strength, let us cut him off from the land of the living, so that his name may be quickly forgotten!'

But you, Lord of hosts, who pronounce a just sentence, who probe the loins and heart, let me see the vengeance you will take on them, for I have committed my cause to you.

### Psalm 7:2-3.9-12. R. v.2

*Lord God, I take refuge in you.*

### John 7:40-52

Several people who had been listening to Jesus said, 'Surely he must be the prophet, ' and some said, 'He is the Christ', but others said, 'Would the Christ be from Galilee? Does not scripture say that the Christ must be descended from David and come from the town of Bethlehem?' So the people could not agree about him. Some would have liked to arrest him, but no one actually laid hands on him.

The police went back to the chief priests and Pharisees who said to them, 'Why haven't you brought him?' The police replied, 'There has never been anybody who has spoken like him.' 'So' the Pharisees answered 'you have been led astray as well? Have any of the authorities believed in him? Any of the Pharisees? This rabble knows nothing about the Law – they are damned.' One of them, Nicodemus – the same man who had come to Jesus earlier – said to them, 'But surely the Law does not allow us to pass judgement on a man without giving him a hearing and discovering what he is about?' To this they answered, 'Are you a Galilean too? Go into the matter, and see for yourself: prophets do not come out of Galilee.'

### Reflection

Today in the Gospel, Nicodemus reminds the Pharisees and the chief priests what the law prohibits – that is, no one should be condemned without a fair hearing. There are some moments when one may be tempted to allow personal dispositions or past experiences to affect a present situation adversely. One should always ensure that laws should not be subverted in order to oppress anyone. Laws should be interpreted to ensure it brings the greatest good to humanity and glory to God.

**5th Sunday of Lent**
**Psalter Week 1**
**Violet**

### Jeremiah 31:31-34

See, the days are coming – it is the Lord who speaks – when I will make a new covenant with the House of Israel and the House of Judah, but not a covenant like the one I made with their ancestors on the day I took them by the hand to bring them out of the land of Egypt. They broke that covenant of mine, so I had to show them who was master. It is the Lord who speaks. No, this is the covenant I will make with the House of Israel when those days arrive – it is the Lord who speaks. Deep within them I will plant my Law, writing it on their hearts. Then I will be their God and they shall be my people. There will be no further need for neighbour to try to teach neighbour, or brother to say to brother, 'Learn to know the Lord!' No, they will all know me, the least no less than the greatest – it is the Lord who speaks – since I will forgive their iniquity and never call their sin to mind.

**Psalm 50:3-4.12-15. R. v.12**

*A pure heart create for me, O God.*

**Hebrews 5:7-9**

During his life on earth, Christ offered up prayer and entreaty, aloud and in silent tears, to the one who had the power to save him out of death, and he submitted so humbly that his prayer was heard. Although he was Son, he learnt to obey through suffering; but having been made perfect, he became for all who obey him the source of eternal salvation.

**John 12:20-30**

Among those who went up to worship at the festival were some Greeks. These approached Philip, who came from Bethsaida in Galilee, and put this request to him, 'Sir, we should like to see Jesus'. Philip went to tell Andrew, and Andrew and Philip together went to tell Jesus. Jesus replied to them: 'Now the hour has come for the Son of Man to be glorified. I tell you, most solemnly, unless a wheat grain falls on the ground and dies, it remains only a single grain; but if it dies, it yields a rich harvest. Anyone who loves his life loses it; anyone who hates his life in this world will keep it for the eternal life. If a man serves me, he must follow me, wherever I am, my servant will be there too. If anyone serves me, my Father will honour him. Now my soul is troubled. What shall I say: Father, save me from this hour? But it was for this very reason that I have come to this hour. Father, glorify your name!'

A voice came from heaven, 'I have glorified it, and I will glorify it again.'

People standing by, who heard this, said it was a clap of thunder; others said, 'It was an angel speaking to him.' Jesus answered, 'It was not for my sake that this voice came, but for yours. 'Now sentence is being passed on this world; now the prince of this world is to be overthrown. And when I am lifted up from the earth, I shall draw all to myself.'

By these words he indicated the kind of death he would die.

**Reflection**

The prophet Jeremiah reminds us of God's willingness to make a new covenant with the House of Israel. This new covenant is to be established with the Passion and death of Jesus Christ and sealed with his precious blood. This new covenant is at a very high cost. Every believer should be grateful to God for giving us this opportunity to be in communion with him at so high a level. May God's grace enable everyone to share fully in the merits of this new covenant.

### Daniel 13:41-62
*(Longer form: Daniel 13:1-9.15-17.19-30.33-62)*
Susanna was condemned to death. She cried out as loud as she could 'Eternal God, you know all secrets and everything before it happens; you know that they have given false evidence against me. And now have I to die, innocent as I am of everything their malice has invented against me?'

The Lord heard her cry and, as she was being led away to die, he roused the holy spirit residing in a young boy named Daniel who began to shout, 'I am innocent of this woman's death!' …
*(See Appendix B-7)*

### Psalm 22. R. v.4
*If I should walk in the valley of darkness, no evil would I fear.*

### John 8:1-11
Jesus went to the Mount of Olives. At daybreak he appeared in the Temple again; and as all the people came to him, he sat down and began to teach them.

The scribes and Pharisees brought a woman along who had been caught committing adultery; and making her stand there in full view of everybody, they said to Jesus, 'Master, this woman was caught in the very act of committing adultery, and Moses has ordered us in the Law to condemn women like this to death by stoning. What have you to say?' They asked him this as a test, looking for something to use against him. But Jesus bent down and started writing on the ground with his finger. As they persisted with their question, he looked up and said, 'If there is one of you who has not sinned, let him be the first to throw a stone at her.' Then he bent down and wrote on the ground again. When they heard this they went away one by one, beginning with the eldest, until Jesus was left alone with the woman, who remained standing there. He looked up and said, 'Woman, where are they? Has no one condemned you?' 'No one, sir' she replied. 'Neither do I condemn you, ' said Jesus 'go away, and don't sin any more.'

### Reflection
Two elders accused Susana wrongly because she refused their immoral requests. Daniel came to judgement and exposed their evil plots. In the Gospel, the scribes and the Pharisees brought a woman before Jesus without the man with whom the immoral act was committed. All believers should shun false accusation and the use of double standards to pervert justice. Everyone should be a rescuer of victims of false accusation and help the weak to be converted and embrace sanctity of life.

## Numbers 21:4-9

The Israelites left Mount Hor by the road to the Sea of Suph, to skirt the land of Edom. On the way the people lost patience. They spoke against God and against Moses, 'Why did you bring us out of Egypt to die in this wilderness? For there is neither bread nor water here; we are sick of this unsatisfying food.'

At this God sent fiery serpents among the people; their bite brought death to many in Israel. The people came and said to Moses, 'We have sinned by speaking against the Lord and against you. Intercede for us with the Lord to save us from these serpents.' Moses interceded for the people, and the Lord answered him, 'Make a fiery serpent and put it on a standard. If anyone is bitten and looks at it, he shall live.' So Moses fashioned a bronze serpent which he put on a standard, and if anyone was bitten by a serpent, he looked at the bronze serpent and lived.

## Psalm 101:2-3.16-21. R. v.2

*O Lord, listen to my prayer and let my cry for help reach you.*

## John 8:21-30

Jesus said to the Pharisees: 'I am going away; you will look for me and you will die in your sin. Where I am going, you cannot come.'

The Jews said to one another, 'Will he kill himself? Is that what he means by saying, "Where I am going, you cannot come"?' Jesus went on: 'You are from below; I am from above. You are of this world; I am not of this world. I have told you already: You will die in your sins. Yes, if you do not believe that I am He, you will die in your sins.'

So they said to him, 'Who are you?' Jesus answered: 'What I have told you from the outset. About you I have much to say and much to condemn; but the one who sent me is truthful, and what I have learnt from him I declare to the world.'

They failed to understand that he was talking to them about the Father. So Jesus said: 'When you have lifted up the Son of Man, then you will know that I am He and that I do nothing of myself: what the Father has taught me is what I preach; he who sent me is with me, and has not left me to myself, for I always do what pleases him.'

As he was saying this, many came to believe in him.

## Reflection

The Israelites spoke against God and Moses as a result of life's difficulties. The good thing is that the Israelites came to Moses and confessed that they had sinned against God. Jesus does not want his followers to draw a battle line between themselves and God, or against one another. Jesus invites all to seek the face of God always and especially in difficult times. Remaining faithful to one another and ultimately to God in times of difficulties is paramount in relationships.

**5th Week of Lent**
Violet
or
**St Turibius of Mogrovejo,**
*bishop*
**(Commemoration)**

### Daniel 3:14-20.24-25.28

King Nebuchadnezzar said, 'Shadrach, Meshach and Abednego, is it true that you do not serve my gods, and that you refuse to worship the golden statue I have erected? When you hear the sound of horn, pipe, lyre, trigon, harp, bagpipe, or any other instrument, are you prepared to prostrate yourselves and worship the statue I have made? If you refuse to worship it, you must be thrown straight away into the burning fiery furnace; and where is the god who could save you from my power?' Shadrach, Meshach and Abednego replied to King Nebuchadnezzar, 'Your question hardly requires an answer: if our God, the one we serve, is able to save us from the burning fiery furnace and from your power, O king, he will save us; and even if he does not, then you must know, O king, that we will not serve your god or worship the statue you have erected.' ...
*(See Appendix B-8)*

### Psalm: Daniel 3:52-56. R. v.52
*To you glory and praise forever more.*

### John 8:31-42

To the Jews who believed in him Jesus said: 'If you make my word your home you will indeed be my disciples, you will learn the truth and the truth will make you free.'

They answered, 'We are descended from Abraham and we have never been the slaves of anyone; what do you mean, "You will be made free"?' Jesus replied: 'I tell you most solemnly, everyone who commits sin is a slave. Now the slave's place in the house is not assured, but the son's place is assured. So if the Son makes you free, you will be free indeed. I know that you are descended from Abraham; but in spite of that you want to kill me because nothing I say has penetrated into you. What I, for my part, speak of is what I have seen with my Father; but you, you put into action the lessons learnt from your father.'

They repeated, 'Our father is Abraham.' Jesus said to them: 'If you were Abraham's children, you would do as Abraham did. As it is, you want to kill me when I tell you the truth as I have learnt it from God; that is not what Abraham did. What you are doing is what your father does.'

'We were not born of prostitution, ' they went on 'we have one father: God.' Jesus answered: 'If God were your father, you would love me, since I have come here from God; yes, I have come from him; not that I came because I chose, no, I was sent, and by him.'

### Reflection

The faith of Shadrach, Meshach and Abednego is a pointer to the fact that every true worship of God begins with a new vision of reality. The three men refused to worship the idol King Nebuchadnezzar erected. Unflinching faith is a basic requirement for every true worshipper of God. In the Gospel, the Jews claim Abraham as their father but do not believe that Jesus was sent by God, and are planning to kill him. "Seasonal faith" is no faith at all.

Isaiah 7:10-14; 8:10
*(See Appendix B–8)*

Psalm 39:7-11 R. vv. 8.9
*Here I am, Lord! I come to do your will.*

**The Annunciation
of the Lord
Solemnity
White**

Hebrews 10:4-10

Bulls' blood and goats' blood are useless for taking away sins, and this is what Christ said, on coming into the world: You who wanted no sacrifice or oblation, prepared a body for me. You took no pleasure in holocausts or sacrifices for sin; then I said, just as I was commanded in the scroll of the book, 'God, here I am! I am coming to obey your will.'

Notice that he says first: You did not want what the Law lays down as the things to be offered, that is: the sacrifices, the oblations, the holocausts and the sacrifices for sin, and you took no pleasure in them; and then he says: Here I am! I am coming to obey your will. He is abolishing the first sort to replace it with the second. And this will was for us to be made holy by the offering of his body made once and for all by Jesus Christ.

Luke 1:26-38

The angel Gabriel was sent by God to a town in Galilee called Nazareth, to a virgin betrothed to a man named Joseph, of the House of David; and the virgin's name was Mary. He went in and said to her, 'Rejoice, so highly favoured! The Lord is with you.' She was deeply disturbed by these words and asked herself what this greeting could mean, but the angel said to her, 'Mary, do not be afraid; you have won God's favour. Listen! You are to conceive and bear a son, and you must name him Jesus. He will be great and will be called Son of the Most High. The Lord God will give him the throne of his ancestor David; he will rule over the House of Jacob for ever and his reign will have no end.' Mary said to the angel, 'But how can this come about, since I am a virgin?' 'The Holy Spirit will come upon you' the angel answered 'and the power of the Most High will cover you with its shadow. And so the child will be holy and will be called Son of God. Know this too: your kinswoman Elizabeth has, in her old age, herself conceived a son, and she whom people called barren is now in her sixth month, for nothing is impossible to God.' 'I am the handmaid of the Lord, ' said Mary 'let what you have said be done to me.' And the angel left her.

Reflection

The Annunciation of the Blessed Virgin Mary commemorates the visit of the Archangel Gabriel to Mary to deliver the message of the Incarnation. God chose Mary and for certain, she is the best of all women ever to live on earth. The Annunciation challenges everyone to always allow God take his rightful position in one's life. When God occupies the rightful position in human and personal history, life gives us the best, just as Mary's "yes" gave us Jesus Christ.

**5th Week of Lent**
**Violet**

### Jeremiah 20:10-13

Jeremiah said: 'I hear so many disparaging me, "Terror from every side! Denounce him! Let us denounce him!" All those who used to be my friends watched for my downfall, "Perhaps he will be seduced into error. Then we will master him and take our revenge!" But the Lord is at my side, a mighty hero; my opponents will stumble, mastered, confounded by their failure; everlasting, unforgettable disgrace will be theirs. But you, Lord of hosts, you who probe with justice, who scrutinise the loins and heart, let me see the vengeance you will take on them, for I have committed my cause to you. Sing to the Lord, praise the Lord, for he has delivered the soul of the needy from the hands of evil men.'

### Psalm 17:2-7. R. cf. v.7

*In my anguish I called to the Lord and he heard my voice.*

### John 10:31-42

The Jews fetched stones to stone him, so Jesus said to them, 'I have done many good works for you to see, works from my Father; for which of these are you stoning me?' The Jews answered him, 'We are not stoning you for doing a good work but for blasphemy: you are only a man and you claim to be God.' Jesus answered: 'Is it not written in your Law: I said, you are gods? So the Law used the word gods of those to whom the word of God was addressed, and scripture cannot be rejected. Yet you say to someone the Father has consecrated and sent into the world, "You are blaspheming, " because he says, "I am the Son of God." If I am not doing my Father's work, there is no need to believe me; but if I am doing it, then even if you refuse to believe in me, at least believe in the work I do; then you will know for sure that the Father is in me and I am in the Father.'

They wanted to arrest him then, but he eluded them.

He went back again to the far side of the Jordan to stay in the district where John had once been baptising. Many people who came to him there said, 'John gave no signs, but all he said about this man was true'; and many of them believed in him.

### Reflection

It does seem that people are sometimes hated no matter what they do, and some people are seemingly loved no matter what they do. Hatred is a strong word but it manifests in people's behaviour. Jesus has not committed any evil at all, yet the Jews are persecuting him for doing his Father's work. Everyone should contribute to the progress of God's mission on earth and not be an obstacle to the growth of God's kingdom. Always identify with God's work.

**Ezekiel 37:21-28**

The Lord says this: 'I am going to take the sons of Israel from the nations where they have gone. I shall gather them together from everywhere and bring them home to their own soil. I shall make them into one nation in my own land and on the mountains of Israel, and one king is to be king of them all; they will no longer form two nations, nor be two separate kingdoms. They will no longer defile themselves with their idols and their filthy practices and all their sins. I shall rescue them from all the betrayals they have been guilty of; I shall cleanse them; they shall be my people and I will be their God. My servant David will reign over them, one shepherd for all; they will follow my observances, respect my laws and practise them. ...

*(See Appendix B-8)*

**5th Week of Lent**
**Violet**

**Psalm: Jeremiah 31:10-13. R. v.10**
*The Lord will guard us as a shepherd guards his flock.*

**John 11:45-56**

Many of the Jews who had come to visit Mary and had seen what Jesus did believed in him, but some of them went to tell the Pharisees what he had done. Then the chief priests and Pharisees called a meeting. 'Here is this man working all these signs' they said 'and what action are we taking? If we let him go on in this way everybody will believe in him, and the Romans will come and destroy the Holy Place and our nation.' One of them, Caiaphas, the high priest that year, said, 'You don't seem to have grasped the situation at all; you fail to see that it is better for one man to die for the people, than for the whole nation to be destroyed.' He did not speak in his own person, it was as high priest that he made this prophecy that Jesus was to die for the nation – and not for the nation only, but to gather together in unity the scattered children of God. From that day they were determined to kill him. So Jesus no longer went about openly among the Jews, but left the district for a town called Ephraim, in the country bordering on the desert, and stayed there with his disciples.

The Jewish Passover drew near, and many of the country people who had gone up to Jerusalem to purify themselves looked out for Jesus, saying to one another as they stood about in the Temple, 'What do you think? Will he come to the festival or not?'

**Reflection**

As some people believed Jesus following the miracle of raising Lazarus from death, the chief priests and the Pharisees were bent on killing Jesus. One man's statement remains indelible in history, Caiaphas, the high priest. Although what he said could be seen to fulfil Old Testament prophecy, one should be cautious in making utterances on issues. Sometimes, people make hurtful statements without remembering them but such words remain indelible in the hearts of the victims.

**Palm Sunday of the
Passion of the Lord
Psalter Week 2
Red**

### Isaiah 50:4-7

The Lord has given me a disciple's tongue. So that I may know how to reply to the wearied, he provides me with speech. Each morning he wakes me to hear, to listen like a disciple. The Lord has opened my ear. For my part, I made no resistance, neither did I turn away. I offered my back to those who struck me, my cheeks to those who tore at my beard; I did not cover my face against insult and spittle. The Lord comes to my help, so that I am untouched by the insults. So, too, I set my face like flint; I know I shall not be shamed.

### Psalm 21:8-9.17-20.23-24. R. v.2

*My God, my God, why have you forsaken me?*

### Philippians 2:6-11

His state was divine, yet Christ Jesus did not cling to his equality with God but emptied himself to assume the condition of a slave, and became as men are; and being as all men are, he was humbler yet, even to accepting death, death on a cross. But God raised him high and gave him

the name which is above all other names so that all beings in the heavens, on earth and in the underworld, should bend the knee at the name of Jesus and that every tongue should acclaim Jesus Christ as Lord, to the glory of God the Father.

## Mark 14:1–15:47
*(Please see the Bible for the Passion reading)*

### Reflection
Today's celebration re-enacts Jesus' triumphant entry into Jerusalem. Jesus takes the place of the Passover Lamb even without the knowledge of the people. Jesus uses a donkey announcing a humble arrival. No one should remain on the high horse. Humility helps one to accept what one cannot change and depend on God, for God always knows the best. Even if one doesn't make it to heart of the people whilst living a humble life, one must make it to the heart of God.

**Monday of Holy Week**
**Violet**

## Isaiah 42:1-7

Here is my servant whom I uphold, my chosen one in whom my soul delights. I have endowed him with my spirit that he may bring true justice to the nations. He does not cry out or shout aloud, or make his voice heard in the streets. He does not break the crushed reed, nor quench the wavering flame. Faithfully he brings true justice; he will neither waver, nor be crushed until true justice is established on earth, for the islands are awaiting his law. Thus says God, the Lord, he who created the heavens and spread them out, who gave shape to the earth and what comes from it, who gave breath to its people and life to the creatures that move in it: I, the Lord, have called you to serve the cause of right; I have taken you by the hand and formed you; I have appointed you as covenant of the people and light of the nations, to open the eyes of the blind, to free captives from prison, and those who live in darkness from the dungeon.

## Psalm 26:1-3.13-14. R. v.1

*The Lord is my light and my help.*

## John 12:1-11

Six days before the Passover, Jesus went to Bethany, where Lazarus was, whom he had raised from the dead. They gave a dinner for him there; Martha waited on them and Lazarus was among those at table. Mary brought in a pound of very costly ointment, pure nard, and with it anointed the feet of Jesus, wiping them with her hair; the house was full of the scent of the ointment. Then Judas Iscariot – one of his disciples, the man who was to betray him – said, 'Why wasn't this ointment sold for three hundred denarii, and the money given to the poor?' He said this, not because he cared about the poor, but because he was a thief; he was in charge of the common fund and used to help himself to the contributions. So Jesus said, 'Leave her alone; she had to keep this scent for the day of my burial. You have the poor with you always, you will not always have me.'

Meanwhile a large number of Jews heard that he was there and came not only on account of Jesus but also to see Lazarus whom he had raised from the dead. Then the chief priests decided to kill Lazarus as well, since it was on his account that many of the Jews were leaving them and believing in Jesus.

## Reflection

Jesus visits the home of Lazarus, Mary and Martha. Mary shows Jesus profound love. Holy week invites us to go a step higher in holiness of life. This could mean going a step higher in responding to God's love. If Mary showed Jesus so much love whilst it was not clear how Jesus would end up, how much are you going to love Jesus now we know that he dies and resurrects for our salvation? No one can ever love God enough.

## Isaiah 49:1-6

Islands, listen to me, pay attention, remotest peoples. The Lord called me before I was born, from my mother's womb he pronounced my name. He made my mouth a sharp sword, and hid me in the shadow of his hand. He made me into a sharpened arrow, and concealed me in his quiver. He said to me, 'You are my servant Israel, in whom I shall be glorified'; while I was thinking, 'I have toiled in vain, I have exhausted myself for nothing'; and all the while my cause was with the Lord, my reward with my God. ...
*(See Appendix B-8)*

**Tuesday of Holy Week**
Violet

## Psalm 70:1-6.15.17. R. v.15
*My lips will tell of your help.*

## John 13:21-33.36-38

While at supper with his disciples, Jesus was troubled in spirit and declared, 'I tell you most solemnly, one of you will betray me.' The disciples looked at one another, wondering which he meant. The disciple Jesus loved was reclining next to Jesus; Simon Peter signed to him and said, 'Ask who it is he means', so leaning back on Jesus's breast he said, 'Who is it, Lord?' 'It is the one' replied Jesus 'to whom I give the piece of bread that I shall dip in the dish.' He dipped the piece of bread and gave it to Judas son of Simon Iscariot. At that instant, after Judas had taken the bread, Satan entered him. Jesus then said, 'What you are going to do, do quickly.' None of the others at table understood the reason he said this. Since Judas had charge of the common fund, some of them thought Jesus was telling him, 'Buy what we need for the festival', or telling him to give something to the poor. As soon as Judas had taken the piece of bread he went out. Night had fallen.

When he had gone Jesus said: 'Now has the Son of Man been glorified, and in him God has been glorified. If God has been glorified in him, God will in turn glorify him in himself, and will glorify him very soon. My little children, I shall not be with you much longer. You will look for me, and, as I told the Jews, where I am going, you cannot come.'

Simon Peter said, 'Lord, where are you going?' Jesus replied, 'Where I am going you cannot follow me now; you will follow me later.' Peter said to him, 'Why can't I follow you now? I will lay down my life for you.' 'Lay down your life for me?' answered Jesus. 'I tell you most solemnly, before the cock crows you will have disowned me three times.'

## Reflection

The Gospel relates that while Jesus was at supper with his disciples, he was troubled in spirit for the primary season that someone was about to betray him. Although Jesus already knew his mission and how it was going to be achieved, yet he was troubled in spirit. Jesus is still betrayed today in our world wherever the Gospel message is put to silence and the expression of faith is clamped down. Let us make Jesus known and alive by our way of life.

### Isaiah 50:4-9

The Lord has given me a disciple's tongue. So that I may know how to reply to the wearied he provides me with speech. Each morning he wakes me to hear, to listen like a disciple. The Lord has opened my ear. For my part, I made no resistance, neither did I turn away. I offered my back to those who struck me, my cheeks to those who tore at my beard; I did not cover my face against insult and spittle. The Lord comes to my help so that I am untouched by the insults. So, too, I set my face like flint; I know I shall not be shamed. My vindicator is here at hand. Does anyone start proceedings against me? Then let us go to court together. Who thinks he has a case against me? Let him approach me. The Lord is coming to my help, who dare condemn me?

### Psalm 68:8-10.21-22.31.33-34. R. v.14

*In your great love, O Lord, answer my prayer for your favour.*

### Matthew 26:14-25

One of the Twelve, the man called Judas Iscariot, went to the chief priests and said, 'What are you prepared to give me if I hand him over to you?' They paid him thirty silver pieces, and from that moment he looked for an opportunity to betray him.

Now on the first day of Unleavened Bread the disciples came to Jesus to say, 'Where do you want us to make the preparations for you to eat the passover?' 'Go to so-and-so in the city' he replied 'and say to him, "The Master says: My time is near. It is at your house that I am keeping Passover with my disciples."' The disciples did what Jesus told them and prepared the Passover.

When evening came he was at table with the twelve disciples. And while they were eating he said, 'I tell you solemnly, one of you is about to betray me.' They were greatly distressed and started asking him in turn, 'Not I, Lord, surely?' He answered, 'Someone who has dipped his hand into the dish with me, will betray me. The Son of Man is going to his fate, as the scriptures say he will, but alas for that man by whom the Son of Man is betrayed! Better for that man if he had never been born!' Judas, who was to betray him, asked in his turn, 'Not I, Rabbi, surely?' 'They are your own words' answered Jesus.

### Reflection

There are gestures that could signal that there is an existing relationship among people, such as eating together regularly. However, this is not always the case. Jesus and his Apostles have on many occasions dined together yet Judas betrayed him. No one should make an exploitative use of his/her closeness to anyone to betray the person. Jesus is betrayed in the person who backbites others. Let everyone support one another and avoid putting anyone down.

Exodus 12:1-8.11-14
*(See Appendix B-9)*

**Psalm 115:12-13.15-18. R. cf. 1 Cor 10:16**
*The blessing-cup that we bless is a communion with the blood of Christ.*

### 1 Corinthians 11:23-26
This is what I received from the Lord, and in turn passed on to you: that on the same night that he was betrayed, the Lord Jesus took some bread, and thanked God for it and broke it, and he said, 'This is my body, which is for you; do this as a memorial of me.' In the same way he took the cup after supper, and said, 'This cup is the new covenant in my blood. Whenever you drink it, do this as a memorial of me.' Until the Lord comes, therefore, every time you eat this bread and drink this cup, you are proclaiming his death.

### John 13:1-15
It was before the festival of the Passover, and Jesus knew that the hour had come for him to pass from this world to the Father. He had always loved those who were his in the world, but now he showed how perfect his love was.

**Holy Thursday
Evening Mass of the
Lord's Supper
White**

They were at supper, and the devil had already put it into the mind of Judas Iscariot son of Simon, to betray him. Jesus knew that the Father had put everything into his hands, and that he had come from God and was returning to God, and he got up from table, removed his outer garment and, taking a towel, wrapped it round his waist; he then poured water into a basin and began to wash the disciples' feet and to wipe them with the towel he was wearing.

He came to Simon Peter, who said to him, 'Lord, are you going to wash my feet?' Jesus answered, 'At the moment you do not know what I am doing, but later you will understand.' 'Never!' said Peter. 'You shall never wash my feet.' Jesus replied, 'If I do not wash you, you can have nothing in common with me.' 'Then, Lord,' said Simon Peter 'not only my feet, but my hands and my head as well!' Jesus said, 'No one who has taken a bath needs washing, he is clean all over. You too are clean, though not all of you are.' He knew who was going to betray him, that was why he said, 'though not all of you are.'

When he had washed their feet and put on his clothes again he went back to the table. 'Do you understand,' he said, 'what I have done to you? You call me Master and Lord, and rightly; so I am. If I, then, the Lord and Master, have washed your feet, you should wash each other's feet. I have given you an example so that you may copy what I have done to you.'

### Reflection
Once more we are invited to enter into the once-for-all-time saving event of Jesus' passion, death and resurrection. The Holy Spirit, who makes the entire Paschal Mystery present at every celebration of the Mass, summons us and calls us to understand, to appreciate and to love this Mystery more deeply than before. And the heart of the Mystery is the limitless Love of God in Jesus Christ which reveals itself in his giving himself wholly to us, pouring out his merciful love as the water is poured over the Apostles' feet. How can we respond, except by pouring out our lives to him and to one another.

**Good Friday
Celebration
of the Lord's Passion
Red**

**Isaiah 52:13–53:12**

See, my servant will prosper, he shall be lifted up, exalted, rise to great heights. As the crowds were appalled on seeing him – so disfigured did he look that he seemed no longer human – so will the crowds be astonished at him, and kings stand speechless before him; for they shall see something never told and witness something never heard before: 'Who could believe what we have heard, and to whom has the power of the Lord been revealed?' Like a sapling he grew up in front of us, like a root in arid ground. Without beauty, without majesty (we saw him), no looks to attract our eyes; a thing despised and rejected by men, a man of sorrows and familiar with suffering, a man to make people screen their faces; he was despised and we took no account of him. And yet ours were the sufferings he bore, ours the sorrows he carried. But we, we thought of him as someone punished, struck by God, and brought low. Yet he was pierced through for our faults, crushed for our sins. …
*(See Appendix B-9)*

**Psalm 30:2.6.12-13.15-17.25. R. Luke 23:46**
*Father, into your hands I commend my spirit.*

**Hebrews 4:14-16; 5:7-9**

Since in Jesus, the Son of God, we have the supreme high priest who has gone through to the highest heaven, we must never let go of the faith that we have professed. For it is not as if we had a high priest who was incapable of feeling our weaknesses with us; but we have one who has been tempted in every way that we are, though he is without sin. Let us be confident, then, in approaching the throne of grace, that we shall have mercy from him and find grace when we are in need of help.

During his life on earth, he offered up prayer and entreaty, aloud and in silent tears, to the one who had the power to save him out of death, and he submitted so humbly that his prayer was heard. Although he was Son, he learnt to obey through suffering; but having been made perfect, he became for all who obey him the source of eternal salvation.

**John 18:1–19:42**
*(Please see the Bible for the Passion reading)*

**Reflection**

God incarnate is betrayed in a garden, that those whose parents had rejected his lordship in a garden might be restored to Paradise. The Word-made-Flesh, at whose command creation sprang to life, remains silent before his earthly judge in order to free sinners from his just judgement. The God-Man who once was tenderly laid on the rough wood of the manger is now mercilessly nailed to the wood of the Cross that those who were without mercy might be shown it. Let us anoint his wounded and outraged Body with the balm of our repentance and gratitude.

**Easter Vigil**
**White**

## Romans 6:3-11

When we were baptised in Christ Jesus we were baptised in his death; in other words, when we were baptised we went into the tomb with him and joined him in death, so that as Christ was raised from the dead by the Father's glory, we too might live a new life.

If in union with Christ we have imitated his death, we shall also imitate him in his resurrection. We must realise that our former selves have been crucified with him to destroy this sinful body and to free us from the slavery of sin. When a man dies, of course, he has finished with sin.

But we believe that having died with Christ we shall return to life with him: Christ, as we know, having been raised from the dead will never die again. Death has no power over him any more. When he died, he died, once for all, to sin, so his life now is life with God; and in that way, you too must consider yourselves to be dead to sin but alive for God in Christ Jesus.

## Psalm 117:1-2.16-17.22-23

*Alleluia, alleluia, alleluia!*

## Mark 16:1-7

When the sabbath was over, Mary of Magdala, Mary the mother of James, and Salome, bought spices with which to go and anoint him. And very early in the morning on the first day of the week they went to the tomb, just as the sun was rising.

They had been saying to one another, 'Who will roll away the stone for us from the entrance to the tomb?' But when they looked they could see that the stone – which was very big – had already been rolled back. On entering the tomb they saw a young man in a white robe seated on the right-hand side, and they were struck with amazement. But he said to them, 'There is no need for alarm. You are looking for Jesus of Nazareth, who was crucified: he has risen, he is not here. See, here is the place where they laid him. But you must go and tell his disciples and Peter, "He is going before you to Galilee; it is there you will see him, just as he told you."'

## Reflection

Human history reaches its climax in the Resurrection of its Lord: the manifestation of the glory which poured from the perfect act of divine love of his Passion and Death. And all of it for us; that we might follow him from darkness to light, from slavery to sin to the freedom of the sons of God. Whatever hardness or blockage there is in us, let us surrender it to the Lord, who will remove it as the stone was removed from the tomb, and fill us with the newness and wonder of his Resurrection. Death, where is thy sting? Grave, where is thy victory? Christ is risen, Alleluia!

### Acts 10:34.37-43

Peter addressed Cornelius and his household: 'You must have heard about the recent happenings in Judaea: about Jesus of Nazareth and how he began in Galilee, after John had been preaching baptism. God had anointed him with the Holy Spirit and with power, and because God was with him, Jesus went about doing good and curing all who had fallen into the power of the devil. Now I, and those with me, can witness to everything he did throughout the countryside of Judaea and in Jerusalem itself: and also to the fact that they killed him by hanging him on a tree, yet three days afterwards God raised him to life and allowed him to be seen, not by the whole people but only by certain witnesses God had chosen beforehand. Now we are those witnesses – we have eaten and drunk with him after his resurrection from the dead – and he has ordered us to proclaim this to his people and to tell them that God has appointed him to judge everyone, alive or dead. It is to him that all the prophets bear this witness: that all who believe in Jesus will have their sins forgiven through his name.'

### Psalm 117:1-2.16-17.22-23. R. v.24

*This day was made by the Lord; we rejoice and are glad.*

### Colossians 3:1-4

*(Alternative reading: 1 Corinthians 5:6-8)*

Since you have been brought back to true life with Christ, you must look for the things that are in heaven, where Christ is, sitting at God's right hand. Let your thoughts be on heavenly things, not on the things that are on the earth, because you have died, and now the life you have is hidden with Christ in God. But when Christ is revealed – and he is your life – you too will be revealed in all your glory with him.

### John 20:1-9

It was very early on the first day of the week and still dark, when Mary of Magdala came to the tomb. She saw that the stone had been moved away from the tomb and came running to Simon Peter and the other disciple, the one Jesus loved. 'They have taken the Lord out of the tomb' she said 'and we don't know where they have put him.'

So Peter set out with the other disciple to go to the tomb. They ran together, but the other disciple, running faster than Peter, reached the tomb first; he bent down and saw the linen cloths lying on the ground, but did not go in. Simon Peter who was following now came up, went right into the tomb, saw the linen cloths on the ground, and also the cloth that had been over his head; this was not with the linen cloths but rolled up in a place by itself. Then the other disciple who had reached the tomb first also went in; he saw and he believed. Till this moment they had failed to understand the teaching of scripture, that he must rise from the dead.

### Reflection
Sometimes we need reminding that Sunday, not Monday, is the first day of the week! The Day of Resurrection, the eighth day of God's great week, having rested in the sleep of death on his saving Sabbath, and risen to never-ending life in his human body. It is the first day of the week of weeks – the fifty days of the Easter Season – in which the glory and the joy of the Resurrection spill-over upon the Church, upon humanity, that we might be caught-up in and transformed by his victory. His glory is the source of our holiness; let us rejoice in it!

**Easter Monday**
White

_____

### Acts 2:14.22-33

On the day of Pentecost, Peter stood up with the Eleven and addressed the crowd in a loud voice: 'Men of Israel, listen to what I am going to say: Jesus the Nazarene was a man commended to you by God by the miracles and portents and signs that God worked through him when he was among you, as you all know. This man, who was put into your power by the deliberate intention and foreknowledge of God, you took and had crucified by men outside the Law. You killed him, but God raised him to life, freeing him from the pangs of Hades; for it was impossible for him to be held in its power since, as David says of him: I saw the Lord before me always, for with him at my right hand nothing can shake me. So my heart was glad and my tongue cried out with joy; my body, too, will rest in the hope that you will not abandon my soul to Hades nor allow your holy one to experience corruption. You have made known the way of life to me, you will fill me with gladness through your presence. *(See Appendix B-9)*

### Psalm 15:1-2.5.7-11. R. v.1

*Preserve me, Lord, I take refuge in you.* (or *Alleluia!*)

### Matthew 28:8-15

Filled with awe and great joy the women came quickly away from the tomb and ran to tell the disciples.

And there, coming to meet them, was Jesus. 'Greetings' he said. And the women came up to him and, falling down before him, clasped his feet. Then Jesus said to them, 'Do not be afraid; go and tell my brothers that they must leave for Galilee; they will see me there.'

While they were on their way, some of the guard went off into the city to tell the chief priests all that had happened. These held a meeting with the elders and, after some discussion, handed a considerable sum of money to the soldiers with these instructions, 'This is what you must say, "His disciples came during the night and stole him away while we were asleep. " And should the governor come to hear of this, we undertake to put things right with him ourselves and to see that you do not get into trouble.' The soldiers took the money and carried out their instructions, and to this day that is the story among the Jews.

### Reflection

Tainted money was exchanged to betray the Son of God into the hands of those who would send him to his death. More money is exchanged in the attempt to silence his conquering death in his rising. Yet priceless and free is the gift of life and freedom the Saving Victim longs to bestow upon those who dare to entrust themselves to him.

**Easter Tuesday**
**White**

## Acts 2:36-41

On the day of Pentecost, Peter spoke to the Jews: 'The whole House of Israel can be certain that God has made this Jesus whom you crucified both Lord and Christ.'

Hearing this, they were cut to the heart and said to Peter and the apostles, 'What must we do, brothers?' 'You must repent,' Peter answered 'and every one of you must be baptised in the name of Jesus Christ for the forgiveness of your sins, and you will receive the gift of the Holy Spirit. The promise that was made is for you and your children, and for all those who are far away, for all those whom the Lord our God will call to himself.' He spoke to them for a long time using many arguments, and he urged them, 'Save yourselves from this perverse generation.' They were convinced by his arguments, and they accepted what he said and were baptised. That very day about three thousand were added to their number.

## Psalm 32:4-5.18-20.22. R. v.5

*The Lord fills the earth with his love.* (or *Alleluia!*)

## John 20:11-18

Mary stayed outside near the tomb, weeping. Then, still weeping, she stooped to look inside, and saw two angels in white sitting where the body of Jesus had been, one at the head, the other at the feet. They said, 'Woman, why are you weeping?' 'They have taken my Lord away,' she replied 'and I don't know where they have put him.' As she said this she turned round and saw Jesus standing there, though she did not recognise him. Jesus said, 'Woman, why are you weeping? Who are you looking for?' Supposing him to be the gardener, she said, 'Sir, if you have taken him away, tell me where you have put him, and I will go and remove him.' Jesus said, 'Mary!' She knew him then and said to him in Hebrew, 'Rabbuni!' – which means Master. Jesus said to her, 'Do not cling to me, because I have not yet ascended to the Father. But go and find the brothers, and tell them: I am ascending to my Father and your Father, to my God and your God.' So Mary of Magdala went and told the disciples that she had seen the Lord and that he had said these things to her.

## Reflection

Mary Magdalene's first encounter with the Risen Jesus, far from being a spectacular scene, is instead steeped in a beautiful tenderness. The intensity of her grief springs from the depth of the love she has for him who loved her first. And already in this exchange there is something new: a grandeur of liberty which enables her to run to the brothers with no fear of ever losing him again. She does not need to cling to him now, for she is held in the embrace of the One who can never die again.

**Easter Wednesday**
**White**

Acts 3:1-10
*(See Appendix B-10)*

Psalm 104:1-4.6-9. R. v.3
*Let the hearts that seek the Lord rejoice.* (or *Alleluia!*)

Luke 24:13-35

Two of the disciples of Jesus were on their way to a village called Emmaus, seven miles from Jerusalem, and they were talking together about all that had happened. Now as they talked this over, Jesus himself came up and walked by their side; but something prevented them from recognising him. He said to them, 'What matters are you discussing as you walk along?' They stopped short, their faces downcast.

Then one of them, called Cleopas, answered him, 'You must be the only person staying in Jerusalem who does not know the things that have been happening there these last few days.' 'What things?' he asked. 'All about Jesus of Nazareth' they answered 'who proved he was a great prophet by the things he said and did in the sight of God and of the whole people; and how our chief priests and our leaders handed him over to be sentenced to death, and had him crucified. Our own hope had been that he would be the one to set Israel free. And this is not all: two whole days have gone by since it all happened; and some women from our group have astounded us: they went to the tomb in the early morning, and when they did not find the body, they came back to tell us they had seen a vision of angels who declared he was alive. Some of our friends went to the tomb and found everything exactly as the women had reported, but of him they saw nothing.'

Then he said to them, 'You foolish men! So slow to believe the full message of the prophets! Was it not ordained that the Christ should suffer and so enter into his glory?' Then, starting with Moses and going through all the prophets, he explained to them the passages throughout the scriptures that were about himself.

When they drew near to the village to which they were going, he made as if to go on; but they pressed him to stay with them. 'It is nearly evening' they said 'and the day is almost over.' So he went in to stay with them. Now while he was with them at table, he took the bread and said the blessing; then he broke it and handed it to them. And their eyes were opened and they recognised him; but he had vanished from their sight. Then they said to each other, 'Did not our hearts burn within us as he talked to us on the road and explained the scriptures to us?' *(See Appendix B-10)*

## Reflection

But he had vanished from their sight. Where did he disappear to? Back to his Father, back to heaven, which he had never left? Disappeared in order to make another resurrection appearance in another place, to other friends? Certainly. But, even more astonishingly, he had disappeared into the Eucharist. And there, in the sacrifice of the Mass and in the consecrated elements, he is present to us, until the day he returns in glory. The Holy Mass, then, is the Beautiful Gate for all those who look expectantly to Jesus for healing and for life, and who long to enter eternal life.

**Acts 3:11-26**

Everyone came running towards Peter and John in great excitement, to the Portico of Solomon, as it is called, where the man was still clinging to them. When Peter saw the people he addressed them, 'Why are you so surprised at this? Why are you staring at us as though we had made this man walk by our own power or holiness? You are Israelites, and it is the God of Abraham, Isaac and Jacob, the God of our ancestors, who has glorified his servant Jesus, the same Jesus you handed over and then disowned in the presence of Pilate, after Pilate had decided to release him. It was you who accused the Holy One, the Just One, you who demanded the reprieve of a murderer while you killed the prince of life. God, however, raised him from the dead, and to that fact we are the witnesses; and it is the name of Jesus which, through our faith in it, has brought back the strength of this man whom you see here and who is well known to you. ... *(See Appendix B-10)*

Easter Thursday
White

**Psalm 8:2.5-9. R. v.2**

*How great is your name, O Lord our God, through all the earth!* (or *Alleluia!*)

**Luke 24:35-48**

The disciples told their story of what had happened on the road and how they had recognised Jesus at the breaking of bread.

They were still talking about this when Jesus himself stood among them and said to them, 'Peace be with you!' In a state of alarm and fright, they thought they were seeing a ghost. But he said, 'Why are you so agitated, and why are these doubts rising in your hearts? Look at my hands and feet; yes, it is I indeed. Touch me and see for yourselves; a ghost has no flesh and bones as you can see I have.' And as he said this he showed them his hands and feet. Their joy was so great that they could not believe it, and they stood there dumbfounded; so he said to them, 'Have you anything here to eat?' And they offered him a piece of grilled fish, which he took and ate before their eyes.

Then he told them, 'This is what I meant when I said, while I was still with you, that everything written about me, in the Law of Moses, in the Prophets and in the Psalms, has to be fulfilled.' He then opened their minds to understand the scriptures, and he said to them, 'So you see how it is written that the Christ would suffer and on the third day rise from the dead, and that, in his name, repentance for the forgiveness of sins would be preached to all the nations, beginning from Jerusalem. You are witnesses to this.'

**Reflection**

The disciples are not so much surprised by joy as shocked by joy! Shocked into a wonder-struck silence as they behold the Prince of Life – their master and best friend – now radiant with the glory of heaven, yet still desiring to eat and drink with them. It is this same joy which is at the heart of his call to repentance to this day. He longs to forgive our sins so that our life might be caught up in his joy.

**Easter Friday**
**White**

### Acts 4:1-12

While Peter and John were talking to the people the priests came up to him, accompanied by the captain of the Temple and the Sadducees. They were extremely annoyed at their teaching the people the doctrine of the resurrection from the dead by proclaiming the resurrection of Jesus. ...
*(See Appendix B-11)*

### Psalm 117:1-2.4.22-27. R. v.22

*The stone which the builders rejected has become the corner stone.* (or *Alleluia!*)

### John 21:1-14

Jesus showed himself again to the disciples. It was by the Sea of Tiberias, and it happened like this: Simon Peter, Thomas called the Twin, Nathanael from Cana in Galilee, the sons of Zebedee and two more of his disciples were together. Simon Peter said, 'I'm going fishing.' They replied, 'We'll come with you.' They went out and got into the boat but caught nothing that night.

It was light by now and there stood Jesus on the shore, though the disciples did not realise that it was Jesus. Jesus called out, 'Have you caught anything, friends?' And when they answered, 'No,' he said, 'Throw the net out to starboard and you'll find something.' So they dropped the net, and there were so many fish that they could not haul it in. The disciple Jesus loved said to Peter, 'It is the Lord.' At these words 'It is the Lord', Simon Peter, who had practically nothing on, wrapped his cloak round him and jumped into the water. The other disciples came on in the boat, towing the net and the fish; they were only about a hundred yards from land.

As soon as they came ashore they saw that there was some bread there, and a charcoal fire with fish cooking on it. Jesus said, 'Bring some of the fish you have just caught.' Simon Peter went aboard and dragged the net to the shore, full of big fish, one hundred and fifty-three of them; and in spite of there being so many the net was not broken. Jesus said to them, 'Come and have breakfast.' None of the disciples was bold enough to ask, 'Who are you?'; they knew quite well it was the Lord. Jesus then stepped forward, took the bread and gave it to them, and the same with the fish. This was the third time that Jesus showed himself to the disciples after rising from the dead.

### Reflection

Jesus called his first disciples at the lakeside and it is there again that he calls them after his rising from the dead. At that first miraculous haul of fish Peter had recoiled from the Lord, aware of his sinfulness and inadequacy. This time he jumps into the water and swims as fast as he can to reach Jesus. Peter is as spontaneous as ever, but something is different. He and the others have entered their maturity as fishers of men, since their ministry will be rooted in the power of Jesus who provides every need – even breakfast!

**Easter Saturday**
**White**

### Acts 4:13-21

The rulers, elders and scribes were astonished at the assurance shown by Peter and John, considering they were uneducated laymen; and they recognised them as associates of Jesus; but when they saw the man who had been cured standing by their side, they could find no answer. So they ordered them to stand outside while the Sanhedrin had a private discussion. 'What are we going to do with these men?' they asked. 'It is obvious to everybody in Jerusalem that a miracle has been worked through them in public, and we cannot deny it. But to stop the whole thing spreading any further among the people, let us caution them never to speak to anyone in this name again.'

So they called them in and gave them a warning on no account to make statements or to teach in the name of Jesus. But Peter and John retorted, 'You must judge whether in God's eyes it is right to listen to you and not to God. We cannot promise to stop proclaiming what we have seen and heard.' The court repeated the warnings and then released them; they could not think of any way to punish them, since all the people were giving glory to God for what had happened.

### Psalm 117:1.14-21. R. v.21

*I will thank you, Lord, for you have given answer.* (or *Alleluia!*)

### Mark 16:9-15

Having risen in the morning on the first day of the week, Jesus appeared first to Mary of Magdala from whom he had cast out seven devils. She then went to those who had been his companions, and who were mourning and in tears, and told them. But they did not believe her when they heard her say that he was alive and that she had seen him.

After this, he showed himself under another form to two of them as they were on their way into the country. These went back and told the others, who did not believe them either.

Lastly, he showed himself to the Eleven themselves while they were at table. He reproached them for their incredulity and obstinacy, because they had refused to believe those who had seen him after he had risen. And he said to them, 'Go out to the whole world; proclaim the Good News to all creation.'

### Reflection

If you were to invent a story of a man coming back from the dead, you most likely would not have it that his chosen friends would refuse to believe that he had risen! Slow to believe as we are, there is an even greater joy when we see the risen Jesus in his sacred humanity reproach and then commission his disciples. Their initial inertia has evaporated in his presence and the rest of their earthly life will be spent ceaselessly proclaiming that he is alive. Their proclamation now is ours.

**2nd Sunday of Easter**
**Divine Mercy Sunday**
**Psalter Week 2**
**White**

**Acts 4:32-35**

The whole group of believers was united, heart and soul; no one claimed for his own use anything that he had, as everything they owned was held in common.

The apostles continued to testify to the resurrection of the Lord Jesus with great power, and they were all given great respect.

None of their members was ever in want, as all those who owned land or houses would sell them, and bring the money from them, to present it to the apostles; it was then distributed to any members who might be in need.

**Psalm 117:2-4.15-18.22-24. R. v.1**
*Give thanks to the Lord for he is good, for his love has no end.* (or *Alleluia!*)

**1 John 5:1-6**

Whoever believes that Jesus is the Christ has been begotten by God; and whoever loves the Father that begot him loves the child whom he begets. We can be sure that we love God's children if we love God himself and do what he has commanded us; this is what loving God is – keeping his commandments; and his commandments are not difficult, because anyone who has been begotten by God has already overcome the world; this is the victory over the world – our faith. Who can overcome the world? Only the man who believes that Jesus is the Son of God; Jesus Christ who came by water and blood, not with water only, but with water and blood; with the Spirit as another witness – since the Spirit is the truth.

**John 20:19-31**

In the evening of that same day, the first day of the week, the doors were closed in the room where the disciples were, for fear of the Jews. Jesus came and stood among them. He said to them, 'Peace be with you,' and showed them his hands and his side. The disciples were filled with joy when they saw the Lord, and he said to them again, 'Peace be with you.

'As the Father sent me, so am I sending you,'

After saying this he breathed on them and said: 'Receive the Holy Spirit. For those whose sins you forgive, they are forgiven; for those whose sins you retain, they are retained.'

Thomas, called the Twin, who was one of the Twelve, was not with them when Jesus came. When the disciples said, 'We have seen the Lord,' he answered, 'Unless I see the holes that the nails made in his hands and can put my finger into the holes they made, and unless I can put my hand into his side, I refuse to believe.' Eight days later the disciples were in the house again and Thomas was with them. The doors were closed, but Jesus came in and stood among them. 'Peace be with you,' he said. Then he spoke to Thomas, 'Put your finger here; look, here are my hands. Give me your hand; put it into my side. Doubt no longer but believe.' Thomas replied, 'My Lord and my God!' Jesus said to him; 'You believe because you can see me. Happy are those who have not seen and yet believe.'

There were many other signs that Jesus worked and the disciples saw, but they are not recorded in this book. These are recorded so that you may believe that Jesus is the Christ, the Son of God, and that believing this you may have life through his name.

## Reflection

True peace is discovered in the healing of our wounds. And it is from the glorious and ever-open wounds of the risen Jesus that all healing flows. The blood and water which still flow mystically from the ascended Christ, through the sacraments of the Church, heal the wounds of sin and bestow the peace which no earthly thing can provide. To live in the Divine Mercy is to return time and again to him, to be washed from our sin, healed of our brokenness and restored to heavenly life.

**2nd Week of Easter**
**White**

### Acts 4:23-31

As soon as Peter and John were released they went to the community and told them everything the chief priests and elders had said to them. When they heard it they lifted up their voice to God all together. 'Master,' they prayed 'it is you who made heaven and earth and sea, and everything in them; you it is who said through the Holy Spirit and speaking through our ancestor David, your servant: Why this arrogance among the nations, these futile plots among the peoples? Kings on earth setting out to war, princes making an alliance, against the Lord and against his Anointed.

'This is what has come true: in this very city Herod and Pontius Pilate made an alliance with the pagan nations and the peoples of Israel, against your holy servant Jesus whom you anointed, but only to bring about the very thing that you in your strength and your wisdom had predetermined should happen. And now, Lord, take note of their threats and help your servants to proclaim your message with all boldness, by stretching out your hand to heal and to work miracles and marvels through the name of your holy servant Jesus.' As they prayed, the house where they were assembled rocked; they were all filled with the Holy Spirit and began to proclaim the word of God boldly.

### Psalm 2:1-9. R. cf. v.13

*Blessed are they who put their trust in God.* (or *Alleluia!*)

### John 3:1-8

There was one of the Pharisees called Nicodemus, a leading Jew, who came to Jesus by night and said, 'Rabbi, we know that you are a teacher who comes from God; for no one could perform the signs that you do unless God were with him.' Jesus answered: 'I tell you most solemnly, unless a man is born from above, he cannot see the kingdom of God.'

Nicodemus said, 'How can a grown man be born? Can he go back into his mother's womb and be born again?' Jesus replied: 'I tell you most solemnly, unless a man is born through water and the Spirit, he cannot enter the kingdom of God: what is born of the flesh is flesh; what is born of the Spirit is spirit. Do not be surprised when I say: You must be born from above. The wind blows wherever it pleases; you hear its sound, but you cannot tell where it comes from or where it is going. That is how it is with all who are born of the Spirit.'

### Reflection

It is ironic that the Greek name Nicodemus means 'Victory of the People', since Nicodemus is at the fringe of understanding that victory is something we cannot achieve for ourselves, since it is a gift. He is a teacher of the Law, but grace and truth are the gift of Jesus. To be born again is to accept the invitation to leave the darkness of doubt and to walk in the light of Christ, who in Baptism immerses us in the life of the Spirit.

## Acts 4:32-37

The whole group of believers was united, heart and soul; no one claimed for his own use anything that he had, as everything they owned was held in common.

The apostles continued to testify to the resurrection of the Lord Jesus with great power, and they were all given great respect.

None of their members was ever in want, as all those who owned land or houses would sell them, and bring the money from them, to present it to the apostles; it was then distributed to any members who might be in need.

There was a Levite of Cypriot origin called Joseph whom the apostles surnamed Barnabas (which means 'son of encouragement'). He owned a piece of land and he sold it and brought the money, and presented it to the apostles.

## Psalm 92:1-2.5. R. v.1

*The Lord is king, with majesty enrobed. (or Alleluia!)*

## John 3:7-15

Jesus said to Nicodemus: 'Do not be surprised when I say: You must be born from above. The wind blows wherever it pleases; you hear its sound, but you cannot tell where it comes from or where it is going. That is how it is with all who are born of the Spirit.' 'How can that be possible?' asked Nicodemus. 'You, a teacher in Israel, and you do not know these things!' replied Jesus. 'I tell you most solemnly, we speak only about what we know and witness only to what we have seen and yet you people reject our evidence. If you do not believe me when I speak about things in this world, how are you going to believe me when I speak to you about heavenly things? No one has gone up to heaven except the one who came down from heaven, the Son of Man who is in heaven; and the Son of Man must be lifted up as Moses lifted up the serpent in the desert, so that everyone who believes may have eternal life in him.'

**2nd Week of Easter**
**White**
**or**
**St Martin I**, *pope, martyr*
**(Optional, Red)**

## Reflection

Already in the first days of the new-born Church a new quality of life is evident amongst the believers, a quality which is born of a paradox. Through faith in Jesus, who was himself lifted up on the Cross, they have been lifted up into heavenly love, yet live with greater ease on earth. Their release from earth-bound concerns displays itself in a remarkable communion of life, where God's generosity towards them inspires their giving of themselves and their goods to one another.

**2nd Week of Easter**
**White**

### Acts 5:17-26

The high priest intervened with all his supporters from the party of the Sadducees. Prompted by jealousy, they arrested the apostles and had them put in the common gaol.

But at night the angel of the Lord opened the prison gates and said as he led them out, 'Go and stand in the Temple, and tell the people all about this new Life.' They did as they were told; they went into the Temple at dawn and began to preach.

When the high priest arrived, he and his supporters convened the Sanhedrin – this was the full Senate of Israel – and sent to the gaol for them to be brought. But when the officials arrived at the prison they found they were not inside, so they went back and reported, 'We found the gaol securely locked and the warders on duty at the gates, but when we unlocked the door we found no one inside.' When the captain of the Temple and the chief priests heard this news they wondered what this could mean. Then a man arrived with fresh news. 'At this very moment,' he said 'the men you imprisoned are in the Temple. They are standing there preaching to the people.' The captain went with his men and fetched them. They were afraid to use force in case the people stoned them.

### Psalm 33:2-9. R. v.7

*This poor man called and the Lord heard him.* (or *Alleluia!*)

### John 3:16-21

Jesus said to Nicodemus: 'God loved the world so much that he gave his only Son, so that everyone who believes in him may not be lost but may have eternal life. For God sent his Son into the world not to condemn the world, but so that through him the world might be saved. No one who believes in him will be condemned; but whoever refuses to believe is condemned already, because he has refused to believe in the name of God's only Son. On these grounds is sentence pronounced: that though the light has come into the world men have shown they prefer darkness to the light because their deeds were evil. And indeed, everybody who does wrong hates the light and avoids it, for fear his actions should be exposed; but the man who lives by the truth comes out into the light, so that it may be plainly seen that what he does is done in God.'

### Reflection

The jealousy which prompted the High Priest and the Sadducees to imprison the apostles betrayed their utter misunderstanding of the God whom they claimed to serve. All Israel longed for the Messiah, yet they are so imprisoned in their self-righteousness that they cannot see him for who he is: the God of love-made-man. It takes courage to stand in the Light of Christ's divine gaze, but liberation is the result for those who humble themselves.

## Acts 5:27-33

When the officials had brought the apostles in to face the Sanhedrin, the high priest demanded an explanation. 'We gave you a formal warning' he said 'not to preach in this name, and what have you done? You have filled Jerusalem with your teaching, and seem determined to fix the guilt of this man's death on us.' In reply Peter and the apostles said, 'Obedience to God comes before obedience to men; it was the God of our ancestors who raised up Jesus, but it was you who had him executed by hanging on a tree. By his own right hand God has now raised him up to be leader and saviour, to give repentance and forgiveness of sins through him to Israel. We are witnesses to all this, we and the Holy Spirit whom God has given to those who obey him.'

This so infuriated them that they wanted to put them to death.

## Psalm 33:2.9.17-20. R. v.7

*This poor man called and the Lord heard him.* (or *Alleluia!*)

## John 3:31-36

John the Baptist said to his disciples: 'He who comes from above is above all others; he who is born of the earth is earthly himself and speaks in an earthly way. He who comes from heaven bears witness to the things he has seen and heard, even if his testimony is not accepted; though all who do accept his testimony are attesting the truthfulness of God, since he whom God has sent speaks God's own words: God gives him the Spirit without reserve. The Father loves the Son and has entrusted everything to him. Anyone who believes in the Son has eternal life, but anyone who refuses to believe in the Son will never see life: the anger of God stays on him.'

**2nd Week of Easter**
**White**

## Reflection

The union of the Father and the Son is such that to refuse the Son is to bring God's anger upon oneself, since to refuse Jesus is to refuse the Father. Upon those who accept him, however, the Holy Spirit is lavished, in whom the believer is lifted into the unimaginable love of God the Trinity.

### Acts 5:34-42
One member of the Sanhedrin, a Pharisee called Gamaliel, who was a doctor of the Law and respected by the whole people, stood up and asked to have the apostles taken outside for a time. Then he addressed the Sanhedrin, 'Men of Israel, be careful how you deal with these people. There was Theudas who became notorious not so long ago. He claimed to be someone important, and he even collected about four hundred followers; but when he was killed, all his followers scattered and that was the end of them. ...
*(See Appendix B-11)*

### Psalm 26:1.4.13-14. R. cf. v.4
*There is one thing I ask of the Lord, to live in the house of the Lord.* (or *Alleluia!*)

### John 6:1-15
Jesus went off to the other side of the Sea of Galilee – or of Tiberias – and a large crowd followed him, impressed by the signs he gave by curing the sick. Jesus climbed the hillside, and sat down there with his disciples. It was shortly before the Jewish feast of Passover.

Looking up, Jesus saw the crowds approaching and said to Philip, 'Where can we buy some bread for these people to eat?' He only said this to test Philip; he himself knew exactly what he was going to do. Philip answered, 'Two hundred denarii would only buy enough to give them a small piece each.' One of his disciples, Andrew, Simon Peter's brother, said, 'There is a small boy here with five barley loaves and two fish; but what is that between so many?' Jesus said to them, 'Make the people sit down.' There was plenty of grass there, and as many as five thousand men sat down. Then Jesus took the loaves, gave thanks, and gave them out to all who were sitting ready; he then did the same with the fish, giving out as much as they wanted. When they had eaten enough he said to the disciples, 'Pick up the pieces left over, so that nothing gets wasted.' So they picked them up, and filled twelve hampers with scraps left over from the meal of five barley loaves. The people, seeing this sign that he had given, said, 'This really is the prophet who is to come into the world.' Jesus, who could see they were about to come and take him by force and make him king, escaped back to the hills by himself.

### Reflection
In the joy of the resurrection the Apostles are indifferent to the threats of the religious authorities, to the point of rejoicing to bear humiliation. The twelve baskets of left-overs at this miraculous foreshadowing of the Eucharist represent the entrusting of the Bread of Life to the care of the Apostles and their successors. Let our love for Jesus in the Eucharist be intensified as we pray for the fidelity and zeal of our shepherds.

**2nd Week of Easter**
**White**

## Acts 6:1-7

About this time, when the number of disciples was increasing, the Hellenists made a complaint against the Hebrews: in the daily distribution their own widows were being overlooked. So the Twelve called a full meeting of the disciples and addressed them 'It would not be right for us to neglect the word of God so as to give out food; you, brothers, must select from among yourselves seven men of good reputation, filled with the Spirit and with wisdom; we will hand over this duty to them, and continue to devote ourselves to prayer and to the service of the word.' The whole assembly approved of this proposal and elected Stephen, a man full of faith and of the Holy Spirit, together with Philip, Prochorus, Nicanor, Timon, Parmenas, and Nicolaus of Antioch, a convert to Judaism. They presented these to the apostles, who prayed and laid their hands on them.

The word of the Lord continued to spread: the number of disciples in Jerusalem was greatly increased, and a large group of priests made their submission to the faith.

## Psalm 32:1-2.4-5.18-19. R. v.22

*May your love be upon us, O Lord, as we place all our hope in you. (or Alleluia!)*

## John 6:16-21

In the evening the disciples went down to the shore of the lake and got into a boat to make for Capernaum on the other side of the lake. It was getting dark by now and Jesus had still not rejoined them. The wind was strong, and the sea was getting rough. They had rowed three or four miles when they saw Jesus walking on the lake and coming towards the boat. This frightened them, but he said, 'It is I. Do not be afraid.' They were for taking him into the boat, but in no time it reached the shore at the place they were making for.

## Reflection

No sooner have the Apostles ministered the miraculous bread to the people than the Lord permits them to experience the forces of nature, over which Jesus will triumph in his death and rising. If we draw upon the heavenly strength of the Eucharist, we too will experience trials, through which – if we rely on him – his love may triumph in us and our journey to our true homeland be strengthened.

**3rd Sunday of Easter**
Psalter Week 3
White

### Acts 3:13-15.17-19

Peter said to the people: 'You are Israelites, and it is the God of Abraham, Isaac and Jacob, the God of our ancestors, who has glorified his servant Jesus, the same Jesus you handed over and then disowned in the presence of Pilate, after Pilate had decided to release him. It was you who accused the Holy One, the Just One, you who demanded the reprieve of a murderer while you killed the prince of life. God, however, raised him from the dead, and to that fact we are the witnesses.

'Now I know, brothers, that neither you nor your leaders had any idea what you were really doing; this was the way God carried out what he had foretold, when he said through all his prophets that his Christ would suffer. Now you must repent and turn to God, so that your sins may be wiped out.'

**Psalm 4:2.4.7.9. R. v.7**

*Lift up the light of your face on us, O Lord.* (or *Alleluia!*)

## 1 John 2:1-5

I am writing this, my children, to stop you sinning; but if anyone should sin, we have our advocate with the Father, Jesus Christ, who is just; he is the sacrifice that takes our sins away, and not only ours, but the whole world's. We can be sure that we know God only by keeping his commandments. Anyone who says, 'I know him', and does not keep his commandments, is a liar, refusing to admit the truth. But when anyone does obey what he has said, God's love comes to perfection in him.

## Luke 24:35-48

The disciples told their story of what had happened on the road and how they had recognised Jesus at the breaking of bread.

They were still talking about all this when Jesus himself stood among them and said to them, 'Peace be with you!' In a state of alarm and fright, they thought they were seeing a ghost. But he said, 'Why are you so agitated, and why are these doubts rising in your hearts? Look at my hands and feet; yes, it is I indeed. Touch me and see for yourselves; a ghost has no flesh and bones as you can see I have.' And as he said this he showed them his hands and feet. Their joy was so great that they could not believe it, and they stood dumbfounded; so he said to them, 'Have you anything here to eat?' And they offered him a piece of grilled fish, which he took and ate before their eyes.

Then he told them, 'This is what I meant when I said, while I was still with you, that everything written about me in the Law of Moses, in the Prophets and in the Psalms, has to be fulfilled.' He then opened their minds to understand the scriptures, and he said to them. 'So you see how it is written that the Christ would suffer and on the third day rise from the dead, and that, in his name, repentance for the forgiveness of sins would be preached to all the nations, beginning from Jerusalem. You are witnesses to this.'

## Reflection

The people of Israel did not know what they were doing when they rejected their Messiah and handed Jesus over to death. It is possible that those who abandon the Church have not really understood what they are leaving behind. The heart of our faith, of the life of the Church, is the good news that Jesus is alive, and in his risen Body we glimpse the future of those who come to him: indestructible life. This is the foundation of our prayer for and witness to those who have not yet understood.

### Acts 6:8-15

Stephen was filled with grace and power and began to work miracles and great signs among the people. But then certain people came forward to debate with Stephen, some from Cyrene and Alexandria who were members of the synagogue called the Synagogue of Freedmen, and others from Cilicia and Asia. They found they could not get the better of him because of his wisdom, and because it was the Spirit that prompted what he said. So they procured some men to say, 'We heard him using blasphemous language against Moses and against God.' Having in this way turned the people against him as well as the elders and scribes, they took Stephen by surprise, and arrested him and brought him before the Sanhedrin. There they put up false witnesses to say, 'This man is always making speeches against this Holy Place and the Law. We have heard him say that Jesus the Nazarene is going to destroy this Place and alter the traditions that Moses handed down to us.' The members of the Sanhedrin all looked intently at Stephen, and his face appeared to them like the face of an angel.

### Psalm 118:23-24.26-27.29-30. R. v.1

*They are happy whose life is blameless.* (or *Alleluia!*)

### John 6:22-29

After Jesus had fed the five thousand, his disciples saw him walking on the water. Next day, the crowd that had stayed on the other side saw that only one boat had been there, and that Jesus had not got into the boat with his disciples, but that the disciples had set off by themselves. Other boats, however, had put in from Tiberias, near the place where the bread had been eaten. When the people saw that neither Jesus nor his disciples were there, they got into those boats and crossed to Capernaum to look for Jesus. When they found him on the other side, they said to him, 'Rabbi, when did you come here?' Jesus answered: 'I tell you most solemnly, you are not looking for me because you have seen the signs but because you had all the bread you wanted to eat. Do not work for food that cannot last, but work for food that endures to eternal life, the kind of food the Son of Man is offering you, for on him the Father, God himself, has set his seal.'

Then they said to him, 'What must we do if we are to do the works that God wants?' Jesus gave them this answer, 'This is working for God: you must believe in the one he has sent.'

### Reflection

One of the great dangers of life is to exhaust ourselves in the pursuit of happiness, all the while seeking it in places where it can never be found. The hunger placed within the human person can never be satisfied by temporary, passing things: it can be satisfied only by the one who placed it there, and who has made himself present and available to us in Jesus Christ.

### Acts 7:51–8:1

Stephen said to the people, the elders and the scribes: 'You stubborn people, with your pagan hearts and pagan ears. You are always resisting the Holy Spirit, just as your ancestors used to do. Can you name a single prophet your ancestors never persecuted? In the past they killed those who foretold the coming of the Just One, and now you have become his betrayers, his murderers. You who had the Law brought to you by angels are the very ones who have not kept it.'

They were infuriated when they heard this, and ground their teeth at him.

But Stephen, filled with the Holy Spirit, gazed into heaven and saw the glory of God, and Jesus standing at God's right hand. 'I can see heaven thrown open' he said 'and the Son of Man standing at the right hand of God.' At this all the members of the council shouted out and stopped their ears with their hands; then they all rushed at him, sent him out of the city and stoned him. The witnesses put down their clothes at the feet of a young man called Saul. As they were stoning him, Stephen said in invocation, 'Lord Jesus, receive my spirit.' Then he knelt down and said aloud, 'Lord, do not hold this sin against them,' and with these words he fell asleep. Saul entirely approved of the killing.

### Psalm 30:3-4.6-8.17.21. R. v.6

*Into your hands, O Lord, I commend my spirit.* (or *Alleluia!*)

### John 6:30-35

The people said to Jesus: 'What sign will you give to show us that we should believe in you? What work will you do? Our fathers had manna to eat in the desert; as scripture says: He gave them bread from heaven to eat.'

Jesus answered: 'I tell you most solemnly, it was not Moses who gave you bread from heaven, it is my Father who gives you the bread from heaven, the true bread; for the bread of God is that which comes down from heaven and gives life to the world.'

'Sir,' they said 'give us that bread always.' Jesus answered: 'I am the bread of life. He who comes to me will never be hungry; he who believes in me will never thirst.'

**3rd Week of Easter**
**White**

### Reflection

It is good sometimes to stop and consider the fact that God has willed for us to live at this precise time in history, in the era of grace. To live in grace is to be freed from the endless cycle of natural events and to enter into the new way of living which tastes already the endless joy of the new heavens and the new earth which we await. And it is in the Bread of Heaven, the Eucharist, that we taste that life.

**3rd Week of Easter**
**White**
or
**St Anselm,** *bishop,*
*doctor*
**(Optional, White)**

## Acts 8:1-8

That day a bitter persecution started against the church in Jerusalem, and everyone except the apostles fled to the country districts of Judaea and Samaria.

There were some devout people, however, who buried Stephen and made great mourning for him.

Saul then worked for the total destruction of the Church; he went from house to house arresting both men and women and sending them to prison.

Those who had escaped went from place to place preaching the Good News. One of them was Philip who went to a Samaritan town and proclaimed the Christ to them. The people united in welcoming the message Philip preached, either because they had heard of the miracles he worked or because they saw them for themselves. There were, for example, unclean spirits that came shrieking out of many who were possessed, and several paralytics and cripples were cured. There was great rejoicing in that town as a result.

## Psalm 65:1-7. R. v.1

*Cry out with joy to God all the earth.* (or *Alleluia!*)

## John 6:35-40

Jesus said to the crowd: 'I am the bread of life. He who comes to me will never be hungry; he who believes in me will never thirst. But, as I have told you, you can see me and still you do not believe. All that the Father gives me will come to me, and whoever comes to me I shall not turn him away; because I have come from heaven, not to do my own will, but to do the will of the one who sent me. Now the will of him who sent me is that I should lose nothing of all that he has given to me, and that I should raise it up on the last day. Yes, it is my Father's will that whoever sees the Son and believes in him shall have eternal life, and that I shall raise him up on the last day.'

## Reflection

We live in a world which is more and more confusing, where even the most fundamental aspects of our personhood and society are questioned, challenged, even rejected. We long for wholeness, which the Christian understands as holiness. Holiness is to be united with God in his incarnate Son, Jesus, and anyone who approaches him will never be turned away. May our finding our home in Jesus be the heart of our witness to others.

**3rd Week of Easter**
**White**

## Acts 8:26-40

The angel of the Lord spoke to Philip saying, 'Be ready to set out at noon along the road that goes from Jerusalem down to Gaza, the desert road.' So he set off on his journey. Now it happened that an Ethiopian had been on pilgrimage to Jerusalem; he was a eunuch and an officer at the court of the kandake, or queen, of Ethiopia, and was in fact her chief treasurer. He was now on his way home; and as he sat in his chariot he was reading the prophet Isaiah. The Spirit said to Philip, 'Go up and meet that chariot.' When Philip ran up, he heard him reading Isaiah the prophet and asked, 'Do you understand what you are reading?' 'How can I' he replied 'unless I have someone to guide me?' So he invited Philip to get in and sit by his side. Now the passage of scripture he was reading was this: Like a sheep that is led to the slaughter-house, like a lamb that is dumb in front of its shearers, like these he never opens his mouth. He has been humiliated and has no one to defend him. Who will ever talk about his descendants, since his life on earth has been cut short!

The eunuch turned to Philip and said, 'Tell me, is the prophet referring to himself or someone else?' Starting, therefore, with this text of scripture Philip proceeded to explain the Good News of Jesus to him.

*(See Appendix B-11)*

## Psalm 65:8-9.16-17.20. R. v.1
*Cry out with joy to God all the earth.* (or *Alleluia!*)

## John 6:44-51

Jesus said to the crowd: 'No one can come to me unless he is drawn by the Father who sent me, and I will raise him up at the last day. It is written in the prophets: They will all be taught by God, and to hear the teaching of the Father, and learn from it, is to come to me. Not that anybody has seen the Father, except the one who comes from God: he has seen the Father. I tell you most solemnly, everybody who believes has eternal life. I am the bread of life. Your fathers ate the manna in the desert and they are dead; but this is the bread that comes down from heaven, so that a man may eat it and not die. I am the living bread which has come down from heaven. Anyone who eats this bread will live for ever; and the bread that I shall give is my flesh, for the life of the world.'

## Reflection
Bread, flesh, life. How wonderful it is that the humblest of all foods, bread, is that which the Lord Jesus chose to become transformed into his Body. The humility with which the Lord of Heaven condescended to come to earth as Man is perfectly mirrored in the divine humility of the Eucharist. Our response, then, can only be one of increasingly humble gratitude.

**3rd Week of Easter**
White
or
**St George,** *martyr*
**England – Solemnity**
*(See Appendix A-7)*

### Acts 9:1-20

Saul was still breathing threats to slaughter the Lord's disciples. He had gone to the high priest and asked for letters addressed to the synagogues in Damascus, that would authorise him to arrest and take to Jerusalem any followers of the Way, men or women, that he could find.

Suddenly, while he was travelling to Damascus and just before he reached the city, there came a light from heaven all round him. He fell to the ground, and then he heard a voice saying, 'Saul, Saul, why are you persecuting me?' 'Who are you, Lord?' he asked, and the voice answered, 'I am Jesus, and you are persecuting me. Get up now and go into the city, and you will be told what you have to do.' The men travelling with Saul stood there speechless, for though they heard the voice they could see no one. Saul got up from the ground, but even with his eyes wide open he could see nothing at all, and they had to lead him into Damascus by the hand. For three days he was without his sight, and took neither food nor drink.
*(See Appendix B-12)*

### Psalm 116. R. Mark 16:15

*Go out to the whole world; proclaim the Good News.*
(or *Alleluia!*)

### John 6:52-59

The Jews started arguing with one another: 'How can this man give us his flesh to eat?' they said. Jesus replied: 'I tell you most solemnly, if you do not eat the flesh of the Son of Man and drink his blood, you will not have life in you. Anyone who does eat my flesh and drink my blood has eternal life, and I shall raise him up on the last day. For my flesh is real food and my blood is real drink. He who eats my flesh and drinks my blood lives in me and I live in him. As I, who am sent by the living Father, myself draw life from the Father, so whoever eats me will draw life from me. This is the bread come down from heaven; not like the bread our ancestors ate: they are dead, but anyone who eats this bread will live for ever.'

He taught this doctrine at Capernaum, in the synagogue.

### Reflection

Today's passage from the Bread of Life Discourse is very confronting for many people – eating flesh and drinking blood. Too easily, we see in it a reference to the real presence of Christ in the Eucharist. We don't stop and think that we have the real presence through his body being broken and his blood being poured out on the cross in unconditional love for us. These stark images refer to the reality of his passion, death and resurrection. In using such shocking and graphic images, the evangelist wants to make it clear that God wants nothing less than to give us eternal life. The cost of that eternal life is paid by his own Son. Is our faith strong enough to enter the depth of union this text demands of us? Or are we fearful of embracing his message and the demands it may place on us? Are we willing to have Jesus live in us, and bring his word to the world through us?

## Acts 9:31-42

The churches throughout Judaea, Galilee and Samaria were now left in peace, building themselves up, living in the fear of the Lord, and filled with the consolation of the Holy Spirit.

Peter visited one place after another and eventually came to the saints living down in Lydda. There he found a man called Aeneas, a paralytic who had been bedridden for eight years. Peter said to him, 'Aeneas, Jesus Christ cures you: get up and fold up your sleeping mat.' Aeneas got up immediately; everybody who lived in Lydda and Sharon saw him, and they were all converted to the Lord.

At Jaffa there was a woman disciple called Tabitha, or Dorcas in Greek, who never tired of doing good or giving in charity. But the time came when she got ill and died, and they washed her and laid her out in a room upstairs. Lydda is not far from Jaffa, so when the disciples heard that Peter was there, they sent two men with an urgent message for him, 'Come and visit us as soon as possible.'
*(See Appendix B-12)*

## Psalm 115:12-17. R. v.12

*How can I repay the Lord for his goodness to me?* (or *Alleluia!*)

## John 6:60-69

After hearing his doctrine, many of the followers of Jesus said, 'This is intolerable language. How could anyone accept it?' Jesus was aware that his followers were complaining about it and said, 'Does this upset you? What if you should see the Son of Man ascend to where he was before? 'It is the spirit that gives life, the flesh has nothing to offer. The words I have spoken to you are spirit and they are life.

'But there are some of you who do not believe.' For Jesus knew from the outset those who did not believe, and who it was that would betray him. He went on, 'This is why I told you that no one could come to me unless the Father allows him.' After this, many of his disciples left him and stopped going with him.

Then Jesus said to the Twelve, 'What about you, do you want to go away too?' Simon Peter answered, 'Lord, who shall we go to? You have the message of eternal life, and we believe; we know that you are the Holy One of God.'

## Reflection

It seems astonishing that Jesus was prepared to let so many of his disciples abandon him. But truth is truth, and not everyone is prepared to accept it. The truth of his Real Presence in the Holy Eucharist is the foundation of the Church and of our life: to believe this is a gift from the Father, and a gift which is to be nurtured and celebrated and given thanks for.

**3rd Week of Easter**
White
or
**St Fidelis of Sigmaringen**, *priest, martyr*
(Optional, Red)

**4th Sunday of Easter**
**Psalter Week 4**
**White**

### Acts 4:8-12

Filled with the Holy Spirit, Peter said: 'Rulers of the people, and elders! If you are questioning us today about an act of kindness to a cripple, and asking us how he was healed, then I am glad to tell you all, and would indeed be glad to tell the whole people of Israel, that it was by the name of Jesus Christ the Nazarene, the one you crucified, whom God raised from the dead, by this name and by no other that this man is able to stand up perfectly healthy, here in your presence today. This is the stone rejected by you the builders, but which has proved to be the keystone. For of all the names in the world given to men, this is the only one by which we can be saved.'

**Psalm 117:1.8-9.21-23.26.28-29. R. v.22**

*The stone which the builders rejected has become the corner stone.* (or *Alleluia!*)

**1 John 3:1-2**

Think of the love that the Father has lavished on us, by letting us be called God's children; and that is what we are. Because the world refused to acknowledge him, therefore it does not acknowledge us. My dear people, we are already the children of God but what we are to be in the future has not yet been revealed; all we know is, that when it is revealed we shall be like him because we shall see him as he really is.

**John 10:11-18**

Jesus said: 'I am the good shepherd: the good shepherd is one who lays down his life for his sheep. The hired man, since he is not the shepherd and the sheep do not belong to him, abandons the sheep and runs away as soon as he sees a wolf coming, and then the wolf attacks and scatters the sheep; this is because he is only a hired man and has no concern for the sheep. I am the good shepherd; I know my own and my own know me, just as the Father knows me and I know the Father; and I lay down my life for my sheep. And there are other sheep I have that are not of this fold, and these I have to lead as well. They too will listen to my voice, and there will be only one flock and one shepherd. The Father loves me, because I lay down my life in order to take it up again. No one takes it from me; I lay it down of my own free will, and as it is in my power to lay it down, so it is in my power to take it up again; and this is the command I have been given by my Father.'

**Reflection**

It is often said that what we all long for is to know and to be known, to love and to be loved. From all eternity Jesus himself has been known, fully and wonderfully, in the bosom of the Father, and the love mutually enjoyed in that divine embrace is the Holy Spirit. Astonishing as it is, this eternal 'being known' is the home to which we are called, and for which we were brought into being. The mission of Jesus, the Good Shepherd, is to bring us into that embrace, and our mission in turn is to share the wonder of knowing and being known with others.

**4th Week of Easter**
**White**

## Acts 11:1-18

The apostles and the brothers in Judaea heard that the pagans too had accepted the word of God, and when Peter came up to Jerusalem the Jews criticised him and said, 'So you have been visiting the uncircumcised and eating with them, have you?' Peter in reply gave them the details point by point: 'One day, when I was in the town of Jaffa,' he began 'I fell into a trance as I was praying and had a vision of something like a big sheet being let down from heaven by its four corners. This sheet reached the ground quite close to me. I watched it intently and saw all sorts of animals and wild beasts – everything possible that could walk, crawl or fly. Then I heard a voice that said to me, "Now, Peter; kill and eat!" But I answered: Certainly not, Lord; nothing profane or unclean has ever crossed my lips. And a second time the voice spoke from heaven. "What God has made clean, you have no right to call profane." This was repeated three times, before the whole of it was drawn up to heaven again. *(See Appendix B-12)*

## Psalm 41:2-3;42:3-4. R. Cf. 41:3

*My soul is thirsting for God, the God of my life.*

## John 10:1-10

Jesus said: 'I tell you most solemnly, anyone who does not enter the sheepfold through the gate, but gets in some other way, is a thief and a brigand. The one who enters through the gate is the shepherd of the flock; the gatekeeper lets him in, the sheep hear his voice, one by one he calls his own sheep and leads them out. When he has brought out his flock, he goes ahead of them, and the sheep follow because they know his voice. They never follow a stranger but run away from him: they do not recognise the voice of strangers.'

Jesus told them this parable but they failed to understand what he meant by telling it to them. So Jesus spoke to them again:

'I tell you most solemnly, I am the gate of the sheepfold. All others who have come are thieves and brigands; but the sheep took no notice of them. I am the gate. Anyone who enters through me will be safe: he will go freely in and out and be sure of finding pasture. The thief comes only to steal and kill and destroy. I have come so that they may have life and have it to the full.'

## Reflection

False Messiahs, false religions and worship, false ideologies; all appear to promise so much – yet deliver nothing, serving only to enslave those who follow them. The temptations and allurements of the Evil One serve only to scatter those who long to be united. Wholeness and integrity of life is given to us only in Christ, because he is the source of life. Life is not easy, but our choice is simple: to follow the one Lord Jesus is to find rest and abundance of life.

**4th Week of Easter**
White
or
**St Louis Grignion de Montfort**, *priest*
(Optional, White)

## Acts 11:19-26

Those who had escaped during the persecution that happened because of Stephen travelled as far as Phoenicia and Cyprus and Antioch, but they usually proclaimed the message only to Jews. Some of them, however, who came from Cyprus and Cyrene, went to Antioch where they started preaching to the Greeks, proclaiming the Good News of the Lord Jesus to them as well. The Lord helped them, and a great number believed and were converted to the Lord.

The church in Jerusalem heard about this and they sent Barnabas to Antioch. There he could see for himself that God had given grace, and this pleased him, and he urged them all to remain faithful to the Lord with heartfelt devotion; for he was a good man, filled with the Holy Spirit and with faith. And a large number of people were won over to the Lord.

Barnabas then left for Tarsus to look for Saul, and when he found him he brought him to Antioch. As things turned out they were to live together in that church a whole year, instructing a large number of people. It was at Antioch that the disciples were first called 'Christians'.

## Psalm 86:1-7. R. Psalm 116:1

*O praise the Lord, all you nations!* (or *Alleluia!*)

## John 10:22-30

It was the time when the feast of Dedication was being celebrated in Jerusalem. It was winter, and Jesus was in the Temple walking up and down in the Portico of Solomon. The Jews gathered round him and said, 'How much longer are you going to keep us in suspense? If you are the Christ, tell us plainly.' Jesus replied: 'I have told you, but you do not believe. The works I do in my Father's name are my witness; but you do not believe, because you are no sheep of mine. The sheep that belong to me listen to my voice; I know them and they follow me. I give them eternal life; they will never be lost and no one will ever steal them from me. The Father who gave them to me is greater than anyone, and no one can steal from the Father. The Father and I are one.'

## Reflection

The Jews' fascination with Jesus has not yet reached the point where they are prepared to let him in: they still are seeking to label him as fulfilling their own expectations. Life in Christ is something different: it is only in the intimacy of listening to his voice – in prayer, in the scriptures, in the sacraments – that we encounter him as he wishes us to know him. And in that embrace, that communion of love, we are already one with the Father.

**4th Week of Easter**
**St Peter Chanel,** *priest,*
*martyr*
**Memorial**
**Red**

## Acts 12:24–13:5

The word of God continued to spread and to gain followers. Barnabas and Saul completed their task and came back from Jerusalem, bringing John Mark with them.

In the church at Antioch the following were prophets and teachers: Barnabas, Simeon called Niger, and Lucius of Cyrene, Manaen, who had been brought up with Herod the tetrarch, and Saul. One day while they were offering worship to the Lord and keeping a fast, the Holy Spirit said, 'I want Barnabas and Saul set apart for the work to which I have called them.' So it was that after fasting and prayer they laid their hands on them and sent them off.

So these two, sent on their mission by the Holy Spirit, went down to Seleucia and from there sailed to Cyprus. They landed at Salamis and proclaimed the word of God in the synagogues of the Jews. John acted as their assistant.

## Psalm 66:2-3.5-6.8. R. v.4

*Let the peoples praise you, O God; let all the peoples praise you.* (or *Alleluia!*)

## John 12:44-50

Jesus declared publicly: 'Whoever believes in me believes not in me but in the one who sent me, and whoever sees me, sees the one who sent me. I, the light, have come into the world, so that whoever believes in me need not stay in the dark any more. If anyone hears my words and does not keep them faithfully, it is not I who shall condemn him, since I have come not to condemn the world, but to save the world: he who rejects me and refuses my words has his judge already: the word itself that I have spoken will be his judge on the last day. For what I have spoken does not come from myself; no, what I was to say, what I had to speak, was commanded by the Father who sent me, and I know that his commands mean eternal life. And therefore what the Father has told me is what I speak.'

## Reflection

Jesus describes the obedience which is at the heart of his eternal relationship with his Father: an unceasing listening to the Father, to the Word of Life, which he himself manifests in his own being. Far above all creatures it is Our Blessed Mother who perfectly shares in this obedience of love and helps us to do the same. As St Louis de Montfort said, 'Devotion to Our Lady is … a means of finding Jesus Christ perfectly, of loving Him tenderly, of serving Him faithfully.'

## 1 John 1:5-2:2

This is what we have heard from Jesus Christ, and the message that we are announcing to you: God is light; there is no darkness in him at all. If we say that we are in union with God while we are living in darkness, we are lying because we are not living the truth. But if we live our lives in the light, as he is in the light, we are in union with one another, and the blood of Jesus, his Son, purifies us from all sin. If we say we have no sin in us, we are deceiving ourselves and refusing to admit the truth; but if we acknowledge our sins, then God who is faithful and just will forgive our sins and purify us from everything that is wrong. To say that we have never sinned is to call God a liar and to show that his word is not in us. I am writing this, my children, to stop you sinning; but if anyone should sin, we have our advocate with the Father, Jesus Christ, who is just; he is the sacrifice that takes our sins away, and not only ours, but the whole world's.

## Psalm 102:1-4.8-9.13-14.17-18

*My soul, give thanks to the Lord.*

## Matthew 11:25-30

Jesus exclaimed, 'I bless you, Father, Lord of heaven and of earth, for hiding these things from the learned and the clever and revealing them to mere children. Yes, Father, for that is what it pleased you to do. Everything has been entrusted to me by my Father; and no one knows the Son except the Father, just as no one knows the Father except the Son and those to whom the Son chooses to reveal him.

'Come to me, all you who labour and are overburdened, and I will give you rest. Shoulder my yoke and learn from me, for I am gentle and humble in heart, and you will find rest for your souls. Yes, my yoke is easy and my burden light.'

**4th Week of Easter
St Catherine of Siena,
*virgin, doctor*
Feast
White**

## Reflection

Within the soul that is not surrendered to God there lies a restlessness and anxiety which underlies everything, even if it is masked with seemingly fruitful activity, even worldly success. St Catherine once wrote, 'The soul always fears until she arrives at true love.' Let us abandon ourselves to the tender love of Jesus, who will restore in us the security and wonder which only the child of God can enjoy.

**4th Week of Easter**
**White**
or
**St Pius V,** *pope*
**(Optional, White)**

### Acts 13:26-33

Paul stood up in the synagogue at Antioch in Pisidia, held up a hand for silence and began to speak: 'My brothers, sons of Abraham's race, and all you who fear God, this message of salvation is meant for you. What the people of Jerusalem and their rulers did, though they did not realise it, was in fact to fulfil the prophecies read on every sabbath. Though they found nothing to justify his death, they condemned him and asked Pilate to have him executed. When they had carried out everything that scripture foretells about him they took him down from the tree and buried him in a tomb. But God raised him from the dead, and for many days he appeared to those who had accompanied him from Galilee to Jerusalem: and it is these same companions of his who are now his witnesses before our people.

'We have come here to tell you the Good News. It was to our ancestors that God made the promise but it is to us, their children, that he has fulfilled it, by raising Jesus from the dead. As scripture says in the first psalm: You are my son: today I have become your father.'

### Psalm 2:6-11. R. v.7

*You are my Son. It is I who have begotten you this day.*
(or *Alleluia!*)

### John 14:1-6

Jesus said to his disciples: 'Do not let your hearts be troubled. Trust in God still, and trust in me. There are many rooms in my Father's house; if there were not, I should have told you. I am going now to prepare a place for you, and after I have gone and prepared you a place, I shall return to take you with me; so that where I am you may be too. You know the way to the place where I am going.'

Thomas said, 'Lord, we do not know where you are going, so how can we know the way?' Jesus said: 'I am the Way, the Truth and the Life. No one can come to the Father except through me.'

### Reflection

These famous words of Jesus are, quite understandably, frequently read at funerals, since they resound with consolation and assurance. But they speak not only of the next life, but of the present. It is wonderful that we are assured of the place Jesus has won for us in heaven, but he himself is the Way there. We do not look to the next life as a positive thought to keep us going, but we choose to live in intimacy of life with Jesus here and now, and in doing so we enter into a living hope which already shines its light on us here and now.

## Acts 13:44-52

The next sabbath almost the whole town of Antioch assembled to hear the word of God. When they saw the crowds, the Jews, prompted by jealousy, used blasphemies and contradicted everything Paul said. Then Paul and Barnabas spoke out boldly. 'We had to proclaim the word of God to you first, but since you have rejected it, since you do not think yourselves worthy of eternal life, we must turn to the pagans. For this is what the Lord commanded us to do when he said: I have made you a light for the nations, so that my salvation may reach the ends of the earth.'

It made the pagans very happy to hear this and they thanked the Lord for his message; all who were destined for eternal life became believers. Thus the word of the Lord spread through the whole countryside.

But the Jews worked upon some of the devout women of the upper classes and the leading men of the city and persuaded them to turn against Paul and Barnabas and expel them from their territory. So they shook the dust from their feet in defiance and went off to Iconium; but the disciples were filled with joy and the Holy Spirit.

## Psalm 97:1-4. R. v.3

*All the ends of the earth have seen the salvation of our God.* (or *Alleluia!*)

## John 14:7-14

Jesus said to his disciples: 'If you know me, you know my Father too. From this moment you know him and have seen him.'

Philip said, 'Lord, let us see the Father and then we shall be satisfied.' 'Have I been with you all this time, Philip,' said Jesus to him, 'and you still do not know me?' 'To have seen me is to have seen the Father, so how can you say, "Let us see the Father"? Do you not believe that I am in the Father and the Father is in me? The words I say to you I do not speak as from myself: it is the Father, living in me, who is doing this work. You must believe me when I say that I am in the Father and the Father is in me; believe it on the evidence of this work, if for no other reason. 'I tell you most solemnly, whoever believes in me will perform the same works as I do myself, he will perform even greater works, because I am going to the Father. Whatever you ask for in my name I will do, so that the Father may be glorified in the Son. If you ask for anything in my name, I will do it.'

## Reflection

In 1955, Pope Pius XII instituted the Feast of St Joseph the Worker, adding to the age-old celebration of Joseph as the Spouse of Mary, on 19 March. Communist leaders across the world celebrate 1 May, known as 'May Day', in honour of workers. Joseph is presented in the Gospels as someone who worked with his hands (Mark 6: 3), and the Church wished to indicate that work is not only associated with productivity, but also with holiness. In the Gospel of John, Jesus regularly speaks of his mission as 'the work' given to him by his Father. He completes this 'work' by the many 'works' that he performs. In today's Gospel Jesus asks that we recognise God's presence among us in his work. Amazingly, he tells us that those who believe in him in this way will do even greater works. The 'work' of the believing Christian continues to make known the goodness and love of God for humankind.

**4th Week of Easter**
White
or
**St Joseph the Worker**
**(Optional, White)**

**5th Sunday of Easter**
Psalter Week 1
White

### Acts 9:26-31

When Saul got to Jerusalem he tried to join the disciples, but they were all afraid of him: they could not believe he was really a disciple. Barnabas, however, took charge of him, introduced him to the apostles, and explained how the Lord had appeared to Saul and spoken to him on his journey, and how he had preached boldly at Damascus in the name of Jesus. Saul now started to go round with them in Jerusalem, preaching fearlessly in the name of the Lord. But after he had spoken to the Hellenists, and argued with them, they became determined to kill him. When the brothers knew, they took him to Caesarea, and sent him off from there to Tarsus.

The churches throughout Judaea, Galilee and Samaria were now left in peace, building themselves up, living in the fear of the Lord, and filled with the consolation of the Holy Spirit.

**Psalm 21:26-28.30-32. R. v.26**
*You, Lord, are my praise in the great assembly.* (or *Alleluia!*)

## 1 John 3:18-24

My children, our love is not to be just words or mere talk, but something real and active; only by this can we be certain that we are the children of the truth and be able to quieten our conscience in his presence, whatever accusations it may raise against us, because God is greater than our conscience and he knows everything. My dear people, if we cannot be condemned by our conscience, we need not be afraid in God's presence, and whatever we ask him, we shall receive, because we keep his commandments and live the kind of life that he wants. His commandments are these: that we believe in the name of his Son Jesus Christ and that we love one another as he told us to. Whoever keeps his commandments lives in God and God lives in him. We know that he lives in us by the Spirit that he has given us.

## John 15:1-8

Jesus said to his disciples: 'I am the true vine, and my Father is the vinedresser. Every branch in me that bears no fruit he cuts away, and every branch that does bear fruit he prunes to make it bear even more. You are pruned already, by means of the word that I have spoken to you. Make your home in me, as I make mine in you. As a branch cannot bear fruit all by itself, but must remain part of the vine, neither can you unless you remain in me. I am the vine, you are the branches. Whoever remains in me, with me in him, bears fruit in plenty; for cut off from me you can do nothing. Anyone who does not remain in me is like a branch that has been thrown away – he withers; these branches are collected and thrown on the fire, and they are burnt. If you remain in me and my words remain in you, you may ask what you will and you shall get it. It is to the glory of my Father that you should bear much fruit, and then you will be my disciples.'

## Reflection

John 15: 1–16: 3 is located at the very heart of John's account of Jesus' final night with his disciples (John 13–17). Today's Gospel, taken from the opening verses of this central passage, uses the model of a vine and its branches to instruct the disciples on the need to maintain union with Jesus. The word that best expresses what Jesus is teaching in these verses is 'remain'. Some translations of the Greek original use the expression 'abide'. The expression appears six times in this Gospel. The relationship between the believer and Jesus should be one of deep intimacy where the life of the believer, described as a branch, draws from the richness of Jesus who identifies himself as the vine.

Jesus tells of two possibilities. Those who remain in Jesus bear fruit, receive all the blessings that they request, and are truly disciples of Jesus. Those who do not remain and fail to bear fruit will be removed from their source, and thus die. Jesus warns: 'Cut off from me you can do nothing'. The opposite is also true: by remaining in Jesus, the disciple can do everything. The theme of 'remaining' does not end as Jesus concludes his references to the vine and the branches. As we will see next Thursday and next Sunday, remaining in Jesus leads to dwelling in his love, but it also generates hatred.

## MAY
# 3
## MONDAY

**Sts Philip and James,**
*apostles*
**Feast**
**Red**

**1 Corinthians 15:1-8**

Brothers, I want to remind you of the Gospel I preached to you, the gospel that you received and in which you are firmly established; because the gospel will save you only if you keep believing exactly what I preached to you – believing anything else will not lead to anything.

Well then, in the first place, I taught you what I had been taught myself, namely that Christ died for our sins, in accordance with the scriptures; that he was buried; and that he was raised to life on the third day, in accordance with the scriptures; that he appeared first to Cephas and secondly to the Twelve. Next he appeared to more than five hundred of the brothers at the same time, most of whom are still alive, though some have died; then he appeared to James, and then to all the apostles; and last of all he appeared to me too; it was as though I was born when no one expected it.

**Psalm 18:2-5. R. v.5**

*Their word goes forth through all the earth.* (or *Alleluia!*)

**John 14:6-14**

Jesus said to Thomas: 'I am the Way, the Truth and the Life. No one can come to the Father except through me. If you know me, you know my Father too. From this moment you know him and have seen him.' Philip said, 'Lord, let us see the Father and then we shall be satisfied'. 'Have I been with you all this time, Philip,' said Jesus to him 'and you still do not know me? 'To have seen me is to have seen the Father, so how can you say, "Let us see the Father?" Do you not believe that I am in the Father and the Father is in me? The words I say to you I do not speak as from myself: it is the Father, living in me, who is doing this work. You must believe me when I say that I am in the Father and the Father is in me; believe it on the evidence of this work if for no other reason. I tell you most solemnly, whoever believes in me will perform the same works as I do myself, he will perform even greater works, because I am going to the Father. Whatever you ask for in my name I will do, so that the Father may be glorified in the Son. If you ask for anything in my name, I will do it.'

**Reflection**

The ongoing daily reading from the Gospel of John leads us back to the Gospel passage used for the celebration of St Joseph the Worker last Saturday (John 14: 7-14). Today the Lectionary adds an extra opening verse. The addition of v. 6 links the passage with Philip the Apostle, as the first reading from St Paul refers to the Apostle James as a witness to the risen Jesus. Philip asks Jesus to explain the 'Way' so that the disciples might be able to follow. Jesus responds by pointing to himself as 'the Way, the Truth, and the Life'. On this feast of two apostles we are drawn back to Jesus. There is only one way to God: Jesus Christ. As the Way, he provides Truth and Life.

## Acts 14:19-28

Some Jews arrived from Antioch and Iconium, and turned the people against the apostles. They stoned Paul and dragged him outside the town, thinking he was dead. The disciples came crowding round him but, as they did so, he stood up and went back to the town. The next day he and Barnabas went off to Derbe.

Having preached the Good News in that town and made a considerable number of disciples, they went back through Lystra and Iconium to Antioch. They put fresh heart into the disciples, encouraging them to persevere in the faith. 'We all have to experience many hardships' they said 'before we enter the kingdom of God.' In each of these churches they appointed elders, and with prayer and fasting they commended them to the Lord in whom they had come to believe.

They passed through Pisidia and reached Pamphylia. Then after proclaiming the word at Perga they went down to Attalia and from there sailed for Antioch, where they had originally been commended to the grace of God for the work they had now completed.

On their arrival they assembled the church and gave an account of all that God had done with them, and how he had opened the door of faith to the pagans. They stayed there with the disciples for some time.

## Psalm 144:10-13.21. R. cf. v.12

*Your friends, O Lord, shall make known the glorious splendour of your reign.* (or *Alleluia!*)

## John 14:27-31

Jesus said to his disciples: 'Peace I bequeath to you, my own peace I give you, a peace the world cannot give, this is my gift to you. Do not let your hearts be troubled or afraid. You heard me say: I am going away, and shall return. If you loved me you would have been glad to know that I am going to the Father, for the Father is greater than I. I have told you this now before it happens, so that when it does happen you may believe. I shall not talk with you any longer, because the prince of this world is on his way. He has no power over me, but the world must be brought to know that I love the Father and that I am doing exactly what the Father told me.'

## Reflection

We continue to read from Jesus' farewell discourse. The task of Jesus is to prepare his disciples of all ages for the long period of time that will endure between his return to the Father and his final coming as judge. He assures us of his gift of an unworldly peace that should guide us through troubled times. The ambiguity of the reception of Paul and Barnabas in today's first reading shows that such times have always existed. One of the guarantees of this peace is the fact that Jesus has instructed us that he must depart, that there will be a time when he does not speak to us face-to-face, when it will appear that 'the prince of this world' will hold sway. We need not fear. God has his own designs, and Jesus responds to them. So should we, as we live the peace that only Jesus Christ can give.

MAY

# 4

**TUESDAY**

**5th Week of Easter**
**White**
or
**The English Martyrs**
**(England – Feast)**
*(See Appendix A-8)*

**5th Week of Easter**
**White**

_____
_____
_____
_____
_____
_____
_____
_____

## Acts 15:1-6

Some men came down from Judaea and taught the brothers, 'Unless you have yourselves circumcised in the tradition of Moses you cannot be saved.' This led to disagreement, and after Paul and Barnabas had had a long argument with these men it was arranged that Paul and Barnabas and others of the church should go up to Jerusalem and discuss the problem with the apostles and elders.

All the members of the church saw them off, and as they passed through Phoenicia and Samaria they told how the pagans had been converted, and this news was received with the greatest satisfaction by the brothers. When they arrived in Jerusalem they were welcomed by the church and by the apostles and elders, and gave an account of all that God had done with them.

But certain members of the Pharisees' party who had become believers objected, insisting that the pagans should be circumcised and instructed to keep the Law of Moses. The apostles and elders met to look into the matter.

## Psalm 121:1-5. R. v.1

_I rejoiced when I heard them say: 'Let us go to God's house.'_ (or _Alleluia!_)

## John 15:1-8

Jesus said to his disciples: 'I am the true vine, and my Father is the vinedresser. Every branch in me that bears no fruit he cuts away, and every branch that does bear fruit he prunes to make it bear even more. You are pruned already, by means of the word that I have spoken to you. Make your home in me, as I make mine in you. As a branch cannot bear fruit all by itself, but must remain part of the vine, neither can you unless you remain in me. I am the vine, you are the branches. Whoever remains in me, with me in him, bears fruit in plenty; for cut off from me you can do nothing. Anyone who does not remain in me is like a branch that has been thrown away – he withers; these branches are collected and thrown on the fire, and they are burnt. If you remain in me and my words remain in you, you may ask what you will and you shall get it. It is to the glory of my Father that you should bear much fruit, and then you will be my disciples.'

## Reflection

At the heart of Jesus' final discourse (John 15: 1–16: 3), Jesus strikes three themes that will determine the way we should live in his absence. The first of these is that we 'remain' or 'abide' in his love. In today's first reading, early Christians argue passionately over who should be admitted to the community. Jesus' use of the image of himself as the true vine, and his Father as the vinedresser guides our understanding of what it means to 'remain' in Jesus. It does not depend on any worldly criterion. Jesus teaches the simple awareness of what happens in the growth and productivity of a branch that depends so much upon its nourishment from the life-giving vine. Jesus, tended by the Father, is our source of life. Without him, we die and will be destroyed. Our awareness of photosynthesis, however, warns us that we must also be active and life-giving agents. Otherwise, the vine will die!

## Acts 15:7-21

After the discussion had gone on a long time, Peter stood up and addressed the apostles and elders.

'My brothers,' he said 'you know perfectly well that in the early days God made his choice among you: the pagans were to learn the Good News from me and so become believers. In fact God, who can read everyone's heart, showed his approval of them by giving the Holy Spirit to them just as he had to us. God made no distinction between them and us, since he purified their hearts by faith. It would only provoke God's anger now, surely, if you imposed on the disciples the very burden that neither we nor our ancestors were strong enough to support? Remember, we believe that we are saved in the same way as they are: through the grace of the Lord Jesus.'

**5th Week of Easter**
**White**

This silenced the entire assembly, and they listened to Barnabas and Paul describing all the signs and wonders God had worked through them among the pagans.

When they had finished it was James who spoke. 'My brothers,' he said 'listen to me. Simon has described how God first arranged to enlist a people for his name out of the pagans. This is entirely in harmony with the words of the prophets, since the scriptures say: After that I shall return and rebuild the fallen House of David; I shall rebuild it from its ruins and restore it. Then the rest of mankind, all the pagans who are consecrated to my name, will look for the Lord, says the Lord who made this known so long ago.

'I rule, then, that instead of making things more difficult for pagans who turn to God, we send them a letter telling them merely to abstain from anything polluted by idols, from fornication, from the meat of strangled animals and from blood. For Moses has always had his preachers in every town, and is read aloud in the synagogues every sabbath.'

## Psalm 95:1-3.10. R. cf. v.3

*Proclaim the wonders of the Lord among all the peoples.* (or *Alleluia!*)

## John 15:9-11

Jesus said to his disciples: 'As the Father has loved me, so I have loved you. Remain in my love. If you keep my commandments you will remain in my love, just as I have kept my Father's commandments and remain in his love. I have told you this so that my own joy may be in you and your joy be complete.'

## Reflection

Jesus communicates the message of 'remaining', that dominates John 15: 1-11, through an initial focus on the image of the necessary symbiotic relationship between the vine and the branches. In v. 9 that image disappears from Jesus' words, because underlying that image is the more fundamental truth of the relationship of love that exists between the Father and the Son. The call to 'remain' continues but is no longer associated with a vine. The believer must 'remain' in Jesus' love. In John's Gospel, Jesus never speaks of the believer's love for God. God's love is made visible in Jesus. Jesus commands that we love him. If that relationship is in place, God will draw us into the love that unites the Father and the Son. Then our joy will be complete. Today's reading from Acts, reporting the so-called Council of Jerusalem, uses the experience of the earliest community to exemplify such unity and joy.

**5th Week of Easter**
**White**

## Acts 15:22-31

The apostles and elders decided to choose delegates to send to Antioch with Paul and Barnabas; the whole church concurred with this. They chose Judas known as Barsabbas and Silas, both leading men in the brotherhood, and gave them this letter to take with them:

'The apostles and elders, your brothers, send greetings to the brothers of pagan birth in Antioch, Syria and Cilicia. We hear that some of our members have disturbed you with their demands and have unsettled your minds. They acted without any authority from us, and so we have decided unanimously to elect delegates and to send them to you with Barnabas and Paul, men we highly respect who have dedicated their lives to the name of our Lord Jesus Christ. Accordingly we are sending you Judas and Silas, who will confirm by word of mouth what we have written in this letter. It has been decided by the Holy Spirit and by ourselves not to saddle you with any burden beyond these essentials: you are to abstain from food sacrificed to idols, from blood, from the meat of strangled animals and from fornication. Avoid these, and you will do what is right. Farewell.'

The party left and went down to Antioch, where they summoned the whole community and delivered the letter. The community read it and were delighted with the encouragement it gave them.

## Psalm 56:8-12. R. v.10

*I will thank you, Lord, among the peoples.* (or *Alleluia!*)

## John 15:12-17

Jesus said to his disciples: 'This is my commandment: love one another, as I have loved you. A man can have no greater love than to lay down his life for his friends. You are my friends, if you do what I command you. I shall not call you servants any more, because a servant does not know his master's business; I call you friends, because I have made known to you everything I have learnt from my Father. You did not choose me, no, I chose you; and I commissioned you to go out and to bear fruit, fruit that will last; and then the Father will give you anything you ask him in my name. What I command you is to love one another.'

## Reflection

Subsequent to the Council of Jerusalem, the apostles send a beautiful message to the Gentile communities. Under the direction of the Holy Spirit, they have decided 'not to saddle you with any burden beyond these essentials'. Such a message delights its recipients. The Gospel brings us to the heart of the last discourse. Jesus has referred to his commandment in John 15: 10. He now states that commandment twice: once at the beginning of the passage and again at its end: 'Love one another as I have loved you.' This message lies at the heart of Christianity. We belong to Jesus and bear much fruit, not because we chose him, but because he chose us. And he has led the way in showing the depths of Christian love: 'A man can have no greater love than to lay down his life for his friends.'

## Acts 16:1-10

From Cilicia Paul went to Derbe, and then on to Lystra. Here there was a disciple called Timothy, whose mother was a Jewess who had become a believer; but his father was a Greek. The brothers at Lystra and Iconium spoke well of Timothy, and Paul, who wanted to have him as a travelling companion, had him circumcised. This was on account of the Jews in the locality where everyone knew his father was a Greek.

As they visited one town after another, they passed on the decisions reached by the apostles and elders in Jerusalem, with instructions to respect them.

So the churches grew strong in the faith, as well as growing daily in numbers.

They travelled through Phrygia and the Galatian country, having been told by the Holy Spirit not to preach the word in Asia. When they reached the frontier of Mysia they thought to cross it into Bithynia, but as the Spirit of Jesus would not allow them, they went through Mysia and came down to Troas.

One night Paul had a vision: a Macedonian appeared and appealed to him in these words, 'Come across to Macedonia and help us.' Once he had seen this vision we lost no time in arranging a passage to Macedonia, convinced that God had called us to bring them the Good News.

## Psalm 99:1-3.5. R. v.1

*Cry out with joy to the Lord, all the earth.* (or *Alleluia!*)

## John 15:18-21

Jesus said to his disciples: 'If the world hates you, remember that it hated me before you. If you belonged to the world, the world would love you as its own; but because you do not belong to the world, because my choice withdrew you from the world, therefore the world hates you. Remember the words I said to you: A servant is not greater than his master. If they persecuted me, they will persecute you too; if they kept my word, they will keep yours as well. But it will be on my account that they will do all this, because they do not know the one who sent me.'

## Reflection

While today's first reading summarises the steady increase in the numbers and the geographical spread of Paul's mission, a different note enters Jesus' last discourse to his disciples on the night before he died. Through John 15: 1-17, the union of 'remaining' and 'loving' has been dominant. These experiences will always be lived out within the context of violence and hatred. Jesus points out why such is the case with a simple but profound truth. The disciples will be hated just as, before their time, Jesus was hated. John uses the expression 'the world' in a number of ways across his Gospel. Here he uses it to indicate those who reject Jesus' message (his word), inviting many to ignore the ways of this negative 'world'. Just as the world has persecuted Jesus because of his saving word, they will persecute all those who accept and attempt to live by his word.

**5th Week of Easter**
**White**

**6th Sunday of Easter**
**Psalter Week 2**
**White**

**Acts 10:25-26.34-35.44-48**
As Peter reached the house Cornelius went out to meet him, knelt at his feet and prostrated himself. But Peter helped him up. 'Stand up,' he said 'I am only a man after all!'

Then Peter addressed them: 'The truth I have now come to realise' he said 'is that God does not have favourites, but that anybody of any nationality who fears God and does what is right is acceptable to him.'

While Peter was still speaking the Holy Spirit came down on all the listeners. Jewish believers who had accompanied Peter were all astonished that the gift of the Holy Spirit should be poured out on the pagans too, since they could hear them speaking strange languages and proclaiming the greatness of God. Peter himself then said, 'Could anyone refuse the water of baptism to these people, now they have received the Holy Spirit just as much as we have?' He then gave orders for them to be baptised in the name of Jesus Christ. Afterwards they begged him to stay on for some days.

**Psalm 97:1-4. R. cf. v.2**
*The Lord has shown his salvation to the nations.*
(or *Alleluia!*)

**1 John 4:7-10**
My dear people, let us love one another since love comes from God and everyone who loves is begotten by God and knows God. Anyone who fails to love can never have known God, because God is love. God's love for us was revealed when God sent into the world his only Son so that we could have life through him; this is the love I mean: not our love for God, but God's love for us when he sent his Son to be the sacrifice that takes our sins away.

**John 15:9-17**
Jesus said to his disciples: 'As the Father has loved me, so have I loved you. Remain in my love. If you keep my commandments you will remain in my love, just as I have kept my Father's commandments and remain in his love. I have told you this so that my own joy may be in you and your joy be complete. This is my commandment: love one another, as I have loved you. A man can have no greater love than to lay down his life for his friends. You are my friends, if you do what I command you. I shall not call you servants any more, because a servant does not know his master's business; I call you friends, because I have made known to you everything I have learnt from my Father. You

did not choose me, no, I chose you; and I commissioned you to go out and to bear fruit, fruit that will last; and then the Father will give you anything you ask him in my name. What I command you is to love one another.'

## Reflection

Peter's visit to Caesarea, the centre of Roman authority in Palestine, and his encounter with the centurion Cornelius marks a turning point in Luke's story of the mission of the early Church. The gift of baptism and participation in the Christian community can no longer be limited to the Jewish-Christians. Peter points out that God has made this clear. Before the administration of baptism, the Spirit had already descended upon the gathering. Rightly has this episode been called 'the Pentecost of the Gentiles'.

The Gospel reading picks up from last Sunday, continuing the theme of 'remaining', describing the nature of the relationship between the believer and Jesus as a relationship of love. A chain of love runs from the Father to the Son, and from the Son to the believer, but only if the believer keeps the commandments of Jesus. The centrepiece of John 15: 1–16: 3 follows in a passage that opens and closes with a description of Jesus' commandment: 'Love one another, as I have loved you'. Jesus tells his disciples of the greatness of his love for them – he lays down his life for them, as they are now his friends. They are dear to him because he has chosen them to be his own. Chosen to live within this communion of love, the believer lives a fruitful life, and receives whatever she or he asks of the Father.

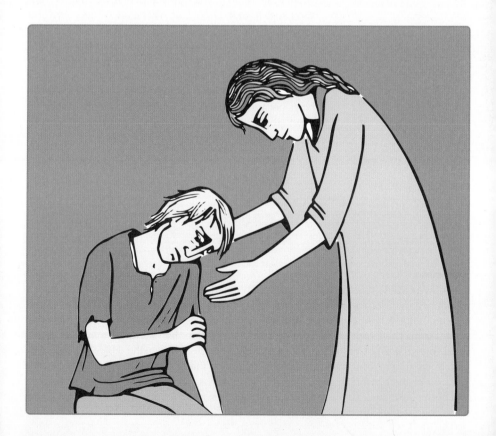

**6th Week of Easter**
**White**

## Acts 16:11-15

Sailing from Troas we made a straight run for Samothrace; the next day for Neapolis, and from there for Philippi, a Roman colony and the principal city of that particular district of Macedonia. After a few days in this city we went along the river outside the gates as it was the sabbath and this was a customary place for prayer. We sat down and preached to the women who had come to the meeting. One of these women was called Lydia, a devout woman from the town of Thyatira who was in the purple-dye trade. She listened to us, and the Lord opened her heart to accept what Paul was saying. After she and her household had been baptised she sent us an invitation: 'If you really think me a true believer in the Lord,' she said 'come and stay with us'; and she would take no refusal.

## Psalm 149:1-6.9. R. v.4

*The Lord takes delight in his people.* (or *Alleluia!*)

## John 15:26–16:4

Jesus said to his disciples: 'When the Advocate comes, whom I shall send to you from the Father, the Spirit of truth who issues from the Father, he will be my witness. And you too will be witnesses, because you have been with me from the outset. I have told you all this so that your faith may not be shaken. They will expel you from the synagogues, and indeed the hour is coming when anyone who kills you will think he is doing a holy duty for God. They will do these things because they have never known either the Father or myself. But I have told you all this, so that when the time for it comes you may remember that I told you.'

## Reflection

The story of Paul's mission takes a further important turn as Paul leaves Asia and comes to European soil for the first time. Arriving in Philippi, his witness produces Europe's first convert, Lydia. A new stage in the Pauline mission has begun as he reaches out to the ends of the earth. The Gospel reading adds a cautionary note, lest we might think that Jesus' word spreads easily. Continuing his instruction of the disciples on the difficulties they will face in the future, Jesus initially comforts them with the promise that the Spirit/Advocate will be with them in their witness to Jesus. Nevertheless, Greek, Roman, and Jewish leaders will persecute them, cast them out of the synagogues, and even slay them, because they do not recognise the Father and Jesus. The future will not be easy.

## Acts 16:22-34

The crowd of Philippians joined in and showed its hostility to Paul and Silas, so the magistrates had them stripped and ordered them to be flogged. They were given many lashes and then thrown into prison, and the gaoler was told to keep a close watch on them. So, following his instructions, he threw them into the inner prison and fastened their feet in the stocks.

**6th Week of Easter**
**White**

Late that night Paul and Silas were praying and singing God's praises, while the other prisoners listened. Suddenly there was an earthquake that shook the prison to its foundations. All the doors flew open and the chains fell from all the prisoners. When the gaoler woke and saw the doors wide open he drew his sword and was about to commit suicide, presuming that the prisoners had escaped. But Paul shouted at the top of his voice, 'Don't do yourself any harm; we are all here.'

The gaoler called for lights, then rushed in, threw himself trembling at the feet of Paul and Silas, and escorted them out, saying, 'Sirs, what must I do to be saved?' They told him 'Become a believer in the Lord Jesus, and you will be saved, and your household too.' Then they preached the word of the Lord to him and to all his family. Late as it was, he took them to wash their wounds, and was baptised then and there with all his household. Afterwards he took them home and gave them a meal, and the whole family celebrated their conversion to belief in God.

## Psalm 137:1-3.7-8. R. v.7

*You stretch out your hand and save me, O Lord.*(or *Alleluia!*)

## John 16:5-11

Jesus said to his disciples: 'Now I am going to the one who sent me. Not one of you has asked, "Where are you going?" Yet you are sad at heart because I have told you this. Still, I must tell you the truth: it is for your own good that I am going because unless I go, the Advocate will not come to you; but if I do go, I will send him to you. And when he comes, he will show the world how wrong it was, about sin, and about who was in the right, and about judgement: about sin: proved by their refusal to believe in me; about who was in the right: proved by my going to the Father and your seeing me no more; about judgement: proved by the prince of this world being already condemned.'

## Reflection

A literary pattern that Luke uses regularly in Acts guides our understanding of the first reading. Paul and his colleagues have arrived in Europe (at Philippi). They are immediately successful in their mission, but opposition emerges, and they are punished and jailed. The mission to the ends of the earth (see Acts 1: 8) often meets opposition. God intervenes in the earthquake, the opening of the doors of the prison, the eventual baptism of the jailer, and the sharing of a community meal. There may be opposition, but the spread of the Good News cannot be stopped. Jesus' farewell discourse takes another turn in today's Gospel passage. Jesus informs his disciples that he must go away if they are to receive the Spirit/Advocate who will lay bare the world's sinfulness and judge its rejection of Jesus. His going away thus affirms the disciples' pursuit of goodness in a sinful world.

# MAY

# 12

## WEDNESDAY

**6th Week of Easter**
White
or
**Sts Nereus and Achilleus,**
*martyrs*
**(Optional, Red)**
**St Pancras,** *martyr*
**(Optional, Red)**

## Acts 17:15.22–18:1

Paul's escort took him as far as Athens, and went back with instructions for Silas and Timothy to rejoin Paul as soon as they could.

Paul stood before the whole Council of the Areopagus and made this speech:

'Men of Athens, I have seen for myself how extremely scrupulous you are in all religious matters, because I noticed, as I strolled round admiring your sacred monuments, that you had an altar inscribed: To An Unknown God. Well, the God whom I proclaim is in fact the one whom you already worship without knowing it.

'Since the God who made the world and everything in it is himself Lord of heaven and earth, he does not make his home in shrines made by human hands. Nor is he dependent on anything that human hands can do for him, since he can never be in need of anything; on the contrary, it is he who gives everything – including life and breath – to everyone. From one single stock he not only created the whole human race so that they could occupy the entire earth, but he decreed how long each nation should flourish and what the boundaries of its territory should be. And he did this so that all nations might seek the deity and, by feeling their way towards him, succeed in finding him. ... *(See Appendix B-13)*

## Psalm 148:1-2.11-14

*Your glory fills all heaven and earth.* (or *Alleluia!*)

## John 16:12-15

Jesus said to his disciples: 'I still have many things to say to you but they would be too much for you now. But when the Spirit of truth comes he will lead you to the complete truth, since he will not be speaking as from himself but will say only what he has learnt; and he will tell you of the things to come. He will glorify me, since all he tells you will be taken from what is mine. Everything the Father has is mine; that is why I said: All he tells you will be taken from what is mine.',

## Reflection

In Athens, Paul uses the language of his listeners. He points out that while the Athenians accept an unknown God, this God is now known. Preaching Jesus' resurrection, he cites a Greek poet (Aratus). Some believe, some ridicule the message of resurrection, while others wish to ponder what they have heard. Jesus' final instruction of the disciples on the gift of the Spirit/Advocate in today's Gospel are among his most important words. He cannot reveal the whole truth about God, his Son, the Spirit, and the many beauties and challenges of the Christian life in one lifetime. The role of the Spirit, across the centuries, gradually unfolds the fulness of the meaning of what God has done for us in Jesus Christ. We never cease learning about God and his Christ, as the Spirit leads us to the complete truth. A Spirit-filled faith community makes that possible.

## Acts 18:1-8

Paul left Athens and went to Corinth, where he met a Jew called Aquila whose family came from Pontus. He and his wife Priscilla had recently left Italy because an edict of Claudius had expelled all the Jews from Rome. Paul went to visit them, and when he found they were tentmakers, of the same trade as himself, he lodged with them, and they worked together. Every sabbath he used to hold debates in the synagogues, trying to convert Jews as well as Greeks.

After Silas and Timothy had arrived from Macedonia, Paul devoted all his time to preaching, declaring to the Jews that Jesus was the Christ. When they turned against him and started to insult him, he took his cloak and shook it out in front of them, saying, 'Your blood be on your own heads; from now on I can go to the pagans with a clear conscience.' Then he left the synagogue and moved to the house next door that belonged to a worshipper of God called Justus. Crispus, president of the synagogue, and his whole household, all became believers in the Lord. A great many Corinthians who had heard him became believers and were baptised.

## Psalm 97:1-4. R. cf. v.2

*The Lord has revealed to the nations his saving power.*
(or *Alleluia!*)

## John 16:16-20

Jesus said to his disciples: 'In a short time you will no longer see me, and then a short time later you will see me again.'

Then some of his disciples said to one another, 'What does he mean, "In a short time you will no longer see me, and then a short time later you will see me again" and, "I am going to the Father?" What is this "short time"? We don't know what he means.' Jesus knew that they wanted to question him, so he said, 'You are asking one another what I meant by saying: In a short time you will no longer see me, and then a short time later you will see me again. 'I tell you most solemnly, you will be weeping and wailing while the world will rejoice; you will be sorrowful, but your sorrow will turn to joy.'

## Reflection

From Athens, Paul journeys to Corinth, where he meets two people who become his fast friends, Aquila and Priscilla. He preaches first to the Jewish community, pointing to Jesus as their Messiah. They reject Paul and his message, and he sets the agenda for his future mission to the Gentiles. As Jesus comes to the end of his farewell discourse with his disciples, they are unable to understand that he must leave them. Jesus introduces a message of 'now' and 'after'. At the present time they are sorrowful because they appear to be losing their Lord, and the world will rejoice because they think that by crucifying him, he has been eliminated. But in a short time their sorrow will be transformed into joy. Jesus' death will be followed by resurrection, return to the Father and the gift of the Holy Spirit. We live in that era, blessed with the joy of life in a believing community.

## MAY
# 13
### THURSDAY

**6th Week of Easter**
**White**
**Our Lady of Fatima**
**(Optional, White)**
**or**
**Ascension of the Lord,**
**(England, Wales &**
**Scotland)**
*(See 16th May)*

**St Matthias,** *apostle*
**Feast**
**Red**

## Acts 1:15-17.20-26

One day Peter stood up to speak to the brothers – there were about a hundred and twenty persons in the congregation: 'Brothers, the passage of scripture has to be fulfilled in which the Holy Spirit, speaking through David, foretells the fate of Judas, who offered himself as a guide to the men who arrested Jesus – after having been one of our number and actually sharing this ministry of ours. Now in the Book of Psalms it says: Let his camp be reduced to ruin, let there be no one to live in it.

And again: Let someone else take his office.

'We must therefore choose someone who has been with us the whole time that the Lord Jesus was travelling round with us, someone who was with us right from the time when John was baptising until the day when he was taken up from us – and he can act with us as a witness to his resurrection.'

Having nominated two candidates, Joseph known as Barsabbas, whose surname was Justus, and Matthias, they prayed, 'Lord, you can read everyone's heart; show us therefore which of these two you have chosen to take over this ministry and apostolate, which Judas abandoned to go to his proper place.' They then drew lots for them, and as the lot fell to Matthias, he was listed as one of the twelve apostles.

## Psalm 112:1-8. R. cf. v.8

*The Lord sets him in the company of the princes of his people.* (or *Alleluia!*)

## John 15:9-17

Jesus said to his disciples: 'As the Father has loved me, so I have loved you. Remain in my love. If you keep my commandments you will remain in my love, just as I have kept my Father's commandments and remain in his love. I have told you this so that my own joy may be in you and your joy be complete. This is my commandment: love one another, as I have loved you. A man can have no greater love than to lay down his life for his friends. You are my friends, if you do what I command you. I shall not call you servants any more, because a servant does not know his master's business; I call you friends, because I have made known to you everything I have learnt from my Father. You did not choose me, no, I chose you; and I commissioned you to go out and to bear fruit, fruit that will last; and then the Father will give you anything you ask him in my name. What I command you is to love one another.'

## Reflection

The completion of the 'Twelve' is an action of the Spirit. As God raised up twelve tribes in Israel, so Jesus founded an inner core of twelve disciples. They are the bedrock of a new people of God. Matthias, who has witnessed Jesus' mission from the time of his baptism till his resurrection, is chosen. The Gospel highlights that a chain of love runs from the Father to the Son, and from the Son to the believer if the believer keeps the commandments of Jesus, explained as 'Love one another, as I have loved you'. Jesus tells his disciples of the greatness of his love for them. They are now his friends, dear to him because he has chosen them. Within this communion of love, the believer lives a fruitful life, receiving whatever she or he asks of the Father.

### Acts 18:23-28

Paul came down to Antioch where he spent a short time before continuing his journey through the Galatian country and then through Phrygia, encouraging all the followers.

An Alexandrian Jew named Apollos now arrived in Ephesus. He was an eloquent man, with a sound knowledge of the scriptures and yet, though he had been given instruction in the Way of the Lord and preached with great earnestness and was accurate in all the details he taught about Jesus, he had only experienced the baptism of John. When Priscilla and Aquila heard him speak boldly in the synagogue, they took an interest in him and gave him further instruction about the Way.

When Apollos thought of crossing over to Achaia, the brothers encouraged him and wrote asking the disciples to welcome him. When he arrived there he was able by God's grace to help the believers considerably by the energetic way he refuted the Jews in public and demonstrated from the scriptures that Jesus was the Christ.

### Psalm 46:2-3.8-10. R. v.8

*God is king of all the earth.* (or *Alleluia!*)

### John 16:23-28

Jesus said to his disciples: 'I tell you most solemnly, anything you ask for from the Father he will grant in my name. Until now you have not asked for anything in my name. Ask and you will receive, and so your joy will be complete. I have been telling you all this in metaphors; the hour is coming when I shall no longer speak to you in metaphors, but tell you about the Father in plain words. When that day comes you will ask in my name; and I do not say that I shall pray to the Father for you, because the Father himself loves you for loving me and believing that I came from God. I came from the Father and have come into the world and now I leave the world to go to the Father.'

**6th Week of Easter**
**White**

### Reflection

Paul sets out again for Asia. Luke tells us that Apollos, a wonderful preacher who knew of 'the Way of the Lord' has appeared in Ephesus. But he did not know of baptism in the Holy Spirit. This situation is rectified by Paul's friends Aquila and Priscilla who instruct him further. On reception of the Holy Spirit Apollos crosses to Greece, and there convincingly proclaims Jesus as the Christ. Knowledge of the Jesus-story is important. But the gift of the Spirit is essential for anyone who wishes to bear witness to Jesus as the Christ. Continuing the theme of 'now' and 'after', Jesus gives the example of a woman expecting a child. On the basis of that powerful image, he instructs the disciples that they too will pass from the pain of 'now' to the joy of 'after'. They will be loved by the Father, and he will grant their prayers, because they have loved his Son.

**The Ascension
of the Lord (Ireland)
Solemnity
or
7th Sunday of Easter
(England, Wales &
Scotland)**
*(See Appendix A-9)*
**Psalter Week 3
White**

## Acts 1:1-11

In my earlier work, Theophilus, I dealt with everything Jesus had done and taught from the beginning until the day he gave his instructions to the apostles he had chosen through the Holy Spirit, and was taken up to heaven. He had shown himself alive to them after his Passion by many demonstrations: for forty days he had continued to appear to them and tell them about the kingdom of God. When he had been at table with them, he had told them not to leave Jerusalem, but to wait there for what the Father had promised. 'It is' he had said 'what you have heard me speak about: John baptised with water but you, not many days from now, will be baptised with the Holy Spirit.'

Now having met together, they asked him, 'Lord, has the time come? Are you going to restore the kingdom of Israel?' He replied, 'It is not for you to know times or dates that the Father has decided by his own authority, but you will receive power when the Holy Spirit comes on you, and then you will be my witnesses not only in Jerusalem but throughout Judaea and Samaria, and indeed to the ends of the earth.'

As he said this he was lifted up while they looked on, and a cloud took him from their sight. They were still staring into the sky when suddenly two men in white were standing near them and they said, 'Why are you men from Galilee standing here looking into the sky? Jesus who has been taken up from you into heaven, this same Jesus will come back in the same way as you have seen him go there.'

**Psalm 46:2-3.6-9. R. v.6**

*God goes up with shouts of joy; the Lord goes up with trumpet blast.* (or *Alleluia!*)

## Ephesians 4:1-13

*(Alternative reading: Ephesians 1:17-23)*

I, the prisoner in the Lord, implore you to lead a life worthy of your vocation. Bear with one another charitably, in complete selflessness, gentleness and patience. Do all you can to preserve the unity of the Spirit by the peace that binds you together. There is one Body, one Spirit, just as you were all called into one and the same hope when you were called. There is one Lord, one faith, one baptism, and one God who is Father of all, over all, through all and within all.

Each one of us, however, has been given his own share of grace, given as Christ allotted it. It was said that he would: When he ascended to the height, he captured prisoners, he gave gifts to men. When it says, 'he ascended', what can it mean if not that he descended right down to the lower regions of the earth? The one who rose higher than all the heavens to fill all things is none other than the one who descended. And to some, his gift was that they should be apostles; to some, prophets; to some, evangelists; to some, pastors and teachers; so that the saints together make a unity in the work of service, building up the body of Christ. In this way we are all to come to unity in our faith and in our knowledge of the Son of God, until we become the perfect Man, fully mature with the fullness of Christ himself.

## Mark 16:15-20

Jesus showed himself to the Eleven, and said to them, 'Go out to the whole world; proclaim the Good News to all creation. He who believes and is baptised will be saved; he who does not believe will be condemned. These are the signs that will be associated with believers: in my name they will cast out devils; they will have the gift of tongues; they will pick up snakes in their hands, and be unharmed should they drink deadly poison; they will lay their hands on the sick, who will recover.'

And so the Lord Jesus, after he had spoken to them, was taken up into heaven: there at the right hand of God he took his place, while they, going out, preached everywhere, the Lord working with them and confirming the word by the signs that accompanied it.

## Reflection

Allowing for the eventual gift of the Spirit on the day of Pentecost, fifty days after the Passover, in the Acts of the Apostles Jesus remains with the earliest Church for forty days. Following his ascension, they must wait in the city of Jerusalem, the centre of God's saving history, to which Jesus travelled, where he suffered and rose, and where the Spirit will be given. They are not to worry about when the end of the world will come as they have a mission ahead of them. As the physical presence of Jesus ends – to be replaced by the Holy Spirit – he commissions his disciples to be his witnesses to the ends of the earth. They do not understand. They stand, gazing into the sky, until the two men in white who were in the empty tomb (see Luke 24: 4) appear and instruct them that they must begin their mission, as one day in the distant future Jesus will return.

The author to the Letter to the Ephesians instructs us on how we are to conduct that mission as Church, until we all reach the perfection for which we were made. The Gospel reading comes from a passage added to the Gospel of Mark late in the second century. The author gathers from various earlier traditions to instruct us on Jesus' ascension, and the wonders that will accompany the faith-filled mission that follows Jesus' departure and the gift of the Spirit that we will celebrate next Sunday.

**7th Week of Easter**
**White**

### Acts 19:1-8

While Apollos was in Corinth, Paul made his way overland as far as Ephesus, where he found a number of disciples. When he asked, 'Did you receive the Holy Spirit when you became believers?' they answered, 'No, we were never even told there was such a thing as a Holy Spirit.' 'Then how were you baptised?' he asked 'With John's baptism' they replied. 'John's baptism' said Paul 'was a baptism of repentance; but he insisted that the people should believe in the one who was to come after him – in other words Jesus.' When they heard this, they were baptised in the name of the Lord Jesus, and the moment Paul had laid hands on them the Holy Spirit came down on them, and they began to speak with tongues and to prophesy. There were about twelve of these men.

He began by going to the synagogue, where he spoke out boldly and argued persuasively about the kingdom of God. He did this for three months.

### Psalm 67:2-7. R. v.33

*Kingdoms of the earth, sing to God.* (or *Alleluia!*)

### John 16:29-33

His disciples said to Jesus, 'Now you are speaking plainly and not using metaphors! Now we see that you know everything, and do not have to wait for questions to be put into words; because of this we believe that you came from God.' Jesus answered them: 'Do you believe at last? Listen; the time will come – in fact it has come already – when you will be scattered, each going his own way and leaving me alone. And yet I am not alone, because the Father is with me. I have told you all this so that you may find peace in me. In the world you will have trouble, but be brave: I have conquered the world.'

### Reflection

Paul arrives in Ephesus, where he will spend some time, only to find that there are disciples in Ephesus who replicate the experience of Apollos: they know the story of Jesus, but have only received the baptism of repentance that comes from John the Baptist. Baptised 'in the name of the Lord Jesus', they are filled with the Spirit and begin to speak in various tongues, like the Apostles on the day of Pentecost (Acts 2: 5-13). As Jesus' final discourse closes, the disciples make an important confession of faith. They now believe that Jesus came from God. He can now point to the difficult times that lie ahead of the Church, comforting them with the assurance that he is never without the presence of his Father. In their faith that Jesus comes from God, they will also have peace because, despite apparent tribulation, Jesus has conquered the world.

## Acts 20:17-27

From Miletus Paul sent for the elders of the church of Ephesus. When they arrived he addressed these words to them:

'You know what my way of life has been ever since the first day I set foot among you in Asia, how I have served the Lord in all humility, with all the sorrows and trials that came to me through the plots of the Jews. I have not hesitated to do anything that would be helpful to you; I have preached to you, and instructed you both in public and in your homes, urging both Jews and Greeks to turn to God and to believe in our Lord Jesus.

'And now you see me a prisoner already in spirit; I am on my way to Jerusalem, but have no idea what will happen to me there, except that the Holy Spirit, in town after town, has made it clear enough that imprisonment and persecution await me. ... *(See Appendix B-13)*

## Psalm 67:10-11.20-21. R. v.33

*Kingdoms of the earth, sing to God.* (or *Alleluia!*)

## John 17:1-11

Jesus raised his eyes to heaven and said: 'Father, the hour has come: glorify your Son so that your Son may glorify you; and, through the power over all mankind that you have given him, let him give eternal life to all those you have entrusted to him. And eternal life is this: to know you, the only true God, and Jesus Christ whom you have sent. I have glorified you on earth and finished the work that you gave me to do. 'Now, Father, it is time for you to glorify me with that glory I had with you before ever the world was. I have made your name known to the men you took from the world to give me. They were yours and you gave them to me, and they have kept your word. Now at last they know that all you have given me comes indeed from you; for I have given them the teaching you gave to me, and they have truly accepted this, that I came from you, and have believed that it was you who sent me. I pray for them; I am not praying for the world but for those you have given me, because they belong to you: all I have is yours and all you have is mine, and in them I am glorified. I am not in the world any longer, but they are in the world, and I am coming to you.'

## Reflection

We have heard Jesus' farewell discourse to his disciples in the Gospel of John. Today, in our ongoing reading of the Acts of the Apostles we encounter the first part of Paul's farewell discourse to the leaders of the Church at Ephesus. In the port city of Miletus, he looks back to all he has encountered during his remarkable missionary journeys. He is aware that a way of suffering lies ahead, and he thanks these early Christian leaders for their affection and support in his bold proclamation of the Gospel of Jesus Christ. The Gospel no longer reports a farewell discourse but the inner world of Jesus' prayer. He asks his Father to glorify him as he has done what the Father has asked him to do. He points to the gathered disciples, who now also belong to the Father. Jesus is about to leave them, and they will remain in the world, responsible for the continuation of Jesus' mission. He will shortly pray for them.

**7th Week of Easter**
**White**
**or**
**St John I,** *pope, martyr*
**(Optional, Red)**

**MAY**

# 19

**WEDNESDAY**

**7th Week of Easter**
**White**

_____

_____

_____

_____

### Acts 20:28-38

Paul addressed these words to the elders of the church of Ephesus: 'Be on your guard for yourselves and for all the flock of which the Holy Spirit has made you the overseers, to feed the Church of God which he bought with his own blood. I know quite well that when I have gone fierce wolves will invade you and will have no mercy on the flock. Even from your own ranks there will be men coming forward with a travesty of the truth on their lips to induce the disciples to follow them. So be on your guard, remembering how night and day for three years I never failed to keep you right, shedding tears over each one of you. And now I commend you to God, and to the word of his grace that has power to build you up and to give you your inheritance among all the sanctified.

'I have never asked anyone for money or clothes; you know for yourselves that the work I did earned enough to meet my needs and those of my companions. I did this to show you that is how we must exert ourselves to support the weak, remembering the words of the Lord Jesus, who himself said, "There is more happiness in giving than in receiving." '

When he had finished speaking he knelt down with them all and prayed. By now they were all in tears; they put their arms round Paul's neck and kissed him; what saddened them most was his saying they would never see his face again. Then they escorted him to the ship.

### Psalm 67:29-30.33-36. R. v.33
_Kingdoms of the earth, sing to God._ (or _Alleluia!_)

### John 17:11-19

Jesus raised his eyes to heaven and said: 'Holy Father, keep those you have given me true to your name, so that they may be one like us. While I was with them, I kept those you had given me true to your name. I have watched over them and not one is lost except the one who chose to be lost, and this was to fulfil the scriptures. But now I am coming to you and while still in the world I say these things to share my joy with them to the full. I passed your word on to them, and the world hated them, because they belong to the world no more than I belong to the world. I am not asking you to remove them from the world, but to protect them from the evil one. They do not belong to the world any more than I belong to the world. Consecrate them in the truth; your word is truth. As you sent me into the world, I have sent them into the world, and for their sake I consecrate myself so that they too may be consecrated in truth.'

### Reflection

Paul continues his farewell discourse to the elders from Ephesus instructing them on their responsibilities to continue witnessing the Gospel of Jesus, despite the challenges that they will encounter on the way. As leaders they are to be wise and caring shepherds of God's flock, never hesitating to show affection and care, as Paul does when he takes their leave. But they must always be wary of the lies and falseness that they will inevitably meet. In the second part of his farewell prayer, Jesus prays for those he has drawn to the Father. Addressing God as 'Holy Father', he first asks that God protect them, to always act as a 'father' to them. Jesus then prays that God might make them 'holy,' as Jesus was holy. Jesus has given himself without condition to the Father's will. He now prays that his disciples will do the same.

## Acts 22:30; 23:6-11

Since the tribune wanted to know what precise charge the Jews were bringing against Paul, he freed him and gave orders for a meeting of the chief priests and the entire Sanhedrin; then he brought Paul down and stood him in front of them.

Now Paul was well aware that one section was made up of Sadducees and the other of Pharisees, so he called out in the Sanhedrin, 'Brothers, I am a Pharisee and the son of Pharisees. It is for our hope in the resurrection of the dead that I am on trial.' As soon as he said this a dispute broke out between the Pharisees and Sadducees, and the assembly was split between the two parties. For the Sadducees say there is neither resurrection, nor angel, nor spirit, while the Pharisees accept all three. ...
*(See Appendix B–13)*

## Psalm 15:1-2.5.7-11. R. v.1

*Preserve me, Lord, I take refuge in you.* (or *Alleluia!*)

## John 17:20-26

Jesus raised his eyes to heaven and said: 'Holy Father, I pray not only for these, but for those also who through their words will believe in me. May they all be one. Father, may they be one in us as you are in me and I am in you, so that the world may believe it was you who sent me. I have given them the glory you gave to me, that they may be one as we are one. With me in them and you in me, may they be so completely one that the world will realise that it was you who sent me and that I have loved them as much as you love me. 'Father, I want those you have given me to be with me where I am, so that they may always see the glory you have given me because you loved me before the foundation of the world. Father, Righteous One, the world has not known you, but I have known you, and these have known that you have sent me. I have made your name known to them and will continue to make it known, so that the love with which you loved me may be in them, and so that I may be in them.'

## Reflection

In Paul's many trials, before Jewish and Roman leaders, he always points to his innocence. Before the Jewish Sanhedrin, he plays upon the divisions between the Sadducees, who did not believe in resurrection after death, and the Pharisees, who did. They cannot come to agreement, as Paul gives witness to Jesus. Even on trial Paul proclaims a great truth: 'It is for our hope in the resurrection of the dead that I am on trial'. This hope remains the bedrock of our faith and the source of trials. Jesus prays for all subsequent generations of believers who will believe in Jesus as a result of the preaching of the first disciples. He prays for unity among all of us, a unity that matches the unity that has always existed between Jesus and his Father. As the prayer ends, Jesus cries out, asking that we all be swept up into the oneness of love that unites the Father and the Son.

**7th Week of Easter**
**White**
**or**
**St Bernardine of Siena,**
*priest*
**(Optional, White)**

**7th Week of Easter**
**White**
or
**St Christopher**
**Magallanes, *priest*, and**
**his companions, *martyrs***
**(Optional, Red)**

### Acts 25:13-21

King Agrippa and Bernice arrived in Caesarea and paid their respects to Festus. Their visit lasted several days, and Festus put Paul's case before the king. 'There is a man here' he said 'whom Felix left behind in custody, and while I was in Jerusalem the chief priests and elders of the Jews laid information against him, demanding his condemnation. But I told them that Romans are not in the habit of surrendering any man, until the accused confronts his accusers and is given an opportunity to defend himself against the charge. So they came here with me, and I wasted no time but took my seat on the tribunal the very next day and had the man brought in. When confronted with him, his accusers did not charge him with any of the crimes I had expected; but they had some argument or other with him about their own religion and about a dead man called Jesus whom Paul alleged to be alive. Not feeling qualified to deal with questions of this sort, I asked him if he would be willing to go to Jerusalem, to be tried there on this issue. But Paul put in an appeal for his case to be reserved for the judgement of the august emperor, so I ordered him to be remanded until I could send him to Caesar.'

### Psalm 102:1-2.11-12.19-20. R. v.19

*The Lord has set his sway in heaven.* (or *Alleluia!*)

### John 21:15-19

Jesus showed himself to his disciples, and after they had eaten he said to Simon Peter, 'Simon son of John, do you love me more than these others do?' He answered, 'Yes Lord, you know I love you.' Jesus said to him, 'Feed my lambs.' A second time he said to him, 'Simon son of John, do you love me?' He replied, 'Yes, Lord, you know I love you.' Jesus said to him, 'Look after my sheep.' Then he said to him a third time, 'Simon son of John, do you love me?' Peter was upset that he asked him the third time, 'Do you love me?' and said, 'Lord, you know everything; you know I love you.' Jesus said to him, 'Feed my sheep. I tell you most solemnly, when you were young you put on your own belt and walked where you liked; but when you grow old you will stretch out your hands, and somebody else will put a belt round you and take you where you would rather not go.' In these words he indicated the kind of death by which Peter would give glory to God. After this he said, 'Follow me.'

### Reflection

In Caesarea, the seat of the Roman administration of Palestine, the governor Festus explains to the Jewish royalty of Agrippa and Bernice that Jewish trials of Paul are unable to convict him of the charges they have tried to bring against him. Paul has decided that he must call upon his privileged status as a Roman citizen from the city of Tarsus. But there is more to it. The Gospel must be preached in Rome – at the ends of the earth. This decision is all part of God's design. Jesus' famous encounter with Simon Peter beside the Lake of Tiberius reverses Peter's earlier failures. Three times he has denied Jesus (see John 18: 12-27); three times he must profess his love for him – 'more than everything else'. Peter will eventually demonstrate the depth of that love by his own crucifixion, a death that glorifies God, just as Jesus' death has glorified God.

## Acts 28:16-20.30-31

On our arrival in Rome Paul was allowed to stay in lodgings of his own with the soldier who guarded him.

After three days he called together the leading Jews. When they had assembled, he said to them, 'Brothers, although I have done nothing against our people or the customs of our ancestors, I was arrested in Jerusalem and handed over to the Romans. They examined me and would have set me free, since they found me guilty of nothing involving the death penalty; but the Jews lodged an objection, and I was forced to appeal to Caesar, not that I had any accusation to make against my own nation. That is why I have asked to see you and talk to you, for it is on account of the hope of Israel that I wear this chain.'

Paul spent the whole of the two years in his own rented lodging. He welcomed all who came to visit him, proclaiming the kingdom of God and teaching the truth about the Lord Jesus Christ with complete freedom and without hindrance from anyone.

## Psalm 10:4-5.7. R. cf. v.7

*The upright shall see your face, O Lord.* (or *Alleluia!*)

## John 21:20-25

Peter turned and saw the disciple Jesus loved following them – the one who had leaned on his breast at the supper and had said to him, 'Lord, who is it that will betray you?' Seeing him, Peter said to Jesus, 'What about him, Lord?' Jesus answered, 'If I want him to stay behind till I come, what does it matter to you? You are to follow me.' The rumour then went out among the brothers that this disciple would not die. Yet Jesus had not said to Peter 'He will not die,' but, 'If I want him to stay behind till I come.'

This disciple is the one who vouches for these things and has written them down, and we know that his testimony is true.

There were many other things that Jesus did; if all were written down, the world itself, I suppose, would not hold all the books that would have to be written.

## Reflection

The Acts of the Apostles must finish in Rome (see Acts 1: 8). Paul witnesses to Jesus at the centre of the then known world by sharing with the Romans his experience of trials and misunderstandings. The Romans have no immediate interest in punishing Paul for something that they do not understand. Thus Luke's second volume concludes with an open ending: Paul courageously proclaims the Kingdom of God and the truth about Jesus Christ. We continue the story as the 'third volume' of God's missionary action at the ends of the earth. As John's Gospel also closes, we find the solution to an important question: who is more important: Peter the Shepherd, or the Beloved Disciple, the witness to God's love? We need both, and we have been blessed on those occasions throughout the Church's history when our Shepherd also shows that he is a Beloved Disciple. We are equally blessed by all Christians whose lives reveal God's loving care for all people and nations.

**7th Week of Easter**
**White**
or
**St Rita of Cascia,**
*religious*
**(Optional, White)**

## MAY
# 23
### SUNDAY

**Pentecost Sunday**
Solemnity
Psalter Week 2
Red

## Acts 2:1-11

When Pentecost day came round, the apostles had all met in one room, when suddenly they heard what sounded like a powerful wind from heaven, the noise of which filled the entire house in which they were sitting; and something appeared to them that seemed like tongues of fire; these separated and came to rest on the head of each of them. They were all filled with the Holy Spirit, and began to speak foreign languages as the Spirit gave them the gift of speech.

Now there were devout men living in Jerusalem from every nation under heaven, and at this sound they all assembled, each one bewildered to hear these men speaking his own language. They were amazed and astonished. 'Surely' they said 'all these men speaking are Galileans? How does it happen that each of us hears them in his own native language? Parthians, Medes and Elamites; people from Mesopotamia, Judaea and Cappadocia, Pontus and Asia, Phrygia and Pamphylia, Egypt and the parts of Libya round Cyrene; as well as visitors from Rome – Jews and proselytes alike – Cretans and Arabs; we hear them preaching in our own language about the marvels of God.'

## Psalm 103:1.24.29-31.34. R. v.30

*Send forth your Spirit, O Lord, and renew the face of the earth.* (or *Alleluia!*)

## Galatians 5:16-25

If you are guided by the Spirit you will be in no danger of yielding to self-indulgence, since self-indulgence is the opposite of the Spirit, the Spirit is totally against such a thing, and it is precisely because the two are so opposed that you do not always carry out your good intentions. If you are led by the Spirit, no law can touch you. When self-indulgence is at work the results are obvious: fornication, gross indecency and sexual irresponsibility; idolatry and sorcery; feuds and wrangling, jealousy, bad temper and quarrels; disagreements, factions, envy; drunkenness, orgies and similar things. I warn you now, as I warned you before: those who behave like this will not inherit the kingdom of God. What the Spirit brings is very different: love, joy, peace, patience, kindness, goodness, trustfulness, gentleness and self-control. There can be no law against things like that, of course. You cannot belong to Christ Jesus unless you crucify all self-indulgent passions and desires.

Since the Spirit is our life, let us be directed by the Spirit.

## John 15:26-27; 16:12-15

Jesus said to his disciples: 'When the Advocate comes, whom I shall send to you from the Father, the Spirit of truth who issues from the Father, he will be my witness. And you too will be witnesses, because you have been with me from the outset. I still have many things to say to you but they would be too much for you now. But when the Spirit of truth comes he will lead you to the complete truth, since he will not be speaking as from himself but will say only what he has learnt; and he will tell you of the things to come. He will glorify me, since all he tells you will be taken from what is mine. Everything the Father has is mine; that is why I said: All he tells you will be taken from what is mine.'

## Reflection

On the Jewish celebration of Pentecost which recalls God's establishment of a covenant with the people of Israel, the gift of the Spirit, 'the power from on high' (Luke 24: 49) opens a new relationship with God and humankind. Signs associated with the event at Sinai are recalled: thunder, lightning, and fire (See Exodus 19: 16-20). The one nation, Israel, is transcended as peoples from many nations understand the disciples who are 'filled with the Holy Spirit', as they speak 'about the marvels of God'.

In the second reading Paul lists the contrasting characteristics of a life without the gift of the Spirit and a life 'guided by the Spirit'. We must examine those characteristics and hear Paul's exhortation: 'Since the Spirit is our life, let us be directed by the Spirit'.

The Gospel reading selects two passages from Jesus' farewell discourse to his disciples. As he returns to the Father, the Spirit/Advocate will continue the presence of the divine among us. Filled with the Spirit, we will continue Jesus' mission of being witnesses to God. However, Jesus has not been able to communicate all the truths of God and God's design for us in the brief period of his ministry. He still has much to teach us. But that will be done down through the Christian ages in and through the presence of the Spirit/Advocate who has learnt from the Father, and 'will tell us of the things to come'.

## Ecclesiasticus 17:20-28

To those who repent, God permits return, and he encourages those who were losing hope. Return to the Lord and leave sin behind, plead before his face and lessen your offence. Come back to the Most High and turn away from iniquity, and hold in abhorrence all that is foul. Who will praise the Most High in Sheol, if the living do not do so by giving glory to him? To the dead, as to those who do not exist, praise is unknown, only those with life and health can praise the Lord. How great is the mercy of the Lord, his pardon on all those who turn towards him!

## Psalm 31:1-2.5-7

*Rejoice, rejoice in the Lord, exult, you just!*

## Mark 10:17-27

Jesus was setting out on a journey when a man ran up, knelt before him and put this question to him, 'Good master, what must I do to inherit eternal life?' Jesus said to him, 'Why do you call me good? No one is good but God alone. You know the commandments: You must not kill; You must not commit adultery; You must not steal; You must not bring false witness; You must not defraud; Honour your father and mother.' And he said to him, 'Master, I have kept all these from my earliest days.' Jesus looked steadily at him and loved him, and he said, 'There is one thing you lack. Go and sell everything you own and give the money to the poor, and you will have treasure in heaven; then come, follow me.' But his face fell at these words and he went away sad, for he was a man of great wealth.

Jesus looked round and said to his disciples, 'How hard it is for those who have riches to enter the kingdom of God!' The disciples were astounded by these words, but Jesus insisted, 'My children,' he said to them 'how hard it is to enter the kingdom of God! It is easier for a camel to pass through the eye of a needle than for a rich man to enter the kingdom of God.' They were more astonished than ever. 'In that case' they said to one another 'who can be saved?' Jesus gazed at them. 'For men' he said 'it is impossible, but not for God: because everything is possible for God.'

## Reflection

Jesus entrusted His beloved mother to the disciples at the culmination of His mission on earth and gave up His life on the cross for the life of humanity. Mary's maternal assistance and guidance helped the disciples to become the extension of Jesus' mission. The role of our Blessed Mother in the Church is once again reinforced when she is honoured as the Mother of the Church. May Mary, the Mother of the Church, intercede for all of us for the grace to be faithful witnesses in the Church.

## Sirach 35:1-12

A man multiplies offerings by keeping the Law; he offers communion sacrifices by following the commandments. By showing gratitude he makes an offering of fine flour, by giving alms he offers a sacrifice of praise. Withdraw from wickedness and the Lord will be pleased, withdraw from injustice and you make atonement. Do not appear empty-handed in the Lord's presence; for all these things are due under the commandment. A virtuous man's offering graces the altar, and its savour rises before the Most High. A virtuous man's sacrifice is acceptable, its memorial will not be forgotten. Honour the Lord with generosity, do not stint the first-fruits you bring. Add a smiling face to all your gifts, and be cheerful as you dedicate your tithes. Give to the Most High as he has given to you, generously as your means can afford; for the Lord is a good rewarder, he will reward you seven times over. Offer him no bribe, he will not accept it, do not put your faith in an unvirtuous sacrifice; since the Lord is a judge who is no respecter of personages.

## Psalm 49:5-8.14.23. R. v.23

*I will show God's salvation to the upright.*

## Mark 10:28-31

'What about us?' Peter asked Jesus. 'We have left everything and followed you.' Jesus said, 'I tell you solemnly, there is no one who has left house, brothers, sisters, father, children or land for my sake and for the sake of the gospel who will not be repaid a hundred times over, houses, brothers, sisters, mothers, children and land – not without persecutions – now in this present time and, in the world to come, eternal life.

'Many who are first will be last, and the last first.'

## Reflection

Translating the wise sayings of his father, about one hundred years before Jesus Christ, Sirach insists on beliefs fundamental to both Judaism and Christianity: the God of Israel judges the performance of human beings. Sirach instructs his audience that God is a just judge. Optimistically, he informs us of the many daily activities that bring God's blessing: keeping the Law, performing our religious duties with love and care, generosity and joy. The Lord rewards good behaviour seven times over. After witnessing Jesus' calling of the rich man and hearing his explanation of the challenges of true discipleship (Mark 10: 17-27), Peter asks Jesus about the situation of those who are following him. They have apparently left everything, as Jesus had requested of the rich man. Pointing beyond the immediate circle in the story, Jesus speaks to all of us as he lists the many challenges that the Christian disciple must face. God and Jesus Christ must be the most important realities in our lives. It is not that the good things listed in the Gospel – houses, family, land – have no value. But they must not take the place of God in our lives.

MAY

# 25

TUESDAY

**8th Week Ordinary Time**
**Green**
or
**St Bede the Venerable,**
*priest, doctor*
**(Optional, White)**
**St Gregory VII,** *pope*
**(Optional, White)**
**St Mary Magdalene de**
**Pazzi,** *virgin*
**(Optional, White)**

**8th Week
in Ordinary Time
St Philip Neri,** *priest*
**Memorial
White**

Sirach 36:1.4-5.10-17
*(See Appendix B-13)*

Psalm 78:8-9.11.13. R. Sirach 36:1
*Have mercy on us, Lord, and look on us.*

Mark 10:32-45
The disciples were on the road, going up to Jerusalem; Jesus was walking on ahead of them; they were in a daze, and those who followed were apprehensive. Once more taking the Twelve aside he began to tell them what was going to happen to him: 'Now we are going up to Jerusalem, and the Son of Man is about to be handed over to the chief priests and the scribes. They will condemn him to death and will hand him over to the pagans, who will mock him and spit at him and scourge him and put him to death; and after three days he will rise again.'

James and John, the sons of Zebedee, approached him. 'Master,' they said to him 'we want you to do us a favour.' He said to them, 'What is it you want me to do for you?' They said to him, 'Allow us to sit one at your right hand and the other at your left in your glory.' 'You do not know what you are asking' Jesus said to them. 'Can you drink the cup that I must drink, or be baptised with the baptism with which I must be baptised?' They replied 'We can.' Jesus said to them, 'The cup that I must drink you shall drink, and with the baptism with which I must be baptised you shall be baptised, but as for seats at my right hand or my left, these are not mine to grant; they belong to those to whom they have been allotted.'

When the other ten heard this they began to feel indignant with James and John, so Jesus called them to him and said to them, 'You know that among the pagans their so-called rulers lord it over them, and their great men make their authority felt. This is not to happen among you. No; anyone who wants to become great among you must be your servant, and anyone who wants to be first among you must be slave to all. For the Son of Man himself did not come to be served but to serve, and to give his life as a ransom for many.'

## Reflection

Sirach insists on God as judge, and Mark's teaching on true discipleship asked that God be the centre of our lives. Sirach insists: 'We have acknowledged that there is no God but you, Lord.' Jesus continues his teaching on the cost of discipleship by announcing his forthcoming death to those who are following him on the road to Jerusalem. But the disciples do not or will not understand his message. The Sons of Zebedee want positions of honour when Jesus establishes a powerful messianic kingdom in Jerusalem. The other ten are annoyed that James and John are jockeying for authority. Jesus teaches them that there is only one way. They must follow his example, 'For the Son of Man himself did not come to be served but to serve, and to give his life and a ransom for many'. Only God will determine who will be on the right and the left of Jesus in Jerusalem: two thieves (Mark 15: 27)!

## Sirach 42:15-25

I will remind you of the works of the Lord, and tell of what I have seen. By the words of the Lord his works come into being and all creation obeys his will. As the sun in shining looks on all things, so the work of the Lord is full of his glory. The Lord has not granted to the holy ones to tell of all his marvels which the Almighty Lord has solidly constructed for the universe to stand firm in his glory. He has fathomed the deep and the heart, and seen into their devious ways; for the Most High knows all the knowledge there is, and has observed the signs of the times. He declares what is past and what will be, and uncovers the traces of hidden things. Not a thought escapes him, not a single word is hidden from him. He has imposed an order on the magnificent works of his wisdom, he is from everlasting to everlasting, nothing can be added to him, nothing taken away, he needs no one's advice. How desirable are all his works, how dazzling to the eye! They all live and last for ever, whatever the circumstances all obey him. All things go in pairs, by opposites, and he has made nothing defective; the one consolidates the excellence of the other, who could ever be sated with gazing at his glory?

## Psalm 32:2-9. R. v.6

*By the word of the Lord the heavens were made.*

## Mark 10:46-52

As Jesus left Jericho with his disciples and a large crowd, Bartimaeus (that is, the son of Timaeus), a blind beggar, was sitting at the side of the road. When he heard that it was Jesus of Nazareth, he began to shout and to say, 'Son of David, Jesus, have pity on me.' And many of them scolded him and told him to keep quiet, but he only shouted all the louder, 'Son of David, have pity on me.' Jesus stopped and said, 'Call him here.' So they called the blind man. 'Courage,' they said 'get up; he is calling you.' So throwing off his cloak, he jumped up and went to Jesus. Then Jesus spoke, 'What do you want me to do for you?' 'Rabbuni,' the blind man said to him 'Master, let me see again.' Jesus said to him, 'Go; your faith has saved you.' And immediately his sight returned and he followed him along the road.

**8th Week
in Ordinary Time
Green
or
St Augustine of
Canterbury,** *bishop*
**(Optional, White)**

**Our Lord Jesus Christ
the Eternal High Priest
(England – Feast)**
*(See Appendix A-10)*

## Reflection

Sirach reminds us of the works of God – our created world that obeys God's will. He provides one of the most moving reflections on creation as the revelation of God's visible presence among us. The Bible calls it 'the glory of God', a driving principle behind Pope Francis' *Laudato Si'*. The account of blind Bartimaeus, sitting by the side of the road in his poverty, calling out to Jesus as he passes by, is a model of what Jesus has been trying to communicate through the instruction of his disciples. Bartimaeus brings nothing to the encounter, but Jesus insists: 'Call him'. Naked before the Lord, he is granted his sight, a recognition of his belief in Jesus. Having nothing of his own, he is filled by God's gracious gift through Jesus. Unlike the disciples, who are frightened as they follow Jesus to Jerusalem (see Mark 10: 32), he 'followed him along the road'.

**8th Week
in Ordinary Time
Green**

**Sirach 44:1.9-13**
*(See Appendix B-14)*

**Psalm 149:1-6.9. R. v.4**
*The Lord takes delight in his people.* (or *Alleluia!*)

**Mark 11:11-26**
After he had been acclaimed by the crowds, Jesus entered Jerusalem and went into the Temple. He looked all round him, but as it was now late, he went out to Bethany with the Twelve.

Next day as they were leaving Bethany, he felt hungry. Seeing a fig tree in leaf some distance away, he went to see if he could find any fruit on it, but when he came up to it he found nothing but leaves; for it was not the season for figs. And he addressed the fig tree. 'May no one ever eat fruit from you again' he said. And his disciples heard him say this.

So they reached Jerusalem and he went into the Temple and began driving out those who were selling and buying there; he upset the tables of the money changers and the chairs of those who were selling pigeons. Nor would he allow anyone to carry anything through the Temple. And he taught them and said, 'Does not scripture say: My house will be called a house of prayer for all the peoples? But you have turned it into a robber's den.' This came to the ears of the chief priests and the scribes, and they tried to find some way of doing away with him; they were afraid of him because the people were carried away by his teaching. And when evening came he went out of the city.

Next morning, as they passed by, they saw the fig tree withered to the roots. Peter remembered. 'Look, Rabbi,' he said to Jesus 'the fig tree you cursed has withered away.' Jesus answered, 'Have faith in God. I tell you solemnly, if anyone says to this mountain, "Get up and throw yourself into the sea," with no hesitation in his heart but believing that what he says will happen, it will be done for him. I tell you therefore: everything you ask and pray for, believe that you have it already, and it will be yours. And when you stand in prayer, forgive whatever you have against anybody, so that your Father in heaven may forgive your failings too. But if you do not forgive, your Father in heaven will not forgive your failings either.'

### Reflection
After his song in praise of all God's creation, Sirach turns to praise many human beings who have also given glory to God. They lived good lives and raised up wonderful families. While many people come and go across history, the names of these figures will endure forever. God can be experienced in good people. As Jesus begins his final days in Jerusalem, he curses a fig-tree that has not born fruit because it has not recognised that this is God's opportune time. He then brings all the cultic activities of the Jerusalem Temple to an end. The commercial side of Temple worship, and even the carrying of vessels in the cult, comes to an end. This 'end' is symbolised by the sight, on the following day, of the withered fig-tree. The era of Israel and its cult has ended. We are to approach God in faith, in prayer and through forgiveness.

## Sirach 51:12-20

I will thank you and praise you, and bless the name of the Lord. When I was still a youth, before I went travelling, in my prayers I asked outright for wisdom. Outside the sanctuary I would pray for her, and to the last I will continue to seek her. From her blossoming to the ripening of her grape my heart has taken its delight in her. My foot has pursued a straight path, I have been following her steps ever since my youth. By bowing my ear a little I have received her, and have found much instruction. Thanks to her I have advanced; the glory be to him who has given me wisdom! For I am determined to put her into practice, have earnestly pursued what is good, I will not be put to shame. My soul has fought to possess her, I have been scrupulous in keeping the Law; I have stretched out my hands to heaven and bewailed my ignorance of her; I have directed my soul towards her, and in purity have found her.

## Psalm 18:8-11. R. v.9

*The precepts of the Lord gladden the heart.*

## Mark 11:27-33

Jesus and his disciples came to Jerusalem, and as Jesus was walking in the Temple, the chief priests and the scribes and the elders came to him, and they said to him, 'What authority have you for acting like this? Or who gave you authority to do these things?' Jesus said to them, 'I will ask you a question, only one; answer me and I will tell you my authority for acting like this. John's baptism: did it come from heaven, or from man? Answer me that.' And they argued it out this way among themselves: 'If we say from heaven, he will say, "Then why did you refuse to believe him?" But dare we say from man?' – they had the people to fear, for everyone held that John was a real prophet. So their reply to Jesus was, 'We do not know.' And Jesus said to them, 'Nor will I tell you my authority for acting like this.'

**8th Week
in Ordinary Time
Green**

## Reflection

Sirach ends his book with the recognition of the glory of God in creation and in the never-to-be forgotten figures from Israel's past. He thanks God for allowing him to search for the revelation of God in Wisdom. Now that he has found Wisdom, he is 'determined to put her into practice'. In the Gospel, the first indications of the passion of Jesus appear as the priests, scribes and elders, representing the leadership of Israel, question the source of his authority to end the cultic activity of the Temple. He reduces them to silence by asking them to name the authority that was behind the ministry of John the Baptist. Too scared to deny the divine origin of John's words and deeds, they are unwilling to answer. Jesus matches their unwillingness, but a conflict has begun that will end on the cross.

**The Most Holy Trinity
Solemnity
Psalter Week 1
White**

### Deuteronomy 4:32-34.39-40

Moses said to the people: 'Put this question to the ages that are past, that went before you, from the time God created man on earth: Was there ever a word so majestic, from one end of heaven to the other? Was anything ever heard? Did ever a people hear the voice of the living God speaking from the heart of the fire, as you heard it, and remain alive? Has any god ventured to take to himself one nation from the midst of another by ordeals, signs, wonders, war with mighty hand and outstretched arm, by fearsome terrors – all this that the Lord your God did for you before your eyes in Egypt?

'Understand this today, therefore, and take it to heart: The Lord is God indeed, in heaven above as on earth beneath, he and no other. Keep his laws and commandments as I give them to you today so that you and your children may prosper and live long in the land that the Lord your God gives you for ever.'

### Psalm 32:4-6.9.18-20.22. R. v.12

*Happy the people the Lord has chosen as his own.*

### Romans 8:14-17

Everyone moved by the Spirit is a son of God. The spirit you received is not the spirit of slaves bringing fear into your lives again; it is the spirit of sons, and it makes us cry out, 'Abba, Father!' The Spirit himself and our spirit bear united witness that we are children of God. And if we are children we are heirs as well: heirs of God and coheirs with Christ, sharing his sufferings so as to share his glory.

### Matthew 28:16-20

The eleven disciples set out for Galilee, to the mountain where Jesus had arranged to meet them. When they saw him they fell down before him, though some hesitated. Jesus came up and spoke to them. He said, 'All authority in heaven and on earth has been given to me. Go therefore, make disciples of all the nations; baptise them in the name of the Father and of the Son and of the Holy Spirit, and teach them to observe all the commands I gave you. And know that I am with you always; yes, to the end of time.'

## Reflection

God's 'mighty hand' shows that there is one true God (Deuteronomy 4: 32-34). However, experience of Jesus' awareness of his Father as the source of all that he was and all that he did, led the early Christians to speak easily of God as the Father, Jesus Christ as the Son, and the gift of the Holy Spirit. Only two decades after the death of Jesus, Paul insists that life in the Spirit enables us to cry out, repeating the words of Jesus: 'Abba, Father' (See also Mark 14: 36). We are united with Christ as children of God, moved by the Spirit. Matthew's Gospel closes with the famous commission of the risen Jesus to his fearful disciples. In a profound development of the Church's Jewish origins, Jesus affirms that all authority, traditionally belonging only to the God of Israel, has been given to him. His disciples can no longer be limited to one people but must come from all nations. The initiation rite of circumcision is to be abandoned. A new people of God will be baptised in the name of the Father, the Son, and the Holy Spirit, and taught to observe what Jesus taught, the perfection of Israel's Law. Difficult days might lie ahead for this community, founded upon the teaching of Jesus, and baptised in Father, Son, and Holy Spirit. But the Risen Lord will be with us always – to the end of time.

## MAY
# 31
## MONDAY

**The Visitation of the
Blessed Virgin Mary**
Feast
White

### Zephaniah 3:14-18
*(Alternative reading: Romans 12: 9-16)*
Shout for joy, daughter of Zion, Israel, shout aloud! Rejoice, exult with all your heart, daughter of Jerusalem! The Lord has repealed your sentence; he has driven your enemies away. The Lord, the king of Israel, is in your midst; you have no more evil to fear. When that day comes, word will come to Jerusalem; Zion, have no fear, do not let your hands fall limp. The Lord your God is in your midst, a victorious warrior. He will exult with joy over you, he will renew you by his love; he will dance with shouts of joy for you as on a day of festival.

### Psalm: Isaiah 12:2-6. R. v.6
*Great in your midst is the Holy One of Israel.*

### Luke 1:39-56
Mary set out and went as quickly as she could to a town in the hill country of Judah. She went into Zechariah's house and greeted Elizabeth. Now as soon as Elizabeth heard Mary's greeting, the child leapt in her womb and Elizabeth was filled with the Holy Spirit. She gave a loud cry and said, 'Of all women you are the most blessed, and blessed is the fruit of your womb. Why should I be honoured with a visit from the mother of my Lord? For the moment your greeting reached my ears, the child in my womb leapt for joy. Yes, blessed is she who believed that the promise made her by the Lord would be fulfilled.'

And Mary said: 'My soul proclaims the greatness of the Lord and my spirit exults in God my saviour; because he has looked upon his lowly handmaid. Yes, from this day forward all generations will call me blessed, for the Almighty has done great things for me. Holy is his name, and his mercy reaches from age to age for those who fear him. He has shown the power of his arm, he has routed the proud of heart. He has pulled down princes from their thrones and exalted the lowly. The hungry he has filled with good things, the rich sent empty away. He has come to the help of Israel his servant, mindful of his mercy – according to the promise he made to our ancestors – of his mercy to Abraham and to his descendants for ever.'

### Reflection
Finally freed from slavery to great nations (Babylon and Egypt), seventh century BC Jerusalem can rejoice in her freedom, proclaims the prophet Zephaniah. The application of the passage to Mary of Nazareth, the first to receive the freedom that only belief in the gift of Jesus Christ (see Luke 1: 38), is appropriate. Luke's account of Jesus' origins begins with two annunciations: one to Zechariah (1: 5-25), and another to Mary of Nazareth (vv. 26-38). Next, the two mothers meet (today's Gospel). The child born of the first annunciation is wonderful, but the child born of the second is more wonderful. Receiving her young kinswoman who has travelled from Galilee to Judea, Elizabeth makes that known. The quickening of her child in her womb leads to the appropriate recognition of Mary as 'the mother of my Lord'. As 'the daughter of Zion', Mary responds with joy: 'My soul proclaims the greatness of the Lord', accepting the wonder of God's graciousness through her song of praise – her *Magnificat*.

## Tobit 2:9-14

I, Tobit, took a bath; then I went into the courtyard and lay down by the courtyard wall. Since it was hot I left my face uncovered. I did not know that there were sparrows in the wall above my head; their hot droppings fell into my eyes. White spots then formed which I was obliged to have treated by the doctors. But the more ointments they tried me with, the more the spots blinded me, and in the end I became blind altogether. I remained without sight four years; all my brothers were distressed; and Ahikar provided for my upkeep for two years, till he left for Elymais.

My wife Anna then undertook woman's work; she would spin wool and take cloth to weave; she used to deliver whatever had been ordered from her and then receive payment. Now on March the seventh she finished a piece of work and delivered it to her customers. They paid her all that was due, and into the bargain presented her with a kid for a meal. When the kid came into my house, it began to bleat. I called to my wife and said, 'Where does this creature come from? Suppose it has been stolen! Quick, let the owners have it back; we have no right to eat stolen goods.' She said, 'No, it was a present given me over and above my wages.' I did not believe her, and told her to give it back to the owners (I blushed at this in her presence). Then she answered, 'What about your own alms? What about your own good works? Everyone knows what return you have had for them.'

## Psalm 111:1-2.7-9. R. cf. v.7

*With a firm heart he trusts in the Lord.*

## Mark 12:13-17

The chief priests and the scribes and the elders sent to Jesus some Pharisees and some Herodians to catch him out in what he said. These came and said to him, 'Master, we know you are an honest man, that you are not afraid of anyone, because a man's rank means nothing to you, and that you teach the way of God in all honesty. Is it permissible to pay taxes to Caesar or not? Should we pay, yes or no?' Seeing through their hypocrisy he said to them, 'Why do you set this trap for me? Hand me a denarius and let me see it.' They handed him one and he said, 'Whose head is this? Whose name?' 'Caesar's' they told him. Jesus said to them, 'Give back to Caesar what belongs to Caesar – and to God what belongs to God.' This reply took them completely by surprise.

## Reflection

Jesus was put in a difficult position by the Pharisees who thought that they were cleverly going to catch Jesus out. What they didn't bargain for was his response. In a master stroke Jesus used his knowledge of the law and scripture to evade their trap. It is St Paul who tells us that scripture can be a sword of defence. How can we spiritually defend ourselves using the tools that God provides?

# 2

**WEDNESDAY**

**9th Week
in Ordinary Time
Green
or
Sts Marcellinus and
Peter, *martyrs*
(Optional, Red)**

**Tobit 3:1-11.16-17**

Sad at heart, I, Tobit, sighed and wept, and began this prayer of lamentation: 'You are just, O Lord, and just are all your works. All your ways are grace and truth, and you are the Judge of the world. Therefore, Lord, remember me, look on me. Do not punish me for my sins or for my heedless faults or for those of my fathers. For we have sinned against you and broken your commandments, and you have given us over to be plundered, to captivity and death, to be the talk, the laughing-stock and scorn of all the nations among whom you have dispersed us. Whereas all your decrees are true when you deal with me as my faults deserve, and those of my fathers, since we have neither kept your commandments nor walked in truth before you; so now, do with me as you will; be pleased to take my life from me; I desire to be delivered from earth and to become earth again. … *(See Appendix B-14)*

**Psalm 24:2-9. R. v.1**

*To you, O Lord, I lift my soul.*

**Mark 12:18-27**

Some Sadducees – who deny that there is a resurrection – came to Jesus and they put this question to him, 'Master, we have it from Moses in writing, if a man's brother dies leaving a wife but no child, the man must marry the widow to raise up children for his brother. Now there were seven brothers. The first married a wife and then died leaving no children. The second married the widow, and he too died leaving no children; with the third it was the same, and none of the seven left any children. Last of all the woman herself died. Now at the resurrection, when they rise again, whose wife will she be, since she had been married to all seven?'

Jesus said to them, 'Is not the reason why you go wrong, that you understand neither the scriptures nor the power of God? For when they rise from the dead, men and women do not marry; no, they are like the angels in heaven. Now about the dead rising again, have you never read in the Book of Moses, in the passage about the Bush, how God spoke to him and said: I am the God of Abraham, the God of Isaac and the God of Jacob? He is God, not of the dead, but of the living. You are very much mistaken.'

**Reflection**

I always feel sad about the Sadducees who did not believe in the resurrection. Where was their hope? They knew the law and the scriptures, as we can see from the structure of their questions in the Gospel today, but it did seem to bring them joy. Knowing God and understanding his word in our lives should animate us and bring life to our whole being. We are people of the resurrection who should be overflowing with God's joy, hope and love.

**Tobit 6:10-11; 7:1.9-14; 8:4-9**

Raphael and Tobias entered Media and had nearly reached Ecbatana when Raphael said to the boy, 'Brother Tobias.' 'Yes?' he answered. The angel went on, 'Tonight we shall be staying with Raguel, who is a kinsman of yours. He has a daughter called Sarah.' As they entered Ecbatana, Tobias said, 'Brother Azarias, take me at once to our brother Raguel's.' And he showed him the way to the house of Raguel, whom they found sitting beside his courtyard door. They greeted him first, and he replied, 'Welcome and greetings, brothers.' And he took them into his house. Raguel killed a sheep from the flock, and he and his wife Edna gave them a warmhearted welcome.

They washed and bathed and sat down to table. Then Tobias said to Raphael, 'Brother Azarias, will you ask Raguel to give me my sister Sarah?' Raguel overheard the words, and said to the young man, 'Eat and drink, and make the most of your evening; no one else has the right to take my daughter Sarah – no one but you, my brother. In any case I, for my own part, am not at liberty to give her to anyone else, since you are her next of kin. ... *(See Appendix B-15)*

**Psalm 127:1-5. R. cf. v.1**
*O blessed are those who fear the Lord.*

**Mark 12:28-34**

One of the scribes came up to Jesus and put a question to him, 'Which is the first of all the commandments?' Jesus replied, 'This is the first: Listen, Israel, the Lord our God is the one Lord, and you must love the Lord your God with all your heart, with all your soul, with all your mind and with all your strength. The second is this: You must love your neighbour as yourself. There is no commandment greater than these.' The scribe said to him, 'Well spoken, Master; what you have said is true: that he is one and there is no other. To love him with all your heart, with all your understanding and strength, and to love your neighbour as yourself, this is far more important than any holocaust or sacrifice.' Jesus, seeing how wisely he had spoken, said, 'You are not far from the kingdom of God.' And after that no one dared to question him any more.

## Reflection

In today's Gospel reading Jesus is asked which is the greatest commandment. He replies by giving the answer as two, love God and love neighbour. The two are completely interconnected. We can't love God if this does not flow into the rest of our lives and situations. This is where Christianity becomes difficult and challenging. It is easy to be holy in church but harder to live that holiness amongst those we find hard to love. The two elements, loving God and loving neighbour, are like wings on a plane. To fly as Christians we need both.

**9th Week in Ordinary Time**
**St Charles Lwanga and companions, *martyrs***
**Memorial**
**Red**

**9th Week
in Ordinary Time
Green**

### Tobit 11:5-17

Anna was sitting, watching the road by which her son would come. She was sure at once it must be he and said to the father, 'Here comes your son, with his companion.'

Raphael said to Tobias before he reached his father, 'I give you my word that your father's eyes will open. You must put the fish's gall to his eyes; the medicine will smart and will draw a filmy white skin off his eyes. And your father will be able to see and look on the light.'

The mother ran forward and threw her arms round her son's neck. 'Now I can die,' she said 'I have seen you again.' And she wept. Tobit rose to his feet and stumbled across the courtyard through the door. Tobias came on towards him (he had the fish's gall in his hand). He blew into his eyes and said, steadying him, 'Take courage, father!' With this he applied the medicine, left it there a while, then with both hands peeled away a filmy skin from the corners of his eyes. Then his father fell on his neck and wept. He exclaimed, 'I can see, my son, the light of my eyes!' And he said: 'Blessed be God! Blessed be his great name! Blessed be all his holy angels! Blessed be his great name for evermore! For he had scourged me and now has had pity on me and I see my son Tobias.'

Tobias went into the house, and with a loud voice joyfully blessed God. Then he told his father everything: how his journey had been successful and he had brought the silver back; how he had married Sarah, the daughter of Raguel; how she was following him now, close behind, and could not be far from the gates of Nineveh.
*(See Appendix B-15)*

### Psalm 145:2.7-10. R. v.2
*My soul, give praise to the Lord.* (or *Alleluia!*)

### Mark 12:35-37

At that time while teaching in the Temple, Jesus said, 'How can the scribes maintain that the Christ is the son of David? David himself, moved by the Holy Spirit, said: The Lord said to my Lord: Sit at my right hand and I will put your enemies under your feet.

David himself calls him Lord, in what way then can he be his son?' And the great majority of the people heard this with delight.

### Reflection

The psalm today takes us to the heart of God, who is the source of all justice. God is unbiased towards the poor and the needy in our world even though we can often lose sight of this at times. To understand God more deeply we should meditate upon this central element of his character. This psalm, like the Magnificat (Mary's Song in Luke's Gospel), is a wonderful and poetic reminder and a good place to start our reflection.

**9th Week
in Ordinary Time
St Boniface, *bishop,
martyr*
Memorial
Red**

## Tobit 12:1.5-15.20

When the feasting was over, Tobit called his son Tobias and said, 'My son, you ought to think about paying the amount due to your fellow traveller; give him more than the figure agreed on.' So Tobias called his companion and said, 'Take half of what you brought back, in payment for all you have done, and go in peace.'

Then Raphael took them both aside and said, 'Bless God, utter his praise before all the living for all the favours he has given you. Bless and extol his name. Proclaim before all men the deeds of God as they deserve, and never tire of giving him thanks. It is right to keep the secret of a king, yet right to reveal and publish the works of God. Thank him worthily. Do what is good, and no evil can befall you.

'Prayer with fasting and alms with right conduct are better than riches with iniquity. Better to practise almsgiving than to hoard up gold. Almsgiving saves from death and purges every kind of sin. Those who give alms have their fill of days; those who commit sin and do evil, bring harm on themselves. *(See Appendix B-16)*

## Psalm: Tobit 13:2.6-8. R. v.1
*Blessed be God, who lives for ever.*

## Mark 12:38-44

In his teaching Jesus said, 'Beware of the scribes who like to walk about in long robes, to be greeted obsequiously in the market squares, to take the front seats in the synagogues and the places of honour at banquets; these are the men who swallow the property of widows, while making a show of lengthy prayers. The more severe will be the sentence they receive.'

He sat down opposite the treasury and watched the people putting money into the treasury, and many of the rich put in a great deal. A poor widow came and put in two small coins, the equivalent of a penny. Then he called his disciples and said to them, 'I tell you solemnly, this poor widow has put more in than all who have contributed to the treasury; for they have all put in money they had over, but she from the little she had has put in everything she possessed, all she had to live on.'

## Reflection

Be the same on the outside as on the inside. This is the theme of today's Gospel. Our outward presentation should reflect our inner reality. As humans we want to present a public face to people and desire to be liked and respected. We may at times feel like contradictions. We need to remember that God sees the inside and the outside and nothing is hidden from him. Part of our growing in holiness is integrating all parts of our lives into a unity in Christ.

## JUNE

# 6

## SUNDAY

**The Most Holy Body
and Blood of Christ
(Corpus Christi)
Solemnity
Psalter Week 2
White**

### Exodus 24:3-8

Moses went and told the people all the commands of the Lord and all the ordinances. In answer, all the people said with one voice, 'We will observe all the commands that the Lord has decreed.' Moses put all the commands of the Lord into writing, and early next morning he built an altar at the foot of the mountain, with twelve standing-stones for the twelve tribes of Israel. Then he directed certain young Israelites to offer holocausts and to immolate bullocks to the Lord as communion sacrifices. Half of the blood Moses took up and put into basins, the other half he cast on the altar. And taking the Book of the Covenant he read it to the listening people, and they said, 'We will observe all that the Lord has decreed; we will obey.' Then Moses took the blood and cast it towards the people. 'This' he said 'is the blood of the Covenant that the Lord has made with you, containing all these rules.'

### Psalm 115:12-13.15-18. R. v.13

*The cup of salvation I will raise; I will call on the Lord's name.* (or *Alleluia!*)

### Hebrews 9:11-15

Now Christ has come, as the high priest of all the blessings which were to come. He has passed through the greater, the more perfect tent, which is better than one made by men's hands because it is not of this created order; and he has entered the sanctuary once and for all, taking with him not the blood of goats and bull calves, but his own blood, having won an eternal redemption for us. The blood of goats and bulls and the ashes of a heifer are sprinkled on those who have incurred defilement and they restore the holiness of their outward lives; how much more effectively the blood of Christ, who offered himself as the perfect sacrifice to God through the eternal Spirit, can purify our inner self from dead actions so that we do our service to the living God.

He brings a new covenant, as the mediator, only so that the people who were called to an eternal inheritance may actually receive what was promised: his death took place to cancel the sins that infringed the earlier covenant.

### Mark 14:12-16.22-26

On the first day of Unleavened Bread, when the Passover lamb was sacrificed, his disciples said to Jesus, 'Where do you want us to go and make the preparations for you to eat the passover?' So he sent two of his disciples, saying to them, 'Go into the city and you will meet a man carrying a pitcher of water. Follow him, and say to the owner of the house which he enters, "The Master says: Where is my dining room in which I can eat the passover with my disciples?" He will show you a large upper room furnished with couches, all prepared. Make the preparations for us there.' The disciples set out and went to the city and found everything as he had told them, and prepared the Passover.

And as they were eating he took some bread, and when he had said the blessing he broke it and gave it to them. 'Take it,' he said 'this is my body.' Then he took a cup, and when he had returned thanks he gave it to them, and all drank from it, and he said to them, 'This is my blood, the blood of the covenant, which is to be poured out for many. I tell you solemnly, I shall not drink any more wine until the day I drink the new wine in the kingdom of God.' After psalms had been sung they left for the Mount of Olives.

### Reflection
We celebrate Jesus in the Blessed Sacrament today. It is God's great gift for his people. We venerate Jesus in the tabernacle and on the altar. But our life in Jesus doesn't stop there. Knowing Jesus in Holy Communion should lead us to grow to know him in our brothers and sisters and recognising his presence in them as people created in his image. We venerate him in the shrine of the Monstrance and in the shrine of the hearts of those around us.

## JUNE

# 7

**MONDAY**

**10th Week
in Ordinary Time
Green**

### 2 Corinthians 1:1-7

From Paul, appointed by God to be an apostle of Christ Jesus, and from Timothy, one of the brothers, to the church of God at Corinth and to all the saints in the whole of Achaia. Grace and peace to you from God our Father and the Lord Jesus Christ.

Blessed be the God and Father of our Lord Jesus Christ, a gentle Father and the God of all consolation, who comforts us in all our sorrows, so that we can offer others, in their sorrows, the consolation that we have received from God ourselves. Indeed, as the sufferings of Christ overflow to us, so, through Christ, does our consolation overflow. When we are made to suffer, it is for your consolation and salvation. When, instead, we are comforted, this should be a consolation to you, supporting you in patiently bearing the same sufferings as we bear. And our hope for you is confident, since we know that, sharing our sufferings, you will also share our consolations.

### Psalm 33:2-9. R. v.9

*Taste and see that the Lord is good.*

### Matthew 5:1-12

Seeing the crowds, Jesus went up the hill. There he sat down and was joined by his disciples. Then he began to speak. This is what he taught them: 'How happy are the poor in spirit; theirs is the kingdom of heaven. Happy the gentle: they shall have the earth for their heritage. Happy those who mourn: they shall be comforted. Happy those who hunger and thirst for what is right: they shall be satisfied. Happy the merciful: they shall have mercy shown them. Happy the pure in heart: they shall see God. Happy the peacemakers: they shall be called sons of God. Happy those who are persecuted in the cause of right: theirs is the kingdom of heaven.

'Happy are you when people abuse you and persecute you and speak all kinds of calumny against you on my account. Rejoice and be glad, for your reward will be great in heaven; this is how they persecuted the prophets before you.'

### Reflection

The world will tell us where to find happiness. Wealth, fame and material things are supposed to solve all our woes and bring us joy. In our Gospel today, Jesus turns this on its head. What Jesus says is completely upside down and back to front from the way the world shows us. He knows where real happiness lies and places this happiness in the context of his Kingdom. In the Beatitudes all this wisdom is placed in the context of eternity.

**10th Week
in Ordinary Time
Green**

## 2 Corinthians 1:18-22

I swear by God's truth, there is no Yes and No about what we say to you. The Son of God, the Christ Jesus that we proclaimed among you – I mean Silvanus and Timothy and I – was never Yes and No: with him it was always Yes, and however many the promises God made, the Yes to them all is in him. That is why it is 'through him' that we answer Amen to the praise of God. Remember it is God himself who assures us all, and you, of our standing in Christ, and has anointed us, marking us with his seal and giving us the pledge, the Spirit, that we carry in our hearts.

## Psalm 118:129-133.135. R. v.135

*Let your face shine on your servant.*

## Matthew 5:13-16

Jesus said to his disciples: 'You are the salt of the earth. But if salt becomes tasteless, what can make it salty again? It is good for nothing, and can only be thrown out to be trampled underfoot by men.

'You are the light of the world. A city built on a hill-top cannot be hidden. No one lights a lamp to put it under a tub; they put it on the lamp-stand where it shines for everyone in the house. In the same way your light must shine in the sight of men, so that, seeing your good works, they may give the praise to your Father in heaven.'

## Reflection

How do we retain our saltiness? As Christians we are called to be conduits for God's healing power in the world. We should breathe his life and love through all that we do. Sadly many Christians can seem dour and lacking in life. We can feel jaded and wearied by all that the world throws at us. Retaining our saltiness and vibrancy comes from being close to Jesus in our prayers and seeing him at work in all that we do.

**10th Week
in Ordinary Time
Green**
or
**Saint Columba
(Colum Cille), Abbot
(Ireland – Feast)**
*(See Appendix A-11)*

### 2 Corinthians 3:4-11

Before God, we are confident of this through Christ: not that we are qualified in ourselves to claim anything as our own work: all our qualifications come from God. He is the one who has given us the qualifications to be the administrators of this new covenant, which is not a covenant of written letters but of the Spirit: the written letters bring death, but the Spirit gives life. Now if the administering of death, in the written letters engraved on stones, was accompanied by such a brightness that the Israelites could not bear looking at the face of Moses, though it was a brightness that faded, then how much greater will be the brightness that surrounds the administering of the Spirit! For if there was any splendour in administering condemnation, there must be very much greater splendour in administering justification. In fact, compared with this greater splendour, the thing that used to have such splendour now seems to have none; and if what was so temporary had any splendour, there must be much more in what is going to last for ever.

### Psalm 98:5-9. R. v.9

*Holy is the Lord our God.*

### Matthew 5:17-19

Jesus said to his disciples: 'Do not imagine that I have come to abolish the Law or the Prophets. I have come not to abolish but to complete them. I tell you solemnly, till heaven and earth disappear, not one dot, not one little stroke, shall disappear from the Law until its purpose is achieved. Therefore, the man who infringes even one of the least of these commandments and teaches others to do the same will be considered the least in the kingdom of heaven; but the man who keeps them and teaches them will be considered great in the kingdom of heaven.'

### Reflection

Jesus comes to fulfil and make whole. We see this expressed by Jesus in the Gospel today. He places this fulfilment in an eternal cosmic context when he speaks of the kingdom. Laws in the world can feel binding and restricting but the law of God frees us to begin to see the reality of the Kingdom of Heaven. By living according to God's ways we open our hearts to new possibilities and fresh ways of being.

## 2 Corinthians 3:15–4:1.3-6

Even today, whenever Moses is read, the veil is over the minds of the Israelites. It will not be removed until they turn to the Lord. Now this Lord is the Spirit, and where the Spirit of the Lord is, there is freedom. And we, with our unveiled faces reflecting like mirrors the brightness of the Lord, all grow brighter and brighter as we are turned into the image that we reflect; this is the work of the Lord who is Spirit.

Since we have by an act of mercy been entrusted with this work of administration, there is no weakening on our part. If our gospel does not penetrate the veil, then the veil is on those who are not on the way to salvation; the unbelievers whose minds the god of this world has blinded, to stop them seeing the light shed by the Good News of the glory of Christ, who is the image of God. For it is not ourselves that we are preaching, but Christ Jesus as the Lord, and ourselves as your servants for Jesus' sake. It is the same God that said, 'Let there be light shining out of darkness,' who has shone in our minds to radiate the light of the knowledge of God's glory, the glory on the face of Christ.

## Psalm 84:9-14. R. cf. v.10

*The glory of the Lord will dwell in our land.*

## Matthew 5:20-26

Jesus said to his disciples: 'If your virtue goes no deeper than that of the scribes and Pharisees, you will never get into the kingdom of heaven.

'You have learnt how it was said to our ancestors: You must not kill; and if anyone does kill he must answer for it before the court. But I say this to you: anyone who is angry with his brother will answer for it before the court; if a man calls his brother "Fool" he will answer for it before the Sanhedrin; and if a man calls him "Renegade" he will answer for it in hell fire. So then, if you are bringing your offering to the altar and there remember that your brother has something against you, leave your offering there before the altar, go and be reconciled with your brother first, and then come back and present your offering. Come to terms with your opponent in good time while you are still on the way to the court with him, or he may hand you over to the judge and the judge to the officer, and you will be thrown into prison. I tell you solemnly, you will not get out till you have paid the last penny.'

## Reflection

Do we come to the Altar whilst we have a grievance with a brother or sister? Jesus tells us to leave our gift at the altar and make up first. Holy Communion expresses our unity with God and each other. We express our family ties with brothers and sisters in the Church throughout the world. Unity is therefore at the heart of all that we do at the altar. Healing relationships in the world is part of restoring the unity that we express in the Church.

**10th Week in Ordinary Time**
**Green**

**The Most Sacred Heart of Jesus**
**Solemnity**
**White**

**Hosea 11:1.3-4.8-9**
*(See Appendix B-16)*

**Psalm Isaiah 12:2-6. R. v.3**
*With joy you will draw water from the wells of salvation.*

**Ephesians 3:8-12.14-19**
I, Paul, who am less than the least of all the saints, have been entrusted with this special grace, not only of proclaiming to the pagans the infinite treasure of Christ but also of explaining how the mystery is to be dispensed. Through all the ages, this has been kept hidden in God, the creator of everything. Why? So that the Sovereignties and Powers should learn only now, through the Church, how comprehensive God's wisdom really is, exactly according to the plan which he had from all eternity in Christ Jesus our Lord. This is why we are bold enough to approach God in complete confidence, through our faith in him.

This then, is what I pray, kneeling before the Father, from whom every family, whether spiritual or natural, takes its name:

Out of his infinite glory, may he give you the power through his Spirit for your hidden self to grow strong, so that Christ may live in your hearts through faith, and then, planted in love and built on love, you will with all the saints have strength to grasp the breadth and the length, the height and the depth; until, knowing the love of Christ, which is beyond all knowledge, you are filled with the utter fullness of God.

**John 19:31-37**
It was Preparation Day, and to prevent the bodies remaining on the cross during the sabbath – since that sabbath was a day of special solemnity – the Jews asked Pilate to have the legs broken and the bodies taken away. Consequently the soldiers came and broke the legs of the first man who had been crucified with him and then of the other. When they came to Jesus, they found he was already dead, and so instead of breaking his legs one of the soldiers pierced his side with a lance; and immediately there came out blood and water. This is the evidence of one who saw it – trustworthy evidence, and he knows he speaks the truth – and he gives it so that you may believe as well. Because all this happened to fulfil the words of scripture: Not one bone of his will be broken; and again, in another place scripture says: They will look on the one whom they have pierced.

**Reflection**
The Passion of Christ is at the heart of our life. Today's reading takes us to the desolation of the cross. We forget how scandalous the death of Jesus is. We wear crosses and have crucifixes in our homes and so we become so used to the image that it can be taken for granted. How would we feel if we saw a noose or an electric chair? We would be shocked by the Cross which for us is a symbol of hope and the pinnacle of love.

## 2 Corinthians 5:14-21

The love of Christ overwhelms us when we reflect that if one man has died for all, then all men should be dead; and the reason he died for all was so that living men should live no longer for themselves, but for him who died and was raised to life for them.

From now onwards, therefore, we do not judge anyone by the standards of the flesh. Even if we did once know Christ in the flesh, that is not how we know him now. And for anyone who is in Christ, there is a new creation; the old creation has gone, and now the new one is here. It is all God's work. It was God who reconciled us to himself through Christ and gave us the work of handing on this reconciliation. In other words, God in Christ was reconciling the world to himself, not holding men's faults against them, and he has entrusted to us the news that they are reconciled. So we are ambassadors for Christ; it is as though God were appealing through us, and the appeal that we make in Christ's name is: be reconciled to God. For our sake God made the sinless one into sin, so that in him we might become the goodness of God.

## Psalm 102:1-4.9-12

*The Lord is compassion and love, slow to anger and rich in mercy.*

## Matthew 5:33-37

Jesus said to his disciples: 'You have learnt how it was said to our ancestors: You must not break your oath, but must fulfil your oaths to the Lord. But I say this to you: do not swear at all, either by heaven, since that is God's throne; or by the earth, since that is his footstool; or by Jerusalem, since that is the city of the great king. Do not swear by your own head either, since you cannot turn a single hair white or black. All you need say is "Yes" if you mean yes, "No" if you mean no; anything more than this comes from the evil one.'

## Reflection

The fear that Mary and Joseph had must have been immense. Losing a child is always a scary thing and panic ensues. Being a parent sometimes means letting go and allowing children to make their own way. Teaching a child to ride a bike means taking off the stabilisers and embracing the risk in order to ride. Mary and Joseph had a special role in nurturing Jesus to be the person that he was called to be and this meant giving him the space needed.

**The Immaculate Heart of the Blessed Virgin Mary**
Memorial
White

## JUNE
# 13
## SUNDAY

**11th Sunday
in Ordinary Time
Psalter Week 3
Green**

### Ezekiel 17:22-24

The Lord says this: 'From the top of the cedar, from the highest branch I will take a shoot and plant it myself on a very high mountain. I will plant it on the high mountain of Israel. It will sprout branches and bear fruit, and become a noble cedar. Every kind of bird will live beneath it, every winged creature rest in the shade of its branches. And every tree of the field will learn that I, the Lord, am the one who stunts tall trees and makes the low ones grow, who withers green trees and makes the withered green. I, the Lord, have spoken, and I will do it.'

### Psalm 91:2-3.13-16. R. cf. v.2

*It is good to give you thanks, O Lord.*

### 2 Corinthians 5:6-10

We are always full of confidence when we remember that to live in the body means to be exiled from the Lord, going as we do by faith and not by sight – we are full of confidence, I say, and actually want to be exiled from the body and make our home with the Lord. Whether we are living in the body or exiled from it, we are intent on pleasing him. For all the truth about us will be brought out in the law court of Christ, and each of us will get what he deserves for the things he did in the body, good or bad.

### Mark 4:26-34

Jesus said to the crowds: 'This is what the kingdom of God is like. A man throws seed on the land. Night and day, while he sleeps, when he is awake, the seed is sprouting and growing; how, he does not know. Of its own accord the land produces first the shoot, then the ear, then the full grain in the ear. And when the crop is ready, he loses no time: he starts to reap because the harvest has come.'

He also said, 'What can we say the kingdom of God is like? What parable can we find for it? It is like a mustard seed which at the time of its sowing in the soil is the smallest of all the seeds on earth; yet once it is sown it grows into the biggest shrub of them all and puts out big branches so that the birds of the air can shelter in its shade.'

Using many parables like these, he spoke the word to them, so far as they were capable of understanding it. He would not speak to them except in parables, but he explained everything to his disciples when they were alone.

## Reflection

Look for the signs. The kingdom of God is unfolding in our midst and the challenge for us is seeing the reality. We are called to be people who should be looking out for indications of the Kingdom around us. It may be small and growing gently but if we are alert we can see the budding of God's new reality all around.  The Kingdom is advancing. Other brasher and noisier Kingdoms rise and fall in our world. The quieter and more subtler unfolding Kingdom is the only one which will endure for ever.

**11th Week
in Ordinary Time
Green**

### 2 Corinthians 6:1-10

As God's fellow workers we beg you once again not to neglect the grace of God that you have received. For he says: At the favourable time, I have listened to you; on the day of salvation I came to your help. Well, now is the favourable time; this is the day of salvation.

We do nothing that people might object to, so as not to bring discredit on our function as God's servants. Instead, we prove we are servants of God by great fortitude in times of suffering: in times of hardship and distress; when we are flogged, or sent to prison, or mobbed; labouring, sleepless, starving. We prove we are God's servants by our purity, knowledge, patience and kindness; by a spirit of holiness, by a love free from affectation; by the word of truth and by the power of God; by being armed with the weapons of righteousness in the right hand and in the left, prepared for honour or disgrace, for blame or praise; taken for impostors while we are genuine; obscure yet famous; said to be dying and here are we alive; rumoured to be executed before we are sentenced; thought most miserable and yet we are always rejoicing; taken for paupers though we make others rich, for people having nothing though we have everything.

### Psalm 97:1-4. R. v.2

*The Lord has made known his salvation.*

### Matthew 5:38-42

Jesus said to his disciples: 'You have learnt how it was said: Eye for eye and tooth for tooth. But I say this to you: offer the wicked man no resistance. On the contrary, if anyone hits you on the right cheek, offer him the other as well; if a man takes you to law and would have your tunic, let him have your cloak as well. And if anyone orders you to go one mile, go two miles with him. Give to anyone who asks, and if anyone wants to borrow, do not turn away.'

### Reflection

In our first reading today St Paul calls us fellow workers. What a privilege and an honour to be considered fellow workers with the creator of heaven and earth. What an amazing God who seeks to be in partnership with us and invites us into such a relationship with him. With this honour also comes great responsibility which St Paul also shares with us through his wisdom today.

## 2 Corinthians 8:1-9

Here, brothers, is the news of the grace of God which was given in the churches in Macedonia; and of how, throughout great trials by suffering, their constant cheerfulness and their intense poverty have overflowed in a wealth of generosity. I can swear that they gave not only as much as they could afford, but far more, and quite spontaneously, begging and begging us for the favour of sharing in this service to the saints and, what was quite unexpected, they offered their own selves first to God and, under God, to us.

Because of this, we have asked Titus, since he has already made a beginning, to bring this work of mercy to the same point of success among you. You always have the most of everything – of faith, of eloquence, of understanding, of keenness for any cause, and the biggest share of our affection – so we expect you to put the most into this work of mercy too. It is not an order that I am giving you; I am just testing the genuineness of your love against the keenness of others. Remember how generous the Lord Jesus was: he was rich, but he became poor for your sake, to make you rich out of his poverty.

## Psalm 145:2.5-9. R. v.2

*My soul, give praise to the Lord.* (or *Alleluia!*)

## Matthew 5:43-48

Jesus said to his disciples: 'You have learnt how it was said: You must love your neighbour and hate your enemy. But I say to you: love your enemies and pray for those who persecute you; in this way you will be sons of your Father in heaven, for he causes his sun to rise on bad men as well as good, and his rain to fall on honest and dishonest men alike. For if you love those who love you, what right have you to claim any credit? Even the tax collectors do as much, do they not? And if you save your greetings for your brothers, are you doing anything exceptional? Even the pagans do as much, do they not? You must therefore be perfect just as your heavenly Father is perfect.'

## Reflection

Isn't Christianity difficult at times? It is easy to love those who love us and our friends but loving our enemies is so hard. Jesus loved his enemies in the most extreme circumstances and so was never asking us to do something which he didn't model through his own life, suffering and passion. When we love our enemies, we share Jesus' great love when he forgave his persecutors from the cross.

## JUNE

# 16

### WEDNESDAY

**11th Week
in Ordinary Time
Green**

### 2 Corinthians 9:6-11

Do not forget: thin sowing means thin reaping; the more you sow, the more you reap. Each one should give what he has decided in his own mind, not grudgingly or because he is made to, for God loves a cheerful giver. And there is no limit to the blessings which God can send you – he will make sure that you will always have all you need for yourselves in every possible circumstance, and still have something to spare for all sorts of good works. As scripture says: He was free in almsgiving, and gave to the poor: his good deeds will never be forgotten.

The one who provides seed for the sower and bread for food will provide you with all the seed you want and make the harvest of your good deeds a larger one, and, made richer in every way, you will be able to do all the generous things which, through us, are the cause of thanksgiving to God.

### Psalm 111:1-4.9. R. v.1

*Happy the man who fears the Lord.* (or *Alleluia!*)

### Matthew 6:1-6.16-18

Jesus said to his disciples: 'Be careful not to parade your good deeds before men to attract their notice; by doing this you will lose all reward from your Father in heaven. So when you give alms, do not have it trumpeted before you; this is what the hypocrites do in the synagogues and in the streets to win men's admiration. I tell you solemnly, they have had their reward. But when you give alms, your left hand must not know what your right is doing; your almsgiving must be secret, and your Father who sees all that is done in secret will reward you.

'And when you pray, do not imitate the hypocrites: they love to say their prayers standing up in the synagogues and at the street corners for people to see them. I tell you solemnly, they have had their reward. But when you pray, go to your private room and, when you have shut your door, pray to your Father who is in that secret place, and your Father who sees all that is done in secret will reward you.

'When you fast do not put on a gloomy look as the hypocrites do: they pull long faces to let men know they are fasting. I tell you solemnly, they have had their reward. But when you fast, put oil on your head and wash your face, so that no one will know you are fasting except your Father who sees all that is done in secret; and your Father who sees all that is done in secret will reward you.'

### Reflection

Do things for the right reasons. When we serve others we should do it as part of our service of God. It is not for others to see but for God alone. So often in our world people do things for recognition. For us the only recognition we should seek is from our loving father. There will be times when others will see our deeds and they will speak of God's love but this should never be our motivation.

## 2 Corinthians 11:1-11

I only wish you were able to tolerate a little foolishness from me. But of course: you are tolerant towards me. You see, the jealousy that I feel for you is God's own jealousy: I arranged for you to marry Christ so that I might give you away as a chaste virgin to this one husband. But the serpent, with his cunning, seduced Eve, and I am afraid that in the same way your ideas may get corrupted and turned away from simple devotion to Christ. Because any newcomer has only to proclaim a new Jesus, different from the one that we preached, or you have only to receive a new spirit, different from the one you have already received, or a new gospel, different from the one you have already accepted – and you welcome it with open arms. As far as I can tell, these arch-apostles have nothing more than I have. I may not be a polished speechmaker, but as for knowledge, that is a different matter; surely we have made this plain, speaking on every subject in front of all of you.

Or was I wrong, lowering myself so as to lift you high, by preaching the gospel of God to you and taking no fee for it? I was robbing other churches, living on them so that I could serve you. When I was with you and ran out of money, I was no burden to anyone; the brothers who came from Macedonia provided me with everything I wanted. I was very careful, and I always shall be, not to be a burden to you in any way, and by Christ's truth in me, this cause of boasting will never be taken from me in the regions of Achaia. Would I do that if I did not love you? God knows I do.

## Psalm 110:1-4.7-8. R. v.7

*Your works, Lord, are justice and truth.* (or *Alleluia!*)

## Matthew 6:7-15

Jesus said to his disciples: 'In your prayers do not babble as the pagans do, for they think that by using many words they will make themselves heard. Do not be like them; your Father knows what you need before you ask him. So you should pray like this: Our Father in heaven, may your name be held holy, your kingdom come, your will be done, on earth as in heaven. Give us today our daily bread. And forgive us our debts, as we have forgiven those who are in debt to us. And do not put us to the test, but save us from the evil one.

'Yes, if you forgive others their failings, your heavenly Father will forgive you yours; but if you do not forgive others, your Father will not forgive your failings either.'

## Reflection

The Lord's Prayer is one of the great prayers of the world. It has shaped our society and it is a wonderfully poetic and expressive prayer. However we say it so often that it becomes familiar and we take it for granted. Why not read it today slowly and prayerfully, in a different language if you can. Rediscover its power and beauty. It is so sad that so many people don't know this prayer any more.

**11th Week
in Ordinary Time
Green**

### 2 Corinthians 11:18.21-30

So many others have been boasting of their worldly achievements, that I will boast myself. But if anyone wants some brazen speaking – I am still talking as a fool – then I can be as brazen as any of them, and about the same things. Hebrews, are they? So am I. Israelites? So am I. Descendants of Abraham? So am I. The servants of Christ? I must be mad to say this, but so am I, and more than they: more, because I have worked harder, I have been sent to prison more often, and whipped so many times more, often almost to death. Five times I had the thirty-nine lashes from the Jews; three times I have been beaten with sticks; once I was stoned; three times I have been shipwrecked and once adrift in the open sea for a night and a day. Constantly travelling, I have been in danger from rivers and in danger from brigands, in danger from my own people and in danger from pagans; in danger in the towns, in danger in the open country, danger at sea and danger from so-called brothers. I have worked and laboured, often without sleep; I have been hungry and thirsty and often starving; I have been in the cold without clothes. And, to leave out much more, there is my daily preoccupation: my anxiety for all the churches. When any man has had scruples, I have had scruples with him; when any man is made to fall, I am tortured.

If I am to boast, then let me boast of my own feebleness.

### Psalm 33:2-7. R. cf. v.18
*The Lord rescues the just in all their distress.*

### Matthew 6:19-23

Jesus said to his disciples: 'Do not store up treasures for yourselves on earth, where moths and woodworms destroy them and thieves can break in and steal. But store up treasures for yourselves in heaven, where neither moth or woodworms destroy them and thieves cannot break in and steal. For where your treasure is, there will your heart be also.

'The lamp of the body is the eye. It follows that if your eye is sound, your whole body will be filled with light. But if your eye is diseased, your whole body will be all darkness. If then, the light inside you is darkness, what darkness that will be!'

### Reflection

Where is your treasure? Is it in worldly possessions or where Jesus envisages it? Jesus knows that this world for us is fleeting and passing. All that we invest our time and energy in passes away. Part of awakening to a life of holiness is recognising that the answers to our searching will not be found in the places of the world. Seeking this Kingdom will allow us to find where the true treasure lies.

JUNE
**19**
SATURDAY

**11th Week
in Ordinary Time
Green
or
St Romuald, *abbot*
(Optional, White)**

## 2 Corinthians 12:1-10

Must I go on boasting, though there is nothing to be gained by it? But I will move on to the visions and revelations I have had from the Lord. I know a man in Christ who, fourteen years ago, was caught up – whether still in the body or out of the body, I do not know; God knows – right into the third heaven. I do know however, that this same person – whether in the body or out of the body, I do not know; God knows – was caught up into paradise and heard things which must not and cannot be put into human language. I will boast about a man like that, but not about anything of my own except my weaknesses. If I should decide to boast, I should not be made to look foolish, because I should only be speaking the truth; but I am not going to, in case anyone should begin to think I am better than he can actually see and hear me to be. *(See Appendix B-16)*

## Psalm 33:8-13. R. v.9

*Taste and see that the Lord is good.*

## Matthew 6:24-34

Jesus said to his disciples: 'No one can be the slave of two masters: he will either hate the first and love the second, or treat the first with respect and the second with scorn. You cannot be the slave both of God and of money.

'That is why I am telling you not to worry about your life and what you are to eat, nor about your body and how you are to clothe it. Surely life means more than food, and the body more than clothing! Look at the birds in the sky. They do not sow or reap or gather into barns; yet your heavenly Father feeds them. Are you not worth much more than they are? Can any of you, for all his worrying, add one single cubit to his span of life? And why worry about clothing? Think of the flowers growing in the fields; they never have to work or spin; yet I assure you that not even Solomon in all his regalia was robed like one of these. Now if that is how God clothes the grass in the field which is there today and thrown into the furnace tomorrow, will he not much more look after you, you men of little faith? So do not worry; do not say, "What are we to eat? What are we to drink? How are we to be clothed?" It is the pagans who set their hearts on all these things. Your heavenly Father knows you need them all. Set your hearts on his kingdom first, and on his righteousness, and all these other things will be given you as well. So do not worry about tomorrow: tomorrow will take care of itself. Each day has enough trouble of its own.'

## Reflection

Don't allow yourselves to be divided. Often we can feel the pressure and pull of competing demands, especially in the hectic cycling days of modern life and society. Jesus recognises that this can so often be futile and shows us that we should only have one master who can provide all that we need in life. If we set our hearts firmly on God everything else is made sense of and falls into place.

## JUNE

# 20

### SUNDAY

**12th Sunday
in Ordinary Time**
Psalter Week 4
Green

### Job 38:1.8-11

From the heart of the tempest the Lord gave Job his answer. He said: Who pent up the sea behind closed doors when it leapt tumultuous out of the womb, when I wrapped it in a robe of mist and made black clouds its swaddling bands; when I marked the bounds it was not to cross and made it fast with a bolted gate? Come thus far, I said, and no farther: here your proud waves shall break.

### Psalm 106:23-26.28-31. R. v.1

*O give thanks to the Lord, for his love endures for ever. (or Alleluia!)*

### 2 Corinthians 5:14-17

The love of Christ overwhelms us when we reflect that if one man has died for all, then all men should be dead; and the reason he died for all was so that living men should live no longer for themselves, but for him who died and was raised to life for them.

From now onwards, therefore, we do not judge anyone by the standards of the flesh. Even if we did once know Christ in the flesh, that is not how we know him now. And for anyone who is in Christ, there is a new creation; the old creation has gone, and now the new one is here.

### Mark 4:35-41

With the coming of evening, Jesus said to his disciples, 'Let us cross over to the other side.' And leaving the crowd behind they took him, just as he was, in the boat; and there were other boats with him. Then it began to blow a gale and the waves were breaking into the boat so that it was almost swamped. But he was in the stern, his head on the cushion, asleep. They woke him and said to him, 'Master, do you not care? We are going down!' And he woke up and rebuked the wind and said to the sea, 'Quiet now! Be calm!' And the wind dropped, and all was calm again. Then he said to them, 'Why are you so frightened? How is it that you have no faith?' They were filled with awe and said to one another, 'Who can this be? Even the wind and the sea obey him.'

## Reflection

St Paul today reminds us of the overwhelming love of Jesus. We find our fullness when we live freely for God and seek the purposes of his kingdom. For Christians in a living relationship with Jesus there is a liberation which nothing else can provide. Christianity should not be a faith which constrains us but rather should be a way of life where we become truly free and enfolded in Jesus' love.

**12th Week
in Ordinary Time
St Aloysius Gonzaga,
*religious*
Memorial
White**

### Genesis 12:1-9

The Lord said to Abram, 'Leave your country, your family and your father's house, for the land I will show you. I will make you a great nation; I will bless you and make your name so famous that it will be used as a blessing. 'I will bless those who bless you: I will curse those who slight you. All the tribes of the earth shall bless themselves by you.'

So Abram went as the Lord told him, and Lot went with him. Abram was seventy-five years old when he left Haran. Abram took his wife Sarai, his nephew Lot, all the possessions they had amassed and the people they had acquired in Haran. They set off for the land of Canaan, and arrived there.

Abram passed through the land as far as Shechem's holy place, the Oak of Moreh. At that time the Canaanites were in the land. The Lord appeared to Abram and said, 'It is to your descendants that I will give this land.' So Abram built there an altar for the Lord who had appeared to him. From there he moved on to the mountainous district east of Bethel, where he pitched his tent, with Bethel to the west and Ai to the east. There he built an altar to the Lord and invoked the name of the Lord. Then Abram made his way stage by stage to the Negeb.

### Psalm 32:12-13.18-20.22. R. v.12

*Happy the people the Lord has chosen as his own.*

### Matthew 7:1-5

Jesus said to his disciples: 'Do not judge, and you will not be judged; because the judgements you give are the judgements you will get, and the amount you measure out is the amount you will be given. Why do you observe the splinter in your brother's eye and never notice the plank in your own? How dare you say to your brother, "Let me take the splinter out of your eye", when all the time there is a plank in your own? Hypocrite! Take the plank out of your own eye first, and then you will see clearly enough to take the splinter out of your brother's eye.'

### Reflection

Today's Gospel reading presents us with wisdom which is both simple and exceptionally challenging for us. Not judging others is one of the most difficult elements of Christian discipleship. We can start off with good intentions and become judgemental without fully realising it. Jesus calls us to remember that we should forgive others because he first forgave us. In this way when we forgive others we share this special love which was given to us first by Christ.

### Genesis 13:2.5-18

Abram was a very rich man, with livestock, silver and gold. Lot, who was travelling with Abram, had flocks and cattle of his own, and tents too. The land was not sufficient to accommodate them both at once, for they had too many possessions to be able to live together. Dispute broke out between the herdsmen of Abram's livestock and those of Lot's. (The Canaanites and the Perizzites were then living in the land. ) Accordingly Abram said to Lot, 'Let there be no dispute between me and you, nor between my herdsmen and yours, for we are brothers. Is not the whole land open before you? Part company with me: if you take the left, I will go right; if you take the right, I will go left.'

Looking round, Lot saw all the Jordan plain, irrigated everywhere – this was before the Lord destroyed Sodom and Gomorrah – like the garden of the Lord or the land of Egypt, as far as Zoar. So Lot chose all the Jordan plain for himself and moved off eastwards. Thus they parted company: Abram settled in the land of Canaan; Lot settled among the towns of the plain, pitching his tents on the outskirts of Sodom. Now the people of Sodom were vicious men, great sinners against the Lord.

*(See Appendix B–16)*

### Psalm 14:2-5. R. v.1

*The just will live in the presence of the Lord.*

### Matthew 7:6.12-14

Jesus said to his disciples: 'Do not give dogs what is holy; and do not throw your pearls in front of pigs, or they may trample them and then turn on you and tear you to pieces.

'So always treat others as you would like them to treat you; that is the meaning of the Law and the Prophets.

'Enter by the narrow gate, since the road that leads to perdition is wide and spacious, and many take it; but it is a narrow gate and a hard road that leads to life, and only a few find it.'

**12th Week
in Ordinary Time**
**Sts John Fisher**, *bishop*,
**and Thomas More**,
*martyrs*, **Memorial
(England – Feast)**
*(See Appendix A-12)*
**Red**

### Reflection

Jesus warns us about false teachers who will come in his name. I am sure that we can all think of examples of such people in history who have come as deceivers and led people off the path of Christ. One important way to protect ourselves from this is to ensure that we know the real and life-giving Christ through scripture, the sacraments and his church. If we truly know who Jesus is we can never be led astray by false teachers.

**12th Week
in Ordinary Time
Green
or
St Paulinus of Nola,
*bishop*
(Optional, White)**

## Genesis 15:1-12.17-18

It happened that the word of the Lord was spoken to Abram in a vision, 'Have no fear, Abram, I am your shield; your reward will be very great.'

'My Lord,' Abram replied 'what do you intend to give me? I go childless. . .' Then Abram said, 'See, you have given me no descendants; some man of my household will be my heir.' And then this word of the Lord was spoken to him, 'He shall not be your heir; your heir shall be of your own flesh and blood.' Then taking him outside he said, 'Look up to heaven and count the stars if you can. Such will be your descendants' he told him. Abram put his faith in the Lord, who counted this as making him justified.

'I am the Lord' he said to him 'who brought you out of Ur of the Chaldaeans to make you heir to this land.' 'My Lord,' Abram replied 'how am I to know that I shall inherit it?' He said to him 'Get me a three-year-old heifer, a three-year-old goat, a three-year-old ram, a turtledove and a young pigeon.' He brought him all these, cut them in half and put half on one side and half facing it on the other; but the birds he did not cut in half. Birds of prey came down on the carcasses but Abram drove them off.

Now as the sun was setting Abram fell into a deep sleep, and terror seized him. When the sun had set and darkness had fallen, there appeared a smoking furnace and a firebrand that went between the halves. That day the Lord made a Covenant with Abram in these terms: 'To your descendants I give this land, from the wadi of Egypt to the Great River, the river Euphrates.'

## Psalm 104:1-4.6-9. R. v.8

*The Lord remembers his covenant for ever.* (or *Alleluia!*)

## Matthew 7:15-20

Jesus said to his disciples: 'Beware of false prophets who come to you disguised as sheep but underneath are ravenous wolves. You will be able to tell them by their fruits. Can people pick grapes from thorns, or figs from thistles? In the same way, a sound tree produces good fruit but a rotten tree bad fruit. A sound tree cannot bear bad fruit, nor a rotten tree bear good fruit. Any tree that does not produce good fruit is cut down and thrown on the fire. I repeat, you will be able to tell them by their fruits.'

## Reflection

Yesterday we heard in the Gospel about false teachers. Today's reading returns with that theme. Here Jesus tells us to look at people's fruits as an indication of their authenticity. This reading also can lead us to think of our own fruits and the ways in which we bear fruit to bless the world around us. What can you tell about you by your fruits?

Isaiah 49:1-6
*(See Appendix B-17)*

Psalm 138:1-3.13-15. R. v.14
*I thank you for the wonder of my being.*

Acts 13:22-26
Paul said: 'God made David the king of our ancestors' of whom he approved in these words, "I have selected David son of Jesse, a man after my own heart, who will carry out my whole purpose." To keep his promise, God has raised up for Israel one of David's descendants, Jesus, as Saviour, whose coming was heralded by John when he proclaimed a baptism of repentance for the whole people of Israel. Before John ended his career he said, "I am not the one you imagine me to be; that one is coming after me and I am not fit to undo his sandal."

'My brothers, sons of Abraham's race, and all you who fear God, this message of salvation is meant for you.'

Luke 1:57-66.80
The time came for Elizabeth to have her child, and she gave birth to a son; and when her neighbours and relations heard that the Lord had shown her so great a kindness, they shared her joy.

Now on the eighth day when they came to circumcise the child, they were going to call him Zechariah after his father, but his mother spoke up. 'No,' she said 'he is to be called John.' They said to her 'But no one in your family has that name', and made signs to his father to find out what he wanted him called. The father asked for a writing tablet and wrote, 'His name is John.' And they were all astonished. At that instant his power of speech returned and he spoke and praised God. All their neighbours were filled with awe and the whole affair was talked about throughout the hill country of Judaea. All those who heard of it treasured it in their hearts. 'What will this child turn out to be?' they wondered. And indeed the hand of the Lord was with him. The child grew up and his spirit matured. And he lived out in the wilderness until the day he appeared openly to Israel.

**JUNE**
**24**
**THURSDAY**

**The Nativity of Saint John the Baptist**
Solemnity
White

**Reflection**
St John the Baptist is a great example for us who seek to live the Christian life. He is someone who remains focused upon the task at hand, even removing himself from the world's distractions so that he can see more clearly the signs of the Kingdom advancing. He never takes the limelight for himself, stepping aside when Jesus finally reveals himself. John today reminds us to look for Jesus and point others to where he is working in the world.

## Genesis 17:1.9-10.15-22

When Abram was ninety-nine years old the Lord appeared to him and said, 'I am El Shaddai. Bear yourself blameless in my presence.

'You shall maintain my Covenant, yourself and your descendants after you, generation after generation. Now this is my Covenant which you are to maintain between myself and you, and your descendants after you: all your males must be circumcised.

'As for Sarai your wife, you shall not call her Sarai, but Sarah. I will bless her and moreover give you a son by her. I will bless her and nations shall come out of her; kings of peoples shall descend from her.' Abraham bowed to the ground, and he laughed, thinking to himself, 'Is a child to be born to a man one hundred years old, and will Sarah have a child at the age of ninety?' Abraham said to God, 'Oh, let Ishmael live in your presence!' But God replied, 'No, but your wife Sarah shall bear you a son whom you are to name Isaac. With him I will establish my Covenant, a Covenant in perpetuity, to be his God and the God of his descendants after him. For Ishmael too I grant you your request: I bless him and I will make him fruitful and greatly increased in numbers. He shall be the father of twelve princes, and I will make him into a great nation. But my Covenant I will establish with Isaac, whom Sarah will bear you at this time next year.' When he had finished speaking to Abraham God went up from him.

## Psalm 127:1-5. R. v.4

*Indeed the man shall be blessed, the man who fears the Lord.*

## Matthew 8:1-4

After Jesus had come down from the mountain large crowds followed him. A leper now came up and bowed low in front of him, 'Sir,' he said 'if you want to, you can cure me.' Jesus stretched out his hand, touched him and said, 'Of course I want to! Be cured!' And his leprosy was cured at once. Then Jesus said to him, 'Mind you do not tell anyone, but go and show yourself to the priest and make the offering prescribed by Moses, as evidence for them.'

## Reflection

Here we see Jesus' compassion demonstrated by his desire to bring healing to the man in the Gospel reading. Jesus not only brings physical healing but restores the man to his place in the human community where previously he had been an outcast. It reminds us that Jesus has no bias towards the marginalised and the poor. How can we seek to bring healing to the disadvantaged in our world today?

**12th Week
in Ordinary Time
Green**

### Genesis 18:1-15

The Lord appeared to Abraham at the Oak of Mamre while he was sitting by the entrance of the tent during the hottest part of the day. He looked up, and there he saw three men standing near him. As soon as he saw them he ran from the entrance of the tent to meet them, and bowed to the ground. 'My lord,' he said 'I beg you, if I find favour with you, kindly do not pass your servant by. A little water shall be brought; you shall wash your feet and lie down under the tree. Let me fetch a little bread and you shall refresh yourselves before going further. That is why you have come in your servant's direction.' They replied, 'Do as you say.' (See Appendix B-17)

### Psalm: Luke 1:46-50.53-55. R. cf. v.54

*The Lord remembered his mercy.*

### Matthew 8:5-17

When Jesus went into Capernaum, a centurion came up and pleaded with him. 'Sir,' he said 'my servant is lying at home paralysed, and in great pain.' 'I will come myself and cure him' said Jesus. The centurion replied, 'Sir, I am not worthy to have you under my roof; just give the word and my servant will be cured. For I am under authority myself, and have soldiers under me; and I say to one man: Go, and he goes; to another: Come here, and he comes; to my servant: Do this, and he does it.' When Jesus heard this he was astonished and said to those following him, 'I tell you solemnly, nowhere in Israel have I found faith like this. And I tell you that many will come from east and west to take their places with Abraham and Isaac and Jacob at the feast in the kingdom of heaven; but the subjects of the kingdom will be turned out into the dark, where there will be weeping and grinding of teeth.' And to the centurion Jesus said, 'Go back, then; you have believed, so let this be done for you.' And the servant was cured at that moment. And going into Peter's house Jesus found Peter's mother-in-law in bed with fever. He touched her hand and the fever left her, and she got up and began to wait on him.

That evening they brought him many who were possessed by devils. He cast out the spirits with a word and cured all who were sick. This was to fulfil the prophecy of Isaiah: He took our sicknesses away and carried our diseases for us.

### Reflection

Submitted to Jesus in faith is a step on the road to truly being a disciple of his. Such abandonment in love is the key to a deeper relationship with God as we open up and make ourselves vulnerable in order to sense his power. This is a great paradox of our faith – Power in weakness and strength in submission. It is another great example about how Christ turns the wisdom of the world on its head.

# JUNE
# 27
## SUNDAY

**13th Sunday
in Ordinary Time
Psalter Week 1
Green**

### Wisdom 1:13-15; 2:23-24

Death was not God's doing, he takes no pleasure in the extinction of the living. To be – for this he created all; the world's created things have health in them, in them no fatal poison can be found, and Hades holds no power on earth; for virtue is undying. Yet God did make man imperishable, he made him in the image of his own nature; it was the devil's envy that brought death into the world, as those who are his partners will discover.

### Psalm 29:2.4-6.11-13. R. v.2

*I will praise you, Lord, you have rescued me.*

### 2 Corinthians 8:7.9.13-15

You always have the most of everything – of faith, of eloquence, of understanding, of keenness for any cause, and the biggest share of our affection – so we expect you to put the most into this work of mercy too. Remember how generous the Lord Jesus was: he was rich, but he became poor for your sake, to make you rich out of his poverty. This does not mean that to give relief to others you ought to make things difficult for yourselves: it is a question of balancing what happens to be your surplus now against their present need, and one day they may have something to spare that will supply your own need. That is how we strike a balance: as scripture says: The man who gathered much had none too much, the man who gathered little did not go short.

## Mark 5:21-43

When Jesus had crossed in the boat to the other side, a large crowd gathered round him and he stayed by the lakeside. Then one of the synagogue officials came up, Jairus by name, and seeing him, fell at his feet and pleaded with him earnestly, saying, 'My little daughter is desperately sick. Do come and lay your hands on her to make her better and save her life.' Jesus went with him and a large crowd followed him; they were pressing all round him.

Now there was a woman who had suffered from a haemorrhage for twelve years; after long and painful treatment under various doctors, she had spent all she had without being any the better for it, in fact, she was getting worse. She had heard about Jesus, and she came up behind him through the crowd and touched his cloak. 'If I can touch even his clothes,' she had told herself 'I shall be well again.' And the source of the bleeding dried up instantly, and she felt in herself that she was cured of her complaint. Immediately aware that power had gone out from him Jesus turned round in the crowd and said, 'Who touched my clothes?' His disciples said to him, 'You see how the crowd is pressing round you and yet you say, "Who touched me?"' But he continued to look all round to see who had done it. Then the woman came forward, frightened and trembling because she knew what had happened to her, and she fell at his feet and told him the whole truth. 'My daughter' he said 'your faith has restored you to health; go in peace and be free from your complaint.'

While he was still speaking some people arrived from the house of the synagogue official to say, 'Your daughter is dead: why put the Master to any further trouble?' But Jesus had overheard this remark of theirs and he said to the official, 'Do not be afraid; only have faith.' And he allowed no one to go with him except Peter and James and John the brother of James.

So they came to the official's house and Jesus noticed all the commotion, with people weeping and wailing unrestrainedly. He went in and said to them, 'Why all this commotion and crying? The child is not dead, but asleep.' But they laughed at him. So he turned them all out and, taking with him the child's father and mother and his own companions, he went into the place where the child lay. And taking the child by the hand he said to her, 'Talitha, kum!' which means, 'Little girl, I tell you to get up.' The little girl got up at once and began to walk about, for she was twelve years old. At this they were overcome with astonishment, and he ordered them strictly not to let anyone know about it, and told them to give her something to eat.

## Reflection

Today's Gospel reading is really two stories. In the middle of the story of the healing of Jairus' daughter is the story of the woman who had experienced great depravations because of her haemorrhage. Here we see that the woman took a great risk to reach out to Jesus but when she did she was rewarded with great healing. This reminds us that we too need to reach out to the God who ultimately reaches out to us.

## JUNE
# 28
## MONDAY

**13th Week
in Ordinary Time**
Saint Irenaeus, *bishop,
martyr*
**Red**

### Genesis 18:16-33

From Mamre the men set out and arrived within sight of Sodom, with Abraham accompanying them to show them the way. Now the Lord had wondered, 'Shall I conceal from Abraham what I am going to do, seeing that Abraham will become a great nation with all the nations of the earth blessing themselves by him? For I have singled him out to command his sons and his household after him to maintain the way of the Lord by just and upright living. In this way the Lord will carry out for Abraham what he has promised him.' Then the Lord said, 'How great an outcry there is against Sodom and Gomorrah! How grievous is their sin! I propose to go down and see whether or not they have done all that is alleged in the outcry against them that has come up to me. I am determined to know.'

The men left there and went to Sodom while Abraham remained standing before the Lord. Approaching him he said, 'Are you really going to destroy the just man with the sinner? Perhaps there are fifty just men in the town. Will you really overwhelm them, will you not spare the place for the fifty just men in it? Do not think of doing such a thing: to kill the just man with the sinner, treating just and sinner alike! Do not think of it! Will the judge of the whole earth not administer justice?' The Lord replied, 'If at Sodom I find fifty just men in the town, I will spare the whole place because of them.' *(See Appendix B-17)*

### Psalm 102:1-4.8-11. R. v.8
*The Lord is compassion and love.*

### Matthew 8:18-22

When Jesus saw the great crowds all about him he gave orders to leave for the other side. One of the scribes then came up and said to him, 'Master, I will follow you wherever you go.' Jesus replied, 'Foxes have holes and the birds of the air have nests, but the Son of Man has nowhere to lay his head.'

Another man, one of his disciples, said to him, 'Sir, let me go and bury my father first.' But Jesus replied, 'Follow me, and leave the dead to bury their dead.'

### Reflection

As Christians we never really belong to this world. Ultimately we are citizens of the Kingdom of Heaven. Whilst we may love our homes, nations, towns and villages these will pass away when the Kingdom of God arrives in its fullness. As Christians we can enjoy the gifts of God in this world, but this needs to be balanced with an awareness that we shouldn't cling too firmly to them or build our identity around them. Such caution is necessary so that we are not blinded by them and left unable to see God.

## Acts 12:1-11

King Herod started persecuting certain members of the Church. He beheaded James the brother of John, and when he saw that this pleased the Jews he decided to arrest Peter as well. This was during the days of Unleavened Bread, and he put Peter in prison, assigning four squads of four soldiers each to guard him in turns. Herod meant to try Peter in public after the end of Passover week. All the time Peter was under guard the Church prayed to God for him unremittingly. *(See Appendix B-18)*

## Psalm 33:2-9. R. v.5

*From all my terrors the Lord set me free.*

## 2 Timothy 4:6-8.17-18

My life is already being poured away as a libation, and the time has come for me to be gone. I have fought the good fight to the end; I have run the race to the finish; I have kept the faith; all there is to come now is the crown of righteousness reserved for me, which the Lord, the righteous judge, will give to me on that Day; and not only to me but to all those who have longed for his Appearing.

The Lord stood by me and gave me power, so that through me the whole message might be proclaimed for all the pagans to hear; and so I was rescued from the lion's mouth. The Lord will rescue me from all evil attempts on me, and bring me safely to his heavenly kingdom. To him be glory for ever and ever. Amen.

## Matthew 16:13-19

When Jesus came to the region of Caesarea Philippi he put this question to his disciples. 'Who do people say the Son of Man is?' And they said, 'Some say he is John the Baptist, some Elijah, and others Jeremiah or one of the prophets.' 'But you,' he said 'who do you say I am?' Then Simon Peter spoke up, 'You are the Christ,' he said 'the Son of the living God.' Jesus replied, 'Simon son of Jonah, you are a happy man! Because it was not flesh and blood that revealed this to you but my Father in heaven. So I now say to you: You are Peter and on this rock I will build my Church. And the gates of the underworld can never hold out against it. I will give you the keys of the kingdom of heaven: whatever you bind on earth shall be considered bound in heaven; whatever you loose on earth shall be considered loosed in heaven.'

## JUNE

# 29

### TUESDAY

**Sts Peter and Paul,**
*apostles*
**Solemnity**
**Red**

## Reflection

When we remember St Peter, it is important to remember that we are in communion with him and his successors. Belonging to the one worldwide Church where all are united through our relationship with St Peter is such a wonderful gift. Being in communion with St Peter ultimately means that we are guaranteed a place in the true Church where we are united in Christ. We are set on the rock, not the shifting sands of the world's concerns.

**13th Week
in Ordinary Time
Green
or
The First Martyrs of the
Holy Roman Church
(Optional, Red)**

### Genesis 21:5.8-20

Abraham was a hundred years old when his son Isaac was born to him. The child grew and was weaned, and Abraham gave a great banquet on the day Isaac was weaned. Now Sarah watched the son that Hagar the Egyptian had borne to Abraham, playing with her son Isaac. 'Drive away that slave-girl and her son,' she said to Abraham; 'this slave-girl's son is not to share the inheritance with my son Isaac.' This greatly distressed Abraham because of his son, but God said to him, 'Do not distress yourself on account of the boy and your slave-girl. Grant Sarah all she asks of you, for it is through Isaac that your name will be carried on. But the slave-girl's son I will also make into a nation, for he is your child too.' Rising early next morning Abraham took some bread and a skin of water and, giving them to Hagar, he put the child on her shoulder and sent her away.

She wandered off into the wilderness of Beersheba. When the skin of water was finished she abandoned the child under a bush. Then she went and sat down at a distance, about a bowshot away, saying to herself, 'I cannot see the child die.' So she sat at a distance; and the child wailed and wept. *(See Appendix B-18)*

### Psalm 33:7-8.10-13. R. v.7
*This poor man called; the Lord heard him.*

### Matthew 8:28-34

When Jesus reached the country of the Gadarenes on the other side of the lake, two demoniacs came towards him out of the tombs – creatures so fierce that no one could pass that way. They stood there shouting, 'What do you want with us, Son of God? Have you come here to torture us before the time?' Now some distance away there was a large herd of pigs feeding, and the devils pleaded with Jesus, 'If you cast us out, send us into the herd of pigs.' And he said to them, 'Go then,' and they came out and made for the pigs; and at that the whole herd charged down the cliff into the lake and perished in the water. The swineherds ran off and made for the town, where they told the whole story, including what had happened to the demoniacs. At this the whole town set out to meet Jesus; and as soon as they saw him they implored him to leave the neighbourhood.

### Reflection

In the Church now we can be wary of talking about spiritual warfare. We always need to approach this subject with great care and caution whilst never forgetting that it is a biblical reality. Today's gospel reading reminds us of this important aspect of the healing ministry of Jesus and his Church. It also highlights that Jesus' love can overpower all forces of darkness. He has won the battle over evil, and his name and grace overpower all.

### Genesis 22:1-19

It happened that God put Abraham to the test. 'Abraham, Abraham,' he called. 'Here I am' he replied. 'Take your son,' God said 'your only child Isaac, whom you love, and go to the land of Moriah. There you shall offer him as a burnt offering on a mountain I will point out to you.'

Rising early next morning Abraham saddled his ass and took with him two of his servants and his son Isaac. He chopped wood for the burnt offering and started on his journey to the place God had pointed out to him. On the third day Abraham looked up and saw the place in the distance. Then Abraham said to his servants, 'Stay here with the donkey. The boy and I will go over there; we will worship and come back to you.'

Abraham took the wood for the burnt offering, loaded it on Isaac, and carried in his own hands the fire and the knife. Then the two of them set out together. Isaac spoke to his father Abraham. 'Father' he said. 'Yes, my son' he replied. 'Look,' he said 'here are the fire and the wood, but where is the lamb for the burnt offering?' Abraham answered, 'My son, God himself will provide the lamb for the burnt offering.' Then the two of them went on together.
*(See Appendix B-18)*

### Psalm 114:1-6.8-9. R. v.9

*I will walk in the presence of the Lord in the land of the living.* (or *Alleluia!*)

### Matthew 9:1-8

Jesus got in the boat, crossed the water and came to his own town. Then some people appeared, bringing him a paralytic stretched out on a bed. Seeing their faith, Jesus said to the paralytic, 'Courage, my child, your sins are forgiven.' And at this some scribes said to themselves, 'This man is blaspheming.' Knowing what was in their minds Jesus said, 'Why do you have such wicked thoughts in your hearts? Now, which of these is easier: to say, "Your sins are forgiven", or to say, "Get up and walk"? But to prove to you that the Son of Man has authority on earth to forgive sins,' – he said to the paralytic – 'get up, and pick up your bed and go off home.' And the man got up and went home. A feeling of awe came over the crowd when they saw this, and they praised God for giving such power to men.

### Reflection

'To err is human, to forgive, divine,' says Alexander Pope. Forgiveness is an attribute of God which flows from the abundance of divine love. Where there is forgiveness, there is love and where there is love, there is forgiveness. God who is the fountain of love cannot contain in his heart anger against his children. Christ manifests God's forgiveness through his preaching, teaching, miracles and most of all his supreme sacrifice on the cross. The scribes accuse him of blasphemy because he makes himself equal to God. But he unequivocally asserts that he has authority on earth to forgive sins because he is both God and human. Forgiveness is an attribute of God. Anyone who extends forgiveness possesses God's divine life because 'to forgive is divine'!

## JULY

# 2

### FRIDAY

**13th Week
in Ordinary Time
Green**

**Genesis 23:1-4.19; 24:1-8.62-67**

The length of Sarah's life was a hundred and twenty-seven years. She died at Kiriath-arba, or Hebron, in the land of Canaan, and Abraham went to mourn and grieve for her.

Then leaving his dead, Abraham spoke to the sons of Heth: 'I am a stranger and a settler among you' he said. 'Let me own a burial-plot among you, so that I may take my dead wife and bury her.'

After this Abraham buried his wife Sarah in the cave of the field of Machpelah opposite Mamre, in the country of Canaan.

By now Abraham was an old man well on in years, and the Lord had blessed him in every way. Abraham said to the eldest servant of his household, the steward of all his property, 'Place your hand under my thigh, I would have you swear by the Lord God of heaven and God of earth, that you will not choose a wife for my son from the daughters of the Canaanites among whom I live. Instead, go to my own land and my own kinsfolk to choose a wife for my son Isaac.' The servant asked him, 'What if the woman does not want to come with me to this country? Must I take your son back to the country from which you came?' Abraham answered, 'On no account take my son back there. …
*(See Appendix B-19)*

**Psalm 105:1-5. R. v.1**

*O give thanks to the Lord for he is good.* (or *Alleluia!*)

## Matthew 9:9-13

As Jesus was walking on he saw a man named Matthew sitting by the customs house, and he said to him, 'Follow me.' And he got up and followed him.

While he was at dinner in the house it happened that a number of tax collectors and sinners came to sit at the table with Jesus and his disciples. When the Pharisees saw this, they said to his disciples, 'Why does your master eat with tax collectors and sinners?' When he heard this he replied, 'It is not the healthy who need the doctor, but the sick. Go and learn the meaning of the words: What I want is mercy, not sacrifice. And indeed I did not come to call the virtuous, but sinners.'

### Reflection

Mathew, like Zacchaeus, was a wealthy tax collector. Because of his profession he was seen by the Jews as belonging to a class of traitors and cheaters. Perhaps it was for this reason that he did not have to think twice when Jesus called him. The words, 'follow me', ignited in him a thirst for joy, peace and hope. He left everything and followed the one who offered him the beauty of a dignified life. His experience of joy and peace produces a ripple effect, as other tax collectors join him in following Jesus and celebrating the experience of discipleship. Jesus, the divine physician, found Matthew and offered him medicine for his soul that brought him true happiness. Jesus heals us too, and brings us joy, peace and hope, no matter what our illness may be.

**Ephesians 2:19-22**
You are no longer aliens or foreign visitors; you are citizens like all the saints, and part of God's household. You are part of a building that has the apostles and prophets for its foundations, and Christ Jesus himself for its main cornerstone. As every structure is aligned on him, all grow into one holy temple in the Lord; and you too, in him, are being built into a house where God lives, in the Spirit.

**St Thomas,** *apostle*
Feast
Red

**Psalm 116. R. Mark 16:15**
*Go out to the whole world; proclaim the Good News.*

**John 20:24-29**
Thomas, called the Twin, who was one of the Twelve, was not with the disciples when Jesus came. When they said, 'We have seen the Lord', he answered, 'Unless I see the holes that the nails made in his hands and can put my finger into the holes they made, and unless I can put my hand into his side, I refuse to believe.' Eight days later the disciples were in the house again and Thomas was with them. The doors were closed, but Jesus came in and stood among them. 'Peace be with you' he said. Then he spoke to Thomas, 'Put your finger here; look, here are my hands. Give me your hand; put it into my side. Doubt no longer but believe.' Thomas replied, 'My Lord and my God!' Jesus said to him: 'You believe because you can see me. Happy are those who have not seen and yet believe.'

**Reflection**
When Jesus appeared to the disciples after his resurrection, Thomas was not with them. Eight days later, Jesus appears to them again and this time Thomas is present. When Thomas was away from the community, he did not experience the risen Christ, but when he was with the community he did. We too can experience the presence of Christ in and through the 'communion of the community'. 'Where two or three are gathered in my name, there am I in their midst', says Jesus (Matthew 18: 20). Thomas had such a powerful experience of the risen Christ in the company of his fellow apostles that he surrendered his life to him with the most profound profession of faith, 'My Lord and my God!' This experience led Thomas in later years to go to distant lands as a missionary and establish Christian communities that exist to this day, bearing significant testimony to Christ. Like Thomas, we do well to remain in communion with the Body of Christ, the Church, so that we experience the power of the risen Lord and are empowered to bear witness to him.

## JULY

# 4

## SUNDAY

**14th Sunday
in Ordinary Time
Psalter Week 2
Green**

### Ezekiel 2:2-5

The spirit came into me and made me stand up, and I heard the Lord speaking to me. He said, 'Son of man, I am sending you to the Israelites, to the rebels who have turned against me. Till now they and their ancestors have been in revolt against me. The sons are defiant and obstinate; I am sending you to them, to say, "The Lord says this." Whether they listen or not, this set of rebels shall know there is a prophet among them.'

### Psalm 122. R. v.2

*Our eyes are on the Lord till he show us his mercy.*

### 2 Corinthians 12:7-10

In view of the extraordinary nature of these revelations, to stop me from getting too proud I was given a thorn in the flesh, an angel of Satan to beat me and stop me from getting too proud! About this thing, I have pleaded with the Lord three times for it to leave me, but he has said, 'My grace is enough for you: my power is at its best in weakness.' So I shall be very happy to make my weaknesses my special boast so that the power of Christ may stay over me, and that is why I am quite content with my weaknesses, and with insults, hardships, persecutions, and the agonies I go through for Christ's sake. For it is when I am weak that I am strong.

### Mark 6:1-6

Jesus went to his home town and his disciples accompanied him. With the coming of the sabbath he began teaching in the synagogue and most of them were astonished when they heard him. They said, 'Where did the man get all this? What is this wisdom that has been granted him, and these miracles that are worked through him? This is the carpenter, surely, the son of Mary, the brother of James and Joset and Jude and Simon? His sisters, too, are they not here with us?' And they would not accept him. And Jesus said to them, 'A prophet is only despised in his own country among his own relations and in his own house'; and he could work no miracle there, though he cured a few sick people by laying his hands on them. He was amazed at their lack of faith.

## Reflection

In the Scripture readings of today, Ezekiel, Paul and Jesus manifest their vocation as God's accredited ambassadors and prophets. Ezekiel is asked by God to go and preach to rebellious Israel. Paul, during his ministry, experiences the power of Satan as he is afflicted with a 'thorn in the flesh'. Jesus was misunderstood and rejected by the people of his own home town. They are prejudiced by their knowledge of him – 'the carpenter, the son of Mary, the brother of James and Joset and Jude and Simon'. They question among themselves: 'Where did the man get all this?'

In all three situations the protagonists are given strength and sustained by the power of God working in them. Jesus was aware of his role as the prophet sent by his Father and was not dissuaded by the opposition and rejection of his townsfolk. Paul experienced the power of Christ who assured him, 'My grace is enough for you'. And God promises Ezekiel that 'Whether they listen or not, this tribe of rebels will know there is a prophet among them.'

When we follow God's precepts and accept to be his messengers, we will experience moments of trial, misunderstanding and rejection. But we will always be strengthened and sustained by the plentiful grace of God.

**14th Week
in Ordinary Time
Green**
or
**St Anthony Zaccaria,**
*priest*
(Optional, White)

**Genesis 28:10-22**
Jacob left Beersheba and set out for Haran. When he had reached a certain place he passed the night there, since the sun had set. Taking one of the stones to be found at that place, he made it his pillow and lay down where he was. He had a dream: a ladder was there, standing on the ground with its top reaching to heaven; and there were angels of God going up it and coming down. And the Lord was there, standing over him, saying, 'I am the Lord, the God of Abraham your father, and the God of Isaac. I will give to you and your descendants the land on which you are lying. Your descendants shall be like the specks of dust on the ground; you shall spread to the west and the east, to the north and the south, and all the tribes of the earth shall bless themselves by you and your descendants. Be sure that I am with you; I will keep you safe wherever you go, and bring you back to this land, for I will not desert you before I have done all that I have promised you.' ...
*(See Appendix B-19)*

**Psalm 90:1-4.14-15. R. cf. v.2**
*My God, in you I trust.*

**Matthew 9:18-26**
While Jesus was speaking, up came one of the officials, who bowed low in front of him and said, 'My daughter has just died, but come and lay your hand on her and her life will be saved.' Jesus rose and, with his disciples, followed him.

Then from behind him came a woman, who had suffered from a haemorrhage for twelve years, and she touched the fringe of his cloak, for she said to herself, 'If I can only touch his cloak I shall be well again.' Jesus turned round and saw her; and he said to her, 'Courage, my daughter, your faith has restored you to health.' And from that moment the woman was well again.

When Jesus reached the official's house, and saw the flute players, with the crowd making a commotion he said, 'Get out of here; the little girl is not dead, she is asleep.' And they laughed at him. But when the people had been turned out he went inside and took the little girl by the hand; and she stood up. And the news spread all round the countryside.

**Reflection**
Jacob experienced the divine presence on his journey. He exclaimed, 'Truly, the Lord is in this place!' He then decided to accept the Lord as his God. In today's Gospel, the official whose daughter has just died and the woman who was suffering from a hemorrhage also experienced in Christ the true presence of God. They knew he had the power to change their miserable situation. They manifested extraordinary faith in the power of Christ. He rewarded the official by raising his daughter from the dead, and the woman by healing her of her haemorrhage. God is in this place, God is in our hearts, as Jacob experienced. The powerful presence of Christ is with us in the sacraments, especially in the Eucharist and in the sacrament of reconciliation. May we today experience anew his power and be transformed, no matter what sufferings assail us.

**14th Week
in Ordinary Time
Green
or
St Maria Goretti,** *virgin,
martyr*
**(Optional, Red)**

## Genesis 32:23-33

Jacob rose, and taking his two wives and his two slave-girls and his eleven children he crossed the ford of the Jabbok. He took them and sent them across the stream and sent all his possessions over too. And Jacob was left alone.

And there was one that wrestled with him until daybreak who, seeing that he could not master him, struck him in the socket of his hip, and Jacob's hip was dislocated as he wrestled with him. He said, 'Let me go, for day is breaking.' But Jacob answered, 'I will not let you go unless you bless me.' He then asked, 'What is your name?' 'Jacob,' he replied. He said, 'Your name shall no longer be Jacob, but Israel; because you have been strong against God, you shall prevail against men.' Jacob then made this request, 'I beg you, tell me your name,' but he replied, 'Why do you ask my name?' And he blessed him there.

Jacob named the place Peniel, 'Because I have seen God face to face,' he said 'and I have survived.' The sun rose as he left Peniel, limping because of his hip. That is the reason why to this day the Israelites do not eat the sciatic nerve which is in the socket of the hip, because he had struck Jacob in the socket of the hip on the sciatic nerve.

## Psalm 16:1-3.6-8.15. R. v.15

*Lord, in my justice I shall see your face.*

## Matthew 9:32-38

A man was brought to Jesus, a dumb demoniac. And when the devil was cast out, the dumb man spoke and the people were amazed. 'Nothing like this has ever been seen in Israel' they said. But the Pharisees said, 'It is through the prince of devils that he casts out devils.'

Jesus made a tour through all the towns and villages, teaching in their synagogues, proclaiming the Good News of the kingdom and curing all kinds of diseases and sickness.

And when he saw the crowds he felt sorry for them because they were harassed and dejected, like sheep without a shepherd. Then he said to his disciples, 'The harvest is rich but the labourers are few, so ask the Lord of the harvest to send labourers to his harvest.'

## Reflection

The Lord wrestles with Jacob and tests his endurance. He is given a new name and a new identity – Israel. This episode changes Jacob. He becomes humble. Jacob's experience is a paradigm for humanity that continuously 'wrestles with God' in prayer. We spend long hours seeking after God, struggling to know him and experience his presence, blessings, conversion and forgiveness. It is a battle that requires faith and perseverance. Paradoxically, in the Gospel we see how Jesus' own life was a battle of another type – a battle with the powers opposed to him. His opponents make the strangest accusation against him – 'It is through the prince of devils that he drives out devils.' Like Jacob, Jesus was struck with the worst blows of his opponents, but in the end his perseverance ensures his triumph. May we experience in a powerful way the presence of God in our battle with the powers of evil and emerge triumphant!

**14th Week
in Ordinary Time
Green
or
Blessed Peter To Rot,**
*martyr*
**(Optional, Red)**

### Genesis 41:55-57; 42:5-7.17-24

When the country of Egypt began to feel the famine, the people cried out to Pharaoh for bread. But Pharaoh told all the Egyptians, 'Go to Joseph and do what he tells you.' – There was famine all over the world. – Then Joseph opened all the granaries and sold grain to the Egyptians. The famine grew worse in the land of Egypt. People came to Egypt from all over the world to buy grain from Joseph, for the famine had grown severe throughout the world.

Israel's sons with others making the same journey went to buy grain, for there was famine in the land of Canaan. It was Joseph, as the man in authority over the country, who sold the grain to all comers. So Joseph's brothers went and bowed down before him, their faces touching the ground. When Joseph saw his brothers he recognised them. Then he kept them all in custody for three days.

On the third day Joseph said to them, 'Do this and you shall keep your lives, for I am a man who fears God. If you are honest men let one of your brothers be kept in the place of your detention; as for you, go and take grain to relieve the famine of your families. ...
*(See Appendix B-19)*

### Psalm 32:2-3.10-11.18-19. R. v.22
*May your love be upon us, O Lord, as we place all our hope in you.*

### Matthew 10:1-7
Jesus summoned his twelve disciples, and gave them authority over unclean spirits with power to cast them out and to cure all kinds of diseases and sickness.

These are the names of the twelve apostles: first, Simon who is called Peter, and his brother Andrew; James the son of Zebedee, and his brother John; Philip and Bartholomew; Thomas, and Matthew the tax collector; James the son of Alphaeus, and Thaddaeus; Simon the Zealot and Judas Iscariot, the one who was to betray him. These twelve Jesus sent out, instructing them as follows:

'Do not turn your steps to pagan territory, and do not enter any Samaritan town; go rather to the lost sheep of the House of Israel. And as you go, proclaim that the kingdom of heaven is close at hand.'

### Reflection
The Patriarch Joseph of the Old Testament is an archetype of Christ. He saved his family and the people of Egypt from a deadly famine. Jesus saved the whole world from sin and death. Joseph was thrown into a well and later sold into slavery. Jesus too was misunderstood, rejected, sold for thirty silver pieces and put to death, but was raised to victory, conquering sin and death and bringing life and salvation to the whole world. The apostles Jesus chose and sent out in today's Gospel share in the saving mission of Jesus, proclaiming that 'the Kingdom of God is at hand'. In the process they too have to go through trials, sufferings, persecutions and even death for the sake of the Good News. But Christ's power and his authority will accompany them every moment of their life.

**Genesis 44:18-21.23-29; 45:1-5**

Judah went up to Joseph and said, 'May it please my lord, let your servant have a word privately with my lord. Do not be angry with your servant, for you are like Pharaoh himself. My lord questioned his servants, "Have you father or brother?" And we said to my lord, "We have an old father, and a younger brother born of his old age. His brother is dead, so he is the only one left of his mother, and his father loves him." Then you said to your servants, "Bring him down to me that my eyes may look on him. If your youngest brother does not come down with you, you will not be admitted to my presence again." When we went back to your servant my father, we repeated to him what my lord had said. So when our father said, "Go back and buy us a little food," we said, "We cannot go down. If our youngest brother is with us, we will go down, for we cannot be admitted to the man's presence unless our youngest brother is with us."

*(See Appendix B-19)*

**Psalm 104:16-21. R. v.5**

*Remember the wonders the Lord has done.* (or *Alleluia!*)

**Matthew 10:7-15**

Jesus instructed the Twelve as follows: 'As you go, proclaim that the kingdom of heaven is close at hand. Cure the sick, raise the dead, cleanse the lepers, cast out devils. You received without charge, give without charge. Provide yourselves with no gold or silver, not even with a few coppers for your purses, with no haversack for the journey or spare tunic or footwear or a staff, for the workman deserves his keep.

'Whatever town or village you go into, ask for someone trustworthy and stay with him until you leave. As you enter his house, salute it, and if the house deserves it, let your peace descend upon it; if it does not, let your peace come back to you. And if anyone does not welcome you or listen to what you have to say, as you walk out of the house or town shake the dust from your feet. I tell you solemnly, on the day of Judgement it will not go as hard with the land of Sodom and Gomorrah as with that town.'

**Reflection**

The instruction given to the apostles by Jesus involves three things: 1. A definition of their mission. It involves the proclamation of the kingdom of God, curing the sick, raising the dead and driving out evil spirits. Jesus gives them a share of his own power and authority to carry out these powerful works. 2. A call for personal commitment to him and total trust. They 'received without charge, give without charge...' They are to be totally committed, fully available and radically free from material baggage and attachment to earthly comforts, trusting solely in divine providence. 3. An awareness of the possibility of rejection. It should not be an occasion for discouragement, but a challenge to move on to other places with the same mission. Even today we have missionaries with the same mandate, going to distant and difficult terrains with the Good News, facing rejection, persecution and danger. Their only strength is the power of Christ that accompanies them.

JULY

# 8

THURSDAY

**14th Week
in Ordinary Time
Green**

## 14th Week
### in Ordinary Time
### Green
### or
### Our Lady of Aberdeen
(Scotland – Feast)
*(See Appendix A-13)*

**Genesis 46:1-7.28-30**

Israel left Canaan with his possessions, and reached Beersheba. There he offered sacrifices to the God of his father Isaac. God spoke to Israel in a vision at night, 'Jacob, Jacob,' he said. 'I am here,' he replied. 'I am God, the God of your father,' he continued. 'Do not be afraid of going down to Egypt, for I will make you a great nation there. I myself will go down to Egypt with you. I myself will bring you back again, and Joseph's hand shall close your eyes.' Then Jacob left Beersheba. Israel's sons conveyed their father Jacob, their little children and their wives in the waggons Pharaoh had sent to fetch him.

Taking their livestock and all that they had acquired in the land of Canaan, they went to Egypt, Jacob and all his family with him: his sons and his grandsons, his daughters and his grand-daughters, in a word, all his children he took with him to Egypt. *(See Appendix B-20)*

**Psalm 36:3-4.18-19.27-28.39-40. R. v.39**
*The salvation of the just comes from the Lord.*

**Matthew 10:16-23**

Jesus instructed the Twelve as follows: 'Remember, I am sending you out like sheep among wolves; so be cunning as serpents and yet as harmless as doves.

'Beware of men: they will hand you over to sanhedrins and scourge you in their synagogues. You will be dragged before governors and kings for my sake, to bear witness before them and the pagans. But when they hand you over, do not worry about how to speak or what to say; what you are to say will be given to you when the time comes; because it is not you who will be speaking; the Spirit of your Father will be speaking in you.

'Brother will betray brother to death, and the father his child; children will rise against their parents and have them put to death. You will be hated by all men on account of my name; but the man who stands firm to the end will be saved. If they persecute you in one town, take refuge in the next; and if they persecute you in that, take refuge in another. I tell you solemnly, you will not have gone the round of the towns of Israel before the Son of Man comes.'

## Reflection

Jesus foresaw and foretold the moments of trial and suffering his disciples would endure. He cautioned them to be prepared for the worst scenario. There will be an atmosphere of hatred, betrayal and even death, as he sends them out 'like sheep among wolves'. He reminds them: 'You will be universally hated on account of my name.' However, he also assures them of the power of the Holy Spirit, guiding them, speaking through them, and empowering them. Anyone who stands firm in the face of trials will be saved, he assures them. Even today persecution of various kinds is a reality. One can explain the bravery and confidence of missionaries only from the viewpoint of their faith and trust in the assurance of Christ: 'Do not worry about how to speak or what to say … the Spirit of your Father will be speaking in you.'

### Genesis 49:29-33; 50:15-26

Jacob gave his sons these instructions, 'I am about to be gathered to my people. Bury me near my fathers, in the cave that is in the field of Ephron the Hittite, in the cave in the field at Machpelah, opposite Mamre, in the land of Canaan, which Abraham bought from Ephron the Hittite as a burial-plot. There Abraham was buried and his wife Sarah. There Isaac was buried and his wife Rebekah. There I buried Leah. I mean the field and the cave in it that were bought from the sons of Heth.'

When Jacob had finished giving his instructions to his sons, he drew his feet up into the bed, and breathing his last was gathered to his people.
*(See Appendix B-20)*

### Psalm 104:1-4.6-7. R. cf. Psalm 68:33

*Seek the Lord, you who are poor, and your hearts will revive.*

### Matthew 10:24-33

Jesus instructed the Twelve as follows: 'The disciple is not superior to his teacher, nor the slave to his master. It is enough for the disciple that he should grow to be like his teacher, and the slave like his master. If they have called the master of the house Beelzebul, what will they not say of his household?

'Do not be afraid of them therefore. For everything that is now covered will be uncovered, and everything now hidden will be made clear. What I say to you in the dark, tell in the daylight; what you hear in whispers, proclaim from the housetops.

'Do not be afraid of those who kill the body but cannot kill the soul; fear him rather who can destroy both body and soul in hell. Can you not buy two sparrows for a penny? And yet not one falls to the ground without your Father knowing. Why, every hair on your head has been counted. So there is no need to be afraid; you are worth more than hundreds of sparrows.

'So if anyone declares himself for me in the presence of men, I will declare myself for him in the presence of my Father in heaven. But the one who disowns me in the presence of men, I will disown in the presence of my Father in heaven.'

### Reflection

Jesus utters the words, 'Do not be afraid' three times in today's Gospel. He is aware of the fierce and deadly persecution his disciples will encounter. Jesus warns them that he himself will be subjected to persecution. They need to face persecution not with fear, but with courage and hope because they are blessed with an immortal soul which no one can destroy even though they may kill the material body. Secondly, the heavenly Father is mindful of every situation, every movement, however small and insignificant they may be. He will not abandon his loved ones. The disciples need to stand firm and declare Christ despite trials. We need not lose faith and hope when the opposing powers strike at us. The power of God's love is always greater than any powers of evil.

**15th Sunday
in Ordinary Time
Psalter Week 3
Green**

## Amos 7:12-15

Amaziah, the priest of Bethel, said to Amos, 'Go away, seer; get back to the land of Judah; earn your bread there, do your prophesying there. We want no more prophesying in Bethel; this is the royal sanctuary, the national temple.' 'I was no prophet, neither did I belong to any of the brotherhoods of prophets,' Amos replied to Amaziah. 'I was a shepherd, and looked after sycamores: but it was the Lord who took me from herding the flock, and the Lord who said, "Go, prophesy to my people Israel."'

## Psalm 84:9-14. R. v.8

*Let us see, O Lord, your mercy and give us your saving help.*

## Ephesians 1:3-10 *(Longer form: Ephesians 1:3-14)*

Blessed be God the Father of our Lord Jesus Christ, who has blessed us with all the spiritual blessings of heaven in Christ. Before the world was made, he chose us, chose us in Christ, to be holy and spotless, and to live through love in his presence, determining that we should become his adopted sons, through Jesus Christ, for his own kind purposes, to make us praise the glory of his grace, his free gift to us in the Beloved, in whom, through his blood, we gain our freedom, the forgiveness of our sins. Such is the richness of the grace which he has showered on us in all wisdom and insight. He has let us know the mystery of his purpose, the hidden plan he so kindly made in Christ from the beginning to act upon when the times had run their course to the end: that he would bring everything together under Christ, as head, everything in the heavens and everything on earth.

## Mark 6:7-13

Jesus summoned the Twelve and began to send them out in pairs giving them authority over the unclean spirits. And he instructed them to take nothing for the journey except a staff – no bread, no haversack, no coppers for their purses. They were to wear sandals but, he added, 'Do not take a spare tunic.' And he said to them, 'If you enter a house anywhere, stay there until you leave the district. And if any place does not welcome you and people refuse to listen to you, as you walk away shake off the dust from under your feet as a sign to them.' So they set off to preach repentance: and they cast out many devils, and anointed many sick people with oil and cured them.

## Reflection

Amos was a herdsman and a dresser of sycamore trees with no prophetic lineage or experience. He preached against the injustice and oppression of the poor by the rich and powerful class. Amazia, the priest of Bethel, asks him to stop preaching and go away. In reply Amos admits his lack of professional qualifications but insists that his call 'to go and prophesy' comes from God. He will not stop speaking the word God gives him to speak.

In the Gospel Jesus summons the twelve apostles and sends them out with a mandate to preach, to heal and to drive out evil spirits. They were mostly uneducated fisher folk. Like Amos, their authority to preach was not based on their qualifications but on the divine calling they received through Jesus. This calling made them ambassadors of God, acting on God's behalf. They had to face challenges and opposition. Yet their mission was amazingly successful because they trusted in the one who called and sent them. They remained faithful to their divine calling regardless of opposition. The secret of their success is explained by Saint Paul, in his Christological hymn of blessing in today's second reading: 'Blessed be God the Father of our Lord Jesus Christ … [who] chose us in Christ before the world was made to be holy and spotless, and to live through love in his presence.'

**Exodus 1:8-14.22**

There came to power in Egypt a new king who knew nothing of Joseph. 'Look,' he said to his subjects 'these people, the sons of Israel, have become so numerous and strong that they are a threat to us. We must be prudent and take steps against their increasing any further, or if war should break out, they might add to the number of our enemies. They might take arms against us and so escape out of the country.' Accordingly they put slave-drivers over the Israelites to wear them down under heavy loads. In this way they built the store-cities of Pithom and Rameses for Pharaoh. But the more they were crushed, the more they increased and spread, and men came to dread the sons of Israel. The Egyptians forced the sons of Israel into slavery, and made their lives unbearable with hard labour, work with clay and with brick, all kinds of work in the fields; they forced on them every kind of labour.

Pharaoh then gave his subjects this command: 'Throw all the boys born to the Hebrews into the river, but let all the girls live.'

**Psalm 123. R. v.8**
*Our help is in the name of the Lord.*

**Matthew 10:34–11:1**

Jesus instructed the Twelve as follows: 'Do not suppose that I have come to bring peace to the earth: it is not peace I have come to bring, but a sword. For I have come to set a man against his father, a daughter against her mother, a daughter-in-law against her mother-in-law. A man's enemies will be those of his own household.

'Anyone who prefers father or mother to me is not worthy of me. Anyone who prefers son or daughter to me is not worthy of me. Anyone who does not take his cross and follow in my footsteps is not worthy of me. Anyone who finds his life will lose it; anyone who loses his life for my sake will find it.

'Anyone who welcomes you welcomes me; and those who welcome me welcome the one who sent me.

'Anyone who welcomes a prophet because he is a prophet will have a prophet's reward; and anyone who welcomes a holy man because he is a holy man will have a holy man's reward.

'If anyone gives so much as a cup of cold water to one of these little ones because he is a disciple, then I tell you solemnly, he will most certainly not lose his reward.'

When Jesus had finished instructing his twelve disciples he moved on from there to teach and preach in their towns.

### Reflection

The concluding part of Jesus' missionary instruction sounds most challenging. He warns his followers of the conflict that will arise on account of their discipleship and mission. Families and communities will be divided on account of the name of Christ. Although such division will happen, Jesus demands a total, radical and steadfast commitment to him and to his cause. No earthly ties or attachments should become a stumbling block to following Christ. Everything is worth sacrificing for the surpassing grace of knowing, following and surrendering to Christ. All those who bear the name of Christ should be prepared to face such conflicting situations in life and when necessary make radical sacrifices to safeguard their relationship with him.

## Exodus 2:1-15

There was a man of the tribe of Levi who had taken a woman of Levi as his wife. She conceived and gave birth to a son and, seeing what a fine child he was, she kept him hidden for three months. When she could hide him no longer, she got a papyrus basket for him; coating it with bitumen and pitch, she put the child inside and laid it among the reeds at the river's edge. His sister stood some distance away to see what would happen to him.

Now Pharaoh's daughter went down to bathe in the river, and the girls attending her were walking along by the riverside. Among the reeds she noticed the basket, and she sent her maid to fetch it. She opened it and looked, and saw a baby boy, crying; and she was sorry for him. 'This is a child of one of the Hebrews' she said. Then the child's sister said to Pharaoh's daughter, 'Shall I go and find you a nurse among the Hebrew women to suckle the child for you?' 'Yes, go' Pharaoh's daughter said to her; and the girl went off to find the baby's own mother. …
*(See Appendix B-20)*

## Psalm 68:3.14.30-31.33-34. R. cf. v.33

*Seek the Lord, you who are poor, and your hearts will revive.*

## Matthew 11:20-24

Jesus began to reproach the towns in which most of his miracles had been worked, because they refused to repent.

'Alas for you, Chorazin! Alas for you, Bethsaida! For if the miracles done in you had been done in Tyre and Sidon, they would have repented long ago in sackcloth and ashes. And still, I tell you that it will not go as hard on Judgement day with Tyre and Sidon as with you. And as for you, Capernaum, did you want to be exalted as high as heaven? You shall be thrown down to hell. For if the miracles done in you had been done in Sodom, it would have been standing yet. And still, I tell you it will not go as hard with the land of Sodom on Judgement day as with you.'

## Reflection

Moses was saved from the genocide of the Hebrew children by a miraculous divine intervention. The subsequent events will show that Moses had his shortcomings and weaknesses, yet he responded to God's plan for him positively. He became the instrument of God in freeing the Hebrew people from Egyptian slavery and he led them through the desert to the threshold of the Promised Land. He was a strong leader and mediator between God and the people. In today's Gospel we see Jesus upbraiding the towns of Chorazin, Bethsaida and Capernaum. Jesus had worked many miracles and signs in these towns but they, unlike Moses, refused to listen and respond positively to the divine presence among them. Our own lives are miracles of God. He intervenes in our lives every day, every moment. God has a plan and a mission for each of us, as he had for Moses. He blesses us as he did those three towns. How do we respond to him? Are our lives a blessing for others?

**15th Week in Ordinary Time**
Green
or
**St Henry**
**(Optional, White)**

**15th Week
in Ordinary Time
Green
or
St Camillus de Lellis,
*priest*
(Optional, White)**

## Exodus 3:1-6.9-12

Moses was looking after the flock of Jethro, his father-in-law, priest of Midian. He led his flock to the far side of the wilderness and came to Horeb, the mountain of God. There the angel of the Lord appeared to him in the shape of a flame of fire, coming from the middle of a bush. Moses looked; there was the bush blazing but it was not being burnt up. 'I must go and look at this strange sight,' Moses said 'and see why the bush is not burnt.' Now the Lord saw him go forward to look, and God called to him from the middle of the bush. 'Moses, Moses!' he said. 'Here I am' he answered. 'Come no nearer' he said. 'Take off your shoes, for the place on which you stand is holy ground. I am the God of your father,' he said 'the God of Abraham, the God of Isaac and the God of Jacob.' At this Moses covered his face, afraid to look at God.

And the Lord said, 'And now the cry of the sons of Israel has come to me, and I have witnessed the way in which the Egyptians oppress them, so come, I send you to Pharaoh to bring the sons of Israel, my people, out of Egypt.'

Moses said to God, 'Who am I to go to Pharaoh and bring the sons of Israel out of Egypt?' 'I shall be with you,' was the answer 'and this is the sign by which you shall know that it is I who have sent you... After you have led the people out of Egypt, you are to offer worship to God on this mountain.'

## Psalm 102:1-4.6-7. R. v.8
*The Lord is compassion and love.*

## Matthew 11:25-27

Jesus exclaimed, 'I bless you, Father, Lord of heaven and of earth, for hiding these things from the learned and the clever and revealing them to mere children. Yes, Father, for that is what it pleased you to do. Everything has been entrusted to me by my Father; and no one knows the Son except the Father, just as no one knows the Father except the Son and those to whom the Son chooses to reveal him.'

## Reflection

The young Moses happened to be at Mount Horeb when God revealed himself to him in the blazing bush: 'I am the God of your ancestors, the God of Abraham, the God of Isaac and the God of Jacob.' The revelation leads to the all-important mission that Moses had to undertake: 'So now I am sending you to Pharaoh, for you to bring my people the Israelites out of Egypt'. Moses responds that he is incapable of doing what God asks, but God assures him: 'I shall be with you'. Moses' limitations and inexperience did not matter to God. God saw his innate ability to lead and guide, and the goodness of his heart. Jesus in today's Gospel exclaims: 'I bless you, Father, Lord of heaven and of earth, for hiding these things from the learned and the clever and revealing them to little children.' The mystery of God's choice is beyond our comprehension. But he chooses whom he wants and whom he chooses he empowers by his very presence.

## Exodus 3:13-20

Moses, hearing the voice of God coming from the middle of the bush, said to him 'I am to go, then, to the sons of Israel and say to them, "The God of your fathers has sent me to you." But if they ask me what his name is, what am I to tell them?' And God said to Moses, 'I Am who I Am. This' he added 'is what you must say to the sons of Israel: "I Am has sent me to you."' And God also said to Moses, 'You are to say to the sons of Israel: "The Lord, the God of your fathers, the God of Abraham, the God of Isaac, and the God of Jacob, has sent me to you." This is my name for all time; by this name I shall be invoked for all generations to come.

'Go and gather the elders of Israel together and tell them, "The Lord, the God of your fathers, has appeared to me, – the God of Abraham, of Isaac, and of Jacob; and he has said to me: I have visited you and seen all that the Egyptians are doing to you. And so I have resolved to bring you up out of Egypt where you are oppressed, into the land of the Canaanites, the Hittites, the Amorites, the Perizzites, the Hivites and the Jebusites, to a land where milk and honey flow." They will listen to your words, and with the elders of Israel you are to go to the king of Egypt and say to him, "The Lord, the God of the Hebrews, has come to meet us. Give us leave, then, to make a three days' journey into the wilderness to offer sacrifice to the Lord our God." For myself, knowing that the king of Egypt will not let you go unless he is forced by a mighty hand, I shall show my power and strike Egypt with all the wonders I am going to work there. After this he will let you go.'

## Psalm 104:1.5.8-9.24-27. R. v.8

*The Lord remembers his covenant for ever.* (or *Alleluia!*)

## Matthew 11:28-30

Jesus said, 'Come to me, all you who labour and are overburdened, and I will give you rest. Shoulder my yoke and learn from me, for I am gentle and humble in heart, and you will find rest for your souls. Yes, my yoke is easy and my burden light.'

## Reflection

The Lord heard the cries of the oppressed and heavily burdened Hebrew people and decided to bring them out of Egypt and lead them to the land flowing with milk and honey. Moses was entrusted with the difficult task of going to Pharaoh and convincing him to free the Hebrew people. The Lord would not take 'no' for an answer from Pharaoh because he was filled with compassion for his suffering people. In today's Gospel we hear Jesus' invitation: 'Come to me, all you who labour and are overburdened and I will give you rest'. We are the new Israel, God's chosen people, his beloved ones redeemed by the blood of Christ. He is mindful of our situation and understands our struggles, trials, sufferings and pains. In the Scriptures and in the sacraments, we are invited to find our rest and experience the freedom of the children of God.

**15th Week
in Ordinary Time
Green
or
Our Lady of Mount
Carmel
(Optional, White)**

**Exodus 11:10–12:14**

Moses and Aaron worked many wonders in the presence of Pharaoh. But the Lord made Pharaoh's heart stubborn, and he did not let the sons of Israel leave his country.

The Lord said to Moses and Aaron in the land of Egypt, 'This month is to be the first of all the others for you, the first month of your year. Speak to the whole community of Israel and say, "On the tenth day of this month each man must take an animal from the flock, one for each family: one animal for each household. If the household is too small to eat the animal, a man must join with his neighbour, the nearest to his house, as the number of persons requires. You must take into account what each can eat in deciding the number for the animal. It must be an animal without blemish, a male one year old; you may take it from either sheep or goats. You must keep it till the fourteenth day of the month when the whole assembly of the community of Israel shall slaughter it between the two evenings. ...

*(See Appendix B-21)*

**Psalm 115:12-13.15-18. R. v.13**

*The cup of salvation I will raise; I will call on the Lord's name.* (or *Alleluia!*)

**Matthew 12:1-8**

Jesus took a walk one sabbath day through the cornfields. His disciples were hungry and began to pick ears of corn and eat them. The Pharisees noticed it and said to him, 'Look, your disciples are doing something that is forbidden on the sabbath.' But he said to them, 'Have you not read what David did when he and his followers were hungry – how he went into the house of God and how they ate the loaves of offering which neither he nor his followers were allowed to eat, but which were for the priests alone? Or again, have you not read in the Law that on the sabbath day the Temple priests break the sabbath without being blamed for it? Now here, I tell you, is something greater than the Temple. And if you had understood the meaning of the words: What I want is mercy, not sacrifice, you would not have condemned the blameless. For the Son of Man is master of the sabbath.'

## Reflection

The central point of the first Passover celebration of the Jews is: 'It is a Passover in the Lord's honour ... When I see the blood, I shall pass over you'. There is a meal eaten in haste on the night of their freedom. The blood of the lamb, sacrificed for the Passover meal, and sprinkled on doorposts, becomes a sign for the angel of death to pass over the houses of the Hebrews. On that night the Hebrew people depart from the slavery of Egypt to journey to the freedom of the Promised Land. Jesus ate the Last Supper in the context of the Passover feast to indicate that he is the new Lamb who would be sacrificed for the redemption of the world, freeing us from sin and eternal death. His body broken and blood shed on Calvary are given sacramentally as our food and drink at the Last Supper becoming the source of our salvation. Every Eucharistic celebration commemorates and makes present the event of our redemption.

## Exodus 12:37-42

The sons of Israel left Rameses for Succoth, about six hundred thousand on the march – all men – not counting their families. People of various sorts joined them in great numbers; there were flocks, too, and herds in immense droves. They baked cakes with the dough which they had brought from Egypt, unleavened because the dough was not leavened; they had been driven out of Egypt, with no time for dallying, and had not provided themselves with food for the journey. The time that the sons of Israel had spent in Egypt was four hundred and thirty years. And on the very day the four hundred and thirty years ended, all the array of the Lord left the land of Egypt. The night, when the Lord kept vigil to bring them out of the land of Egypt, must be kept as a vigil in honour of the Lord for all their generations.

## Psalm 135:1.10-15.23-24

*Great is his love, love without end.* (or *Alleluia!*)

## Matthew 12:14-21

The Pharisees went out and began to plot against Jesus, discussing how to destroy him.

Jesus knew this and withdrew from the district. Many followed him and he cured them all, but warned them not to make him known. This was to fulfil the prophecy of Isaiah: Here is my servant whom I have chosen, my beloved, the favourite of my soul. I will endow him with my spirit, and he will proclaim the true faith to the nations. He will not brawl or shout, nor will anyone hear his voice in the streets. He will not break the crushed reed, nor put out the smouldering wick till he has led the truth to victory: in his name the nations will put their hope.

## Reflection

Jesus, knowing of the plot to destroy him, withdraws from the district, but continues his mission of curing the sick. A simple, itinerant preacher, the son, as people thought, of a carpenter and followed by a few fishermen, has no place to lay his head, no power, no authority, no weaponry and no wealth. As the prophet Isaiah writes, 'He will not brawl or cry out, his voice is not heard in the streets; he will not break the crushed reed or snuff the faltering wick' (Isaiah 42: 2). And yet, he becomes a threat to the establishment and inconvenient to the ruling and religious classes. His new brand of teaching threatens their positions of power. They think it best to do away with him. The only power that Jesus exercises is power from God; as Isaiah also foretells: 'I will put my Spirit on him, and he will bring true justice to the nations' (Isaiah 42: 1). Jesus becomes the hope of the nations by the power of God. Our life and destiny depend on him.

**16th Sunday
in Ordinary Time
Psalter Week 4
Green**

### Jeremiah 23:1-6

'Doom for the shepherds who allow the flock of my pasture to be destroyed and scattered – it is the Lord who speaks! This, therefore, is what the Lord, the God of Israel says about the shepherds in charge of my people: You have let my flock be scattered and go wandering and have not taken care of them. Right, I will take care of you for your misdeeds – it is the Lord who speaks! But the remnant of my flock I myself will gather from all the countries where I have dispersed them, and will bring them back to their pastures: they shall be fruitful and increase in numbers. I will raise up shepherds to look after them and pasture them; no fear, no terror for them any more; not one shall be lost – it is the Lord who speaks!

'See, the days are coming – it is the Lord who speaks – when I will raise a virtuous Branch for David, who will reign as true king and be wise, practising honesty and integrity in the land. In his days Judah will be saved and Israel dwell in confidence. And this is the name he will be called: The Lord-our-integrity.'

### Psalm 22. R. v.2

*The Lord is my shepherd; there is nothing I shall want.*

### Ephesians 2:13-18

In Christ Jesus, you that used to be so far apart from us have been brought very close, by the blood of Christ. For he is the peace between us, and has made the two into one and broken down the barrier which used to keep them apart, actually destroying in his own person the hostility caused by the rules and decrees of the Law. This was to create one single New Man in himself out of the two of them and by restoring peace through the cross, to unite them both in a single Body and reconcile them with God. In his own person he killed the hostility. Later he came to bring the good news of peace, peace to you who were far away and peace to those who were near at hand. Through him, both of us have in the one Spirit our way to come to the Father.

### Mark 6:30-34

The apostles rejoined Jesus and told him all they had done and taught. Then he said to them, 'You must come away to some lonely place all by yourselves and rest for a while'; for there were so many coming and going that the apostles had no time even to eat. So they went off in a boat to a lonely place where they could be by themselves. But people saw them going, and many could guess where; and from every town they all hurried to the place on foot and reached it before them. So as he stepped ashore he saw a large crowd; and he took pity on them because they were like sheep without a shepherd, and he set himself to teach them at some length.

## Reflection

Today's readings compare the people of God to sheep and their leaders to shepherds. Jeremiah the Prophet expresses the Lord's disappointment with the shepherds: 'You have scattered my flock; you have driven them away and have not taken care of them.' But the Lord will not abandon them. Speaking through the prophet, the Lord says, 'I myself shall gather them from all the countries where I have dispersed them and will bring them back to their pastures; they shall be fruitful and increase in numbers.' To gather his sheep the Lord will raise up for David's branch an upright and just shepherd. This prophecy points to Jesus, the incarnate Son of God. Saint Paul refers to him thus: 'He is the peace between us and has made the two into one and broken down the barrier... restoring peace through the cross, to unite [all] in a single body and reconcile them with God. In his own person he killed the hostility.'

Jesus the Good Shepherd appears in today's Gospel as having compassion for the crowd, 'because they were like sheep without a shepherd, and he set himself to teach them at some length.' In Jesus we have the shepherd who laid down his life for us in order to save us and lead us to the green pastures of the kingdom of heaven.

## JULY
# 19
### MONDAY

**16th Week
in Ordinary Time
Green**

**Exodus 14:5-18**

When Pharaoh, king of Egypt, was told that the Israelites had made their escape, he and his courtiers changed their minds about the people. 'What have we done,' they said 'allowing Israel to leave our service?' So Pharaoh had his chariot harnessed and gathered his troops about him, taking six hundred of the best chariots and all the other chariots in Egypt, each manned by a picked team. The Lord made Pharaoh, king of Egypt, stubborn, and he gave chase to the sons of Israel as they made their triumphant escape. So the Egyptians gave chase and came up with them where they lay encamped beside the sea – all the horses, the chariots of Pharaoh, his horsemen, his army – near Pi-hahiroth, facing Baal-zephon. And as Pharaoh approached, the sons of Israel looked round – and there were the Egyptians in pursuit of them! The sons of Israel were terrified and cried out to the Lord. To Moses they said, 'Were there no graves in Egypt that you must lead us out to die in the wilderness? What good have you done us, bringing us out of Egypt? We spoke of this in Egypt, did we not? Leave us alone, we said, we would rather work for the Egyptians! Better to work for the Egyptians than die in the wilderness!' Moses answered the people, 'Have no fear! Stand firm, and you will see what the Lord will do to save you today: the Egyptians you see today, you will never see again. The Lord will do the fighting for you: you have only to keep still.'
*(See Appendix B-21)*

**Psalm: Exodus 15:1-6. R. v.1**
*I will sing to the Lord, glorious his triumph!*

**Matthew 12:38-42**
Some of the scribes and Pharisees spoke up. 'Master,' they said 'we should like to see a sign from you.' Jesus replied, 'It is an evil and unfaithful generation that asks for a sign! The only sign it will be given is the sign of the prophet Jonah. For as Jonah was in the belly of the sea-monster for three days and three nights, so will the Son of Man be in the heart of the earth for three days and three nights. On Judgement day the men of Nineveh will stand up with this generation and condemn it, because when Jonah preached they repented; and there is something greater than Jonah here. On Judgement day the Queen of the South will rise up with this generation and condemn it, because she came from the ends of the earth to hear the wisdom of Solomon; and there is something greater than Solomon here.'

**Reflection**
The Hebrew people conveniently forget all the mighty works of God when they see the Egyptian army pursuing them. They begin to murmur against God and complain against Moses. Instead of trusting in the Lord's power to deliver them, they give themselves over to fear. Despite their complete lack of faith, the Lord promises to save them: 'Do not be afraid, stand firm, and see the deliverance that the Lord will accomplish for you today; for the Egyptians whom you see today you shall never see again…' The Pharisees in today's Gospel behave the same way as the faithless Hebrews. They ask for yet another sign from Jesus. He calls them an evil and ungrateful generation. Today's psalm reminds us that we need to recognise the wonders of God in our life and sing his praise: 'I will sing to the Lord, glorious his triumph!'

## Exodus 14:21–15:1

Moses stretched out his hand over the sea. The Lord drove back the sea with a strong easterly wind all night, and he made dry land of the sea. The waters parted and the sons of Israel went on dry ground right into the sea, walls of water to right and to left of them. The Egyptians gave chase: after them they went, right into the sea, all Pharaoh's horses, his chariots, and his horsemen. In the morning watch, the Lord looked down on the army of the Egyptians from the pillar of fire and of cloud, and threw the army into confusion. He so clogged their chariot wheels that they could scarcely make headway. 'Let us flee from the Israelites,' the Egyptians cried 'the Lord is fighting for them against the Egyptians!' 'Stretch out your hand over the sea,' the Lord said to Moses 'that the waters may flow back on the Egyptians and their chariots and their horsemen.' Moses stretched out his hand over the sea and, as day broke, the sea returned to its bed. The fleeing Egyptians marched right into it, and the Lord overthrew the Egyptians in the very middle of the sea. The returning waters overwhelmed the chariots and the horsemen of Pharaoh's whole army, which had followed the Israelites into the sea; not a single one of them was left. But the sons of Israel had marched through the sea on dry ground, walls of water to right and to left of them. That day, the Lord rescued Israel from the Egyptians, and Israel saw the Egyptians lying dead on the shore. Israel witnessed the great act that the Lord had performed against the Egyptians, and the people venerated the Lord; they put their faith in the Lord and in Moses, his servant.

It was then that Moses and the sons of Israel sang this song in honour of the Lord.

**16th Week in Ordinary Time**
**Green**
**or**
**St Apollinaris, *bishop, martyr***
**(Optional, Red)**

## Psalm Exodus 15:8-10.12.17. R. v.1

*I will sing to the Lord, glorious his triumph!*

## Matthew 12:46-50

Jesus was speaking to the crowds when his mother and his brothers appeared; they were standing outside and were anxious to have a word with him. But to the man who told him this Jesus replied, 'Who is my mother? Who are my brothers?' And stretching out his hand towards his disciples he said, 'Here are my mother and my brothers. Anyone who does the will of my Father in heaven, he is my brother and sister and mother.'

## Reflection

The Israelites, during their exodus from Egypt, experience the power of God yet again. He overthrows the Egyptians in the middle of the sea while the Israelites march on dry ground to safety: 'That day, the Lord rescued Israel from the clutches of the Egyptians.' The Lord's presence was made visible to them by fire at night and a cloud by day. God's power always accompanies us and rescues us, regardless of how powerful the enemy, how hard the struggle, how hopeless the situation and how insurmountable the problem. He is present within our hearts, in the Word of God, in the sacraments and in our fellow believers. We need to discover his presence, do his will and trust in his power. With the people of Israel we too shall 'sing to the Lord, glorious his triumph!'

**16th Week
in Ordinary Time
Green
or
St Lawrence of Brindisi,
priest, doctor
(Optional, White)**

## Exodus 16:1-5.9-15

From Elim they set out, and the whole community of the sons of Israel reached the wilderness of Sin – between Elim and Sinai – on the fifteenth day of the second month after they had left Egypt. And the whole community of the sons of Israel began to complain against Moses and Aaron in the wilderness and said to them, 'Why did we not die at the Lord's hand in the land of Egypt, when we were able to sit down to pans of meat and could eat bread to our heart's content! As it is, you have brought us to this wilderness to starve this whole company to death!'

Then the Lord said to Moses, 'Now I will rain down bread for you from the heavens. Each day the people are to go out and gather the day's portion; I propose to test them in this way to see whether they will follow my law or not. On the sixth day, when they prepare what they have brought in, this will be twice as much as the daily gathering.'

Moses said to Aaron, 'To the whole community of the sons of Israel say this, "Present yourselves before the Lord, for he has heard your complaints."' ...
*(See Appendix B-21)*

## Psalm 77:18-19.23-28. R. v.24
*The Lord gave them bread from heaven.*

## Matthew 13:1-9

Jesus left the house and sat by the lakeside, but such crowds gathered round him that he got into a boat and sat there. The people all stood on the beach, and he told them many things in parables.

He said, 'Imagine a sower going out to sow. As he sowed, some seeds fell on the edge of the path, and the birds came and ate them up. Others fell on patches of rock where they found little soil and sprang up straight away, because there was no depth of earth; but as soon as the sun came up they were scorched and, not having any roots, they withered away. Others fell among thorns, and the thorns grew up and choked them. Others fell on rich soil and produced their crop, some a hundredfold, some sixty, some thirty. Listen, anyone who has ears!'

## Reflection

The Israelites yet again indulge in what they know best: murmur and complaint! With every experience of hardship, they lose faith in the Lord and Moses. They forget all the good they have experienced. But the Lord still comes to their rescue: 'At twilight you will eat meat, and in the morning you will have bread to your heart's content.' Sometimes we allow the soil of our hearts to become too hardened, too preoccupied with our own concerns and too vulnerable to the evil one, that we, like the Israelites, forget God's mighty deeds in our lives and block the growth of the kingdom of God in us. We forget that God gives us the air to breathe, water to drink and food to eat every day; he sustains us and protects us from the evil one. The manna of the desert foreshadows the Eucharistic meal. May we never forget the surpassing value of this precious food that he gives us for our spiritual life.

**Song 3:1-4**

*(Alternative Reading: 2 Corinthians 5: 14-17)*

The bride says this: On my bed, at night, I sought him whom my heart loves. I sought but did not find him. So I will rise and go through the City; in the streets and the squares I will seek him whom my heart loves. I sought but did not find him. The watchmen came upon me on their rounds in the City: 'Have you seen him whom my heart loves?' Scarcely had I passed them than I found him whom my heart loves.

**Psalm 62:2-6.8-9. R. v.2**

*For you my soul is thirsting, O Lord my God.*

**St Mary Magdalene**
**Feast**
**White**

**John 20:1-2.11-18**

It was very early on the first day of the week and still dark, when Mary of Magdala came to the tomb. She saw that the stone had been moved away from the tomb and came running to Simon Peter and the other disciple, the one Jesus loved. 'They have taken the Lord out of the tomb' she said 'and we don't know where they have put him.'

Mary stayed outside near the tomb, weeping. Then, still weeping, she stooped to look inside, and saw two angels in white sitting where the body of Jesus had been, one at the head, the other at the feet. They said, 'Woman, why are you weeping?' 'They have taken my Lord away' she replied 'and I don't know where they have put him.' As she said this she turned round and saw Jesus standing there, though she did not recognise him. Jesus said, 'Woman, why are you weeping? Who are you looking for?' Supposing him to be the gardener, she said, 'Sir, if you have taken him away, tell me where you have put him, and I will go and remove him.' Jesus said, 'Mary!' She knew him then and said to him in Hebrew, 'Rabbuni!' – which means Master. Jesus said to her, 'Do not cling to me, because I have not yet ascended to the Father. But go and find the brothers, and tell them: I am ascending to my Father and your Father, to my God and your God.' So Mary of Magdala went and told the disciples that she had seen the Lord and that he had said these things to her.

## Reflection

Mary Magdalene loved Jesus much. That is why even before sunrise she does a lot of running! First, she goes to the tomb where Jesus was buried. Then she runs back to tell Peter that the body has been removed. Then again, she rushes back to the tomb and finds two angels in white sitting near the tomb, and subsequently she meets the risen Jesus himself standing nearby. She then runs back to Peter and other disciples to declare, 'I have seen the Lord'. Doesn't all this activity indicate how much she loved Jesus? As a reward, she is given the privilege of being the first to meet and recognise the risen Lord, and to announce to the apostles that Jesus is risen. She becomes an apostle to the apostles. Mary is a model disciple filled with the love of the Lord. Through her intercession may we deepen our love for the risen Jesus.

**St Bridget of Sweden,
Patroness of Europe**
*Feast*
*White*

### Galatians 2:19-20

Through the Law I am dead to the Law, so that now I can live with God. I have been crucified with Christ, and I live now not with my own life but with the life of Christ who lives in me. The life I now live in this body I live in faith: faith in the Son of God who loved me and who sacrificed himself for my sake.

### Psalm 33:2-11. R. v.2

*I will bless the Lord at all times.*

### John 15:1-8

Jesus said to his disciples:

'I am the true vine, and my Father is the vinedresser. Every branch in me that bears no fruit he cuts away, and every branch that does bear fruit he prunes to make it bear even more. You are pruned already, by means of the word that I have spoken to you. Make your home in me, as I make mine in you. As a branch cannot bear fruit all by itself, but must remain part of the vine, neither can you unless you remain in me. I am the vine, you are the branches. Whoever remains in me, with me in him, bears fruit in plenty; for cut off from me you can do nothing. Anyone who does not remain in me is like a branch that has been thrown away – he withers; these branches are collected and thrown on the fire, and they are burnt. If you remain in me and my words remain in you, you may ask what you will and you shall get it. It is to the glory of my Father that you should bear much fruit, and then you will be my disciples.'

### Reflection

"Without me, you can do nothing!" This statement of the Lord includes both a message of hope and a dire warning. In every situation of our lives we can and should depend on him. Jesus the true Vine exhorts us to continually foster and nourish our relationship with him and to show forth the fruits of this relationship in our daily lives.

## Exodus 24:3-8

Moses went and told the people all the commands of the Lord and all the ordinances. In answer, all the people said with one voice, 'We will observe all the commands that the Lord has decreed.' Moses put all the commands of the Lord into writing, and early next morning he built an altar at the foot of the mountain, with twelve standing-stones for the twelve tribes of Israel. Then he directed certain young Israelites to offer holocausts and to immolate bullocks to the Lord as communion sacrifices. Half of the blood Moses took up and put into basins, the other half he cast on the altar. And taking the Book of the Covenant he read it to the listening people, and they said, 'We will observe all that the Lord has decreed; we will obey.' Then Moses took the blood and cast it towards the people. 'This' he said 'is the blood of the Covenant that the Lord has made with you, containing all these rules.'

## Psalm 49:1-2.5-6.14-15. R. v.14

*Pay your sacrifice of thanksgiving to God.*

## Matthew 13:24-30

Jesus put a parable before the crowds, 'The kingdom of heaven may be compared to a man who sowed good seed in his field. While everybody was asleep his enemy came, sowed darnel all among the wheat, and made off. When the new wheat sprouted and ripened, the darnel appeared as well. The owner's servants went to him and said, "Sir, was it not good seed that you sowed in your field? If so, where does the darnel come from?" "Some enemy has done this" he answered. And the servants said, "Do you want us to go and weed it out?" But he said, "No, because when you weed out the darnel you might pull up the wheat with it. Let them both grow till the harvest; and at harvest time I shall say to the reapers: First collect the darnel and tie it in bundles to be burnt, then gather the wheat into my barn."'

**16th Week in Ordinary Time**
**Green**
or
**St Sharbel Makhluf,**
*priest*
**(Optional, White)**

## Reflection

The Lord has given the law to Moses who in turn not only announces it to the people but puts it in writing for the people to remember. Most importantly, these words are to be imprinted in their hearts so that they may never forget. The people are also told to teach them diligently to their children, and to talk of them when they sit in their house, when they walk by the way, when they lie down and when they rise (see Deuteronomy 6: 7). The Gospel reminds us that God sows good seed that produces good fruit in the hearts of the people. But the devil sows bad seed and as a result there is evil in the world against which we must struggle. But in the end we will witness the total triumph of good and the destruction of evil.

## JULY
# 25
**SUNDAY**

**17th Sunday
in Ordinary Time**
Psalter Week 1
Green

**2 Kings 4:42-44**
A man came from Baal-shalishah, bringing Elisha, the man of God, bread from the first-fruits, twenty barley loaves and fresh grain in the ear. 'Give it to the people to eat,' Elisha said. But his servant replied, 'How can I serve this to a hundred men?' 'Give it to the people to eat' he insisted 'for the Lord says this, "They will eat and have some left over."' He served them; they ate and had some over, as the Lord had said.

**Psalm 144:10-11.15-18. R. v.16**
*You open wide your hand, O Lord, and grant our desires.*

**Ephesians 4:1-6**
I, the prisoner in the Lord, implore you to lead a life worthy of your vocation. Bear with one another charitably, in complete selflessness, gentleness and patience. Do all you

can to preserve the unity of the Spirit by the peace that binds you together. There is one Body, one Spirit, just as you were all called into one and the same hope when you were called. There is one Lord, one faith, one baptism, and one God who is Father of all, through all and within all.

## John 6:1-15
Jesus went off to the other side of the Sea of Galilee – or of Tiberias – and a large crowd followed him, impressed by the signs he gave by curing the sick. Jesus climbed the hillside, and sat down there with his disciples. It was shortly before the Jewish feast of Passover.

Looking up, Jesus saw the crowds approaching and said to Philip, 'Where can we buy some bread for these people to eat?' He only said this to test Philip; he himself knew exactly what he was going to do. Philip answered, 'Two hundred denarii would only buy enough to give them a small piece each.' One of his disciples, Andrew, Simon Peter's brother, said, 'There is a small boy here with five barley loaves and two fish; but what is that between so many?' Jesus said to them, 'Make the people sit down.' There was plenty of grass there, and as many as five thousand men sat down. Then Jesus took the loaves, gave thanks, and gave them out to all who were sitting ready; he then did the same with the fish, giving out as much as was wanted. When they had eaten enough he said to the disciples, 'Pick up the pieces left over, so that nothing gets wasted.' So they picked them up, and filled twelve hampers with scraps left over from the meal of five barley loaves. The people, seeing this sign that he had given, said, 'This really is the prophet who is to come into the world.' Jesus, who could see they were about to come and take him by force and make him king, escaped back to the hills by himself.

## Reflection
The first reading and the Gospel of today speak about the reality of hunger and the food that satisfies. In both instances people were hungry and in need of food. In the Gospel episode, the crowd is large and far from any town. By human standards they are in an impossible situation for they have no way to obtain food. But what is impossible for humans is possible for the God of compassion and love. Jesus challenges the disciples to come up with a solution: 'Where can we buy some bread for these people to eat?' Andrew's half-hearted initiative and the boy's generosity are blessed by Jesus with remarkable results. The small boy's 'five barley loaves and two fish' are enough to feed well over 5000 people, with plenty left over!

God works wonders when we are willing to cooperate with him. Complaining and murmuring about the enormity of a problem won't solve it. But if we are willing and generous enough to place our small contribution at the Lord's feet, remarkable results can come. St Paul exhorts us today to lead a life worthy of the vocation to which we are called, and to support one another in love, with complete selflessness, gentleness and patience. Humility, gentleness, patience in all situations and loving support for each other are hallmarks of the Christian life.

**17th Week
in Ordinary Time
Sts Joachim and Anne,
parents of
Blessed Virgin Mary
Memorial
White**

## Exodus 32:15-24.30-34

Moses made his way back down the mountain with the two tablets of the Testimony in his hands, tablets inscribed on both sides, inscribed on the front and on the back. These tablets were the work of God, and the writing on them was God's writing engraved on the tablets. Joshua heard the noise of the people shouting. 'There is the sound of battle in the camp', he told Moses. Moses answered him: 'No song of victory is this sound, no wailing for defeat this sound; it is the sound of chanting that I hear.' As he approached the camp and saw the calf and the groups dancing, Moses' anger blazed. He threw down the tablets he was holding and broke them at the foot of the mountain. He seized the calf they had made and burned it, grinding it into powder which he scattered on the water; and he made the sons of Israel drink it. To Aaron Moses said, 'What has this people done to you, for you to bring such a great sin on them?' 'Let not my lord's anger blaze like this' Aaron answered. 'You know yourself how prone this people is to evil. They said to me, "Make us a god to go at our head; this Moses, the man who brought us up from Egypt, we do not know what has become of him." So I said to them, "Who has gold?," and they took it off and brought it to me. I threw it into the fire and out came this calf.' On the following day Moses said to the people, 'You have committed a grave sin. But now I shall go up to the Lord: perhaps I can make atonement for your sin.' And Moses returned to the Lord. 'I am grieved,' he cried 'this people has committed a grave sin, making themselves a god of gold. And yet, if it pleased you to forgive this sin of theirs...! But if not, then blot me out from the book that you have written.' The Lord answered Moses, "It is the man who has sinned against me that I shall blot out from my book. Go now, lead the people to the place of which I told you. My angel shall go before you but, on the day of my visitation, I shall punish them for their sin.'

## Psalm 105:19-23. R. v.1
*O give thanks to the Lord for he is good.*

## Matthew 13:31-35

Jesus put a parable before the crowds: 'The kingdom of heaven is like a mustard seed which a man took and sowed in his field. It is the smallest of all the seeds, but when it has grown it is the biggest shrub of all and becomes a tree so that the birds of the air come and shelter in its branches.' He told them another parable: 'The kingdom of heaven is like the yeast a woman took and mixed in with three measures of flour till it was leavened all through.' In all this Jesus spoke to the crowds in parables; indeed, he would never speak to them except in parables. This was to fulfil the prophecy:

I will speak to you in parables
and expound things hidden since the foundation of the world.

## Reflection

We know little about Joachim and Anne, the parents of the Virgin Mary. But we can surmise that they were people of great faith who longed for the coming of the Saviour. Unbeknown to them, they were to be agents of the arrival of that great day, and for that we praise them still. The mundane tasks that we fulfil each day, in faith, hope and love, may in fact be remarkable channels through which the grace of God flows into our world. Future generations may not know our names, but the good we do can live on long after we have left this earth.

**17th Week
in Ordinary Time
Green**

### Exodus 33:7-11; 34:5-9.28

Moses used to take the Tent and pitch it outside the camp, at some distance from the camp. He called it the Tent of Meeting. Anyone who had to consult the Lord would go out to the Tent of Meeting, outside the camp. Whenever Moses went out to the Tent, all the people would rise. Every man would stand at the door of his tent and watch Moses until he reached the Tent; the pillar of cloud would come down and station itself at the entrance to the Tent, and the Lord would speak with Moses. When they saw the pillar of cloud stationed at the entrance to the Tent, all the people would rise and bow low, each at the door of his tent. The Lord would speak with Moses face to face, as a man speaks with his friend. Then Moses would turn back to the camp, but the young man who was his servant, Joshua son of Nun, would not leave the Tent.

Moses stood with the Lord on the mountain. He called on the name of the Lord. The Lord passed before him and proclaimed, 'The Lord, the Lord, a God of tenderness and compassion, slow to anger, rich in kindness and faithfulness; ... *(See Appendix B-22)*

### Psalm 102:6-13. R. v.8
*The Lord is compassion and love.*

### Matthew 13:36-43

Leaving the crowds, Jesus went to the house, and his disciples came to him and said, 'Explain the parable about the darnel in the field to us.' He said in reply, 'The sower of the good seed is the Son of Man. The field is the world; the good seed is the subjects of the kingdom; the darnel, the subjects of the evil one; the enemy who sowed them, the devil; the harvest is the end of the world; the reapers are the angels. Well then, just as the darnel is gathered up and burnt in the fire, so it will be at the end of time. The Son of Man will send his angels and they will gather out of his kingdom all things that provoke offences and all who do evil, and throw them into the blazing furnace, where there will be weeping and grinding of teeth. Then the virtuous will shine like the sun in the kingdom of their Father. Listen, anyone who has ears!'

### Reflection

So many characters and elements feature in Jesus' explanation of the parable of the wheat and the darnel – the Father, the Son of Man, the devil, the angels, the subjects of the kingdom and the subjects of the evil one. Each has a specific role to play. Jesus, through this explanation, addresses the age-old problem of evil in the world. Where does evil come from? Why does evil coexist with good? What is God's approach to evil? The struggle between good and evil will continue until the end of time, and during that time we all need to do what we can to decrease the influence of evil in our world and multiply the good. May we be heartened in this struggle by God's promise that the ultimate and complete triumph will be with the good. At the end of time the virtuous will shine like the sun in the kingdom of their Father.

**17th Week
in Ordinary Time
Green**

### Exodus 34:29-35

When Moses came down from the mountain of Sinai – as he came down from the mountain, Moses had the two tablets of the Testimony in his hands – he did not know that the skin on his face was radiant after speaking with the Lord. And when Aaron and all the sons of Israel saw Moses, the skin on his face shone so much that they would not venture near him. But Moses called to them, and Aaron with all the leaders of the community came back to him; and he spoke to them. Then all the sons of Israel came closer, and he passed on to them all the orders that the Lord had given him on the mountain of Sinai. And when Moses had finished speaking to them, he put a veil over his face. Whenever he went into the Lord's presence to speak with him, Moses would remove the veil until he came out again. And when he came out, he would tell the sons of Israel what he had been ordered to pass on to them, and the sons of Israel would see the face of Moses radiant. Then Moses would put the veil back over his face until he returned to speak with the Lord.

### Psalm 98:5-7.9. R. cf. v.9
*You are holy, O Lord our God.*

### Matthew 13:44-46

Jesus said to the crowds: 'The kingdom of heaven is like treasure hidden in a field which someone has found; he hides it again, goes off happy, sells everything he owns and buys the field.

'Again, the kingdom of heaven is like a merchant looking for fine pearls; when he finds one of great value he goes and sells everything he owns and buys it.'

### Reflection

Jesus tells us in today's Gospel that the kingdom of God is like a treasure hidden in a field. In fact, it is the greatest treasure we can ever possess or even think of! Once discovered and possessed, nothing else could be of greater value than this. Saint Paul puts it bluntly: 'Indeed I count everything as loss because of the surpassing worth of knowing Christ Jesus my Lord' (Philippians 3: 8). How do we discover and possess the kingdom of God? We must follow the example of the farmer and the merchant – one finding the treasure by chance and the other searching and finding a pearl of great value. On finding the most valuable treasure, they are willing to give up everything to possess it. Personal study, prayer and meditation will lead us to the discovery of the treasure hidden within us and among us – Christ Jesus, our Lord. Finding it will enable us to detach ourselves from all treasures of lesser value.

## Exodus 40:16-21.34-38

Moses did exactly as the Lord had directed him. The tabernacle was set up on the first day of the first month in the second year. Moses erected the tabernacle. He fixed the sockets for it, put up its frames, put its crossbars in position, set up its posts. He spread the tent over the tabernacle and on top of this the covering for the tent, as the Lord had directed Moses. He took the Testimony and placed it inside the ark. He set the shafts to the ark and placed the throne of mercy on it. He brought the ark into the tabernacle and put the screening veil in place; thus he screened the ark of the Lord, as the Lord had directed Moses.

The cloud covered the Tent of Meeting and the glory of the Lord filled the tabernacle. Moses could not enter the Tent of Meeting because of the cloud that rested on it and because of the glory of the Lord that filled the tabernacle.

At every stage of their journey, whenever the cloud rose from the tabernacle the sons of Israel would resume their march. If the cloud did not rise, they waited and would not march until it did. For the cloud of the Lord rested on the tabernacle by day, and a fire shone within the cloud by night, for all the House of Israel to see. And so it was for every stage of their journey.

## Psalm 83:3-6.8.11. R. v.2

*How lovely is your dwelling-place, Lord, God of hosts.*

## John 11:19-27

Many Jews had come to Martha and Mary to sympathise with them over their brother. When Martha heard that Jesus had come she went to meet him. Mary remained sitting in the house. Martha said to Jesus, 'If you had been here, my brother would not have died, but I know that, even now, whatever you ask of God, he will grant you.' 'Your brother' said Jesus to her 'will rise again.' Martha said, 'I know he will rise again at the resurrection on the last day.' Jesus said: 'I am the resurrection and the life. If anyone believes in me, even though he dies he will live, and whoever lives and believes in me will never die. Do you believe this?' 'Yes, Lord,' she said 'I believe that you are the Christ, the Son of God, the one who was to come into this world.'

## Reflection

The Church today keeps the memory of Martha of Bethany, the sister of Mary and Lazarus. She, together with her siblings, was a close friend of Jesus. On one occasion when Jesus visited their home (Luke 10: 38-42), Martha complains to Jesus about her sister Mary: 'Lord, do you not care that my sister has left me to serve alone? Tell her then to help me.' Martha, of course, was a diligent and hardworking host but did not have her priorities right. Jesus reminds her that while she is distracted about many things it is Mary who has chosen the better part – sitting in the company of Jesus and listening to him. In the alternative Gospel passage Martha places her total trust in Jesus, saying: 'Yes, Lord; I believe that you are the Christ, the Son of God, who is coming into the world.' Let us learn from Martha to place our trust in the Son of God and in his saving power.

**17th Week
in Ordinary Time
St Martha
Memorial
White**

**17th Week
in Ordinary Time
Green
or
St Peter Chrysologus,
*bishop, doctor*
(Optional, White)**

**Leviticus 23:1.4-11.15-16.27.34-37**
The Lord spoke to Moses; he said:

'These are the Lord's solemn festivals, the sacred assemblies to which you are to summon the sons of Israel on the appointed day.

'The fourteenth day of the first month, between the two evenings, is the Passover of the Lord; and the fifteenth day of the same month is the feast of Unleavened Bread for the Lord. For seven days you shall eat bread without leaven. On the first day you are to hold a sacred assembly; you must do no heavy work. For seven days you shall offer a burnt offering to the Lord. The seventh day is to be a day of sacred assembly; you must do no work.'

The Lord spoke to Moses; he said: 'Speak to the sons of Israel and say to them:

"When you enter the land that I give you, and gather in the harvest there, you must bring the first sheaf of your harvest to the priest, and he is to present it to the Lord with the gesture of offering, so that you may be acceptable. The priest shall make this offering on the day after the sabbath.

"From the day after the sabbath, the day on which you bring the sheaf of offering, you are to count seven full weeks. You are to count fifty days, to the day after the seventh sabbath, and then you are to offer the Lord a new oblation. *(See Appendix B-22)*

**Psalm 80:3-6.10-11. R. v.2**
*Ring out your joy to God our strength.*

**Matthew 13:54-58**
Coming to his home town, Jesus taught the people in their synagogue in such a way that they were astonished and said, 'Where did the man get this wisdom and these miraculous powers? This is the carpenter's son, surely? Is not his mother the woman called Mary, and his brothers James and Joseph and Simon and Jude? His sisters, too, are they not all here with us? So where did the man get it all?' And they would not accept him. But Jesus said to them, 'A prophet is only despised in his own country and in his own house,' and he did not work many miracles there because of their lack of faith.

**Reflection**
The Gospel of today shows how dreadful prejudice can be. The people of Jesus' own home town could not accept him because he was the 'carpenter's son' and a brother of the people they know so well. They could not accept that someone so familiar and ordinary could be a prophet of God. As a result, Jesus 'did not work many miracles there because of their lack of faith.' The people of his hometown are not the only ones guilty of such prejudice. Jesus' words that 'a prophet is despised only in his own country and in his own house' have a universal application. Prejudice can prevent us also from knowing, believing and trusting someone. On the contrary an attitude of openness and acceptance helps us grow in knowledge, faith and love. Are we blinded by prejudice in our attitude to people and events? Do we reject people because of their appearance, background or familiarity?

## Leviticus 25:1.8-17

The Lord spoke to Moses on Mount Sinai; he said: 'You are to count seven weeks of years – seven times seven years, that is to say a period of seven weeks of years, forty-nine years. And on the tenth day of the seventh month you shall sound the trumpet; on the Day of Atonement you shall sound the trumpet throughout the land. You will declare this fiftieth year sacred and proclaim the liberation of all the inhabitants of the land. This is to be a jubilee for you; each of you will return to his ancestral home, each to his own clan. This fiftieth year is to be a jubilee for you: you will not sow, you will not harvest the ungathered corn, you will not gather from the untrimmed vine. The jubilee is to be a holy thing to you, you will eat what comes from the fields. *(See Appendix B-22)*

**17th Week
in Ordinary Time
St Ignatius Loyola,** *priest*
**Memorial
White**

## Psalm 66:2-3.5.7-8. R. v.4

*Let the peoples praise you, O God, let all the peoples praise you.*

## Matthew 14:1-12

Herod the tetrarch heard about the reputation of Jesus, and said to his court, 'This is John the Baptist himself; he has risen from the dead, and that is why miraculous powers are at work in him.'

Now it was Herod who had arrested John, chained him up and put him in prison because of Herodias, his brother Philip's wife. For John had told him, 'It is against the Law for you to have her.' He had wanted to kill him but was afraid of the people, who regarded John as a prophet. Then, during the celebrations for Herod's birthday, the daughter of Herodias danced before the company, and so delighted Herod that he promised on oath to give her anything she asked. Prompted by her mother she said, 'Give me John the Baptist's head, here, on a dish.' The king was distressed but, thinking of the oaths he had sworn and of his guests, he ordered it to be given her, and sent and had John beheaded in the prison. The head was brought in on a dish and given to the girl who took it to her mother. John's disciples came and took the body and buried it; then they went off to tell Jesus.

## Reflection

Herod hears about Jesus' fame and mistakenly concludes that 'this is John the Baptist himself'. His subconscious mind is reminding him of the dreadful crime he committed against John by having him beheaded. Haunted by fear and guilt, he reveals himself to be a coward despite his great power and wealth. This is what happens to people when they refuse to acknowledge the wrong they have done and repent. Their guilt, even if denied, deprives them of true peace, joy and freedom. Like Herod they can be weighed down by fear and guilt. The only way out is to encounter Christ and repent, for 'the Lord is gracious and merciful, slow to anger and abounding in steadfast love' (Psalm 145: 8). Saint Ignatius of Loyola teaches us that one can indeed surrender one's life to Christ and his cause, no matter what may have happened in the past!

### Exodus 16:2-4.12-15

The whole community of the sons of Israel began to complain against Moses and Aaron in the wilderness and said to them, 'Why did we not die at the Lord's hand in the land of Egypt, when we were able to sit down to pans of meat and could eat bread to our heart's content! As it is, you have brought us to this wilderness to starve this whole company to death!'

Then the Lord said to Moses, 'Now I will rain down bread for you from the heavens. Each day the people are to go out and gather the day's portion; I propose to test them in this way to see whether they will follow my law or not.'

'I have heard the complaints of the sons of Israel. Say this to them, "Between the two evenings you shall eat meat, and in the morning you shall have bread to your heart's content. Then you will learn that I, the Lord, am your God."' And so it came about: quails flew up in the evening, and they covered the camp; in the morning there was a coating of dew all round the camp. When the coating of dew lifted, there on the surface of the desert was a thing delicate, powdery, as fine as hoarfrost on the ground. When they saw this, the sons of Israel said to one another, 'What is that?' not knowing what it was. 'That' said Moses to them 'is the bread the Lord gives you to eat.'

**Psalm 77:3-4.23-25.54. R. v.24**

*The Lord gave them bread from heaven.*

## Ephesians 4:17.20-24

I want to urge you in the name of the Lord, not to go on living the aimless kind of life that pagans live. Now that is hardly the way you have learnt from Christ, unless you failed to hear him properly when you were taught what the truth is in Jesus. You must give up your old way of life; you must put aside your old self, which gets corrupted by following illusory desires. Your mind must be renewed by a spiritual revolution so that you can put on the new self that has been created in God's way, in the goodness and holiness of the truth.

## John 6:24-35

When the people saw that neither Jesus nor his disciples were there, they got into boats and crossed to Capernaum to look for Jesus. When they found him on the other side, they said to him, 'Rabbi, when did you come here?' Jesus answered: 'I tell you most solemnly, you are not looking for me because you have seen the signs but because you had all the bread you wanted to eat. Do not work for food that cannot last, but work for food that endures to eternal life, the kind of food the Son of Man is offering you, for on him the Father, God himself, has set his seal.'

Then they said to him, 'What must we do if we are do the works that God wants?' Jesus gave them this answer, 'This is working for God: you must believe in the one he has sent.' So they said, 'What sign will you give to show us that we should believe in you? What work will you do? Our fathers had manna to eat in the desert; as scripture says: He gave them bread from heaven to eat.'

Jesus answered: 'I tell you most solemnly, it was not Moses who gave you bread from heaven, it is my Father who gives you the bread from heaven, the true bread; for the bread of God is that which comes down from heaven and gives life to the world.'

'Sir,' they said 'give us that bread always.' Jesus answered: 'I am the bread of life. He who comes to me will never be hungry; he who believes in me will never thirst.'

## Reflection

When Scripture speaks of 'bread', it can bring to mind not only physical food, but the experience of human hunger and contentment, as well as God's providence, spiritual nourishment, and the work of human hands. Pause to consider 'bread' in your life, including the deepest hungers and satisfactions of your heart; the blessings in your life and the work of your own hands.

Today's readings bring together all these dimensions. In John's Gospel Jesus reminds his listeners that the miraculous *manna* of the Exodus story is God's gift, given to strengthen them spiritually and physically. Amid harsh desert conditions the miracle serves to call the Israelites to trust God who feeds them with 'bread from heaven' (Psalm 77). Flowing from this sacred memory, something new and extraordinary is taking place for Jesus' listeners. The Father's gift come down from heaven and into the world to feed, nourish and give life, is Jesus himself, 'the bread of life'. To receive Jesus is to receive the Father, to be enlivened with the very life of God. As Catholics we hear in this Gospel a powerful summons to eucharistic faith.

# AUGUST
# 2
## MONDAY

**18th Week
in Ordinary Time
Green
or
St Eusebius of Vercelli,**
*bishop*
**(Optional, White)
St Peter Julian Eymard,**
*priest*
**(Optional, White)**

### Numbers 11:4-15

The sons of Israel began to wail, 'Who will give us meat to eat?' they said. 'Think of the fish we used to eat free in Egypt, the cucumbers, melons, leeks, onions and garlic! Here we are wasting away, stripped of everything; there is nothing but manna for us to look at!'

The manna was like coriander seed, and had the appearance of bdellium. The people went round gathering it, and ground it in a mill or crushed it with a pestle; it was then cooked in a pot and made into pancakes. It tasted like cake made with oil. When the dew fell on the camp at night-time, the manna fell with it.

Moses heard the people wailing, every family at the door of its tent. The anger of the Lord flared out, and Moses greatly worried over this. And he spoke to the Lord: …
*(See Appendix B-22)*

### Psalm 80:12-17. R. v.2
*Ring out your joy to God our strength.*

### Matthew 14:13-21

When Jesus received the news of John the Baptist's death he withdrew by boat to a lonely place where they could be by themselves. But the people heard of this and, leaving the towns, went after him on foot. So as he stepped ashore he saw a large crowd; and he took pity on them and healed their sick.

When evening came, the disciples went to him and said, 'This is a lonely place, and the time has slipped by; so send the people away, and they can go to the villages to buy themselves some food.' Jesus replied, 'There is no need for them to go: give them something to eat yourselves.' But they answered, 'All we have with us is five loaves and two fish.' 'Bring them here to me,' he said. He gave orders that the people were to sit down on the grass; then he took the five loaves and the two fish, raised his eyes to heaven and said the blessing. And breaking the loaves he handed them to his disciples who gave them to the crowds. They all ate as much as they wanted, and they collected the scraps remaining, twelve baskets full. Those who ate numbered about five thousand men, to say nothing of women and children.

### Reflection

The burden of leadership weighs heavily on Moses. He cries out to the Lord for help, likening his dilemma to a woman fatigued by the demands of childbearing, breastfeeding and whinging children. In the Gospel we see Jesus also struggling with the demands of his mission, unable to withdraw from the crowds, such is their hunger for healing, hope and food. Both readings depict the complexities of the life of faith. Assailed as we are by complaint, fatigue, frustration, grief and anxiety, there is still to be found blessing, miracle, divine presence and wondrous events. As Christians, we don't seek an easy life but life lived with hearts open to God and hands ready to serve. Fed by the bread of life, we are to be 'bread for the world'.

## Numbers 12:1-13

Miriam, and Aaron too, spoke against Moses in connection with the Cushite woman he had taken. (For he had married a Cushite woman. ) They said, 'Has the Lord spoken to Moses only? Has he not spoken to us too?' The Lord heard this. Now Moses was the most humble of men, the humblest man on earth.

Suddenly, the Lord said to Moses and Aaron and Miriam 'Come, all three of you, to the Tent of Meeting.' They went, all three of them, and the Lord came down in a pillar of cloud and stood at the entrance of the Tent. ...
*(See Appendix B-23)*

## Psalm 50:3-7.12-13. R. cf. v.3

*Have mercy on us, Lord, for we have sinned.*

## Matthew 14:22-36

Jesus made the disciples get into the boat and go on ahead to the other side while he would send the crowds away. After sending the crowds away he went up into the hills by himself to pray. When evening came, he was there alone, while the boat, by now far out on the lake, was battling with a heavy sea, for there was a head-wind. In the fourth watch of the night he went towards them, walking on the lake, and when the disciples saw him walking on the lake they were terrified. 'It is a ghost' they said, and cried out in fear. But at once Jesus called out to them, saying, 'Courage! It is I! Do not be afraid.' It was Peter who answered. 'Lord,' he said 'if it is you, tell me to come to you across the water.' 'Come' said Jesus. Then Peter got out of the boat and started walking towards Jesus across the water, but as soon as he felt the force of the wind, he took fright and began to sink. 'Lord! Save me!' he cried. Jesus put out his hand at once and held him. 'Man of little faith,' he said 'why did you doubt?' And as they got into the boat the wind dropped. The men in the boat bowed down before him and said, 'Truly, you are the Son of God.'

Having made the crossing, they came to land at Gennesaret. When the local people recognised him they spread the news through the whole neighbourhood and took all that were sick to him, begging him just to let them touch the fringe of his cloak. And all those who touched it were completely cured.

## Reflection

Who is a person of faith? Someone who has no doubts about God? Constantly trusting, loving, praying? Rather, like St Peter, sometimes we walk on water; next minute we are sinking in the sea. Like Miriam and Aaron, sometimes we are cooperative leaders; next minute we are squabbling siblings. Flawed and faithful, we are ever mindful of God's mercy. Indeed, the life of faith is often about *remembering* those times we walked on water. Such memories help us as we struggle through times when it seems like we're drowning. Healthy attitudes, good habits, and daily rituals can strengthen our resolve and anchor our commitment. Most importantly, we need community: good people of faith who will 'hold' us within the body of Christ, and love us from that place, whether or not we are our best selves.

**18th Week
in Ordinary Time
St Dominic,** *priest*
**Memorial
White**

**18th Week
in Ordinary Time**
St John Vianney, priest
Memorial
White

**Numbers 13:1-2.25–14:1.26-29.34-35**

The Lord spoke to Moses in the wilderness of Paran and said, 'Send out men, one from each tribe, to make a reconnaissance of this land of Canaan which I am giving to the sons of Israel. Send the leader of each tribe.' At the end of forty days, they came back from their reconnaissance of the land. They sought out Moses, Aaron and the whole community of Israel, in the wilderness of Paran, at Kadesh. They made their report to them, and to the whole community, and showed them the produce of the country.

They told them this story, 'We went into the land to which you sent us. It does indeed flow with milk and honey; this is its produce. At the same time, its inhabitants are a powerful people; the towns are fortified and very big; yes, and we saw the descendants of Anak there. The Amalekite holds the Negeb area, the Hittite, Amorite and Jebusite the highlands, and the Canaanite the sea coast and the banks of the Jordan.'

Caleb harangued the people gathered about Moses: 'We must march in,' he said 'and conquer this land: we are well able to do it.' … *(See Appendix B-23)*

**Psalm 105:6-7.13-14.21-23. R. v.4**

*O Lord, remember me out of the love you have for your people.* (or *Alleluia!*)

**Matthew 15:21-28**

Jesus left Gennesaret and withdrew to the region of Tyre and Sidon. Then out came a Canaanite woman from that district and started shouting, 'Sir, Son of David, take pity on me. My daughter is tormented by a devil.' But he answered her not a word. And his disciples went and pleaded with him. 'Give her what she wants,' they said 'because she is shouting after us.' He said in reply, 'I was sent only to the lost sheep of the House of Israel.' But the woman had come up and was kneeling at his feet. 'Lord,' she said 'help me.' He replied, 'It is not fair to take the children's food and throw it to the house-dogs.' She retorted, 'Ah yes, sir, but even house-dogs can eat the scraps that fall from their master's table.' Then Jesus answered her, 'Woman, you have great faith. Let your wish be granted.' And from that moment her daughter was well again.

**Reflection**

The story of the scouts (first reading) can be interpreted as a failure of nerve as the Israelites draw near to the promised land. Their dilemma is ours. Should we step out, or retreat? Enter the unknown, or stay within familiar terrain? Is this what God wants of us? Are we ready? We may never be sure. Yet risk-taking is part of the journey of faith. In today's Gospel we see Jesus himself pulled beyond his comfort zone. He is clear about his mission: he is sent first to his own people. But the Canaanite woman challenges him to engage, right now, with herself, a foreigner, and Jesus accepts this challenge. What a lesson for us when we feel secure in our ordered worldview! Can we be responsive to those who unsettle and stretch us?

## Numbers 20:1-13

The sons of Israel, the whole community, arrived in the first month at the desert of Zin. The people settled at Kadesh. It was there that Miriam died and was buried.

There was no water for the community, and they were all united against Moses and Aaron. The people challenged Moses: 'We would rather have died,' they said 'as our brothers died before the Lord! Why did you bring the assembly of the Lord into this wilderness, only to let us die here, ourselves and our cattle? Why did you lead us out of Egypt, only to bring us to this wretched place? It is a place unfit for sowing, it has no figs, no vines, no pomegranates, and there is not even water to drink!'
*(See Appendix B-23)*

**18th Week
in Ordinary Time
Green
or
Dedication of the
Basilica of St Mary Major
(Optional, White)**

## Psalm 94:1-2.6-9. R. v.8

*O that today you would listen to his voice! 'Harden not your hearts.'*

## Matthew 16:13-23

When Jesus came to the region of Caesarea Philippi he put this question to his disciples, 'Who do people say the Son of Man is?' And they said, 'Some say he is John the Baptist, some Elijah, and others Jeremiah or one of the prophets.' 'But you,' he said 'who do you say I am?' Then Simon Peter spoke up, 'You are the Christ,' he said 'the Son of the living God.' Jesus replied, 'Simon son of Jonah, you are a happy man! Because it was not flesh and blood that revealed this to you but my Father in heaven. So I now say to you: You are Peter and on this rock I will build my Church. And the gates of the underworld can never hold out against it. I will give you the keys of the kingdom of heaven; whatever you bind on earth shall be considered bound in heaven; whatever you loose on earth shall be considered loosed in heaven.' Then he gave the disciples strict orders not to tell anyone that he was the Christ.

From that time Jesus began to make it clear to his disciples that he was destined to go to Jerusalem and suffer grievously at the hands of the elders and chief priests and scribes, to be put to death and to be raised up on the third day. Then, taking him aside, Peter started to remonstrate with him. 'Heaven preserve you, Lord,' he said 'this must not happen to you.' But he turned and said to Peter, 'Get behind me, Satan! You are an obstacle in my path, because the way you think is not God's way but man's.'

## Reflection

Today we hear of a crisis point for Moses' leadership. Miriam dies, and the people are without water. While their thirst-driven complaints are not new, Miriam's death appears to unhinge Moses. He responds badly, with serious consequences, showing that he no longer has what it takes to lead God's people. Meanwhile, the Gospel depicts a critical turning point in the life of Jesus. 'Who do you say I am?' he asks his disciples. The dramatic geographical backdrop for this question is Caesarea Philippi, a place associated with mighty powers, both pagan and political. Peter's inspired answer cuts through, revealing the true face of power and authority: 'You are the Christ, the Son of the living God'. Confronted by many demands that can unhinge us as Christian disciples, may we discern the lifegiving presence of the risen Christ.

**Transfiguration
of the Lord**
Feast
White

Daniel 7:9-10.13-14
*(See Appendix B–24)*

Psalm 96:1-2.5-6.9. R. vv. 1.9
*The Lord is king, most high above all the earth.*

2 Peter 1:16-19
It was not any cleverly invented myths that we were repeating when we brought you the knowledge of the power and the coming of our Lord Jesus Christ; we had seen his majesty for ourselves. He was honoured and glorified by God the Father, when the Sublime Glory itself spoke to him and said, 'This is my Son, the Beloved; he enjoys my favour.' We heard this ourselves, spoken from heaven, when we were with him on the holy mountain.

So we have confirmation of what was said in prophecies; and you will be right to depend on prophecy and take it as a lamp for lighting a way through the dark until the dawn comes and the morning star rises in your minds.

Mark 9:2-10
Jesus took with him Peter and James and John and led them up a high mountain where they could be alone by themselves. There in their presence he was transfigured; his clothes became dazzlingly white, whiter than any earthly bleacher could make them. Elijah appeared to them with Moses; and they were talking with Jesus. Then Peter spoke to Jesus: 'Rabbi,' he said 'it is wonderful for us to be here; so let's make three tents, one for you, one for Moses and one for Elijah.' He did not know what to say; they were so frightened. And a cloud came, covering them in shadow; and there came a voice from the cloud, 'This is my Son, the Beloved. Listen to him.' Then suddenly, when they looked round, they saw no one with them any more but only Jesus.

As they came down the mountain he warned them to tell no one what they had seen, until after the Son of Man had risen from the dead. They observed the warning faithfully, though among themselves they discussed what 'rising from the dead' could mean.

### Reflection
At the Transfiguration the disciples glimpse the glory that belongs to Jesus in his unique relationship with the Father. It is a manifestation that takes the disciples beyond what they know and points to future events. At the same time, the Transfiguration affirms what has gone before in salvation history. The transfigured Jesus converses intently with Moses and Elijah, towering biblical figures representing the two great pillars of Judaism: the Law and the Prophets. In his personal identity Jesus is both the Son of God and 'an authentic son of Israel' (St John Paul II). In our own lives, God's grace does not obliterate our human identity, but reveals its deepest truth. In the words of St Irenaeus, 'The glory of God is a human being fully alive'!

## Deuteronomy 6:4-13

Moses said to the people: 'Listen, Israel: the Lord our God is the one Lord. You shall love the Lord your God with all your heart, with all your soul, with all your strength. Let these words I urge on you today be written on your heart. You shall repeat them to your children and say them over to them whether at rest in your house or walking abroad, at your lying down or at your rising; you shall fasten them on your hands as a sign and on your forehead as a circlet; you shall write them on the doorposts of your house and on your gates.

'When the Lord has brought you into the land which he swore to your fathers Abraham, Isaac and Jacob that he would give you, with great and prosperous cities not of your building, houses full of good things not furnished by you, wells you did not dig, vineyards and olives you did not plant, when you have eaten these and had your fill, then take care you do not forget the Lord who brought you out of the land of Egypt, out of the house of slavery. You must fear the Lord your God, you must serve him, by his name you must swear.'

## Psalm 17:2-4.47.51. R. v.2

*I love you, Lord, my strength.*

## Matthew 17:14-20

A man came up to Jesus and went down on his knees before him. 'Lord,' he said 'take pity on my son: he is a lunatic and in a wretched state; he is always falling into the fire or into the water. I took him to your disciples and they were unable to cure him.' 'Faithless and perverse generation!' Jesus said in reply. 'How much longer must I be with you? How much longer must I put up with you? Bring him here to me.' And when Jesus rebuked it the devil came out of the boy who was cured from that moment.

Then the disciples came privately to Jesus. 'Why were we unable to cast it out?' they asked. He answered, 'Because you have little faith. I tell you solemnly, if your faith were the size of a mustard seed you could say to this mountain "Move from here to there", and it would move; nothing would be impossible for you.'

## Reflection

Jesus issues a strong critique for a 'faithless generation' and for his own disciples who 'have little faith'. In keeping with the words of Moses (first reading), this Gospel reminds us that faith is not something we can 'measure' by works, possessions or achievements. Rather, it is our willingness to wholeheartedly love and trust God in every breath and at every step. It is easy to forget this. We can be tempted to judge the faith of people by certain worldly standards masked by a veneer of piety, making calculations based on religious productivity or theological knowledge. The psalmist sums up the authentic voice of faith: 'I love you, Lord, my strength' (Psalm 17). From this fundamental orientation all moral power and good works flow.

**18th Week
in Ordinary Time
Green
or
St Sixtus II, *pope*, and
companions, *martyrs*
(Optional, Red)
St Cajetan, *priest*
(Optional, White)**

## AUGUST

# 8

### SUNDAY

**19th Sunday
in Ordinary Time
Psalter Week 3
White**

**1 Kings 19:4-8**
Elijah went into the wilderness, a day's journey, and sitting under a furze bush wished he were dead. 'Lord', he said 'I have had enough. Take my life; I am no better than my ancestors.' Then he lay down and went to sleep. But an angel touched him and said, 'Get up and eat.' He looked round, and there at his head was a scone baked on hot stones, and a jar of water. He ate and drank and then lay down again. But the angel of the Lord came back a second time and touched him and said, 'Get up and eat, or the journey will be too long for you.' So he got up and ate and drank, and strengthened by that food he walked for forty days and forty nights until he reached Horeb, the mountain of God.

**Psalm 33:2-9**
*Taste and see that the Lord is good.*

**Ephesians 4:30-5:2**
Do not grieve the Holy Spirit of God who has marked you with his seal for you to be set free when the day comes. Never have grudges against others, or lose your temper, or raise your voice to anybody, or call each other names, or allow any sort of spitefulness. Be friends with one another, and kind, forgiving each other as readily as God forgave you in Christ.

Try, then, to imitate God, as children of his that he loves, and follow Christ by loving as he loved you, giving himself up in our place as a fragrant offering and a sacrifice to God.

**John 6:41-51**
The Jews were complaining to each other about Jesus, because he had said, 'I am the bread that came down from heaven.' 'Surely this is Jesus son of Joseph' they said. 'We know his father and mother. How can he now say, "I have come down from heaven"?' Jesus said in reply, 'Stop complaining to each other.

'No one can come to me unless he is drawn by the Father who sent me, and I will raise him up at the last day. It is written in the prophets: They will all be taught by God, and to hear the teaching of the Father, and learn from it, is to come to me. Not that anybody has seen the Father, except the one who comes from God: he has seen the Father. I tell you most solemnly, everybody who believes has eternal life. I am the bread of life. Your fathers ate the manna in the desert and they are dead; but this is the bread that comes down from heaven, so that a man may eat it and not die. I am the living bread which has come down from heaven. Anyone who eats this bread will live for ever; and the bread that I shall give is my flesh, for the life of the world.'

## Reflection

The Liturgy of the Word invites us to focus on Jesus who continues to draw us to Himself so that we can be nourished and strengthened like Elijah in the desert. Jesus chose to be the bread and wine to be in communion with humanity. Those who partake in the consumption of the body and blood of Christ establish a close relationship with him. Hence to eat of Christ's body and drink of His blood is to share in His life.

## AUGUST

# 9

## MONDAY

**St Theresa Benedicta of the Cross,** *virgin, martyr*
**Feast**
**Red**

### Hosea 2:16.17.21-22

The Lord says this:

I am going to lead her out into the wilderness and speak to her heart. There she will respond to me as she did when she was young, as she did when she came out of the land of Egypt. I will betroth you to myself for ever, betroth you with integrity and justice, with tenderness and love; I will betroth you to myself with faithfulness, and you will come to know the Lord.

### Psalm 44:11-12.14-17. R. v.11

*Listen, O daughter, give ear to my words.*

### Matthew 25:1-13

Jesus told this parable to his disciples: 'The kingdom of heaven will be like this: Ten bridesmaids took their lamps and went to meet the bridegroom. Five of them were foolish and five were sensible: the foolish ones did take their lamps, but they brought no oil, whereas the sensible ones took flasks of oil as well as their lamps. The bridegroom was late, and they all grew drowsy and fell asleep. But at midnight there was a cry, "The bridegroom is here! Go out and meet him." At this, all those bridesmaids woke up and trimmed their lamps, and the foolish ones said to the sensible ones, "Give us some of your oil: our lamps are going out." But they replied, "There may not be enough for us and for you; you had better go to those who sell it and buy some for yourselves." They had gone off to buy it when the bridegroom arrived. Those who were ready went in with him to the wedding hall and the door was closed. The other bridesmaids arrived later. "Lord, Lord," they said "open the door for us." But he replied, "I tell you solemnly, I do not know you." So stay awake, because you do not know either the day or the hour.'

### Reflection

Today's Gospel reminds us to make use of every opportunity that life offers and to be ever-prepared in receiving the coming of the Lord. The unpreparedness of the foolish virgins costs them dearly. The Lord offers many opportunities to deepen our faith, strengthen our relationships, etc. Saint Teresa Benedicta of the Cross, whom we celebrate today, received the oil of faith from the writings of Saint Teresa of Avila and kept her lamp of faith burning until her martyrdom. Let us keep our lamps ever ready to meet the Lord!

**St Lawrence,** *deacon, martyr*
**Feast**
**Red**

### 2 Corinthians 9:6-10

Do not forget: thin sowing means thin reaping; the more you sow, the more you reap. Each one should give what he has decided in his own mind, not grudgingly or because he is made to, for God loves a cheerful giver. And there is no limit to the blessings which God can send you – he will make sure that you will always have all you need for yourselves in every possible circumstance, and still have something to spare for all sorts of good works. As scripture says: He was free in almsgiving, and gave to the poor: his good deeds will never be forgotten.

The one who provides seed for the sower and bread for food will provide you with all the seed you want and make the harvest of your good deeds a larger one.

### Psalm 111:1-2.5-9. R. v.5

*Happy the merciful who give to those in need.*

### John 12:24-26

Jesus said to his disciples: 'I tell you, most solemnly, unless a wheat grain falls on the ground and dies, it remains only a single grain; but if it dies, it yields a rich harvest. Anyone who loves his life loses it; anyone who hates his life in this world will keep it for the eternal life. If a man serves me, he must follow me, wherever I am, my servant will be there too. If anyone serves me, my Father will honour him.'

### Reflection

Seed sown in the ground, dying to give way to a harvest which becomes lifegiving bread, is a fitting image for the feast of a martyr. The cycle of dying and rising is familiar to each of us as we go through life, experiencing both suffering and joy. It is never easy, and at times we are tempted to lose hope. Yet, as Pope Francis is fond of saying, we believe in 'the God of surprises'. We trust in the testimony of Scripture and the witness of the saints, that even in the darkest of nights there flickers a tiny flame, lighting our way and calling us on: another step, and one more, until we are moving again, and rediscovering the One who walks with us.

**19th Week
in Ordinary Time
St Clare, *virgin*
Memorial
White**

### Deuteronomy 34:1-12

Leaving the plains of Moab, Moses went up Mount Nebo, the peak of Pisgah opposite Jericho, and the Lord showed him the whole land; Gilead as far as Dan, all Naphtali, the land of Ephraim and Manasseh, all the land of Judah as far as the Western Sea, the Negeb, and the stretch of the Valley of Jericho, city of palm trees, as far as Zoar. The Lord said to him, 'This is the land I swore to give to Abraham, Isaac and Jacob, saying: I will give it to your descendants. I have let you see it with your own eyes, but you shall not cross into it.' There in the land of Moab, Moses the servant of the Lord died as the Lord decreed; he buried him in the valley, in the land of Moab, opposite Beth-peor; but to this day no one has ever found his grave. Moses was a hundred and twenty years old when he died, his eye undimmed, his vigour unimpaired. The sons of Israel wept for Moses in the plains of Moab for thirty days. The days of weeping for the mourning rites of Moses came to an end. Joshua son of Nun was filled with the spirit of wisdom, for Moses had laid his hands on him. It was he that the sons of Israel obeyed, carrying out the order that the Lord had given to Moses.

Since then, never has there been such a prophet in Israel as Moses, the man the Lord knew face to face. What signs and wonders the Lord caused him to perform in the land of Egypt against Pharaoh and all his servants and his whole land! How mighty the hand and great the fear that Moses wielded in the sight of all Israel!

### Psalm 65:1-3.5.16-17. R. cf. vv. 20.9

*Blessed be God, who gave life to my soul.*

### Matthew 18:15-20

Jesus said to his disciples: 'If your brother does something wrong, go and have it out with him alone, between your two selves. If he listens to you, you have won back your brother. If he does not listen, take one or two others along with you: the evidence of two or three witnesses is required to sustain any charge. But if he refuses to listen to these, report it to the community; and if he refuses to listen to the community, treat him like a pagan or a tax collector.

'I tell you solemnly, whatever you bind on earth shall be considered bound in heaven; whatever you loose on earth shall be considered loosed in heaven.

'I tell you solemnly once again, if two of you on earth agree to ask anything at all, it will be granted to you by my Father in heaven. For where two or three meet in my name, I shall be there with them.'

### Reflection

Our God works marvellous deeds! (cf. Psalm 65: 3) And God enlists our participation in these works. Thus, Scripture speaks not only of God, but of God's partners: creation, individuals, families, the people of Israel, and the emerging Christian communities. Both today's first reading and Gospel highlight the role of the community in our relationship with God. Just as the time came for Moses to surrender his leadership to Joshua in order for God to continue to lead the people forward, so must we as Christians think and act and pray with the life of the community in mind. We come to the Lord not as lone-ranger activists, but as members of the body of Christ.

**19th Week
in Ordinary Time
Green
or
St Jane Frances de
Chantal, *religious*
(Optional, White)**

## Joshua 3:7-11.13-17

The Lord said to Joshua, 'This very day I will begin to make you a great man in the eyes of all Israel, to let them be sure that I am going to be with you even as I was with Moses. As for you, give this order to the priests carrying the ark of the covenant: "When you have reached the brink of the waters of the Jordan, you are to stand still in the Jordan itself."' ...
*(See Appendix B-24)*

## Psalm 113A: 1-6

*Alleluia!*

## Matthew 18:21–19:1

Peter went up to Jesus and said, 'Lord, how often must I forgive my brother if he wrongs me? As often as seven times?' Jesus answered, 'Not seven, I tell you, but seventy-seven times.

'And so the kingdom of heaven may be compared to a king who decided to settle his accounts with his servants. When the reckoning began, they brought him a man who owed ten thousand talents; but he had no means of paying, so his master gave orders that he should be sold, together with his wife and children and all his possessions, to meet the debt. At this, the servant threw himself down at his master's feet. "Give me time" he said "and I will pay the whole sum." And the servant's master felt so sorry for him that he let him go and cancelled the debt. Now as this servant went out, he happened to meet a fellow servant who owed him one hundred denarii; and he seized him by the throat and began to throttle him. "Pay what you owe me" he said. His fellow servant fell at his feet and implored him, saying, "Give me time and I will pay you." But the other would not agree; on the contrary, he had him thrown into prison till he should pay the debt. His fellow servants were deeply distressed when they saw what had happened, and they went to their master and reported the whole affair to him. Then the master sent for him. "You wicked servant," he said. "I cancelled all that debt of yours when you appealed to me. Were you not bound, then, to have pity on your fellow servant just as I had pity on you?" And in his anger the master handed him over to the torturers till he should pay all his debt. And that is how my heavenly Father will deal with you unless you each forgive your brother from your heart.'

Jesus had now finished what he wanted to say, and he left Galilee and came into the part of Judaea which is on the far side of the Jordan.

### Reflection

Under Joshua's leadership, the Jordan waters part, and 'the whole nation' of Israelites cross into the promised land. This climactic image of homecoming has powerful currency for the Church. It fires the Christian imagination to view redemption through Christ as the journey from the slavery of sin into the freedom of right relations with God, from the wilderness of fear to the security of God's forgiveness and peace. Viewed from the perspective of Christian discipleship, reconciliation with God and one another is a journey of faithful steps, compassionate choices, merciful actions repeated 'seventy-seven times' (i.e., continually). God journeys with us as we walk the way of Christ, guided by the Holy Spirit, in the company of the saints.

**19th Week
in Ordinary Time**
Green
or
**Sts Pontian, *pope*, and
Hippolytus, *priest*,
*martyrs***
(Optional, Red)

## Joshua 24:1-13

Joshua gathered all the tribes of Israel together at Shechem; then he called the elders, leaders, judges and scribes of Israel, and they presented themselves before God. Then Joshua said to all the people:

'The Lord the God of Israel says this, "In ancient days your ancestors lived beyond the River – such was Terah the father of Abraham and of Nahor – and they served other gods. Then I brought your father Abraham from beyond the River and led him through all the land of Canaan. I increased his descendants and gave him Isaac. To Isaac I gave Jacob and Esau. To Esau I gave the mountain country of Seir as his possession. Jacob and his sons went down into Egypt. Then I sent Moses and Aaron and plagued Egypt with the wonders that I worked there. …
*(See Appendix B-24)*

## Psalm 135:1-3.16-18.21-22.24

*O give thanks to the Lord for he is good.*

## Matthew 19:3-12

Some Pharisees approached Jesus, and to test him they said, 'Is it against the Law for a man to divorce his wife on any pretext whatever?' He answered, 'Have you not read that the creator from the beginning made them male and female and that he said: This is why a man must leave father and mother, and cling to his wife, and the two become one body? They are no longer two, therefore, but one body. So then, what God has united, man must not divide.'

They said to him, 'Then why did Moses command that a writ of dismissal should be given in cases of divorce?' 'It was because you were so unteachable' he said 'that Moses allowed you to divorce your wives, but it was not like this from the beginning. Now I say this to you: the man who divorces his wife – I am not speaking of fornication – and marries another, is guilty of adultery.'

The disciples said to him, 'If that is how things are between husband and wife, it is not advisable to marry.' But he replied, 'It is not everyone who can accept what I have said, but only those to whom it is granted. There are eunuchs born that way from their mother's womb, there are eunuchs made so by men and there are eunuchs who have made themselves that way for the sake of the kingdom of heaven. Let anyone accept this who can.'

## Reflection

Think back over your life. Can you see the hand of God at work? Do you recognise your maturation over time? In today's first reading, Joshua remembers the great events and personalities of Israel's history. His listeners are not the Hebrew slaves who left Egypt but a new generation of Israelites; they need to hear their ancestral story! In the Gospel, too, we find Jesus remembering and interpreting his people's biblical story. He affirms that marriage was ordained at creation, while acknowledging that, in a different time and place, Moses taught in a way that responded to the needs of the people under his care. Jesus himself teaches boldly in a way that takes his listeners forward. In our own journey, are we willing to remember, grow and change as the Holy Spirit leads?

## Joshua 24:14-29

Joshua said to all the people: 'Fear the Lord and serve him perfectly and sincerely; put away the gods that your ancestors served beyond the River and in Egypt, and serve the Lord. But if you will not serve the Lord, choose today whom you wish to serve, whether the gods that your ancestors served beyond the River, or the gods of the Amorites in whose land you are now living. As for me in my House, we will serve the Lord.'

The people answered, 'We have no intention of deserting the Lord and serving other gods! Was it not the Lord our God who brought us and our ancestors out of the land of Egypt, the house of slavery, who worked those great wonders before our eyes and preserved us all along the way we travelled and among all the peoples through whom we journeyed? What is more, the Lord drove all those peoples out before us, as well as the Amorites who used to live in this country. We too will serve the Lord, for he is our God.'

**19th Week
in Ordinary Time
St Maximilian Kolbe,
*priest, martyr*
Memorial
Red**

Then Joshua said to the people, 'You cannot serve the Lord, because he is a holy God, he is a jealous God who will not forgive your transgressions or your sins. If you desert the Lord to follow alien gods he in turn will afflict and destroy you after the goodness he has shown you.' The people answered Joshua, 'No, it is the Lord we wish to serve.' Then Joshua said to the people, 'You are witnesses against yourselves that you have chosen the Lord, to serve him.' They answered, 'We are witnesses.' 'Then cast away the alien gods among you and give your hearts to the Lord the God of Israel!' The people answered Joshua, 'It is the Lord our God we choose to serve; it is his voice that we will obey.' *(See Appendix B-25)*

## Psalm 15:1-2.5.7-8.11. R. cf. v.5
*You are my inheritance, O Lord.*

## Matthew 19:13-15

People brought little children to Jesus, for him to lay his hands on them and say a prayer. The disciples turned them away, but Jesus said, 'Let the little children alone, and do not stop them coming to me; for it is to such as these that the kingdom of heaven belongs.' Then he laid his hands on them and went on his way.

## Reflection

Do today's readings strike you as contradictory? Joshua's long speech, a serious testing of the Israelites' allegiance to God, sounds very different to Jesus' brief exhortation to 'Let the little children come to me.' The first case depicts obedience to God as a difficult challenge. Not to be pursued lightly! Yet, in the Gospel, the path to Jesus is portrayed as uncomplicated, inviting, easy for a mere child. Which, then, best describes the path of faith? How about both! Often we experience the call of discipleship as sobering, difficult. At other times, Christian life is simply delightful. We need not be surprised at this. The faith journey is as complex as human beings and life itself. Religious teachings and traditional practices firmly anchor our course, while the open hearts of mere children also show us the way.

**The Assumption of the
Blessed Virgin Mary
Solemnity
Psalter Week 4
White**

**Apocalypse 11:19; 12:1-6.10**
The sanctuary of God in heaven opened, and the ark of the covenant could be seen inside it.

Now a great sign appeared in heaven: a woman, adorned with the sun, standing on the moon, and with the twelve stars on her head for a crown. She was pregnant, and in labour, crying aloud in the pangs of childbirth. Then a second sign appeared in the sky, a huge red dragon which had seven heads and ten horns, and each of the seven heads crowned with a coronet. Its tail dragged a third of the stars from the sky and dropped them to the earth, and the dragon stopped in front of the woman as she was having the child, so that he could eat it as soon as it was born from its mother. The woman brought a male child into the world, the son who was to rule all the nations with an iron sceptre, and the child was taken straight up to God and to his throne, while the woman escaped into the desert, where God had made a place of safety ready. Then I heard a voice shout from heaven, 'Victory and power and empire for ever have been won by our God, and all authority for his Christ.'

**Psalm 44:10-12.16. R. v.10**
*On your right stands the queen, in garments of gold.*

**1 Corinthians 15:20-26**
Christ has been raised from the dead, the first-fruits of all who have fallen asleep. Death came through one man and in the same way the resurrection of the dead has come through one man. Just as all die in Adam, so all will be brought to life in Christ; but all of them in their proper order: Christ as the first-fruits and then, after the coming of Christ, those who belong to him. After that will come the end, when he hands over the kingdom to God the Father, having done away with every sovereignty, authority and power. For he must be king until he has put all his enemies under his feet and the last of the enemies to be destroyed is death, for everything is to be put under his feet.

**Luke 1:39-56**
Mary set out and went as quickly as she could to a town in the hill country of Judah. She went into Zechariah's house and greeted Elizabeth. Now as soon as Elizabeth heard Mary's greeting, the child leapt in her womb and Elizabeth was filled with the Holy Spirit. She gave a loud cry and said, 'Of all women you are the most blessed, and blessed is the fruit of your womb. Why should I be honoured with a visit from the mother of my Lord? For the moment your greeting reached my ears, the child in my womb leapt for

joy. Yes, blessed is she who believed that the promise made to her by the Lord would be fulfilled.'

And Mary said: 'My soul proclaims the greatness of the Lord and my spirit exults in God my saviour; because he has looked upon his lowly handmaid. Yes, from this day forward all generations will call me blessed, for the Almighty has done great things for me. Holy is his name, and his mercy reaches from age to age for those who fear him. He has shown the power of his arm, he has routed the proud of heart. He has pulled down princes from their thrones and exalted the lowly. The hungry he has filled with good things, the rich sent empty away. He has come to the help of Israel his servant, mindful of his mercy – according to the promise he made to our ancestors – of his mercy to Abraham and to his descendants for ever.'

Mary stayed with Elizabeth about three months and then went back home.

## Reflection

What do we Catholics mean when we express our conviction that, at the end of her earthly life, Mary was taken up body and soul into heavenly glory? Are we simply heaping praises upon Mary for her 'specialness'? Or is there something deeper at stake? In fact, like all Marian teachings, the Assumption speaks of the saving love of Christ that envelops our human lives. 'For the Son of God became human, so that we might become God' is a saying of the Church Fathers (cf. *Catechism*, 460). Mary, the 'first disciple' of Jesus Christ, walks with and before us in our own path of Christian discipleship. Her singular participation in her Son's resurrection is an anticipation of *our* resurrection. *Who Mary is, we are becoming.* One day we, too, will live forever with God in heavenly glory. The Assumption is a compelling celebration of Christian hope, an affirmation of the human body, and deep-down encouragement in our earthly struggles.

# AUGUST
# 16
## MONDAY

**20th Week
in Ordinary Time
Green
or
St Stephen of Hungary
(Optional, White)**

### Judges 2:11-19

The sons of Israel did what displeases the Lord and served the Baals. They deserted the Lord, the God of their ancestors, who had brought them out of the land of Egypt, and followed other gods from the gods of the peoples round them. They bowed down to these; they provoked the Lord; they deserted the Lord to serve Baal and Astarte. Then the Lord's anger flamed out against Israel. He handed them over to pillagers who plundered them; he delivered them to the enemies surrounding them, and they were not able to resist them. In every warlike venture, the hand of the Lord was there to foil them, as the Lord had warned, as the Lord had sworn to them. Thus he reduced them to dire distress.

Then the Lord appointed judges for them, and rescued the men of Israel from the hands of their plunderers. But they would not listen to their judges. They prostituted themselves to other gods, and bowed down before these. Very quickly they left the path their ancestors had trodden in obedience to the orders of the Lord; they did not follow their example. When the Lord appointed judges for them, the Lord was with the judge and rescued them from the hands of their enemies as long as the judge lived, for the Lord felt pity for them as they groaned under the iron grip of their oppressors. But once the judge was dead, they relapsed and behaved even worse than their ancestors. They followed other gods; they served them and bowed before them, and would not give up the practices and stubborn ways of their ancestors at all.

### Psalm 105:34-37.39-40.43-44. R. v.4

*O Lord, remember me out of the love you have for your people.*

### Matthew 19:16-22 *(See front cover of this book)*

There was a man who came to Jesus and asked, 'Master, what good deed must I do to possess eternal life?' Jesus said to him, 'Why do you ask me about what is good? There is one alone who is good. But if you wish to enter into life, keep the commandments.' He said, 'Which?' 'These,' Jesus replied. 'You must not kill. You must not commit adultery. You must not bring false witness. Honour your father and mother, and: You must love your neighbour as yourself.' The young man said to him, 'I have kept all these. What more do I need to do?' Jesus said, 'If you wish to be perfect, go and sell what you own and give the money to the poor, and you will have treasure in heaven; then come, follow me.' But when the young man heard these words he went away sad, for he was a man of great wealth.

### Reflection

Today's Gospel is the story of the restless searchings of a young man's heart. The rich young man senses a connection between the meaning of life and doing what is 'good'. His search draws him closer to the person of Jesus. The young man is attracted to 'the Good' because he is made in the image and likeness of 'the one alone who is good'. Sensitive to the young man's yearnings for more, Jesus challenges him to extend himself in an act of radical self-giving. Why did the young man go away sad? Because the answer is not what he expected? Because he was about to part with his many possessions? The Gospel does not actually tell us, but we are invited to explore its subtleties and possible interpretations.

**Judges 6:11-24**

The angel of the Lord came and sat under the terebinth at Ophrah which belonged to Joash of Abiezer. Gideon his son was threshing wheat inside the winepress to keep it hidden from Midian, when the angel of the Lord appeared to him and said, 'The Lord is with you, valiant warrior!' Gideon answered him, 'Forgive me, my lord, but if the Lord is with us, then why is it that all this is happening to us now? And where are all the wonders our ancestors tell us of when they say, "Did not the Lord bring us out of Egypt?" But now the Lord has deserted us; he has abandoned us to Midian.'

At this the Lord turned to him and said, 'Go in the strength now upholding you, and you will rescue Israel from the power of Midian. Do I not send you myself?' Gideon answered him, 'Forgive me, my lord, but how can I deliver Israel? My clan, you must know, is the weakest in Manasseh and I am the least important in my family.' The Lord answered him, 'I will be with you and you shall crush Midian as though it were a single man.' ...
*(See Appendix B-25)*

**20th Week
in Ordinary Time
Green
or
Our Lady of Knock
(Ireland – Memorial)**

**Psalm 84:9.11-14. R. v.9**
*The Lord speaks of peace to his people.*

**Matthew 19:23-30**

Jesus said to his disciples, 'I tell you solemnly, it will be hard for a rich man to enter the kingdom of heaven. Yes, I tell you again, it is easier for a camel to pass through the eye of a needle than for a rich man to enter the kingdom of heaven.' When the disciples heard this they were astonished. 'Who can be saved, then?' they said. Jesus gazed at them. 'For men' he told them 'this is impossible; for God everything is possible.'

Then Peter spoke. 'What about us?' he said to him. 'We have left everything and followed you. What are we to have, then?' Jesus said to him, 'I tell you solemnly, when all is made new and the Son of Man sits on his throne of glory, you will yourselves sit on twelve thrones to judge the twelve tribes of Israel. And everyone who has left houses, brothers, sisters, father, mother, children or land for the sake of my name will be repaid a hundred times over, and also inherit eternal life.

'Many who are first will be last, and the last, first.'

**Reflection**

We Christians have faith in Jesus Christ, who is 'God-with-us'. Yet often life feels like 'God-far-from-us'. We are like Gideon in today's first reading: 'If the Lord is with us, then why is all this [disaster] happening to us?' And Peter in the Gospel: 'What about us? We have left everything ... What are we to have?' Such questions need not suggest a lack of faith or resolve. It is normal and healthy to express to God our concerns and misgivings, our grief and anger. It signifies a real, authentic relationship. Even Mary questioned God's angel: 'How can this be ...?' In good times and bad, let us unhesitatingly come, honest and open, before God who wants to hear us; just as we in turn 'will hear what the Lord God has to say' (Psalm 84: 1).

**20th Week
in Ordinary Time
Green**

### Judges 9:6-15

All the leading men of Shechem and all Bethmillo gathered, and proclaimed Abimelech king by the terebinth of the pillar at Shechem.

News of this was brought to Jotham. He came and stood on the top of Mount Gerizim and shouted aloud for them to hear: 'Hear me, leaders of Shechem, that God may also hear you! One day the trees went out to anoint a king to rule over them. They said to the olive tree, "Be our king!" The olive tree answered them, "Must I forego my oil which gives honour to gods and men, to stand swaying above the trees?" ... *(See Appendix B-26)*

### Psalm 20:2-7. R. v.2

*O Lord, your strength gives joy to the king.*

### Matthew 20:1-16

Jesus said to his disciples: 'The kingdom of heaven is like a landowner going out at daybreak to hire workers for his vineyard. He made an agreement with the workers for one denarius a day, and sent them to his vineyard. Going out at about the third hour he saw others standing idle in the market place and said to them, "You go to my vineyard too and I will give you a fair wage." So they went. At about the sixth hour and again at about the ninth hour, he went out and did the same. Then at about the eleventh hour he went out and found more men standing round, and he said to them, "Why have you been standing here idle all day?" "Because no one has hired us" they answered. He said to them, "You go into my vineyard too." In the evening, the owner of the vineyard said to his bailiff, "Call the workers and pay them their wages, starting with the last arrivals and ending with the first." So those who were hired at about the eleventh hour came forward and received one denarius each. When the first came, they expected to get more, but they too received one denarius each. They took it, but grumbled at the landowner. "The men who came last" they said "have done only one hour, and you have treated them the same as us, though we have done a heavy day's work in all the heat." He answered one of them and said, "My friend, I am not being unjust to you; did we not agree on one denarius? Take your earnings and go. I choose to pay the last-comer as much as I pay you. Have I no right to do what I like with my own? Why be envious because I am generous?" Thus the last will be first, and the first, last.'

### Reflection

It may help to read today's Gospel in the context of Jesus' response to Peter (Matthew 19: 27-30). Peter has just said: *Hey, we've given up everything for you; what's in it for us?* To which Jesus tells the parable of the generous landowner whose employment practices are accused of being unfair. As Christians we like to think that our commitment flows from the pure motive of following Christ. And, at some level, it probably does. But, like Peter, we are also prone to seeking personal reward and comparing ourselves with others. Have you ever felt envious at seeing someone reap benefits, wages, prizes or praises which you believe you deserve? If so, Jesus' parable is for you! As it was for Peter, a great apostle and saint.

## Judges 11:29-39

The spirit of the Lord came on Jephthah, who crossed Gilead and Manasseh, passed through to Mizpah in Gilead and from Mizpah in Gilead made his way to the rear of the Ammonites. And Jephthah made a vow to the Lord, 'If you deliver the Ammonites into my hands, then the first person to meet me from the door of my house when I return in triumph from fighting the Ammonites shall belong to the Lord, and I will offer him up as a holocaust.' Jephthah marched against the Ammonites to attack them, and the Lord delivered them into his power. He harassed them from Aroer almost to Minnith (twenty towns) and to Abel-keramim. It was a very severe defeat, and the Ammonites were humbled before the Israelites.
(See Appendix B-26)

## Psalm 39:5.7-10. R. vv. 8-9

*Here I am, Lord! I come to do your will.*

## Matthew 22:1-14

Jesus began to speak to the chief priests and the elders of the people in parables, 'The kingdom of heaven may be compared to a king who gave a feast for his son's wedding.

He sent his servants to call those who had been invited, but they would not come. Next he sent some more servants. "Tell those who have been invited" he said "that I have my banquet all prepared, my oxen and fattened cattle have been slaughtered, everything is ready. Come to the wedding." But they were not interested: one went off to his farm, another to his business, and the rest seized his servants, maltreated them and killed them. The king was furious. He despatched his troops, destroyed those murderers and burnt their town. Then he said to his servants, "The wedding is ready; but as those who were invited proved to be unworthy, go to the crossroads in the town and invite everyone you can find to the wedding." So these servants went out on to the roads and collected together everyone they could find, bad and good alike, and the wedding hall was filled with guests. When the king came in to look at the guests he noticed one man who was not wearing a wedding garment, and said to him, "How did you get in here, my friend, without a wedding garment?" And the man was silent. Then the king said to the attendants, "Bind him hand and foot and throw him out into the dark, where there will be weeping and grinding of teeth." For many are called, but few are chosen.'

## Reflection

When God sends invitations and opportunities my way, I'd better be ready to respond with an unreserved 'Yes'! That's one interpretation of today's Gospel. In Scripture, the wedding banquet is a messianic image. The reign of God is a personal summons to each of us: Come to the feast! This is not the time for lame excuses or half-hearted appearances. God wants me there, now! We are to be dressed and ready, an active participant saying, 'Here am I, Lord: I come to do your will' (Psalm 39). Can you feel the urgent demand of this teaching on discipleship? Very different from the 'come as you are' message we hear in other parts of Scripture. We need *all* of Scripture to grasp the fullness of what it means to follow Christ and walk in God's ways.

**20th Week in Ordinary Time**
**Green**
**or**
**St John Eudes,** *priest*
**(Optional, White)**

**20th Week
in Ordinary Time**
St Bernard, *abbot,
doctor*
Memorial
White

## Ruth 1:1.3-6.14-16.22

In the days of the Judges famine came to the land and a certain man from Bethlehem of Judah went – he, his wife and his two sons – to live in the country of Moab. Elimelech, Naomi's husband, died, and she and her two sons were left. These married Moabite women: one was named Orpah and the other Ruth. They lived there about ten years. Then both Mahlon and Chilion also died and the woman was bereft of her two sons and her husband. So she and her daughters-in-law prepared to return from the country of Moab, for she had heard that the Lord had visited his people and given them food. Then Orpah kissed her mother-in-law and went back to her people. But Ruth clung to her.

Naomi said to her, 'Look, your sister-in-law has gone back to her people and to her god. You must return too; follow your sister-in-law.' But Ruth said, 'Do not press me to leave you and turn back from your company, for 'wherever you go, I will go, wherever you live, I will live. Your people shall be my people, and your God, my God.'

This was how Naomi, she who returned from the country of Moab, came back with Ruth the Moabitess her daughter-in-law. And they came to Bethlehem at the beginning of the barley harvest.

## Psalm 145:5-10. R. v.2
*My soul, give praise to the Lord.*

## Matthew 22:34-40

When the Pharisees heard that Jesus had silenced the Sadducees they got together and, to disconcert him, one of them put a question, 'Master, which is the greatest commandment of the Law?' Jesus said, 'You must love the Lord your God with all your heart, with all your soul, and with all your mind. This is the greatest and the first commandment. The second resembles it: you must love your neighbour as yourself. On these two commandments hang the whole Law, and the Prophets also.'

## Reflection

'To love another person is to see the face of God' (*Les Miserables*). From ancient times, love of God and love of neighbour have been central tenets of both Jewish and Christian traditions. This twofold relational orientation is beautifully expressed in the story of Ruth. In her commitment to her Israelite mother-in-law, Ruth is at once committing herself to the God of Israel. We can also say that every Christian parent or grandparent who steadfastly loves their children or grandchildren, is enveloping them in the embrace of Christ and his Church. It is good to remember this when we grieve for younger generations who do not seem to value the religious practices we hold dear. When we love God, we are empowered to love our families. And when we love our families, God is embracing them through us.

## Ruth 2:1-3.8-11; 4:13-17

Naomi had a kinsman on her husband's side, well-to-do and of Elimelech's clan. His name was Boaz.

Ruth the Moabitess said to Naomi, 'Let me go into the fields and glean among the ears of corn in the footsteps of some man who will look on me with favour.' And she said to her, 'Go, my daughter.' So she set out and went to glean in the fields after the reapers. And it chanced that she came to that part of the fields which belonged to Boaz of Elimelech's clan.

Boaz said to Ruth, 'Listen, my daughter, and understand this. You are not to glean in any other field, do not leave here but stay with my servants. Keep your eyes on whatever part of the field they are reaping and follow behind. I have ordered my servants not to molest you. And if you are thirsty, go to the pitchers and drink what the servants have drawn.' Then she fell on her face, bowing to the ground. And she said to him, 'How have I so earned your favour that you take notice of me, even though I am a foreigner?'…
*(See Appendix B-26)*

## Psalm 127:1-5. R. v.4

*Indeed thus shall be blessed the man who fears the Lord.*

## Matthew 23:1-12

Addressing the people and his disciples Jesus said, 'The scribes and the Pharisees occupy the chair of Moses. You must therefore do what they tell you and listen to what they say; but do not be guided by what they do: since they do not practise what they preach. They tie up heavy burdens and lay them on men's shoulders, but will they lift a finger to move them? Not they! Everything they do is done to attract attention, like wearing broader phylacteries and longer tassels, like wanting to take the place of honour at banquets and the front seats in the synagogues, being greeted obsequiously in the market squares and having people call them Rabbi.

'You, however, must not allow yourselves to be called Rabbi, since you have only one Master, and you are all brothers. You must call no one on earth your father, since you have only one Father, and he is in heaven. Nor must you allow yourselves to be called teachers, for you have only one Teacher, the Christ. The greatest among you must be your servant. Anyone who exalts himself will be humbled, and anyone who humbles himself will be exalted.'

## Reflection

We may have met teachers and preachers who give excellent lectures or homilies but do not practise what they preach. A similar scenario is presented where Jesus urges his listeners to be discerning regarding certain scribes and Pharisees. On the one hand he affirms their legitimate authority, as they 'occupy the Chair of Moses'. The problem is not their teaching, but their actual example, for they are not good role models. The human fragility of religious leaders is a reality in all communities, including our own Church. But we cannot use the failings of others as an excuse to opt out of our tradition or give up on God. Public office is but one form of influence and service. We each have a sphere of influence. Amidst our own fragilities, God can accomplish wondrous things through our willing service.

**20th Week
in Ordinary Time
St Pius X,** *pope*
**Memorial
White**

## AUGUST

# 22

## SUNDAY

**21st Sunday
in Ordinary Time
Psalter Week 1
Green**

### Joshua 24:1-2.15-18

Joshua gathered all the tribes of Israel together at Shechem; then he called the elders, leaders, judges and scribes of Israel, and they presented themselves before God. Then Joshua said to all the people: 'If you will not serve the Lord, choose today whom you wish to serve, whether the gods that your ancestors served beyond the River, or the gods of the Amorites in whose land you are now living. As for me and my House, we will serve the Lord.'

The people answered, 'We have no intention of deserting the Lord our God who brought us and our ancestors out of the land of Egypt, the house of slavery, who worked those great wonders before our eyes and preserved us all along the way we travelled and among all the peoples through whom we journeyed. We too will serve the Lord, for he is our God.'

### Psalm 33:2-3.16-23. R. v.9

*Taste and see that the Lord is good.*

### Ephesians 5:21-32

Give way to one another in obedience to Christ. Wives should regard their husbands as they regard the Lord, since as Christ is head of the Church and saves the whole body, so is a husband the head of his wife; and as the Church submits to Christ, so should wives to their husbands, in everything. Husbands should love their wives just as Christ loved the Church and sacrificed himself for her to make her holy. He made her clean by washing her in water with a form of words, so that when he took her to himself she would be glorious, with no speck or wrinkle or anything like that, but holy and faultless. In the same way, husbands must love their wives as they love their own bodies; for a man to love his wife is for him to love himself. A man never hates his own body, but he feeds it and looks after it; and that is the way Christ treats the Church, because it is his body – and we are its living parts. For this reason, a man must leave his father and mother and be joined to his wife, and the two will become one body. This mystery has many implications; but I am saying it applies to Christ and the Church.

### John 6:60-69

After hearing his doctrine many of the followers of Jesus said, 'This is intolerable language. How could anyone accept it?' Jesus was aware that his followers were complaining about it and said, 'Does this upset you? What if you should see the Son of Man ascend to where he was before?

'It is the spirit that gives life, the flesh has nothing to offer. The words I have spoken to you are spirit and they are life.

'But there are some of you who do not believe.' For Jesus knew from the outset those who did not believe, and who it was that would betray him. He went on, 'This is why I told you that no one could come to me unless the Father allows him.' After this, many of his disciples left him and stopped going with him.

Then Jesus said to the Twelve, 'What about you, do you want to go away too?' Simon Peter answered, 'Lord, who shall we go to? You have the message of eternal life, and we believe; we know that you are the Holy One of God.'

## Reflection

Today's first reading and Gospel present 'crossroads' scenes. Just as the tribes of Israel must decide whether they will persist in following the Lord God, so must Jesus' disciples consider their future in the face of a difficult teaching. In both cases, the memory of divine fidelity is integral to their decision to stay the course. The Israelites remember the faithful God who delivered them from slavery. Meanwhile, Simon Peter admits that their only authentic option is to trust what they have already come to believe: Jesus has the message of eternal life; he is the Holy One of God. Crossroads are part of our lives too. On those days when being faithful involves a difficult or unpopular choice, may the deep memory of God's steadfast love anchor our commitment and see us through.

**21st Week
in Ordinary Time
Green
or
St Rose of Lima, virgin
(Optional, White)**

### 1 Thessalonians 1:1-5.8-10

From Paul, Silvanus, and Timothy, to the Church in Thessalonika which is in God the Father and the Lord Jesus Christ; wishing you grace and peace from God the Father and the Lord Jesus Christ.

We always mention you in our prayers and thank God for you all, and constantly remember before God our Father how you have shown your faith in action, worked for love and persevered through hope, in our Lord Jesus Christ. *(See Appendix B-26)*

### Psalm 149:1-6.9. R. v.4
*The Lord takes delight in his people.*

### Matthew 23:13-22

Jesus said: 'Alas for you, scribes and Pharisees, you hypocrites! You who shut up the kingdom of heaven in men's faces, neither going in yourselves nor allowing others to go in who want to.

'Alas for you, scribes and Pharisees, you hypocrites! You who travel over sea and land to make a single proselyte, and when you have him you make him twice as fit for hell as you are.

'Alas for you, blind guides! You who say, "If a man swears by the Temple, it has no force; but if a man swears by the gold of the Temple, he is bound." Fools and blind! For which is of greater worth, the gold or the Temple that makes the gold sacred? Or else, "If a man swears by the altar it has no force; but if a man swears by the offering that is on the altar, he is bound." You blind men! For which is of greater worth, the offering or the altar that makes the offering sacred? Therefore, when a man swears by the altar he is swearing by that and by everything on it. And when a man swears by the Temple he is swearing by that and by the One who dwells in it. And when a man swears by heaven he is swearing by the throne of God and by the One who is seated there.'

### Reflection

If we were ever tempted to view Jesus as a harmless 'nice guy', today's Gospel dispels such a mirage. Passages like this which present Jesus in conflict with certain Jewish authorities must be interpreted carefully, however; especially given the toxic way they have often been misused by Christians in centuries past to condemn Judaism. Vatican II repudiated this anti-Jewish conditioning, and subsequent Vatican statements issued guidelines for teachers and homilists. These guidelines warn us not to pit Jesus *against* his own Jewish tradition, nor to set the New Testament against the Old Testament as if the latter depicts a religion of fear and legalism (cf. CRRJ, *Guidelines*). Rather, today's Gospel serves as a lens to examine the hypocritical tendencies of our own Christian lives, to lay bare our hearts to God who searches and knows our human depths (Psalm 137).

### Apocalypse 21:9-14

The angel came to speak to me, and said, 'Come here and I will show you the bride that the Lamb has married.' In the spirit he took me to the top of an enormous high mountain and showed me Jerusalem, the holy city, coming down from God out of heaven. It had all the radiant glory of God and glittered like some precious jewel of crystal-clear diamond. The walls of it were of a great height, and had twelve gates; at each of the twelve gates there was an angel, and over the gates were written the names of the twelve tribes of Israel; on the east there were three gates, on the north three gates, on the south three gates, and on the west three gates. The city walls stood on twelve foundation stones, each one of which bore the name of one of the twelve apostles of the Lamb.

### Psalm 144:10-13.17-18. R. cf. v.12

*Your friends, O Lord, make known the glorious splendour of your reign.*

### John 1:45-51

Philip found Nathanael and said to him, 'We have found the one Moses wrote about in the Law, the one about whom the prophets wrote: he is Jesus son of Joseph, from Nazareth,' 'From Nazareth?' said Nathanael. 'Can anything good come from that place?' 'Come and see' replied Philip. When Jesus saw Nathanael coming he said of him, 'There is an Israelite who deserves the name, incapable of deceit.' 'How do you know me?' said Nathanael. 'Before Philip came to call you,' said Jesus 'I saw you under the fig tree.' Nathanael answered, 'Rabbi, you are the Son of God, you are the King of Israel.' Jesus replied, 'You believe that just because I said: I saw you under the fig tree. You will see greater things than that.' And then he added, 'I tell you most solemnly, you will see heaven laid open and, above the Son of Man, the angels of God ascending and descending.'

### Reflection

The episode of Nathanael's call to discipleship is rich in Old Testament motifs, and invites us to ponder Jesus as both Son of God and a son of Israel. It also suggests a creative tension between two strong personalities. Nathanael's retort ('Can anything good come out of Nazareth?') is not so much a hesitation as a testing of Jesus' mettle; and Jesus seems to relish the challenge! Nathanael is no fence sitter; he is a 'stand-up' guy with a thirst for authenticity and zero tolerance of nonsense. This, Jesus seems to be saying, is the character of a true believer, one who does his faith family proud! In our own lives, can we recognise those 'Nathanael' moments – when 'push back' and 'scepticism' signal, not an adversary, but the determined questions of an authentic spiritual searcher?

**St Bartholomew,** *apostle* Feast Red

# AUGUST
# 25
## WEDNESDAY

**21st Week
in Ordinary Time
Green
or
St Louis
(Optional, White)
St Joseph Calasanz,
*priest*
(Optional, White)**

### 1 Thessalonians 2:9-13

Let me remind you, brothers, how hard we used to work, slaving night and day so as not to be a burden on any one of you while we were proclaiming God's Good News to you. You are witnesses, and so is God, that our treatment of you, since you became believers, has been impeccably right and fair. You can remember how we treated every one of you as a father treats his children, teaching you what was right, encouraging you and appealing to you to live a life worthy of God, who is calling you to share the glory of his kingdom.

Another reason why we constantly thank God for you is that as soon as you heard the message that we brought you as God's message, you accepted it for what it really is, God's message and not some human thinking; and it is still a living power among you who believe it.

### Psalm 138:7-12. R. v.1
*O Lord, you search me and you know me.*

### Matthew 23:27-32

Jesus said, 'Alas for you, scribes and Pharisees, you hypocrites! You who are like whitewashed tombs that look handsome on the outside, but inside are full of dead men's bones and every kind of corruption. In the same way you appear to people from the outside like good honest men, but inside you are full of hypocrisy and lawlessness.

'Alas for you, scribes and Pharisees, you hypocrites! You who build the sepulchres of the prophets and decorate the tombs of holy men, saying, "We would never have joined in shedding the blood of the prophets, had we lived in our fathers' day." So! Your own evidence tells against you! You are the sons of those who murdered the prophets! Very well then, finish off the work that your fathers began.'

### Reflection

The image of whitewashed tombs in today's Gospel is indeed confronting. Hypocrisy is a deathly character trait, and no external veneer of religiosity can hide it from the penetrating gaze of God (Psalm 138). The hypocrisy highlighted here is the lip service given to the tombs of revered prophets while being complicit in the rejection of present-day prophets. Contrast this with the honest labour, familial love and gospel responsiveness praised by St Paul. Where do we find ourselves within these readings? Perhaps falling to our knees in view of our sins, yet also reassured that God knows our honest efforts to live faithfully, mercifully, and ethically. So, let's neither wallow in our sins nor become complacent in our goodness. We are hypocrites and disciples, sinners and saints. God knows it all, loves us still, and calls us on.

**21st Week
in Ordinary Time
Green**

## 1 Thessalonians 3:7-13

Brothers, your faith has been a great comfort to us in the middle of our own troubles and sorrows; now we can breathe again, as you are still holding firm in the Lord. How can we thank God enough for you, for all the joy we feel before our God on your account? We are earnestly praying night and day to be able to see you face to face again and make up any shortcomings in your faith.

May God our Father himself, and our Lord Jesus Christ, make it easy for us to come to you. May the Lord be generous in increasing your love and make you love one another and the whole human race as much as we love you. And may he so confirm your hearts in holiness that you may be blameless in the sight of our God and Father when our Lord Jesus Christ comes with all his saints.

## Psalm 89:3-4.12-14.17. R. v.14

*Fill us with your love that we may rejoice.*

## Matthew 24:42-51

Jesus said to his disciples: 'Stay awake, because you do not know the day when your master is coming. You may be quite sure of this, that if the householder had known at what time of the night the burglar would come, he would have stayed awake and would not have allowed anyone to break the wall of his house. Therefore, you too must stand ready because the Son of Man is coming at an hour you do not expect.

'What sort of servant, then, is faithful and wise enough for the master to place him over his household to give them their food at the proper time? Happy that servant if his master's arrival finds him at this employment. I tell you solemnly, he will place him over everything he owns. But as for the dishonest servant who says to himself, "My master is taking his time," and sets about beating his fellow servants and eating and drinking with drunkards, his master will come on a day he does not expect and at an hour he does not know. The master will cut him off and send him to the same fate as the hypocrites, where there will be weeping and grinding of teeth.'

## Reflection

What does it mean to 'stay awake' in a gospel sense? It can mean living in the present moment, not caught up in past regrets and negative memories that blind us to the gracious opportunities of the 'now'. Similarly, to be fully 'awake' is to resist being consumed by anxieties about the future. Staying awake, then, means entrusting both the past and the future to God, sensitive to divine presence encountered in the unexpected people and events of any given day. We can be assisted in this 'wakefulness' by Catholic mindfulness practices and contemplative daily exercises such as the Ignatian Awareness Examen. Tools like these teach discernment, attentiveness to the true self and to the footprints of grace in our lives.

**21st Week
in Ordinary Time
St Monica
Memorial
White**

**1 Thessalonians 4:1-8**

Brothers, we urge you and appeal to you in the Lord Jesus to make more and more progress in the kind of life that you are meant to live: the life that God wants, as you learnt from us, and as you are already living it. You have not forgotten the instructions we gave you on the authority of the Lord Jesus.

What God wants is for you all to be holy. He wants you to keep away from fornication, and each one of you to know how to use the body that belongs to him in a way that is holy and honourable, not giving way to selfish lust like the pagans who do not know God. He wants nobody at all ever to sin by taking advantage of a brother in these matters; the Lord always punishes sins of that sort, as we told you before and assured you. We have been called by God to be holy, not to be immoral; in other words, anyone who objects is not objecting to a human authority, but to God, who gives you his Holy Spirit.

**Psalm 96:1-2.5-6.10-12. R. v.12**

*Rejoice, you just, in the Lord.*

**Matthew 25:1-13**

Jesus said to his disciples: 'The kingdom of heaven will be like this: Ten bridesmaids took their lamps and went to meet the bridegroom. Five of them were foolish and five were sensible: the foolish ones did take their lamps, but they brought no oil, whereas the sensible ones took flasks of oil as well as their lamps. The bridegroom was late, and they all grew drowsy and fell asleep. But at midnight there was a cry, "The bridegroom is here! Go out and meet him." At this, all those bridesmaids woke up and trimmed their lamps, and the foolish ones said to the sensible ones, "Give us some of your oil: our lamps are going out." But they replied, "There may not be enough for us and for you; you had better go to those who sell it and buy some for yourselves." They had gone off to buy it when the bridegroom arrived. Those who were ready went in with him to the wedding hall and the door was closed. The other bridesmaids arrived later. "Lord, Lord," they said "open the door for us." But he replied, "I tell you solemnly, I do not know you." So stay awake, because you do not know either the day or the hour.'

**Reflection**

The parable of the ten bridesmaids speaks of spiritual 'readiness'. What are the 'oil stores' to be kept at hand? We can rightly name traditional practices like Scripture study, worship, sacraments, service, and the fostering of lifegiving relationships. Another way of naming the fuel source in this parable is this: *a keen sensitivity to the Holy Spirit at work in the secular world.* Sometimes the Church finds itself well-equipped within a familiar religious framework, but empty-handed when caught off guard by an unexpected secular development. The response is sometimes 'too little, too late'. The capacity to 'discern and act' in a timely manner is an 'oil flask' that allows us to be 'God-ready' at any given moment, and 'to make more and more progress in the kind of life that we are meant to live'.

1 Thessalonians 4:9-11
*(See Appendix B–27)*

Psalm 97:1.7-9. R. v.9
*The Lord comes to rule the people with fairness.*

## Matthew 25:14-30

Jesus told his disciples this parable: 'A man on his way abroad summoned his servants and entrusted his property to them. To one he gave five talents, to another two, to a third one; each in proportion to his ability. Then he set out. The man who had received the five talents promptly went and traded with them and made five more. The man who had received two made two more in the same way. But the man who had received one went off and dug a hole in the ground and hid his master's money. Now a long time after, the master of those servants came back and went through his accounts with them. The man who had received the five talents came forward bringing five more. "Sir," he said "you entrusted me with five talents; here are five more that I have made." His master said to him, "Well done, good and faithful servant; you have shown you can be faithful in small things, I will trust you with greater; come and join in your master's happiness." Next the man with the two talents came forward. "Sir," he said "you entrusted me with two talents; here are two more that I have made." His master said to him, "Well done, good and faithful servant; you have shown you can be faithful in small things, I will trust you with greater; come and join in your master's happiness." Last came forward the man who had the one talent. "Sir," said he "I had heard you were a hard man, reaping where you have not sown and gathering where you have not scattered; so I was afraid, and I went off and hid your talent in the ground. Here it is; it was yours, you have it back." But his master answered him, "You wicked and lazy servant! So you knew that I reap where I have not sown and gather where I have not scattered? Well then, you should have deposited my money with the bankers, and on my return I would have recovered my capital with interest. So now, take the talent from him and give it to the man who has the five talents. For to everyone who has will be given more, and he will have more than enough; but from the man who has not, even what he has will be taken away. As for this good-for-nothing servant, throw him out into the dark, where there will be weeping and grinding of teeth."'

**21st Week
in Ordinary Time**
**St Augustine, *bishop,
doctor***
**Memorial
White**

## Reflection

Do you empathise with the servant who buried his one talent? After all, he didn't lose or embezzle his master's resource; he preserved it perfectly. Why the harsh judgement? Perhaps this parable highlights the devasting effects of fear. The unfruitful servant is ruled by fear. Presumably the other two servants also had their share of problems and anxieties. But they didn't allow their fear to gain the upper hand. They focused on what they could do, rather than agonising over what might go wrong. The 'weeping and grinding of teeth' is what we inflict upon ourselves when we approach life 'small and miserly', rather than 'giving it all we've got'. Life is a gift, to be fully lived and shared for the glory of God and the blessing of others.

### Deuteronomy 4:1-2.6-8

Moses said to the people: 'Now, Israel, take notice of the laws and customs that I teach you today, and observe them, that you may have life and may enter and take possession of the land that the Lord the God of your fathers is giving you. You must add nothing to what I command you, and take nothing from it, but keep the commandments of the Lord your God just as I lay them down for you. Keep them, observe them and they will demonstrate to the peoples your wisdom and understanding. When they come to know of all these laws they will exclaim, "No other people is as wise and prudent as this great nation." And indeed, what great nation is there that has its gods so near as the Lord our God is to us whenever we call to him? And what great nation is there that has laws and customs to match this whole Law that I put before you today?'

### Psalm 14:2-5. R. v.1

*The just will live in the presence of the Lord.*

### James 1:17-18.21-22.27

It is all that is good, everything that is perfect, which is given us from above; it comes down from the Father of all light; with him there is no such thing as alteration, no shadow of a change. By his own choice he made us his children by the message of the truth so that we should be a sort of first-fruits of all that he had created.

Accept and submit to the word which has been planted in you and can save your souls. But you must do what the word tells you, and not just listen to it and deceive yourselves.

Pure unspoilt religion, in the eyes of God our Father is this: coming to the help of orphans and widows when they need it, and keeping oneself uncontaminated by the world.

### Mark 7:1-8.14-15.21-23

The Pharisees and some of the scribes who had come from Jerusalem gathered round Jesus, and they noticed that some of his disciples were eating with unclean hands, that is, without washing them. For the Pharisees, and the Jews in general, follow the tradition of the elders and never eat without washing their arms as far as the elbow; and on returning from the market place they never eat without first sprinkling themselves. There are also many other observances which have been handed down to them concerning the washing of cups and pots and bronze dishes. So these Pharisees and scribes asked him, 'Why do your disciples not respect the tradition of the elders but eat their food with unclean hands?' He answered, 'It was of you hypocrites that Isaiah so rightly prophesied in this passage of scripture: This people honours me only with lip-service, while their hearts are far from me. The worship they offer me is worthless, the doctrines they teach are only human regulations.

You put aside the commandment of God to cling to human traditions.'

He called the people to him again and said, 'Listen to me, all of you, and understand. Nothing that goes into a man from outside can make him unclean; it is the things that come out of a man that make him unclean. For it is from within, from men's hearts, that evil intentions emerge: fornication, theft, murder, adultery, avarice, malice, deceit, indecency, envy, slander, pride, folly. All these evil things come from within and make a man unclean.'

## Reflection

Which is more defining of a Christian disciple? Inner thoughts or outer actions? The heartfelt faith conviction, or the act of service or worship which gives it expression? How about both! As Christ's body, we are an incarnational, sacramental people. Our existence is more than bodily activity, we have rich spiritual depths. Yet we do not aspire to be angelic spiritual beings; we are human beings immersed in the physical world and its history. The love of God and neighbour in our hearts is to be embodied and enacted on earth. But what if we start to bear inner resentments, grudges, hatreds? No matter how privately held, these seeds (if left unattended) will grow and infect the conduct of our outward, visible lives. Today, make an examination of conscience. Uproot a toxic attitude; plant and nurture a seed of love and gratitude.

# AUGUST
# 30
## MONDAY

**22nd Week
in Ordinary Time
Green**

**1 Thessalonians 4:13-18**
*(See Appendix B-27)*

**Psalm 95:1.3-5.11-13. R. v.13**
*The Lord comes to rule the earth.*

## Luke 4:16-30

Jesus came to Nazara, where he had been brought up, and went into the synagogue on the sabbath day as he usually did. He stood up to read, and they handed him the scroll of the prophet Isaiah. Unrolling the scroll he found the place where it is written: The spirit of the Lord has been given to me, for he has anointed me. He has sent me to bring the good news to the poor, to proclaim liberty to captives and to the blind new sight, to set the downtrodden free, to proclaim the Lord's year of favour.

He then rolled up the scroll, gave it back to the assistant and sat down. And all eyes in the synagogue were fixed on him. Then he began to speak to them, 'This text is being fulfilled today even as you listen.' And he won the approval of all, and they were astonished by the gracious words that came from his lips.

They said, 'This is Joseph's son, surely?' But he replied, 'No doubt you will quote me the saying, "Physician, heal yourself" and tell me, "We have heard all that happened in Capernaum, do the same here in your own countryside."' And he went on, 'I tell you solemnly, no prophet is ever accepted in his own country.

'There were many widows in Israel, I can assure you, in Elijah's day, when heaven remained shut for three years and six months and a great famine raged throughout the land, but Elijah was not sent to any one of these: he was sent to a widow at Zarephath, a Sidonian town. And in the prophet Elisha's time there were many lepers in Israel, but none of these was cured, except the Syrian, Naaman.'

When they heard this everyone in the synagogue was enraged. They sprang to their feet and hustled him out of the town; and they took him up to the brow of the hill their town was built on, intending to throw him down the cliff, but he slipped through the crowd and walked away.

### Reflection

Writing to the Thessalonians, St Paul is expectant that Christ is soon to return in glory. But we know that this did not occur as expected. Further, we remember that Jesus himself received a mixed, and eventually violent, reaction to his public ministry; we should not be surprised by our own difficulties in proclaiming the Good News. Christians have always lived their faith in this 'in-between' time: the reign of God is 'now', and 'not yet'; Christ has come, and 'will come again'. Carrying this tension is not easy, and we should not gloss over its challenges. It takes courage to live gratefully knowing that Christian life is already on earth a participation in the death and resurrection of Christ; and it takes courage to live hopefully (there is more to come!) as active participants in the unfolding of God's kingdom.

**22nd Week
in Ordinary Time
Green**

## 1 Thessalonians 5:1-6.9-11

You will not be expecting us to write anything to you, brothers, about 'times and seasons', since you know very well that the Day of the Lord is going to come like a thief in the night. It is when people are saying, 'How quiet and peaceful it is' that the worst suddenly happens, as suddenly as labour pains come on a pregnant woman; and there will be no way for anybody to evade it.

But it is not as if you live in the dark, my brothers, for that Day to overtake you like a thief. No, you are all sons of light and sons of the day: we do not belong to the night or to darkness, so we should not go on sleeping, as everyone else does, but stay wide awake and sober. God never meant us to experience the Retribution, but to win salvation through our Lord Jesus Christ, who died for us so that, alive or dead, we should still live united to him. So give encouragement to each other, and keep strengthening one another, as you do already.

## Psalm 26:1.4.13-14. R. v.13

*I am sure I shall see the Lord's goodness in the land of the living.*

## Luke 4:31-37

Jesus went down to Capernaum, a town in Galilee, and taught them on the sabbath. And his teaching made a deep impression on them because he spoke with authority.

In the synagogue there was a man who was possessed by the spirit of an unclean devil, and it shouted at the top of its voice, 'Ha! What do you want with us, Jesus of Nazareth? Have you come to destroy us? I know who you are: the Holy One of God.' But Jesus said sharply, 'Be quiet! Come out of him!' And the devil, throwing the man down in front of everyone, went out of him without hurting him at all. Astonishment seized them and they were all saying to one another, 'What teaching! He gives orders to unclean spirits with authority and power and they come out.' And reports of him went all through the surrounding countryside.

## Reflection

In the Old Testament, one of the expected signs of the dawning of the messianic age is the healing of physical disability and the defeat of evil. In today's Gospel, a man considered possessed is dramatically confronted by Jesus' healing power. The scene provides a clue to Jesus' messianic identity. In the healing act, note the role of Jesus' *words* and their authoritative power. We might consider the power of our own words to heal, save, encourage and console. As Christians, what we do and what we say shapes a twofold witness to the risen Christ. May we speak with the confidence of the gospel. May our activities bring a healing presence, firm and loving in the face of moral darkness and human misery.

**22nd Week
in Ordinary Time
Green**

### Colossians 1:1-8

From Paul, appointed by God to be an apostle of Christ Jesus, and from our brother Timothy to the saints in Colossae, our faithful brothers in Christ: Grace and peace to you from God our Father.

We have never failed to remember you in our prayers and to give thanks for you to God, the Father of our Lord Jesus Christ, ever since we heard about your faith in Christ Jesus and the love that you show towards all the saints because of the hope which is stored up for you in heaven. It is only recently that you heard of this, when it was announced in the message of the truth. The Good News which has reached you is spreading all over the world and producing the same results as it has among you ever since the day when you heard about God's grace and understood what this really is. Epaphras, who taught you, is one of our closest fellow workers and a faithful deputy for us as Christ's servant, and it was he who told us all about your love in the Spirit.

### Psalm 51:10-11. R. v.10

*I trust in the goodness of God for ever and ever.*

### Luke 4:38-44

Leaving the synagogue Jesus went to Simon's house. Now Simon's mother-in-law was suffering from a high fever and they asked him to do something for her. Leaning over her he rebuked the fever and it left her. And she immediately got up and began to wait on them.

At sunset all those who had friends suffering from diseases of one kind or another brought them to him, and laying his hands on each he cured them. Devils too came out of many people, howling, 'You are the Son of God.' But he rebuked them and would not allow them to speak because they knew that he was the Christ.

When daylight came he left the house and made his way to a lonely place. The crowds went to look for him, and when they had caught up with him they wanted to prevent him leaving them, but he answered, 'I must proclaim the Good News of the kingdom of God to the other towns too, because that is what I was sent to do.' And he continued his preaching in the synagogues of Judaea.

### Reflection

Why didn't Jesus want the devils to reveal his identity as the Christ? We can understand better when we read that the crowds wanted to prevent him from leaving them. Jesus had work to do, he still needed to go out and heal and proclaim the Good News. Just as at the Transfiguration on the mountain, or with Mary when she saw him in the garden after the resurrection... people wanted to hold onto Jesus, but he wants us to share him.

**22nd Week
in Ordinary Time
Green**

### Colossians 1:9-14

Ever since the day we heard about you, we have never failed to pray for you, and what we ask God is that through perfect wisdom and spiritual understanding you should reach the fullest knowledge of his will. So you will be able to lead the kind of life which the Lord expects of you, a life acceptable to him in all its aspects; showing the results in all the good actions you do and increasing your knowledge of God. You will have in you the strength, based on his own glorious power, never to give in, but to bear anything joyfully, thanking the Father who has made it possible for you to join the saints and with them to inherit the light.

Because that is what he has done: he has taken us out of the power of darkness and created a place for us in the kingdom of the Son that he loves, and in him, we gain our freedom, the forgiveness of our sins.

### Psalm 97:2-6. R. v.2

*The Lord has made known his salvation.*

### Luke 5:1-11

Jesus was standing one day by the lake of Gennesaret, with the crowd pressing round him listening to the word of God, when he caught sight of two boats close to the bank. The fishermen had gone out of them and were washing their nets. He got into one of the boats – it was Simon's – and asked him to put out a little from the shore. Then he sat down and taught the crowds from the boat.

When he had finished speaking he said to Simon, 'Put out into deep water and pay out your nets for a catch.' 'Master,' Simon replied 'we worked hard all night long and caught nothing, but if you say so, I will pay out the nets.' And when they had done this they netted such a huge number of fish that their nets began to tear, so they signalled to their companions in the other boat to come and help them; when these came, they filled the two boats to sinking point.

When Simon Peter saw this he fell at the knees of Jesus saying 'Leave me, Lord; I am a sinful man.' For he and all his companions were completely overcome by the catch they had made; so also were James and John, sons of Zebedee, who were Simon's partners. But Jesus said to Simon, 'Do not be afraid, from now on it is men you will catch.' Then, bringing their boats back to land, they left everything and followed him.

### Reflection

The gospel today shows us the miracle that can happen in our everyday lives. Jesus invites himself into Simon's life, he gets into his day-job, and it was one of those disappointing days when he had worked all night for nothing – no fish! Then, Simon, the experienced tradesman, is humble enough to be led by this carpenter from Nazareth, and a miracle happens. What might happen in our lives if we listened more to the Lord?

**St Gregory the Great,**
*pope, doctor*
**Feast**
**White**

### 1 Thessalonians 2:2-8

It was our God who gave us the courage to proclaim his Good News to you in the face of great opposition. We have not taken to preaching because we are deluded, or immoral, or trying to deceive anyone; it was God who decided that we were fit to be entrusted with the Good News, and when we are speaking, we are not trying to please men but God, who can read our inmost thoughts. You know very well, and we can swear it before God, that never at any time have our speeches been simply flattery, or a cover for trying to get money; nor have we ever looked for any special honour from men, either from you or anybody else, when we could have imposed ourselves on you with full weight, as apostles of Christ.

Instead, we were unassuming. Like a mother feeding and looking after her own children, we felt so devoted and protective towards you, and had come to love you so much, that we were eager to hand over to you not only the Good News but our whole lives as well.

### Psalm 95:1-3.7-8.10

*Proclaim the wonders of the Lord among all the peoples.*

### Matthew 16:13-19

When Jesus came to the region of Caesarea Philippi he put this question to his disciples, 'Who do people say the Son of Man is?' And they said, 'Some say he is John the Baptist, some Elijah, and others Jeremiah or one of the prophets.' 'But you,' he said 'who do you say I am?' Then Simon Peter spoke up, 'You are the Christ,' he said 'the Son of the living God.' Jesus replied, 'Simon son of Jonah, you are a happy man! Because it was not flesh and blood that revealed this to you but my Father in heaven. So I now say to you: You are Peter and on this rock I will build my Church. And the gates of the underworld can never hold out against it. I will give you the keys of the kingdom of heaven: whatever you bind on earth shall be considered bound in heaven; whatever you loose on earth shall be considered loosed in heaven.'

### Reflection

People thought Jesus was another prophet... seems a compliment! It is good to be in the company of great men like John the Baptist, Elijah or any of the great prophets, but Simon Peter knew deep within himself; Jesus was more than a great prophet, he was the Son of God. Peter had an insight that was so unimaginable, that it had to be an inspiration from the Father. Because Peter understood God's purpose, Jesus entrusts his Church – us – to him, because he knows how to listen to God.

**22nd Week
in Ordinary Time
Green**

### Colossians 1:21-23

Not long ago, you were foreigners and enemies, in the way that you used to think and the evil things that you did; but now God has reconciled you, by Christ's death in his mortal body. Now you are able to appear before him holy, pure and blameless – as long as you persevere and stand firm on the solid base of the faith, never letting yourselves drift away from the hope promised by the Good News, which you have heard, which has been preached to the whole human race, and of which I, Paul, have become the servant.

### Psalm 53:3-4.6.8. R. v.6

*I have God for my help.*

### Luke 6:1-5

One sabbath Jesus happened to be taking a walk through the cornfields, and his disciples were picking ears of corn, rubbing them in their hands and eating them. Some of the Pharisees said, 'Why are you doing something that is forbidden on the sabbath day?' Jesus answered them, 'So you have not read what David did when he and his followers were hungry – how he went into the House of God, took the loaves of offering and ate them and gave them to his followers, loaves which only the priests are allowed to eat?' And he said to them, 'The Son of Man is master of the sabbath.'

### Reflection

'The son of man' can be interpreted in two ways; as being Jesus, because that is what he sometimes called himself, or it can mean Son of Adam, so that is essentially human beings. The law of God, in both the old and the new testament, is supposed to bring life. It's supposed to be good for us. So perhaps Jesus is telling the Pharisees (the lawyers) that what's important is people, not rules.

**23rd Sunday
in Ordinary Time
Psalter Week 3
Green**

### Isaiah 35:4-7

Say to all faint hearts, 'Courage! Do not be afraid. 'Look, your God is coming, vengeance is coming, the retribution of God; he is coming to save you.' Then the eyes of the blind shall be opened, the ears of the deaf unsealed, then the lame shall leap like a deer and the tongues of the dumb sing for joy; for water gushes in the desert, streams in the wasteland, the scorched earth becomes a lake, the parched land springs of water.

### Psalm 145:7-10. R. v.1

*My soul, give praise to the Lord.*

### James 2:1-5

My brothers, do not try to combine faith in Jesus Christ, our glorified Lord, with the making of distinctions between classes of people. Now suppose a man comes into your synagogue, beautifully dressed and with a gold ring on, and at the same time a poor man comes in, in shabby clothes, and you take notice of the well-dressed man, and say, 'Come this way to the best seats;' then you tell the poor man, 'Stand over there' or 'You can sit on the floor by my foot-rest.' Can't you see that you have used two different standards in your mind, and turned yourselves into judges, and corrupt judges at that?

Listen, my dear brothers: it was those who are poor according to the world that God chose, to be rich in faith and to be the heirs to the kingdom which he promised to those who love him.

### Mark 7:31-37

Returning from the district of Tyre, Jesus went by way of Sidon towards the Sea of Galilee, right through the Decapolis region. And they brought him a deaf man who had an impediment in his speech; and they asked him to lay his hand on him. He took him aside in private, away from the crowd, put his fingers into the man's ears and touched his tongue with spittle. Then looking up to heaven he sighed; and he said to him, 'Ephphatha,' that is, 'Be opened.' And his ears were opened, and the ligament of his tongue was loosened and he spoke clearly. And Jesus ordered them to tell no one about it, but the more he insisted, the more widely they published it. Their admiration was unbounded. 'He has done all things well,' they said 'he makes the deaf hear and the dumb speak.'

## Reflection

Who are "they" who brought the deaf man with a speech impediment to Jesus to be healed? Why did Jesus take him aside "in private away from the crowd" to heal him? Perhaps Jesus was afraid that his was becoming a celebrity trick-show, with all these crowds wanting to see a miracle, bringing him a vulnerable person to prompt his show. The crowd were amazed, but why? Jesus wanted to heal because he cares about us, not because he wanted to be famous.

**23rd Week
in Ordinary Time
Green**

### Colossians 1:24-2:3

It makes me happy to suffer for you, as I am suffering now, and in my own body to do what I can to make up all that has still to be undergone by Christ for the sake of his body, the Church. I became the servant of the Church when God made me responsible for delivering God's message to you, the message which was a mystery hidden for generations and centuries and has now been revealed to his saints. It was God's purpose to reveal it to them and to show all the rich glory of this mystery to pagans. The mystery is Christ among you, your hope of glory: this is the Christ we proclaim, this is the wisdom in which we thoroughly train everyone and instruct everyone, to make them all perfect in Christ. It is for this I struggle wearily on, helped only by his power driving me irresistibly.

Yes, I want you to know that I do have to struggle hard for you, and for those in Laodicea, and for so many others who have never seen me face to face. It is all to bind you together in love and to stir your minds, so that your understanding may come to full development, until you really know God's secret in which all the jewels of wisdom and knowledge are hidden.

### Psalm 61:6-7.9. R. v.8

*In God is my safety and glory.*

### Luke 6:6-11

On the sabbath Jesus went into the synagogue and began to teach, and a man was there whose right hand was withered. The scribes and the Pharisees were watching him to see if he would cure a man on the sabbath, hoping to find something to use against him. But he knew their thoughts; and he said to the man with the withered hand, 'Stand up! Come out into the middle.' And he came out and stood there. Then Jesus said to them, 'I put it to you: is it against the law on the sabbath to do good, or to do evil; to save life, or to destroy it?' Then he looked round at them all and said to the man, 'Stretch out your hand.' He did so, and his hand was better. But they were furious, and began to discuss the best way of dealing with Jesus.

### Reflection

In the bible, 7 is the sign of completeness and perfection. This day was the Sabbath, the day God commanded us to keep holy and not to work. If we look at this another way, the woman's hand was withered; it wasn't the way it should be. Perhaps Jesus wanted to continue doing his father's work and bring the woman to the full glory of a human person, which is praising God, bringing her into the Sabbath rest.

## Colossians 2:6-15

You must live your whole life according to the Christ you have received – Jesus the Lord; you must be rooted in him and built on him and held firm by the faith you have been taught, and full of thanksgiving.

Make sure that no one traps you and deprives you of your freedom by some secondhand, empty, rational philosophy based on the principles of this world instead of on Christ.

In his body lives the fullness of divinity, and in him you too find your own fulfilment, in the one who is the head of every Sovereignty and Power.

In him you have been circumcised, with circumcision not performed by human hand, but by the complete stripping of your body of flesh. This is circumcision according to Christ. You have been buried with him, when you were baptised; and by baptism, too, you have been raised up with him through your belief in the power of God who raised him from the dead. … *(See Appendix B-27)*

## Psalm 144:1-2.8-11. R. v.9
*How good is the Lord to all.*

## Luke 6:12-19

Jesus went out into the hills to pray; and he spent the whole night in prayer to God. When day came he summoned his disciples and picked out twelve of them; he called them 'apostles': Simon whom he called Peter, and his brother Andrew; James, John, Philip, Bartholomew, Matthew, Thomas, James son of Alphaeus, Simon called the Zealot, Judas son of James, and Judas Iscariot who became a traitor.

He then came down with them and stopped at a piece of level ground where there was a large gathering of his disciples with a great crowd of people from all parts of Judaea and from Jerusalem and from the coastal region of Tyre and Sidon who had come to hear him and to be cured of their diseases. People tormented by unclean spirits were also cured, and everyone in the crowd was trying to touch him because power came out of him that cured them all.

## Reflection
The call of the apostles is the fruit of the prayer of Jesus. He didn't just take time-out to plan everything. He spoke to his father and discerned what his will was. God's will is always for good, and see, Judas was one of the chosen. But Judas "became a traitor" he didn't start out that way. God invites us all to participate in his wonderful creation, we are always free to help or to mess it up.

**The Nativity
of the Blessed
Virgin Mary
Feast
White**

**Micah 5:1-4**
*(Alternative Reading: Romans 8: 28-30)*
The Lord says this: 'You, Bethlehem Ephrathah, the least of the clans of Judah, out of you will be born for me the one who is to rule over Israel; his origin goes back to the distant past, to the days of old. The Lord is therefore going to abandon them till the time when she who is to give birth gives birth. Then the remnant of his brothers will come back to the sons of Israel. He will stand and feed his flock with the power of the Lord, with the majesty of the name of his God. They will live secure, for from then on he will extend his power to the ends of the land. He himself will be peace.'

**Psalm 12:6-7. R. Isaiah 61:10**
*I exult for joy in the Lord.*

**Mathew 1:18-23** *(Longer Form: Mathew 1:1-16.18-23)*
This is how Jesus Christ came to be born. His mother Mary was betrothed to Joseph; but before they came to live together she was found to be with child through the Holy Spirit. Her husband Joseph, being a man of honour and wanting to spare her publicity, decided to divorce her informally. He had made up his mind to do this when the angel of the Lord appeared to him in a dream and said, 'Joseph, son of David, do not be afraid to take Mary home as your wife, because she has conceived what is in her by the Holy Spirit. She will give birth to a son and you must name him Jesus, because he is the one who is to save his people from their sins.' Now all this took place to fulfil the words spoken by the Lord through the prophet:

The virgin will conceive and give birth to a son and they will call him Emmanuel, a name which means 'God-is-with-us.'

**Reflection**
From Mary was born into the world, God-with-us, but look how many people, how many generations played a part in this, and there were many more whose names are not written in the book. Mary was the specially graced woman, but we too can have our part in the story of salvation just like those saints and sinners before us. We just need to follow God's will in our lives and wonderful things will happen, just perhaps not in our lifetime.

### Colossians 3:12-17

You are God's chosen race, his saints; he loves you, and you should be clothed in sincere compassion, in kindness and humility, gentleness and patience. Bear with one another; forgive each other as soon as a quarrel begins. The Lord has forgiven you; now you must do the same. Over all these clothes, to keep them together and complete them, put on love. … *(See Appendix B-27)*

### Psalm 150:1-6. R. v.6

*Let everything that lives and that breathes give praise to the Lord.*

### Luke 6:27-38

Jesus said to his disciples: 'I say this to you who are listening: Love your enemies, do good to those who hate you, bless those who curse you, pray for those who treat you badly. To the man who slaps you on one cheek, present the other cheek too; to the man who takes your cloak from you, do not refuse your tunic. Give to everyone who asks you, and do not ask for your property back from the man who robs you. Treat others as you would like them to treat you. If you love those who love you, what thanks can you expect? Even sinners love those who love them. And if you do good to those who do good to you, what thanks can you expect? For even sinners do that much. And if you lend to those from whom you hope to receive, what thanks can you expect? Even sinners lend to get back the same amount. Instead, love your enemies and do good, and lend without any hope of return. You will have a great reward, and you will be sons of the Most High, for he himself is kind to the ungrateful and the wicked.

'Be compassionate as your Father is compassionate. Do not judge, and you will not be judged yourselves; do not condemn, and you will not be condemned yourselves; grant pardon, and you will be pardoned. Give, and there will be gifts for you: a full measure, pressed down, shaken together, and running over, will be poured into your lap; because the amount you measure out is the amount you will be given back.'

**23rd Week
in Ordinary Time
Green
or
St Peter Claver, *priest*
(Optional, White)**

### Reflection

This surely is the measure of a spiritual person. Many will say how they go to church or pray for so long or so often, but the fruit of genuine devotion is charity. To love those who cannot or will not love you in return is the sign of godliness. The first reading reminds us that this is our vocation as Christians, as saints. "Let the message of Christ, in all its richness, find a home with you."

**23rd Week
in Ordinary Time
Green**

## 1 Timothy 1:1-2.12-14

From Paul, apostle of Christ Jesus appointed by the command of God our saviour and of Christ Jesus our hope, to Timothy, true child of mine in the faith; wishing you grace, mercy and peace from God the Father and from Christ Jesus our Lord.

I thank Christ Jesus our Lord, who has given me strength, and who judged me faithful enough to call me into his service even though I used to be a blasphemer and did all I could to injure and discredit the faith. Mercy, however, was shown me, because until I became a believer I had been acting in ignorance; and the grace of our Lord filled me with faith and with the love that is in Christ Jesus.

## Psalm 15:1-2.5.7-8.11. R. cf. v.5

*You are my inheritance, O Lord.*

## Luke 6:39-42

Jesus told a parable to the disciples, 'Can one blind man guide another? Surely both will fall into a pit? The disciple is not superior to his teacher; the fully trained disciple will always be like his teacher. Why do you observe the splinter in your brother's eye and never notice the plank in your own? How can you say to your brother, "Brother, let me take out the splinter that is in your eye," when you cannot see the plank in your own? Hypocrite! Take the plank out of your own eye first, and then you will see clearly enough to take out the splinter that is in your brother's eye.'

## Reflection

What do you aspire to? Who do you hope to be? Studious or not, we are always learning, always changing. There are two ways to learn; trial and error or learning from another. The splinter in the eye is an easy lesson to understand, but we can overlook another lesson in this gospel... "the fully trained disciple will always be like his teacher." The important thing, therefore, is to choose our teacher well. Jesus is the Divine teacher, "the Way, Truth and Life."

## 1 Timothy 1:15-17

Here is a saying that you can rely on and nobody should doubt: that Christ Jesus came into the world to save sinners. I myself am the greatest of them; and if mercy has been shown to me, it is because Jesus Christ meant to make me the greatest evidence of his inexhaustible patience for all the other people who would later have to trust in him to come to eternal life. To the eternal King, the undying, invisible and only God, be honour and glory for ever and ever. Amen.

## Psalm 112:1-7. R. v.2

*May the name of the Lord be blessed for evermore!*

## Luke 6:43-49

Jesus said to his disciples: 'There is no sound tree that produces rotten fruit, nor again a rotten tree that produces sound fruit. For every tree can be told by its own fruit: people do not pick figs from thorns, nor gather grapes from brambles. A good man draws what is good from the store of goodness in his heart; a bad man draws what is bad from the store of badness. For a man's words flow out of what fills his heart.

'Why do you call me, "Lord, Lord" and not do what I say?

'Everyone who comes to me and listens to my words and acts on them – I will show you what he is like. He is like the man who when he built his house dug, and dug deep, and laid the foundations on rock; when the river was in flood it bore down on that house but could not shake it, it was so well built. But the one who listens and does nothing is like the man who built his house on soil, with no foundations: as soon as the river bore down on it, it collapsed; and what a ruin that house became!'

## Reflection

Today's gospel is not suggesting a method for judging others, because Jesus tells us not to judge, so it must be about how we see ourselves. It's hard to see ourselves in a balanced way, as God sees us. If we reflect on our lives, our time, our relationships, then we can more easily see, we might not be as bad as we think, or perhaps, see where we need to change for the better. The only sure way to measure ourselves, is against the Gospel.

## SEPTEMBER
# 12
### SUNDAY

**24th Sunday
in Ordinary Time
Psalter Week 4
Green**

### Isaiah 50:5-9

The Lord has opened my ear. For my part, I made no resistance, neither did I turn away. I offered my back to those who struck me, my cheeks to those who tore at my beard; I did not cover my face against insult and spittle. The Lord comes to my help, so that I am untouched by the insults. So, too, I set my face like flint; I know I shall not be shamed. My vindicator is here at hand. Does anyone start proceedings against me? Then let us go to court together. Who thinks he has a case against me? Let him approach me. The Lord is coming to my help, who dare condemn me?

### Psalm 114:1-6.8-9. R. v.9

*I will walk in the presence of the Lord, in the land of the living.*

### James 2:14-18

Take the case, my brothers, of someone who has never done a single good act but claims that he has faith. Will that faith save him? If one of the brothers or one of the sisters is in need of clothes and has not enough food to live on, and one of you says to them, 'I wish you well; keep yourself warm and eat plenty,' without giving them these bare necessities of life, then what good is that? Faith is like that: if good works do not go with it, it is quite dead.

This is the way to talk to people of that kind: 'You say you have faith and I have good deeds; I will prove to you that I have faith by showing you my good deeds – now you prove to me that you have faith without any good deeds to show.'

### Mark 8:27-35

Jesus and his disciples left for the villages round Caesarea Philippi. On the way he put this question to his disciples, 'Who do people say I am?' And they told him. 'John the Baptist,' they said, 'others Elijah; others again, one of the prophets.' 'But you,' he asked 'who do you say I am?' Peter spoke up and said to him, 'You are the Christ.' And he gave them strict orders not to tell anyone about him.

And he began to teach them that the Son of Man was destined to suffer grievously, to be rejected by the elders and the chief priests and the scribes, and to be put to death, and after three days to rise again; and he said all this quite openly. Then, taking him aside, Peter started to remonstrate with him. But, turning and seeing his disciples, he rebuked Peter and said to him, 'Get behind me, Satan! Because the way you think is not God's way but man's.'

He called the people and his disciples to him and said, 'If anyone wants to be a follower of mine, let him renounce himself and take up his cross and follow me. For anyone who wants to save his life will lose it; but anyone who loses his life for my sake, and for the sake of the gospel, will save it.'

## Reflection

After hearing how highly people thought of him, Jesus points out how temporary this is – telling them how he will suffer and be rejected by his own people. This can happen to us too, in our everyday lives, especially in social media. It happens to people we care about. Jesus teaches us never to hold on to what others are telling about us, but to dedicate our energy instead to forget ourselves and live the gospel.

**24th Week
in Ordinary Time
St John Chrysostom,
bishop, doctor
Memorial
White**

### 1 Timothy 2:1-8

My advice is that, first of all, there should be prayers offered for everyone – petitions, intercessions and thanksgiving – and especially for kings and others in authority, so that we may be able to live religious and reverent lives in peace and quiet. To do this is right, and will please God our saviour: he wants everyone to be saved and reach full knowledge of the truth. For there is only one God, and there is only one mediator between God and mankind, himself a man, Christ Jesus, who sacrificed himself as a ransom for them all. He is the evidence of this, sent at the appointed time, and I have been named a herald and apostle of it and – I am telling the truth and no lie – a teacher of the faith and the truth to the pagans.

In every place, then, I want the men to lift their hands up reverently in prayer, with no anger or argument.

### Psalm 27:2.7-9. R. v.6

*Blessed be the Lord, for he has heard my cry.*

### Luke 7:1-10

When Jesus had come to the end of all he wanted the people to hear, he went into Capernaum. A centurion there had a servant, a favourite of his, who was sick and near death. Having heard about Jesus he sent some Jewish elders to him to ask him to come and heal his servant. When they came to Jesus they pleaded earnestly with him. 'He deserves this of you' they said 'because he is friendly towards our people; in fact, he is the one who built the synagogue.' So Jesus went with them, and was not very far from the house when the centurion sent word to him by some friends: 'Sir,' he said 'do not put yourself to trouble; because I am not worthy to have you under my roof; and for this same reason I did not presume to come to you myself; but give the word and let my servant be cured. For I am under authority myself, and have soldiers under me; and I say to one man: Go, and he goes; to another: Come here, and he comes; to my servant: Do this, and he does it.' When Jesus heard these words he was astonished at him and, turning round, said to the crowd following him, 'I tell you, not even in Israel have I found faith like this.' And when the messengers got back to the house they found the servant in perfect health.

### Reflection

This centurion knew his place in the world, he did not expect Jesus to come to him and help, but the prayers of his friends, the Jewish elders, brought Jesus to him. Even at that, the centurion, knowing the order of the world, believed it would be the same for heavenly things. Orders are orders. We learn that faith doesn't need to be a special gift, it just needs simplicity of heart.

## Numbers 21:4-9

On the way through the wilderness the people lost patience. They spoke against God and against Moses, 'Why did you bring us out of Egypt to die in this wilderness? For there is neither bread nor water here: we are sick of this unsatisfying food.'

At this God sent fiery serpents among the people; their bite brought death to many in Israel. The people came and said to Moses, 'We have sinned by speaking against the Lord and against you. Intercede for us with the Lord to save us from these serpents.' Moses interceded for the people, and the Lord answered him, 'Make a fiery serpent and put it on a standard. If anyone is bitten and looks at it, he shall live.' So Moses fashioned a bronze serpent which he put on a standard, and if anyone was bitten by a serpent, he looked at the bronze serpent and lived.

## Psalm 77:1-2.34-38. R. v.7

*Never forget the deeds of the Lord.*

## Philippians 2:6-11

The state of Jesus Christ was divine, yet he did not cling to his equality with God but emptied himself to assume the condition of a slave, and became as men are: and being as all men are, he was humbler yet, even to accepting death, death on a cross. But God raised him high and gave him the name which is above all other names so that all beings in the heavens, on earth and in the underworld, should bend the knee at the name of Jesus and that every tongue should acclaim Jesus Christ as Lord, to the glory of God the Father.

## John 3:13-17

Jesus said to Nicodemus: 'No one has gone up to heaven except the one who came down from heaven, the Son of Man who is in heaven; and the Son of Man must be lifted up as Moses lifted up the serpent in the desert, so that everyone who believes may have eternal life in him. Yes, God loved the world so much that he gave his only Son, so that everyone who believes in him may not be lost but may have eternal life. For God sent his Son into the world not to condemn the world, but so that through him the world might be saved.'

**The Exaltation
of the Holy Cross
Feast
Red**

## Reflection

This is a consoling gospel, a glorious day when we are reassured of salvation through our Lord Jesus. The first reading is a key to understanding the gospel. That which we expect to bring us most pain – death – if we face it in Christ, it will not harm us but bring us to eternal life. We must face death every day and turn to Christ who will save us.

**24th Week
in Ordinary Time
Our Lady of Sorrows
Memorial
White**

### 1 Timothy 3:14-16

At the moment of writing to you, I am hoping that I may be with you soon; but in case I should be delayed, I wanted you to know how people ought to behave in God's family – that is, in the Church of the living God, which upholds the truth and keeps it safe. Without any doubt, the mystery of our religion is very deep indeed:

He was made visible in the flesh,
attested by the Spirit,
seen by angels,
proclaimed to the pagans,
believed in by the world,
taken up in glory.

### Psalm 110:1-6

*Great are the works of the Lord.*

### John 19:25-27

Near the cross of Jesus stood his mother and his mother's sister, Mary the wife of Clopas, and Mary of Magdala. Seeing his mother and the disciple he loved standing near her, Jesus said to his mother, 'Woman, this is your son.' Then to the disciple he said, 'This is your mother.' And from that moment the disciple made a place for her in his home.

### Reflection

Now, as baptised in Christ, Jesus' followers, we receive the sorrowful mother as our mother. What if we were to care for her as the beloved disciple did? Mary now depends on John, on the Church, to care for her in her sorrow. They have each other to lean on now. The first reading reminds us that we are family and now we should behave: uphold truth and proclaim the mystery of Jesus the Christ.

1 Timothy 4:12-16
*(See Appendix B-27)*

Psalm 110:7-10. R. v.2
*How great are the works of the Lord!* (or *Alleluia!*)

Luke 7:36-50
One of the Pharisees invited Jesus to a meal. When he arrived at the Pharisee's house and took his place at table, a woman came in, who had a bad name in the town. She had heard he was dining with the Pharisee and had brought with her an alabaster jar of ointment. She waited behind him at his feet, weeping, and her tears fell on his feet, and she wiped them away with her hair; then she covered his feet with kisses and anointed them with the ointment.

When the Pharisee who had invited him saw this, he said to himself, 'If this man were a prophet, he would know who this woman is that is touching him and what a bad name she has.' Then Jesus took him up and said, 'Simon, I have something to say to you.' 'Speak, Master' was the reply. 'There was once a creditor who had two men in his debt; one owed him five hundred denarii, the other fifty. They were unable to pay, so he pardoned them both. Which of them will love him more?' 'The one who was pardoned more, I suppose' answered Simon. Jesus said, 'You are right.'

Then he turned to the woman. 'Simon,' he said 'you see this woman? I came into your house, and you poured no water over my feet, but she has poured out her tears over my feet and wiped them away with her hair. You gave me no kiss, but she has been covering my feet with kisses ever since I came in. You did not anoint my head with oil, but she has anointed my feet with ointment. For this reason I tell you that her sins, her many sins, must have been forgiven her, or she would not have shown such great love. It is the man who is forgiven little who shows little love.' Then he said to her, 'Your sins are forgiven.' Those who were with him at the table began to say to themselves, 'Who is this man, that he even forgives sins?' But he said to the woman, 'Your faith has saved you; go in peace.'

**24th Week
in Ordinary Time**
Sts Cornelius, *pope*, and
Cyprian, *bishop, martyrs*
**Memorial**
**Red**
or
**Saint Ninian, Bishop
(Scotland – Feast)**
*(See Appendix A-14)*

Reflection
One of the lessons from today's gospel is perhaps how easy it is for us to judge people in one light and assume that they are all bad and there is nothing we can learn from them. We therefore strip them of humanity in our mind's eye and become heartless and inhuman ourselves. Jesus teaches us to open our eyes and learn from others what we have closed our eyes to.

**24th Week
in Ordinary Time
Green
or
St Robert Bellarmine,
*bishop, doctor*
(Optional, White)**

**1 Timothy 6:2-12**
This is what you are to teach the brothers to believe and persuade them to do. Anyone who teaches anything different, and does not keep to the sound teaching which is that of our Lord Jesus Christ, the doctrine which is in accordance with true religion, is simply ignorant and must be full of self-conceit – with a craze for questioning everything and arguing about words. All that can come of this is jealousy, contention, abuse and wicked mistrust of one another; and unending disputes by people who are neither rational nor informed and imagine that religion is a way of making a profit. Religion, of course, does bring large profits, but only to those who are content with what they have. We brought nothing into the world, and we can take nothing out of it; but as long as we have food and clothing, let us be content with that. People who long to be rich are a prey to temptation; they get trapped into all sorts of foolish and dangerous ambitions which eventually plunge them into ruin and destruction. 'The love of money is the root of all evils' and there are some who, pursuing it, have wandered away from the faith, and so given their souls any number of fatal wounds.

But, as a man dedicated to God, you must avoid all that. You must aim to be saintly and religious, filled with faith and love, patient and gentle. Fight the good fight of the faith and win for yourself the eternal life to which you were called when you made your profession and spoke up for the truth in front of many witnesses.

**Psalm 48:6-10.17-20. R. Matthew 5:3**
*How happy are the poor in spirit: theirs is the kingdom of heaven.*

**Luke 8:1-3**
Jesus made his way through towns and villages preaching, and proclaiming the Good News of the kingdom of God. With him went the Twelve, as well as certain women, who had been cured of evil spirits and ailments: Mary surnamed the Magdalene, from whom seven demons had gone out, Joanna the wife of Herod's steward Chuza, Susanna, and several others who provided for them out of their own resources.

**Reflection**
Today we are reminded, that Jesus not only called twelve men to follow him and learn from him, but he also called women too. It is also important that some of these women were transformed by Jesus as he came into their lives. This is what happens when we follow Jesus – and then, when we do, we open all we must share with him and his other followers.

**24th Week
in Ordinary Time
Green**

## 1 Timothy 6:13-16

Before God the source of all life and before Jesus Christ, who spoke up as a witness for the truth in front of Pontius Pilate, I put to you the duty of doing all that you have been told, with no faults or failures, until the Appearing of our Lord Jesus Christ, who at the due time will be revealed by God, the blessed and only Ruler of all, the King of kings and the Lord of lords, who alone is immortal, whose home is in inaccessible light, whom no man has seen and no man is able to see: to him be honour and everlasting power. Amen.

## Psalm 99. R. v.2

*Come before the Lord, singing for joy.*

## Luke 8:4-15

With a large crowd gathering and people from every town finding their way to him, Jesus used this parable:

'A sower went out to sow his seed. As he sowed, some fell on the edge of the path and was trampled on; and the birds of the air ate it up. Some seed fell on rock, and when it came up it withered away, having no moisture. Some seed fell amongst thorns and the thorns grew with it and choked it. And some seed fell into rich soil and grew and produced its crop a hundredfold.' Saying this he cried, 'Listen, anyone who has ears to hear!'

His disciples asked him what this parable might mean, and he said, 'The mysteries of the kingdom of God are revealed to you; for the rest there are only parables, so that they may see but not perceive, listen but not understand.

'This, then, is what the parable means: the seed is the word of God. Those on the edge of the path are people who have heard it, and then the devil comes and carries away the word from their hearts in case they should believe and be saved. Those on the rock are people who, when they first hear it, welcome the word with joy. But these have no root; they believe for a while, and in time of trial they give up. As for the part that fell into thorns, this is people who have heard, but as they go on their way they are choked by the worries and riches and pleasures of life and do not reach maturity. As for the part in the rich soil, this is people with a noble and generous heart who have heard the word and take it to themselves and yield a harvest through their perseverance.'

## Reflection

The gospel today reminds us of the complexity of our lives. The Word of God – the seed – is the same, but the conditions of the soil are different. Some of those conditions we can manage, some of them are beyond our control. It is funny though, how Jesus tells the disciples that these mysteries are revealed to them – but he must explain them still! Perhaps we need to learn that we can do nothing without Jesus' help.

**25th Sunday
in Ordinary Time
Psalter Week 1
Green**

### Wisdom 2:12.17-20

The godless say to themselves, 'Let us lie in wait for the virtuous man, since he annoys us and opposes our way of life, reproaches us for our breaches of the law and accuses us of playing false to our upbringing. Let us see if what he says is true, let us observe what kind of end he himself will have. If the virtuous man is God's son, God will take his part and rescue him from the clutches of his enemies. Let us test him with cruelty and with torture, and thus explore this gentleness of his and put his endurance to the proof. Let us condemn him to a shameful death since he will be looked after – we have his word for it.'

### Psalm 53:3-6.8. R. v.6
*The Lord upholds my life.*

### James 3:16–4:3

Wherever you find jealousy and ambition, you find disharmony, and wicked things of every kind being done; whereas the wisdom that comes down from above is essentially something pure; it also makes for peace, and is kindly and considerate; it is full of compassion and shows itself by doing good; nor is there any trace of partiality or hypocrisy in it. Peacemakers, when they work for peace, sow the seeds which will bear fruit in holiness.

Where do these wars and battles between yourselves first start? Isn't it precisely in the desires fighting inside your own selves? You want something and you haven't got it; so you are prepared to kill. You have an ambition that you cannot satisfy; so you fight to get your way by force. Why you don't have what you want is because you don't pray for it; when you do pray and don't get it, it is because you have not prayed properly, you have prayed for something to indulge your own desires.

### Mark 9:30-37

After leaving the mountain Jesus and his disciples made their way through Galilee; and he did not want anyone to know, because he was instructing his disciples; he was telling them, 'The Son of Man will be delivered into the hands of men; they will put him to death; and three days after he has been put to death he will rise again.' But they did not understand what he said and were afraid to ask him.

They came to Capernaum, and when he was in the house he asked them, 'What were you arguing about on the road?' They said nothing because they had been arguing which of them was the greatest. So he sat down, called the Twelve to him and said, 'If anyone wants to be first, he must make himself last of all and servant of all.' He then took a little child, set him in front of them, put his arms round him, and said to them, 'Anyone who welcomes one of these little children in my name, welcomes me; and anyone who welcomes me welcomes not me but the one who sent me.'

## Reflection

Anybody who observes children closely knows that they can be cute – but also manipulative and greedy – so this can't be a lesson in innocence. It must be a lesson on power. The disciples were arguing over status – one seeking to be better than another, but Jesus invites them to be humble – simply honest and welcome the helpless and unimportant people and serve them in his name. Jesus asks them to welcome those who will not bring them power.

## SEPTEMBER
# 20
## MONDAY

**25th Week
in Ordinary Time
Sts Andrew Kim
Tae-gŏn,** *priest, martyr*
**and Paul Chŏng Ha-sang
& Companions,** *martyrs*
**Memorial
Red**

### Ezra 1:1-6

In the first year of Cyrus king of Persia, to fulfil the word of the Lord that was spoken through Jeremiah, the Lord roused the spirit of Cyrus king of Persia to issue a proclamation and to have it publicly displayed throughout his kingdom: 'Thus speaks Cyrus king of Persia, "The Lord, the God of heaven, has given me all the kingdoms of the earth; he has ordered me to build him a Temple in Jerusalem, in Judah. Whoever there is among you of all his people, may his God be with him! Let him go up to Jerusalem in Judah to build the Temple of the Lord, the God of Israel – he is the God who is in Jerusalem. And let each survivor, wherever he lives, be helped by the people of that place with silver and gold, with goods and cattle, as well as voluntary offerings for the Temple of God which is in Jerusalem."'

Then the heads of families of Judah and of Benjamin, the priests and the Levites, in fact all whose spirit had been roused by God, prepared to go and rebuild the Temple of the Lord in Jerusalem; and all their neighbours gave them every assistance with silver, gold, goods, cattle, quantities of costly gifts and with voluntary offerings of every kind.

### Psalm 125. R. v.3
*What marvels the Lord worked for us.*

### Luke 8:16-18

Jesus said to the crowds: 'No one lights a lamp to cover it with a bowl or to put it under a bed. No, he puts it on a lamp-stand so that people may see the light when they come in. For nothing is hidden but it will be made clear, nothing secret but it will be known and brought to light. So take care how you hear; for anyone who has will be given more; from anyone who has not, even what he thinks he has will be taken away.'

### Reflection
We must ask ourselves, what has God given me? Because this gospel reminds us that if we are given something, it's because we are to share it with others. The first reading throws light on this – that the temple of the Lord should be built high in Jerusalem, but with the contributions of the faithful and their friends, so that it would be for all to see and take delight and ownership in.

**St Matthew**, *apostle, evangelist*
**Feast**
**Red**

### Ephesians 4:1-7.11-13

I, the prisoner in the Lord, implore you to lead a life worthy of your vocation. Bear with one another charitably, in complete selflessness, gentleness and patience. Do all you can to preserve the unity of the Spirit by the peace that binds you together. There is one Body, one Spirit, just as you were all called into one and the same hope when you were called. There is one Lord, one faith, one baptism, and one God who is Father of all, over all, through all and within all.

Each one of us, however, has been given his own share of grace, given as Christ allotted it. And to some, his gift was that they should be apostles; to some, prophets; to some, evangelists; to some, pastors and teachers; so that the saints together make a unity in the work of service, building up the body of Christ. In this way we are all to come to unity in our faith and in our knowledge of the Son of God, until we become the perfect Man, fully mature with the fullness of Christ himself.

### Psalm 18:2-5. R. v.5

*Their word goes forth through all the earth.*

### Matthew 9:9-13

As Jesus was walking on he saw a man named Matthew sitting by the customs house, and he said to him, 'Follow me.' And he got up and followed him.

While he was at dinner in the house it happened that a number of tax collectors and sinners came to sit at the table with Jesus and his disciples. When the Pharisees saw this, they said to his disciples, 'Why does your master eat with tax collectors and sinners?' When he heard this he replied, 'It is not the healthy who need the doctor, but the sick. Go and learn the meaning of the words: What I want is mercy, not sacrifice. And indeed I did not come to call the virtuous, but sinners.'

### Reflection

Matthew was by the customs house because he was a tax collector. He would have been considered a greedy man, or an extortionist or a bringer of misery. He would not have been considered a godly man. However, being invited by Jesus to follow him, many other ungodly men were inspired by this, and they felt free to approach Jesus. Sometimes we just don't invite people to the table that we should.

## SEPTEMBER

# 22

**WEDNESDAY**

**25th Week
in Ordinary Time
Green**

### Ezra 9:5-9

At the evening sacrifice I, Ezra, came out of my stupor and falling on my knees, with my garment and cloak torn, I stretched out my hands to the Lord my God, and said:

'My God, I am ashamed, I blush to lift my face to you, my God. For our crimes have increased, until they are higher than our heads, and our sin has piled up to heaven. From the days of our ancestors until now our guilt has been great; on account of our crimes we, our kings and our priests, were given into the power of the kings of other countries, given to the sword, to captivity, to pillage and to shame, as is the case today. But now, suddenly, the Lord our God by his favour has left us a remnant and granted us a refuge in his holy place; this is how our God has cheered our eyes and given us a little respite in our slavery. For we are slaves: but God has not forgotten us in our slavery; he has shown us kindness in the eyes of the kings of Persia, obtaining permission for us to rebuild the Temple of our God and restore its ruins, and he has found us safety and shelter in Judah and in Jerusalem.'

### Psalm: Tobit 13:2.4.6-8. R. v.1

*Blessed be God, who lives for ever.*

### Luke 9:1-6

Jesus called the Twelve together and gave them power and authority over all devils and to cure diseases, and he sent them out to proclaim the kingdom of God and to heal. He said to them, 'Take nothing for the journey: neither staff, nor haversack, nor bread, nor money; and let none of you take a spare tunic. Whatever house you enter, stay there; and when you leave, let it be from there. As for those who do not welcome you, when you leave their town shake the dust from your feet as a sign to them.' So they set out and went from village to village proclaiming the Good News and healing everywhere.

### Reflection

Jesus was giving his disciples the power to do wonderful things in his name, but with the indispensable condition that they should go vulnerable and powerless. God's work is only accomplished when we remove all barriers and don't present ourselves as arrogant benefactors – we need to take off our shoes and walk the earth as fellow-wounded and needy human beings. We cannot witness to this Good News if we do not show it in our own flesh.

## Haggai 1:1-8

In the second year of King Darius, on the first day of the sixth month, the word of the Lord was addressed through the prophet Haggai to Zerubbabel son of Shealtiel, high commissioner of Judah, and to Joshua son of Jehozadak, the high priest, as follows, 'The Lord of hosts says this, "This people says: The time has not yet come to rebuild the Temple of the Lord. (And the word of the Lord was addressed through the prophet Haggai, as follows: ) Is this a time for you to live in your panelled houses, when this House lies in ruins? So now, the Lord of hosts says this: Reflect carefully how things have gone for you. You have sown much and harvested little; you eat but never have enough, drink but never have your fill, put on clothes but do not feel warm. The wage earner gets his wages only to put them in a purse riddled with holes. Reflect carefully how things have gone for you. So go to the hill country, fetch wood, and rebuild the House: I shall then take pleasure in it, and be glorified there, says the Lord."'

## Psalm 149:1-6.9. R. v.4

*The Lord takes delight in his people.*

## Luke 9:7-9

Herod the tetrarch had heard about all that was being done by Jesus; and he was puzzled, because some people were saying that John had risen from the dead, others that Elijah had reappeared, still others that one of the ancient prophets had come back to life. But Herod said, 'John? I beheaded him. So who is this I hear such reports about?' And he was anxious to see Jesus.

**25th Week
in Ordinary Time
St Pius of Pietrelcina,
*priest*
Memorial
White**

## Reflection

Who knows what was going through Herod's mind? It would be normal for him to be puzzled. People were saying various things about Jesus, none of them even knew him; it was all gossip and hearsay. We can never really know persons until we meet them at a profound level, and the same is true for us today. We must encounter the risen Jesus for us to be able to tell others – this is our work of evangelisation today.

## SEPTEMBER
# 24
### FRIDAY

**25th Week
in Ordinary Time
Green**

### Haggai 1:15–2:9

In the second year of King Darius, on the twenty-first day of the seventh month, the word of the Lord was addressed through the prophet Haggai, as follows, 'You are to speak to Zerubbabel son of Shealtiel, the high commissioner of Judah, to Joshua son of Jehozadak, the high priest, and to all the remnant of the people. Say this, "Who is there left among you that saw this Temple in its former glory? And how does it look to you now? Does it seem nothing to you? But take courage now, Zerubbabel – it is the Lord who speaks. Courage, High Priest Joshua son of Jehozadak. Courage, all you people of the country! – it is the Lord who speaks. To work! I am with you – it is the Lord of hosts who speaks – and my spirit remains among you. Do not be afraid! For the Lord of hosts says this: A little while now, and I am going to shake the heavens and the earth, the sea and the dry land. I will shake all the nations and the treasures of all the nations shall flow in, and I will fill this Temple with glory, says the Lord of hosts. Mine is the silver, mine the gold! – it is the Lord of hosts who speaks. The new glory of this Temple is going to surpass the old, says the Lord of hosts, and in this place I will give peace – it is the Lord of hosts who speaks."'

### Psalm 42:1-4. R. cf. v.5

*Hope in God; I will praise him still, my saviour and my God.*

### Luke 9:18-22

One day when Jesus was praying alone in the presence of his disciples he put this question to them, 'Who do the crowds say I am?' And they answered, 'John the Baptist; others Elijah; and others say one of the ancient prophets come back to life.' 'But you,' he said 'who do you say I am?' It was Peter who spoke up. 'The Christ of God' he said. But he gave them strict orders not to tell anyone anything about this.

'The Son of Man' he said 'is destined to suffer grievously, to be rejected by the elders and chief priests and scribes and to be put to death, and to be raised up on the third day.'

### Reflection

How did Jesus pray? Jesus was praying, in the presence of his disciples. That means, he didn't always go off to be alone. How did he pray, what was going through his mind if it popped into his head to ask this question of his disciples? He must have been reflecting on himself, or his life. Perhaps reflecting on our life with God is prayer too.

## Zechariah 2:5-9.14-15

Raising my eyes, I saw a vision. It was this: there was a man with a measuring line in his hand. I asked him, 'Where are you going?' He said, 'To measure Jerusalem, to find out her breadth and her length.' And then, while the angel who was talking to me stood still, another angel came forward to meet him. He said to him, 'Run, and tell that young man this, "Jerusalem is to remain unwalled, because of the great number of men and cattle there will be in her. But I – it is the Lord who speaks – I will be a wall of fire for her all round her, and I will be her glory in the midst of her."'

Sing, rejoice, daughter of Zion; for I am coming to dwell in the middle of you – it is the Lord who speaks. Many nations will join the Lord, on that day; they will become his people.

## Psalm: Jeremiah 31:10-13. R. v.10

*The Lord will guard us, as a shepherd guards his flock.*

## Luke 9:43-45

At a time when everyone was full of admiration for all he did, Jesus said to his disciples, 'For your part, you must have these words constantly in your mind: The Son of Man is going to be handed over into the power of men.' But they did not understand him when he said this; it was hidden from them so that they should not see the meaning of it, and they were afraid to ask him about what he had just said.

**25th Week in Ordinary Time**
**Green**

## Reflection

In God giving us his only son, he did it with no strings attached. Jesus did not come with power or glory or riches or position. He was "handed over" to the power of men. Jesus even today is handed over to us – what do we do with him? No matter what, as we have learned, God will turn all things for the good in the end, because his mercy is our salvation.

**26th Sunday
in Ordinary Time
Psalter Week 2
Green**

### Numbers 11:25-29

The Lord came down in the Cloud. He spoke with Moses, but took some of the spirit that was on him and put it on the seventy elders. When the spirit came on them they prophesied, but not again.

Two men had stayed back in the camp; one was called Eldad and the other Medad. The spirit came down on them; though they had not gone to the Tent, their names were enrolled among the rest. These began to prophesy in the camp. The young man ran to tell this to Moses, 'Look,' he said, 'Eldad and Medad are prophesying in the camp.' Then said Joshua the son of Nun, who had served Moses from his youth, 'My Lord Moses, stop them!' Moses answered him, 'Are you jealous on my account? If only the whole people of the Lord were prophets, and the Lord gave his Spirit to them all!'

## Psalm 18:8.10.12-14. R. v.9

*The precepts of the Lord gladden the heart.*

## James 5:1-6

An answer for the rich. Start crying, weep for the miseries that are coming to you. Your wealth is all rotting, your clothes are all eaten up by moths. All your gold and your silver are corroding away, and the same corrosion will be your own sentence, and eat into your body. It was a burning fire that you stored up as your treasure for the last days. Labourers mowed your fields, and you cheated them – listen to the wages that you kept back, calling out; realise that the cries of the reapers have reached the ears of the Lord of hosts. On earth you have had a life of comfort and luxury; in the time of slaughter you went on eating to your heart's content. It was you who condemned the innocent and killed them; they offered you no resistance.

## Mark 9:38-43.45.47-48

John said to Jesus, 'Master, we saw a man who is not one of us casting out devils in your name; and because he was not one of us we tried to stop him.' But Jesus said, 'You must not stop him: no one who works a miracle in my name is likely to speak evil of me. Anyone who is not against us is for us.

'If anyone gives you a cup of water to drink just because you belong to Christ, then I tell you solemnly, he will most certainly not lose his reward.

'But anyone who is an obstacle to bring down one of these little ones who have faith, would be better thrown into the sea with a great millstone round his neck. And if your hand should cause you to sin, cut it off; it is better for you to enter into life crippled, than to have two hands and go to hell, into the fire that cannot be put out. And if your foot should cause you to sin, cut it off; it is better for you to enter into life lame, than to have two feet and be thrown into hell. And if your eye should cause you to sin, tear it out; it is better for you to enter into the kingdom of God with one eye, than to have two eyes and be thrown into hell where their worm does not die nor their fire go out.'

## Reflection

The gospel today is explaining that in the grand scale of things, there are only two positions – working in communion with God, through Jesus in the Holy Spirit, or not, and not doing so is the disastrous choice. It's a bad choice because of what it does to others – it robs them of the inheritance promised; that God's kingdom will come, and they can live with him in happiness forever.

**26th Week
in Ordinary Time
St Vincent de Paul, *priest*
Memorial
White**

### Zechariah 8:1-8

The word of the Lord of hosts was addressed to me as follows: 'The Lord of hosts says this. I am burning with jealousy for Zion, with great anger for her sake. 'The Lord of hosts says this. I am coming back to Zion and shall dwell in the middle of Jerusalem. Jerusalem will be called Faithful City and the mountain of the Lord of hosts, the Holy Mountain. 'The Lord of hosts says this. Old men and old women will again sit down in the squares of Jerusalem; every one of them staff in hand because of their great age. And the squares of the city will be full of boys and girls playing in the squares. 'The Lord of hosts says this. If this seems a miracle to the remnant of this people (in those days), will it seem one to me? It is the Lord of hosts who speaks. The Lord of hosts says this. Now I am going to save my people from the countries of the East and from the countries of the West. I will bring them back to live inside Jerusalem. They shall be my people and I will be their God in faithfulness and integrity.'

### Psalm 101:16-21.29.22-23. R. v.17

*The Lord shall build up Zion again and appear in all his glory.*

### Luke 9:46-50

An argument started between the disciples about which of them was the greatest. Jesus knew what thoughts were going through their minds, and he took a little child and set him by his side and then said to them, 'Anyone who welcomes this little child in my name welcomes me; and anyone who welcomes me welcomes the one who sent me. For the least among you all, that is the one who is great.'

John spoke up. 'Master,' he said 'we saw a man casting out devils in your name, and because he is not with us we tried to stop him.' But Jesus said to him, 'You must not stop him: anyone who is not against you is for you.'

### Reflection

Again today, Jesus teaches us that he is one of communion – communion with his heavenly father, with the little children whom the world regards as powerless, and with all those who do the mission of God. In communion there can be no competition of wills, only mutual attentiveness and service. This communion is open to us all, we only need to lay down control and enter in. This is intimacy with God.

**26th Week
in Ordinary Time
Green
or
St Wenceslaus, *martyr*
(Optional, Red)
St Lawrence Ruiz and
companions, *martyrs*
(Optional, Red)**

### Zechariah 8:20-23

The Lord of hosts says this. 'There will be other peoples yet, and citizens of great cities. And the inhabitants of one city will go to the next and say, "Come, let us go and entreat the favour of the Lord, and seek the Lord of hosts; I am going myself." And many peoples and great nations will come to seek the Lord of hosts in Jerusalem and to entreat the favour of the Lord.'

The Lord of hosts says this. 'In those days, ten men of nations of every language will take a Jew by the sleeve and say, "We want to go with you, since we have learnt that God is with you."'

### Psalm 86. R. Zechariah 8:23
*God is with us.*

### Luke 9:51-56

As the time drew near for him to be taken up to heaven, Jesus resolutely took the road for Jerusalem and sent messengers ahead of him. These set out, and they went into a Samaritan village to make preparations for him, but the people would not receive him because he was making for Jerusalem. Seeing this, the disciples James and John said, 'Lord, do you want us to call down fire from heaven to burn them up?' But he turned and rebuked them, and they went off to another village.

### Reflection

Jesus was focused on his mission; that the culmination of his self-giving would be fulfilled. Then two of his closest disciples – whom he'd taken up the mountain at the transfiguration – let him see how little they had understood about him. This is perhaps true of some of us disciples today, we must always be careful not to fall on the side of anger and retribution in the name of Jesus, who was meek and humble to death for everybody.

**Sts Michael, Gabriel, Raphael,** *archangels*
**Feast**
**White**

**Daniel 7:9-10.13-14**
*(Alternative Reading: Apocalypse 12: 7-12)*

As I watched: Thrones were set in place and one of great age took his seat. His robe was white as snow, the hair of his head as pure as wool. His throne was a blaze of flames, its wheels were a burning fire. A stream of fire poured out, issuing from his presence. A thousand thousand waited on him, ten thousand times ten thousand stood before him. A court was held and the books were opened. I gazed into the visions of the night. And I saw, coming on the clouds of heaven, one like a son of man. He came to the one of great age and was led into his presence. On him was conferred sovereignty, glory and kingship, and men of all peoples, nations and languages became his servants. His sovereignty is an eternal sovereignty which shall never pass away, nor will his empire ever be destroyed.

**Psalm 137:1-5. R. v.1**
*In the presence of the angels I will bless you, O Lord.*

**John 1:47-51**

When Jesus saw Nathanael coming he said of him, 'There is an Israelite who deserves the name, incapable of deceit.' 'How do you know me?' said Nathanael. 'Before Philip came to call you,' said Jesus, 'I saw you under the fig tree.' Nathanael answered, 'Rabbi, you are the Son of God, you are the King of Israel.' Jesus replied, 'You believe that just because I said: I saw you under the fig tree. You will see greater things than that.' And then he added, 'I tell you most solemnly, you will see heaven laid open and, above the Son of Man, the angels of God ascending and descending.'

**Reflection**
Today we remember the archangels – God's messengers. Whatever happened under the fig-tree that made Jesus say he was incapable of deceit, must have been related to the truth. The truth, Jesus tells us, will also be revealed one day, and in that truth, there are angels of God – messengers that go up and down, carrying God's word. Nathanael and all those of us who live in the truth will see that wonderful sight.

## Nehemiah 8:1-12

When the seventh month came, all the people gathered as one man on the square before the Water Gate. They asked Ezra the scribe to bring the Book of the Law of Moses which the Lord had prescribed for Israel. Accordingly Ezra the priest brought the Law before the assembly, consisting of men, women, and children old enough to understand. This was the first day of the seventh month. On the square before the Water Gate, in the presence of the men and women, and children old enough to understand, he read from the book from early morning till noon; all the people listened attentively to the Book of the Law.

Ezra the scribe stood on a wooden dais erected for the purpose. In full view of all the people – since he stood higher than all the people – Ezra opened the book; and when he opened it all the people stood up. ...
*(See Appendix B-28)*

## Psalm 18:8-11. R. v.9
*The precepts of the Lord gladden the heart.*

## Luke 10:1-12

The Lord appointed seventy-two others and sent them out ahead of him, in pairs, to all the towns and places he himself was to visit. He said to them, 'The harvest is rich but the labourers are few, so ask the Lord of the harvest to send labourers to his harvest. Start off now, but remember, I am sending you out like lambs among wolves. Carry no purse, no haversack, no sandals. Salute no one on the road. Whatever house you go into, let your first words be, "Peace to this house!" And if a man of peace lives there, your peace will go and rest on him; if not, it will come back to you. Stay in the same house, taking what food and drink they have to offer, for the labourer deserves his wages; do not move from house to house. Whenever you go into a town where they make you welcome, eat what is set before you. Cure those in it who are sick, and say, "The kingdom of God is very near to you." But whenever you enter a town and they do not make you welcome, go out into its streets and say, "We wipe off the very dust of your town that clings to our feet, and leave it with you. Yet be sure of this: the kingdom of God is very near." I tell you, on that day it will not go as hard with Sodom as with that town.'

## Reflection

36 pairs went out to prepare places where Jesus intended to go. It is interesting that they were not sent alone. Perhaps because Jewish law needs two witnesses, or because it might have been dangerous, or simply because we all need support. Genesis reminds us, "It is not good that man be alone." God doesn't want us to do it ourselves. God wants us poor, simple peacemakers who witness to communion. That is how we prepare the way for Jesus.

**26th Week
in Ordinary Time
St Jerome, *priest, doctor*
Memorial
White**

**26th Week
in Ordinary Time
St Therese of the Child
Jesus, *virgin, doctor*
Memorial
White**

### Baruch 1:15-22

Integrity belongs to the Lord our God; to us the look of shame we wear today, to us, the people of Judah and the citizens of Jerusalem, to our kings and princes, our priests, our prophets, as to our ancestors, because we have sinned in the sight of the Lord, have disobeyed him, and have not listened to the voice of the Lord our God telling us to follow the commandments which the Lord had ordained for us. From the day when the Lord brought our ancestors out of the land of Egypt until today we have been disobedient to the Lord our God, we have been disloyal, refusing to listen to his voice. And so the disasters, and the curse which the Lord pronounced through his servant Moses the day he brought our fathers out of Egypt to give us a land where milk and honey flow, have seized on us, disasters we experience today. Despite all the words of those prophets whom he sent us, we have not listened to the voice of the Lord our God, but, each following the dictates of his evil heart, we have taken to serving alien gods, and doing what is displeasing to the Lord our God.

### Psalm 78:1-5.8-9. R. v.9

*Rescue us, O Lord, for the glory of your name.*

### Luke 10:13-16

Jesus said to his disciples: 'Alas for you, Chorazin! Alas for you, Bethsaida! For if the miracles done in you had been done in Tyre and Sidon, they would have repented long ago, sitting in sackcloth and ashes. And still, it will not go as hard with Tyre and Sidon at the Judgement as with you. And as for you, Capernaum, did you want to be exalted high as heaven? You shall be thrown down to hell.

'Anyone who listens to you listens to me; anyone who rejects you rejects me, and those who reject me reject the one who sent me.'

### Reflection

As Jesus is witness of God, the disciples go as witnesses of Christ. St Therese left behind a concrete way of witnessing, an example of heroic virtue, childlike faith and affectionate sympathy, which in so many mysterious ways fulfilled her cherished resolution of always "doing good on earth". The quality of discipleship is embedded in deep spirituality, which is expressed in the life of service and selflessness, the life that asks nothing for itself and is willing to give all that others may benefit. This is possible because of one's total trust and deep surrender to God's providence.

## Baruch 4:5-12.27-29

Take courage, my people, constant reminder of Israel. You were sold to the nations, but not for extermination. You provoked God; and so were delivered to your enemies, since you had angered your creator by offering sacrifices to demons, not to God. You had forgotten the eternal God who reared you. You had also grieved Jerusalem who nursed you, for when she saw the anger fall on you from God, she said: Listen, you neighbours of Zion: God has sent me great sorrow. I have seen my sons and daughters taken into captivity, to which they have been sentenced by the Eternal. I had reared them joyfully; in tears, in sorrow, I watched them go away. Do not, any of you, exult over me, a widow, deserted by so many; I suffer loneliness because of the sins of my own children, who turned away from the Law of God. Take courage, my children, call on God: he who brought disaster on you will remember you. As by your will you first strayed away from God, so now turn back and search for him ten times as hard; for as he brought down those disasters on you, so will he rescue you and give you eternal joy.

## Psalm 68:33-37

*The Lord listens to the needy.*

## Matthew 18:1-5.10

The disciples came to Jesus and said, 'Who is the greatest in the kingdom of heaven?' So he called a little child to him and set the child in front of them. Then he said, 'I tell you solemnly, unless you change and become like little children you will never enter the kingdom of heaven. And so, the one who makes himself as little as this little child is the greatest in the kingdom of heaven.

'Anyone who welcomes a little child like this in my name welcomes me. See that you never despise any of these little ones, for I tell you that their angels in heaven are continually in the presence of my Father in heaven.'

**26th Week
in Ordinary Time
The Holy
Guardian Angels
Memorial
White**

## Reflection

The reality of the guardian angels is one of the most consoling and inspiring truths of our faith. Angels played an active role in the Old Testament, in the life of Jesus and of the Church. God entrusts each human being to the guidance and protection of a guardian angel. "From infancy to death human life is surrounded by their watchful care and intercession" (CCC 336). It is essential to have a heart of a child to be open to the signs of God's love through our guardian angels.

### Genesis 2:18-24

The Lord God said, 'It is not good that the man should be alone. I will make him a helpmate.' So from the soil the Lord God fashioned all the wild beasts and all the birds of heaven. These he brought to the man to see what he would call them; each one was to bear the name the man would give it. The man gave names to all the cattle, all the birds of heaven and all the wild beasts. But no helpmate suitable for man was found for him. So the Lord God made the man fall into a deep sleep. And while he slept, he took one of his ribs and enclosed it in flesh. The Lord built the rib he had taken from the man into a woman, and brought her to the man. The man exclaimed:

'This at last is bone from my bones, and flesh from my flesh! This is to be called woman, for this was taken from man.'

This is why a man leaves his father and mother and joins himself to his wife, and they become one body.

### Psalm 127. R. v.5

*May the Lord bless us all the days of our life.*

### Hebrews 2:9-11

We see in Jesus one who was for a short while made lower than the angels and is now crowned with glory and splendour because he submitted to death; by God's grace he had to experience death for all mankind.

As it was his purpose to bring a great many of his sons into glory, it was appropriate that God, for whom everything exists and through whom everything exists, should make perfect, through suffering, the leader who would take them to their salvation. For the one who sanctifies, and the ones who are sanctified, are of the same stock; that is why he openly calls them brothers.

### Mark 10:1-12 *(Longer Form: Mark 10:2-16)*

Some Pharisees approached Jesus and asked, 'Is it against the law for a man to divorce his wife?' They were testing him. He answered them, 'What did Moses command you?' 'Moses allowed us' they said 'to draw up a writ of dismissal and so to divorce.' Then Jesus said to them, 'It was because you were so unteachable that he wrote this commandment for you. But from the beginning of creation God made them male and female. This is why a man must leave father and mother, and the two become one body. They are no longer two, therefore, but one body. So then, what God has united, man must not divide.' Back in the house the disciples questioned him again about this, and he said to them, 'The man who divorces his wife and marries another is guilty of adultery against her. And if a woman divorces her husband and marries another she is guilty of adultery too.'

## Reflection

Is it lawful for a man to divorce his wife? Jesus grabs this as an opportunity to instruct his disciples about the character and cost of discipleship. Marriage like discipleship requires absolute commitment and fidelity. Sons and daughters of the kingdom see the divine will in marriage because it is part of God's plan and will in creating the human race. The relationship between the husband and the wife reflects God's relationship with his people. Our relationship with God is based on freedom and love and not on law.

**27th Week
in Ordinary Time
St Francis of Assisi
Memorial
White**

Jonah 1:1-2:1.11

*(See Appendix B-28)*

Psalm Jon 2:3-5.8. R. v.7
*You lifted my life from the pit, O Lord.*

## Luke 10:25-37

There was a lawyer who, to disconcert Jesus, stood up and said to him, 'Master, what must I do to inherit eternal life?' He said to him, 'What is written in the Law? What do you read there?' He replied, 'You must love the Lord your God with all your heart, with all your soul, with all your strength, and with all your mind, and your neighbour as yourself.' 'You have answered right,' said Jesus 'do this and life is yours.'

But the man was anxious to justify himself and said to Jesus, 'And who is my neighbour?' Jesus replied, 'A man was once on his way down from Jerusalem to Jericho and fell into the hands of brigands; they took all he had, beat him and then made off, leaving him half dead. Now a priest happened to be travelling down the same road, but when he saw the man, he passed by on the other side. In the same way a Levite who came to the place saw him, and passed by on the other side. But a Samaritan traveller who came upon him was moved with compassion when he saw him. He went up and bandaged his wounds, pouring oil and wine on them. He then lifted him on to his own mount, carried him to the inn and looked after him. Next day, he took out two denarii and handed them to the innkeeper. "Look after him," he said "and on my way back I will make good any extra expense you have." Which of these three, do you think, proved himself a neighbour to the man who fell into the brigands' hands?' 'The one who took pity on him' he replied. Jesus said to him, 'Go, and do the same yourself.'

## Reflection

In this parable Jesus shows that neighbourliness is something which cuts across all-natural barriers and hatreds. The Samaritan is the embodiment of someone the Jews despise and dislike, the person with whom they would have no dealings and would least wish to be in any way indebted. The heart of the story tells us that the person whom you must love is not the person whom you can help (victim), but the person who can help you personified by the Samaritan – the person you ostracise and exclude from your life. The subtle message of this parable is to show us the beauty not of charity but of humility, that most elusive of all virtues.

**27th Week
in Ordinary Time
Green
or
St Faustina Kowalska,
*virgin*
(Optional, White)**

## Jonah 3:1-10

The word of the Lord was addressed to Jonah: 'Up!' he said, 'Go to Nineveh, the great city, and preach to them as I told you to.' Jonah set out and went to Nineveh in obedience to the word of the Lord. Now Nineveh was a city great beyond compare: it took three days to cross it. Jonah went on into the city, making a day's journey. He preached in these words, 'Only forty days more and Nineveh is going to be destroyed.' And the people of Nineveh believed in God; they proclaimed a fast and put on sackcloth, from the greatest to the least. The news reached the king of Nineveh, who rose from his throne, took off his robe, put on sackcloth and sat down in ashes. A proclamation was then promulgated throughout Nineveh, by decree of the king and his ministers, as follows: 'Men and beasts, herds and flocks, are to taste nothing; they must not eat, they must not drink water. All are to put on sackcloth and call on God with all their might; and let everyone renounce his evil behaviour and the wicked things he has done. Who knows if God will not change his mind and relent, if he will not renounce his burning wrath, so that we do not perish?' God saw their efforts to renounce their evil behaviour. And God relented: he did not inflict on them the disaster which he had threatened.

## Psalm 129:1-4.7-8. R. v.3

*If you, O Lord, should mark our guilt: Lord, who would survive?*

## Luke 10:38-42

Jesus came to a village, and a woman named Martha welcomed him into her house. She had a sister called Mary, who sat down at the Lord's feet and listened to him speaking. Now Martha who was distracted with all the serving said, 'Lord, do you not care that my sister is leaving me to do the serving all by myself? Please tell her to help me.' But the Lord answered: 'Martha, Martha,' he said 'you worry and fret about so many things, and yet few are needed, indeed only one. It is Mary who has chosen the better part; it is not to be taken from her.'

## Reflection

It is easy to sympathise with Martha and be sorry that the Lord rebukes her, the heart of the story is not the contrast between Martha and Mary or the roles they play. The distinction should be between sitting at the feet of the Lord and listening to the word and the perishable food being served with anxiety and worry. This little incident has special significance in our time, when we worry about the demands and pressures of life that we have no time to listen or to think. Life is more than food, and the body more than the clothing (Lk 12:22-23). When we do things out of love for God, they become source of joy instead of a burden..

**27th Week
in Ordinary Time
Green
or
St Bruno,** *priest*
**(Optional, White)**

### Jonah 4:1-11

Jonah was very indignant; he fell into a rage. He prayed to the Lord and said, 'Ah! Lord, is not this just as I said would happen when I was still at home? That was why I went and fled to Tarshish: I knew that you were a God of tenderness and compassion, slow to anger, rich in graciousness, relenting from evil. So now Lord, please take away my life, for I might as well be dead as go on living.' The Lord replied, 'Are you right to be angry?' Jonah then went out of the city and sat down to the east of the city. There he made himself a shelter and sat under it in the shade, to see what would happen to the city. Then the Lord God arranged that a castor-oil plant should grow up over Jonah to give shade for his head and soothe his ill-humour; Jonah was delighted with the castor-oil plant. But at dawn the next day, God arranged that a worm should attack the castor-oil plant – and it withered. Next, when the sun rose, God arranged that there should be a scorching east wind; the sun beat down so hard on Jonah's head that he was overcome and begged for death, saying, 'I might as well be dead as go on living.' God said to Jonah, 'Are you right to be angry about the castor-oil plant?' He replied, 'I have every right to be angry, to the point of death.' The Lord replied, 'You are only upset about a castor-oil plant which cost you no labour, which you did not make grow, which sprouted in a night and has perished in a night. And am I not to feel sorry for Nineveh, the great city, in which there are more than a hundred and twenty thousand people who cannot tell their right hand from their left, to say nothing of all the animals?'

### Psalm 85:3-6.9-10. R. v.15

*You, O Lord, have mercy and compassion.*

### Luke 11:1-4

Once Jesus was in a certain place praying, and when he had finished, one of his disciples said, 'Lord, teach us to pray, just as John taught his disciples.' He said to them, 'Say this when you pray:

"Father, may your name be held holy, your kingdom come; give us each day our daily bread, and forgive us our sins, for we ourselves forgive each one who is in debt to us. And do not put us to the test."'

### Reflection

Take note that all the pronouns in the prayer are in the plural. We pray not only for ourselves but also for the world. We ask for daily bread not only for ourselves, but also for all the starving poor of the world. We ask for forgiveness not only for ourselves, but also for all sinners who cannot pray for themselves. In prayer we approach God as a loving parent. Prayer ultimately is placing before God our absolute nothingness.

**27th Week
in Ordinary Time
Our Lady of the Rosary
Memorial
White**

## Malachi 3:13-20

You say harsh things about me, says the Lord. You ask, 'What have we said against you?' You say, 'It is useless to serve God; what is the good of keeping his commands or of walking mournfully before the Lord of hosts? Now we have reached the point when we call the arrogant blessed; yes, they prosper, these evildoers; they try God's patience and yet go free.' This is what those who fear the Lord used to say to one another. But the Lord took note and heard them: a book of remembrance was written in his presence recording those who fear him and take refuge in his name. On the day which I am preparing, says the Lord of hosts, they are going to be my own special possession. ...
*(See Appendix B-29)*

## Psalm 1. R. Psalm 39:5

*Happy the man who has placed his trust in the Lord.*

## Luke 11:5-13

Jesus said to his disciples: 'Suppose one of you has a friend and goes to him in the middle of the night to say, "My friend, lend me three loaves, because a friend of mine on his travels has just arrived at my house and I have nothing to offer him"; and the man answers from inside the house, "Do not bother me. The door is bolted now, and my children and I are in bed; I cannot get up to give it you." I tell you, if the man does not get up and give it him for friendship's sake, persistence will be enough to make him get up and give his friend all he wants.

'So I say to you: Ask, and it will be given to you; search, and you will find; knock, and the door will be opened to you. For the one who asks always receives; the one who searches always finds; the one who knocks will always have the door opened to him. What father among you would hand his son a stone when he asked for bread? Or hand him a snake instead of a fish? Or hand him a scorpion if he asked for an egg? If you then, who are evil, know how to give your children what is good, how much more will the heavenly Father give the Holy Spirit to those who ask him!'

## Reflection

If our relationship with God is really that of a child and his loving father then we have nothing to fear. The God to whom we pray is not a distant potentate to be approached only through intermediaries, or a tyrant to be appeased by gifts and flattering remarks, but a loving father who is interested in even the smallest details of our lives, who takes pride in our achievements, sorrows over our failures, and hungers for our love.

**27th Week
in Ordinary Time
Green**

### Joel 1:13-15; 2:1-2

Priests, put on sackcloth and lament. Ministers of the altar, wail. Come, pass the night in sackcloth, you ministers of my God. For the house of our God has been deprived of oblation and libation. Order a fast, proclaim a solemn assembly; elders, call together all the inhabitants of the country to the house of the Lord your God. Cry out to the Lord, 'Oh, what a day! For the day of the Lord is near, it comes as a devastation from Shaddai.' Sound the trumpet in Zion, give the alarm on my holy mountain! Let all the inhabitants of the country tremble, for the day of the Lord is coming, yes, it is near. Day of darkness and gloom, day of cloud and blackness. Like the dawn there spreads across the mountains a vast and mighty host, such as has never been before, such as will never be again to the remotest ages.

### Psalm 9:2-3.6.16.8-9. R. v.9

*The Lord will judge the world with justice.*

### Luke 11:15-26

When Jesus had cast out a devil, some of the people said, 'It is through Beelzebul, the prince of devils, that he casts out devils.' Others asked Jesus, as a test, for a sign from heaven; but, knowing what they were thinking, he said to them, 'Every kingdom divided against itself is heading for ruin, and a household divided against itself collapses. So too with Satan: if he is divided against himself, how can his kingdom stand? – since you assert that it is through Beelzebul that I cast out devils. Now if it is through Beelzebul that I cast out devils, through whom do your own experts cast them out? Let them be your judges, then. But if it is through the finger of God that I cast out devils, then know that the kingdom of God has overtaken you. So long as a strong man fully armed guards his own palace, his goods are undisturbed; but when someone stronger than he is attacks and defeats him, the stronger man takes away all the weapons he relied on and shares out his spoil.

'He who is not with me is against me; and he who does not gather with me scatters.

'When an unclean spirit goes out of a man it wanders through waterless country looking for a place to rest, and not finding one it says, "I will go back to the home I came from." But on arrival, finding it swept and tidied, it then goes off and brings seven other spirits more wicked than itself, and they go in and set up house there, so that the man ends up by being worse than he was before.'

### Reflection

Jesus' detractors are afflicted with spiritual myopia and are oblivious to the divine presence through his miracles. They see good as evil and evil as good. In Jesus, God has accomplished a self-disclosure with all of the simplicity and completeness we require. We only need to open our eyes and recognise the inbreaking of God's reign through the little miracles we encounter every day. We must choose for God and pay our obedience and allegiance to God.

**27th Week
in Ordinary Time
Green
or
St Denis, *bishop*, and
companions, *martyrs*
(Optional, Red)
St John Leonardi, *priest*
(Optional, White)**

### Joel 4:12-21

The Lord says this: 'Let the nations rouse themselves, let them march to the Valley of Jehoshaphat, for I am going to sit in judgement there on all the nations round. Put the sickle in: the harvest is ripe; come and tread: the winepress is full, the vats are overflowing, so great is their wickedness!' Host on host in the Valley of Decision! For the day of the Lord is near in the Valley of Decision! Sun and moon grow dark, the stars lose their brilliance. The Lord roars from Zion, makes his voice heard from Jerusalem; heaven and earth tremble. But the Lord will be a shelter for his people, a stronghold for the sons of Israel. 'You will learn then that I am the Lord your God, dwelling in Zion, my holy mountain. Jerusalem will be a holy place, no alien will ever pass through it again.' When that day comes, the mountains will run with new wine and the hills flow with milk, and all the river beds of Judah will run with water. A fountain will spring from the house of the Lord to water the wadi of Acacias. Egypt will become a desolation, Edom a desert waste on account of the violence done to the sons of Judah whose innocent blood they shed in their country. But Judah will be inhabited for ever, Jerusalem from age to age. 'I will avenge their blood and let none go unpunished,' and the Lord shall make his home in Zion.

### Psalm 96:1-2.5-6.11-12. R. v.12

*Rejoice, you just, in the Lord.*

### Luke 11:27-28

As Jesus was speaking, a woman in the crowd raised her voice and said, 'Happy the womb that bore you and the breasts you sucked!' But he replied, 'Still happier those who hear the word of God and keep it!'

### Reflection

Biological relationship wilts before the relationship in the kingdom which is based on response to the Word of God. Jesus' reply to the woman's praise of his eloquence is no rejection of his mother. Rather he points beyond mere physical relationship with him to a deeper faith relationship. Our knowledge of Jesus should lead to authentic faith that does justice in the here and now.

**28th Sunday
in Ordinary Time
Psalter Week 4
Green**

### Wisdom 7:7-11

I prayed, and understanding was given me; I entreated, and the spirit of Wisdom came to me. I esteemed her more than sceptres and thrones; compared with her, I held riches as nothing. I reckoned no priceless stone to be her peer, for compared with her, all gold is a pinch of sand, and beside her silver ranks as mud. I loved her more than health or beauty, preferred her to the light, since her radiance never sleeps. In her company all good things came to me, at her hands riches not to be numbered.

### Psalm 89:12-17. R. v.14

*Fill us with your love that we may rejoice.*

### Hebrews 4:12-13

The word of God is something alive and active: it cuts like any double-edged sword but more finely: it can slip through the place where the soul is divided from the spirit, or joints from the marrow; it can judge the secret emotions and thoughts. No created thing can hide from him; everything is uncovered and open to the eyes of the one to whom we must give account of ourselves.

### Mark 10:17-27 *(Longer Form: Mark 10:17-30)*

Jesus was setting out on a journey when a man ran up, knelt before him and put this question to him, 'Good master, what must I do to inherit eternal life?' Jesus said to him, 'Why do you call me good? No one is good but God alone. You know the commandments: You must not kill; You must not commit adultery; You must not steal; You must not bring false witness; You must not defraud; Honour your father and mother.' And he said to him, 'Master, I have kept all these from my earliest days.' Jesus looked steadily at him and loved him, and he said, 'There is one thing you lack. Go and sell everything you own and give the money to the poor, and you will have treasure in heaven; then come, follow me.' But his face fell at these words and he went away sad, for he was a man of great wealth.

Jesus looked round and said to his disciples, 'How hard it is for those who have riches to enter the kingdom of God!' The disciples were astounded by these words, but Jesus insisted, 'My children,' he said to them, 'how hard it is to enter the kingdom of God! It is easier for a camel to pass through the eye of a needle than for a rich man to enter the kingdom of God.' They were more astonished than ever. 'In that case' they said to one another 'who can be saved?' Jesus gazed at them. 'For men' he said 'it is impossible, but not for God: because everything is possible for God.'

## Reflection

The young man is shocked after Jesus challenges him to sell his possessions, give to the poor, and follow him. Jesus asks him to make a radical decision to love, one that does not know of accommodation and compromise. The young man fails the greatest challenge of his life because his wealth, instead of being a blessing, becomes a stumbling block to his gaining eternal life. In this story, Jesus defines discipleship not as a spiteful scorn for material goods but as a life of supreme love. The story has much to say to a world bedevilled by materialism. Riches signify so many things: proud self-sufficiency, the supremacy of the law of the profit over that of morality, the utter inequality in the use of the earth's goods, the search for pleasure and vanity. But all these are empty, all vanity!

*You may like to reflect on the painting of this episode on the front cover of this book, and the comment of the painter on page 2.*

## OCTOBER

# 11

### MONDAY

**28th Week
in Ordinary Time
Green
or
St John XXIII, *pope*
(Optional, White)**

### Romans 1:1-7

From Paul, a servant of Christ Jesus who has been called to be an apostle, and specially chosen to preach the Good News that God promised long ago through his prophets in the scriptures.

This news is about the Son of God who, according to the human nature he took, was a descendant of David: it is about Jesus Christ our Lord who, in the order of the spirit, the spirit of holiness that was in him, was proclaimed Son of God in all his power through his resurrection from the dead. Through him we received grace and our apostolic mission to preach the obedience of faith to all pagan nations in honour of his name. You are one of these nations, and by his call belong to Jesus Christ. To you all, then, who are God's beloved in Rome, called to be saints, may God our Father and the Lord Jesus Christ send grace and peace.

### Psalm 97:1-4. R. v.2

*The Lord has made known his salvation.*

### Luke 11:29-32

The crowds got even bigger and Jesus addressed them, 'This is a wicked generation; it is asking for a sign. The only sign it will be given is the sign of Jonah. For just as Jonah became a sign to the Ninevites, so will the Son of Man be to this generation. On Judgement day the Queen of the South will rise up with the men of this generation and condemn them, because she came from the ends of the earth to hear the wisdom of Solomon, and there is something greater than Solomon here. On Judgement day the men of Nineveh will stand up with this generation and condemn it, because when Jonah preached they repented; and there is something greater than Jonah here.'

### Reflection

Jesus extols the Queen of Sheba because she recognised the divine wisdom in Solomon and took the trouble and expense to put herself in the presence of that wisdom. By contrast, in Jesus, a more transparent personification of divine wisdom has come to the present generation of people, and they are for the most part oblivious to or indifferent to the presence. Jesus calls the crowd gathered around him an evil generation because they fail to see the entry of God's kingdom in his ministry, which calls for conversion of hearts and minds. They demand for more miracles other than what they have already seen Jesus doing.

## Romans 1:16-25

I am not ashamed of the Good News: it is the power of God saving all who have faith – Jews first, but Greeks as well – since this is what reveals the justice of God to us: it shows how faith leads to faith, or as scripture says: The upright man finds life through faith.

The anger of God is being revealed from heaven against all the impiety and depravity of men who keep truth imprisoned in their wickedness. For what can be known about God is perfectly plain to them since God himself has made it plain. Ever since God created the world his everlasting power and deity – however invisible – have been there for the mind to see in the things he has made. That is why such people are without excuse: they knew God and yet refused to honour him as God or to thank him; instead, they made nonsense out of logic and their empty minds were darkened. The more they called themselves philosophers, the more stupid they grew, until they exchanged the glory of the immortal God for a worthless imitation, for the image of mortal man, of birds, of quadrupeds and reptiles. That is why God left them to their filthy enjoyments and the practices with which they dishonour their own bodies, since they have given up divine truth for a lie and have worshipped and served creatures instead of the creator, who is blessed for ever. Amen!

## Psalm 18:2-5. R. v.2

*The heavens proclaim the glory of God.*

## Luke 11:37-41

Jesus had just finished speaking when a Pharisee invited him to dine at his house. He went in and sat down at the table. The Pharisee saw this and was surprised that he had not first washed before the meal. But the Lord said to him, 'Oh, you Pharisees! You clean the outside of cup and plate, while inside yourselves you are filled with extortion and wickedness. Fools! Did not he who made the outside make the inside too? Instead, give alms from what you have and then indeed everything will be clean for you.'

## Reflection

It is easy to equate the external appearance as more important than building up an authentic character or to link external piety with internal conversion. Jesus denounces the Pharisees for their excessive concern for ritual purity and the rigour of trivialities to appear good, but their interiority is full of the dirt of plunder and evil. Christian life is summarised as love of God and neighbour. We love God in our neighbour not for the benefit of onlookers. Today the Lord challenges you to walk the path of authentic conversion.

**28th Week
in Ordinary Time
Green**

### Romans 2:1-11

No matter who you are, if you pass judgement you have no excuse. In judging others you condemn yourself, since you behave no differently from those you judge. We know that God condemns that sort of behaviour impartially: and when you judge those who behave like this while you are doing exactly the same, do you think you will escape God's judgement? Or are you abusing his abundant goodness, patience and toleration, not realising that this goodness of God is meant to lead you to repentance? Your stubborn refusal to repent is only adding to the anger God will have towards you on that day of anger when his just judgements will be made known. He will repay each one as his works deserve. For those who sought renown and honour and immortality by always doing good there will be eternal life; for the unsubmissive who refused to take truth for their guide and took depravity instead, there will be anger and fury. Pain and suffering will come to every human being who employs himself in evil – Jews first, but Greeks as well; renown, honour and peace will come to everyone who does good – Jews first, but Greeks as well. God has no favourites.

### Psalm 61:2-3.6-7.9. R. v.13

*Lord, you repay each man according to his deeds.*

### Luke 11:42-46

The Lord said to the Pharisees: 'Alas for you Pharisees! You who pay your tithe of mint and rue and all sorts of garden herbs and overlook justice and the love of God! These you should have practised, without leaving the others undone. Alas for you Pharisees who like taking the seats of honour in the synagogues and being greeted obsequiously in the market squares! Alas for you, because you are like the unmarked tombs that men walk on without knowing it!'

A lawyer then spoke up. 'Master,' he said 'when you speak like this you insult us too.' 'Alas for you lawyers also,' he replied 'because you load on men burdens that are unendurable, burdens that you yourselves do not move a finger to lift.'

### Reflection

Jesus is blunt in his words of calling a spade a spade with regard to the abuses of the religious authorities. Their concern for outward purity hides a deep bankruptcy within. In Mt 23:33 Jesus has even harsher words for them: they are "serpents or brood of vipers" for turning religion an opportunity to suck out the blood of the poor. The heart of our Christian faith is righteousness and love of God. What pleases God is when we learn to live our whole lives as gifts, as a thanksgiving offering.

**28th Week
in Ordinary Time
Green
or
St Callistus I,** *pope,
martyr*
**(Optional, White)**

## Romans 3:21-30

God's justice that was made known through the Law and the Prophets has now been revealed outside the Law, since it is the same justice of God that comes through faith to everyone, Jew and pagan alike, who believes in Jesus Christ. Both Jew and pagan sinned and forfeited God's glory, and both are justified through the free gift of his grace by being redeemed in Christ Jesus who was appointed by God to sacrifice his life so as to win reconciliation through faith. In this way God makes his justice known; first, for the past, when sins went unpunished because he held his hand, then, for the present age, by showing positively that he is just, and that he justifies everyone who believes in Jesus.

So what becomes of our boasts? There is no room for them. What sort of law excludes them? The sort of law that tells us what to do? On the contrary, it is the law of faith, since, as we see it, a man is justified by faith and not by doing something the Law tells him to do. Is God the God of Jews alone and not of the pagans too? Of the pagans too, most certainly, since there is only one God.

## Psalm 129:1-6. R. v.7

*With the Lord there is mercy, and fullness of redemption.*

## Luke 11:47-54

Jesus said: 'Alas for you who build the tombs of the prophets, the men your ancestors killed! In this way you both witness what your ancestors did and approve it; they did the killing, you do the building.

'And that is why the Wisdom of God said, "I will send them prophets and apostles; some they will slaughter and persecute, so that this generation will have to answer for every prophet's blood that has been shed since the foundation of the world, from the blood of Abel to the blood of Zechariah, who was murdered between the altar and the sanctuary." Yes, I tell you, this generation will have to answer for it all.

'Alas for you lawyers who have taken away the key of knowledge! You have not gone in yourselves, and have prevented others going in who wanted to.'

When he left the house, the scribes and the Pharisees began a furious attack on him and tried to force answers from him on innumerable questions, setting traps to catch him out in something he might say.

## Reflection

Jesus attacks two privileged exclusive clubs: the Pharisees and the lawyers. He has openly accused them of the murder of the prophets and in making sure that the people were left in the darkness of ignorance to keep up their dignity and authority. This gives us a glimpse of why Jesus' public ministry has ended up on the cross. Knowledge is power. The Lord enjoins us to grab the opportunities to share the light with those who are in darkness or to bring freedom to those who are trapped.

**28th Week
in Ordinary Time
St Teresa of Jesus,
*virgin, doctor*
Memorial
White**

### Romans 4:1-8

What shall we say about Abraham, the ancestor from whom we are all descended? If Abraham was justified as a reward for doing something, he would really have had something to boast about, though not in God's sight because scripture says: Abraham put his faith in God, and this faith was considered as justifying him. If a man has work to show, his wages are not considered as a favour but as his due; but when a man has nothing to show except faith in the one who justifies sinners, then his faith is considered as justifying him. And David says the same: a man is happy if God considers him righteous, irrespective of good deeds: Happy those whose crimes are forgiven, whose sins are blotted out; happy the man whom the Lord considers sinless.

### Psalm 31:1-2.5.11. R. cf. v.7

*You are my refuge, O Lord; you fill me with the joy of salvation.*

### Luke 12:1-7

The people had gathered in their thousands so that they were treading on one another. And Jesus began to speak, first of all to his disciples. 'Be on your guard against the yeast of the Pharisees – that is, their hypocrisy. Everything that is now covered will be uncovered, and everything now hidden will be made clear. For this reason, whatever you have said in the dark will be heard in the daylight, and what you have whispered in hidden places will be proclaimed on the housetops.

'To you my friends I say: Do not be afraid of those who kill the body and after that can do no more. I will tell you whom to fear: fear him who, after he has killed, has the power to cast into hell. Yes, I tell you, fear him. Can you not buy five sparrows for two pennies? And yet not one is forgotten in God's sight. Why, every hair on your head has been counted. There is no need to be afraid: you are worth more than hundreds of sparrows.'

### Reflection

Generally, the New Testament associates the leaven with "fermentation" and with political and moral corruption. Jesus warns his disciples of the leaven of the Pharisees –hypocrisy – an evil thing which can grow and affect the whole society. It is a hidden yet powerful force beneath their virtuous appearance. One cannot hide anything from God for there is nothing concealed that will not be revealed, nor secret that will not be known. The way to discipleship is to be transparent in one's conviction.

## Romans 4:13.16-18

The promise of inheriting the world was not made to Abraham and his descendants on account of any law but on account of the righteousness which consists in faith. That is why what fulfils the promise depends on faith, so that it may be a free gift and be available to all of Abraham's descendants, not only those who belong to the Law but also those who belong to the faith of Abraham who is the father of all of us. As scripture says: I have made you the ancestor of many nations – Abraham is our father in the eyes of God, in whom he put his faith, and who brings the dead to life and calls into being what does not exist.

Though it seemed Abraham's hope could not be fulfilled, he hoped and he believed, and through doing so he did become the father of many nations exactly as he had been promised: Your descendants will be as many as the stars.

## Psalm 104:6-9.42-43. R. v.8

*The Lord remembers his covenant for ever.*

## Luke 12:9-12

Jesus said to his disciples: 'I tell you, if anyone openly declares himself for me in the presence of men, the Son of Man will declare himself for him in the presence of God's angels. But the man who disowns me in the presence of men will be disowned in the presence of God's angels.

'Everyone who says a word against the Son of Man will be forgiven, but he who blasphemes against the Holy Spirit will not be forgiven.

'When they take you before synagogues and magistrates and authorities, do not worry about how to defend yourselves or what to say, because when the time comes, the Holy Spirit will teach you what you must say.'

**28th Week
in Ordinary Time
Green
or
St Hedwig, *religious*
(Optional, White)
St Margaret Mary
Alacoque, *virgin*
(Optional, White)**

## Reflection

The sin against the Holy Spirit is not the uttering of any form of words, but the conscious and wicked rejection of the saving power and grace of God towards the human person. This resistance and denial of the power of the Holy Spirit to guide is described as "blasphemy against the Holy Spirit" because it denies the power of God to declare what is just and true. In Mark 3:28-30, Jesus is accused of being in league with the devil, and that what appears to be good deeds are in fact bad ones. The ultimate sin here is to call good evil and evil good. Once this continuing attitude has been reached in one's life there can be no forgiveness of sins because they will not appear to him as sins at all but as good deeds. A person in such a situation no longer has the capacity to repent and seek forgiveness because he or she lacks a sense of sin. Today let us surrender ourselves completely to the Holy Spirit for guidance and spiritual nourishment.

# OCTOBER
# 17
## SUNDAY

**29th Sunday
in Ordinary Time**
Psalter Week 1
**Green**

### Isaiah 53:10-11

The Lord has been pleased to crush his servant with suffering. If he offers his life in atonement, he shall see his heirs, he shall have a long life and through him what the Lord wishes will be done. His soul's anguish over he shall see the light and be content. By his sufferings shall my servant justify many, taking their faults on himself.

### Psalm 32:4-5.18-20.22. R. v.22

*May your love be upon us, O Lord, as we place all our hope in you.*

### Hebrews 4:14-16

Since in Jesus, the Son of God, we have the supreme high priest who has gone through to the highest heaven, we must never let go of the faith that we have professed. For it is not as if we had a high priest who was incapable of feeling our weaknesses with us; but we have one who has been tempted in every way that we are, though he is without sin. Let us be confident, then in approaching the throne of grace, that we shall have mercy from him and find grace when we are in need of help.

### Mark 10:35-45 *(Shorter Form: Mark 10:42-45)*

James and John, the sons of Zebedee, approached Jesus. 'Master,' they said to him, 'we want you to do us a favour.' He said to them, 'What is it you want me to do for you?' They said to him, 'Allow us to sit one at your right hand and the other at your left in your glory.' 'You do not know what you are asking' Jesus said to them. 'Can you drink the cup that I must drink, or be baptised with the baptism with which I must be baptised?' They replied, 'We can.' Jesus said to them, 'The cup that I must drink you shall drink, and with the baptism with which I must be baptised you shall be baptised, but as for seats at my right hand or my left, these are not mine to grant; they belong to those to whom they have been allotted.'

When the other ten heard this they began to feel indignant with James and John, so Jesus called them to him and said to them, 'You know that among the pagans their so-called rulers lord it over them, and their great men make their authority felt. This is not to happen among you. No; anyone who wants to become great among you must be your servant, and anyone who wants to be first among you must be slave to all. For the Son of Man himself did not come to be served but to serve, and to give his life as a ransom for many.

## Reflection

The two brothers aptly represent the attitude of worldly rulers characterised by their lust for authority and power and prestige. Jesus seizes the occasion to teach a lesson on power and authority not only to the two brothers but also to the other ten disciples who behave no better, getting jealous of the two. Jesus inculcates in them that true power is shown by a person's ability to stoop down and serve; the greatest are those who forget their position so as to minister to the needs of all. St Augustine, reflecting on his position as a bishop wrote: "What I am with you gives me joy, what I am for you frightens me. For with you, I am a Christian; for you I am a bishop. The former is grace, the latter is an office. The former is salvation, the latter a temptation."

**St Luke,** *evangelist*
**Feast**
**Red**

**2 Timothy 4:10-17**
Demas has deserted me for love of this life and gone to Thessalonika, Crescens has gone to Galatia and Titus to Dalmatia; only Luke is with me. Get Mark to come and bring him with you; I find him a useful helper in my work. I have sent Tychicus to Ephesus. When you come, bring the cloak I left with Carpus in Troas, and the scrolls, especially the parchment ones. Alexander the coppersmith has done me a lot of harm; the Lord will repay him for what he has done. Be on your guard against him yourself, because he has been bitterly contesting everything that we say.

The first time I had to present my defence, there was not a single witness to support me. Everyone of them deserted me – may they not be held accountable for it. But the Lord stood by me and gave me power, so that through me the whole message might be proclaimed for all the pagans to hear.

**Psalm 144:10-13.17-18. R. v.12**
*Your friends, O Lord, shall make known the glorious splendour of your reign.*

**Luke 10:1-9**
The Lord appointed seventy-two others and sent them out ahead of him, in pairs, to all the towns and places he himself was to visit. He said to them, 'The harvest is rich but the labourers are few, so ask the Lord of the harvest to send labourers to his harvest. Start off now, but remember, I am sending you out like lambs among wolves. Carry no purse, no haversack, no sandals. Salute no one on the road. Whatever house you go into, let your first words be, "Peace to this house!" And if a man of peace lives there, your peace will go and rest on him; if not, it will come back to you. Stay in the same house, taking what food and drink they have to offer, for the labourer deserves his wages; do not move from house to house. Whenever you go into a town where they make you welcome, eat what is set before you. Cure those in it who are sick, and say, "The kingdom of God is very near to you."'

**Reflection**
The rapid spread of Christianity is due not only to the Twelve but also to the many and active "apostles and evangelists" symbolised by the 72 disciples sent by Jesus. Many of them were fearful, entirely average, and sinners, often the least ideal candidates to do something for God. God likes using men and women who know that they do not know. God sees pride as a barrier to discipleship. Today God can do something incredible through you if you are open to the promptings of God's Spirit, because a heart oriented towards God can accomplish far more than wisdom and experience can. Your mission is something only you can do in your unique way.

### Romans 5:12.15.17-21

Sin entered the world through one man, and through sin death, and thus death has spread through the whole human race because everyone has sinned.

If it is certain that through one man's fall so many died, it is even more certain that divine grace, coming through the one man, Jesus Christ, came to so many as an abundant free gift. If it is certain that death reigned over everyone as the consequence of one man's fall, it is even more certain that one man, Jesus Christ, will cause everyone to reign in life who receives the free gift that he does not deserve, of being made righteous. Again, as one man's fall brought condemnation on everyone, so the good act of one man brings everyone life and makes them justified. As by one man's disobedience many were made sinners, so by one man's obedience many will be made righteous. But however great the number of sins committed, grace was even greater; and so, just as sin reigned wherever there was death, so grace will reign to eternal life, thanks to the righteousness that comes through Jesus Christ our Lord.

### Psalm 39:7-10.17. R. cf. vv. 8.9

*Here I am, Lord! I come to do your will.*

### Luke 12:35-38

Jesus said to his disciples: 'See that you are dressed for action and have your lamps lit. Be like men waiting for their master to return from the wedding feast, ready to open the door as soon as he comes and knocks. Happy those servants whom the master finds awake when he comes. I tell you solemnly, he will put on an apron, sit them down at table and wait on them. It may be in the second watch he comes, or in the third, but happy those servants if he finds them ready.'

**29th Week
in Ordinary Time
Green
or
Sts John of Brebeuf and
Isaac Jogues, *priests*,
and companions, *martyrs*
(Optional, Red)
St Paul of the Cross,
*priest*
(Optional, White)**

### Reflection

Christian existence is always in the context of waiting for and anticipating the Master – Jesus. Part of active waiting is letting go of worldly concerns and values. The prepared person will not be attached to the concerns of this life, even though she or he may be immersed in the midst of them. Moreover, Jesus' followers are ready to face the crises of life in the spirit of true discipleship.

**29th Week
in Ordinary Time
Green**

## Romans 6:12-18

You must not let sin reign in your mortal bodies or command your obedience to bodily passions, you must not let any part of your body turn into an unholy weapon fighting on the side of sin; you should, instead, offer yourselves to God, and consider yourselves dead men brought back to life; you should make every part of your body into a weapon fighting on the side of God; and then sin will no longer dominate your life, since you are living by grace and not by law. *(See Appendix B-29)*

## Psalm 123. R. v.8

*Our help is in the name of the Lord.*

## Luke 12:39-48

Jesus said to his disciples: 'You may be quite sure of this, that if the householder had known at what hour the burglar would come, he would not have let anyone break through the wall of his house. You too must stand ready, because the Son of Man is coming at an hour you do not expect.'

Peter said, 'Lord, do you mean this parable for us, or for everyone?' The Lord replied, 'What sort of steward, then, is faithful and wise enough for the master to place him over his household to give them their allowance of food at the proper time? Happy that servant if his master's arrival finds him at this employment. I tell you truly, he will place him over everything he owns. But as for the servant who says to himself, "My master is taking his time coming," and sets about beating the menservants and the maids, and eating and drinking and getting drunk, his master will come on a day he does not expect and at an hour he does not know. The master will cut him off and send him to the same fate as the unfaithful.

'The servant who knows what his master wants, but has not even started to carry out those wishes, will receive very many strokes of the lash. The one who did not know, but deserves to be beaten for what he has done, will receive fewer strokes. When a man has had a great deal given him, a great deal will be demanded of him; when a man has had a great deal given him on trust, even more will be expected of him.'

## Reflection

The Lord's coming will be sudden and unexpected "like a thief in the night". Its timing is unknown. Therefore the attitudes of vigilance are required, even if the return of the Master appears "delayed". The servant must make every effort to find out what God's will is and do it. All are accountable according to the responsibility one has received. Authority is meant to serve others. Today the Lord charges us to be vigilant while attending to our duties with a sense of responsibility.

**29th Week
in Ordinary Time
Green**

**Romans 6:19-23**

If I may use human terms to help your natural weakness: as once you put your bodies at the service of vice and immorality, so now you must put them at the service of righteousness for your sanctification.

When you were slaves of sin, you felt no obligation to righteousness, and what did you get from this? Nothing but experiences that now make you blush, since that sort of behaviour ends in death. Now, however, you have been set free from sin, you have been made slaves of God, and you get a reward leading to your sanctification and ending in eternal life. For the wage paid by sin is death; the present given by God is eternal life in Christ Jesus our Lord.

**Psalm 1:1-4.6. R. Psalm 39:5**

*Happy the man who has placed his trust in the Lord.*

**Luke 12:49-53**

Jesus said to his disciples: 'I have come to bring fire to the earth, and how I wish it were blazing already! There is a baptism I must still receive, and how great is my distress till it is over!

'Do you suppose that I am here to bring peace on earth? No, I tell you, but rather division. For from now on a household of five will be divided: three against two and two against three; the father divided against the son, son against father, mother against daughter, daughter against mother, mother-in-law against daughter-in-law, daughter-in-law against mother-in-law.'

**Reflection**

Jesus uses three words of great symbolic meaning in reference to his coming: fire, baptism and division. Fire symbolises purification and judgement. Jesus finds so much rubbish to be burned in men's lives – ideas, and in the religion of the day the ways it has become a burden. *Baptism* with the Holy Spirit and fire, that is, Jesus communicates God's love as a transforming power. *Division* ensues when people could not discern whether Jesus' miracles are the signal from God or whether he is a minion of Satan, a charlatan, a deceiver of the people. People must make a decision for or against God.

**29th Week
in Ordinary Time
Green
or
St John Paul II,** *pope*
**(Optional, White)**

### Romans 7:18-25

I know of nothing good living in me – living, that is, in my unspiritual self – for though the will to do what is good is in me, the performance is not, with the result that instead of doing the good things I want to do, I carry out the sinful things I do not want. When I act against my will, then, it is not my true self doing it, but sin which lives in me.

In fact, this seems to be the rule, that every single time I want to do good it is something evil that comes to hand. In my inmost self I dearly love God's Law, but I can see that my body follows a different law that battles against the law which my reason dictates. This is what makes me a prisoner of that law of sin which lives inside my body.

What a wretched man I am! Who will rescue me from this body doomed to death? Thanks be to God through Jesus Christ our Lord!

### Psalm 118:66.68.76-77.93-94. R. v.68

*Lord, teach me your statutes.*

### Luke 12:54-59

Jesus said to the crowds, 'When you see a cloud looming up in the west you say at once that rain is coming, and so it does. And when the wind is from the south you say it will be hot, and it is. Hypocrites! You know how to interpret the face of the earth and the sky. How is it you do not know how to interpret these times?

'Why not judge for yourselves what is right? For example: when you go to court with your opponent, try to settle with him on the way, or he may drag you before the judge and the judge hand you over to the bailiff and the bailiff have you thrown into prison. I tell you, you will not get out till you have paid the very last penny.'

### Reflection

Jesus chastises the crowds as hypocrites because they focus only on the external and superficial. They understand the winds of the earth, but not the winds of God; they could discern the sky, but not the heavens. Their religious externalism prevents them from seeing the significance of the coming of Jesus. And while they refuse to heed Jesus' call to conversion, they put their trust on false prophets and self-proclaimed messiahs. We are also like them when we expect God in spectacular events and fail to see God's presence in the littlest things that happen in every moment of our lives. Every moment is a call to conversion – no ifs, no buts, no tomorrow – the time for God is now!

## Romans 8:1-11

The reason why those who are in Christ Jesus are not condemned, is that the law of the spirit of life in Christ Jesus has set you free from the law of sin and death. God has done what the Law, because of our unspiritual nature, was unable to do. God dealt with sin by sending his own Son in a body as physical as any sinful body, and in that body God condemned sin. He did this in order that the Law's just demands might be satisfied in us, who behave not as our unspiritual nature but as the spirit dictates.

The unspiritual are interested only in what is unspiritual, but the spiritual are interested in spiritual things. It is death to limit oneself to what is unspiritual; life and peace can only come with concern for the spiritual. ...
*(See Appendix B-29)*

## Psalm 23:1-6. R. v.6
*Such are the men who seek your face, O Lord.*

## Luke 13:1-9

Some people arrived and told Jesus about the Galileans whose blood Pilate had mingled with that of their sacrifices. At this he said to them, 'Do you suppose these Galileans who suffered like that were greater sinners than any other Galileans? They were not, I tell you. No; but unless you repent you will all perish as they did. Or those eighteen on whom the tower at Siloam fell and killed them? Do you suppose that they were more guilty than all the other people living in Jerusalem? They were not, I tell you. No; but unless you repent you will all perish as they did.'

He told this parable: 'A man had a fig tree planted in his vineyard, and he came looking for fruit on it but found none. He said to the man who looked after the vineyard, "Look here, for three years now I have been coming to look for fruit on this fig tree and finding none. Cut it down: why should it be taking up the ground?" "Sir," the man replied "leave it one more year and give me time to dig round it and manure it: it may bear fruit next year; if not, then you can cut it down."'

## Reflection

Jesus refuses to see the Galileans' untimely death as a punishment for sin, or at least he does not pronounce any judgement on the matter. One cannot argue from sudden and violent death to the enormity of sin. Rather, he directs the people's attention to something else. The disasters should make them conscious of their own sinfulness. Opportunities to repent are offered as the parable of the barren fig tree shows. There is no room for self-complacency because patience has its limits, and when disaster or judgement comes, the "barren person" has only himself or herself to blame. The 'time of grace' given us must be used fruitfully.

**29th Week
in Ordinary Time
Green
or
St John of Capistrano,
priest
(Optional, White)**

**30th Sunday
in Ordinary Time
Psalter Week 2
Green**

### Jeremiah 31:7-9

The Lord says this: Shout with joy for Jacob! Hail the chief of nations! Proclaim! Praise! Shout: 'The Lord has saved his people, the remnant of Israel!' See, I will bring them back from the land of the North and gather them from the far ends of earth; all of them: the blind and the lame, women with child, women in labour: a great company returning here. They had left in tears, I will comfort them as I lead them back; I will guide them to streams of water, by a smooth path where they will not stumble. For I am a father to Israel, and Ephraim is my first-born son.

### Psalm 125. R. v.3

*What marvels the Lord worked for us! Indeed we were glad.*

### Hebrews 5:1-6

Every high priest has been taken out of mankind and is appointed to act for men in their relations with God, to offer gifts and sacrifices for sins; and so he can sympathise with those who are ignorant or uncertain because he too lives in the limitations of weakness. That is why he has to make sin offerings for himself as well as for the people. No one takes this honour on himself, but each one is called by God, as Aaron was. Nor did Christ give himself the glory of becoming high priest, but he had it from the one who said to him: You are my son, today I have become your father, and in another text: You are a priest of the order of Melchizedek, and for ever.

### Mark 10:46-52

As Jesus left Jericho with his disciples and a large crowd, Bartimaeus (that is, the son of Timaeus), a blind beggar, was sitting at the side of the road. When he heard that it was Jesus of Nazareth, he began to shout and to say, 'Son of David, Jesus, have pity on me.' And many of them scolded him and told him to keep quiet, but he only shouted all the louder, 'Son of David, have pity on me.' Jesus stopped and said, 'Call him here.' So they called the blind man. 'Courage,' they said, 'get up; he is calling you.' So throwing off his cloak, he jumped up and went to Jesus. Then Jesus spoke, 'What do you want me to do for you?' 'Rabbuni,' the blind man said to him, 'Master, let me see again.' Jesus said to him, 'Go; your faith has saved you.' And immediately his sight returned and he followed him along the road.

## Reflection

For the disciples, Jesus is not to be inconvenienced by the desperate needs of a poor blind man. However, no one is too insignificant to Jesus. He stops on his tracks and commands Bartimaeus to come to him. Bartimaeus has received the gift of sight and sets out on the way of Jesus: the way that leads to Jerusalem. Bartimaeus is a symbol of every human who has suffered a lot. Most likely he has been to every quack doctor or faith-healer, tried every magical potion and holy well. Some of us might have reached the depths of desperation in unbearable illness, in a losing battle with addiction or a compulsive humiliation. We are all blind in one way or another before God. Today let our prayer be: "Jesus, Son of David, have mercy on me!"

**30th Week
in Ordinary Time
Green
or
The Six Welsh Martyrs
and their Companions
(Wales – Feast)**
*(See Appendix A-15)*

### Romans 8:12-17

My brothers, there is no necessity for us to obey our unspiritual selves or to live unspiritual lives. If you do live in that way, you are doomed to die; but if by the Spirit you put an end to the misdeeds of the body you will live.

Everyone moved by the Spirit is a son of God. The spirit you received is not the spirit of slaves bringing fear into your lives again; it is the spirit of sons, and it makes us cry out, 'Abba, Father!' The Spirit himself and our spirit bear united witness that we are children of God. And if we are children we are heirs as well: heirs of God and coheirs with Christ, sharing his sufferings so as to share his glory.

### Psalm 67:2.4.6-7.20-21. R. v.21

*This God of ours is a God who saves.*

### Luke 13:10-17

One sabbath day Jesus was teaching in one of the synagogues, and a woman was there who for eighteen years had been possessed by a spirit that left her enfeebled; she was bent double and quite unable to stand upright. When Jesus saw her he called her over and said, 'Woman, you are rid of your infirmity' and he laid his hands on her. And at once she straightened up, and she glorified God.

But the synagogue official was indignant because Jesus had healed on the sabbath, and he addressed the people present. 'There are six days' he said 'when work is to be done. Come and be healed on one of those days and not on the sabbath.' But the Lord answered him. 'Hypocrites!' he said 'Is there one of you who does not untie his ox or his donkey from the manger on the sabbath and take it out for watering? And this woman, a daughter of Abraham whom Satan has held bound these eighteen years – was it not right to untie her bonds on the sabbath day?' When he said this, all his adversaries were covered with confusion, and all the people were overjoyed at all the wonders he worked.

### Reflection

The synagogue leader is indignant that Jesus cures a crippled woman on a Sabbath. He is more interested in the Law than in the state of the woman. She may be only a "woman" and may be sick, but for Jesus she enjoys the privilege of being a "daughter of Abraham", and should therefore be released from the bondage of Satan any time – even on a Sabbath. Indeed, faced with such a human need, it is compulsory to heal even on the Sabbath! Today Jesus tells us to respect and affirm the inviolable inherent dignity of every human person.

**30th Week
in Ordinary Time
Green**

## Romans 8:18-25

I think that what we suffer in this life can never be compared to the glory, as yet unrevealed, which is waiting for us. The whole creation is eagerly waiting for God to reveal his sons. It was not for any fault on the part of creation that it was made unable to attain its purpose, it was made so by God; but creation still retains the hope of being freed, like us, from its slavery to decadence, to enjoy the same freedom and glory as the children of God. From the beginning till now the entire creation, as we know, has been groaning in one great act of giving birth; and not only creation, but all of us who possess the first-fruits of the Spirit, we too groan inwardly as we wait for our bodies to be set free. For we must be content to hope that we shall be saved – our salvation is not in sight, we should not have to be hoping for it if it were – but, as I say, we must hope to be saved since we are not saved yet – it is something we must wait for with patience.

## Psalm 125. R. v.3

*What marvels the Lord worked for us.*

## Luke 13:18-21

Jesus said, 'What is the kingdom of God like? What shall I compare it with? It is like a mustard seed which a man took and threw into his garden: it grew and became a tree, and the birds of the air sheltered in its branches.'

Another thing he said, 'What shall I compare the kingdom of God with? It is like the yeast a woman took and mixed in with three measures of flour till it was leavened all through.'

## Reflection

The two short parables contrast small beginnings with powerful results: the tiny seed shoots into a tree; the yeast leavens a whole lump. The tiny seed and leaven work quietly and unseen – the kingdom of God despite its insignificant beginnings in the person and ministry of Jesus will eventually expand to all peoples of the earth. The parables encourage us to share our little contribution in the building up of God's kingdom in the here and now by living our lives according to its values.

### Romans 8:26-30

The Spirit comes to help us in our weakness. For when we cannot choose words in order to pray properly, the Spirit himself expresses our plea in a way that could never be put into words, and God who knows everything in our hearts knows perfectly well what he means, and that the pleas of the saints expressed by the Spirit are according to the mind of God.

We know that by turning everything to their good God co-operates with all those who love him, with all those that he has called according to his purpose. They are the ones he chose specially long ago and intended to become true images of his Son, so that his Son might be the eldest of many brothers. He called those he intended for this; those he called he justified, and with those he justified he shared his glory.

### Psalm 12:4-6. R. v.6

*Lord, I trust in your mercy.*

### Luke 13:22-30

Through towns and villages Jesus went teaching, making his way to Jerusalem. Someone said to him, 'Sir, will there be only a few saved?' He said to them, 'Try your best to enter by the narrow door, because, I tell you, many will try to enter and will not succeed.

'Once the master of the house has got up and locked the door, you may find yourself knocking on the door, saying, "Lord, open to us" but he will answer, "I do not know where you come from." Then you will find yourself saying, "We once ate and drank in your company; you taught in our streets" but he will reply, "I do not know where you come from. Away from me, all you wicked men!"

'Then there will be weeping and grinding of teeth, when you see Abraham and Isaac and Jacob and all the prophets in the kingdom of God, and yourselves turned outside. And men from east and west, from north and south, will come to take their places at the feast in the kingdom of God.

'Yes, there are those now last who will be first, and those now first who will be last.'

### Reflection

Jesus does not answer the question in terms of numbers but focuses more on what is important. Jesus admonishes all to "try your best to enter by the narrow door," a path that is difficult but not impossible. The lesson is directed to those who drag along their accomplishments, their religious or social status, or their material possessions in seeking easy access to salvation. There is an emphasis on the urgency to enter now rather than later. It is interesting to note that the entrance to the kingdom is already open now and not in the future. The time to be converted and to live according to the values of the kingdom is NOW before it is too late.

### Ephesians 2:19-22

You are no longer aliens or foreign visitors: you are citizens like all the saints, and part of God's household. You are part of a building that has the apostles and prophets for its foundations, and Christ Jesus himself for its main cornerstone. As every structure is aligned on him, all grow into one holy temple in the Lord; and you too, in him, are being built into a house where God lives, in the Spirit.

### Psalm 18:2-5. R. v.5

*Their word goes forth through all the earth.*

### Luke 6:12-19

Jesus went out into the hills to pray; and he spent the whole night in prayer to God. When day came he summoned his disciples and picked out twelve of them; he called them 'apostles': Simon whom he called Peter, and his brother Andrew; James, John, Philip, Bartholomew, Matthew, Thomas, James son of Alphaeus, Simon called the Zealot, Judas son of James, and Judas Iscariot who became a traitor.

He then came down with them and stopped at a piece of level ground where there was a large gathering of his disciples with a great crowd of people from all parts of Judaea and from Jerusalem and from the coastal region of Tyre and Sidon who had come to hear him and to be cured of their diseases. People tormented by unclean spirits were also cured, and everyone in the crowd was trying to touch him because power came out of him that cured them all.

**Sts Simon and Jude,**
*apostles*
**Feast**
**Red**

### Reflection

It is interesting to note that before Jesus chooses the Twelve to be part of his inner circle and to continue his mission of proclaiming the kingdom, he spends the whole night in prayer. Jesus is aware that his ministry would be a short one. Much would depend upon this inner circle whose education and edification must now be one of the Lord's tasks. Today we celebrate the feast of the two apostles: Simon, nicknamed "Zealot" – tradition relates his mission to Egypt and Persia (Iran) followed by his martyrdom. Jude is also known as Thaddeus. Ancient legends mention his work in Mesopotamia and Persia. He has become the object of a popular devotion as a patron and helper of hopeless causes.

## OCTOBER
# 29
### FRIDAY

**30th Week
in Ordinary Time
Green**

### Romans 9:1-5

What I want to say is no pretence; I say it in union with Christ – it is the truth – my conscience in union with the Holy Spirit assures me of it too. What I want to say is this: my sorrow is so great, my mental anguish so endless, I would willingly be condemned and be cut off from Christ if it could help my brothers of Israel, my own flesh and blood. They were adopted as sons, they were given the glory and the covenants; the Law and the ritual were drawn up for them, and the promises were made to them. They are descended from the patriarchs and from their flesh and blood came Christ who is above all, God for ever blessed! Amen.

### Psalm 147:12-15.19-20. R. v.12
*O praise the Lord, Jerusalem!*

### Luke 14:1-6

Now on a sabbath day Jesus had gone for a meal to the house of one of the leading Pharisees; and they watched him closely. There in front of him was a man with dropsy, and Jesus addressed the lawyers and Pharisees, 'Is it against the law' he asked 'to cure a man on the sabbath, or not?' But they remained silent, so he took the man and cured him and sent him away. Then he said to them, 'Which of you here, if his son falls into a well, or his ox, will not pull him out on a sabbath day without hesitation?' And to this they could find no answer.

### Reflection

Moved by compassion, Jesus takes the initiative to cure the man suffering with dropsy or edema even if he did not ask for it. The Pharisees and the lawyers are not happy when Jesus heals this poor suffering man. Jesus exposes their spiritual illness – while the poor man has a physical swelling of his body, they are swollen with spiritual pride and hypocrisy. Jesus invites us to see the intimate link between our faith and works of charity.

## Romans 11:1-2.11-12.25-29

Let me put a question: is it possible that God has rejected his people? Of course not. I, an Israelite, descended from Abraham through the tribe of Benjamin, could never agree that God had rejected his people, the people he chose specially long ago.

Let me put another question then: have the Jews fallen for ever, or have they just stumbled? Obviously they have not fallen for ever: their fall, though, has saved the pagans in a way the Jews may now well emulate. Think of the extent to which the world, the pagan world, has benefited from their fall and defection – then think how much more it will benefit from the conversion of them all.

There is a hidden reason for all this, brothers, of which I do not want you to be ignorant, in case you think you know more than you do. One section of Israel has become blind, but this will last only until the whole pagan world has entered, and then after this the rest of Israel will be saved as well. As scripture says: The liberator will come from Zion, he will banish godlessness from Jacob. And this is the covenant I will make with them when I take their sins away.

The Jews are enemies of God only with regard to the Good News, and enemies only for your sake; but as the chosen people, they are still loved by God, loved for the sake of their ancestors. God never takes back his gifts or revokes his choice.

## Psalm 93:12-15.17-18. R. v.14

*The Lord will not abandon his people.*

## Luke 14:1.7-11

Now on a Sabbath day Jesus had gone for a meal to the house of one of the leading Pharisees; and they watched him closely.

He then told the guests a parable, because he had noticed how they picked the places of honour. He said this, 'When someone invites you to a wedding feast, do not take your seat in the place of honour. A more distinguished person than you may have been invited, and the person who invited you both may come and say, "Give up your place to this man." And then, to your embarrassment, you would have to go and take the lowest place. No; when you are a guest, make your way to the lowest place and sit there, so that, when your host comes, he may say, "My friend, move up higher." In that way, everyone with you at the table will see you honoured. For everyone who exalts himself will be humbled, and the man who humbles himself will be exalted.'

## Reflection

Today Jesus teaches us a simple lesson on humility: First, we should let go of our self-importance and entitlement because it makes us think we have the right to occupy seats of honour. Second, our accomplishments or connections, blood relations, and office position should not lead us to think we are special in any event. Third, the way to get to the top is to start at the bottom. The truly humble person will finish up where she or he ought to be and receive the honour that is due. Jesus chose to be born in a humble family and in a lowly place in solidarity with the poor and ordinary people.

**30th Week
in Ordinary Time
Green**

# OCTOBER
# 31
## SUNDAY

**31st Sunday
in Ordinary Time
Green
or
All Saints (England)
Solemnity**
*(See 1 November)*

### Deuteronomy 6:2-6

Moses said to the people: 'If you fear the Lord your God all the days of your life and if you keep all his laws and commandments which I lay on you, you will have a long life, you and your son and your grandson. Listen then, Israel, keep and observe what will make you prosper and give you great increase, as the Lord God of your fathers has promised you, giving you a land where milk and honey flow.

'Listen, Israel: The Lord our God is the one Lord. You shall love the Lord your God with all your heart, with all your soul, with all your strength. Let these words I urge on you today be written on your heart.'

### Psalm 17:2-4.47.51. R. v.2
*I love you, Lord, my strength.*

### Hebrews 7:23-28

There used to be a great number of priests under the former covenant, because death put an end to each one of them; but this one, Christ, because he remains for ever, can never lose his priesthood. It follows then, that his power to save is utterly certain, since he is living for ever to intercede for all who come to God through him.

To suit us, the ideal high priest would have to be holy, innocent and uncontaminated, beyond the influence of sinners, and raised up above the heavens; one who would not need to offer sacrifices every day, as the other high priests do for their own sins and then for those of the people, because he has done this once and for all by offering himself. The Law appoints high priests who are men subject to weakness; but the promise on oath, which came after the Law, appointed the Son who is made perfect for ever.

### Mark 12:28-34

One of the scribes came up to Jesus and put a question to him, 'Which is the first of all the commandments?' Jesus replied, 'This is the first: Listen, Israel, the Lord our God is the one Lord, and you must love the Lord your God with all your heart, with all your soul, with all your mind and with all your strength. The second is this: You must love your neighbour as yourself. There is no commandment greater than these.' The scribe said to him, 'Well spoken, Master; what you have said is true: that he is one and there is no other. To love with all your heart, with all your understanding and strength and to love your neighbour as yourself, this is far more important than any holocaust or sacrifice.' Jesus, seeing how wisely he had spoken said, 'You are not far from the kingdom of God.' And after that no one dared to question him any more.

## Reflection

It is common understanding among the Jews that their relationship with God as taught by their religious leaders rests on three pillars: the Law, the worship (or sacrifices) and the works of love. The Law came first and it gave the direction to worship and love. Jesus challenges this traditional order or priorities. He argues that love comes first because it comes from God. The other two, Law and worship, only have meaning if they are a response to God's love. In essence, there is only one commandment – love of God and neighbour. When the New Testament speaks of love of God it hardly ever refers to our efforts. Mostly it means God's love for us (cf 1 Jn 4:10). It is when we find God's love in ourselves that we discover our self-worth. When we find God in our hearts we will find him in others. God empowers us to cease projecting all our self-hatred out onto others.

**All Saints Day**
Solemnity
White
or
Monday of
31st Week in Ordinary
Time (England)
*(See Appendix A-16)*

### Apocalypse 7:2-4.9-14

I, John, saw another angel rising where the sun rises, carrying the seal of the living God; he called in a powerful voice to the four angels whose duty was to devastate land and sea, 'Wait before you do any damage on land or at sea or to the trees, until we have put the seal on the foreheads of the servants of our God.' Then I heard how many were sealed: a hundred and forty-four thousand, out of all the tribes of Israel.
*(See Appendix B-29)*

### Psalm 23:1-6. R. cf. v.6

*Lord, this is the people that longs to see your face.*

### 1 John 3:1-3

Think of the love that the Father has lavished on us, by letting us be called God's children; and that is what we are. Because the world refused to acknowledge him, therefore it does not acknowledge us. My dear people, we are already the children of God but what we are to be in the future has not yet been revealed; all we know is, that when it is revealed we shall be like him because we shall see him as he really is. Surely everyone who entertains this hope must purify himself, must try to be as pure as Christ.

### Matthew 5:1-12

Seeing the crowds, Jesus went up the hill. There he sat down and was joined by his disciples. Then he began to speak. This is what he taught them: 'How happy are the poor in spirit; theirs is the kingdom of heaven. Happy the gentle: they shall have the earth for their heritage. Happy those who mourn: they shall be comforted. Happy those who hunger and thirst for what is right: they shall be satisfied. Happy the merciful: they shall have mercy shown them. Happy the pure in heart: they shall see God. Happy the peacemakers: they shall be called sons of God. Happy those who are persecuted in the cause of right: theirs is the kingdom of heaven.

'Happy are you when people abuse you and persecute you and speak all kinds of calumny against you on my account. Rejoice and be glad, for your reward will be great in heaven.'

### Reflection

Surely the passage we call 'The Beatitudes' is one of the best known and most loved sections of Jesus' teaching in the Gospels. Jesus affirms each of us no matter how we are feeling or what we are experiencing. Jesus does not deny life's struggles but reminds us that all who stand for him will be 'blessed', will be 'happy' – not at some shallow superficial level, but at our core, day by day, and finally be rewarded with a place in heaven (the heart of God). On this 'All Saints Day', John the Evangelist also affirms us when he tells us that 'we are already the children of God', and that in the future 'we shall see God, as he really is'! Today honours the fact that the saints in heaven intercede for us, while All Souls Day (tomorrow) affirms that we pray for all who have died.

Isaiah 25:6-9
*(See Appendix B–30)*

**Psalm 22. R. v.1**
*The Lord is my shepherd; there is nothing I shall want.*

**Romans 5:5-11**

Hope is not deceptive, because the love of God has been poured into our hearts by the Holy Spirit which has been given to us. We were still helpless when at his appointed moment Christ died for sinful men. It is not easy to die even for a good man – though of course for someone really worthy, a man might be prepared to die – but what proves that God loves us is that Christ died for us while we were still sinners. Having died to make us righteous, is it likely that he would now fail to save us from God's anger? When we were reconciled to God by the death of his Son, we were still enemies; now that we have been reconciled, surely we may count on being saved by the life of his Son? Not merely because we have been reconciled but because we are filled with joyful trust in God, through our Lord Jesus Christ, through whom we have already gained our reconciliation.

**Mark 15:33-39; 16:1-6**

When the sixth hour came there was darkness over the whole land until the ninth hour. And at the ninth hour Jesus cried out in a loud voice, 'Eloi, Eloi, lama sabachthani?' which means, 'My God, my God, why have you deserted me?' When some of those who stood by heard this, they said, 'Listen, he is calling on Elijah'. Someone ran and soaked a sponge in vinegar and, putting it on a reed, gave it him to drink saying, 'Wait and see if Elijah will come to take him down'. But Jesus gave a loud cry and breathed his last. And the veil of the Temple was torn in two from top to bottom. The centurion, who was standing in front of him, had seen how he had died, and he said, 'In truth this man was a son of God'.

When the sabbath was over, Mary of Magdala, Mary the mother of James, and Salome, bought spices with which to go and anoint him. And very early in the morning on the first day of the week they went to the tomb, just as the sun was rising.

They had been saying to one another, 'Who will roll away the stone for us from the entrance to the tomb?' But when they looked they could see that the stone – which was very big – had already been rolled back. On entering the tomb they saw a young man in a white robe seated on the right-hand side, and they were struck with amazement. But he said to them, 'There is no need for alarm. You are looking for Jesus of Nazareth, who was crucified: he is risen, he is not here. See, here is the place where they laid him.'

**Reflection**

Death hurts! Death is an ending of life as we know it. Death is also inevitable. All that has life must die … and yet today's readings encourage us to see beyond the pain of loss. Yes, we must grieve the deaths of those we love with honesty, but as people of faith we live with the promise of 'the more' than we can ever imagine or know in this life. In the first reading the prophet Isaiah tells the people that God will destroy death forever. In the second reading St Paul reminds us that 'we are filled with joyful trust in God', and the Gospel tells us that Jesus who died 'is risen'. How can this be? We have no neat answers, but by faith we believe that death has become a doorway into greater life as only those who have died can know – and they wait to welcome us.

**31st Week
in Ordinary Time
Green
or
St Martin de Porres,**
*religious*
**(Optional, White)**

## Romans 13:8-10

Avoid getting into debt, except the debt of mutual love. If you love your fellow men you have carried out your obligations. All the commandments: You shall not commit adultery, you shall not kill, you shall not steal, you shall not covet, and so on, are summed up in this single command: You must love your neighbour as yourself. Love is the one thing that cannot hurt your neighbour; that is why it is the answer to every one of the commandments.

## Psalm 111:1-2.4-5.9. R. v.5

*Happy the man who takes pity and lends.*

## Luke 14:25-33

Great crowds accompanied Jesus on his way and he turned and spoke to them. 'If any man comes to me without hating his father, mother, wife, children, brothers, sisters, yes and his own life too, he cannot be my disciple. Anyone who does not carry his cross and come after me cannot be my disciple.

'And indeed, which of you here, intending to build a tower, would not first sit down and work out the cost to see if he had enough to complete it? Otherwise, if he laid the foundation and then found himself unable to finish the work, the onlookers would all start making fun of him and saying, "Here is a man who started to build and was unable to finish." Or again, what king marching to war against another king would not first sit down and consider whether with ten thousand men he could stand up to the other who advanced against him with twenty thousand? If not, then while the other king was still a long way off, he would send envoys to sue for peace. So in the same way, none of you can be my disciple unless he gives up all his possessions.'

## Reflection

So much of the Bible speaks of love. Today's first reading is no exception for St Paul reminds us of Jesus' words: 'You must love your neighbour as yourself.' So, it comes as a shock when the Gospel begins with Jesus saying: 'If anyone comes to me without hating...' 'To hate' in the Jewish tradition didn't carry the same hurtful and negative emotions as it does now. Jesus was really suggesting that those who follow him must get their priorities right. To choose his way (of love) was most important because it means that the love we offer others doesn't have its roots in any obsessive attachments. We need courage to come to Jesus free from a love of possessions. When we do, we truly are his disciples.

**Romans 14:7-12**

The life and death of each of us has its influence on others; if we live, we live for the Lord; and if we die, we die for the Lord, so that alive or dead we belong to the Lord. This explains why Christ both died and came to life, it was so that he might be Lord both of the dead and of the living. This is also why you should never pass judgement on a brother or treat him with contempt, as some of you have done. We shall all have to stand before the judgement seat of God; as scripture says: By my life – it is the Lord who speaks – every knee shall bend before me, and every tongue shall praise God. It is to God, therefore, that each of us must give an account of himself.

**Psalm 26:1.4.13-14. R. v.13**

*I am sure I shall see the Lord's goodness in the land of the living.*

**Luke 15:1-10**

The tax collectors and the sinners were all seeking the company of Jesus to hear what he had to say, and the Pharisees and the scribes complained. 'This man' they said 'welcomes sinners and eats with them.' So he spoke this parable to them:

'What man among you with a hundred sheep, losing one, would not leave the ninety-nine in the wilderness and go after the missing one till he found it? And when he found it, would he not joyfully take it on his shoulders and then, when he got home, call together his friends and neighbours? "Rejoice with me," he would say "I have found my sheep that was lost." In the same way, I tell you, there will be more rejoicing in heaven over one repentant sinner than over ninety-nine virtuous men who have no need of repentance.

'Or again, what woman with ten drachmas would not, if she lost one, light a lamp and sweep out the house and search thoroughly till she found it? And then, when she had found it, call together her friends and neighbours? "Rejoice with me," she would say "I have found the drachma I lost." In the same way, I tell you, there is rejoicing among the angels of God over one repentant sinner.'

**Reflection**

Both parables in today's Gospel end with expressions of joy. One is about a man and the other about a woman which highlights the Gospel's inclusiveness. Both parables are about vulnerability and grace. Though the first focuses on the man who lost the sheep, our attention is also drawn to the lost sheep itself – its fear, its aloneness, and then its delight in being carried home on the man's shoulders. And like the woman who lost the ten drachmas, we are in distress when we lose something precious. Both the woman and the man search until they find what they have lost. We are both the lost and the found – we lose our way and Jesus comes seeking us. Oh, the rejoicing! In the 18th century, John Newton, a former slave trader, wrote of his experience: 'Amazing grace, how sweet the sound … I once was lost, but now am found'.

**NOVEMBER**

# 4

**THURSDAY**

**31st Week in Ordinary Time**
**St Charles Borromeo, *bishop***
**Memorial**
**White**

31st Week
in Ordinary Time
Green

**Romans 15:14-21**

My brothers, I am quite certain that you are full of good intentions, perfectly well instructed and able to advise each other. The reason why I have written to you, and put some things rather strongly, is to refresh your memories, since God has given me this special position. He has appointed me as a priest of Jesus Christ, and I am to carry out my priestly duty by bringing the Good News from God to the pagans, and so make them acceptable as an offering, made holy by the Holy Spirit.

*(See Appendix B-30)*

**Psalm 97:1-4. R. cf. v.2**

*The Lord has shown his salvation to the nations.*

**Luke 16:1-8**

Jesus said to his disciples: 'There was a rich man and he had a steward who was denounced to him for being wasteful with his property. He called for the man and said, "What is this I hear about you? Draw me up an account of your stewardship because you are not to be my steward any longer." Then the steward said to himself, "Now that my master is taking the stewardship from me, what am I to do? Dig? I am not strong enough. Go begging? I should be too ashamed. Ah, I know what I will do to make sure that when I am dismissed from office there will be some to welcome me into their homes."

'Then he called his master's debtors one by one. To the first he said, "How much do you owe my master?" "One hundred measures of oil" was the reply. The steward said, "Here, take your bond; sit down straight away and write fifty." To another he said, "And you, sir, how much do you owe?" "One hundred measures of wheat" was the reply. The steward said, "Here, take your bond and write eighty."

'The master praised the dishonest steward for his astuteness. For the children of this world are more astute in dealing with their own kind than are the children of light.'

**Reflection**

Jesus and his disciples are heading for Jerusalem. As they walk Jesus tells many parables to those they meet along the way. However, the parable in today's Gospel is told only to his disciples. While Jesus' parables are generally cryptic, this one, in which he seems to be commending a man whom he calls dishonest, seems very strange. Yet, because it is a parable, all is not as it seems! Jesus is neither commending nor condemning the man – he is acknowledging that all of us are a mix of good and not so good. He is telling his disciples that money is not the key to life, rather it is choosing to be 'children of light'. While self-preservation is a somewhat natural response to life's circumstances, it is only the 'children of this world' who choose the path of dishonesty and manipulation over honesty. A child of the light will always endeavour to live with integrity.

### Romans 16:3-9.16.22-27

My greetings to Prisca and Aquila, my fellow workers in Christ Jesus, who risked death to save my life: I am not the only one to owe them a debt of gratitude, all the churches among the pagans do as well. My greetings also to the church that meets at their house.

Greetings to my friend Epaenetus, the first of Asia's gifts to Christ; greetings to Mary who worked so hard for you; to those outstanding apostles Andronicus and Junias, my compatriots and fellow prisoners who became Christians before me, to Ampliatus, my friend in the Lord; to Urban, my fellow worker in Christ; to my friend Stachys. Greet each other with a holy kiss. All the churches of Christ send greetings.

I, Tertius, who wrote out this letter, greet you in the Lord. Greetings from Gaius, who is entertaining me and from the whole church that meets in his house. Erastus, the city treasurer, sends his greetings; so does our brother Quartus.
*(See Appendix B-30)*

### Psalm 144:2-5.10-11. R. v.1
*I will bless your name for ever, O Lord.*

### Luke 16:9-15

Jesus said to his disciples: 'I tell you this: use money, tainted as it is, to win you friends, and thus make sure that when it fails you, they will welcome you into the tents of eternity. The man who can be trusted in little things can be trusted in great; the man who is dishonest in little things will be dishonest in great. If then you cannot be trusted with money, that tainted thing, who will trust you with genuine riches? And if you cannot be trusted with what is not yours, who will give you what is your very own?

'No servant can be the slave of two masters: he will either hate the first and love the second, or treat the first with respect and the second with scorn. You cannot be the slave both of God and of money.'

The Pharisees, who loved money, heard all this and laughed at him. He said to them, 'You are the very ones who pass yourselves off as virtuous in people's sight, but God knows your hearts. For what is thought highly of by men is loathsome in the sight of God.'

### Reflection

It is almost a shock to hear Jesus suggesting that to buy friendship with 'money, tainted as it is', is okay. Fortunately, he doesn't leave it at that! In referring to dishonesty, Jesus implies that friendship 'won' this way is not to be trusted. If friendship is secured with money, the so-called friend is no friend at all. Friendship is a wonderful gift to offer. As a gift, it can only be offered freely. Elsewhere Jesus says we are no longer slaves or servants but friends (John 15: 15) and we know the value Jesus placed on that friendship – his life because of love. Jesus does remind us that 'God know our hearts', so checking out our priorities is a good exercise!

**31st Week in Ordinary Time**
**Green**
or
**All Saints of Ireland (Ireland – Feast)**
*(See Appendix A-17)*

**32nd Sunday
in Ordinary Time
Psalter Week 4
Green**

### 1 Kings 17:10-16

Elijah the Prophet went off to Sidon. And when he reached the city gate, there was a widow gathering sticks; addressing her he said, 'Please bring a little water in a vessel for me to drink.' She was setting off to bring it when he called after her. 'Please' he said, 'bring me a scrap of bread in your hand.' 'As the Lord your God lives,' she replied, 'I have no baked bread, but only a handful of meal in a jar and a little oil in a jug; I am just gathering a stick or two to go and prepare this for myself and my son to eat, and then we shall die.' But Elijah said to her, 'Do not be afraid, go and do as you have said; but first make a little scone of it for me and bring it to me, and then make some for yourself and for your son. For thus the Lord speaks, the God of Israel:

"Jar of meal shall not be spent, jug of oil shall not be emptied, before the day when the Lord sends rain on the face of the earth." '

The woman went and did as Elijah told her and they ate the food, she, himself and her son. The jar of meal was not spent nor the jug of oil emptied, just as the Lord had foretold through Elijah.

### Psalm 145:7-10. R. v.2

*My soul, give praise to the Lord.*

## Hebrews 9:24-28

It is not as though Christ had entered a man-made sanctuary which was only modelled on the real one; but it was heaven itself, so that he could appear in the actual presence of God on our behalf. And he does not have to offer himself again and again, like the high priest going into the sanctuary year after year with the blood that is not his own, or else he would have had to suffer over and over again since the world began. Instead of that, he has made his appearance once and for all, now at the end of the last age, to do away with sin by sacrificing himself. Since men only die once, and after that comes judgement, so Christ, too, offers himself only once to take the faults of many on himself, and when he appears a second time, it will not be to deal with sin but to reward with salvation those who are waiting for him.

## Mark 12:38-44

In his teaching Jesus said, 'Beware of the scribes who like to walk about in long robes, to be greeted obsequiously in the market squares, to take the front seats in the synagogues and the places of honour at banquets; these are the men who swallow the property of widows, while making a show of lengthy prayers. The more severe will be the sentence they receive.'

He sat down opposite the treasury and watched the people putting money into the treasury, and many of the rich put in a great deal. A poor widow came and put in two small coins, the equivalent of a penny. Then he called his disciples and said to them, 'I tell you solemnly, this poor widow has put more in than all who have contributed to the treasury; for they have all put in money they had over, but she from the little she had has put in everything she possessed, all she had to live on.'

## Reflection

The widow in the first reading responded to Elijah's request with honesty – she was about to prepare the last meal she and her son would have before they starved to death. Nevertheless, she did as she was asked and shared the last of their food with Elijah. And the three of them lived because of God's provision. In the Gospel, Jesus drew the disciples' attention to another widow as a way of enabling them to see discipleship in action. He highlighted the innate goodness which leads to generous giving. Goodness is quiet – literally so in the case of the widow, for the tiny coins she dropped into the treasury would not have made a sound. Goodness is not showy – she didn't seek to attract attention with lengthy prayers or elaborate clothing. Goodness is generous. It's almost impossible to get one's mind around the fact that she gave '*all* she had to live on'. To give is to return to God what God has given us because of his innate goodness for, as the poem says:

To give and give, and give again,
what God has given thee;
to spend thyself nor count the cost;
to serve right gloriously
the God who gave all worlds that are,
and all that are to be.

*(From:* Awake, Awake to Love and Work, *GAS Kennedy, 1921)*

### Wisdom 1:1-7

Love virtue, you who are judges on earth, let honesty prompt your thinking about the Lord, seek him in simplicity of heart; since he is to be found by those who do not put him to the test, he shows himself to those who do not distrust him. But selfish intentions divorce from God; and Omnipotence, put to the test, confounds the foolish. No, Wisdom will never make its way into a crafty soul nor stay in a body that is in debt to sin; the holy spirit of instruction shuns deceit, it stands aloof from reckless purposes, is taken aback when iniquity appears. Wisdom is a spirit, a friend to man, though she will not pardon the words of a blasphemer, since God sees into the innermost parts of him, truly observes his heart, and listens to his tongue. The Spirit of the Lord, indeed, fills the whole world, and that which holds all things together knows every word that is said.

### Psalm 138:1-10. R. v.24

*Lead me, O Lord, in the path of life eternal.*

### Luke 17:1-6

Jesus said to his disciples; 'Obstacles are sure to come, but alas for the one who provides them! It would be better for him to be thrown into the sea with a millstone put round his neck than that he should lead astray a single one of these little ones. Watch yourselves!

'If your brother does something wrong, reprove him and, if he is sorry, forgive him. And if he wrongs you seven times a day and seven times comes back to you and says, "I am sorry," you must forgive him.'

The apostles said to the Lord, 'Increase our faith.' The Lord replied, 'Were your faith the size of a mustard seed you could say to this mulberry tree, "Be uprooted and planted in the sea," and it would obey you.'

### Reflection

Jesus' three sayings are instructions to his disciples about how to live in harmony with each other and all they encounter. The first is a reminder that it is often personal pig-headedness which becomes an obstacle – perhaps not listening to another's view, or not being willing to change course. The second is about having the courage to correct another – being able to do so in a manner which is not an obstacle in itself, and then the willingness to accept an apology – *and* to forgive! The third saying begins with the apostles asking for more faith! They wouldn't be apostles if they had no faith, so Jesus reminds them to live the possibilities of their faith. It is this faith, in itself, which will enable them to do great things.

**The Dedication of the
Lateran Basilica
Feast
White**

### Ezekiel 47:1-2.8-9.12

The angel brought me to the entrance of the Temple, where a stream came out from under the Temple threshold and flowed eastwards, since the Temple faced east. The water flowed from under the right side of the Temple, south of the altar. He took me out by the north gate and led me right round outside as far as the outer east gate where the water flowed out on the right-hand side. …
*(See Appendix B-30)*

### Psalm 45:2-3.5-6.8-9. R. v.5

*The waters of a river give joy to God's city, the holy place where the Most High dwells.*

### 1 Corinthians 3:9-11.16-17

You are God's building. By the grace God gave me, I succeeded as an architect and laid the foundations, on which someone else is doing the building. Everyone doing the building must work carefully. For the foundation, nobody can lay any other than the one which has already been laid, that is, Jesus Christ.

Didn't you realise that you were God's temple and that the Spirit of God was living among you? If anybody should destroy the temple of God, God will destroy him, because the temple of God is sacred; and you are that temple.

### John 2:13-22

Just before the Jewish Passover Jesus went up to Jerusalem, and in the Temple he found people selling cattle and sheep and pigeons, and the money changers sitting at their counters there. Making a whip out of some cord, he drove them all out of the Temple, cattle and sheep as well, scattered the money changers' coins, knocked their tables over and said to the pigeon-sellers, 'Take all this out of here and stop turning my Father's house into a market.' Then his disciples remembered the words of scripture: Zeal for your house will devour me. The Jews intervened and said, 'What sign can you show us to justify what you have done?' Jesus answered, 'Destroy this sanctuary, and in three days I will raise it up.' The Jews replied, 'It has taken forty-six years to build this sanctuary: are you going to raise it up in three days?' But he was speaking of the sanctuary that was his body, and when Jesus rose from the dead, his disciples remembered that he had said this, and they believed the scripture and the words he had said.

### Reflection

The Lateran Basilica is the Cathedral Church of the Diocese of Rome and as such is the seat (*cathedra*) of the Bishop of Rome, the Pope. We grieve, or even become angry, when a church is desecrated. Jesus was so angry about abuses in the temple that he made a whip and drove out those violating the sacred place. Then he spoke of building a sacred place in three days! Shock! Horror! 'Impossible!' said the Jews. But Jesus knew what he was on about – he was speaking about his own person. St Paul reminds us that we are 'God's building, God's temple and the dwelling place of the Holy Spirit'. While all life is sacred, human life is considered 'the temple of God' thus worthy of respect. How do we honour our bodies? How do we nurture our spirit, and honour our Creator?

**32nd Week
in Ordinary Time
St Leo the Great,
pope, doctor
Memorial
White**

### Wisdom 6:1-11

Listen, kings, and understand; rulers of remotest lands, take warning; hear this, you who have thousands under your rule, who boast of your hordes of subjects. For power is a gift to you from the Lord, sovereignty is from the Most High; he himself will probe your acts and scrutinise your intentions. If, as administrators of his kingdom, you have not governed justly nor observed the law, nor behaved as God would have you behave, he will fall on you swiftly and terribly. Ruthless judgement is reserved for the high and mighty; the lowly will be compassionately pardoned, the mighty will be mightily punished. For the Lord of All does not cower before a personage, he does not stand in awe of greatness, since he himself has made small and great and provides for all alike; but strict scrutiny awaits those in power. Yes, despots, my words are for you, that you may learn what wisdom is and not transgress; for they who observe holy things holily will be adjudged holy, and, accepting instruction from them, will find their defence in them. Look forward, therefore, to my words; yearn for them, and they will instruct you.

### Psalm 81:3-4.6-7. R. v.8

*Arise, O God, to judge the earth.*

### Luke 17:11-19

On the way to Jerusalem Jesus travelled along the border between Samaria and Galilee. As he entered one of the villages, ten lepers came to meet him. They stood some way off and called to him, 'Jesus! Master! Take pity on us.' When he saw them he said, 'Go and show yourselves to the priests.' Now as they were going away they were cleansed. Finding himself cured, one of them turned back praising God at the top of his voice and threw himself at the feet of Jesus and thanked him. The man was a Samaritan. This made Jesus say, 'Were not all ten made clean? The other nine, where are they? It seems that no one has come back to give praise to God, except this foreigner.' And he said to the man, 'Stand up and go on your way. Your faith has saved you.'

### Reflection

How was Jesus feeling as he drew closer and closer to Jerusalem? He knew his life was in danger so no doubt he was troubled, yet this did not stop him responding to the unfortunate lepers cast out from their communities because of their disease. He responded to their plea by telling them to show themselves to the priests because only the priests could return a healed leper to the community. As they were going away they found themselves healed. Only one, the Samaritan, who was effectively a double-outcast being both a leper and a pagan, was so filled with joy that he rushed back to Jesus to express his gratitude. Was Jesus saddened because the others didn't say 'thank you'? He may have been but to the grateful one he gave an added blessing: 'Your faith has saved you.' Only Jesus understood the price of this added blessing – his death on the cross. May we always be grateful for the blessings we receive!

**32nd of Week
in Ordinary Time
St Martin of Tours,
*bishop*
Memorial
White**

## Wisdom 7:22–8:1

Within Wisdom is a spirit intelligent, holy, unique, manifold, subtle, active, incisive, unsullied, lucid, invulnerable, benevolent, sharp, irresistible, beneficent, loving to man, steadfast, dependable, unperturbed, almighty, all-surveying, penetrating all intelligent, pure and most subtle spirits; for Wisdom is quicker to move than any motion; she is so pure, she pervades and permeates all things. She is a breath of the power of God, pure emanation of the glory of the Almighty; hence nothing impure can find a way into her. She is a reflection of the eternal light, untarnished mirror of God's active power, image of his goodness. Although alone, she can do all; herself unchanging, she makes all things new. In each generation she passes into holy souls, she makes them friends of God and prophets; for God loves only the man who lives with Wisdom. She is indeed more splendid than the sun, she outshines all the constellations; compared with light, she takes first place, for light must yield to night, but over Wisdom evil can never triumph. She deploys her strength from one end of the earth to the other, ordering all things for good.

## Psalm 118:89-91.130.135.175. R. v.89
*Your word, O Lord, stands for ever.*

## Luke 17:20-25

Asked by the Pharisees when the kingdom of God was to come, Jesus gave them this answer, 'The coming of the kingdom of God does not admit of observation and there will be no one to say, "Look here! Look there!" For, you must know, the kingdom of God is among you.'

He said to the disciples, 'A time will come when you will long to see one of the days of the Son of Man and will not see it. They will say to you, "Look there!" or, "Look here!" Make no move; do not set off in pursuit; for as the lightning flashing from one part of heaven lights up the other, so will be the Son of Man when his day comes. But first he must suffer grievously and be rejected by this generation.'

## Reflection

The Pharisees put a question to Jesus for which they want a definitive answer – when will God's kingdom come? In reply Jesus tells them, 'it's already among you'. Jesus doesn't say how it is present! Then he tells the disciples that it is not a matter of looking for startling signs, rather it is being aware that the kingdom is present in the quietness of lives lived lovingly, in the goodness of caring for our neighbour and the attention paid to care of the earth and all life forms. Even though today's Gospel does not spell out how we are to live, a cursory reading of Luke offers a Christ-like life model. Being too focused on the future negates the precious gift of each day (even though frequently each of us will experience pain-filled days). However, we continue to live with the promise: Christ will come again!

**32nd of Week
in Ordinary Time
St Josaphat,
*bishop, martyr*
Memorial
Red**

## Wisdom 13:1-9

Naturally stupid are all men who have not known God and who, from the good things that are seen, have not been able to discover Him-who-is, or, by studying the works, have failed to recognise the Artificer. Fire however, or wind, or the swift air, the sphere of the stars, impetuous water, heaven's lamps, are what they have held to be the gods who govern the world. If, charmed by their beauty, they have taken things for gods, let them know how much the Lord of these excels them, since the very Author of beauty has created them. And if they have been impressed by their power and energy, let them deduce from these how much mightier is he that has formed them, since through the grandeur and beauty of the creatures we may, by analogy, contemplate their Author. Small blame, however, attaches to these men, for perhaps they only go astray in their search for God and their eagerness to find him; living among his works, they strive to comprehend them and fall victim to appearances, seeing so much beauty. Even so, they are not to be excused: if they are capable of acquiring enough knowledge to be able to investigate the world, how have they been so slow to find its Master?

## Psalm 18:2-5. R. v.2

*The heavens proclaim the glory of God.*

## Luke 17:26-37

Jesus said to the disciples: 'As it was in Noah's day, so will it also be in the days of the Son of Man. People were eating and drinking, marrying wives and husbands, right up to the day Noah went into the ark, and the Flood came and destroyed them all. It will be the same as it was in Lot's day: people were eating and drinking, buying and selling, planting and building, but the day Lot left Sodom, God rained fire and brimstone from heaven and it destroyed them all. It will be the same when the day comes for the Son of Man to be revealed.

'When that day comes, anyone on the housetop, with his possessions in the house, must not come down to collect them, nor must anyone in the fields turn back either. Remember Lot's wife. Anyone who tries to preserve his life will lose it; and anyone who loses it will keep it safe. I tell you, on that night two will be in one bed: one will be taken, the other left, two women will be grinding corn together: one will be taken, the other left.' The disciples interrupted. 'Where Lord?' they asked. He said, 'Where the body is, there too will the vultures gather.'

## Reflection

Today's Gospel rounds off chapter 17 of Luke's Gospel which began with a warning not to be an obstacle and ends with Jesus' refusal to predict when 'the end' will come. Rather he reminds the disciples that, even though people have always lived in similar ways (eating, marrying etc), there have been unpredictable events. The important thing is to live! The psalmist tells us that whether it be day or night, all we have to do is look and listen and we will experience the wonder of God – then, we will live! 'The heavens proclaim the glory of God and the firmament shows forth the work of his hands. Day unto day takes up the story, and night unto night makes known the message'. The message is Love – 'I am with you always' sharing your joys and sorrows.

**Wisdom 18:14-16; 19:6-9**

When peaceful silence lay over all, and night had run the half of her swift course, down from the heavens, from the royal throne, leapt your all-powerful Word; into the heart of a doomed land the stern warrior leapt. Carrying your unambiguous command like a sharp sword, he stood, and filled the universe with death; he touched the sky, yet trod the earth. For, to keep your children from all harm, the whole creation, obedient to your commands, was once more, and newly, fashioned in its nature. Overshadowing the camp there was the cloud, where water had been, dry land was seen to rise, the Red Sea became an unimpeded way, the tempestuous flood a green plain; sheltered by your hand, the whole nation passed across, gazing at these amazing miracles. They were like horses at pasture, they skipped like lambs, singing your praises, Lord, their deliverer.

**Psalm 104:2-3.36-37.42-43. R. v.5**
*Remember the wonders the Lord has done.*

**Luke 18:1-8**

Jesus told his disciples a parable about the need to pray continually and never lose heart. 'There was a judge in a certain town' he said 'who had neither fear of God nor respect for man. In the same town there was a widow who kept on coming to him and saying, "I want justice from you against my enemy!" For a long time he refused, but at last he said to himself, "Maybe I have neither fear of God nor respect for man, but since she keeps pestering me I must give this widow her just rights, or she will persist in coming and worry me to death."'

And the Lord said, 'You notice what the unjust judge has to say? Now will not God see justice done to his chosen who cry to him day and night even when he delays to help them? I promise you, he will see justice done to them, and done speedily. But when the Son of Man comes, will he find any faith on earth?'

## Reflection

Jesus wants his disciples to be very sure about two things: i) God is on the side of the poor and always acts justly, and ii) we need to be persistent in our prayers and never lose heart. The judge was not carrying out his responsibilities properly and only gave the widow justice because she was tiring him. God does hear our prayers – and God does respond. However, there are times when we wonder whether God is listening because it seems we are getting no response. What we forget is that God's answer may not be what we are expecting, it may not come immediately, and for us to hear God's voice amid our noisy world, we need to listen attentively and always with faith and trust. The Son of Man will find faith when he comes again if we trust God in all things.

**33rd Sunday
in Ordinary Time
Psalter Week 3
Green**

### Daniel 12:1-13

'At that time Michael will stand up, the great prince who mounts guard over your people. There is going to be a time of great distress, unparalleled since nations first came into existence. When that time comes, your own people will be spared, all those whose names are found written in the Book. Of those who lie sleeping in the dust of the earth many will awake, some to everlasting life, some to shame and everlasting disgrace. The learned will shine as brightly as the vault of heaven, and those who have instructed many in virtue, as bright as stars for all eternity.'

### Psalm 15:5.8-11

*Preserve me, God, I take refuge in you.*

### Hebrews 10:11-14.18

All the priests stand at their duties every day, offering over and over again the same sacrifices which are quite incapable of taking sins away. Christ, on the other hand, has offered one single sacrifice for sins, and then taken his place for ever, at the right hand of God, where he is now waiting until his enemies are made into a footstool for him. By virtue of that one single offering, he has achieved the eternal perfection of all whom he is sanctifying. When all sins have been forgiven, there can be no more sin offerings.

### Mark 13:24-32

Jesus said to his disciples: 'In those days, after the time of distress, the sun will be darkened, the moon will lose its brightness, the stars will come falling from heaven and the powers in the heavens will be shaken. And then they will see the Son of Man coming in the clouds with great power and glory; then too he will send the angels to gather his chosen from the four winds, from the ends of the world to the ends of heaven.

'Take the fig tree as a parable: as soon as its twigs grow supple and its leaves come out, you know that summer is near. So with you, when you see these things happening: know that he is near, at the very gates. I tell you solemnly, before this generation has passed away all these things will have taken place. Heaven and earth will pass away, but my words will not pass away.

'But as for that day or hour, nobody knows it, neither the angels of heaven, nor the Son; no one but the Father.

### Reflection

Hope is a powerful motivating force for life, and both the first reading and the Gospel offer hope. In Daniel's day, the people were being persecuted and put to death for their beliefs. In Mark's time, those who chose Jesus were also being driven from the temple, persecuted and killed. Both readings offer hope to the people – and to all who presently choose to follow God. Persecution of Christians continues, and we know that life can be tough: illness, violence, loneliness, etc. Wherein lives hope for us? Well, from Daniel, 'your own people (those whose names are recorded in the Book) will be spared', and from Mark: 'my words will not pass away', and that he, the Son of Man 'will send his angels to gather his chosen'. And even though there are frequent prophecies about the ending of all we know, Jesus says that 'nobody knows it, neither the angels of heaven, nor the Son; only the Father'. Hope reminds us that by being attentive to the signs of the times, we will recognise that 'he is near' – in the changing seasons, in the presence of those we love and in the wonder of all of creation.

**33rd Week
in Ordinary Time
Green
or
St Albert the Great,
bishop, doctor
(Optional, White)**

**1 Maccabees 1:10-15.41-43.54-57.62-64**

There grew a sinful offshoot, Antiochus Epiphanes, son of King Antiochus; once a hostage in Rome, he became king in the one hundred and thirty-seventh year of the kingdom of the Greeks. It was then that there emerged from Israel a set of renegades who led many people astray. 'Come,' they said 'let us reach an understanding with the pagans surrounding us, for since we separated ourselves from them many misfortunes have overtaken us.' This proposal proved acceptable, and a number of the people eagerly approached the king, who authorised them to practise the pagan observances. So they built a gymnasium in Jerusalem, such as the pagans have, disguised their circumcision, and abandoned the holy covenant, submitting to the heathen rule as willing slaves of impiety.

Then the king issued a proclamation to his whole kingdom that all were to become a single people, each renouncing his particular customs. All the pagans conformed to the king's decree, and many Israelites chose to accept his religion, sacrificing to idols and profaning the sabbath. …
*(See Appendix B-31)*

**Psalm 118:53.61.134.150.155.158. R. cf. v.88**
*Give me life, O Lord, and I will do your will.*

**Luke 18:35-43**

As Jesus drew near to Jericho there was a blind man sitting at the side of the road begging. When he heard the crowd going past he asked what it was all about, and they told him that Jesus the Nazarene was passing by. So he called out, 'Jesus, Son of David, have pity on me.' The people in front scolded him and told him to keep quiet, but he shouted all the louder, 'Son of David, have pity on me.' Jesus stopped and ordered them to bring the man to him, and when he came up, asked him, 'What do you want me to do for you?' 'Sir,' he replied 'let me see again.' Jesus said to him, 'Receive your sight. Your faith has saved you.' And instantly his sight returned and he followed him praising God, and all the people who saw it gave praise to God for what had happened.

## Reflection

In Jesus' 'mission statement' (Luke 4: 18-19) he says he has come to bring sight to the blind (among other gifts). Knowing Jesus is nearby, the blind man in today's Gospel is persistent in his desire to be heard. He calls to Jesus addressing him with his messianic title, Son of David, which means that he truly *sees* Jesus for who he is. Jesus doesn't say 'what do you want?' Rather his question is relational: 'what do *you* want *me* to do for *you*?' The blind man wants to see, and instantly he does! However, Jesus gives him more than sight: 'your faith has saved you.' The man who can now see follows Jesus praising God – and all present praise God (a community of praise). The Gospel acclamation links following Jesus with the gift of life: 'whoever follows me will have the light of life.' *Seeing + following + persistence* = LIFE!

**33rd Week
in Ordinary Time
Green
or
St Margaret of Scotland
(Scotland – Feast)**
*(See Appendix A-18)*

## 2 Maccabees 6:18-31

Eleazar, one of the foremost teachers of the Law, a man already advanced in years and of most noble appearance, was being forced to open his mouth wide to swallow pig's flesh. But he, resolving to die with honour rather than to live disgraced, went to the block of his own accord, spitting the stuff out, the plain duty of anyone with the courage to reject what it is not lawful to taste, even from a natural tenderness for his own life. Those in charge of the impious banquet, because of their long-standing friendship with him, took him aside and privately urged him to have meat brought of a kind he could properly use, prepared by himself, and only pretend to eat the portions of sacrificial meat as prescribed by the king; this action would enable him to escape death, by availing himself of an act of kindness prompted by their long friendship. But having taken a noble decision worthy of his years and the dignity of his great age and the well earned distinction of his grey hairs, worthy too of his impeccable conduct from boyhood, and above all of the holy legislation established by God himself, he publicly stated his convictions, telling them to send him at once to Hades. ... *(See Appendix B-31)*

## Psalm 3:2-7. R. v.6
*The Lord upholds me.*

## Luke 19:1-10

Jesus entered Jericho and was going through the town when a man whose name was Zacchaeus made his appearance; he was one of the senior tax collectors and a wealthy man. He was anxious to see what kind of man Jesus was, but he was too short and could not see him for the crowd; so he ran ahead and climbed a sycamore tree to catch a glimpse of Jesus who was to pass that way. When Jesus reached the spot he looked up and spoke to him: 'Zacchaeus, come down. Hurry, because I must stay at your house today.' And he hurried down and welcomed him joyfully. They all complained when they saw what was happening. 'He has gone to stay at a sinner's house' they said. But Zacchaeus stood his ground and said to the Lord, 'Look, sir, I am going to give half my property to the poor, and if I have cheated anybody I will pay him back four times the amount.' And Jesus said to him, 'Today salvation has come to this house, because this man too is a son of Abraham; for the Son of Man has come to seek out and save what was lost.'

## Reflection

My name is Zacchaeus. When Jesus came to Jericho, I was a tax collector for the Romans and became rich because I was not honourable. In stature I am a short man. I was also short of self-worth and self-esteem. I'd heard about Jesus and the changes he wrought in peoples' lives, so I was determined to see him. As I had no dignity, I climbed a tree to see him – I had nothing to lose. And Jesus *saw* me! He looked into my eyes. He saw my heart. He said, 'come down, I want to stay with you.' I was out of that tree and home faster than I've ever moved. I told Jesus I'd stop cheating and repay fourfold my ill-gotten wealth. And do you know what? Jesus gave me the greatest gift imaginable – salvation! I was lost, and now I am saved – I have changed!

**33rd Week
in Ordinary Time
St Elizabeth of Hungary,**
*religious*
**Memorial
White**

_____

_____

_____

_____

_____

**2 Maccabees 7:1.20-31**
There were seven brothers who were arrested with their mother. The king tried to force them to taste pig's flesh, which the Law forbids, by torturing them with whips and scourges. *(See Appendix B-31)*

**Psalm 16:1.5-6.8.15. R. v.15**
*I shall be filled, when I awake, with the sight of your glory, O Lord.*

**Luke 19:11-28**
While the people were listening, Jesus went on to tell a parable, because he was near Jerusalem and they imagined that the kingdom of God was going to show itself then and there. Accordingly he said, 'A man of noble birth went to a distant country to be appointed king and afterwards return. He summoned ten of his servants and gave them ten pounds. "Do business with these" he told them "until I get back." But his compatriots detested him and sent a delegation to follow him with this message, "We do not want this man to be our king."

'Now on his return, having received his appointment as king, he sent for those servants to whom he had given the money, to find out what profit each had made. The first came in and said, "Sir, your one pound has brought in ten." "Well done, my good servant!" he replied. "Since you have proved yourself faithful in a very small thing, you shall have the government of ten cities." Then came the second and said, "Sir, your one pound has made five." To this one also he said, "And you shall be in charge of five cities." Next came the other and said, "Sir, here is your pound. I put it away safely in a piece of linen because I was afraid of you; for you are an exacting man: you pick up what you have not put down and reap what you have not sown." "You wicked servant!" he said "Out of your own mouth I condemn you. So you knew I was an exacting man, picking up what I have not put down and reaping what I have not sown? Then why did you not put my money in the bank? On my return I could have drawn it out with interest." And he said to those standing by, "Take the pound from him and give it to the man who has ten pounds." And they said to him, "But, sir, he has ten pounds …" "I tell you, to everyone who has will be given more; but from the man who has not, even what he has will be taken away. '"But as for my enemies who did not want me for their king, bring them here and execute them in my presence."'

When he had said this he went on ahead, going up to Jerusalem.

### Reflection

'Use it or lose it'! The parable Jesus tells seems rather harsh, but is it really, or is it simply a fact of life? God gives us gifts – not just for the sake of gifting, but gifts to use which will increase the quality of life for everyone and everything. This means we are accountable for the gifts we receive and have the responsibility to use them wisely. Gifts are not to be taken for granted. Sometimes we need to work hard in order to use the gifts to their full advantage. The words of the parable, which could well be understood as 'to those who use well their gifts, more will be given; from those who don't use them, they will be taken away' (see Luke 8: 18), are frequently prophetic. Ponder the words of the Gospel acclamation: 'go and bear fruit that will last'.

**1 Maccabees 2:15-29**

The commissioners of King Antiochus who were enforcing the apostasy came to the town of Modein to make them sacrifice. Many Israelites gathered round them, but Mattathias and his sons drew apart. The king's commissioners then addressed Mattathias as follows, 'You are a respected leader, a great man in this town; you have sons and brothers to support you. Be the first to step forward and conform to the king's decree, as all the nations have done, and the leaders of Judah and the survivors in Jerusalem; you and your sons shall be reckoned among the Friends of the King, you and your sons shall be honoured with gold and silver and many presents.' Raising his voice, Mattathias retorted, 'Even if every nation living in the king's dominions obeys him, each forsaking its ancestral religion to conform to his decrees, I, my sons and my brothers will still follow the covenant of our ancestors. Heaven preserve us from forsaking the Law and its observances. As for the king's orders, we will not follow them: we will not swerve from our own religion either to right or to left.' As he finished speaking, a Jew came forward in the sight of all to offer sacrifice on the altar in Modein as the royal edict required. When Mattathias saw this, he was fired with zeal; stirred to the depth of his being, he gave vent to his legitimate anger, threw himself on the man and slaughtered him on the altar. ...

*(See Appendix B-32)*

**33rd Week
in Ordinary Time
Green
or
Dedication of the
Basilicas of Sts Peter
and Paul, *apostles*
(Optional, White)**

**Psalm 49:1-2.5-6.14-15. R. v.23**

*I will show God's salvation to the upright.*

**Luke 19:41-44**

As Jesus drew near Jerusalem and came in sight of the city he shed tears over it and said, 'If you in your turn had only understood on this day the message of peace! But, alas, it is hidden from your eyes! Yes, a time is coming when your enemies will raise fortifications all round you, when they will encircle you and hem you in on every side; they will dash you and the children inside your walls to the ground; they will leave not one stone standing on another within you – and all because you did not recognise your opportunity when God offered it!'

**Reflection**

When Luke wrote his Gospel, Jesus' lament had come true. The Prince of Peace had 'foreseen' the fall of the 'city of peace' (the popular meaning of Jerusalem), not only because there were those in Jerusalem who had sought his death, but also as a consequence of people not choosing the path of peace. Jesus lamented over Jerusalem on that day long ago, that is, he looked with love and anguish, with grief and sorrow, and possibly even anger that he could not convince the people that peace is the only way. What about now – does he still lament as he looks over cities and nations, including ours, when we do not recognise what God offers us? Individually, do we seek peace and work for peace? Does 'peace' mean more than the absence of war?

## NOVEMBER
# 19
### FRIDAY

**33rd Week
in Ordinary Time
Green**

### 1 Maccabees 4:36-37.52-59

Judas and his brothers said, 'Now that our enemies have been defeated, let us go up to purify the sanctuary and dedicate it.' So they marshalled the whole army, and went up to Mount Zion.

On the twenty-fifth of the ninth month, Chislev, in the year one hundred and forty-eight, they rose at dawn and offered a lawful sacrifice on the new altar of holocausts which they had made. The altar was dedicated, to the sound of zithers, harps and cymbals, at the same time of year and on the same day on which the pagans had originally profaned it. The whole people fell prostrate in adoration, praising to the skies him who had made them so successful. For eight days they celebrated the dedication of the altar, joyfully offering holocausts, communion sacrifices and thanksgivings. They ornamented the front of the Temple with crowns and bosses of gold, repaired the gates and the storerooms and fitted them with doors. There was no end to the rejoicing among the people, and the reproach of the pagans was lifted from them. Judas, with his brothers and the whole assembly of Israel, made it a law that the days of the dedication of the altar should be celebrated yearly at the proper season, for eight days beginning on the twenty-fifth of the month Chislev, with rejoicing and gladness.

### Psalm 1 Chronicles 29:10-12. R. v.13
*We praise your glorious name, O Lord.*

### Luke 19:45-48

Jesus went into the Temple and began driving out those who were selling. 'According to scripture,' he said 'my house will be a house of prayer. But you have turned it into a robbers' den.'

He taught in the Temple every day. The chief priests and the scribes, with the support of the leading citizens, tried to do away with him, but they did not see how they could carry this out because the people as a whole hung on his words.

### Reflection

Jesus does not have anything against the temple itself. His anger is directed at those who are abusing its purpose as a house of prayer by turning it into a place of business. In accordance with the Law of Moses, the child Jesus was presented in the temple (Luke 2: 22-36). There, two people of great faith, Simeon and Anna, recognise him for who he really is. Simeon warns Mary, his mother, that there will be many who will oppose him. His words prove to be true. Jesus, now in Jerusalem, is in the temple teaching daily. The ordinary people hang on his words. The authorities – the chief priests, scribes and leading citizens – begin to look for a way 'to do away with him' because they fear the people will turn to Jesus and they will lose their authority. After all, the record shows that Jesus spoke with authority (Luke 4: 32; 5: 24).

**33rd Week
in Ordinary Time
Green**

## 1 Maccabees 6:1-13

King Antiochus was making his way across the upper provinces; he had heard that in Persia there was a city called Elymais, renowned for its riches, its silver and gold, and its very wealthy temple containing golden armour, breastplates and weapons, left there by Alexander son of Philip, the king of Macedon, the first to reign over the Greeks. He therefore went and attempted to take the city and pillage it, but without success, since the citizens learnt of his intention, and offered him a stiff resistance, whereupon he turned about and retreated, disconsolate, in the direction of Babylon. ...
*(See Appendix B-32)*

## Psalm 9:2-4.6.16.19. R. cf. v.16

*I will rejoice in your saving help, O Lord.*

## Luke 20:27-40

Some Sadducees – those who say that there is no resurrection – approached Jesus and they put this question to him, 'Master, we have it from Moses in writing, that if a man's married brother dies childless, the man must marry the widow to raise up children for his brother. Well then, there were seven brothers. The first, having married a wife, died childless. The second and then the third married the widow. And the same with all seven, they died leaving no children. Finally the woman herself died. Now, at the resurrection, to which of them will she be wife since she had been married to all seven?'

Jesus replied, 'The children of this world take wives and husbands, but those who are judged worthy of a place in the other world and in the resurrection from the dead do not marry because they can no longer die, for they are the same as the angels, and being children of the resurrection they are sons of God. And Moses himself implies that the dead rise again, in the passage about the bush where he calls the Lord the God of Abraham, the God of Isaac and the God of Jacob. Now he is God, not of the dead, but of the living; for to him all men are in fact alive.'

Some scribes then spoke up. 'Well put, Master' they said – because they would not dare to ask him any more questions.

## Reflection

The Sadducees, a small wealthy group of Jews whose belief system was based solely on the Pentateuch (the five books of Moses) didn't believe in resurrection. Moses didn't mention it. They came up with a convoluted argument to ridicule Jesus, not because they wanted an answer! However, Jesus was not fazed. He told them that life after death is not a continuation of the 'here and now', which Moses implied when he spoke of the Lord as 'the God of Abraham, Isaac and Jacob'. Jesus didn't describe resurrected life, but he did say the relationship with God is forever – 'for to him all are in fact alive'. He affirmed resurrection: 'because I live, you also will live' (John 14: 19). This keystone of Christian hope is acknowledged in the funeral liturgy: 'life is changed, not ended' and stated in the Creed: 'we believe in the resurrection of the dead...'.

## NOVEMBER
# 21
### SUNDAY

**Our Lord Jesus Christ,
King of the Universe
Psalter Week 2
Solemnity
White**

### Daniel 7:13-14

I gazed into the visions of the night. And I saw, coming on the clouds of heaven, one like a son of man. He came to the one of great age and was led into his presence. On him was conferred sovereignty, glory and kingship, and men of all peoples, nations and languages became his servants. His sovereignty is an eternal sovereignty which shall never pass away, nor will his empire ever be destroyed.

### Psalm 92:1-2.5. R. v.1

*The Lord is king, with majesty enrobed.*

### Apocalypse 1:5-8

Jesus Christ is the faithful witness, the First-born from the dead, the Ruler of the kings of the earth. He loves us and has washed away our sins with his blood, and made us a line of kings, priests to serve his God and Father; to him, then, be glory and power for ever and ever. Amen. It is he who is coming on the clouds; everyone will see him, even those who pierced him, and all the races of the earth will mourn over him. This is the truth. Amen. 'I am the Alpha and the Omega' says the Lord God, who is, who was, and who is to come, the Almighty.

### John 18:33-37

'Are you the king of the Jews?' Pilate asked. Jesus replied, 'Do you ask this of your own accord, or have others spoken to you about me?' Pilate answered, 'Am I a Jew? It is your own people and the chief priests who have handed you over to me: what have you done?' Jesus replied, 'Mine is not a kingdom of this world; if my kingdom were of this world, my men would have fought to prevent my being surrendered to the Jews. But my kingdom is not of this kind.' 'So you are a king then?' said Pilate. 'It is you who say it' answered Jesus. 'Yes, I am a king. I was born for this, I came into the world for this: to bear witness to the truth; and all who are on the side of truth listen to my voice.'

## Reflection

The last Sunday of the Church's Year celebrates the universal kingship of Christ, with encouraging and hope-filled readings! Daniel reminds us that Christ's sovereignty and empire are eternal and everlasting. The psalm affirms our king's trustworthiness is forever. The second reading assures us that Jesus Christ loves us and calls us to service. Before reading the Gospel, pause a moment to imagine Jesus in the harrowing hours before he faced Pilate: being arrested, knowing he'd been betrayed by his companions; being struck, bound and dragged before the ruling authority because the Jewish leaders feared how he stood with and for the people. Coming to today's Gospel, Pilate asks Jesus a question which seems out of 'left field': 'Are you the king of the Jews?' When Jesus affirms this, we learn what kingship means to him. We are blessed to be 'subjects' of the king who does not choose power for the sake of 'power over' and does not seek possessions or fame. Jesus desires only to empower the hearts of those he loves with truth ('I am the truth', John 14: 6) while asking that we bear witness to the truth and listen to his voice. In doing this, we live enabled by our king who is Love.

**34th Week
in Ordinary Time**
St Cecilia, *virgin, martyr*
**Memorial
Red**

### Daniel 1:1-6.8-20

In the third year of the reign of Jehoiakim king of Judah, Nebuchadnezzar king of Babylon marched on Jerusalem and besieged it. The Lord delivered Jehoiakim king of Judah into his hands, with some of the furnishings of the Temple of God. He took them away to the land of Shinar, and stored the sacred vessels in the treasury of his own gods.

The king ordered Ashpenaz, his chief eunuch, to select from the Israelites a certain number of boys of either royal or noble descent; they had to be without any physical defect, of good appearance, trained in every kind of wisdom, well-informed, quick at learning, suitable for service in the palace of the king. Ashpenaz himself was to teach them the language and literature of the Chaldaeans. The king assigned them a daily allowance of food and wine from his own royal table. They were to receive an education lasting for three years, after which they were expected to be fit for the king's society. Among them were Daniel, Hananiah, Mishael and Azariah, who were Judaeans. Daniel, who was most anxious not to defile himself with the food and wine from the royal table, begged the chief eunuch to spare him this defilement; and by the grace of God Daniel met goodwill and sympathy on the part of the chief eunuch. But he warned Daniel, 'I am afraid of my lord the king: he has assigned you food and drink, and if he sees you looking thinner in the face than the other boys of your age, my head will be in danger with the king because of you.' At this Daniel turned to the guard whom the chief eunuch had assigned to Daniel, Hananiah, Mishael and Azariah. …
*(See Appendix B-33)*

**Psalm: Daniel 3:52-56. R. v.52**
*To you glory and praise for evermore.*

### Luke 21:1-4

As Jesus looked up he saw rich people putting their offerings into the treasury; then he happened to notice a poverty-stricken widow putting in two small coins, and he said, 'I tell you truly, this poor widow has put in more than any of them; for these have all contributed money they had over, but she from the little she had has put in all she had to live on.'

### Reflection

Immediately prior to this Gospel, Jesus condemned the scribes because they 'devour widow's houses' (Luke 20: 47). He stands with and for the poor and deplores systems which perpetuate injustice. He watched as the rich gave their offerings to the treasury and noted they gave from their abundance – giving to receive praise from others. But the poverty-stricken widow, an outcast with no one to provide for her (perhaps she tried to keep to the shadows so as not to be noticed), chose to give all she had. And this was at the time when Jesus was on his way to giving his all on the cross. Jesus is not saying everyone must give their all, rather that we consider thoughtfully why we give – our money, our gifts, ourselves. Is it to be noticed or are we motivated by love?

## Daniel 2:31-45

Daniel said to Nebuchadnezzar, 'You have had a vision, O king; this is what you saw: a statue, a great statue of extreme brightness, stood before you, terrible to see. The head of this statue was of fine gold, its chest and arms were of silver, its belly and thighs of bronze, its legs of iron, its feet part iron, part earthenware. While you were gazing, a stone broke away, untouched by any hand, and struck the statue, struck its feet of iron and earthenware and shattered them. And then, iron and earthenware, bronze, silver, gold all broke into small pieces as fine as chaff on the threshing-floor in summer. The wind blew them away, leaving not a trace behind. And the stone that had struck the statue grew into a great mountain, filling the whole earth. This was the dream; now we will explain to the king what it means. You, O king, king of kings, to whom the God of heaven has given sovereignty, power, strength and glory – the sons of men, the beasts of the field, the birds of heaven, wherever they live, he has entrusted to your rule, making you king of them all – you are the golden head. ...
*(See Appendix B-33)*

**34th Week in Ordinary Time**
Green
or
St Clement I, *pope, martyr*
(Optional, Red)
St Columban, *abbot*
(Optional, White)

### Psalm: Daniel 3:57-61. R. v.59
*Give glory and eternal praise to him!*

### Luke 21:5-11

When some were talking about the Temple, remarking how it was adorned with fine stonework and votive offerings, Jesus said, 'All these things you are staring at now – the time will come when not a single stone will be left on another: everything will be destroyed.' And they put to him this question: 'Master,' they said 'when will this happen, then, and what sign will there be that this is about to take place?'

'Take care not to be deceived,' he said 'because many will come using my name and saying, "I am he" and, "The time is near at hand." Refuse to join them. And when you hear of wars and revolutions, do not be frightened, for this is something that must happen but the end is not so soon.' Then he said to them, 'Nation will fight against nation, and kingdom against kingdom. There will be great earthquakes, and plagues and famines here and there; there will be fearful sights and great signs from heaven.'

### Reflection

By the time Luke had written his Gospel, the temple the people were admiring had been destroyed, as Jesus prophesied. The people who heard Jesus make this prophecy would have experienced great confusion and, no doubt, fear. Humankind generally wants information: what will happen, when will it happen, how will it happen? Jesus does say there will be signs, and even people claiming to be him. Many of the signs Jesus mentioned have been experienced century after century. Even today wars are ongoing, as are earthquakes, famines, fires and floods. We can choose to live in constant fear or to live each day to the full appreciating the gifts we have, the gift we are to others, and the gift they are to us. May God enable us to have the courage to live the 'sacrament of the present moment' (*de Chardin*).

**34th Week
in Ordinary Time
St Andrew Dung-Lac,
priest and Companions,
martyrs
Memorial
Red**

**Daniel 5:1-6.13-14.16-17.23-28**

King Belshazzar gave a great banquet for his noblemen; a thousand of them attended, and he drank wine in company with this thousand. As he sipped his wine, Belshazzar gave orders for the gold and silver vessels to be brought which his father Nebuchadnezzar had looted from the sanctuary in Jerusalem, so that the king, his noblemen, his wives and his singing women could drink out of them. The gold and silver vessels looted from the sanctuary of the Temple of God in Jerusalem were brought in, and the king, his noblemen, his wives and his singing women drank out of them. They drank their wine and praised their gods of gold and silver, of bronze and iron, of wood and stone. Suddenly the fingers of a human hand appeared, and began to write on the plaster of the palace wall, directly behind the lampstand; and the king could see the hand as it wrote. The king turned pale with alarm: his thigh-joints went slack and his knees began to knock. Daniel was brought into the king's presence; the king said to Daniel, 'Are you the Daniel who was one of the Judaean exiles brought by my father the king from Judah? I am told that the spirit of God Most Holy lives in you, and that you are known for your perception, intelligence and marvellous wisdom. ...
*(See Appendix B-34)*

**Psalm: Daniel 3:62-67. R. v.59**
*Give glory and eternal praise to him!*

**Luke 21:12-19**

Jesus said to his disciples: 'Men will seize you and persecute you; they will hand you over to the synagogues and to imprisonment, and bring you before kings and governors because of my name – and that will be your opportunity to bear witness. Keep this carefully in mind: you are not to prepare your defence, because I myself shall give you an eloquence and a wisdom that none of your opponents will be able to resist or contradict. You will be betrayed even by parents and brothers, relations and friends; and some of you will be put to death. You will be hated by all men on account of my name, but not a hair of your head will be lost. Your endurance will win you your lives.'

**Reflection**

With Jesus' birth, God's love became incarnate on earth. Jesus lived love in ways we still seek to emulate. He knew people who honoured him may come up against the forces of evil simply because they chose to follow him. He told his disciples 2000 years ago that, if this happened, he would give them an 'eloquence and wisdom' their opponents would not be able to fault. Sadly, sometimes those who are against Jesus' followers are family and friends. While those who oppose the followers of Jesus may not be able to fault their eloquence and wisdom, they can still choose to imprison them and even put them to death. Goodness shows up evil for what it is! Since Jesus' time thousands have been martyred. Today's Gospel fits well with the Memorial of Andrew Dung-Lac and his companions. It offers words of hope to those facing martyrdom and to everyone who struggles – 'your endurance will win you your lives'.

## Daniel 6:12-28

The presidents and satraps came along in a body and found Daniel praying and pleading with God. They then came to the king and said, 'Have you not just signed an edict forbidding any man for the next thirty days to pray to anyone, god or man, other than to yourself, O king, on pain of being thrown into the lions' den?' 'The decision stands,' the king replied 'as befits the law of the Medes and the Persians, which cannot be revoked.' Then they said to the king, 'O king, this man Daniel, one of the exiles from Judah, disregards both you and the edict which you have signed: he is at his prayers three times each day.' When the king heard these words he was deeply distressed, and determined to save Daniel; he racked his brains until sunset to find some way out. But the men came back in a body to the king and said, 'O king, remember that in conformity with the law of the Medes and the Persians, no edict or decree can be altered when once issued by the king.'

The king then ordered Daniel to be fetched and thrown into the lion pit. The king said to Daniel, 'Your God himself, whom you have served so faithfully, will have to save you.' … *(See Appendix B–34)*

## Psalm: Daniel 3:68-74. R. v.59
*Give glory and eternal praise to him!*

## Luke 21:20-28

Jesus said to his disciples: 'When you see Jerusalem surrounded by armies, you must realise that she will soon be laid desolate. Then those in Judaea must escape to the mountains, those inside the city must leave it, and those in country districts must not take refuge in it. For this is the time of vengeance when all that scripture says must be fulfilled. Alas for those with child, or with babies at the breast, when those days come!

'For great misery will descend on the land and wrath on this people. They will fall by the edge of the sword and be led captive to every pagan country; and Jerusalem will be trampled down by the pagans until the age of the pagans is completely over.

'There will be signs in the sun and moon and stars; on earth nations in agony, bewildered by the clamour of the ocean and its waves; men dying of fear as they await what menaces the world, for the powers of heaven will be shaken. And then they will see the Son of Man coming in a cloud with power and great glory. When these things begin to take place, stand erect, hold your heads high, because your liberation is near at hand.'

## Reflection

How would each of us chose to live today if we knew our life would end tomorrow? Would we do things differently, or would we live the gift of the day delighting in the fact that we have been gifted life? Today's Gospel seems rather scary! In fact, it is scary! But, embedded in it is a message of hope and encouragement for all who align themselves with Christ: whatever happens – whether we die before the Son of Man comes again – in and through Christ we will find liberation. Check out Colossians 1: 9-20 and enjoy life in all its fullness.

**34th Week
in Ordinary Time
Green
or
St Catherine
of Alexandria,
*virgin, martyr*
(Optional, Red)**

### Daniel 7:2-14

I, Daniel, have been seeing visions in the night. I saw that the four winds of heaven were stirring up the great sea; four great beasts emerged from the sea, each different from the other. The first was like a lion with eagle's wings; and as I looked its wings were torn off, and it was lifted from the ground and set standing on its feet like a man; and it was given a human heart. The second beast I saw was different, like a bear, raised up on one of its sides, with three ribs in its mouth, between its teeth. 'Up!' came the command 'Eat quantities of flesh!' After this I looked, and saw another beast, like a leopard, and with four bird's wings on its flanks; it had four heads, and power was given to it. Next I saw another vision in the visions of the night: I saw a fourth beast, fearful, terrifying, very strong; it had great iron teeth, and it ate, crushed and trampled underfoot what remained. It was different from the previous beasts and had ten horns.

While I was looking at these horns, I saw another horn sprouting among them, a little one; three of the original horns were pulled out by the roots to make way for it; and in this horn I saw eyes like human eyes, and a mouth that was full of boasts. As I watched: Thrones were set in place and one of great age took his seat. His robe was white as snow, the hair of his head as pure as wool. His throne was a blaze of flames, its wheels were a burning fire. A stream of fire poured out, issuing from his presence. A thousand thousand waited on him, ten thousand times ten thousand stood before him. A court was held and the books were opened. *(See Appendix B-34)*

**Psalm: Daniel 3:75-81. R. v.59**
*Give glory and eternal praise to him!*

### Luke 21:29-33

Jesus told his disciples a parable, 'Think of the fig tree and indeed every tree. As soon as you see them bud, you know that summer is now near. So with you when you see these things happening: know that the kingdom of God is near. I tell you solemnly, before this generation has passed away all will have taken place. Heaven and earth will pass away, but my words will never pass away.'

### Reflection

The kingdom of God has many signs. Hope has been restored for many a farmer during a drought when a ring is seen around the moon – a sign that rain will come soon. The leaves of trees changing from green to hues of reds and yellows point to a long hot summer giving way to the coolness of autumn. Winter's end is announced when tiny shoots poke through the soil and fresh green leaves sprout on bare brown branches. Nature offers us countless signs of changing seasons and, if we are observant, each sign is a reminder of the creativity of God. Jesus says that while life as we know it will pass away, his words will not! And as for now, well, 'the kingdom of God is near'!

## Daniel 7:15-27

I, Daniel, was deeply disturbed and the visions that passed through my head alarmed me. So I approached one of those who were standing by and asked him to tell me the truth about all this. And in reply he revealed to me what these things meant. 'These four great beasts are four kings who will rise from the earth. Those who are granted sovereignty are the saints of the Most High, and the kingdom will be theirs for ever, for ever and ever.' Then I asked to know the truth about the fourth beast, different from all the rest, very terrifying, with iron teeth, and bronze claws, eating, crushing and trampling underfoot what remained; and the truth about the ten horns on its head – and why the other horn sprouted and the three original horns fell, and why this horn had eyes and a mouth that was full of boasts, and why it made a greater show than the other horns. This was the horn I had watched making war on the saints and proving the stronger, until the coming of the one of great age who gave judgement in favour of the saints of the Most High, when the time came for the saints to take over the kingdom. This is what he said:

'The fourth beast is to be a fourth kingdom on earth, different from all other kingdoms. It will devour the whole earth, trample it underfoot and crush it. As for the ten horns: from this kingdom will rise ten kings, and another after them; this one will be different from the previous ones and will bring down three kings; he is going to speak words against the Most High, and harass the saints of the Most High. He will consider changing seasons and the Law, and the saints will be put into his power for a time, two times, and half a time. But a court will be held and his power will be stripped from him, consumed, and utterly destroyed. And sovereignty and kingship, and the splendours of all the kingdoms under heaven will be given to the people of the saints of the Most High. His sovereignty is an eternal sovereignty and every empire will serve and obey him.'

## Psalm: Daniel 3:82-87. R. v.59

*Sons of men! bless the Lord.*

## Luke 21:34-36

Jesus said to his disciples: 'Watch yourselves, or your hearts will be coarsened with debauchery and drunkenness and the cares of life, and that day will be sprung on you suddenly, like a trap. For it will come down on every living man on the face of the earth. Stay awake, praying at all times for the strength to survive all that is going to happen, and to stand with confidence before the Son of Man.'

## Reflection

In the Gospel for the last day of Ordinary Time, Jesus offers his disciples, then and now, some pertinent advice. There are three key phrases: i) Watch yourselves – don't get bogged down in the seeming pleasures or the worries which are part of life; ii) Stay awake – and this doesn't mean 'don't sleep', rather, be aware of all that is going on around you in the daily events and your relationships with others; iii) Pray constantly – nurture your relationship with God remembering that prayer is not only pouring out words, it is also listening for God's voice in the midst of chaos or pleasure. Through prayer God will enable us to live fully regardless of life's circumstances until Christ, the Son of Man, should call or come again.

**1st Sunday of Advent
(Year C)
Psalter Week 1
Violet**

### Jeremiah 33:14-16

See, the days are coming – it is the Lord who speaks – when I am going to fulfil the promise I made to the House of Israel and the House of Judah: 'In those days and at that time, I will make a virtuous Branch grow for David, who shall practise honesty and integrity in the land. In those days Judah shall be saved and Israel shall dwell in confidence. And this is the name the city will be called: The Lord-our-integrity.'

### Psalm 24:4-5.8-9.10.14. R. v.1

*To you, O Lord, I lift up my soul.*

### 1 Thessalonians 3:12–4:2

May the Lord be generous in increasing your love and make you love one another and the whole human race as much as we love you. And may he so confirm your hearts in holiness that you may be blameless in the sight of our God and Father when our Lord Jesus Christ comes with all his saints.

Finally, brothers, we urge you and appeal to you in the Lord Jesus to make more and more progress in the kind of life that you are meant to live: the life that God wants, as you learnt from us, and as you are already living it. You have not forgotten the instructions we gave you on the authority of the Lord Jesus.

### Luke 21:25-28.34-36

Jesus said to his disciples: 'There will be signs in the sun and moon and stars; on earth nations in agony, bewildered by the clamour of the ocean and its waves; men dying of fear as they await what menaces the world, for the powers of heaven will be shaken. And then they will see the Son of Man coming in a cloud with power and great glory. When these things begin to take place, stand erect, hold your heads high, because your liberation is near at hand.'

'Watch yourselves, or your hearts will be coarsened with debauchery and drunkenness and the cares of life, and that day will be sprung on you suddenly, like a trap. For it will come down on every living man on the face of the earth. Stay awake, praying at all times for the strength to survive all that is going to happen, and to stand with confidence before the Son of Man.'

## Reflection

Another liturgical year has ended, and we stand at a new beginning. Advent has a two-pronged message. Firstly we remember and celebrate, and secondly we look forward to Christ's coming in glory. What wonderful readings we have to lead us into this season! Jeremiah reminds us of the Lord's long-ago promise that 'a virtuous branch' from David's line would come to 'practise honesty and integrity'. This immediately encourages us to ponder the wonder of Christ's birth which we celebrate at Christmas. The Gospel reminds us that Christ will come again and calls on us to trust in God at all times and in all circumstances. Between these two readings the psalm confidently asks for God's help, trusting in the Lord's goodness and uprightness, faithfulness and love. In the second reading Paul prays for the Thessalonians asking the Lord to increase their love and to help them live as God desires. Perhaps 'the keys' to the joy of Advent are to live with anticipation, with love, and to fulfil another of God's promises: 'you shall be holy, for I am holy' (Leviticus 11: 45; 1 Peter 1: 16).

## Isaiah 2:1-5

The vision of Isaiah son of Amoz, concerning Judah and Jerusalem. In the days to come the mountain of the Temple of the Lord shall tower above the mountains and be lifted higher than the hills. All the nations will stream to it, peoples without number will come to it; and they will say: 'Come, let us go up to the mountain of the Lord, to the Temple of the God of Jacob that he may teach us his ways so that we may walk in his paths; since the Law will go out from Zion, and the oracle of the Lord from Jerusalem.' He will wield authority over the nations and adjudicate between many peoples; these will hammer their swords into ploughshares, their spears into sickles. Nation will not lift sword against nation, there will be no more training for war. O House of Jacob, come, let us walk in the light of the Lord.

## Psalm 121:1-2.4-5.6-9. R. cf. v.1

*I rejoiced when I heard them say: 'Let us go to God's house.'*

## Matthew 8:5-11

When Jesus went into Capernaum a centurion came up and pleaded with him. 'Sir,' he said 'my servant is lying at home paralysed, and in great pain.' 'I will come myself and cure him' said Jesus. The centurion replied, 'Sir, I am not worthy to have you under my roof; just give the word and my servant will be cured. For I am under authority myself, and have soldiers under me; and I say to one man: Go, and he goes; to another: Come here, and he comes; to my servant: Do this, and he does it.' When Jesus heard this he was astonished and said to those following him, 'I tell you solemnly, nowhere in Israel have I found faith like this. And I tell you that many will come from east and west to take their places with Abraham and Isaac and Jacob at the feast in the kingdom of heaven.'

## Reflection

Chapter 8 in Matthew begins with three healings by Jesus. Today we read the second. Given that any healing is a marvel, a miracle, in itself, these three healings reveal that the kingdom is inclusive – all people are welcome. Each of the healings is an example that Jesus' compassion is not restricted by social norms. In the first and third, Jesus heals by touch: he touches a leper who is an outcast, and he touches a sick woman which is definitely not permitted! We read about a Roman centurion (a Gentile) who came pleading for his sick servant. This too is unusual: a person with power pleading for a slave who many would consider of no consequence. Jesus' response is also amazing. He doesn't talk about healing. He speaks about the Gentile's depth of faith – and he heals the servant.

## Romans 10:9-18

If your lips confess that Jesus is Lord and if you believe in your heart that God raised him from the dead, then you will be saved. By believing from the heart you are made righteous; by confessing with your lips you are saved. When scripture says: those who believe in him will have no cause for shame, it makes no distinction between Jew and Greek: all belong to the same Lord who is rich enough however many ask his help, for everyone who calls on the name of the Lord will be saved.

But they will not ask his help unless they believe in him, and they will not believe in him unless they have heard of him, and they will not hear of him unless they get a preacher, and they will never have a preacher unless one is sent, but as scripture says: The footsteps of those who bring good news are a welcome sound. Not everyone, of course, listens to the Good News. As Isaiah says: Lord, how many believed what we proclaimed? So faith comes from what is preached, and what is preached comes from the word of Christ.

Let me put the question: is it possible that they did not hear? Indeed they did; in the words of the psalm, their voice has gone out through all the earth, and their message to the ends of the world.

## Psalm 18:2-5. R. v.5

*Their message goes out through all the earth.*

## Matthew 4:18-22

As Jesus was walking by the Sea of Galilee he saw two brothers, Simon, who was called Peter, and his brother Andrew; they were making a cast in the lake with their net, for they were fishermen. And he said to them, 'Follow me and I will make you fishers of men.' And they left their nets at once and followed him. Going on from there he saw another pair of brothers, James son of Zebedee and his brother John; they were in their boat with their father Zebedee, mending their nets, and he called them. At once, leaving the boat and their father, they followed him.

## Reflection

Imagine yourself doing what you normally do each day when, completely unexpectedly, someone says to you, 'follow me'. What would you do? Matthew gives no indication that Peter and Andrew, James and John, knew Jesus. John's Gospel (1: 35-43) which records that Andrew brought his brother to Jesus, suggests that they may have known him. Probably they 'knew of' rather than 'knew' Jesus. Regardless, these men respond instantly to Jesus' request to follow him! They leave what they know and set out on an uncertain path. They were seemingly ordinary men, and yet, they gave to Jesus the greatest gift they had – they gave themselves. How do we respond when Jesus says, 'follow me'? It is in the following that we come, not to know of, but to know the One who is Love who calls us.

**St Andrew,** *apostle*
Feast
Red
**(Scotland – Solemnity)**
*(See Appendix A-20)*

# DECEMBER
# 1
## WEDNESDAY

**1st Week of Advent**
Violet

### Isaiah 25:6-10

On this mountain, the Lord of hosts will prepare for all peoples a banquet of rich food, a banquet of fine wines, of food rich and juicy, of fine strained wines. On this mountain he will remove the mourning veil covering all peoples, and the shroud enwrapping all nations, he will destroy Death for ever. The Lord God will wipe away the tears from every cheek; he will take away his people's shame everywhere on earth, for the Lord has said so. That day, it will be said: See, this is our God in whom we hoped for salvation; the Lord is the one in whom we hoped. We exult and we rejoice that he has saved us; for the hand of the Lord rests on this mountain.

### Psalm 22. R. v.6

*In the Lord's own house shall I dwell for ever and ever.*

### Matthew 15:29-37

Jesus reached the shores of the Sea of Galilee, and he went up into the hills. He sat there, and large crowds came to him bringing the lame, the crippled, the blind, the dumb and many others; these they put down at his feet, and he cured them. The crowds were astonished to see the dumb speaking, the cripples whole again, the lame walking and the blind with their sight, and they praised the God of Israel.

But Jesus called his disciples to him and said, 'I feel sorry for all these people; they have been with me for three days now and have nothing to eat. I do not want to send them off hungry, they might collapse on the way.' The disciples said to him, 'Where could we get enough bread in this deserted place to feed such a crowd?' Jesus said to them, 'How many loaves have you?' 'Seven' they said 'and a few small fish.' Then he instructed the crowd to sit down on the ground, and he took the seven loaves and the fish, and he gave thanks and broke them and handed them to the disciples who gave them to the crowds. They all ate as much as they wanted, and they collected what was left of the scraps, seven baskets full.

### Reflection

Today's psalm is perhaps the best known of all of the 150 psalms. It's a text known by name and in popular melody: *The Lord's My Shepherd,* often sung to the tune Crimond. Set to one of its many popular melodies, this psalm is a classic at funerals, partly because people of all faiths and of none can easily join in, but also because grieving people know their need to be gently carried through the 'valley of darkness and death' to 'God's dwelling place forevermore'. But more often the words of this prayer give us direction and hope in the midst of daily routines and demands. When we pray with this psalm, we see that it is not about death at all, but about life both now and eternally. That's the kind of good news that we need every day.

**1st Week of Advent**
**Violet**

### Isaiah 26:1-6

That day, this song will be sung in the land of Judah: We have a strong city; to guard us he has set wall and rampart about us. Open the gates! Let the upright nation come in, she, the faithful one whose mind is steadfast, who keeps the peace, because she trusts in you. Trust in the Lord for ever, for the Lord is the everlasting Rock; he has brought low those who lived high up in the steep citadel; he brings it down, brings it down to the ground, flings it down in the dust: the feet of the lowly, the footsteps of the poor trample on it.

### Psalm 117:1.8-9.19-21.25-27. R. v.26

*Blessed in the name of the Lord is he who comes.*

### Matthew 7:21.24-27

Jesus said to his disciples: 'It is not those who say to me, "Lord, Lord", who will enter the kingdom of heaven, but the person who does the will of my Father in heaven.

'Therefore, everyone who listens to these words of mine and acts on them will be like a sensible man who built his house on rock. Rain came down, floods rose, gales blew and hurled themselves against that house, and it did not fall: it was founded on rock. But everyone who listens to these words of mine and does not act on them will be like a stupid man who built his house on sand. Rain came down, floods rose, gales blew and struck that house, and it fell; and what a fall it had!'

### Reflection

Words are important. We chatter all day without thinking, responding to comments in casual interactions. Our prayer too can become chatter when it is superficial. Jesus warns us about prayer that has become little more than lip-service, when we call out 'Lord, Lord' as a superficial cry that does not reflect our inner life. If prayer is to grow into relationship rather than remain as obligation it needs to reflect the reality of our lives and the life of our heart. In this way prayer becomes foundational as a personal relationship with Jesus Christ who is God-with-us. This divine relationship enables us to not only survive life's storms, but to grow and even thrive through the experiences that may be unwelcome, helping us to remember, in the words of the popular song, that even though the mountains may fall and the hills turn to dust, the love of God is our sure foundation.

# DECEMBER
# 3
## FRIDAY

**1st Week of Advent**
St Francis Xavier,
*priest*
Memorial
White

## Isaiah 29:17-24

The Lord says this: In a short time, a very short time, shall not Lebanon become fertile land and fertile land turn into forest? The deaf, that day, will hear the words of a book and, after shadow and darkness, the eyes of the blind will see. But the lowly will rejoice in the Lord even more and the poorest exult in the Holy One of Israel; for tyrants shall be no more, and scoffers vanish, and all be destroyed who are disposed to do evil: those who gossip to incriminate others, those who try at the gate to trip the arbitrator and get the upright man's case dismissed for groundless reasons. Therefore the Lord speaks, the God of the House of Jacob, Abraham's redeemer: No longer shall Jacob be ashamed, no more shall his face grow pale, for he shall see what my hands have done in his midst, he shall hold my name holy. They will hallow the Holy One of Jacob, stand in awe of the God of Israel. Erring spirits will learn wisdom and murmurers accept instruction.

## Psalm 26:1.4.13-14. R. v.1

*The Lord is my light and my help.*

## Matthew 9:27-31

As Jesus went on his way two blind men followed him shouting, 'Take pity on us, Son of David.' And when Jesus reached the house the blind men came up with him and he said to them, 'Do you believe I can do this?' They said, 'Sir, we do.' Then he touched their eyes saying, 'Your faith deserves it, so let this be done for you.' And their sight returned. Then Jesus sternly warned them, 'Take care that no one learns about this.' But when they had gone, they talked about him all over the countryside.

## Reflection

Many people cope with the miraculous by reducing it to what they can understand, perhaps suggesting that Jesus just increased the blind men's psychological vision or opened their eyes of faith rather than actually restoring their physical sight. The gospel truth is that Jesus did give them physical sight. But the really good news is that this is not the best thing that happened to these men that day. Deep within, the healthy human is a longing for much more than sight and sound and legs and arms and houses and land and money. This deep desire is planted in every human heart. This longing is the question to which Jesus is the answer. And this is the great miracle we see Jesus working in today's Gospel reading. In the same way Christ enables us to look beyond our present struggles and anxieties to the real answer to all our human desires. This is the fact that gives a person vision.

## Isaiah 30:19-21.23-26

Thus says the Lord God, the Holy One of Israel:

People of Zion, you will live in Jerusalem and weep no more. He will be gracious to you when he hears your cry; when he hears he will answer. When the Lord has given you the bread of suffering and the water of distress, he who is your teacher will hide no longer, and you will see your teacher with your own eyes. Whether you turn to right or left, your ears will hear these words behind you, 'This is the way, follow it.' He will send rain for the seed you sow in the ground, and the bread that the ground provides will be rich and nourishing. Your cattle will graze, that day, in wide pastures. Oxen and donkeys that till the ground will eat a salted fodder, winnowed with shovel and fork. On every lofty mountain, on every high hill there will be streams and watercourses, on the day of the great slaughter when the strongholds fall. Then moonlight will be bright as sunlight and sunlight itself be seven times brighter – like the light of seven days in one – on the day the Lord dresses the wound of his people and heals the bruises his blows have left.

## Psalm 146:1-6. R. Isaiah 30:18

*Happy are all who hope in the Lord.*

## Matthew 9:35–10:1.6-8

Jesus made a tour through all the towns and villages, teaching in their synagogues, proclaiming the Good News of the kingdom and curing all kinds of diseases and sickness.

And when he saw the crowds he felt sorry for them because they were harassed and dejected, like sheep without a shepherd. Then he said to his disciples, 'The harvest is rich but the labourers are few, so ask the Lord of the harvest to send labourers to his harvest.'

He summoned his twelve disciples, and gave them authority over unclean spirits with power to cast them out and to cure all kinds of diseases and sickness. These twelve Jesus sent out, instructing them as follows: 'Go rather to the lost sheep of the House of Israel. And as you go, proclaim that the kingdom of heaven is close at hand. Cure the sick, raise the dead, cleanse the lepers, cast out devils. You received without charge, give without charge.'

## Reflection

As people who strive to live in relationship with Christ, taking every opportunity to deepen our relationship with him, we can fall into thinking that we have already been called and now must share what we have received: that now we are the labourers in the great harvest seeking the lost sheep. While this is true of course, we also need to remember that while we are disciples and labourers alongside Christ, we also remain at every moment a lost sheep in need of salvation. The best response to the question 'have you been saved' is not a past tense 'yes, I have been saved', but a present experience 'I am being saved'. How are you experiencing the saving action of Jesus Christ in your life this week?

DECEMBER

4

SATURDAY

**1st Week of Advent**
Violet
or
St John Damascene,
*priest, doctor*
(Optional, White)

**2nd Sunday of Advent**
Psalter Week 2
Violet

## Baruch 5:1-9

Jerusalem, take off your dress of sorrow and distress, put on the beauty of the glory of God for ever, wrap the cloak of the integrity of God around you, put the diadem of the glory of the Eternal on your head: since God means to show your splendour to every nation under heaven, since the name God gives you for ever will be, 'Peace through integrity, and honour through devotedness.' Arise, Jerusalem, stand on the heights and turn your eyes to the east: see your sons reassembled from west and east at the command of the Holy One, jubilant that God has remembered them. Though they left you on foot, with enemies for an escort, now God brings them back to you like royal princes carried back in glory. For God has decreed the flattening of each high mountain, of the everlasting hills, the filling of the valleys to make the ground level so that Israel can walk in safety under the glory of God. And the forests and every fragrant tree will provide shade for Israel at the command of God; for God will guide Israel in joy by the light of his glory with his mercy and integrity for escort.

## Psalm 125. R. v.3

*What marvels the Lord worked for us! Indeed we were glad.*

## Philippians 1:3-6.8-11

Every time I pray for all of you, I pray with joy, remembering how you have helped to spread the Good News from the day you first heard it right up to the present. I am quite certain that the One who began this good work in you will see that it is finished when the Day of Christ Jesus comes. God knows how much I miss you all, loving you as Christ Jesus loves you. My prayer is that your love for each other may increase more and more and never stop improving your knowledge and deepening your perception so that you can always recognise what is best. This will help you to become pure and blameless, and prepare you for the Day of Christ, when you will reach the perfect goodness which Jesus Christ produces in us for the glory and praise of God.

## Luke 3:1-6

In the fifteenth year of Tiberius Caesar's reign, when Pontius Pilate was governor of Judaea, Herod tetrarch of Galilee, his brother Philip tetrarch of the lands of Ituraea and Trachonitis, Lysanias tetrarch of Abilene, during the pontificate of Annas and Caiaphas, the word of God came to John son of Zechariah, in the wilderness. He went through the whole Jordan district proclaiming a baptism of repentance for the forgiveness of sins, as it is written in the book of the sayings of the prophet Isaiah: A voice cries in the wilderness: Prepare a way for the Lord, make his paths straight. Every valley will be filled in, every mountain and hill be laid low, winding ways will be straightened and rough roads made smooth. And all mankind shall see the salvation of God.

## Reflection

Today, the Second Sunday of Advent, we meet John the Baptist. Note the details in the Gospel reading: John the Baptist 'went throughout the whole Jordan district proclaiming a baptism of repentance…' The word in the original Greek that is often translated as repentance is 'metanoia' literally meaning 'change of heart'. One commentary adds that this kind of repentance is not about regret or guilt or shame but implies making a decision to turn around, to face a new direction. When we face away from the light, all we can see is our own shadow. When we turn towards the light our shadow and the darkness are behind us. Repentance means not only turning from what is bad, but also from many things that are good, but just not for us at this time, or turning from good things to which we have become inordinately attached and which, therefore, restrict our ability to be truly free.

### Isaiah 35:1-10

Let the wilderness and the dry-lands exult, let the wasteland rejoice and bloom, let it bring forth flowers like the jonquil, let it rejoice and sing for joy. The glory of Lebanon is bestowed on it, the splendour of Carmel and Sharon; they shall see the glory of the Lord, the splendour of our God. Strengthen all weary hands, steady all trembling knees and say to all faint hearts, 'Courage! Do not be afraid. Look, your God is coming, vengeance is coming, the retribution of God; he is coming to save you.' …
*(See Appendix B-35)*

### Psalm 84:9-14. R. Isaiah 35:4

*Look, our God is coming to save us.*

### Luke 5:17-26

Jesus was teaching one day, and among the audience there were Pharisees and doctors of the Law who had come from every village in Galilee, from Judaea and from Jerusalem. And the Power of the Lord was behind his works of healing. Then some men appeared, carrying on a bed a paralysed man whom they were trying to bring in and lay down in front of him. But as the crowd made it impossible to find a way of getting him in, they went up on to the flat roof and lowered him and his stretcher down through the tiles into the middle of the gathering, in front of Jesus. Seeing their faith he said, 'My friend, your sins are forgiven you.' The scribes and the Pharisees began to think this over. 'Who is this man talking blasphemy? Who can forgive sins but God alone?' But Jesus, aware of their thoughts, made them this reply, 'What are these thoughts you have in your hearts? Which of these is easier: to say, "Your sins are forgiven you" or to say, "Get up and walk"? But to prove to you that the Son of Man has authority on earth to forgive sins' – he said to the paralysed man – 'I order you: get up, and pick up your stretcher and go home.' And immediately before their very eyes he got up, picked up what he had been lying on and went home praising God.

They were all astounded and praised God, and were filled with awe, saying, 'We have seen strange things today.'

### Reflection

Some Bible translations begin today's Gospel with these words: 'And it came to pass on a certain day that Jesus was teaching …'. The phrase 'it came to pass' is worth pondering. Jesus often spent time simply responding to the things that 'came to pass'. So much of my time and energy is about working to complete the good things that I plan to do, so much so that I hardly notice the opportunities that come to pass. Yet when I look back on a day or a week, I notice that many of the things I plan seem to bear little fruit and my most powerful encounters with the divine are unexpected and certainly unplanned. While good planning is necessary, I find unexpected abundance in life when I practise sensitivity to the presence of Jesus in the things that simply come to pass.

**2nd Week of Advent**
St Ambrose,
*bishop, doctor*
Memorial
White

### Isaiah 40:1-11

'Console my people, console them' says your God. 'Speak to the heart of Jerusalem and call to her that her time of service is ended, that her sin is atoned for, that she has received from the hand of the Lord double punishment for all her crimes.' A voice cries, 'Prepare in the wilderness a way for the Lord. Make a straight highway for our God across the desert. Let every valley be filled in, every mountain and hill be laid low, let every cliff become a plain, and the ridges a valley; then the glory of the Lord shall be revealed and all mankind shall see it; for the mouth of the Lord has spoken.' A voice commands: 'Cry!' and I answered, 'What shall I cry?' – 'All flesh is grass and its beauty like the wild flower's. The grass withers, the flower fades when the breath of the Lord blows on them. (The grass is without doubt the people. ) The grass withers, the flower fades, but the word of our God remains for ever.' Go up on a high mountain, joyful messenger to Zion. Shout with a loud voice, joyful messenger to Jerusalem. Shout without fear, say to the towns of Judah, 'Here is your God.' Here is the Lord coming with power, his arms subduing all things to him. The prize of his victory is with him, his trophies all go before him. He is like a shepherd feeding his flock, gathering lambs in his arms, holding them against his breast and leading to their rest the mother ewes.

### Psalm 95:1-3.10-13. R. cf. Isaiah 40:9-10

*Here is our God coming with power.*

### Matthew 18:12-14

Jesus said to his disciples: 'Tell me. Suppose a man has a hundred sheep and one of them strays; will he not leave the ninety-nine on the hillside and go in search of the stray? I tell you solemnly, if he finds it, it gives him more joy than do the ninety-nine that did not stray at all. Similarly, it is never the will of your Father in heaven that one of these little ones should be lost.'

### Reflection

I'm not sure I would leave the ninety-nine (sheep or dollars) to go in search of the one. My fear would be that I end up with only one and the ninety-nine would vanish and I'm sure most farmers and investors would agree with me. But Jesus is inviting us to see ourselves as the lost ones remembering that he is the one who is seeking us. Those who go tramping in the bush or climbing in the mountains are given a very clear instruction as they set out: If you think you are lost, stay still and you will increase your chance of being found. The same is true in our faith. Rather than rushing about trying to feel found, be still and the one who seeks us will find us and come to us, gathering us into his arms and feeding us.

**The Immaculate
Conception of the
Blessed Virgin Mary
Solemnity
White**

**Genesis 3:9-15.20**
*(See Appendix B-35)*

**Psalm 97:1-4. R. v.1**
*Sing a new song to the Lord for he has worked wonders.*

**Ephesians 1:3-6.11-12**
Blessed be God the Father of our Lord Jesus Christ, who has blessed us with all the spiritual blessings of heaven in Christ. Before the world was made, he chose us, chose us in Christ, to be holy and spotless, and to live through love in his presence, determining that we should become his adopted sons, through Jesus Christ for his own kind purposes, to make us praise the glory of his grace, his free gift to us in the Beloved. And it is in him that we were claimed as God's own, chosen from the beginning, under the predetermined plan of the one who guides all things as he decides by his own will; chosen to be, for his greater glory, the people who would put their hopes in Christ before he came.

**Luke 1:26-38**
The angel Gabriel was sent by God to a town in Galilee called Nazareth, to a virgin betrothed to a man named Joseph, of the House of David; and the virgin's name was Mary. He went in and said to her, 'Rejoice, so highly favoured! The Lord is with you.' She was deeply disturbed by these words and asked herself what this greeting could mean, but the angel said to her, 'Mary, do not be afraid; you have won God's favour. Listen! You are to conceive and bear a son, and you must name him Jesus. He will be great and will be called Son of the Most High. The Lord God will give him the throne of his ancestor David; he will rule over the House of Jacob for ever and his reign will have no end.' Mary said to the angel, 'But how can this come about, since I am a virgin?' 'The Holy Spirit will come upon you,' the angel answered, 'and the power of the Most High will cover you with its shadow. And so the child will be holy and will be called Son of God. Know this too: your kinswoman Elizabeth has, in her old age, herself conceived a son, and she whom people called barren is now in her sixth month, for nothing is impossible to God.' 'I am the handmaid of the Lord,' said Mary, 'let what you have said be done to me.' And the angel left her.

### Reflection
Without the intervention of God to free Mary from the effects of Original Sin, she would have suffered the same inclination to sin that is ours before we fruitfully receive the sacrament of baptism. Once the beauty of human freedom in uncontaminated relationship with God had been disrupted by the first experience of sin it becomes more difficult for us to live in harmony with God. We all know what this is like from our experience in human relationships. Once we say one 'no' we open a door to a pattern that easily becomes a habit and we then struggle to give a whole-hearted 'yes'.

The Old Testament begins with a rejection of God. Adam's first response when he meets God after his 'no' is to hide. This is our problem too when our shame and guilt mean we foolishly keep our distance from the love we most deeply and desperately seek. The New Testament begins with a 'YES'. This new era is ours when we allow the grace given in baptism to take root and grow to maturity within us. Without this practice of the presence of Jesus, baptismal grace (while still present) struggles to bear fruit.

## Isaiah 41:13-20

I, the Lord, your God, I am holding you by the right hand; I tell you, 'Do not be afraid, I will help you.' Do not be afraid, Jacob, poor worm, Israel, puny mite. I will help you – it is the Lord who speaks – the Holy One of Israel is your redeemer. See, I turn you into a threshing-sled, new, with doubled teeth; you shall thresh and crush the mountains, and turn the hills to chaff. You shall winnow them and the wind will blow them away, the gale will scatter them. But you yourself will rejoice in the Lord, and glory in the Holy One of Israel. The poor and the needy ask for water, and there is none, their tongue is parched with thirst. I, the Lord, will answer them, I, the God of Israel, will not abandon them. I will make rivers well up on barren heights, and fountains in the midst of valleys; turn the wilderness into a lake, and dry ground into waterspring. In the wilderness I will put cedar trees, acacias, myrtles, olives. In the desert I will plant juniper, plane tree and cypress side by side; so that men may see and know, may all observe and understand that the hand of the Lord has done this, that the Holy One of Israel has created it.

## Psalm 144:1.9-13. R. v.8

*The Lord is kind and full of compassion, slow to anger, abounding in love.*

## Matthew 11:11-15

Jesus spoke to the crowds: 'I tell you solemnly, of all the children born of women, a greater than John the Baptist has never been seen; yet the least in the kingdom of heaven is greater than he is. Since John the Baptist came, up to this present time, the kingdom of heaven has been subjected to violence and the violent are taking it by storm. Because it was towards John that all the prophecies of the prophets and of the Law were leading; and he, if you will believe me, is the Elijah who was to return. If anyone has ears to hear, let him listen!'

**2nd Week of Advent**
Violet
or
**St Juan Diego Cuauhtlatoatzin
(Optional, White)**

## Reflection

The conclusion of today's Gospel reading caught my attention: they who have ears to hear, let them listen. Our physical senses connect us with the world that surrounds us. We see, we touch, we taste, we smell and we hear. These physical senses can also entice us to a deeper reality. Just as we have physical senses, we have deeper spiritual senses which are the window to the life of the soul. Ignatius of Loyola in his *Spiritual Exercises* invites us to use our physical senses in prayer as a way of becoming more sensitive to the voice of Jesus, an invitation to hear with the ears of the heart and to see with the vision of faith, moving beyond our own blinkered perceptions and fear-filled prejudices to truly hear his voice, receive his gaze and experience his touch. In this most sensible of methods we soon find that we are living more deliberately and abundantly.

## DECEMBER

# 10

**FRIDAY**

**2nd Week of Advent**
**Violet**

### Isaiah 48:17-19

Thus says the Lord, your redeemer, the Holy One of Israel: I, the Lord, your God, teach you what is good for you, I lead you in the way that you must go. If only you had been alert to my commandments, your happiness would have been like a river, your integrity like the waves of the sea. Your children would have been numbered like the sand, your descendants as many as its grains. Never would your name have been cut off or blotted out before me.

### Psalm 1:1-4.6. R. cf. John 8:12

*Anyone who follows you, O Lord, will have the light of life.*

### Matthew 11:16-19

Jesus spoke to the crowds: 'What description can I find for this generation? It is like children shouting to each other as they sit in the market place: "We played the pipes for you, and you wouldn't dance; we sang dirges, and you wouldn't be mourners."

'For John came, neither eating nor drinking, and they say, "He is possessed." The Son of Man came, eating and drinking, and they say, "Look, a glutton and a drunkard, a friend of tax collectors and sinners." Yet wisdom has been proved right by her actions.'

### Reflection

Have you ever worked hard to please or appease someone doing the very thing you knew they wanted you to do – and they still weren't happy? With some people it seems you can't win whatever you do. Then there are other people who are so generous of spirit that it is hard to upset them. A friend of mine quotes one of his mentors who speaks about the importance of living by an internal score card. It's good advice. If we rely on the opinions of others and the fashions and fears of our time to determine what we say and do we will fall victim to every voice and sell our soul for any quick ego-boost. When we live in relationship with Jesus listening to his voice and guidance in the depth of our heart, we show the face of personal integrity to the world.

## Sirach 48:1-4.9-11

The prophet Elijah arose like a fire, his word flaring like a torch. It was he who brought famine on them, and who decimated them in his zeal. By the word of the Lord, he shut up the heavens, he also, three times, brought down fire. How glorious you were in your miracles, Elijah! Has anyone reason to boast as you have? – taken up in the whirlwind of fire, in a chariot with fiery horses; designated in the prophecies of doom to allay God's wrath before the fury breaks, to turn the hearts of fathers towards their children, and to restore the tribes of Jacob. Happy shall they be who see you, and those who have fallen asleep in love.

## Psalm 79:2-3.15-16.18-19. R. v.4

*Lord of hosts, bring us back; let your face shine on us and we shall be saved.*

## Matthew 17:10-13

As they came down from the mountain the disciples put this question to Jesus, 'Why do the scribes say that Elijah has to come first?' 'True', he replied; 'Elijah is to come to see that everything is once more as it should be; however, I tell you that Elijah has come already and they did not recognise him but treated him as they pleased; and the Son of Man will suffer similarly at their hands.' The disciples understood then that he had been speaking of John the Baptist.

## Reflection

We know that Jesus often exhorts his disciples to go forth telling everyone what they have seen and heard, that all may come to believe. We forget that there are times when Jesus calls those who have experienced his power to be silent and to tell no one. This is a call to be discerning about not only how to share what we have received but also about how much to share and when to share. Earlier in Matthew's Gospel Jesus warns his disciples not to cast pearls before swine. We know that Jesus Christ, received in the Eucharist, is real food, and not everyone is able to digest real food. So too the message and miracles of Jesus are too much for some people and it may be unwise or even careless and harmful to give someone a message they are not asking for or ready for. As we journey closer to Christmas the wisdom of Mary reminds us to speak and act when necessary, and often to ponder what we have experienced in our hearts.

**3rd Sunday of Advent**
**Psalter Week 2**
**Violet (or Rose)**

### Zephaniah 3:14-18

Shout for joy, daughter of Zion, Israel, shout aloud! Rejoice, exult with all your heart, daughter of Jerusalem! The Lord has repealed your sentence; he has driven your enemies away. The Lord, the king of Israel, is in your midst; you have no more evil to fear. When that day comes, word will come to Jerusalem: Zion, have no fear, do not let your hands fall limp. The Lord your God is in your midst, a victorious warrior. He will exult with joy over you, he will renew you by his love; he will dance with shouts of joy for you as on a day of festival.

### Psalm: Isaiah 12:2-6. R. v.6

*Sing and shout for joy for great in your midst is the Holy One of Israel.*

### Philippians 4:4-7

I want you to be happy, always happy in the Lord; I repeat, what I want is your happiness. Let your tolerance be evident to everyone: the Lord is very near. There is no need to worry; but if there is anything you need, pray for it, asking God for it with prayer and thanksgiving, and that peace of God, which is so much greater than we can understand, will guard your hearts and your thoughts, in Christ Jesus.

### Luke 3:10-18

When all the people asked John, 'What must we do? he answered, 'If anyone has two tunics he must share with the man who has none, and the one with something to eat must do the same.' There were tax collectors too who came for baptism, and these said to him, 'Master, what must we do?' He said to them, 'Exact no more than your rate.' Some soldiers asked him in their turn, 'What must we do?' He said to them, 'No intimidation! No extortion! Be content with your pay!'

A feeling of expectancy had grown among the people, who were beginning to think that John might be the Christ, so John declared before them all, 'I baptise you with water, but someone is coming, someone who is more powerful than I am, and I am not fit to undo the strap of his sandals; he will baptise you with the Holy Spirit and fire. His winnowing-fan is in his hand to clear his threshing-floor and to gather the wheat into his barn; but the chaff he will burn in a fire that will never go out.' As well as this, there were many other things he said to exhort the people and to announce the Good News to them.

## Reflection

One of the four candles on an Advent wreath is usually rose-coloured. This is the candle lit today, the Third Sunday of Advent, the Sunday also named Gaudete or 'rejoicing' Sunday, a name taken from the opening word of the Entrance Antiphon for today's Mass.

Before the birth of Christ people often seemed to be at a loss about how to live in harmony with God. While they received the law through Moses as a gift, they soon tragically reduced this life-giving direction to little rules that served to bind rather than free. Those who are captive struggle to sing songs of rejoicing. Such directionless people flock to John asking: What must we do then? At this point John presents the first clear social teaching of the Christian era, firstly to the people, then tax collectors, then the soldiers. Afterwards John declares before them all that Christ whom they had awaited was immanent and the era they had long awaited had arrived.

The risk we face is to see the arrival of the Messiah only as an historical event. The reality is that Jesus Christ, who overcame death, is present in our world today, and wherever there is love, there is God. There is no greater cause for rejoicing than awareness of this fact.

**3rd Week of Advent**
St Lucy, *virgin, martyr*
**Memorial**
**Red**

## Numbers 24:2-7.15-17

Raising his eyes Balaam saw Israel, encamped by tribes; the spirit of God came on him and he declaimed his poem. He said: 'The oracle of Balaam son of Beor, the oracle of the man with far-seeing eyes, the oracle of one who hears the word of God. He sees what Shaddai makes him see, receives the divine answer, and his eyes are opened. How fair are your tents, O Jacob! How fair your dwellings, Israel! Like valleys that stretch afar, like gardens by the banks of a river, like aloes planted by the Lord, like cedars beside the waters! A hero arises from their stock, he reigns over countless peoples. His king is greater than Agag, his majesty is exalted.' Then Balaam declaimed his poem again. He said: 'The oracle of Balaam son of Beor, the oracle of the man with far-seeing eyes, the oracle of the one who hears the word of God, of one who knows the knowledge of the Most High. He sees what Shaddai makes him see, receives the divine answer, and his eyes are opened. I see him – but not in the present, I behold him – but not close at hand: a star from Jacob takes the leadership, a sceptre arises from Israel.'

## Psalm 24:4-9. R. v.4

*Lord, make me know your ways.*

## Matthew 21:23-27

Jesus had gone into the Temple and was teaching, when the chief priests and the elders of the people came to him and said, 'What authority have you for acting like this? And who gave you this authority?' 'And I' replied Jesus 'will ask you a question, only one; if you tell me the answer to it, I will then tell you my authority for acting like this. John's baptism: where did it come from: heaven or man?' And they argued it out this way among themselves, 'If we say from heaven, he will retort, "Then why did you refuse to believe him?"; but if we say from man, we have the people to fear, for they all hold that John was a prophet.' So their reply to Jesus was, 'We do not know.' And he retorted, 'Nor will I tell you my authority for acting like this.'

## Reflection

When Moses came down the mountain bringing the Ten Commandments the people welcomed the law since it was a direct communication from God who they knew to be their creator and therefore their ultimate authority. Today our reaction to law might not be as positive. We do all we can to avoid a traffic ticket. We forget that it is the law that makes it safe to leave the house and to drive on the road. While many cultures value independence and personal power, a healthy human will acknowledge the beauty of submission to a higher power and divine authority. This was the wisdom of John the Baptist. Just as his own followers were growing in numbers, he pointed away from himself to the One who gives all life.

## Zephaniah 3:1-2.9-13

Trouble is coming to the rebellious, the defiled, the tyrannical city! She would never listen to the call, would never learn the lesson; she has never trusted in the Lord, never drawn near to her God. Yes, I will then give the peoples lips that are clean, so that all may invoke the name of the Lord and serve him under the same yoke. From beyond the banks of the rivers of Ethiopia my suppliants will bring me offerings. When that day comes you need feel no shame for all the misdeeds you have committed against me, for I will remove your proud boasters from your midst; and you will cease to strut on my holy mountain. In your midst I will leave a humble and lowly people, and those who are left in Israel will seek refuge in the name of the Lord. They will do no wrong, will tell no lies; and the perjured tongue will no longer be found in their mouths. But they will be able to graze and rest with no one to disturb them.

## Psalm 33:2-3.6-7.16.18-19.23. R. v.7

*This poor man called; the Lord heard him.*

## Matthew 21:28-32

Jesus said to the chief priests and the elders of the people, 'What is your opinion? A man had two sons. He went and said to the first, "My boy, you go and work in the vineyard today." He answered, "I will not go," but afterwards thought better of it and went. The man then went and said the same thing to the second who answered, "Certainly, sir," but did not go. Which of the two did the father's will? 'The first' they said. Jesus said to them, 'I tell you solemnly, tax collectors and prostitutes are making their way into the kingdom of God before you. For John came to you, a pattern of true righteousness, but you did not believe him, and yet the tax collectors and prostitutes did. Even after seeing that, you refused to think better of it and believe in him.'

## Reflection

I imagine the father standing with his two sons surrounded by many workers. One son sought to keep the peace and lied to his father 'yes I will go', but had no intention of going to the vineyard. The second son honestly said he would not do what his father wanted. Christians are often accused of being hypocrites, saying one thing and doing another. I know I am a bit like this since I profess belief in Christ and too often fail to live this belief. There is some integrity in acknowledging this resistance to the will of the father. Note that the turning point in this encounter was when the second son, moved with repentance, changed his mind and decided to do what the father asked. In this turning he becomes an example of what it is to have faith.

**3rd Week of Advent**
**Violet**

## Isaiah 45:6-8.18.21-26

Apart from me, all is nothing. I am the Lord, unrivalled, I form the light and create the dark. I make good fortune and create calamity, it is I, the Lord, who do all this. Send victory like a dew, you heavens, and let the clouds rain it down. Let the earth open for salvation to spring up. Let deliverance, too, bud forth which I, the Lord, shall create. Yes, thus says the Lord, creator of the heavens, who is God, who formed the earth and made it, who set it firm, created it no chaos, but a place to be lived in: 'I am the Lord, unrivalled. There is no other god besides me, a God of integrity and a saviour; there is none apart from me. Turn to me and be saved, all the ends of the earth, for I am God unrivalled. 'By my own self I swear it; what comes from my mouth is truth, a word irrevocable; before me every knee shall bend, by me every tongue shall swear, saying, "From the Lord alone come victory and strength." To him shall come, ashamed, all who raged against him. Victorious and glorious through the Lord shall be all the descendants of Israel.'

## Psalm 84:9-14. R. cf. Isaiah 45:8

*Send victory like a dew, you heavens, and let the clouds rain it down.*

## Luke 7:19-23

John, summoning two of his disciples, sent them to the Lord to ask, 'Are you the one who is to come, or must we wait for someone else?' When the men reached Jesus they said, 'John the Baptist has sent us to you, to ask, "Are you the one who is to come or have we to wait for someone else?"' It was just then that he cured many people of diseases and afflictions and of evil spirits, and gave the gift of sight to many who were blind. Then he gave the messengers their answer, 'Go back and tell John what you have seen and heard: the blind see again, the lame walk, lepers are cleansed, and the deaf hear, the dead are raised to life, the Good News is proclaimed to the poor and happy is the man who does not lose faith in me.'

## Reflection

Perhaps we all carry the tendency to never be satisfied and to seek more than we have. This restlessness is a characteristic of healthy humanity. We are restless until we rest in God and the dis-ease that impinges even on our happiest moments is a sign that our humanity is alive and pressing us forward.

The disciples of John encountered Jesus and noticed that he appeared to be an adequate response to their inner longing. They ask him if he is the One. Rather than give a simple doctrinal answer Jesus directs them to look at the evidence of their experience. They recall that those who encounter Jesus are able to see with renewed vision, to listen with more finely attuned hearing, to observe that the lame walk, the sick are healed and the dead are restored to life. This is enough. They have found the Christ and there is no need to search for another.

## Isaiah 54:1-10

Shout for joy, you barren women who bore no children! Break into cries of joy and gladness, you who were never in labour! For the sons of the foresaken one are more in number than the sons of the wedded wife, says the Lord. Widen the space of your tent, stretch out your hangings freely, lengthen your ropes, make your pegs firm; for you will burst out to right and to left. Your race will take possession of the nations, and people the abandoned cities. Do not be afraid, you will not be put to shame, do not be dismayed, you will not be disgraced; for you will forget the shame of your youth and no longer remember the curse of your widowhood. For now your creator will be your husband, his name, the Lord of hosts; your redeemer will be the Holy One of Israel, he is called the God of the whole earth. Yes, like a forsaken wife, distressed in spirit, the Lord calls you back. ...
*(See Appendix B–35)*

### Psalm 29:2.4-6.11-13. R. v.2
*I will praise you, Lord, you have rescued me.*

### Luke 7:24-30
When John's messengers had gone Jesus began to talk to the people about John, 'What did you go out into the wilderness to see? A reed swaying in the breeze? No? Then what did you go out to see? A man dressed in fine clothes? Oh no, those who go in for fine clothes and live luxuriously are to be found at court! Then what did you go out to see? A prophet? Yes, I tell you, and much more than a prophet: he is the one of whom scripture says: See, I am going to send my messenger before you; he will prepare the way before you. I tell you, of all the children born of women, there is no greater than John; yet the least in the kingdom of God is greater than he is. All the people who heard him, and the tax collectors too, acknowledged God's plan by accepting baptism from John; but by refusing baptism from him the Pharisees and the lawyers had thwarted what God had in mind for them.'

**DECEMBER 16 THURSDAY**

**3rd Week of Advent**
**Violet**

### Reflection
The refrain we pray to the responsorial psalm at Mass often provides a key to understanding the scripture readings and also provides a useful mantra for a day's prayer. Today we pray: 'I will praise you Lord, for you have rescued me.' Notice that 'rescued' is past tense – it has already happened and now we are more or less open to receiving the rescue and living the grace of this gift. Our love and praise of God comes from this knowledge. And it is this knowledge that changes everything, not only the addition of a program to our already full hard-drive, or a reboot, but the offer of life with a new and default setting. And in this confident knowledge we realise that we are happier. We are freer because we are living more intentionally and more abundantly. Because you are rescuing me Lord, I am praising you.

**3rd Week of Advent**
**Violet**

**Genesis 49:2.8-10**
*(See Appendix B-36)*

**Psalm 71:1-4.7-8.17. R. cf. v.7**
*In his days justice shall flourish and peace till the moon fails.*

**Matthew 1:1-17**
A genealogy of Jesus Christ, son of David, son of Abraham: Abraham was the father of Isaac, Isaac the father of Jacob, Jacob the father of Judah and his brothers, Judah was the father of Perez and Zerah, Tamar being their mother, Perez was the father of Hezron, Hezron the father of Ram, Ram was the father of Amminadab, Amminadab the father of Nahshon, Nahshon the father of Salmon, Salmon was the father of Boaz, Rahab being his mother, Boaz was the father of Obed, Ruth being his mother, Obed was the father of Jesse; and Jesse was the father of King David. David was the father of Solomon, whose mother had been Uriah's wife, Solomon was the father of Rehoboam, Rehoboam the father of Abijah, Abijah the father of Asa, Asa was the father of Jehoshaphat, Jehoshaphat the father of Joram, Joram the father of Azariah, Azariah was the father of Jotham, Jotham the father of Ahaz, Ahaz the father of Hezekiah, Hezekiah was the father of Manasseh, Manasseh the father of Amon, Amon the father of Josiah; and Josiah was the father of Jechoniah and his brothers. Then the deportation to Babylon took place. After the deportation to Babylon: Jechoniah was the father of Shealtiel, Shealtiel the father of Zerubbabel, Zerubbabel was the father of Abiud, Abiud the father of Eliakim, Eliakim the father of Azor, Azor was the father of Zadok, Zadok the father of Achim, Achim the father of Eliud, Eliud was the father of Eleazar, Eleazar the father of Matthan, Matthan the father of Jacob; and Jacob was the father of Joseph the husband of Mary; of her was born Jesus who is called Christ.

The sum of generations is therefore: fourteen from Abraham to David; fourteen from David to the Babylonian deportation; and fourteen from the Babylonian deportation to Christ.

**Reflection**
We might wonder why at this important stage of preparation for Christmas an entire Gospel reading is given to the genealogy of Jesus listing forty-two generations concluding with 'Jacob the father of Joseph the husband of Mary of whom Jesus was born.' It is hardly an exciting read and most will stumble through the pronunciation of names wondering why it is read at all. Well it is all about flesh and blood, beginning with the promise to Abraham and culminating in the fulfilment of the covenant with the birth of Jesus the Messiah.

These opening verses of Matthew's Gospel remind us in every name mentioned of a unique human person who lived and breathed and walked this earth, every one of them with their exits and entrances, playing many parts from infancy to earthly death, each human life a creation of God, at times resistant and at times co-operative. And, most important, God used them all as God uses each of us to sow a seed that may only bear fruit in generations to come.

**Jeremiah 23:5-8**

'See, the days are coming – it is the Lord who speaks – when I will raise a virtuous Branch for David, who will reign as true king and be wise, practising honesty and integrity in the land. In his days Judah will be saved and Israel dwell in confidence. And this is the name he will be called: The Lord-our-integrity.

'So, then, the days are coming – it is the Lord who speaks – when people will no longer say, "As the Lord lives who brought the sons of Israel out of the land of Egypt!" but, "As the Lord lives who led back and brought home the descendants of the House of Israel out of the land of the North and from all the countries to which he had dispersed them, to live on their own soil."'

**Psalm 71:1-2.12-13.18-19. R. cf. v.7**

*In his days justice shall flourish and peace till the moon fails.*

**Matthew 1:18-24**

This is how Jesus Christ came to be born. His mother Mary was betrothed to Joseph, but before they came to live together she was found to be with child through the Holy Spirit. Her husband Joseph, being a man of honour and wanting to spare her publicity, decided to divorce her informally. He had made up his mind to do this when the angel of the Lord appeared to him in a dream and said, 'Joseph son of David, do not be afraid to take Mary home as your wife, because she has conceived what is in her by the Holy Spirit. She will give birth to a son and you must name him Jesus, because he is the one who is to save his people from their sins.' Now all this took place to fulfil the words spoken by the Lord through the prophet:

The virgin will conceive and give birth to a son and they will call him Emmanuel, a name which means 'God-is-with-us'. When Joseph woke up he did what the angel of the Lord had told him to do: he took his wife to his home.

**Reflection**

Joseph is an often overlooked but central protagonist in the account of the birth of Jesus. I like the way he struggles to understand when Mary informs him that she is pregnant by the Holy Spirit. And I'm moved by his sensitivity to the nudgings and communications of God to him through the inner voices of dreams and conscience. Clearly he was a just and holy man. I also like the way he is a bit sidelined in the gospel accounts. It is in the nature of a child to want centre stage, and perhaps in our teenage dreams we seek to be a hero, making the headlines and achieving fame in work and sport. Then, for the healthy person on the path to maturity, something shifts and we seek more solitude. Without Christ this solitude risks becoming loneliness and isolation. With Christ we find our true place and realise that our happiness is found when it is no longer I who live, but Christ who lives through me.

# DECEMBER
# 19
## SUNDAY

**4th Sunday of Advent**
**Psalter Week 4**
**Violet**

## Micah 5:1-4

The Lord says this: You, Bethlehem Ephrathah, the least of the clans of Judah, out of you will be born for me the one who is to rule over Israel; his origin goes back to the distant past, to the days of old. The Lord is therefore going to abandon them till the time when she who is to give birth gives birth. Then the remnant of his brothers will come back to the sons of Israel. He will stand and feed his flock with the power of the Lord, with the majesty of the name of his God. They will live secure, for from then on he will extend his power to the ends of the land. He himself will be peace.

## Psalm 79:2-3.15-16.18-19. R. v.4

*God of hosts, bring us back; let your face shine on us and we shall be saved.*

## Hebrews 10:5-10

This is what Christ said, on coming into the world: You who wanted no sacrifice or oblation, prepared a body for me. You took no pleasure in holocausts or sacrifices for sin; then I said, just as I was commanded in the scroll of the book, 'God, here I am! I am coming to obey your will.'

Notice that he says first: You did not want what the Law lays down as the things to be offered, that is: the sacrifices, the oblations, the holocausts and the sacrifices for sin, and you took no pleasure in them; and then he says: Here I am! I am coming to obey your will. He is abolishing the first sort to replace it with the second. And this will was for us to be made holy by the offering of his body made once and for all by Jesus Christ.

## Luke 1:39-44

Mary set out and went as quickly as she could to a town in the hill country of Judah. She went into Zechariah's house and greeted Elizabeth. Now as soon as Elizabeth heard Mary's greeting, the child leapt in her womb and Elizabeth was filled with the Holy Spirit. She gave a loud cry and said, 'Of all women you are the most blessed, and blessed is the fruit of your womb. Why should I be honoured with a visit from the mother of my Lord? For the moment your greeting reached my ears, the child in my womb leapt for joy. Yes, blessed is she who believed that the promise made her by the Lord would be fulfilled.'

## Reflection

I imagine a lot of love and humour in the visit of Mary to Elizabeth. It's likely that the situations of both women would have fuelled gossip in their little villages and among family and friends, and now we meet Mary seeking solidarity and refuge in the home of her cousin Elizabeth. It's helpful to recall the enthusiasm and excitement of their greeting: the child Jesus in Mary's womb 'leaped' for joy and Elizabeth was 'filled with the Holy Spirit'. Perhaps these two didn't meet all that often, but when they did it was as friends and conversation would have carried on where they had left off at the last visit.

The humour I imagine is in the fact that the man of the house, Zechariah, was silent giving Mary and Elizabeth space to laugh and chat thus making his house their own. All of this during what must have been difficult circumstances for each of them. Their shared humour comes from their confidence that in their unexpected pregnancies God is at work.

And don't miss the Opening Prayer of today's Mass, familiar to us as the concluding prayer of the great Angelus: The word became flesh, and dwells amongst us.

**4th Week of Advent**
**Violet**

### Isaiah 7:10-14

The Lord spoke to Ahaz and said, 'Ask the Lord your God for a sign for yourself coming either from the depths of Sheol or from the heights above.' 'No,' Ahaz answered, 'I will not put the Lord to the test.'

Then Isaiah said: 'Listen now, House of David: are you not satisfied with trying the patience of men without trying the patience of my God, too? The Lord himself, therefore, will give you a sign. It is this: the maiden is with child and will soon give birth to a son whom she will call Emmanuel, a name which means "God-is-with-us"'.

### Psalm 23:1-6. R. cf. v.7.10

*Let the Lord enter! He is the king of glory.*

### Luke 1:26-38

The angel Gabriel was sent by God to a town in Galilee called Nazareth, to a virgin betrothed to a man named Joseph, of the House of David; and the virgin's name was Mary. He went in and said to her, 'Rejoice, so highly favoured! The Lord is with you.' She was deeply disturbed by these words and asked herself what this greeting could mean, but the angel said to her, 'Mary, do not be afraid; you have won God's favour. Listen! You are to conceive and bear a son, and you must name him Jesus. He will be great and will be called Son of the Most High. The Lord God will give him the throne of his ancestor David; he will rule over the House of Jacob for ever and his reign will have no end.' Mary said to the angel, 'But how can this come about, since I am a virgin?' 'The Holy Spirit will come upon you', the angel answered, 'and the power of the Most High will cover you with its shadow. And so the child will be holy and will be called Son of God. Know this too: your kinswoman Elizabeth has, in her old age, herself conceived a son, and she whom people called barren is now in her sixth month, for nothing is impossible to God.' 'I am the handmaid of the Lord,' said Mary, 'let what you have said be done to me.' And the angel left her.

### Reflection

It's a bit of an insult to call someone an angel. Angels are not human. They do not make their home in earthly time and space. I would rather be called a human since that is what I am created to be. But I hope I am always ready to listen to anyone who (like an angel) delivers a personal message from God to me. It is usual in a Scriptural account of the appearance of an angel for the messenger to speak first encouraging a person to not be afraid. Gabriel greets Mary warmly: 'Greetings, favoured one! The Lord is with you.' The conversation continues with Mary able to honestly express her confusion as she pondered the meaning and the message of the visit. It's helpful to remember that every message from God, whoever or whatever the messenger, is for our good, and the one who desires to live in relationship with Christ will welcome even the most unlikely or unexpected messenger.

**4th Week of Advent**
**Violet**
or
**St Peter Canisius,**
*priest, doctor*
**(Commemoration)**

## Song 2:8-14
*(Alternative Reading: Zephaniah 3: 14-18)*

I hear my Beloved. See how he comes leaping on the mountains, bounding over the hills. My Beloved is like a gazelle, like a young stag. See where he stands behind our wall. He looks in at the window, he peers through the lattice. My Beloved lifts up his voice, he says to me, 'Come then, my love, my lovely one, come. For see, winter is past, the rains are over and gone. The flowers appear on the earth. The season of glad songs has come, the cooing of the turtledove is heard in our land. The fig tree is forming its first figs and the blossoming vines give out their fragrance. Come then, my love, my lovely one, come. My dove, hiding in the clefts of the rock, in the coverts of the cliff, show me your face, let me hear your voice; for your voice is sweet and your face is beautiful.'

## Psalm 32:2-3.11-12.20-21. R. vv. 1.3
*Ring out your joy to the Lord, O you just; O sing him a song that is new.*

## Luke 1:39-45

Mary set out and went as quickly as she could to a town in the hill country of Judah. She went into Zechariah's house and greeted Elizabeth. Now as soon as Elizabeth heard Mary's greeting, the child leapt in her womb and Elizabeth was filled with the Holy Spirit. She gave a loud cry and said, 'Of all women you are the most blessed, and blessed is the fruit of your womb. Why should I be honoured with a visit from the mother of my Lord? For the moment your greeting reached my ears, the child in my womb leapt for joy. Yes, blessed is she who believed that the promise made her by the Lord would be fulfilled.'

## Reflection

I am moved by the often-overlooked closing words of this passage: 'blessed is she who believed that the promise made her by the Lord would be fulfilled.' Even if we do not accept that God has spoken to us personally and directly through an event, a person or an inner communication, the fact is that the Lord has made specific promises of love, mercy, and present and eternal life to all people. There comes a point when we realise that we, like Mary, must make a decision, responding 'Yes' to all that God is offering. At this point as we re-orient ourselves to Christ a new clarity pervades every moment of our life. We no longer wander about directionless wondering whether to respond. From this point of decision, we have responded, and we have said 'yes'. Now we are able to enjoy the clarity and freedom of this new life: the promise spoken to us by the Lord is now being fulfilled in us.

**4th Week of Advent**
**Violet**

## 1 Samuel 1:24-28

When Hannah had weaned Samuel, she took him up with her together with a three-year old bull, an ephah of flour and a skin of wine, and she brought him to the temple of the Lord at Shiloh; and the child was with them. They slaughtered the bull and the child's mother came to Eli. She said, 'If you please, my lord. As you live, my lord, I am the woman who stood here beside you, praying to the Lord. This is the child I prayed for, and the Lord granted me what I asked him. Now I make him over to the Lord for the whole of his life. He is made over to the Lord.'

There she left him, for the Lord.

## Psalm: 1 Samuel 2:1.4-8. R. v.1
*My heart exults in the Lord my Saviour.*

## Luke 1:46-56

Mary said: 'My soul proclaims the greatness of the Lord and my spirit exults in God my saviour; because he has looked upon his lowly handmaid. Yes, from this day forward all generations will call me blessed, for the Almighty has done great things for me. Holy is his name, and his mercy reaches from age to age for those who fear him. 'He has shown the power of his arm, he has routed the proud of heart. He has pulled down princes from their thrones and exalted the lowly. The hungry he has filled with good things, the rich sent empty away. He has come to the help of Israel his servant, mindful of his mercy – according to the promise he made to our ancestors – of his mercy to Abraham and to his descendants for ever.' Mary stayed with Elizabeth about three months and then went back home.

## Reflection

History credits the Polish astronomer Copernicus with being the first to confidently announce that the earth is not the centre of the universe. Today this is widely accepted and our knowledge of the cosmos continues to grow. Centuries before Copernicus, Jesus taught that there was life beyond our limited personal and communal perceptions and reminded us that there will come a time when the earth on which we are so focussed will pass away. Mary understood this and communicates this new era in her revolutionary canticle of praise announcing a God who is looking on the lowly with favour, scattering the proud, tipping the mighty from their thrones and lifting up the lowly, filling the hungry and sending the rich away empty. This great prayer is a daily Gospel Canticle of the Church prayed at every Evening Prayer concluding with the life-giving reminder that the promise made to Abraham is for us, his descendants in the family of faith in the one God.

## Malachi 3:1-4.23-24

The Lord God says this: Look, I am going to send my messenger to prepare a way before me. And the Lord you are seeking will suddenly enter his Temple; and the angel of the covenant whom you are longing for, yes, he is coming, says the Lord of hosts. Who will be able to resist the day of his coming? Who will remain standing when he appears? For he is like the refiner's fire and the fullers' alkali. He will take his seat as refiner and purifier; he will purify the sons of Levi and refine them like gold and silver, and then they will make the offering to the Lord as it should be made. The offering of Judah and Jerusalem will be welcomed by the Lord as in former days, as in the years of old.

Know that I am going to send you Elijah the prophet before my day comes, that great and terrible day. He shall turn the hearts of fathers towards their children and the hearts of the children towards their fathers, lest I come and strike the land with a curse.

## Psalm 24:4-5.8-9.10.14. R. Luke 21:28

*Stand erect, hold your heads high, because your liberation is near at hand.*

## Luke 1:57-66

The time came for Elizabeth to have her child, and she gave birth to a son; and when her neighbours and relations heard that the Lord had shown her so great a kindness, they shared her joy.

Now on the eighth day they came to circumcise the child; they were going to call him Zechariah after his father, but his mother spoke up. 'No,' she said 'he is to be called John.' They said to her, 'But no one in your family has that name,' and made signs to his father to find out what he wanted him called. The father asked for a writing-tablet and wrote, 'His name is John.' And they were all astonished. At that instant his power of speech returned and he spoke and praised God. All their neighbours were filled with awe and the whole affair was talked about throughout the hill country of Judaea. All those who heard of it treasured it in their hearts. 'What will this child turn out to be?' they wondered. And indeed the hand of the Lord was with him.

## Reflection

We are not sure how long Zechariah was without speech, but no doubt it provided hours of reflective time for him while his wife and Mary enjoyed each other's company. It seems a bit tough for the good and upright priest Zechariah to be silenced simply for struggling to understand the angel's promise that he and his wife would bear a son who would prepare the way for the Christ. A good life-coach will notice the students who show potential, challenging them even more than the rest. But these are the students who, if they respond to the extra attention and challenge, become the highest achievers. God as life-coach for Zechariah – already one who served faithfully in the temple – gave him an opportunity for silent reflection. Then 'his mouth opened and his tongue freed, and he began to speak praising God' in a way that was fresh and powerful so that all who heard his words pondered them.

**4th Week of Advent**
Violet
or
**St John of Kanty, *priest*
(Commemoration)**

### 2 Samuel 7:1-5.8-12.14.16

Once David had settled into his house and the Lord had given him rest from all the enemies surrounding him, the king said to the prophet Nathan, 'Look, I am living in a house of cedar while the ark of God dwells in a tent.' Nathan said to the king, 'Go and do all that is in your mind, for the Lord is with you.'

But that very night the word of the Lord came to Nathan: 'Go and tell my servant David, "Thus the Lord speaks: Are you the man to build me a house to dwell in? I took you from the pasture, from following the sheep, to be leader of my people Israel; I have been with you on all your expeditions; I have cut off all your enemies before you. I will give you fame as great as the fame of the greatest on earth. …
(See Appendix B–36)

### Psalm 88:2-5.27.29. R. cf. v.2

*I will sing forever of your love, O Lord.*

### Luke 1:67-79

John's father Zechariah was filled with the Holy Spirit and spoke this prophecy:

'Blessed be the Lord, the God of Israel, for he has visited his people, he has come to their rescue and he has raised up for us a power for salvation in the House of his servant David, even as he proclaimed, by the mouth of his holy prophets from ancient times, that he would save us from our enemies and from the hands of all who hate us. Thus he shows mercy to our ancestors, thus he remembers his holy covenant, the oath he swore to our father Abraham that he would grant us, free from fear, to be delivered from the hands of our enemies, to serve him in holiness and virtue in his presence, all our days. And you, little child, you shall be called Prophet of the Most High, for you will go before the Lord to prepare the way for him. To give his people knowledge of salvation through the forgiveness of their sins, this by the tender mercy of our God who from on high will bring the rising Sun to visit us, to give light to those who live in darkness and the shadow of death, and to guide our feet into the way of peace.'

### Reflection

The Scriptures remind us that God can speak to us in many ways and through many means. But in the new era of divine communication the Word of God became flesh and God's normal way of communicating becomes people, beginning with the flesh and blood presence of God in the world through Jesus Christ. There are moments when I sense the closeness and the communication of Jesus to me in my own life. Sometimes this is an inner sense of the direction I should or should not take. But people are most often the prime communicators of the voice of Jesus directly to me, sometimes friends and family, sometimes strangers, and even people I don't like and circumstances I would rather avoid. In these hours of preparation for the feast of the birth of the Lord let's be open to every moment, every circumstance and every person as a potential Christ-bearer for us.

Isaiah 52:7-10
*(See Appendix B-36)*

**Psalm 97:1-6. R. v.3**
*All the ends of the earth have seen the salvation of our God.*

**The Nativity
of the Lord
(Mass During the Day)
Solemnity
White**

**Hebrews 1:1-6**
At various times in the past and in various different ways, God spoke to our ancestors through the prophets; but in our own time, the last days, he has spoken to us through his Son, the Son that he has appointed to inherit everything and through whom he made everything there is. He is the radiant light of God's glory and the perfect copy of his nature, sustaining the universe by his powerful command; and now that he has destroyed the defilement of sin, he has gone to take his place in heaven at the right hand of divine Majesty. So he is now as far above the angels as the title which he has inherited is higher than their own name.

God has never said to any angel: You are my Son, today I have become your father, or: I will be a father to him and he a son to me. Again, when he brings the First-born into the world, he says: Let all the angels of God worship him.

**A Grace before
Christmas Dinner**
Before we share this
    Christmas meal together,
let us take a moment of
    silent prayer
to give God thanks
for all the blessings
we have received this year.

**John 1:1-5.9-14** *(Longer Form: John 1:1-18)*
In the beginning was the Word: the Word was with God and the Word was God. He was with God in the beginning. Through him all things came to be, not one thing had its being but through him. All that came to be had life in him and that life was the light of men, a light that shines in the dark, a light that darkness could not overpower.

The Word was the true light that enlightens all men; and he was coming into the world. He was in the world that had its being through him, and the world did not know him. He came to his own domain and his own people did not accept him. But to all who did accept him he gave power to become children of God, to all who believe in the name of him who was born not out of human stock or urge of the flesh or will of man but of God himself. The Word was made flesh, he lived among us, and we saw his glory, the glory that is his as the only Son of the Father, full of grace and truth.

Let us remember those
we have shared Christmas
    with in past years,
those who have died,
and also those who are not
    able to be with us today
because of distance and
    illness.
Let us now share aloud
the names of those
we especially wish to
remember.

May the light of this candle
lead us to Christ
who overcomes every
    darkness.
And for what we receive in
    this meal,
the food, drink, and family
    and friendship,
let us be deeply grateful.
Amen.

**The Holy Family
of Jesus, Mary
and Joseph**
Psalter Week 1
Feast
White

### 1 Samuel 1:20-22.24-28

Hannah conceived and gave birth to a son, and called him Samuel 'since' she said 'I asked the Lord for him.'

When a year had gone by, the husband Elkanah went up again with all his family to offer the annual sacrifice to the Lord and to fulfil his vow. Hannah, however, did not go up, having said to her husband, 'Not before the child is weaned. Then I will bring him and present him before the Lord and he shall stay there for ever.'

When she had weaned him, she took him up with her together with a three-year old bull, an ephah of flour and a skin of wine, and she brought him to the temple of the Lord at Shiloh; and the child was with them. They slaughtered the bull and the child's mother came to Eli. She said, 'If you please, my lord. As you live, my lord, I am the woman who stood here beside you, praying to the Lord. This is the child I prayed for, and the Lord granted me what I asked him. Now I make him over to the Lord for the whole of his life. He is made over to the Lord.'

There she left him, for the Lord.

### Psalm 127:1-5

*O blessed are those who fear the Lord and walk in his ways!*

## Colossians 3:12-21

You are God's chosen race, his saints; he loves you, and you should be clothed in sincere compassion, in kindness and humility, gentleness and patience. Bear with one another; forgive each other as soon as a quarrel begins. The Lord has forgiven you; now you must do the same. Over all these clothes, to keep them together and complete them, put on love. And may the peace of Christ reign in your hearts, because it is for this that you were called together as parts of one body. Always be thankful.

Let the message of Christ, in all its richness, find a home with you. Teach each other, and advise each other, in all wisdom. With gratitude in your hearts sing psalms and hymns and inspired songs to God; and never say or do anything except in the name of the Lord Jesus, giving thanks to God the Father through him.

Wives, give way to your husbands, as you should in the Lord. Husbands, love your wives and treat them with gentleness. Children, be obedient to your parents always, because that is what will please the Lord. Parents, never drive your children to resentment or you will make them feel frustrated.

## Luke 2:41-52

Every year the parents of Jesus used to go to Jerusalem for the feast of the Passover. When he was twelve years old, they went up for the feast as usual. When they were on their way home after the feast, the boy Jesus stayed behind in Jerusalem without his parents knowing it. They assumed he was with the caravan, and it was only after a day's journey that they went to look for him among their relations and acquaintances. When they failed to find him they went back to Jerusalem looking for him everywhere.

Three days later, they found him in the Temple, sitting among the doctors, listening to them and asking them questions; and all those who heard him were astounded at his intelligence and his replies. They were overcome when they saw him, and his mother said to him, 'My child, why have you done this to us? See how worried your father and I have been, looking for you.' 'Why were you looking for me?' he replied. 'Did you not know that I must be busy with my Father's affairs?' But they did not understand what he meant.

He then went down with them and came to Nazareth and lived under their authority. His mother stored up all these things in her heart. And Jesus increased in wisdom, in stature, and in favour with God and men.

## Reflection

For most of the history of human civilisation the term family has been used to speak of a community of love: parents and children, with a complex and diverse range of relationship connections through blood, legal contract and friendship ties.

Jesus was raised in a family of love which doesn't meet the narrow understanding of nuclear family: this without even taking into account the active role of the Holy Spirit in the birth of Jesus. Healthy families have always been 'extended' and include not only biological relations but friends and those who are in need.

The ministry of Jesus institutes a new form of family. God is now Our Father and even (in the intimate language of Jesus) our 'abba', our papa and our daddy. Now we are literally the children of God. We speak of Mary as our mother, and our sisters and brothers are those who with us look to the one Christ.

**St John,**
*apostle,*
*evangelist*
**Feast**
**White**

## 1 John 1:1-4

Something which has existed since the beginning, that we have heard, and we have seen with our own eyes; that we have watched and touched with our hands: the Word, who is life – this is our subject. That life was made visible: we saw it and we are giving our testimony, telling you of the eternal life which was with the Father and has been made visible to us. What we have seen and heard we are telling you so that you too may be in union with us, as we are in union with the Father and with his Son Jesus Christ. We are writing this to you to make our own joy complete.

**Psalm 96:1-2.5-6.11-12. R. v.12**

*Rejoice, you just, in the Lord.*

## John 20:2-8

On the first day of the week Mary of Magdala came running to Simon Peter and the other disciple, the one Jesus loved. 'They have taken the Lord out of the tomb' she said 'and we don't know where they have put him.'

So Peter set out with the other disciple to go to the tomb. They ran together, but the other disciple, running faster than Peter, reached the tomb first; he bent down and saw the linen cloths lying on the ground, but did not go in. Simon Peter who was following now came up, went right into the tomb, saw the linen cloths on the ground, and also the cloth that had been over his head; this was not with the linen cloths but rolled up in a place by itself. Then the other disciple who had reached the tomb first also went in; he saw and he believed.

## Reflection

There is a wonderful work of art by Eugène Burnand (1898) illustrating the opening verses of the Gospel for today's feast of the evangelist and apostle John: 'Peter and John running to the tomb on the morning of the resurrection' captures the hope of the disciple John, the beloved, and the mixed feelings of Peter who is at once excited at the report of the women that Jesus was alive, and at the same time fearful at having to face the one whom he had betrayed.

In the opening of his first letter, John writes: 'We declare ... what we have heard, what we have seen with our eyes, what we have looked at and touched with our hands...' Following John's example let's pray that we will hear and see and touch the living presence of Jesus evidenced in the routines and demands of our daily experience.

**The Holy Innocents,**
*martyrs*
**Feast**
**Red**

## 1 John 1:5–2:2

This is what we have heard from Jesus Christ, and the message that we are announcing to you: God is light; there is no darkness in him at all. If we say that we are in union with God while we are living in darkness, we are lying because we are not living the truth. But if we live our lives in the light, as he is in the light, we are in union with one another, and the blood of Jesus, his Son, purifies us from all sin. If we say we have no sin in us, we are deceiving ourselves and refusing to admit the truth; but if we acknowledge our sins, then God who is faithful and just will forgive our sins and purify us from everything that is wrong. To say that we have never sinned is to call God a liar and to show that his word is not in us. I am writing this, my children, to stop you sinning; but if anyone should sin, we have our advocate with the Father, Jesus Christ, who is just; he is the sacrifice that takes our sins away, and not only ours, but the whole world's.

## Psalm 123:2-5.7-8. R. v.7

*Our life, like a bird, has escaped from the snare of the fowler.*

## Matthew 2:13-18

After the wise men had left, the angel of the Lord appeared to Joseph in a dream and said, 'Get up, take the child and his mother with you, and escape into Egypt, and stay there until I tell you, because Herod intends to search for the child and do away with him.' So Joseph got up and, taking the child and his mother with him, left that night for Egypt, where he stayed until Herod was dead. This was to fulfil what the Lord had spoken through the prophet:

I called my son out of Egypt.

Herod was furious when he realised that he had been outwitted by the wise men, and in Bethlehem and its surrounding district he had all the male children killed who were two years old or under, reckoning by the date he had been careful to ask the wise men. It was then that the words spoken through the prophet Jeremiah were fulfilled: A voice was heard in Ramah, sobbing and loudly lamenting: it was Rachel weeping for her children, refusing to be comforted because they were no more.

## Reflection

Surrounded by presents and tinsel, peaceful nativity scenes and Christmas goodwill, it is easy to forget the full reality of the Christmas event. Today's feast of the Holy Innocents reminds us of the most significant trial this new family faced. As Herod set out to kill the newborn 'King of the Jews', Joseph and Mary were forced to flee with Jesus to the safety of Egypt. Herod's evil action in killing the innocents had tragic consequences – for the children, their families and their little town. Perhaps Herod too could not cope with his action for within a year he was dead. The taking of innocent life always has traumatic consequences.

**5th Day within the Octave of Christmas**
White
or
**St Thomas Becket,**
*bishop, martyr*
**(England – Feast)**
*(See Appendix A-21)*

**1 John 2:3-11**

We can be sure that we know Jesus only by keeping his commandments. Anyone who says, 'I know him', and does not keep his commandments, is a liar, refusing to admit the truth. But when anyone does obey what he has said, God's love comes to perfection in him. We can be sure that we are in God only when the one who claims to be living in him is living the same kind of life as Christ lived. ...
*(See Appendix B-36)*

**Psalm 95:1-3.5-6. R. v.11**

*Let the heavens rejoice and earth be glad.*

**Luke 2:22-35**

When the day came for them to be purified as laid down by the Law of Moses, the parents of Jesus took him up to Jerusalem to present him to the Lord – observing what stands written in the Law of the Lord: Every first-born male must be consecrated to the Lord – and also to offer in sacrifice, in accordance with what is said in the Law of the Lord, a pair of turtledoves or two young pigeons. Now in Jerusalem there was a man named Simeon. He was an upright and devout man; he looked forward to Israel's comforting and the Holy Spirit rested on him. It had been revealed to him by the Holy Spirit that he would not see death until he had set eyes on the Christ of the Lord. Prompted by the Spirit he came to the Temple: and when the parents brought in the child Jesus to do for him what the Law required, he took him into his arms and blessed God; and he said: 'Now, Master, you can let your servant go in peace, just as you promised; because my eyes have seen the salvation which you have prepared for all the nations to see, a light to enlighten the pagans and the glory of your people Israel.'

As the child's father and mother stood there wondering at the things that were being said about him, Simeon blessed them and said to Mary his mother, 'You see this child: he is destined for the fall and for the rising of many in Israel, destined to be a sign that is rejected – and a sword will pierce your own soul too – so that the secret thoughts of many may be laid bare.'

## Reflection

Another of the great Gospel canticles is at the heart of today's Gospel, the account of Mary and Joseph bringing Jesus to Jerusalem to present him to the Lord. Simeon was devout and righteous and had spent his life looking forward to the presence of the Messiah. Now, as an old man who knew that he would not see death before he had seen the Messiah, the moment is finally here. His moment of encounter with Jesus heralded the end of his earthly life, and he is ready for death since he not only knew his life's purpose but recognised when this had been achieved. He responds in the canticle we now pray at Night Prayer: 'At last, all powerful Master, you give leave to your servant...' The disciple is one who seeks to recognise the presence and action of Jesus through us, especially in daily moments which feel deathly.

**6th Day within the Octave of Christmas**
**White**

### 1 John 2:12-17

I am writing to you, my own children, whose sins have already been forgiven through his name; I am writing to you, fathers, who have come to know the one who has existed since the beginning; I am writing to you, young men, who have already overcome the Evil One; I have written to you, children, because you already know the Father; I have written to you, fathers, because you have come to know the one who has existed since the beginning; I have written to you, young men, because you are strong and God's word has made its home in you, and you have overcome the Evil One. You must not love this passing world or anything that is in the world. The love of the Father cannot be in any man who loves the world, because nothing the world has to offer – the sensual body, the lustful eye, pride in possessions – could ever come from the Father but only from the world; and the world, with all it craves for, is coming to an end; but anyone who does the will of God remains for ever.

### Psalm 95:7-10. R. v.11

*Let the heavens rejoice and earth be glad.*

### Luke 2:36-40

There was a prophetess, Anna the daughter of Phanuel, of the tribe of Asher. She was well on in years. Her days of girlhood over, she had been married for seven years before becoming a widow. She was now eighty-four years old and never left the Temple, serving God night and day with fasting and prayer. She came by just at that moment and began to praise God; and she spoke of the child to all who looked forward to the deliverance of Jerusalem. When they had done everything the Law of the Lord required, they went back to Galilee, to their own town of Nazareth. Meanwhile the child grew to maturity, and he was filled with wisdom; and God's favour was with him.

### Reflection

I'm moved today by the witness of the wonderful woman Anna, a widow for more than sixty years who worshipped in the temple night and day. To lose a husband was the loss of love and security. Perhaps it was this suffering over many years that now enabled her to immediately recognise Jesus as the long-expected One when Mary and Joseph presented their son in the temple. It is significant that so many of those who became the intimate friends of Jesus in the Gospels first encountered him because of their suffering. These were the sinners, the sick, the abandoned, the helpless and the hopeless whose need brought them to Jesus. In this experience of intimacy with Jesus they were forgiven, healed and transformed, becoming apostles, disciples and saints. Anna's expectation enabled her to live every moment fully focused on the life that was yet to come. In her immediate welcome and recognition of the Messiah we see the central characteristics of the Christian apostle, disciple and saint.

**7th Day within the
Octave of Christmas
White
or
St Sylvester I, *pope*
(Commemoration)**

**1 John 2:18-21**

Children, these are the last days; you were told that an Antichrist must come, and now several antichrists have already appeared; we know from this that these are the last days. Those rivals of Christ came out of our own number, but they had never really belonged; if they had belonged, they would have stayed with us; but they left us, to prove that not one of them ever belonged to us. But you have been anointed by the Holy One, and have all received the knowledge. It is not because you do not know the truth that I am writing to you but rather because you know it already and know that no lie can come from the truth.

**Psalm 95:1-2.11-13. R. v.11**

*Let the heavens rejoice and earth be glad.*

**John 1:1-18**

In the beginning was the Word: the Word was with God and the Word was God. He was with God in the beginning. Through him all things came to be, not one thing had its being but through him. All that came to be had life in him and that life was the light of men, a light that shines in the dark, a light that darkness could not overpower. A man came, sent by God. His name was John. He came as a witness, as a witness to speak for the light, so that everyone might believe through him. He was not the light, only a witness to speak for the light. The Word was the true light that enlightens all men; and he was coming into the world. He was in the world that had its being through him, and the world did not know him. He came to his own domain and his own people did not accept him. But to all who did accept him he gave power to become children of God, to all who believe in the name of him who was born not out of human stock or urge of the flesh or will of man but of God himself. The Word was made flesh, he lived among us, and we saw his glory, the glory that is his as the only Son of the Father, full of grace and truth. John appears as his witness. He proclaims: 'This is the one of whom I said: He who comes after me ranks before me because he existed before me.' Indeed, from his fullness we have, all of us, received – yes, grace in return for grace, since, though the Law was given through Moses, grace and truth have come through Jesus Christ. No one has ever seen God; it is the only Son, who is nearest to the Father's heart, who has made him known.

## Reflection

Those who are familiar with the Extraordinary Form of the Mass will appreciate the five-hundred-year tradition of hearing the opening verses of John's Gospel read at the end of every Mass. This tradition reminds us that we focus on the Word because we are people of the Eucharist (God-with-us and God in us) and we focus on the Eucharistic presence of Jesus because we are people of the Word who is Jesus-with-us, a Word who was 'in the beginning' and who brought all things into being. The Word who is the light shining in the darkness. The Word who has made God known to us. It's appropriate that this 'Last Gospel' is given for the eve of a new year. I'm reminded of T. S. Eliot: 'What we call the beginning is often the end. And to make an end is to make a beginning. The end is where we start from.' (*Little Gidding*)

**Isaiah 52:7-10**

How beautiful on the mountains, are the feet of one who brings good news, who heralds peace, brings happiness, proclaims salvation, and tells Zion, 'Your God is king!' Listen! Your watchmen raise their voices, they shout for joy together, for they see the Lord face to face, as he returns to Zion. Break into shouts of joy together, you ruins of Jerusalem; for the Lord is consoling his people, redeeming Jerusalem. The Lord bares his holy arm in the sight of all the nations, and all the ends of the earth shall see the salvation of our God.

**Psalm 95:1-3.7-8.10**

*Proclaim the wonders of the Lord among all the peoples.*

**2 Timothy 4:1-5**

Before God and before Christ Jesus who is to be judge of the living and the dead, I put this duty to you, in the name of his Appearing and of his kingdom: proclaim the message and, welcome or unwelcome, insist on it. Refute falsehood, correct error, call to obedience – but do all with patience and with the intention of teaching. The time is sure to come when, far from being content with sound teaching, people will be avid for the latest novelty and collect themselves a whole series of teachers according to their own tastes; and then, instead of listening to the truth, they will turn to myths. Be careful always to choose the right course; be brave under trials; make the preaching of the Good News your life's work, in thoroughgoing service.

**Luke 5:1-11**

Jesus was standing one day by the Lake of Gennesaret, with the crowd pressing round him listening to the word of God, when he caught sight of two boats close to the bank. The fishermen had gone out of them and were washing their nets. He got into one of the boats – it was Simon's – and asked him to put out a little from the shore. Then he sat down and taught the crowds from the boat.

When he had finished speaking he said to Simon, 'Put out into deep water and pay out your nets for a catch.' 'Master,' Simon replied, 'we worked hard all night long and caught nothing, but if you say so, I will pay out the nets.' And when they had done this they netted such a huge number of fish that their nets began to tear, so they signalled to their companions in the other boat to come and help them; when these came, they filled the two boats to sinking point.

When Simon Peter saw this he fell at the knees of Jesus saying, 'Leave me, Lord; I am a sinful man.' For he and all his companions were completely overcome by the catch they had made; so also were James and John, sons of Zebedee, who were Simon's partners. But Jesus said to Simon, 'Do not be afraid; from now on it is men you will catch.' Then, bringing their boats back to land, they left everything and followed him.

## FEBRUARY

# 1

### MONDAY

**Saint Brigid, Abbess,
Secondary Patron of
Ireland**
Feast
White

### Job 31:16-20.24-25.31-32

Have I been insensible to poor men's needs, or let a widow's eyes grow dim? Or taken my share of bread alone, not giving a share to the orphan? I, whom God has fostered father-like, from childhood, and guided since I left my mother's womb. Have I ever seen a wretch in need of clothing, or a beggar going naked, without his having cause to bless me from his heart, as he felt the warmth of the fleece from my lambs? Have I put all my trust in gold, from finest gold sought my security? Have I ever gloated over my great wealth, or the riches that my hands have won? The people of my tent, did they not say, 'Is there a man he has not filled with meat'? No stranger ever had to sleep outside, my door was always open to the traveller.

### Psalm 106

*Give thanks to the Lord for he is good; for his love has no end.*

### Luke 6:32-38

Jesus said to his disciples:

'If you love those who love you, what thanks can you expect? Even sinners love those who love them. And if you do good to those who do good to you, what thanks can you expect? For even sinners do that much. And if you lend to those from whom you hope to receive, what thanks can you expect? Even sinners lend to sinners to get back the same amount. Instead, love your enemies and do good, and lend without any hope of return. You will have a great reward, and you will be sons of the Most High, for he himself is kind to the ungrateful and the wicked.

'Be compassionate as your Father is compassionate. Do not judge, and you will not be judged yourselves; do not condemn, and you will not be condemned yourselves; grant pardon, and you will be pardoned. Give, and there will be gifts for you: a full measure, pressed down, shaken together, and running over, will be poured into your lap; because the amount you measure out is the amount you will be given back.'

**Saint David, Bishop
(Wales – Solemnity)
White**

### Isaiah 61:1-3.10-11
The spirit of the Lord has been given to me, for the Lord has anointed me. He has sent me to bring good news to the poor, to bind up hearts that are broken; to proclaim liberty to captives, freedom to those in prison; to proclaim a year of favour from the Lord, a day of vengeance for our God, to comfort all those who mourn and to give them for ashes a garland; for mourning robe the oil of gladness, for despondency, praise. 'I exult for joy in the Lord, my soul rejoices in my God, for he has clothed me in the garments of salvation, he has wrapped me in the cloak of integrity, like a bridegroom wearing his wreath, like a bride adorned in her jewels. 'For as the earth makes fresh things grow, as a garden makes seeds spring up, so will the Lord make both integrity and praise spring up in the sight of the nations.'

### Psalm 1:1-4.6
*Happy the man who has placed his trust in the Lord.*

### Philippians 3:8-14
I believe nothing can happen that will outweigh the supreme advantage of knowing Christ Jesus my Lord. For him I have accepted the loss of everything, and I look on everything as so much rubbish if only I can have Christ and be given a place in him. I am no longer trying for perfection by my own efforts, the perfection that comes from the Law, but I want only the perfection that comes through faith in Christ, and is from God and based on faith. All I want is to know Christ and the power of his resurrection and to share his sufferings by reproducing the pattern of his death. That is the way I can hope to take my place in the resurrection of the dead. Not that I have become perfect yet: I have not yet won, but I am still running, trying to capture the prize for which Christ Jesus captured me. I can assure you my brothers, I am far from thinking that I have already won. All I can say is that I forget the past and I strain ahead for what is still to come; I am racing for the finish, for the prize to which God calls us upwards to receive in Christ Jesus.

### Matthew 5:13-16
Jesus said to his disciples: 'You are the salt of the earth. But if salt becomes tasteless, what can make it salty again? It is good for nothing, and can only be thrown out to be trampled underfoot by men.

'You are the light of the world. A city built on a hill-top cannot be hidden. No one lights a lamp to put it under a tub; they put it on the lamp-stand where it shines for everyone in the house. In the same way your light must shine in the sight of men, so that, seeing your good works, they may give the praise to your Father in heaven.'

## MARCH

# 1

### WEDNESDAY

**Saint David, Bishop
(England – Feast)
White**

### Philippians 3:8-14

I believe nothing can happen that will outweigh the supreme advantage of knowing Christ Jesus my Lord. For him I have accepted the loss of everything, and I look on everything as so much rubbish if only I can have Christ and be given a place in him. I am no longer trying for perfection by my own efforts, the perfection that comes from the Law, but I want only the perfection that comes through faith in Christ, and is from God and based on faith. All I want is to know Christ and the power of his resurrection and to share his sufferings by reproducing the pattern of his death. That is the way I can hope to take my place in the resurrection of the dead. Not that I have become perfect yet: I have not yet won, but I am still running, trying to capture the prize for which Christ Jesus captured me. I can assure you my brothers, I am far from thinking that I have already won. All I can say is that I forget the past and I strain ahead for what is still to come; I am racing for the finish, for the prize to which God calls us upwards to receive in Christ Jesus.

### Psalm 1 R. Ps 39:5

*Happy the man who has placed his trust in the Lord.*

### Matthew 5:13-16

Jesus said to his disciples: 'You are the salt of the earth. But if salt becomes tasteless, what can make it salty again? It is good for nothing, and can only be thrown out to be trampled underfoot by men.

'You are the light of the world. A city built on a hill-top cannot be hidden. No one lights a lamp to put it under a tub; they put it on the lamp-stand where it shines for everyone in the house. In the same way your light must shine in the sight of men, so that, seeing your good works, they may give the praise to your Father in heaven.'

### Isaiah 50:5-9

The Lord has opened my ear. For my part, I made no resistance, neither did I turn away. I offered my back to those who struck me, my cheeks to those who tore at my beard; I did not cover my face against insult and spittle. The Lord comes to my help, so that I am untouched by the insults. So, too, I set my face like flint; I know I shall not be shamed. My vindicator is here at hand. Does anyone start proceedings against me? Then let us go to court together. Who thinks he has a case against me? Let him approach me. The Lord is coming to my help, who will dare to condemn me?

### Psalm 76:12-16,21

*I remember the deeds of the Lord.*

### 1 Corinthians 1:3-7

May God our Father and the Lord Jesus Christ send you grace and peace.

I never stop thanking God for all the graces you have received through Jesus Christ. I thank him that you have been enriched in so many ways, especially in your teachers and preachers; the witness to Christ has indeed been strong among you so that you will not be without any of the gifts of the Spirit while you are waiting for our Lord Jesus Christ to be revealed.

### John 12:24-26

Jesus said to his disciples: 'I tell you, most solemnly, unless a wheat grain falls on the ground and dies, it remains only a single grain; but if it dies, it yields a rich harvest.

Anyone who loves his life loses it; anyone who hates his life in this world will keep it for the eternal life. If a man serves me, he must follow me, wherever I am, my servant will be there too. If anyone serves me, my Father will honour him.'

## MARCH
# 17
### FRIDAY

**St Patrick**
**(Ireland – Solemnity)**
**White**

### Jeremiah 1:1.4-9

The word of the Lord was addressed to me, saying, 'Before I formed you in the womb I knew you; before you came to birth I consecrated you; I have appointed you as prophet to the nations. I said, 'Ah, Lord God; look, I do not know how to speak: I am a child!' But the Lord replied, 'Do not say, "I am a child." Go now to those to whom I send you and say whatever I command you. Do not be afraid of them, for I am with you to protect you – it is the Lord who speaks!' Then the Lord put out his hand and touched my mouth and said to me: 'There! I am putting my words into your mouth.'

### Psalm 116

*Go out to the whole world: proclaim the Good News.*

### Romans 10:9-18

If your lips confess that Jesus is Lord and if you believe in your heart that God raised him from the dead, then you will be saved. By believing from the heart you are made righteous; by confessing with your lips you are saved. When scripture says: those who believe in him will have no cause for shame, it makes no distinction between Jew and Greek: all belong to the same Lord who is rich enough, however many ask his help, for everyone who calls on the name of the Lord will be saved.

But they will not ask his help unless they believe in him, and they will not believe in him unless they have heard of him, and they will not hear of him unless they get a preacher, and they will never have a preacher unless one is sent, but as scripture says: The footsteps of those who bring good news are a welcome sound. Not everyone, of course, listens to the Good News. As Isaiah says: Lord, how many believed what we proclaimed? So faith comes from what is preached, and what is preached comes from the word of Christ.

Let me put the question: is it possible that they did not hear? Indeed they did; in the words of the psalm, their voice has gone out through all the earth, and their message to the ends of the world.

### Mark 16:15-20

Jesus showed himself to the Eleven, and he said to them, 'Go out to the whole world; proclaim the Good News to all creation. He who believes and is baptised will be saved; he who does not believe will be condemned. These are the signs that will be associated with believers: in my name they will cast out devils; they will have the gift of tongues; they will pick up snakes in their hands, and be unharmed should they drink deadly poison; they will lay their hands on the sick, who will recover.'

And so the Lord Jesus, after he had spoken to them, was taken up into heaven: there at the right hand of God he took his place, while they, going out, preached everywhere, the Lord working with them and confirming the word by the signs that accompanied it.

**St George, Martyr
(England – Solemnity)
White**

### Apocalypse 12:10-12

I, John, heard a voice shout from heaven, 'Victory and power and empire for ever have been won by our God, and all authority for his Christ, now that the persecutor, who accused our brothers day and night before our God, has been brought down. They have triumphed over him by the blood of the Lamb and by the witness of their martyrdom, because even in the face of death they would not cling to life. Let the heavens rejoice and all who live there.'

### Psalm 125

*Those who are sowing in tears will sing when they reap.*

### John 15:18-21

Jesus said to his disciples:

'If the world hates you, remember that it hated me before you. If you belonged to the world, the world would love you as its own; but because you do not belong to the world, because my choice withdrew you from the world, therefore the world hates you. Remember the words I said to you: A servant is not greater than his master. If they persecuted me, they will persecute you too; if they kept my word, they will keep yours as well. But it will be on my account that they will do this, because they do not know the one who sent me.'

## MAY
# 4
### TUESDAY

**The English Martyrs
(England – Feast)
White**

### Acts 7:55-60

Stephen, filled with the Holy Spirit, gazed into heaven and saw the glory of God, and Jesus standing at God's right hand. 'I can see heaven thrown open' he said 'and the Son of Man standing at the right hand of God.' At this all the members of the council shouted out and stopped their ears with their hands; then they all rushed at him, sent him out of the city and stoned him. The witnesses put down their clothes at the feet of a young man called Saul. As they were stoning him, Stephen said in invocation, 'Lord Jesus, receive my spirit.' Then he knelt down and said aloud, 'Lord, do not hold this sin against them'; and with these words he fell asleep.

### Psalm 30:3-4.6.8.17.21

*Into your hands, O Lord, I commend my spirit.*

### Matthew 10:17-20

Jesus said to his disciples: 'Beware of men: they will hand you over to sanhedrins and scourge you in their synagogues. You will be dragged before governors and kings for my sake, to bear witness before them and the pagans. But when they hand you over, do not worry about how to speak or what to say; what you are to say will be given to you when the time comes; because it is not you who will be speaking; the Spirit of your Father will be speaking in you.'

### Acts 1:15-17.20-26

One day Peter stood up to speak to the brothers – there were about a hundred and twenty persons in the congregation: 'Brothers, the passage of scripture had to be fulfilled in which the Holy Spirit, speaking through David, foretells the fate of Judas, who offered himself as a guide to the men who arrested Jesus – after having been one of our number and actually sharing this ministry of ours. Now in the Book of Psalms it says:

Let someone else take his office.

'We must therefore choose someone who has been with us the whole time that the Lord Jesus was travelling round with us, someone who was with us right from the time when John was baptising until the day when he was taken up from us – and he can act with us as a witness to his resurrection.'

Having nominated two candidates, Joseph known as Barsabbas, whose surname was Justus, and Matthias, they prayed, 'Lord, you can read everyone's heart; show us therefore which of these two you have chosen to take over this ministry and apostolate, which Judas abandoned to go to his proper place.' They then drew lots for them, and as the lot fell to Matthias, he was listed as one of the twelve apostles.

### Psalm 102:1-2.11-12.19-20

*The Lord has set his sway in heaven.*

### 1 John 4:11-16

My dear people, since God has loved us so much, we too should love one another. No one has ever seen God; but as long as we love one another God will live in us and his love will be complete in us. We can know that we are living in him and he is living in us because he lets us share his Spirit. We ourselves saw and we testify that the Father sent his Son as saviour of the world. If anyone acknowledges that Jesus is the Son of God, God lives in him, and he in God. We ourselves have known and put our faith in God's love towards ourselves. God is love and anyone who lives in love lives in God, and God lives in him.

### John 17:11-19

Jesus raised his eyes to heaven and said:

'Holy Father, keep those you have given me true to your name, so that they may be one like us. While I was with them, I kept those you had given me true to your name. I have watched over them and not one is lost except the one who chose to be lost, and this was to fulfil the scriptures. But now I am coming to you and while still in the world I say these things to share my joy with them to the full. I passed your word on to them, and the world hated them, because they belong to the world no more than I belong to the world. I am not asking you to remove them from the world, but to protect them from the evil one. They do not belong to the world any more than I belong to the world. Consecrate them in the truth; your word is truth. As you sent me into the world, I have sent them into the world, and for their sake I consecrate myself so that they too may be consecrated in truth.'

**7th Sunday of Easter (England, Scotland & Wales)**
**White**

## MAY
# 27
### WEDNESDAY

**Our Lord Jesus Christ
the Eternal High Priest
(England & Wales –
Feast)
White**

### Jeremiah 31:31-34

See, the days are coming – it is the Lord who speaks – when I will make a new covenant with the House of Israel (and the House of Judah), but not a covenant like the one I made with their ancestors on the day I took them by the hand to bring them out of the land of Egypt. They broke that covenant of mine, so I had to show them who was master. It is the Lord who speaks. No, this is the covenant I will make with the House of Israel when those days arrive – it is the Lord who speaks. Deep within them I will plant my Law, writing it on their hearts. Then I will be their God and they shall be my people. There will be no further need for neighbour to try to teach neighbour, or brother to say to brother, 'Learn to know the Lord!' No, they will all know me, the least no less than the greatest – it is the Lord who speaks – since I will forgive their iniquity and never call their sin to mind.

### Psalm 109:1-4

*You are a priest for ever, a priest like Melchizedek of old.*

### Mark 14:22-25

As they were eating he took some bread, and when he had said the blessing he broke it and gave it to them. 'Take it,' he said 'this is my body.' Then he took a cup, and when he had returned thanks he gave it to them, and all drank from it, and he said to them, 'This is my blood, the blood of the covenant, which is to be poured out for many. I tell you solemnly, I shall not drink any more wine until the day I drink the new wine in the kingdom of God.'

## Romans 12:1-2.9-13

Think of God's mercy, my brothers, and worship him, I beg you, in a way that is worthy of thinking beings, by offering your living bodies as a holy sacrifice, truly pleasing to God. Do not model yourselves on the behaviour of the world around you, but let your behaviour change, modelled by your new mind. This is the only way to discover the will of God and know what is good, what it is that God wants, what is the perfect thing to do.

Do not let your love be a pretence, but sincerely prefer good to evil. Love each other as much as brothers should, and have a profound respect for each other. Work for the Lord with untiring effort and with great earnestness of spirit. If you have hope, this will make you cheerful. Do not give up if trials come; and keep on praying. If any of the saints are in need you must share with them; and you should make hospitality your special care.

## Psalm 33:2-3.10-15

*Taste and see that the Lord is good.*

## Matthew 8:18-27

When Jesus saw the great crowds all about him he gave orders to leave for the other side. One of the scribes then came up and said to him, 'Master, I will follow you wherever you go.' Jesus replied, 'Foxes have holes and the birds of the air have nests, but the Son of Man has nowhere to lay his head.'

Another man, one of his disciples, said to him, 'Sir, let me go and bury my father first.' But Jesus replied, 'Follow me, and leave the dead to bury their dead.'

Jesus got into the boat followed by his disciples. Without warning a storm broke over the lake, so violent that the waves were breaking right over the boat. But he was asleep. So they went to him and woke him saying, 'Save us, Lord, we are going down!' And he said to them, 'Why are you so frightened, you men of little faith?' And with that he stood up and rebuked the winds and the sea; and all was calm again. The men were astounded and said, 'Whatever kind of man is this? Even the winds and the sea obey him.'

**St Columba
(Ireland – Feast)
White**

## JUNE
# 22
### TUESDAY

**Saints John Fisher And Tomas More, Martyrs (England – Feast)**
**White**

**2 Maccabees 6:18.21.24-31**

Eleazar, one of the foremost teachers of the Law, a man already advanced in years and of most noble appearance, was being forced to open his mouth wide to swallow pig's flesh. Those in charge of the impious banquet, because of their long-standing friendship with him, took him aside and privately urged him to have meat brought of a kind he could properly use, prepared by himself, and only pretend to eat the portions of sacrificial meat as prescribed by the king. 'Such pretence' he said 'does not square with our time of life; many young people would suppose that Eleazar at the age of ninety had conformed to the foreigners' way of life, and because I had played this part for the sake of a paltry brief spell of life might themselves be led astray on my account; I should only bring defilement and disgrace on my old age. Even though for the moment I avoid execution by man, I can never, living or dead, elude the grasp of the Almighty. Therefore if I am man enough to quit this life here and now I shall prove myself worthy of my old age, and I shall have left the young a noble example of how to make a good death, eagerly and generously, for the venerable and holy laws.' With these words he went straight to the block. His escorts, so recently well disposed towards him, turned against him after this declaration, which they regarded as sheer madness. Just before he died under the blows, he groaned aloud and said, 'The Lord whose knowledge is holy sees clearly that, though I might have escaped death, whatever agonies of body I now endure under this bludgeoning, in my soul I am glad to suffer, because of the awe which he inspires in me.' This was how he died, leaving his death as an example of nobility and a record of virtue not only for the young but for the great majority of the nation.

**Psalm 30:2.6.8-9.1517.25 R. Lk 23:46**
*Father, into your hands I commend my spirit.*

### Matthew 24:4-13

Jesus said to his disciples: 'Take care that no one deceives you; because many will come using my name and saying, "I am the Christ," and they will deceive many. You will hear of wars and rumours of wars; do not be alarmed, for this is something that must happen, but the end will not be yet. For nation will fight against nation, and kingdom against kingdom. There will be famines and earthquakes here and there. All this is only the beginning of the birth-pangs.

'Then they will hand you over to be tortured and put to death; and you will be hated by all the nations on account of my name. And then many will fall away; men will betray one another and hate one another. Many false prophets will arise; they will deceive many, and with the increase of lawlessness, love in most men will grow cold; but the man who stands firm to the end will be saved.'

### Genesis 3:9-15.20

After Adam had eaten of the tree the Lord God called to him. 'Where are you?' he asked. 'I heard the sound of you in the garden;' he replied 'I was afraid because I was naked, so I hid.' 'Who told you that you were naked?' he asked 'Have you been eating of the tree I forbade you to eat?' The man replied, 'It was the woman you put with me; she gave me the fruit, and I ate it.' Then the Lord God asked the woman, 'What is this you have done?' The woman replied, 'The serpent tempted me and I ate.' Then the Lord God said to the serpent, 'Because you have done this, 'Be accursed beyond all cattle, all wild beasts. You shall crawl on your belly and eat dust every day of your life. I will make you enemies of each other: you and the woman, your offspring and her offspring. It will crush your head and you will strike its heel.' The man named his wife 'Eve' because she was the mother of all those who live.

**Our Lady of Aberdeen
(Scotland – Feast)
White**

### Psalm 1 Samuel 2:1.4-8

*My heart exults in the Lord my Saviour.*

### Matthew 1:1-16.18-23

A genealogy of Jesus Christ, son of David, son of Abraham:

Abraham was the father of Isaac, Isaac the father of Jacob, Jacob the father of Judah and his brothers, Judah was the father of Perez and Zerah, Tamar being their mother, Perez was the father of Hezron, Hezron the father of Ram, Ram was the father of Amminadab, Amminadab the father of Nahshon, Nahshon the father of Salmon, Salmon was the father of Boaz, Rahab being his mother, Boaz was the father of Obed, Ruth being his mother, Obed was the father of Jesse; and Jesse was the father of King David. David was the father of Solomon, whose mother had been Uriah's wife, Solomon was the father of Rehoboam, Rehoboam the father of Abijah, Abijah the father of Asa, Asa was the father of Jehoshaphat, Jehoshaphat the father of Joram, Joram the father of Azariah, Azariah was the father of Jotham, Jotham the father of Ahaz, Ahaz the father of Hezekiah, Hezekiah was the father of Manasseh, Manasseh the father of Amon, Amon the father of Josiah; and Josiah was the father of Jechoniah and his brothers. Then the deportation to Babylon took place. After the deportation to Babylon: Jechoniah was the father of Shealtiel, Shealtiel the father of Zerubbabel, Zerubbabel was the father of Abiud, Abiud the father of Eliakim, Eliakim the father of Azor, Azor was the father of Zadok, Zadok the father of Achim, Achim the father of Eliud, Eliud was the father of Eleazar, Eleazar the father of Matthan, Matthan the father of Jacob; and Jacob was the father of Joseph the husband of Mary; of her was born Jesus who is called Christ.

This is how Jesus Christ came to be born. His mother Mary was betrothed to Joseph; but before they came to live together she was found to be with child through the Holy Spirit. Her husband Joseph; being a man of honour and wanting to spare her publicity, decided to divorce her informally. He had made up his mind to do this when the angel of the Lord appeared to him in a dream and said, 'Joseph son of David, do not be afraid to take Mary home as your wife, because she has conceived what is in her by the Holy Spirit. She will give birth to a son and you must name him Jesus, because he is the one who is to save his people from their sins.' Now all this took place to fulfil the words spoken by the Lord through the prophet:

The virgin will conceive and give birth to a son and they will call him Emmanuel, a name which means 'God-is-with-us.'

## SEPTEMBER

# 16

### THURSDAY

**St Ninian
(Scotland – Feast)
White**

**Exodus 32:7-14 ·**

The Lord spoke to Moses, 'Go down now, because your people whom you brought out of Egypt have apostatised. They have been quick to leave the way I marked out for them; they have made themselves a calf of molten metal and have worshipped it and offered it sacrifice. "Here is your God, Israel," they have cried "who brought you up from the land of Egypt!"' the Lord said to Moses, 'I can see how headstrong these people are! Leave me, now, my wrath shall blaze out against them and devour them; of you, however, I will make a great nation.'

But Moses pleaded with the Lord his God. 'Lord,' he said 'why should your wrath blaze out against this people of yours whom you brought out of the land of Egypt with arm outstretched and mighty hand? Why let the Egyptians say, "Ah, it was in treachery that he brought them out, to do them to death in the mountains and wipe them off the face of the earth"? Leave your burning wrath; relent and do not bring this disaster on your people. Remember Abraham, Isaac and Jacob, your servants to whom by your own self you swore and made this promise: I will make your offspring as many as the stars of heaven, and all this land which I promised I will give to your descendants, and it shall be their heritage for ever.'

So the Lord relented and did not bring on his people the disaster he had threatened.

**Psalm 88:2-5.21-22.25.27**
*I will sing for ever of your love, O Lord.*

**Matthew 9:35-37**
Jesus made a tour through all the towns and villages, teaching in their synagogues, proclaiming the Good News of the kingdom and curing all kinds of diseases and sickness.

And when he saw the crowds he felt sorry for them because they were harassed and dejected, like sheep without a shepherd. Then he said to his disciples, 'The harvest is rich but the labourers are few, so ask the Lord of the harvest to send labourers to his harvest.'

## OCTOBER
# 25
### DAY

**Six Welsh Martyrs and
Their Companions
(Wales – Feast)
Red**

### Hebrews 11:33-40

The prophets were men who through faith conquered kingdoms, did what is right and earned the promises. They could keep a lion's mouth shut, put out blazing fires and emerge unscathed from battle. They were weak people who were given strength, to be brave in war and drive back foreign invaders. Some came back to their wives from the dead, by resurrection; and others submitted to torture, refusing release so that they would rise again to a better life. Some had to bear being pilloried and flogged, or even chained up in prison. They were stoned, or sawn in half, or beheaded; they were homeless, and dressed in the skins of sheep and goats; they were penniless and were given nothing but ill-treatment. They were too good for the world and they went out to live in deserts and mountains and in caves and ravines. These are all heroes of faith, but they did not receive what was promised, since God had made provision for us to have something better, and they were not to reach perfection except with us.

### Psalm 15:1-2.5.7-11

*Preserve me, Lord, I take refuge in you.*

### John 12:24-26

Jesus said to his disciples: 'I tell you, most solemnly, unless a wheat grain falls on the ground and dies, it remains only a single grain; but if it dies, it yields a rich harvest. Anyone who loves his life loses it; anyone who hates his life in this world will keep it for the eternal life. If a man serves me, he must follow me, wherever I am, my servant will be there too. If anyone serves me, my Father will honour him.'

## NOVEMBER

# 1

### MONDAY

**31st Week
in Ordinary Time
(England)
Green**

**Romans 11:29-36**
God never takes back his gifts or revokes his choice.

Just as you changed from being disobedient to God, and now enjoy mercy because of their disobedience, so those who are disobedient now – and only because of the mercy shown to you – will also enjoy mercy eventually. God has imprisoned all men in their own disobedience only to show mercy to all mankind.

How rich are the depths of God – how deep his wisdom and knowledge – and how impossible to penetrate his motives or understand his methods! Who could ever know the mind of the Lord? Who could ever be his counsellor? Who could ever give him anything or lend him anything?

All that exists comes from him; all is by him and for him. To him be glory for ever! Amen.

**Psalm 68:30-31.33-34.36-37**
*In your great love, answer me, O God.*

**Luke 14:12-14**
Jesus said to his host, one of the leading Pharisees, 'When you give a lunch or a dinner, do not ask your friends, brothers, relations or rich neighbours, for fear they repay your courtesy by inviting you in return. No; when you have a party, invite the poor, the crippled, the lame, the blind; that they cannot pay you back means that you are fortunate, because repayment will be made to you when the virtuous rise again.'

### Ecclesiasticus 44:1-15
Let us praise illustrious men, our ancestors in their successive generations. The Lord has created an abundance of glory, and displayed his greatness from earliest times. Some wielded authority as kings and were renowned for their strength; others were intelligent advisers and uttered prophetic oracles. Others directed the people by their advice, by their understanding of the popular mind, and by the wise words of their teaching; others composed musical melodies, and set down ballads; others were rich and powerful, living peacefully in their homes. All these were honoured by their contemporaries, and were the glory of their day. Some of them left a name behind them, so that their praises are still sung. While others have left no memory, and disappeared as though they had not existed, they are now as though they had never been, and so too, their children after them.

But here is a list of generous men whose good works have not been forgotten. In their descendants there remains a rich inheritance born of them. Their descendants stand by the covenants and, thanks to them, so do their children's children. Their offspring will last for ever, their glory will not fade. Their bodies have been buried in peace, and their name lives on for all generations. The peoples will proclaim their wisdom, the assembly will celebrate their praises.

### Psalm 14:2-5. R. v.1
*The just will live in the presence of the Lord.*

### Luke 6:17-23
Jesus came down with the Twelve and stopped at a piece of level ground where there was a large gathering of his disciples with a great crowd of people from all parts of Judaea and from Jerusalem and from the coastal region of Tyre and Sidon who had come to hear him and to be cured of their diseases. People tormented by unclean spirits were also cured, and everyone in the crowd was trying to touch him because power came out of him that cured them all.

Then fixing his eyes on his disciples he said: 'How happy are you who are poor: yours is the kingdom of God. Happy you who are hungry now: you shall be satisfied. Happy you who weep now: you shall laugh.

Happy are you when people hate you, drive you out, abuse you, denounce your name as criminal, on account of the Son of Man. Rejoice when that day comes and dance for joy, for then your reward will be great in heaven. This was the way their ancestors treated the prophets.

## NOVEMBER

# 16

**TUESDAY**

**St Margaret of Scotland
(Scotland – Feast)
White**

### Proverbs 31:10-13.19-20.30-31

A perfect wife – who can find her? She is far beyond the price of pearls. Her husband's heart has confidence in her, from her he will derive no little profit. Advantage and not hurt she brings him all the days of her life. She is always busy with wool and with flax, she does her work with eager hands. She sets her hands to the distaff, her fingers grasp the spindle. She holds out her hand to the poor, she opens her arms to the needy. Charm is deceitful, and beauty empty; the woman who is wise is the one to praise. Give her a share in what her hands have worked for, and let her works tell her praises at the city gates.

### Psalm 127:1-5

*O blessed are those who fear the Lord.*

### 1 Corinthians 12:31-13:13

Be ambitious for the higher gifts. And I am going to show you a way that is better than any of them.

If I have all the eloquence of men or of angels, but speak without love, I am simply a gong booming or a cymbal clashing. If I have the gift of prophecy, understanding all the mysteries there are, and knowing everything, and if I have faith in all its fullness, to move mountains, but without love, then I am nothing at all. If I give away all that I possess, piece by piece, and if I even let them take my body to burn it, but am without love, it will do me no good whatever.

Love is always patient and kind; it is never jealous; love is never boastful or conceited; it is never rude or selfish; it does not take offence, and is not resentful. Love takes no pleasure in other people's sins but delights in the truth; it is always ready to excuse, to trust, to hope, and to endure whatever comes.

Love does not come to an end. But if there are gifts of prophecy, the time will come when they must fail; or the gift of languages, it will not continue for ever; and knowledge – for this, too, the time will come when it must fail. For our knowledge is imperfect and our prophesying is imperfect; but once perfection comes, all imperfect things will disappear. When I was a child, I used to talk like a child, and think like a child, and argue like a child, but now I am a man, all childish ways are put behind me. Now we are seeing a dim reflection in a mirror; but then we shall be seeing face to face. The knowledge that I have now is imperfect; but then I shall know as fully as I am known.

In short, there are three things that last: faith, hope and love; and the greatest of these is love.

**Matthew 25:31-46**

Jesus said to his disciples: 'When the Son of Man comes in his glory, escorted by all the angels, then he will take his seat on his throne of glory. All the nations will be assembled before him and he will separate men one from another as the shepherd separates sheep from goats. He will place the sheep on his right hand and the goats on his left.

'Then the King will say to those on his right hand, "Come, you whom my Father has blessed, take for your heritage the kingdom prepared for you since the foundation of the world. For I was hungry and you gave me food; I was thirsty and you gave me drink; I was a stranger and you made me welcome; naked and you clothed me, sick and you visited me, in prison and you came to see me." Then the virtuous will say to him in reply, "Lord, when did we see you hungry and feed you; or thirsty and give you drink? When did we see you a stranger and make you welcome; naked and clothe you; sick or in prison and go to see you?" And the King will answer, "I tell you solemnly, in so far as you did this to one of the least of these brothers of mine, you did it to me."

'Next he will say to those on his left hand, "Go away from me, with your curse upon you, to the eternal fire prepared for the devil and his angels. For I was hungry and you never gave me food; I was thirsty and you never gave me anything to drink; I was a stranger and you never made me welcome, naked and you never clothed me, sick and in prison and you never visited me." Then it will be their turn to ask, "Lord, when did we see you hungry or thirsty, a stranger or naked, sick or in prison, and did not come to your help?" Then he will answer, "I tell you solemnly, in so far as you neglected to do this to one of the least of these, you neglected to do it to me."

'And they will go away to eternal punishment, and the virtuous to eternal life.'

# NOVEMBER
# 30
### FRIDAY

**Saint Andrew, Apostle
(Scotland – Solemnity)
Green**

_____

**Wisdom 3:1-9**

The souls of the virtuous are in the hands of God, no torment shall ever touch them.

In the eyes of the unwise, they did appear to die, their going looked like a disaster,

their leaving us, like annihilation; but they are in peace.

If they experienced punishment as men see it, their hope was rich with immortality; slight was their affliction, great will their blessings be.

God has put them to the test and proved them worthy to be with him; he has tested them like gold in a furnace, and accepted them as a holocaust.

When the time comes for his visitation they will shine out; as sparks run through the stubble, so will they.

They shall judge nations, rule over peoples, and the Lord will be their king for ever.

They who trust in him will understand the truth, those who are faithful will live with him in love; for grace and mercy await those he has chosen.

**Psalm 30:3-4.6.8.17.21**

*Into your hands, O Lord, I commend my spirit.*

**Romans 10:9-18**

If your lips confess that Jesus is Lord and if you believe in your heart that God raised him from the dead, then you will be saved. By believing from the heart you are made righteous; by confessing with your lips you are saved. When scripture says: those who believe in him will have no cause for shame, it makes no distinction between Jew and Greek: all belong to the same Lord who is rich enough, however many ask his help, for everyone who calls on the name of the Lord will be saved.

But they will not ask his help unless they believe in him, and they will not believe in him unless they have heard of him, and they will not hear of him unless they get a preacher, and they will never have a preacher unless one is sent, but as scripture says: The footsteps of those who bring good news are a welcome sound. Not everyone, of course, listens to the Good News. As Isaiah says: Lord, how many believed what we proclaimed? So faith comes from what is preached, and what is preached comes from the word of Christ. Let me put the question: is it possible that they did not hear? Indeed they did; in the words of the psalm, their voice has gone out through all the earth, and their message to the ends of the world.

**Matthew 4:18-22**

As Jesus was walking by the Sea of Galilee, he saw two brothers, Simon, who was called Peter, and his brother Andrew; they were making a cast in the lake with their net, for they were fishermen. And he said to them, 'Follow me and I will make you fishers of men.' And they left their nets at once and followed him. Going on from there he saw another pair of brothers, James son of Zebedee and his brother John; they were in their boat with their father Zebedee, mending their nets, and he called them. At once, leaving the boat and their father, they followed him.

**Saint Thomas Becket
(England – Feast)
Red**

## Colossians 1:24-29

It makes me happy to suffer for you, as I am suffering now, and in my own body to do what I can to make up all that has still to be undergone by Christ for the sake of his body, the Church. I became the servant of the Church when God made me responsible for delivering God's message to you, the message which was a mystery hidden for generations and centuries and has now been revealed to his saints. It was God's purpose to reveal it to them and to show all the rich glory of this mystery to pagans. The mystery is Christ among you, your hope of glory: this is the Christ we proclaim, this is the wisdom in which we thoroughly train everyone and instruct everyone, to make them all perfect in Christ. It is for this I struggle wearily on, helped only by his power driving me irresistibly.

## Psalm 22

*The Lord is my shepherd: there is nothing I shall want.*

## Luke 22:24-30

A dispute arose between the disciples about which should be reckoned the greatest, but Jesus said to them:

'Among pagans it is the kings who lord it over them, and those who have authority over them are given the title Benefactor. This must not happen with you. No; the greatest among you must behave as if he were the youngest, the leader as if he were the one who serves. For who is the greater: the one at table or the one who serves? The one at table, surely? Yet here am I among you as one who serves!

'You are the men who have stood by me faithfully in my trials; and now I confer a kingdom on you, just as my Father conferred one on me: you will eat and drink at my table in my kingdom, and you will sit on thrones to judge the twelve tribes of Israel.'

### January 27 Wednesday: 3rd Week in Ordinary Time
### Hebrews 10:11-18

All the priests stand at their duties every day, offering over and over again the same sacrifices which are quite incapable of taking sins away. Jesus, on the other hand, has offered one single sacrifice for sins, and then taken his place for ever, at the right hand of God, where he is now waiting until his enemies are made into a footstool for him. By virtue of that one single offering, he has achieved the eternal perfection of all whom he is sanctifying.

The Holy Spirit assures us of this; for he says, first: This is the covenant I will make with them when those days arrive; and the Lord then goes on to say: I will put my laws into their hearts and write them on their minds. I will never call their sins to mind, or their offences.

When all sins have been forgiven, there can be no more sin offerings.

### January 30 Saturday: 3rd Week in Ordinary Time
### Hebrews 11:1-2.8-19

All these died in faith, before receiving any of the things that had been promised, but they saw them in the far distance and welcomed them, recognising that they were only strangers and nomads on earth. People who use such terms about themselves make it quite plain that they are in search of their real homeland. They can hardly have meant the country they came from, since they had the opportunity to go back to it; but in fact they were longing for a better homeland, their heavenly homeland. That is why God is not ashamed to be called their God, since he has founded the city for them.

It was by faith that Abraham, when put to the test, offered up Isaac. He offered to sacrifice his only son even though the promises had been made to him and he had been told: It is through Isaac that your name will be carried on. He was confident that God had the power even to raise the dead; and so, figuratively speaking, he was given back Isaac from the dead.

### February 1 Monday: 4th Week in Ordinary Time
### Hebrews 11:32-40

Gideon, Barak, Samson, Jephthah, David, Samuel and the prophets – these were men who through faith conquered kingdoms, did what is right and earned the promises. They could keep a lion's mouth shut, put out blazing fires and emerge unscathed from battle. They were weak people who were given strength, to be brave in war and drive back foreign invaders. Some came back to their wives from the dead, by resurrection; and others submitted to torture, refusing release so that they would rise again to a better life. Some had to bear being pilloried and flogged, or even chained up in prison. They were stoned, or sawn in half, or beheaded, they were homeless, and dressed in the skins of sheep and goats; they were penniless and were given nothing but ill-treatment. They were too good for the world and they went out to live in deserts and mountains and in caves and ravines. These are all heroes of faith, but they did not receive what was promised, since God had made provision for us to have something better, and they were not to reach perfection except with us.

### February 2 Tuesday: The Presentation of the Lord
### Malachi 3:1-4

The Lord God says this: Look, I am going to send my messenger to prepare a way before me. And the Lord you are seeking will suddenly enter his Temple; and the angel of the covenant whom you are longing for, yes, he is coming, says the Lord of hosts. Who will be able to resist the day of his coming? Who will remain standing when he appears? For he is like the refiner's fire and the fullers' alkali. He will take his seat as refiner and purifier; he will purify the sons of Levi and refine them like gold and silver, and then they will make the offering to the Lord as it should be made. The offering of Judah and Jerusalem will then be welcomed by the Lord as in former days, as in the years of old.

### February 5 Friday: 4th Week in Ordinary Time
### Hebrews 13:1-8

Continue to love each other like brothers, and remember always to welcome strangers, for by doing this, some people have entertained angels without knowing it. Keep in mind those who are in prison, as though you were in prison with them; and those who are being badly treated, since you too are in the one body. Marriage is to be honoured by all, and marriages are to be kept undefiled, because fornicators and adulterers will come under God's judgement. Put greed out of your lives and be content with whatever you have; God himself has said: I will not fail you or desert you, and so we can say with confidence: With the Lord to help me, I fear nothing: what can man do to me?

Remember your leaders, who preached the word of God to you, and as you reflect on the outcome of their lives, imitate their faith. Jesus Christ is the same today as he was yesterday and as he will be for ever.

### February 8 Monday: 5th Week in Ordinary Time
### Genesis 1:1-19

God said, 'Let there be lights in the vault of heaven to divide day from night, and let them indicate festivals, days and years. Let them be lights in the vault of heaven to shine on the earth.' And so it was. God made the two great lights: the greater light to govern the day, the smaller light to govern the night, and the stars. God set them in the vault of heaven to shine on the earth, to govern the day and the night and to divide light from darkness. God saw that it was good. Evening came and morning came: the fourth day.

### February 9 Tuesday: 5th Week in Ordinary Time
### Genesis 1:20-2:4

God said, 'Let the waters teem with living creatures, and let birds fly above the earth within the vault of heaven.' And so it was. God created great sea-serpents and every kind of living creature with which the waters teem, and every kind of winged creature. God saw that it was good. God blessed them, saying, 'Be fruitful, multiply, and fill the waters of the seas; and let the birds multiply upon the earth.' Evening came and morning came: the fifth day.

God said, 'Let the earth produce every kind of living creature: cattle, reptiles, and every kind of wild beast.' And so it was. God made every kind of wild beast, every kind of cattle, and every kind of land reptile. God saw that it was good.

God said, 'Let us make man in our own image, in the likeness of ourselves, and let them be masters of the fish of the sea, the birds of heaven, the cattle, all the wild beasts and all the reptiles that crawl upon the earth.'

God created man in the image of himself, in the image of God he created him, male and female he created them.

God blessed them, saying to them, 'Be fruitful, multiply, fill the earth and conquer it. Be masters of the fish of the sea, the birds of heaven and all living animals on the earth.' God said, 'See, I give you all the seed-bearing plants that are upon the whole earth, and all the trees with seed-bearing fruit; this shall be your food. To all wild beasts, all birds of heaven and all living reptiles on the earth I give all the foliage of plants for food.' And so it was. God saw all he had made, and indeed it was very good. Evening came and morning came: the sixth day.

Thus heaven and earth were completed with all their array. On the seventh day God completed the work he had been doing. He rested on the seventh day after all the work he had been doing. God blessed the seventh day and made it holy, because on that day he had rested after all his work of creating.

Such were the origins of heaven and earth when they were created.

### February 13 Saturday: 5th Week in Ordinary Time
### Genesis 3:9-24

To the woman he said: 'I will multiply your pains in childbearing, you shall give birth to your children in pain. Your yearning shall be for your husband, yet he will lord it over you.'

To the man he said, 'Because you listened to the voice of your wife and ate from the tree of which I had forbidden you to eat, 'Accursed be the soil because of you. With suffering shall you get your food from it every day of your life. It shall yield you brambles and thistles, and you shall eat wild plants. With sweat on your brow shall you eat your bread, until you return to the soil, as you were taken from it. For dust you are and to dust you shall return.'

The man named his wife 'Eve' because she was the mother of all those who live. The Lord God made clothes out of skins for the man and his wife, and they put them on. Then the Lord God said, 'See, the man has become like one of us, with his knowledge of good and evil. He must not be allowed to stretch his hand out next and pick from the tree of life also, and eat some and live for ever.' So the Lord God expelled him from the garden of Eden, to till the soil from which he had been taken. He banished the man, and in front of the garden of Eden he posted the cherubs, and the flame of a flashing sword, to guard the way to the tree of life.

### February 15 Monday: 6th Week in Ordinary Time
### Genesis 4:1-15.25

… You shall be a fugitive and a wanderer over the earth.' Then Cain said to the Lord, 'My punishment is greater than I can bear. See! Today you drive me from this ground. I must hide from you, and be a fugitive and a wanderer over the earth. Why, whoever comes across me will kill me!' 'Very well, then,' the Lord replied 'if anyone kills Cain, sevenfold vengeance shall be taken from him.' So the Lord put a mark on Cain, to prevent whoever might come across him from striking him down.

Adam had intercourse with his wife, and she gave birth to a son whom she named Seth, 'because God has granted me other offspring' she said 'in place of Abel, since Cain has killed him.'

### February 17 Wednesday: Ash Wednesday
### Joel 2:12-18

'Now, now – it is the Lord who speaks – come back to me with all your heart, fasting, weeping, mourning.' Let your hearts be broken not your garments torn, turn to the Lord your God again, for he is all tenderness and compassion, slow to anger, rich in graciousness, and ready to relent. Who knows if he will not turn again, will not relent, will not leave a blessing as he passes, oblation and libation for the Lord your God? Sound the trumpet in Zion! Order a fast, proclaim a solemn assembly, call the people together, summon the community, assemble the elders, gather the children, even the infants at the breast. Let the bridegroom leave his bedroom and the bride her alcove. Between vestibule and altar let the priests, the ministers of the Lord, lament. Let them say, 'Spare your people, Lord! Do not make your heritage a thing of shame, a byword for the nations. Why should it be said among the nations, "Where is their God?"' Then the Lord, jealous on behalf of his land, took pity on his people.

### March 4 Thursday: 2nd Week of Lent
### Jeremiah 17:5-10

… He is like a tree by the waterside that thrusts its roots to the stream: when the heat comes it feels no alarm, its foliage stays green; it has no worries in a year of drought, and never ceases to bear fruit. 'The heart is more devious than any other thing, perverse too: who can pierce its secrets? I, the Lord, search the heart, I probe the loins, to give each man what his conduct and actions deserve.'

### March 5 Friday: 2nd Week of Lent
### Genesis 37:3-4.12-13.17-28

They saw him in the distance, and before he reached them they made a plot among themselves to put him to death. 'Here comes the man of dreams' they said to one another. 'Come on, let us kill him and throw him into some well; we can say that a wild beast devoured him. Then we shall see what becomes of his dreams.'

But Reuben heard, and he saved him from their violence. 'We must not take his life' he said. 'Shed no blood,' said Reuben to them 'throw him into this well in the wilderness, but do not lay violent hands on him' – intending to save him from them and to restore him to his father. So, when Joseph reached his brothers, they pulled off his coat, the coat with long sleeves that he was wearing, and catching hold of him they threw him into the well, an empty well with no water in it. They then sat down to eat.

Looking up they saw a group of Ishmaelites who were coming from Gilead, their camels laden with gum, tragacanth, balsam and resin, which they were taking down into Egypt. Then Judah said to his brothers, 'What do we gain by killing our brother and covering up his blood? Come, let us sell him to the Ishmaelites, but let us not do any harm to him. After all, he is our brother, and our own flesh.' His brothers agreed.

Now some Midianite merchants were passing, and they drew Joseph up out of the well. They sold Joseph to the Ishmaelites for twenty silver pieces, and these men took Joseph to Egypt.

## March 6 Saturday: 2nd Week of Lent
## Micah 7:14-15.18-20

With shepherd's crook, O Lord, lead your people to pasture, the flock that is your heritage, living confined in a forest with meadow land all around. Let them pasture in Bashan and Gilead as in the days of old. As in the days when you came out of Egypt grant us to see wonders. What god can compare with you: taking fault away, pardoning crime, not cherishing anger for ever but delighting in showing mercy? Once more have pity on us, tread down our faults, to the bottom of the sea throw all our sins. Grant Jacob your faithfulness, and Abraham your mercy, as you swore to our fathers from the days of long ago.

## Luke 15:1-3.11-32

… "Your brother has come" replied the servant "and your father has killed the calf we had fattened because he has got him back safe and sound." He was angry then and refused to go in, and his father came out to plead with him; but he answered his father, "Look, all these years I have slaved for you and never once disobeyed your orders, yet you never offered me so much as a kid for me to celebrate with my friends. But, for this son of yours, when he comes back after swallowing up your property – he and his women – you kill the calf we had been fattening."

'The father said, "My son, you are with me always and all I have is yours. But it is only right we should celebrate and rejoice, because your brother here was dead and has come to life; he was lost and is found."'

## March 8 Monday: 3rd Week of Lent
## 2 Kings 5:1-15

When Elisha heard that the king of Israel had torn his garments he sent word to the king, 'Why did you tear your garments? Let him come to me, and he will find there is a prophet in Israel.' So Naaman came with his team and chariot and drew up at the door of Elisha's house. And Elisha sent him a messenger to say, 'Go and bathe seven times in the Jordan, and your flesh will become clean once more.' But Naaman was indignant and went off, saying, 'Here was I thinking he would be sure to come out to me, and stand there, and call on the name of the Lord his God, and wave his hand over the spot and cure the leprous part. Surely Abana and Pharpar, the rivers of Damascus, are better than any water in Israel? Could I not bathe in them and become clean?' And he turned round and went off in a rage. But his servants approached him and said, 'My father, if the prophet had asked you to do something difficult, would you not have done it? All the more reason, then, when he says to you, "Bathe, and you will become clean."' So he went down and immersed himself seven times in the Jordan, as Elisha had told him to do. And his flesh became clean once more like the flesh of a little child.

Returning to Elisha with his whole escort, he went in and stood before him. 'Now I know' he said 'that there is no God in all the earth except in Israel.'

### March 9 Tuesday: 3rd Week of Lent
### Daniel 3: 25, 34-43

Azariah stood in the heart of the fire, and he began to pray: Oh! Do not abandon us for ever, for the sake of your name; do not repudiate your covenant, do not withdraw your favour from us, for the sake of Abraham, your friend, of Isaac your servant, and of Israel your holy one, to whom you promised descendants as countless as the stars of heaven and as the grains of sand on the seashore. Lord, now we are the least of all the nations, now we are despised throughout the world, today because of our sins. We have at this time no leader, no prophet, no prince, no holocaust, no sacrifice, no oblation, no incense, no place where we can offer you the first-fruits and win your favour. But may the contrite soul, the humbled spirit be as acceptable to you as holocausts of rams and bullocks, as thousands of fattened lambs: such let our sacrifice be to you today, and may it be your will that we follow you wholeheartedly, since those who put their trust in you will not be disappointed. And now we put our whole heart into following you, into fearing you and seeking your face once more. Do not disappoint us: treat us gently, as you yourself are gentle and very merciful. Grant us deliverance worthy of your wonderful deeds, let your name win glory, Lord.

### March 16 Tuesday: 4th Week of Lent
### Ezekiel 47:1-9.12

… The man went to the east holding his measuring line and measured off a thousand cubits; he then made me wade across the stream; the water reached my ankles. He measured off another thousand and made me wade across the stream again; the water reached my knees. He measured off another thousand and made me wade across again; the water reached my waist. He measured off another thousand; it was now a river which I could not cross; the stream had swollen and was now deep water, a river impossible to cross. He then said, 'Do you see, son of man?' He took me further, then brought me back to the bank of the river. When I got back, there were many trees on each bank of the river. He said, 'This water flows east down to the Arabah and to the sea; and flowing into the sea it makes its waters wholesome. Whenever the river flows, all living creatures teeming in it will live. Fish will be very plentiful, for wherever the water goes it brings health, and life teems wherever the river flows. Along the river, on either bank, will grow every kind of fruit tree with leaves that never wither and fruit that never fails; they will bear new fruit every month, because this water comes from the sanctuary. And their fruit will be good to eat and the leaves medicinal.'

### March 18 Thursday: 4th Week of Lent
### Exodus 32:7-14

But Moses pleaded with the Lord his God. 'Lord,' he said 'why should your wrath blaze out against this people of yours whom you brought out of the land of Egypt with arm outstretched and mighty hand? Why let the Egyptians say, "Ah, it was in treachery that he brought them out, to do them to death in the mountains and wipe them off the face of the earth"? Leave your burning wrath; relent and do not bring this disaster on your people. Remember Abraham, Isaac and Jacob, your servants to whom by your own self you swore and made this promise: I will make your offspring as many as the stars of heaven, and all this land which I promised I will give to your descendants, and it shall be their heritage for ever.' So the Lord relented and did not bring on his people the disaster he had threatened.

## March 19 Friday: St Joseph
## 2 Samuel 7:4-5.12-14.16

The word of the Lord came to Nathan: 'Go and tell my servant David, "Thus the Lord speaks: When your days are ended and you are laid to rest with your ancestors, I will preserve the offspring of your body after you and make his sovereignty secure. (It is he who shall build a house for my name, and I will make his royal throne secure for ever.) I will be a father to him and he a son to me. Your House and your sovereignty will always stand secure before me and your throne be established for ever."'

## March 22 Monday: 5th Week of Lent
## Daniel 13:41-62

… At which all the people turned to him and asked, 'What do you mean by these words?' Standing in the middle of the crowd he replied, 'Are you so stupid, sons of Israel, as to condemn a daughter of Israel unheard, and without troubling to find out the truth? Go back to the scene of the trial: these men have given false evidence against her.'

All the people hurried back, and the elders said to Daniel, 'Come and sit with us and tell us what you mean, since God has given you the gifts that elders have.' Daniel said, 'Keep the men well apart from each other for I want to question them.' When the men had been separated, Daniel had one of them brought to him. 'You have grown old in wickedness,' he said 'and now the sins of your earlier days have overtaken you, you with your unjust judgements, your condemnation of the innocent, your acquittal of guilty men, when the Lord has said, "You must not put the innocent and the just to death." Now then, since you saw her so clearly, tell me what tree you saw them lying under?' He replied, 'Under a mastic tree.' Daniel said, 'True enough! Your lie recoils on your own head: the angel of God has already received your sentence from him and will slash you in half.' He dismissed the man, ordered the other to be brought and said to him, 'Spawn of Canaan, not of Judah, beauty has seduced you, lust has led your heart astray! This is how you have been behaving with the daughters of Israel and they were too frightened to resist; but here is a daughter of Judah who could not stomach your wickedness! Now then, tell me what tree you surprised them under?' He replied, 'Under a holm oak.' Daniel said, 'True enough! Your lie recoils on your own head: the angel of God is waiting, with a sword to drive home and split you, and destroy the pair of you.'

Then the whole assembly shouted, blessing God, the saviour of those who trust in him. And they turned on the two elders whom Daniel had convicted of false evidence out of their own mouths. As prescribed in the Law of Moses, they sentenced them to the same punishment as they had intended to inflict on their neighbour. They put them to death; the life of an innocent woman was spared that day.

### March 24 Wednesday: 5th Week of Lent
### Daniel 3:14-20.24-25.28

… These words infuriated King Nebuchadnezzar; his expression was very different now as he looked at Shadrach, Meshach and Abednego. He gave orders for the furnace to be made seven times hotter than usual, and commanded certain stalwarts from his army to bind Shadrach, Meshach and Abednego and throw them into the burning fiery furnace.

Then King Nebuchadnezzar sprang to his feet in amazement. He said to his advisers, 'Did we not have these three men thrown bound into the fire?' They replied, 'Certainly, O king.' 'But,' he went on 'I can see four men walking about freely in the heart of the fire without coming to any harm. And the fourth looks like a son of the gods.'

Nebuchadnezzar exclaimed, 'Blessed be the God of Shadrach, Meshach and Abednego: he has sent his angel to rescue his servants who, putting their trust in him, defied the order of the king, and preferred to forfeit their bodies rather than serve or worship any god but their own.'

### March 25 Thursday: The Annunciation of the Lord
### Isaiah 7:10-14; 8:10

The Lord spoke to Ahaz and said, 'Ask the Lord your God for a sign for yourself coming either from the depths of Sheol or from the heights above.' 'No,' Ahaz answered 'I will not put the Lord to the test.'

Then Isaiah said: 'Listen now, House of David: are you not satisfied with trying the patience of men without trying the patience of God, too? The Lord himself, therefore, will give you a sign. It is this: the maiden is with child and will soon give birth to a son whom she will call Emmanuel, a name which means "God-is-with-us".'

### March 27 Saturday: 5th Week of Lent
### Ezekiel 37:21-28

… They will live in the land that I gave my servant Jacob, the land in which your ancestors lived. They will live in it, they, their children, their children's children, for ever. David my servant is to be their prince for ever. I shall make a covenant of peace with them, an eternal covenant with them. I shall resettle them and increase them; I shall settle my sanctuary among them for ever. I shall make my home above them; I will be their God, they shall be my people. And the nations will learn that I am the Lord the sanctifier of Israel, when my sanctuary is with them for ever.'

### March 30 Tuesday: Tuesday of Holy Week
### Isaiah 49:1-6

… I was honoured in the eyes of the Lord, my God was my strength. And now the Lord has spoken, he who formed me in the womb to be his servant, to bring Jacob back to him, to gather Israel to him: 'It is not enough for you to be my servant, to restore the tribes of Jacob and bring back the survivors of Israel; I will make you the light of the nations so that my salvation may reach to the ends of the earth.'

## April 1 Thursday: Holy Thursday
### Exodus 12:1-8.11-14

The Lord said to Moses and Aaron in the land of Egypt, 'This month is to be the first of all the others for you, the first month of your year. Speak to the whole community of Israel and say, "On the tenth day of this month each man must take an animal from the flock, one for each family: one animal for each household. If the household is too small to eat the animal, a man must join with his neighbour, the nearest to his house, as the number of persons requires. You must take into account what each can eat in deciding the number for the animal. It must be an animal without blemish, a male one year old; you may take it from either sheep or goats. You must keep it till the fourteenth day of the month when the whole assembly of the community of Israel shall slaughter it between the two evenings. Some of the blood must then be taken and put on the two doorposts and the lintel of the houses where it is eaten. That night, the flesh is to be eaten, roasted over the fire; it must be eaten with unleavened bread and bitter herbs. You shall eat it like this: with a girdle round your waist, sandals on your feet, a staff in your hand. You shall eat it hastily: it is a passover in honour of the Lord. That night, I will go through the land of Egypt and strike down all the first-born in the land of Egypt, man and beast alike, and I shall deal out punishment to all the gods of Egypt, I am the Lord. The blood shall serve to mark the houses that you live in. When I see the blood I will pass over you and you shall escape the destroying plague when I strike the land of Egypt. This day is to be a day of remembrance for you, and you must celebrate it as a feast in the Lord's honour. For all generations you are to declare it a day of festival, for ever."'

## April 2 Friday: Good Friday
### Isaiah 52:13–53:12

… On him lies a punishment that brings us peace, and through his wounds we are healed. We had all gone astray like sheep, each taking his own way, and the Lord burdened him with the sins of all of us. Harshly dealt with, he bore it humbly, he never opened his mouth, like a lamb that is led to the slaughter-house, like a sheep that is dumb before its shearers never opening its mouth. By force and by law he was taken; would anyone plead his cause? Yes, he was torn away from the land of the living; for our faults struck down in death. They gave him a grave with the wicked, a tomb with the rich, though he had done no wrong and there had been no perjury in his mouth. The Lord has been pleased to crush him with suffering. If he offers his life in atonement, he shall see his heirs, he shall have a long life and through him what the Lord wishes will be done. His soul's anguish over he shall see the light and be content. By his sufferings shall my servant justify many, taking their faults on himself. Hence I will grant whole hordes for his tribute, he shall divide the spoil with the mighty, for surrendering himself to death and letting himself be taken for a sinner, while he was bearing the faults of many and praying all the time for sinners.

## April 5 Monday: Easter Monday
### Acts 2:14.22-33

'Brothers, no one can deny that the patriarch David himself is dead and buried: his tomb is still with us. But since he was a prophet, and knew that God had sworn him an oath to make one of his descendants succeed him on the throne, what he foresaw and spoke about was the resurrection of the Christ: he is the one who was not abandoned to Hades, and whose body did not experience corruption. God raised this man Jesus to life, and all of us are witnesses to that.

'Now raised to the heights by God's right hand, he has received from the Father the Holy Spirit, who was promised, and what you see and hear is the outpouring of that Spirit.'

### April 7 Wednesday: Easter Wednesday
### Acts 3:1-10

Once, when Peter and John were going up to the Temple for the prayers at the ninth hour, it happened that there was a man being carried past. He was a cripple from birth; and they used to put him down every day near the Temple entrance called the Beautiful Gate so that he could beg from the people going in. When this man saw Peter and John on their way into the Temple he begged from them. Both Peter and John looked straight at him and said, 'Look at us.' He turned to them expectantly, hoping to get something from them, but Peter said, 'I have neither silver nor gold, but I will give you what I have: in the name of Jesus Christ the Nazarene, walk!' Peter then took him by the hand and helped him to stand up. Instantly his feet and ankles became firm, he jumped up, stood, and began to walk, and he went with them into the Temple, walking and jumping and praising God. Everyone could see him walking and praising God, and they recognised him as the man who used to sit begging at the Beautiful Gate of the Temple. They were all astonished and unable to explain what had happened to him.

### Luke 24:13-35

They set out that instant and returned to Jerusalem. There they found the Eleven assembled together with their companions, who said to them, 'Yes, it is true. The Lord has risen and has appeared to Simon.' Then they told their story of what had happened on the road and how they had recognised him at the breaking of bread.

### April 8 Thursday: Easter Thursday
### Acts 3:11-26

… It is faith in that name that has restored this man to health, as you can all see.

'Now I know, brothers, that neither you nor your leaders had any idea what you were really doing; this was the way God carried out what he had foretold, when he said through all his prophets that Christ would suffer. Now you must repent and turn to God, so that your sins may be wiped out, and so that the Lord may send the time of comfort. Then he will send you the Christ he has predestined, that is Jesus, whom heaven must keep till the universal restoration comes which God proclaimed, speaking through his holy prophets. Moses, for example, said: The Lord God will raise up a prophet like myself for you, from among your own brothers; you must listen to whatever he tells you. The man who does not listen to that prophet is to be cut off from the people. In fact, all the prophets that have ever spoken, from Samuel onwards, have predicted these days.

'You are the heirs of the prophets, the heirs of the covenant God made with our ancestors when he told Abraham: in your offspring all the families of the earth will be blessed. It was for you in the first place that God raised up his servant and sent him to bless you by turning every one of you from your wicked ways.'

### April 9 Friday: Easter Friday
Acts 4:1-12

… They arrested them, but as it was already late, they held them till the next day. But many of those who had listened to their message became believers, the total number of whom had now risen to something like five thousand.

The next day the rulers, elders and scribes had a meeting in Jerusalem with Annas the high priest, Caiaphas, Jonathan, Alexander and all the members of the high-priestly families. They made the prisoners stand in the middle and began to interrogate them, 'By what power, and by whose name have you men done this?' Then Peter, filled with the Holy Spirit, addressed them, 'Rulers of the people, and elders! If you are questioning us today about an act of kindness to a cripple, and asking us how he was healed, then I am glad to tell you all, and would indeed be glad to tell the whole people of Israel, that it was by the name of Jesus Christ the Nazarene, the one you crucified, whom God raised from the dead, by this name and by no other that this man is able to stand up perfectly healthy, here in your presence today. This is the stone rejected by you the builders, but which has proved to be the keystone. For of all the names in the world given to men, this is the only one by which we can be saved.'

### April 16 Friday: 2nd Week of Easter
Acts 5:34-42

… And then there was Judas the Galilean, at the time of the census, who attracted crowds of supporters; but he got killed too, and all his followers dispersed. What I suggest, therefore, is that you leave these men alone and let them go. If this enterprise, this movement of theirs, is of human origin it will break up of its own accord; but if it does in fact come from God you will not only be unable to destroy them, but you might find yourselves fighting against God.'

His advice was accepted; and they had the apostles called in, gave orders for them to be flogged, warned them not to speak in the name of Jesus and released them. And so they left the presence of the Sanhedrin glad to have had the honour of suffering humiliation for the sake of the name.

They preached every day both in the Temple and in private houses, and their proclamation of the Good News of Christ Jesus was never interrupted.

### April 22 Thursday: 3rd Week of Easter
Acts 8:26-40

Further along the road they came to some water, and the eunuch said, 'Look, there is some water here; is there anything to stop me being baptised?' He ordered the chariot to stop, then Philip and the eunuch both went down to the water and Philip baptised him. But after they had come up out of the water again Philip was taken away by the Spirit of the Lord, and the eunuch never saw him again but went on his way rejoicing. Philip found that he had reached Azotus and continued his journey proclaiming the Good News in every town as far as Caesarea.

## April 23 Friday: 3rd Week of Easter
### Acts 9:1-20

A disciple called Ananias who lived in Damascus had a vision in which he heard the Lord say to him, 'Ananias!' When he replied, 'Here I am, Lord,' the Lord said, 'You must go to Straight Street and ask at the house of Judas for someone called Saul, who comes from Tarsus. At this moment he is praying, having had a vision of a man called Ananias coming in and laying hands on him to give him back his sight.'

When he heard that, Ananias said, 'Lord, several people have told me about this man and all the harm he has been doing to your saints in Jerusalem. He has only come here because he holds a warrant from the chief priests to arrest everybody who invokes your name.' The Lord replied, 'You must go all the same, because this man is my chosen instrument to bring my name before pagans and pagan kings and before the people of Israel; I myself will show him how much he himself must suffer for my name.' Then Ananias went. He entered the house, and at once laid his hands on Saul and said, 'Brother Saul, I have been sent by the Lord Jesus who appeared to you on your way here so that you may recover your sight and be filled with the Holy Spirit.' Immediately it was as though scales fell away from Saul's eyes and he could see again. So he was baptised there and then, and after taking some food he regained his strength.

After he had spent only a few days with the disciples in Damascus, he began preaching in the synagogues, 'Jesus is the Son of God.'

## April 24 Saturday: 3rd Week of Easter
### Acts 9:31-42

Peter went back with them straightaway, and on his arrival they took him to the upstairs room, where all the widows stood round him in tears, showing him tunics and other clothes Dorcas had made when she was with them. Peter sent them all out of the room and knelt down and prayed. Then he turned to the dead woman and said, 'Tabitha, stand up.' She opened her eyes, looked at Peter and sat up. Peter helped her to her feet, then he called in the saints and widows and showed them she was alive. The whole of Jaffa heard about it and many believed in the Lord.

## April 26 Monday: 4th Week of Easter
### Acts 11:1-18

'Just at that moment, three men stopped outside the house where we were staying; they had been sent from Caesarea to fetch me, and the Spirit told me to have no hesitation about going back with them. The six brothers here came with me as well, and we entered the man's house. He told us he had seen an angel standing in his house who said, "Send to Jaffa and fetch Simon known as Peter; he has a message for you that will save you and your entire household."

'I had scarcely begun to speak when the Holy Spirit came down on them in the same way as it came on us at the beginning, and I remembered that the Lord had said, "John baptised with water, but you will be baptised with the Holy Spirit." I realised then that God was giving them the identical thing he gave to us when we believed in the Lord Jesus Christ; and who was I to stand in God's way?'

This account satisfied them, and they gave glory to God. 'God' they said 'can evidently grant even the pagans the repentance that leads to life.'

### May 12 Wednesday: 6th Week of Easter
### Acts 17:15.22–18:1

... Yet in fact he is not far from any of us, since it is in him that we live, and move, and exist, as indeed some of your own writers have said:

"We are all his children."

'Since we are the children of God, we have no excuse for thinking that the deity looks like anything in gold, silver or stone that has been carved and designed by a man.

'God overlooked that sort of thing when men were ignorant, but now he is telling everyone everywhere that they must repent, because he has fixed a day when the whole world will be judged, and judged in righteousness, and he has appointed a man to be the judge. And God has publicly proved this by raising this man from the dead.'

At this mention of rising from the dead, some of them burst out laughing; others said, 'We would like to hear you talk about this again.' After that Paul left them, but there were some who attached themselves to him and became believers, among them Dionysius the Areopagite and a woman called Damaris, and others besides. After this Paul left Athens and went to Corinth.

### May 18 Tuesday: 7th Week of Easter
### Acts 20:17-27

... But life to me is not a thing to waste words on, provided that when I finish my race I have carried out the mission the Lord Jesus gave me – and that was to bear witness to the Good News of God's grace.

'I now feel sure that none of you among whom I have gone about proclaiming the kingdom will ever see my face again. And so here and now I swear that my conscience is clear as far as all of you are concerned, for I have without faltering put before you the whole of God's purpose.'

### May 20 Thursday: 7th Week of Easter
### Acts 22:30;23:6-11

... The shouting grew louder, and some of the scribes from the Pharisees' party stood up and protested strongly, 'We find nothing wrong with this man. Suppose a spirit has spoken to him, or an angel?' Feeling was running high, and the tribune, afraid that they would tear Paul to pieces, ordered his troops to go down and haul him out and bring him into the fortress.

Next night, the Lord appeared to him and said, 'Courage! You have borne witness for me in Jerusalem, now you must do the same in Rome.'

### May 26 Wednesday: 8th Week in Ordinary Time
### Sirach 36:1.4-5.10-17

Have mercy on us, Master, Lord of all, and look on us, cast the fear of yourself over every nation. Let them acknowledge you, just as we have acknowledged that there is no God but you, Lord. Send new portents, do fresh wonders, win glory for your hand and your right arm. Gather together all the tribes of Jacob, restore them their inheritance as in the beginning. Have mercy, Lord, on the people who have invoked your name, on Israel whom you have treated as a first-born. Show compassion on your holy city, on Jerusalem the place of your rest. Fill Zion with songs of your praise, and your sanctuary with your glory. Bear witness to those you created in the beginning, and bring about what has been prophesied in your name. Give those who wait for you their reward, and let your prophets be proved worthy of belief. Grant, Lord, the prayer of your servants, in accordance with Aaron's blessing on your people, so that all the earth's inhabitants may acknowledge that you are the Lord, the everlasting God.

### May 28 Friday: 8th Week in Ordinary Time
### Sirach 44:1.9-13

Let us praise illustrious men, our ancestors in their successive generations. While others have left no memory, and disappeared as though they had not existed, they are now as though they had never been, and so too, their children after them. But here is a list of generous men whose good works have not been forgotten. In their descendants there remains a rich inheritance born of them. Their descendants stand by the covenants and, thanks to them, so do their children's children. Their offspring will last for ever, their glory will not fade.

### June 2 Wednesday: 9th Week in Ordinary Time
### Tobit 3:1-11.16-17

… For death is better for me than life. I have been reviled without a cause and I am distressed beyond measure. 'Lord, I wait for the sentence you will give to deliver me from this affliction. Let me go away to my everlasting home; do not turn your face from me, O Lord. For it is better to die than still to live in the face of trouble that knows no pity; I am weary of hearing myself traduced.'

It chanced on the same day that Sarah the daughter of Raguel, who lived in Media at Ecbatana, also heard insults from one of her father's maids. You must know that she had been given in marriage seven times, and that Asmodeus, that worst of demons, had killed her bridegrooms one after another before ever they had slept with her as man with wife. The servant-girl said, 'Yes, you kill your bridegrooms yourself. That makes seven already to whom you have been given, and you have not once been in luck yet. Just because your bridegrooms have died, that is no reason for punishing us. Go and join them, and may we be spared the sight of any child of yours!' That day, she grieved, she sobbed, and went up to her father's room intending to hang herself. But then she thought, 'Suppose they blamed my father! They will say, "You had an only daughter whom you loved, and now she has hanged herself for grief." I cannot cause my father a sorrow which would bring down his old age to the dwelling of the dead. I should do better not to hang myself, but to beg the Lord to let me die and not live to hear any more insults.'

This time the prayer of each of them found favour before the glory of God, and Raphael was sent to bring remedy to them both.

### June 3 Thursday: 9th Week in Ordinary Time
### Tobit 6:10-11; 7:1.9-14; 8:4-9

… However, my boy, I must be frank with you: I have tried to find a husband for her seven times among our kinsmen, and all of them have died the first evening, on going to her room. But for the present, my boy, eat and drink; the Lord will grant you his grace and peace.' Tobias spoke out, 'I will not hear of eating and drinking till you have come to a decision about me.' Raguel answered. 'Very well. Since, as prescribed by the Book of Moses, she is given to you, heaven itself decrees she shall be yours. I therefore entrust your sister to you. From now you are her brother and she is your sister. She is given to you from today for ever. The Lord of heaven favour you tonight, my child, and grant you his grace and peace.' Raguel called for his daughter Sarah, took her by the hand and gave her to Tobias with these words, 'I entrust her to you; the law and the ruling recorded in the Book of Moses assign her to you as your wife. Take her; take her home to your father's house with a good conscience. The God of heaven grant you a good journey in peace.' Then he turned to her mother and asked her to fetch him writing paper. He drew up the marriage contract, how he gave his daughter as bride to Tobias according to the ordinance in the Law of Moses.

After this they began to eat and drink. The parents meanwhile had gone out and shut the door behind them. Tobias said to Sarah, 'Get up, my sister! You and I must pray and petition our Lord to win his grace and his protection.' She stood up, and they began praying for protection, and this was how he began:

'You are blessed, O God of our fathers; blessed, too, is your name for ever and ever. Let the heavens bless you and all things you have made for evermore. It was you who created Adam, you who created Eve his wife to be his help and support; and from these two the human race was born. It was you who said, "It is not good that the man should be alone; let us make him a helpmate like himself." And so I do not take my sister for any lustful motive; I do it in singleness of heart. Be kind enough to have pity on her and on me and bring us to old age together.'

And together they said, 'Amen, Amen', and lay down for the night.

### June 4 Friday: 9th Week in Ordinary Time
### Tobit 11:5-17

Tobit set off to the gates of Nineveh to meet his daughter-in-law, giving joyful praise to God as he went. When the people of Nineveh saw him walking without a guide and stepping forward as briskly as of old, they were astonished. Tobit described to them how God had taken pity on him and had opened his eyes. Then Tobit met Sarah, the bride of his son Tobias, and blessed her in these words, 'Welcome, daughter! Blessed be your God for sending you to us, my daughter. Blessings on your father, blessings on my son Tobias, blessings on yourself, my daughter. Welcome now to your own house in joyfulness and in blessedness. Come in, my daughter.' He held a feast that day for all the Jews of Nineveh.

### June 5 Saturday: 9th Week in Ordinary Time
### Tobit 12:1.5-15.20

'I am going to tell you the whole truth, hiding nothing from you. I have already told you that it is right to keep the secret of a king, yet right too to reveal in worthy fashion the works of God. So you must know that when you and Sarah were at prayer, it was I who offered your supplications before the glory of the Lord and who read them; so too when you were burying the dead. When you did not hesitate to get up and leave the table to go and bury a dead man, I was sent to test your faith, and at the same time God sent me to heal you and your daughter-in-law Sarah. I am Raphael, one of the seven angels who stand ever ready to enter the presence of the glory of the Lord.

'Now bless the Lord on earth and give thanks to God. I am about to return to him above who sent me.'

### June 11 Friday: The Most Sacred Heart of Jesus
### Hosea 11:1.3-4.8-9

Listen to the word of the Lord: When Israel was a child I loved him, and I called my son out of Egypt. I myself taught Ephraim to walk, I took them in my arms; yet they have not understood that I was the one looking after them. I led them with reins of kindness, with leading-strings of love. I was like someone who lifts an infant close against his cheek; stooping down to him I gave him his food. How could I treat you like Admah, or deal with you like Zeboiim? My heart recoils from it, my whole being trembles at the thought. I will not give rein to my fierce anger, I will not destroy Ephraim again, for I am God, not man: I am the Holy One in your midst and have no wish to destroy.

### June 19 Saturday: 11th Week in Ordinary Time
### 2 Corinthians 12:1-10

In view of the extraordinary nature of these revelations, to stop me from getting too proud I was given a thorn in the flesh, an angel of Satan to beat me and stop me from getting too proud! About this thing, I have pleaded with the Lord three times for it to leave me, but he has said, 'My grace is enough for you: my power is at its best in weakness.' So I shall be very happy to make my weaknesses my special boast so that the power of Christ may stay over me, and that is why I am quite content with my weaknesses, and with insults, hardships, persecutions, and the agonies I go through for Christ's sake. For it is when I am weak that I am strong.

### June 22 Tuesday: 12th Week in Ordinary Time
### Genesis 13:2.5-18

The Lord said to Abram after Lot had parted company with him, 'Look all round from where you are towards the north and the south, towards the east and the west. All the land within sight I will give to you and your descendants for ever. I will make your descendants like the dust on the ground: when men succeed in counting the specks of dust on the ground, then they will be able to count your descendants! Come, travel through the length and breadth of the land, for I mean to give it to you.'

So Abram went with his tents to settle at the Oak of Mamre, at Hebron, and there he built an altar to the Lord.

## June 24 Thursday: The Nativity of Saint John the Baptist
### Isaiah 49: 1-6

Islands, listen to me, pay attention, remotest peoples. The Lord called me before I was born, from my mother's womb he pronounced my name. He made my mouth a sharp sword, and hid me in the shadow of his hand. He made me into a sharpened arrow, and concealed me in his quiver. He said to me, 'You are my servant (Israel) in whom I shall be glorified'; while I was thinking, 'I have toiled in vain, I have exhausted myself for nothing'; and all the while my cause was with the Lord, my reward with my God. I was honoured in the eyes of the Lord, my God was my strength. And now the Lord has spoken, he who formed me in the womb to be his servant, to bring Jacob back to him, to gather Israel to him: 'It is not enough for you to be my servant, to restore the tribes of Jacob and bring back the survivors of Israel; I will make you the light of the nations so that my salvation may reach to the ends of the earth.'

## June 26 Saturday: 12th Week in Ordinary Time
### Genesis 18:1-15

Abraham hastened to the tent to find Sarah. 'Hurry,' he said 'knead three bushels of flour and make loaves.' Then running to the cattle Abraham took a fine and tender calf and gave it to the servant, who hurried to prepare it. Then taking cream, milk and the calf he had prepared, he laid all before them, and they ate while he remained standing near them under the tree.

'Where is your wife Sarah?' they asked him. 'She is in the tent' he replied. Then his guest said, 'I shall visit you again next year without fail, and your wife will then have a son.' Sarah was listening at the entrance of the tent behind him. Now Abraham and Sarah were old, well on in years, and Sarah had ceased to have her monthly periods. So Sarah laughed to herself, thinking, 'Now that I am past the age of child-bearing, and my husband is an old man, is pleasure to come my way again!' But the Lord asked Abraham, 'Why did Sarah laugh and say, "Am I really going to have a child now that I am old?" Is anything too wonderful for the Lord? At the same time next year I shall visit you again and Sarah will have a son.' 'I did not laugh' Sarah said, lying because she was afraid. But he replied, 'Oh yes, you did laugh.'

## June 28 Monday: 13th Week in Ordinary Time
### Genesis 18:16-33

Abraham replied, 'I am bold indeed to speak like this to my Lord, I who am dust and ashes. But perhaps the fifty just men lack five: will you destroy the whole city for five?' 'No,' he replied 'I will not destroy it if I find forty-five just men there.' Again Abraham said to him, 'Perhaps there will only be forty there.' 'I will not do it' he replied 'for the sake of the forty.'

Abraham said, 'I trust my Lord will not be angry, but give me leave to speak: perhaps there will only be thirty there.' 'I will not do it' he replied 'if I find thirty there.' He said, 'I am bold indeed to speak like this, but perhaps there will only be twenty there.' 'I will not destroy it' he replied 'for the sake of the twenty.' He said, 'I trust my Lord will not be angry if I speak once more: perhaps there will only be ten.' 'I will not destroy it' he replied 'for the sake of the ten.' When he had finished talking to Abraham the Lord went away, and Abraham returned home.

### June 29 Tuesday: Sts Peter and Paul
### Acts 12:1-11

On the night before Herod was to try him, Peter was sleeping between two soldiers, fastened with double chains, while guards kept watch at the main entrance to the prison. Then suddenly the angel of the Lord stood there, and the cell was filled with light. He tapped Peter on the side and woke him. 'Get up!' he said 'Hurry!' – and the chains fell from his hands. The angel then said, 'Put on your belt and sandals.' After he had done this, the angel next said, 'Wrap your cloak round you and follow me.' Peter followed him, but had no idea that what the angel did was all happening in reality; he thought he was seeing a vision. They passed through two guard posts one after the other, and reached the iron gate leading to the city. This opened of its own accord; they went through it and had walked the whole length of the street when suddenly the angel left him. It was only then that Peter came to himself. 'Now I know it is all true,' he said. 'The Lord really did send his angel and has saved me from Herod and from all that the Jewish people were so certain would happen to me.'

### June 30 Wednesday: 13th Week in Ordinary Time
### Genesis 21:5.8-20

But God heard the boy wailing, and the angel of God called to Hagar from heaven. 'What is wrong, Hagar?' he asked. 'Do not be afraid, for God has heard the boy's cry where he lies. Come pick up the boy and hold him safe, for I will make him into a great nation.' Then God opened Hagar's eyes and she saw a well, so she went and filled the skin with water and gave the boy a drink.

God was with the boy. He grew up and made his home in the wilderness, and he became a bowman.

### July 1 Thursday: 13th Week in Ordinary Time
### Genesis 22:1-19

When they arrived at the place God had pointed out to him, Abraham built an altar there, and arranged the wood. Then he bound his son Isaac and put him on the altar on top of the wood. Abraham stretched out his hands and seized the knife to kill his son.

But the angel of the Lord called to him from heaven. 'Abraham, Abraham' he said. 'I am here' he replied. 'Do not raise your hand against the boy' the angel said. 'Do not harm him, for now I know you fear God. You have not refused me your son, your only son.' Then looking up, Abraham saw a ram caught by its horns in a bush. Abraham took the ram and offered it as a burnt-offering in place of his son. Abraham called this place 'The Lord provides', and hence the saying today: On the mountain the Lord provides.

The angel of the Lord called Abraham a second time from heaven. 'I swear by my own self – it is the Lord who speaks – because you have done this, because you have not refused me your son, your only son, I will shower blessings on you, I will make your descendants as many as the stars of heaven and the grains of sand on the seashore. Your descendants shall gain possession of the gates of their enemies. All the nations of the earth shall bless themselves by your descendants, as a reward for your obedience.'

Abraham went back to his servants, and together they set out for Beersheba, and he settled in Beersheba.

### July 2 Friday: 13th Week in Ordinary Time
**Genesis 23:1-4.19; 24:1-8.62-67**

… The Lord, God of heaven and God of earth, took me from my father's home, and from the land of my kinsfolk, and he swore to me that he would give this country to my descendants. He will now send his angel ahead of you, so that you may choose a wife for my son there. And if the woman does not want to come with you, you will be free from this oath of mine. Only do not take my son back there.'

Isaac, who lived in the Negeb, had meanwhile come into the wilderness of the well of Lahai Roi. Now Isaac went walking in the fields as evening fell, and looking up saw camels approaching. And Rebekah looked up and saw Isaac. She jumped down from her camel, and asked the servant 'Who is that man walking through the fields to meet us?' The servant replied, 'That is my master'; then she took her veil and hid her face. The servant told Isaac the whole story, and Isaac led Rebekah into his tent and made her his wife; and he loved her. And so Isaac was consoled for the loss of his mother.

### July 5 Monday: 14th Week in Ordinary Time
**Genesis 28:10-22**

… Then Jacob awoke from his sleep and said, 'Truly, the Lord is in this place and I never knew it!' He was afraid and said, 'How awe-inspiring this place is! This is nothing less than a house of God; this is the gate of heaven!' Rising early in the morning, Jacob took the stone he had used for his pillow, and set it up as a monument, pouring oil over the top of it. He named the place Bethel, but before that the town was called Luz.

Jacob made this vow, 'If God goes with me and keeps me safe on this journey I am making, if he gives me bread to eat and clothes to wear, and if I return home safely to my father, then the Lord shall be my God. This stone I have set up as a monument shall be a house of God.'

### July 7 Wednesday: 14th Week in Ordinary Time
**Genesis 41:55-57; 42:5-7.17-24**

… You shall bring me your youngest brother; this way your words will be proved true, and you will not have to die!' This they did. They said to one another, 'Truly we are being called to account for our brother. We saw his misery of soul when he begged our mercy, but we did not listen to him and now this misery has come home to us.' Reuben answered them, 'Did I not tell you not to wrong the boy? But you did not listen, and now we are brought to account for his blood.' They did not know that Joseph understood, because there was an interpreter between them. He left them and wept.

### July 8 Thursday: 14th Week in Ordinary Time
**Genesis 44:18-21.23-29; 45:1-5**

… So your servant our father said to us, "You know that my wife bore me two children. When one left me, I said that he must have been torn to pieces. And I have not seen him to this day. If you take this one from me too and any harm comes to him, you will send me down to Sheol with my white head bowed in misery."'

Then Joseph could not control his feelings in front of all his retainers, and he exclaimed, 'Let everyone leave me.' No one therefore was present with him while Joseph made himself known to his brothers, but he wept so loudly that all the Egyptians heard, and the news reached Pharaoh's palace.

Joseph said to his brothers, 'I am Joseph. Is my father really still alive?' His brothers could not answer him, they were so dismayed at the sight of him. Then Joseph said to his brothers, 'Come closer to me.' When they had come closer to him he said, 'I am your brother Joseph whom you sold into Egypt. But now, do not grieve, do not reproach yourselves for having sold me here, since God sent me before you to preserve your lives.'

### July 9 Friday: 14th Week in Ordinary Time
### Genesis 46:1-7.28-30

Israel sent Judah ahead to Joseph, so that the latter might present himself to him in Goshen. When they arrived in the land of Goshen, Joseph had his chariot made ready and went up to meet his father Israel in Goshen. As soon as he appeared he threw his arms round his neck and for a long time wept on his shoulder. Israel said to Joseph, 'Now I can die, now that I have seen you again, and seen you still alive.'

### July 10 Saturday: 14th Week in Ordinary Time
### Genesis 49:29-33; 50:15-26

Seeing that their father was dead, Joseph's brothers said, 'What if Joseph intends to treat us as enemies and repay us in full for all the wrong we did him?' So they sent this message to Joseph: 'Before your father died he gave us this order: "You must say to Joseph: Oh forgive your brothers their crime and their sin and all the wrong they did you." Now therefore, we beg you, forgive the crime of the servants of your father's God.' Joseph wept at the message they sent to him.

His brothers came themselves and fell down before him. 'We present ourselves before you' they said 'as your slaves.' But Joseph answered them, 'Do not be afraid; is it for me to put myself in God's place? The evil you planned to do me has by God's design been turned to good, that he might bring about, as indeed he has, the deliverance of a numerous people. So you need not be afraid; I myself will provide for you and your dependants.' In this way he reassured them with words that touched their hearts.

So Joseph stayed in Egypt with his father's family; and Joseph lived a hundred and ten years. Joseph saw the third generation of Ephraim's children, as also the children of Machir, Manasseh's son, who were born on Joseph's lap. At length Joseph said to his brothers, 'I am about to die; but God will be sure to remember you kindly and take you back from this country to the land that he promised on oath to Abraham, Isaac and Jacob.' And Joseph made Israel's sons swear an oath, 'When God remembers you with kindness be sure to take my bones from here.'

Joseph died at the age of hundred and ten; they embalmed him and laid him in his coffin in Egypt.

### July 13 Tuesday: 15th Week in Ordinary Time
### Exodus 2:1-15

… To her the daughter of Pharaoh said, 'Take this child away and suckle it for me. I will see you are paid.' So the woman took the child and suckled it. When the child grew up, she brought him to Pharaoh's daughter who treated him like a son; she named him Moses because, she said, 'I drew him out of the water.'

Moses, a man by now, set out at this time to visit his countrymen, and he saw what a hard life they were having; and he saw an Egyptian strike a Hebrew, one of his countrymen.

Looking round he could see no one in sight, so he killed the Egyptian and hid him in the sand. On the following day he came back, and there were two Hebrews, fighting. He said to the man who was in the wrong, 'What do you mean by hitting your fellow countryman?' 'And who appointed you' the man retorted 'to be prince over us, and judge? Do you intend to kill me as you killed the Egyptian?' Moses was frightened. 'Clearly that business has come to light' he thought. When Pharaoh heard of the matter he would have killed Moses, but Moses fled from Pharaoh and made for the land of Midian.

### July 16 Friday: 15th Week in Ordinary Time
### Exodus 11:10–12:14

… Some of the blood must then be taken and put on the two doorposts and the lintel of the houses where it is eaten. That night, the flesh is to be eaten, roasted over the fire; it must be eaten with unleavened bread and bitter herbs. Do not eat any of it raw or boiled, but roasted over the fire, head, feet and entrails. You must not leave any over till the morning: whatever is left till morning you are to burn. You shall eat it like this: with a girdle round your waist, sandals on your feet, a staff in your hand. You shall eat it hastily: it is a passover in honour of the Lord. That night, I will go through the land of Egypt and strike down all the first-born in the land of Egypt, man and beast alike, and I shall deal out punishment to all the gods of Egypt. I am the Lord! The blood shall serve to mark the houses that you live in. When I see the blood I will pass over you and you shall escape the destroying plague when I strike the land of Egypt. This day is to be a day of remembrance for you, and you must celebrate it as a feast in the Lord's honour. For all generations you are to declare it a day of festival, for ever.'

### July 19 Monday: 16th Week in Ordinary Time
### Exodus 14:5-18

The Lord said to Moses, 'Why do you cry to me so? Tell the sons of Israel to march on. For yourself, raise your staff and stretch out your hand over the sea and part it for the sons of Israel to walk through the sea on dry ground. I for my part will make the heart of the Egyptians so stubborn that they will follow them. So shall I win myself glory at the expense of Pharaoh, of all his army, his chariots, his horsemen. And when I have won glory for myself, at the expense of Pharaoh and his chariots and his army, the Egyptians will learn that I am the Lord.'

### July 21 Wednesday: 16th Week in Ordinary Time
### Exodus 16:1-5.9-15

… As Aaron was speaking to the whole community of the sons of Israel, they turned towards the wilderness, and there was the glory of the Lord appearing in the form of a cloud. Then the Lord spoke to Moses and said, 'I have heard the complaints of the sons of Israel. Say this to them, "Between the two evenings you shall eat meat, and in the morning you shall have bread to your heart's content. Then you will learn that I, the Lord, am your God."' And so it came about: quails flew up in the evening, and they covered the camp; in the morning there was a coating of dew all round the camp. When the coating of dew lifted, there on the surface of the desert was a thing delicate, powdery, as fine as hoarfrost on the ground. When they saw this, the sons of Israel said to one another, 'What is that?' not knowing what it was. 'That' said Moses to them 'is the bread the Lord gives you to eat.'

### July 27 Tuesday: 17th Week in Ordinary Time
### Exodus 33:7-11; 34:5-9.28

… for thousands he maintains his kindness, forgives faults, transgression, sin; yet he lets nothing go unchecked, punishing the father's fault in the sons and in the grandsons to the third and fourth generation.' And Moses bowed down to the ground at once and worshipped. 'If I have indeed won your favour, Lord,' he said 'let my Lord come with us, I beg. True, they are a headstrong people, but forgive us our faults and our sins, and adopt us as your heritage.'

He stayed there with the Lord for forty days and forty nights, eating and drinking nothing. He inscribed on the tablets the words of the Covenant – the Ten Words.

### July 30 Friday: 17th Week in Ordinary Time
### Leviticus 23:1.4-11.15-16.27.34-37

"But the tenth day of this seventh month shall be the Day of Atonement. You are to hold a sacred assembly. You must fast, and you must offer a burnt offering to the Lord.

"The fifteenth day of this seventh month shall be the feast of Tabernacles for the Lord, lasting seven days. The first day is a day of sacred assembly; you must do no heavy work. For seven days you must offer a burnt offering to the Lord. On the eighth day you are to hold a sacred assembly, you must offer a burnt offering to the Lord. It is a day of solemn meeting; you must do no heavy work.

"These are the solemn festivals of the Lord to which you are to summon the children of Israel, sacred assemblies for the purpose of offering burnt offerings, holocausts, oblations, sacrifices and libations to the Lord, according to the ritual of each day."'

### July 31 Saturday: 17th Week in Ordinary Time
### Leviticus 25:1.8-17

'In this year of jubilee each of you is to return to his ancestral home. If you buy or sell with your neighbour, let no one wrong his brother. If you buy from your neighbour, this must take into account the number of years since the jubilee: according to the number of productive years he will fix the price. The greater the number of years, the higher shall be the price demanded; the less the number of years, the greater the reduction; for what he is selling you is a certain number of harvests. Let none of you wrong his neighbour, but fear your God; I am the Lord your God.'

### August 2 Monday: 18th Week in Ordinary Time
### Numbers 11:4-15

… 'Why do you treat your servant so badly? Why have I not found favour with you, so that you load on me the weight of all this nation? Was it I who conceived all this people, was it I who gave them birth, that you should say to me, "Carry them in your bosom, like a nurse with a baby at the breast, to the land that I swore to give their fathers?" Where am I to find meat to give to all this people, when they come worrying me so tearfully and say, "Give us meat to eat"? I am not able to carry this nation by myself alone; the weight is too much for me. If this is how you want to deal with me, I would rather you killed me! If only I had found favour in your eyes, and not lived to see such misery as this!'

### August 3 Tuesday: 18th Week in Ordinary Time
### Numbers 12:1-13

… He called Aaron and Miriam and they both came forward. The Lord said, 'Listen now to my words: If any man among you is a prophet I make myself known to him in a vision, I speak to him in a dream. Not so with my servant Moses: he is at home in my house; I speak with him face to face, plainly and not in riddles, and he sees the form of the Lord. How then have you dared to speak against my servant Moses?'

The anger of the Lord blazed out against them. He departed and as soon as the cloud withdrew from the Tent, there was Miriam a leper, white as snow! Aaron turned to look at her; she had become a leper.

Aaron said to Moses: 'Help me, my lord! Do not punish us for a sin committed in folly of which we are guilty. I entreat you, do not let her be like a monster, coming from its mother's womb with flesh half corrupted.'

Moses cried to the Lord, 'O God,' he said 'please heal her, I beg you!'

### August 4 Wednesday: 18th Week in Ordinary Time
### Numbers 13:1-2.25–14:1.26-29.34-35

… But the men who had gone up with him answered, 'We are not able to march against this people; they are stronger than we are.' And they began to disparage the country they had reconnoitred to the sons of Israel, 'The country we went to reconnoitre is a country that devours its inhabitants. Every man we saw there was of enormous size. Yes, and we saw giants there (the sons of Anak, descendants of the Giants). We felt like grasshoppers, and so we seemed to them.'

At this, the whole community raised their voices and cried aloud, and the people wailed all that night. The Lord spoke to Moses and Aaron. He said:

'How long does this perverse community complain against me? I have heard the complaints which the sons of Israel make against me. Say to them, "As I live – it is the Lord who speaks – I will deal with you according to the very words you have used in my hearing. In this wilderness your dead bodies will fall, all you men of the census, all you who were numbered from the age of twenty years and over, you who have complained against me. For forty days you reconnoitred the land. Each day shall count for a year: for forty years you shall bear the burden of your sins, and you shall learn what it means to reject me." I, the Lord have spoken: this is how I will deal with this perverse community that has conspired against me. Here in this wilderness, to the last man, they shall die.'

### August 5 Thursday: 18th Week in Ordinary Time
### Numbers 20:1-13

Leaving the assembly, Moses and Aaron went to the door of the Tent of Meeting. They threw themselves face downward on the ground, and the glory of the Lord appeared to them. The Lord spoke to Moses and said, 'Take the branch and call the community together, you and your brother Aaron. Then, in full view of them, order this rock to give water. You will make water flow for them out of the rock, and provide drink for the community and their cattle.'

Moses took up the branch from before the Lord, as he had directed him. Then Moses and Aaron called the assembly together in front of the rock and addressed them, 'Listen now, you rebels. Shall we make water gush from this rock for you?' And Moses raised his hand and struck the rock twice with the branch; water gushed in abundance, and the community drank and their cattle too.

Then the Lord said to Moses and Aaron, 'Because you did not believe that I could proclaim my holiness in the eyes of the sons of Israel, you shall not lead this assembly into the land I am giving them.'

These are the waters of Meribah, where the sons of Israel challenged the Lord and he proclaimed his holiness.

### August 6 Friday: Transfiguration of the Lord
### Daniel 7:9-10.13-14

As I watched: Thrones were set in place and one of great age took his seat. His robe was white as snow, the hair of his head as pure as wool. His throne was a blaze of flames, its wheels were a burning fire. A stream of fire poured out, issuing from his presence. A thousand thousand waited on him, ten thousand times ten thousand stood before him. A court was held and the books were opened. I gazed into the visions of the night. And I saw, coming on the clouds of heaven, one like a son of man. He came to the one of great age and was led into his presence. On him was conferred sovereignty, glory and kingship and men of all peoples, nations and languages became his servants. His sovereignty is an eternal sovereignty which shall never pass away, nor will his empire ever be destroyed.

### August 12 Thursday: 19th Week in Ordinary Time
### Joshua 3:7-11.13-17

… Then Joshua said to the Israelites, 'Come closer and hear the words of the Lord your God.' Joshua said, 'By this you shall know that a living God is with you and without a doubt will expel the Canaanite. Look, the ark of the Lord, the Lord of the whole earth, is about to cross the Jordan at your head. As soon as the priests with the ark of the Lord, the Lord of the whole earth, have set their feet in the waters of the Jordan, the upper waters of the Jordan flowing down will be stopped in their course and stand still in one mass.'

Accordingly, when the people struck camp to cross the Jordan, the priests carried the ark of the covenant in front of the people. As soon as the bearers of the ark reached the Jordan and the feet of the priests who carried it touched the waters (the Jordan overflows the whole length of its banks throughout the harvest season) the upper waters stood still and made one heap over a wide space – from Adam to the fortress of Zarethan – while those flowing down to the Sea of the Arabah, that is, the Salt Sea, stopped running altogether. The people crossed opposite Jericho. The priests who carried the ark of the covenant of the Lord stood still on dry ground in mid-Jordan, and all Israel continued to cross dry-shod till the whole nation had finished its crossing of the river.

### August 13 Friday: 19th Week in Ordinary Time
### Joshua 24:1-13

… So I brought you out of it. I brought your ancestors out of Egypt, and you came to the Sea; the Egyptians pursued your ancestors with chariots and horsemen as far as the Sea of Reeds. There they called to the Lord, and he spread a thick fog between you and the Egyptians, and made the sea go back on them and cover them. You saw with your own eyes the things I did in Egypt. Then for a long time you lived in the wilderness, until I brought you into the land of the Amorites who lived beyond the Jordan; they made war on you and I gave them into your hands; you took possession of their country because I destroyed them before you. Next, Balak son of Zippor the king of Moab arose to make war on Israel, and sent for Balaam son of Beor to come and curse you. But I would not listen to Balaam; instead, he had to bless you, and I saved you from his hand.

'"When you crossed the Jordan and came to Jericho, those who held Jericho fought against you, as did the Amorites and Perizzites, the Canaanites, Hittites, Girgashites, Hivites and Jebusites, but I put them all into your power. I sent out hornets in front of you, which drove the two Amorite kings before you; this was not the work of your sword or your bow. I gave you a land where you never toiled, you live in towns you never built; you eat now from vineyards and olive groves you never planted."'

### August 14 Saturday: 19th Week in Ordinary Time
### Joshua 24:14-29

That day, Joshua made a covenant for the people; he laid down a statute and ordinance for them at Shechem. Joshua wrote these words in the Book of the Law of God. Then he took a great stone and set it up there, under the oak in the sanctuary of the Lord, and Joshua said to all the people, 'See! This stone shall be a witness against us because it has heard all the words that the Lord has spoken to us: it shall be a witness against you in case you deny your God.' Then Joshua sent the people away, and each returned to his own inheritance.

After these things Joshua son of Nun, the servant of the Lord, died; he was a hundred and ten years old.

### August 17 Tuesday: 20th Week in Ordinary Time
### Judges 6:11-24

… Gideon said to him, 'If I have found favour in your sight, give me a sign that it is you who speak to me. I beg you, do not go away until I come back. I will bring you my offering and set it down before you.' And he answered, 'I will stay until you return.'

Gideon went away and prepared a young goat and made unleavened cakes with an ephah of flour. He put the meat into a basket and the broth into a pot, then brought it all to him under the terebinth. As he came near, the angel of the Lord said to him, 'Take the meat and unleavened cakes, put them on this rock and pour the broth over them.' Gideon did so. Then the angel of the Lord reached out the tip of the staff in his hand and touched the meat and unleavened cakes. Fire sprang from the rock and consumed the meat and unleavened cakes, and the angel of the Lord vanished before his eyes. Then Gideon knew this was the angel of the Lord, and he said, 'Alas, my Lord! I have seen the angel of the Lord face to face!' The Lord answered him, 'Peace be with you; have no fear; you will not die.' Gideon built an altar there to the Lord and called it The-Lord-is-Peace.

### August 18 Wednesday: 20th Week in Ordinary Time
### Judges 9:6-15

…Then the trees said to the fig tree, "Come now, you be our king!" The fig tree answered them, "Must I forego my sweetness, forego my excellent fruit, to stand swaying above the trees?" Then the trees said to the vine, "Come now, you be our king!" The vine answered them, "Must I forego my wine which cheers the heart of gods and men, to stand swaying above the trees?" Then all the trees said to the thorn bush, "Come now, you be our king!" And the thorn bush answered the trees, "If in all good faith you anoint me king to reign over you, then come and shelter in my shade. If not, fire will come from the thorn bush and devour the cedars of Lebanon."'

### August 19 Thursday: 20th Week in Ordinary Time
### Judges 11:29-39

As Jephthah returned to his house at Mizpah, his daughter came out from it to meet him; she was dancing to the sound of timbrels. This was his only child; apart from her he had neither son nor daughter. When he saw her, he tore his clothes and exclaimed, 'Oh my daughter, what sorrow you are bringing me! Must it be you, the cause of my ill-fortune! I have given a promise to the Lord, and I cannot unsay what I have said.' She answered him, 'My father, you have given a promise to the Lord: treat me as the vow you took binds you to, since the Lord has given you vengeance on your enemies the Ammonites.' Then she said to her father, 'Grant me one request. Let me be free for two months. I shall go and wander in the mountains, and with my companions bewail my virginity.' He answered, 'Go,' and let her depart for two months. So she went away with her companions and bewailed her virginity in the mountains. When the two months were over, she returned to her father, and he treated her as the vow he had uttered bound him.

### August 21 Saturday: 20th Week in Ordinary Time
### Ruth 2:1-3.8-11; 4:13-17

… And Boaz answered her, 'I have been told all you have done for your mother-in-law since your husband's death, and how you left your own father and mother and the land where you were born to come among a people whom you knew nothing about before you came here.'

So Boaz took Ruth and she became his wife. And when they came together, the Lord made her conceive and she bore a son. And the woman said to Naomi, 'Blessed be the Lord who has not left the dead man without next of kin this day to perpetuate his name in Israel. The child will be a comfort to you and the prop of your old age, for your daughter-in-law who loves you and is more to you than seven sons has given him birth.' And Naomi took the child to her own bosom and she became his nurse.

And the women of the neighbourhood gave him a name. 'A son has been born for Naomi' they said; and they named him Obed. This was the father of David's father, Jesse.

### August 23 Monday: 21st Week in Ordinary Time
### 1 Thessalonians 1:1-5.8-10

We know, brothers, that God loves you and that you have been chosen, because when we brought the Good News to you, it came to you not only as words, but as power and as the Holy Spirit and as utter conviction. And you observed the sort of life we lived when we were with you, which was for your instruction. We do not need to tell other people about it: other people tell us how we started the work among you, how you broke with idolatry when you were converted to God and became servants of the real, living God; and how you are now waiting for Jesus, his Son, whom he raised from the dead, to come from heaven to save us from the retribution which is coming.

### August 28 Saturday: 21st Week in Ordinary Time
### 1 Thessalonians 4:9-11

As for loving our brothers, there is no need for anyone to write to you about that, since you have learnt from God yourselves to love one another, and in fact this is what you are doing with all the brothers throughout the whole of Macedonia. However, we do urge you, brothers, to go on making even greater progress and to make a point of living quietly, attending to your own business and earning your living, just as we told you to.

### August 30 Monday: 22nd Week in Ordinary Time
### 1 Thessalonians 4:13-18

We want you to be quite certain, brothers, about those who have died, to make sure that you do not grieve about them, like the other people who have no hope. We believe that Jesus died and rose again, and that it will be the same for those who have died in Jesus: God will bring them with him. We can tell you this from the Lord's own teaching, that any of us who are left alive until the Lord's coming will not have any advantage over those who have died. At the trumpet of God, the voice of the archangel will call out the command and the Lord himself will come down from heaven; those who have died in Christ will be the first to rise, and then those of us who are still alive will be taken up in the clouds, together with them, to meet the Lord in the air. So we shall stay with the Lord for ever. With such thoughts as these you should comfort one another.

### September 7 Tuesday: 23rd Week in Ordinary Time
### Colossians 2:6-15

… You were dead, because you were sinners and had not been circumcised: he has brought you to life with him, he has forgiven us all our sins.

He has overridden the Law, and cancelled every record of the debt that we had to pay; he has done away with it by nailing it to the cross; and so he got rid of the Sovereignties and the Powers, and paraded them in public, behind him in his triumphal procession.

### September 9 Thursday: 23rd Week in Ordinary Time
### Colossians 3:12-17

… And may the peace of Christ reign in your hearts, because it is for this that you were called together as parts of one body. Always be thankful.

Let the message of Christ, in all its richness, find a home with you. Teach each other, and advise each other, in all wisdom. With gratitude in your hearts sing psalms and hymns and inspired songs to God; and never say or do anything except in the name of the Lord Jesus, giving thanks to God the Father through him.

### September 16 Thursday: 24th Week in Ordinary Time
### 1 Timothy 4:12-16

Do not let people disregard you because you are young, but be an example to all the believers in the way you speak and behave, and in your love, your faith and your purity. Make use of the time until I arrive by reading to the people, preaching and teaching.

You have in you a spiritual gift which was given to you when the prophets spoke and the body of elders laid their hands on you; do not let it lie unused. Think hard about all this, and put it into practice, and everyone will be able to see how you are advancing. Take great care about what you do and what you teach; always do this, and in this way you will save both yourself and those who listen to you.

## September 30 Thursday: 26th Week in Ordinary Time
## Nehemiah 8:1-12

… Then Ezra blessed the Lord, the great God, and all the people raised their hands and answered, 'Amen! Amen!'; then they bowed down and, face to the ground, prostrated themselves before the Lord.

The Levites explained the Law to the people while the people remained standing. And Ezra read from the Law of God, translating and giving the sense, so that the people understood what was read.

Then Nehemiah – His Excellency – and Ezra, priest and scribe (and the Levites who were instructing the people) said to all the people, 'This day is sacred to the Lord your God. Do not be mournful, do not weep.' For the people were all in tears as they listened to the words of the Law.

He then said, 'Go, eat the fat, drink the sweet wine, and send a portion to the man who has nothing prepared ready. For this day is sacred to our Lord. Do not be sad: the joy of the Lord is your stronghold.' And the Levites calmed all the people, saying, 'Be at ease; this is a sacred day. Do not be sad.' And all the people went off to eat and drink and give shares away and begin to enjoy themselves since they had understood the meaning of what had been proclaimed to them.

## October 4 Monday: 27th Week in Ordinary Time
## Jonah 1:1–2:1.11

The word of the Lord was addressed to Jonah son of Amittai:

'Up!' he said 'Go to Nineveh, the great city, and inform them that their wickedness has become known to me.' Jonah decided to run away from the Lord, and to go to Tarshish. He went down to Joppa and found a ship bound for Tarshish; he paid his fare and went aboard, to go with them to Tarshish, to get away from the Lord. But the Lord unleashed a violent wind on the sea, and there was such a great storm at sea that the ship threatened to break up. The sailors took fright, and each of them called on his own god, and to lighten the ship they threw the cargo overboard. Jonah, however, had gone below and lain down in the hold and fallen fast asleep. The boatswain came upon him and said, 'What do you mean by sleeping? Get up! Call on your god! Perhaps he will spare us a thought, and not leave us to die.' Then they said to each other, 'Come on, let us draw lots to find out who is responsible for bringing this evil on us.' So they cast lots, and the lot fell to Jonah. Then they said to him, 'Tell us, what is your business? Where do you come from? What is your country? What is your nationality?' He replied, 'I am a Hebrew, and I worship the Lord, the God of heaven, who made the sea and the land.' The sailors were seized with terror at this and said, 'What have you done?' They knew that he was trying to escape from the Lord, because he had told them so. They then said, 'What are we to do with you, to make the sea grow calm for us?' For the sea was growing rougher and rougher. He replied, 'Take me and throw me into the sea, and then it will grow calm for you. For I can see it is my fault this violent storm has happened to you.' The sailors rowed hard in an effort to reach the shore, but in vain, since the sea grew still rougher for them. They then called on the Lord and said, 'O Lord, do not let us perish for taking this man's life; do not hold us guilty of innocent blood; for you, the Lord, have acted as you have thought right.' And taking hold of Jonah they threw him into the sea; and the sea grew calm again. At this the men were seized with dread of the Lord; they offered a sacrifice to the Lord and made vows.

The Lord had arranged that a great fish should be there to swallow Jonah; and Jonah remained in the belly of the fish for three days and three nights. The Lord spoke to the fish, which then vomited Jonah on to the shore.

### October 7 Thursday: 27th Week in Ordinary Time
### Malachi 3:13-20

… I will make allowances for them as a man makes allowances for the son who obeys him. Then once again you will see the difference between an upright man and a wicked one, between the one who serves God and the one who does not serve him. For the day is coming now, burning like a furnace; and all the arrogant and the evildoers will be like stubble. The day that is coming is going to burn them up, says the Lord of hosts, leaving them neither root nor stalk. But for you who fear my name, the sun of righteousness will shine out with healing in its rays.

### October 20 Wednesday: 29th Week in Ordinary Time
### Romans 6:12-18

Does the fact that we are living by grace and not by law mean that we are free to sin? Of course not. You know that if you agree to serve and obey a master you become his slaves. You cannot be slaves of sin that leads to death and at the same time slaves of obedience that leads to righteousness. You were once slaves of sin, but thank God you submitted without reservation to the creed you were taught. You may have been freed from the slavery of sin, but only to become 'slaves' of righteousness.

### October 23 Saturday: 29th Week in Ordinary Time
### Romans 8:1-11

… That is because to limit oneself to what is unspiritual is to be at enmity with God: such a limitation never could and never does submit to God's law. People who are interested only in unspiritual things can never be pleasing to God. Your interests, however, are not in the unspiritual, but in the spiritual, since the Spirit of God has made his home in you. In fact, unless you possessed the Spirit of Christ you would not belong to him. Though your body may be dead it is because of sin, but if Christ is in you then your spirit is life itself because you have been justified; and if the Spirit of him who raised Jesus from the dead is living in you, then he who raised Jesus from the dead will give life to your own mortal bodies through his Spirit living in you.

### November 1 Monday: All Saints Day
### Apocalypse 7:2-4.9-14

After that I saw a huge number, impossible to count, of people from every nation, race, tribe and language; they were standing in front of the throne and in front of the Lamb, dressed in white robes and holding palms in their hands. They shouted aloud, 'Victory to our God, who sits on the throne, and to the Lamb!' And all the angels who were standing in a circle round the throne, surrounding the elders and the four animals, prostrated themselves before the throne, and touched the ground with their foreheads, worshipping God with these words: 'Amen. Praise and glory and wisdom and thanksgiving and honour and power and strength to our God for ever and ever. Amen.'

One of the elders then spoke, and asked me, 'Do you know who these people are, dressed in white robes, and where they have come from?' I answered him, 'You can tell me, my Lord.' Then he said, 'These are the people who have been through the great persecution, and they have washed their robes white again in the blood of the Lamb.'

### November 2 Tuesday: The Commemoration of all the Faithful Departed
### Isaiah 25:6-9

On this mountain, the Lord of hosts will prepare for all peoples a banquet of rich food. On this mountain he will remove the mourning veil covering all peoples, and the shroud enwrapping all nations, he will destroy Death for ever. The Lord will wipe away the tears from every cheek; he will take away his people's shame everywhere on earth, for the Lord has said so. That day, it will be said: See, this is our God in whom we hoped for salvation; the Lord is the one in whom we hoped. We exult and we rejoice that he has saved us.

### November 5 Friday: 31st Week in Ordinary Time
### Romans 15:14-21

I think I have some reason to be proud of what I, in union with Christ Jesus, have been able to do for God. What I am presuming to speak of, of course, is only what Christ himself has done to win the allegiance of the pagans, using what I have said and done by the power of signs and wonders, by the power of the Holy Spirit. Thus, all the way along, from Jerusalem to Illyricum, I have preached Christ's Good News to the utmost of my capacity. I have always, however, made it an unbroken rule never to preach where Christ's name has already been heard. The reason for that was that I had no wish to build on other men's foundations; on the contrary, my chief concern has been to fulfil the text: Those who have never been told about him will see him, and those who have never heard about him will understand.

### November 6 Saturday: 31st Week in Ordinary Time
### Romans 16:3-9.16.22-27

Glory to him who is able to give you the strength to live according to the Good News I preach, and in which I proclaim Jesus Christ, the revelation of a mystery kept secret for endless ages, but now so clear that it must be broadcast to pagans everywhere to bring them to the obedience of faith. This is only what scripture has predicted, and it is all part of the way the eternal God wants things to be. He alone is wisdom; give glory therefore to him through Jesus Christ for ever and ever. Amen.

### November 9 Tuesday: The Dedication of the Lateran Basilica
### Ezekiel 47:1-2.8-9.12

… He then said, 'Do you see, son of man?' He took me further, then brought me back to the bank of the river. When I got back, there were many trees on each bank of the river. He said, 'This water flows east down to the Arabah and to the sea; and flowing into the sea it makes its waters wholesome. Wherever the river flows, all living creatures teeming in it will live. Fish will be very plentiful, for wherever the water goes it brings health, and life teems wherever the river flows. Along the river, on either bank, will grow every kind of fruit tree with leaves that never wither and fruit that never fails, they will bear new fruit every month, because this water comes from the sanctuary. And their fruit will be good to eat and the leaves medicinal.'

## November 15 Monday: 33rd Week in Ordinary Time
## 1 Maccabees 1:10-15.41-43.54-57.62-64

… On the fifteenth day of Chislev in the year one hundred and forty-five the king erected the abomination of desolation above the altar; and altars were built in the surrounding towns of Judah and incense offered at the doors of houses and in the streets. Any books of the Law that came to light were torn up and burned. Whenever anyone was discovered possessing a copy of the covenant or practising the Law, the king's decree sentenced him to death.

Yet there were many in Israel who stood firm and found the courage to refuse unclean food. They chose death rather than contamination by such fare or profanation of the holy covenant, and they were executed. It was a dreadful wrath that visited Israel.

## November 16 Tuesday: 33rd Week in Ordinary Time
## 2 Maccabees 6:18-31

… 'Such pretence' he said 'does not square with our time of life; many young people would suppose that Eleazar at the age of ninety had conformed to the foreigners' way of life, and because I had played this part for the sake of a paltry brief spell of life might themselves be led astray on my account; I should only bring defilement and disgrace on my old age. Even though for the moment I avoid execution by man, I can never, living or dead, elude the grasp of the Almighty. Therefore if I am man enough to quit this life here and now I shall prove myself worthy of my old age, and I shall have left the young a noble example of how to make a good death, eagerly and generously, for the venerable and holy laws.'

With these words he went straight to the block. His escorts, so recently well disposed towards him, turned against him after his declaration, which they regarded as sheer madness. Just before he died under the blows, he groaned aloud and said, 'The Lord whose knowledge is holy sees clearly that, though I might have escaped death, whatever agonies of body I now endure under this bludgeoning, in my soul I am glad to suffer, because of the awe which he inspires in me.'

This was how he died, leaving his death as an example of nobility and a record of virtue not only for the young but for the great majority of the nation.

## November 17 Wednesday: 33rd Week in Ordinary Time
## 2 Maccabees 7:1.20-31

The mother was especially admirable and worthy of honourable remembrance, for she watched the death of seven sons in the course of a single day, and endured it resolutely because of her hopes in the Lord. Indeed she encouraged each of them in the language of their ancestors; filled with noble conviction, she reinforced her womanly argument with manly courage, saying to them, 'I do not know how you appeared in my womb; it was not I who endowed you with breath and life, I had not the shaping of your every part. It is the creator of the world, ordaining the process of man's birth and presiding over the origin of all things, who in his mercy will most surely give you back both breath and life, seeing that you now despise your own existence for the sake of his laws.'

Antiochus thought he was being ridiculed, suspecting insult in the tone of her voice; and as the youngest was still alive he appealed to him not with mere words but with promises on oath to make him both rich and happy if he would abandon the traditions of his ancestors; he would make him his Friend and entrust him with public office. The young man took no notice at all, and so the king then appealed to the mother, urging her to advise the youth to save his life. After a great deal of urging on his part she agreed to try persuasion on her son. Bending over him, she fooled the cruel tyrant with these words, uttered in the language of their ancestors, 'My son, have pity on me; I carried you nine months in my womb and suckled you three years, fed you and reared you to the age you are now and cherished you. I implore you, my child, observe heaven and earth, consider all that is in them, and acknowledge that God made them out of what did not exist, and that mankind comes into being in the same way. Do not fear this executioner, but prove yourself worthy of your brothers, and make death welcome, so that in the day of mercy I may receive you back in your brothers' company.'

She had scarcely ended when the young man said, 'What are you all waiting for? I will not comply with the king's ordinance; I obey the ordinance of the Law given to our ancestors through Moses. As for you, sir, who have contrived every kind of evil against the Hebrews, you will certainly not escape the hands of God.'

## November 18 Thursday: 33rd Week in Ordinary Time
## 1 Maccabees 2:15-29

… At the same time he killed the king's commissioner who was there to enforce the sacrifice, and tore down the altar. In his zeal for the Law he acted as Phinehas did against Zimri son of Salu. Then Mattathias went through the town, shouting at the top of his voice, 'Let everyone who has a fervour for the Law and takes his stand on the covenant come out and follow me.' Then he fled with his sons into the hills, leaving all their possessions behind in the town.

At this many who were concerned for virtue and justice went down to the desert and stayed there.

## November 20 Saturday: 33rd Week in Ordinary Time
## 1 Maccabees 6:1-13

… But while he was still in Persia news reached him that the armies that had invaded the land of Judah had been defeated, and that Lysias in particular had advanced in massive strength, only to be forced to turn and flee before the Jews; these had been strengthened by the acquisition of arms, supplies and abundant spoils from the armies they had cut to pieces; they had overthrown the abomination he had erected over the altar in Jerusalem, and had encircled the sanctuary with high walls as in the past, and had fortified Bethzur, one of his cities. When the king heard this news he was amazed and profoundly shaken; he threw himself on his bed and fell into a lethargy from acute disappointment, because things had not turned out for him as he had planned. And there he remained for many days, subject to deep and recurrent fits of melancholy, until he understood that he was dying. Then summoning all his Friends, he said to them, 'Sleep evades my eyes, and my heart is cowed by anxiety. I have been asking myself how I could have come to such a pitch of distress, so great a flood as that which now engulfs me – I who was so generous and well-loved in my heyday. But now I remembered the wrong I did in Jerusalem when I seized all the vessels of silver and gold there, and ordered the extermination of the inhabitants of Judah for no reason at all. This, I am convinced, is why these misfortunes have overtaken me, and why I am dying of melancholy in a foreign land.'

## November 22 Monday: 34th Week in Ordinary Time
## Daniel 1:1-6.8-20

… He said, 'Please allow your servants a ten days' trial, during which we are given only vegetables to eat and water to drink. You can then compare our looks with those of the boys who eat the king's food; go by what you see, and treat your servants accordingly.' The man agreed to do what they asked and put them on ten days' trial. When the ten days were over they looked and were in better health than any of the boys who had eaten their allowance from the royal table; so the guard withdrew their allowance of food and the wine they were to drink, and gave them vegetables. And God favoured these four boys with knowledge and intelligence in everything connected with literature, and in wisdom; while Daniel had the gift of interpreting every kind of vision and dream. When the period stipulated by the king for the boys' training was over, the chief eunuch presented them to Nebuchadnezzar. The king conversed with them, and among all the boys found none to equal Daniel, Hananiah, Mishael and Azariah. So they became members of the king's court, and on whatever point of wisdom or information he might question them, he found them ten times better than all the magicians and enchanters in his entire kingdom.

## November 23 Tuesday: 34th Week in Ordinary Time
## Daniel 2:31-45

… And after you another kingdom will rise, not so great as you, and then a third, of bronze, which will rule the whole world. There will be a fourth kingdom, hard as iron, as iron that shatters and crushes all. Like iron that breaks everything to pieces, it will crush and break all the earlier kingdoms. The feet you saw, part earthenware, part iron, are a kingdom which will be split in two, but which will retain something of the strength of iron, just as you saw the iron and the clay of the earthenware mixed together. The feet were part iron, part earthenware: the kingdom will be partly strong and partly weak. And just as you saw the iron and the clay of the earthenware mixed together, so the two will be mixed together in the seed of man; but they will not hold together any more than iron will blend with earthenware. In the time of these kings the God of heaven will set up a kingdom which shall never be destroyed, and this kingdom will not pass into the hands of another race: it will shatter and absorb all the previous kingdoms, and itself last for ever – just as you saw the stone untouched by hand break from the mountain and shatter iron, bronze, earthenware, silver and gold. The great God has shown the king what is to take place. The dream is true, the interpretation exact.'

## November 24 Wednesday: 34th Week in Ordinary Time
### Daniel 5:1-6.13-14.16-17.23-28

… As I am told that you are able to give interpretations and to unravel difficult problems, if you can read the writing and tell me what it means, you shall be dressed in purple, and have a chain of gold put round your neck, and be third in rank in the kingdom.'

Then Daniel spoke up in the presence of the king. 'Keep your gifts for yourself,' he said 'and give your rewards to others. I will read the writing to the king without them, and tell him what it means. You have defied the Lord of heaven, you have had the vessels from his Temple brought to you, and you, your noblemen, your wives and your singing women have drunk your wine out of them. You have praised gods of gold and silver, of bronze and iron, of wood and stone, which cannot either see, hear or understand; but you have given no glory to the God who holds your breath and all your fortunes in his hands. That is why he has sent the hand which, by itself, has written these words. The writing reads: Mene, Mene, Tekel and Parsin. The meaning of the words is this: Mene: God has measured your sovereignty and put an end to it; Tekel: you have been weighed in the balance and found wanting; Parsin: your kingdom has been divided and given to the Medes and the Persians.'

## November 25 Thursday: 34th Week in Ordinary Time
### Daniel 6: 12-28

… A stone was then brought and laid over the mouth of the pit; and the king sealed it with his own signet and with that of his noblemen, so that there could be no going back on the original decision about Daniel. The king returned to his palace, spent the night in fasting and refused to receive any of his concubines. Sleep eluded him, and at the first sign of dawn he was up, and hurried off to the lion pit. As he approached the pit he shouted in anguished tones, 'Daniel, servant of the living God! Has your God, whom you serve so faithfully, been able to save you from the lions?' Daniel replied, 'O king, live for ever! My God sent his angel who sealed the lions' jaws, they did me no harm, since in his sight I am blameless, and I have never done you any wrong either, O king.' The king was overjoyed, and ordered Daniel to be released from the pit. Daniel was released from the pit, and found to be quite unhurt, because he had trusted in his God. The king sent for the men who had accused Daniel and had them thrown into the lion pit, they, their wives and their children: and they had not reached the floor of the pit before the lions had seized them and crushed their bones to pieces.

King Darius then wrote to men of all nations, peoples and languages throughout the world. 'May peace be always with you! I decree: in every kingdom of my empire let all tremble with fear before the God of Daniel:

'He is the living God, he endures for ever, his sovereignty will never be destroyed and his kingship never end. He saves, sets free, and works signs and wonders in the heavens and on earth; he has saved Daniel from the power of the lions.'

## November 26 Friday: 34th Week in Ordinary Time
### Daniel 7:2-14

The great things the horn was saying were still ringing in my ears, and as I watched, the beast was killed, and its body destroyed and committed to the flames. The other beasts were deprived of their power, but received a lease of life for a season and a time.

I gazed into the visions of the night. And I saw, coming on the clouds of heavens, one like a son of man. He came to the one of great age and was led into his presence. On him was conferred sovereignty, glory and kingship, and men of all peoples, nations and languages became his servants. His sovereignty is an eternal sovereignty which shall never pass away, nor will his empire ever be destroyed.

### December 6 Monday: 2nd Week of Advent
### Isaiah 35:1-10

… Then the eyes of the blind shall be opened, the ears of the deaf unsealed, then the lame shall leap like a deer and the tongues of the dumb sing for joy; for water gushes in the desert, streams in the wasteland, the scorched earth becomes a lake, the parched land springs of water. The lairs where the jackals used to live become thickets of reed and papyrus. And through it will run a highway undefiled which shall be called the Sacred Way; the unclean may not travel by it, nor fools stray along it. No lion will be there nor any fierce beast roam about it, but the redeemed will walk there, for those the Lord has ransomed shall return. They will come to Zion shouting for joy, everlasting joy on their faces; joy and gladness will go with them and sorrow and lament be ended.

### December 8 Wednesday: The Immaculate Conception of the Blessed Virgin Mary
### Genesis 3:9-15.20

After Adam had eaten of the tree, the Lord God called to him. 'Where are you?' he asked. 'I heard the sound of you in the garden', he replied. 'I was afraid because I was naked, so I hid.' 'Who told you that you were naked?' he asked. 'Have you been eating of the tree I forbade you to eat?' The man replied, 'It was the woman you put with me; she gave me the fruit, and I ate it.' Then the Lord God asked the woman, 'What is this you have done?' The woman replied, 'The serpent tempted me and I ate.'

Then the Lord God said to the serpent, 'Because you have done this, be accursed beyond all cattle, all wild beasts. You shall crawl on your belly and eat dust every day of your life. I will make you enemies of each other: you and the woman, your offspring and her offspring. It will crush your head and you will strike its heel.' The man named his wife 'Eve' because she was the mother of all those who live.

### December 16 Thursday: 3rd Week of Advent
### Isaiah 54:1-10

… Does a man cast off the wife of his youth? says your God. I did forsake you for a brief moment, but with great love will I take you back. In excess of anger, for a moment I hid my face from you. But with everlasting love I have taken pity on you, says the Lord, your redeemer. I am now as I was in the days of Noah when I swore that Noah's waters should never flood the world again. So now I swear concerning my anger with you and the threats I made against you; for the mountains may depart, the hills be shaken, but my love for you will never leave you and my covenant of peace with you will never be shaken, says the Lord who takes pity on you.

### December 17 Friday: 3rd Week of Advent
### Genesis 49:2.8-10

Jacob called his sons and said, 'Gather round, sons of Jacob, and listen, listen to Israel your father. Judah, your brothers shall praise you: you grip your enemies by the neck, your father's sons shall do you homage, Judah is a lion cub, you climb back, my son, from your kill; like a lion he crouches and lies down, or a lioness: who dare rouse him? The sceptre shall not pass from Judah, nor the mace from between his feet, until he come to whom it belongs, to whom the peoples shall render obedience.'

### December 24 Friday: 4th Week of Advent
### 2 Samuel 7:1-5.8-12.14.16

… I will provide a place for my people Israel; I will plant them there and they shall dwell in that place and never be disturbed again; nor shall the wicked continue to oppress them as they did, in the days when I appointed judges over my people Israel; I will give them rest from all their enemies. The Lord will make you great; the Lord will make you a House. And when your days are ended and you are laid to rest with your ancestors, I will preserve the offspring of your body after you and make his sovereignty secure. I will be a father to him and he a son to me. Your House and your sovereignty will always stand secure before me and your throne be established for ever."'

### December 25 Saturday: The Nativity of the Lord
### Isaiah 52:7-10

How beautiful on the mountains, are the feet of one who brings good news, who heralds peace, brings happiness, proclaims salvation, and tells Zion, 'Your God is king!' Listen! Your watchmen raise their voices, they shout for joy together, for they see the Lord face to face, as he returns to Zion. Break into shouts of joy together, you ruins of Jerusalem; for the Lord is consoling his people, redeeming Jerusalem. The Lord bares his holy arm in the sight of all the nations, and all the ends of the earth shall see the salvation of our God.

### December 29 Wednesday: 5th Day within the Octave of Christmas
### 1 John 2:3-11

… My dear people, this is not a new commandment that I am writing to tell you, but an old commandment that you were given from the beginning, the original commandment which was the message brought to you. Yet in another way, what I am writing to you, and what is being carried out in your lives as it was in his, is a new commandment; because the night is over and the real light is already shining. Anyone who claims to be in the light but hates his brother is still in the dark. But anyone who loves his brother is living in the light and need not be afraid of stumbling; unlike the man who hates his brother and is in the darkness, not knowing where he is going, because it is too dark to see.

# THE CHAPLET OF THE DIVINE MERCY

## OPENING PRAYER

*First, make the Sign of the Cross. Touch the forehead, then the chest, then the left shoulder, then the right shoulder, while saying:*

**In the Name of the Father,** and of the Son, and of the Holy Spirit. Amen.

*Recite this opening prayer once:*

**You expired,** O Jesus, but the Source of Life gushed forth for souls and the Ocean of Mercy opened up for the whole world. O Fount of Life, unfathomable Divine Mercy, envelop the whole world and empty Yourself out upon us.

*Recite the following prayer three times:*

**O Blood and Water,** which gushed forth from the Heart of Jesus as a fount of mercy for us, I trust in You.

*Then recite one Our Father, one Hail Mary, and the Apostles' Creed:*

**Our Father,** who art in Heaven, hallowed be thy name. Thy kingdom come, thy will be done, on earth as it is in Heaven. Give us this day our daily bread. And forgive us our trespasses, as we forgive those who trespass against us. And lead us not into temptation, but deliver us from evil. Amen.

**Hail Mary,** full of grace, the Lord is with thee. Blessed art thou among women, and blessed is the fruit of thy womb Jesus. Holy Mary, Mother of God, pray for us sinners, now and at the hour of our death. Amen.

APPENDIX C–1

**Apostles Creed:** I believe in God, the Father almighty, Creator of heaven and earth.

I believe in Jesus Christ, his only Son, our Lord, who was conceived by the power of the Holy Spirit, born of the Virgin Mary, suffered under Pontius Pilate, was crucified, died, and was buried. He descended to the dead. On the third day, he rose again. He ascended into Heaven and is seated at the right hand of the Father. He will come again to judge the living and the dead.

I believe in the Holy Spirit, the holy catholic Church, the communion of saints, the forgiveness of sins, the resurrection of the body, and the life everlasting. Amen.

## THE DECADES OF THE CHAPLET

*After the Opening Prayers, the next prayers are said in sets of ten, called 'decades.' A set of five decades is called a 'chaplet.' The prayers are said using ordinary Rosary beads.*

*On the single large bead (before each set of ten smaller beads) recite:*

**Eternal Father,** I offer You the Body and Blood, Soul and Divinity of Your dearly beloved Son, our Lord Jesus Christ, in atonement for our sins and those of the whole world.

*Then, on each of the ten smaller beads, recite:*

**For the sake** of His sorrowful Passion,
have mercy on us and on the whole world.

*(Alternate version of this prayer: For the sake of Jesus Christ's sorrowful Passion and death on the Cross, have mercy on us and on the whole world.)*

*After each set of ten prayers, many persons add:*

**O Blood and Water,** which gushed forth from the Heart of Jesus as a fount of mercy for us, I trust in You.

*Repeat the above set of prayers, called a decade, five times to complete one Divine Mercy Chaplet.*

## CLOSING PRAYERS

*Recite the following prayer three times:*

**Holy God,** Holy Mighty One, Holy Immortal One, have mercy on us and on the whole world.

*Then recite this closing prayer:*

**Eternal God,** Your Mercy is endless, and Your treasury of compassion is inexhaustible. Look with kindness upon us and increase Your Mercy within us, so that, in difficult moments, we may not despair, nor become despondent, but may, with great confidence, submit ourselves to Your Holy Will, which is Love and Mercy itself. Amen.

*Finally, make the Sign of the Cross again:*

**In the Name of the Father**, and of the Son, and of the Holy Spirit. Amen.

## INTENTIONS FOR EACH DAY OF THE NOVENA

### FIRST DAY

Today bring to Me ALL MANKIND, ESPECIALLY ALL SINNERS

Most Merciful Jesus, whose very nature it is to have compassion on us and to forgive us, do not look upon our sins but upon our trust which we place in Your infinite goodness. Receive us all into the abode of Your Most Compassionate Heart, and never let us escape from it. We beg this of You by Your love which unites You to the Father and the Holy Spirit.

Eternal Father, turn Your merciful gaze upon all mankind and especially upon poor sinners, all enfolded in the Most Compassionate Heart of Jesus. For the sake of His sorrowful Passion show us Your mercy, that we may praise the omnipotence of Your mercy for ever and ever. Amen.

### SECOND DAY

Today bring to Me THE SOULS OF PRIESTS AND RELIGIOUS

Most Merciful Jesus, from whom comes all that is good, increase Your grace in men and women consecrated to Your service, that they may perform worthy works of mercy; and that all who see them may glorify the Father of Mercy who is in heaven.

Eternal Father, turn Your merciful gaze upon the company of chosen ones in Your vineyard—upon the souls of priests and religious; and endow them with the strength of Your blessing. For the love of the Heart of Your Son in which they are enfolded, impart to them Your power and light, that they may be able to guide others in the way of salvation and with one voice sing praise to Your boundless mercy for ages without end. Amen.

### THIRD DAY

Today bring to Me ALL DEVOUT AND FAITHFUL SOULS

Most Merciful Jesus, from the treasury of Your mercy You impart Your graces in great abundance to each and all. Receive us into the abode of Your Most Compassionate Heart and never let us escape from it. We beg this of You by that most wondrous love for the heavenly Father with which Your Heart burns so fiercely.

Eternal Father, turn Your merciful gaze upon faithful souls, as upon the inheritance of Your Son. For the sake of His sorrowful Passion, grant them Your blessing and surround them with Your constant protection. Thus may they never fail in love or lose the treasure of the holy faith, but rather, with all the hosts of Angels and Saints, may they glorify your boundless mercy for endless ages. Amen.

## FOURTH DAY

Today bring to Me THOSE WHO DO NOT BELIEVE IN GOD AND THOSE WHO DO NOT YET KNOW ME

Most compassionate Jesus, You are the Light of the whole world. Receive into the abode of Your Most Compassionate Heart the souls of those who do not believe in God and of those who as yet do not know You. Let the rays of Your grace enlighten them that they, too, together with us, may extol Your wonderful mercy; and do not let them escape from the abode which is Your Most Compassionate Heart.

Eternal Father, turn Your merciful gaze upon the souls of those who do not believe in You, and of those who as yet do not know You, but who are enclosed in the Most Compassionate Heart of Jesus. Draw them to the light of the Gospel. These souls do not know what great happiness it is to love You. Grant that they, too, may extol the generosity of Your mercy for endless ages. Amen.

## FIFTH DAY

Today bring to Me THE SOULS OF THOSE WHO HAVE SEPARATED THEMSELVES FROM MY CHURCH

Most Merciful Jesus, Goodness Itself, You do not refuse light to those who seek it of You. Receive into the abode of Your Most Compassionate Heart the souls of those who have separated themselves from Your Church. Draw them by Your light into the unity of the Church, and do not let them escape from the abode of Your Most Compassionate Heart; but bring it about that they, too, come to glorify the generosity of Your mercy.

Eternal Father, turn Your merciful gaze upon the souls of those who have separated themselves from Your Son's Church, who have squandered Your blessings and misused Your graces by obstinately persisting in their errors. Do not look upon their errors, but upon the love of Your own Son and upon His bitter Passion, which He underwent for their sake, since they, too, are enclosed in His Most Compassionate Heart. Bring it about that they also may glorify Your great mercy for endless ages. Amen.

## SIXTH DAY

Today bring to Me THE MEEK AND HUMBLE SOULS AND THE SOULS OF LITTLE CHILDREN

Most Merciful Jesus, You yourself have said, 'Learn from Me for I am meek and humble of heart.' Receive into the abode of Your Most Compassionate Heart all meek and humble souls and the souls of little children. These souls send all heaven into ecstasy and they are the heavenly Father's favorites. They are a sweet-smelling bouquet before the throne of God; God himself takes delight in their fragrance. These souls have a permanent abode in Your Most Compassionate Heart, O Jesus, and they unceasingly sing out a hymn of love and mercy.

Eternal Father, turn Your merciful gaze upon meek souls, upon humble souls, and upon little children who are enfolded in the abode which is the Most Compassionate Heart of Jesus. These souls bear the closest resemblance to Your Son. Their fragrance rises from the earth and reaches Your very throne. Father of mercy and of all goodness, I beg You by the love You bear these souls and by the delight You take in them: Bless the whole world, that all souls together may sing out the praises of Your mercy for endless ages. Amen.

## SEVENTH DAY

Today bring to Me THE SOULS WHO ESPECIALLY VENERATE AND GLORIFY MY MERCY

Most Merciful Jesus, whose Heart is Love Itself, receive into the abode of Your Most Compassionate Heart the souls of those who particularly extol and venerate the greatness of Your mercy. These souls are mighty with the very power of God Himself. In the midst of all afflictions and adversities they go forward, confident of Your mercy; and united to You, O Jesus, they carry all mankind on their shoulders. These souls will not be judged severely, but Your mercy will embrace them as they depart from this life.

Eternal Father, turn Your merciful gaze upon the souls who glorify and venerate Your greatest attribute, that of Your fathomless mercy, and who are enclosed in the Most Compassionate Heart of Jesus. These souls are a living Gospel; their hands are full of deeds of mercy, and their hearts, overflowing with joy, sing a canticle of mercy to You, O Most High! I beg You O God: Show them Your mercy according to the hope and trust they have placed in You. Let there be accomplished in them the promise of Jesus, who said to them that during their life, but especially at the hour of death, the souls who will venerate this fathomless mercy of His, He, Himself, will defend as His glory. Amen.

## EIGHTH DAY

Today bring to Me THE SOULS WHO ARE DETAINED IN PURGATORY

Most Merciful Jesus, You Yourself have said that You desire mercy; so I bring into the abode of Your Most Compassionate Heart the souls in Purgatory, souls who are very dear to You, and yet, who must make retribution to Your justice. May the streams of Blood and Water which gushed forth from Your Heart put out the flames of Purgatory, that there, too, the power of Your mercy may be celebrated.

Eternal Father, turn Your merciful gaze upon the souls suffering in Purgatory, who are enfolded in the Most Compassionate Heart of Jesus. I beg You, by the sorrowful Passion of Jesus Your Son, and by all the bitterness with which His most sacred Soul was flooded: Manifest Your mercy to the souls who are under Your just scrutiny. Look upon them in no other way but only through the Wounds of Jesus, Your dearly beloved Son; for we firmly believe that there is no limit to Your goodness and compassion. Amen.

**NINTH DAY**

Today bring to Me SOULS WHO HAVE BECOME LUKEWARM

Most compassionate Jesus, You are Compassion Itself. I bring lukewarm souls into the abode of Your Most Compassionate Heart. In this fire of Your pure love let these tepid souls, who like corpses, filled You with such deep loathing, be once again set aflame. O Most Compassionate Jesus, exercise the omnipotence of Your mercy and draw them into the very ardor of Your love, and bestow upon them the gift of holy love, for nothing is beyond Your power.

Eternal Father, turn Your merciful gaze upon lukewarm souls who are nonetheless enfolded in the Most Compassionate Heart of Jesus. Father of Mercy, I beg You by the bitter Passion of Your Son and by His three-hour agony on the Cross: Let them, too, glorify the abyss of Your mercy. Amen.

# PRAYER BEFORE HOLY COMMUNION

Almighty and everlasting God,
behold I come to the Sacrament of
of your only-Begotten Son, our Lord Jesus Christ,
as one infirm to the physician of life,
as one unclean to the fountain of mercy,
 as one blind to the light of everlasting brightness,
as one poor and needy to the Lord of heaven and earth.
I ask, therefore, for the abundance of your infinite generosity,
that you may graciously cure my sickness,
wash away my defilement, enlighten my blindness,
enrich my poverty, clothe my nakedness,
that I may receive the bread of Angels,
the King of kings, the Lord of lords,
with such reverence and humility, contrition and devotion,
purity and faith, and purpose and intention
as may be conducive to my soul's salvation.
Grant I pray, that I may receive
not only the Sacrament of our Lord's Body and Blood,
but also the grace and power of the Sacrament.
O most gracious God, grant me so to receive
the Body of your only-begotten Son, our Lord Jesus Christ,

which He took from the Virgin Mary,

that I may be worthy to be incorporated into his Mystical Body,

and to be numbered amongst his members.

O most loving Father,

Grant that I may at last gaze forever

upon the unveiled face of your beloved Son,

whom I, a wayfarer, propose to receive now veiled under these species

who lives and reigns with you forever and ever. Amen.

# EUCHARISTIC CELEBRATION

## THE INTRODUCTORY RITES

*The Entrance Procession and Song*

**Celebrant:** In the name of the Father, and of the Son, and of the Holy Spirit.

**All:** Amen.

*Greeting*

**C:** The grace of our Lord Jesus Christ, and the love of God, and the communion of the Holy Spirit be with you all.

**All:** And with your spirit.

## PENITENTIAL RITE

**C:** Brethren (brothers and sisters), let us acknowledge our sins, and so prepare ourselves to celebrate the sacred mysteries. *(a brief silence)*

**All:** I confess to almighty God and to you, my brothers and sisters, that I have greatly sinned, in my thoughts and in my words, in what I have done and in what I have failed to do, (and, striking their breast, they say:)  through my fault, through my fault, through my most grievous fault; therefore I ask blessed Mary ever-Virgin, all the Angels and Saints, and you, my brothers and sisters, to pray for me to the Lord our God.

**C:** May almighty God have mercy on us, forgive us our sins, and bring us to everlasting life.

**All:** Amen.

**C:** Lord, have mercy.   **All:** Lord, have mercy.

**C:** Christ, have mercy.   **All:** Christ, have mercy.

**C:** Lord, have mercy.   **All:** Lord, have mercy.

## THE HYMN "GLORIA" *(When prescribed)*

Glory to God in the highest,
and on earth peace to people of good will.
We praise you, we bless you, we adore you,
we glorify you, we give you thanks
for your great glory,
Lord God, heavenly King,
O God, almighty Father.
Lord Jesus Christ, Only Begotten Son,
Lord God, Lamb of God, Son of the Father,
you take away the sins of the world, have mercy on us;
you take away the sins of the world, receive our prayer;
you are seated at the right hand of the Father,
have mercy on us.
For you alone are the Holy One,
you alone are the Lord,
you alone are the Most High, Jesus Christ,
with the Holy Spirit, in the glory of God the Father. Amen.

## OPENING PRAYER

## THE LITURGY OF THE WORD

*First Reading*

*The Responsorial Psalm*

*The Second Reading (when prescribed).*

*The Acclamation before the Gospel*

*The Gospel*

*The homily*

*The Profession of Faith (when prescribed)*

## THE APOSTLES' CREED

I believe in God, the Father almighty, Creator of heaven and earth, and in Jesus Christ, his only Son, our Lord, *(At the words that follow, up to and including the Virgin Mary, all bow.)* who was conceived by the Holy Spirit, born of the Virgin Mary, suffered under Pontius Pilate, was crucified, died and was buried; he descended into hell; on the third day he rose again from the dead; he ascended into heaven, and is seated at the right hand of God the Father almighty; from there he will come to judge the living and the dead. I believe in the Holy Spirit, the holy catholic Church, the communion of saints, the forgiveness of sins, the resurrection of the body, and life everlasting. Amen.

## THE PRAYER OF THE FAITHFUL *(Universal Prayer)*

## THE LITURGY OF THE EUCHARIST

### THE PREPARATION OF THE GIFTS

*The offertory procession and song*

*Presenting the bread:*

**C:** Blessed are you, Lord, God of all creation, for through your goodness we have received the bread we offer you: fruit of the earth and work of human hands, it will become for us the bread of life.

**All:** Blessed be God for ever.

*Presenting the chalice:*

**C:** Blessed are you, Lord, God of all creation, for through your goodness we have received the wine we offer you: fruit of the vine and work of human hands, it will become our spiritual drink.

**All:** Blessed be God for ever.

**C:** Pray, brethren (brothers and sisters), that my sacrifice and yours may be acceptable to God, the almighty Father.

**All:** May the Lord accept the sacrifice at your hands/ for the praise and glory of his name,/ for our good and the good of all his holy Church.

### THE PRAYER OVER THE OFFERINGS

### THE EUCHARISTIC PRAYER

### EUCHARISTIC PRAYER – II

**C:** It is truly right and just, our duty and our salvation, always and everywhere to give you thanks, Father most holy, through your beloved Son, Jesus Christ, your Word through whom you made all things, whom you sent as our Saviour and Redeemer, incarnate by the Holy Spirit and born of the Virgin. Fulfilling your will and gaining for you a holy people, he stretched out his hands as he endured his Passion, so as to break the bonds of death and manifest the Resurrection.

And so, with the Angels and all the Saints we declare your glory, as with one voice we acclaim:

**All:** Holy, Holy, Holy...

**C:** You are indeed Holy, O Lord, the fount of all holiness.

**CC:** Make holy, therefore, these gifts, we pray,
by sending down your Spirit upon them
like the dewfall,
so that they may become for us
the Body and ✠ Blood
of our Lord Jesus Christ.
At the time he was betrayed

and entered willingly into his Passion,
he took bread and, giving thanks, broke it,
and gave it to his disciples, saying:

**TAKE THIS, ALL OF YOU, AND EAT OF IT,**
**FOR THIS IS MY BODY,**
**WHICH WILL BE GIVEN UP FOR YOU.**

In a similar way, when supper was ended,
he took the chalice
and, once more giving thanks,
he gave it to his disciples, saying:
TAKE THIS, ALL OF YOU,

**AND DRINK FROM IT,**
**FOR THIS IS THE CHALICE OF MY BLOOD,**
**THE BLOOD OF THE NEW**
**AND ETERNAL COVENANT,**
**WHICH WILL BE POURED OUT FOR YOU**
**AND FOR MANY**
**FOR THE FORGIVENESS OF SINS.**
**DO THIS IN MEMORY OF ME.**

**C:** The mystery of faith.
**All:** We proclaim your Death, O Lord,
and profess your Resurrection
until you come again.

**CC:** Therefore, as we celebrate
the memorial of his Death and Resurrection,
we offer you, Lord,
the Bread of life and the Chalice of salvation,
giving thanks that you have held us worthy
to be in your presence and minister to you.
Humbly we pray
that, partaking of the Body and Blood of Christ,
we may be gathered into one by the Holy Spirit.

**C1:** Remember, Lord, your Church,
spread throughout the world,
and bring her to the fullness of charity,
together with N. our Pope and N. our Bishop
and all the clergy.

*In Masses for the Dead, the following may be added:*

Remember your servant N.,
whom you have called (today)
from this world to yourself.
Grant that he (she) who was united
with your Son in a death like his,

may also be one with him
in his Resurrection.

**C2:** Remember also our brothers and sisters
who have fallen asleep
in the hope of the resurrection,
and all who have died in your mercy:
welcome them into the light of your face.
Have mercy on us all, we pray,
that with the Blessed Virgin Mary,
Mother of God, with blessed Joseph,
her spouse, with the blessed Apostles,
and all the Saints
who have pleased you throughout the ages,
we may merit to be coheirs to eternal life,
and may praise and glorify you
through your Son, Jesus Christ.

**CC:** Through him, and with him, and in him,
O God, almighty Father,
in the unity of the Holy Spirit,
all glory and honour is yours,
for ever and ever.

**All:** Amen.

## THE LORD'S PRAYER

**C:** At the Saviour's command and formed by divine teaching, we dare to say:

**All:** Our Father, who art in heaven, / hallowed be thy name; / thy Kingdom come, / thy will be done on earth as it is in heaven. / Give us this day our daily bread, / and forgive us our trespasses, / as we forgive those who trespass against us; / and lead us not into temptation,/ but deliver us from evil.

**C:** Deliver us, Lord, we pray, from every evil, graciously grant peace in our days, that, by the help of your mercy, we may be always free from sin and safe from all distress, as we await the blessed hope and the coming of our Saviour, Jesus Christ.

**All:** For the kingdom, / the power and the glory are yours / now and for ever.

## THE RITE OF PEACE

**C:** Lord Jesus Christ, who said to your Apostles: Peace I leave you, my peace I give you, look not on our sins, but on the faith of your Church, and graciously grant her peace and unity in accordance with your will. Who live and reign for ever and ever.

**All:** Amen.

**C:** The peace of the Lord be with you always.

**All:** And with your spirit.

*Then the deacon (or the priest) adds:*

**Let us offer each other the sign of peace.**

## THE BREAKING OF THE BREAD

*Meanwhile the following is sung or said:*

> Lamb of God, you take away the sins of the world,
> have mercy on us.
> Lamb of God, you take away the sins of the world,
> have mercy on us.
> Lamb of God, you take away the sins of the world,
> grant us peace.

## COMMUNION

> *The Priest, with hands joined, says one of the following prayers in a low voice:*

May the receiving of your Body and Blood, Lord Jesus Christ, not bring me to judgement and condemnation, but through your loving mercy be for me protection in mind and body and a healing remedy.

*The Priest genuflects, takes the host and, holding it slightly raised above the paten or above the chalice, says:*

**C:** Behold the Lamb of God,
beholds him who takes away
the sins of the world.
Blessed are those called to the supper
of the Lamb.

**All:** Lord, I am not worthy
that you should enter under my roof,
but only say the word
and my soul shall be healed.

## THE PRAYER AFTER COMMUNION

## THE DISMISSAL
**C:** The Lord be with you.

**All:** And with your spirit.

**C:** May almighty God bless you, the Father, and the Son, ✠ and the Holy Spirit.

**All:** Amen.

**C:** Go forth, the Mass is ended.

**All:** Thanks be to God.

# VARIOUS PRAYERS

## THANKSGIVING AFTER MASS

I adore You present in my heart,
O Incarnate Word,
only Son and splendour of the Father,
born of Mary.
I thank You, sole Master and Truth by essence,
for Your immense goodness in coming to me,
an ignorant person and a sinner.
With Mary I offer You to the Father:
through You, with You, in You,
may there be eternal praise,
thanksgiving and supplication
for peace among people.
Enlighten my mind;
render me a docile disciple of the Church;
grant that I may live by faith;
give me an understanding of the Scriptures.
Make me Your ardent apostle.
Let the light of Your Gospel, O Divine Master,
shine on the farthest bounds of the world.

## ANIMA CHRISTI

Soul of Christ, sanctify me.
Body of Christ, save me.
Blood of Christ, inebriate me.
Water from the side of Christ, wash me.
Passion of Christ, strengthen me.
O good Jesus, hear me.
Within Your wounds, hide me.
Suffer me not to be separated from You.
From the evil enemy defend me.
And bid me come unto You –
That with Your saints I may praise You
Forever and ever.
Amen.

## PRAYER FOR PRIESTS

O Jesus, eternal Priest,
keep those Your servants
within the shelter of Your Sacred Heart
where no one may harm them.
Keep unstained their anointed hands
which daily touch Your Sacred Body.
Keep unsullied their lips
purpled with Your Precious Blood.
Keep pure and unworldly their hearts
sealed with the sublime marks of Your glorious Priesthood.
Let Your holy love surround them
and shield them from the world's contagion.
Bless their labours with abundant fruit and
may the souls to whom they minister here below,
be their joy and consolation
and in heaven their beautiful and everlasting crown. Amen.
Jesus, Saviour of the world,
make Your priests and their helpers holy.
Mary, Queen of priests, pray for priests.

## PRAYER FOR CONSECRATED PEOPLE

God, Father and Source of all that is good,
in every age and place,
You called forth women and men to consecrate
their lives to You.
Cognizant of the privilege of this call
and its accompanying graces,
we praise and thank You
for the consecrated lives of priests, sisters and brothers
throughout the world
and in particular those living and
serving within our own Diocese.
Your call to holiness extends to
every man, woman and child.
May the goodness and holiness of those for whom we pray
serve as beacons lighting the path for all
who seek a closer walk with You.
We ask this of You, through Jesus, Your Son,
and in the power of the Holy Spirit,
One God dwelling in everlasting glory.
Amen.

## PRAYER FOR THE LAITY

Heavenly Father,
you have called us all to holiness,
by sharing in Your divine life.
Fill us with a sense of true dignity
as Your daughters and sons in the world
and Your ambassadors of justice, love and peace.
May we be witnesses to Your love in our families,
places of work, institutions of learning and recreation.
Give us the desire to be worthy of this great calling
and the courage to live up to it.
We ask this through Christ, Our Lord.
Amen.

## PRAYER TO THE HOLY SPIRIT

Come, Holy Spirit,
Replace the tension within us with a holy relaxation.
Replace the turbulence within us
with a quiet confidence.
Replace the fear within us with a strong faith.
Replace the bitterness within us
with the sweetness of grace.
Replace the darkness within us with a gentle light.
Replace the coldness within us with a living warmth.
Replace the night within us with Your light
Replace the winter within us with Your spring.
Straighten our crookedness, fill our emptiness.
Blunt the edge of our pride,
sharpen the edge of our humility.
Light the fires of our love,
quench the flames of our lust.
Let us see ourselves as You see us,
that we may see You as You have promised
and be fortunate according to Your word:
"Blessed are the pure of heart, for they shall see God."

## PRAYER FOR DIVINE GUIDANCE

Grant me, I beseech You, almighty
and most merciful God, fervently to desire,
wisely to search out, and perfectly to fulfil
all that is well pleasing unto You.
Order my worldly condition to the glory of Your name;

grant me the knowledge, desire and ability
to do that which You require of me,
so that I may walk with You unto my perfect end.
Give me, O Lord, a steadfast heart
which no unworthy affection may debase;
give me an enduring heart
which no tribulation can wear out;
give me an upright heart
which no unworthy purpose may tempt aside.
Bestow upon me, O Lord my God,
understanding to know You, diligence to seek You,
wisdom to find You,
and a faithfulness that may finally posses You.

## PRAYER FOR DELIVERANCE

In the name of God, the Father Almighty,
Creator of heaven and earth,
in the name of Jesus Christ, His only-begotten Son
and our Lord and Saviour,
in the name of the Holy Spirit who dwells in our hearts,
through the intercession of Mary,
the Immaculate Virgin Mother of God,
and of St Michael the Archangel
and of all the Angels and Saints,
I take authority, and bind all demonic powers
and forces that have come against me.
I resist the devil, all his pressures, his attacks,
his deceptions, every instrument or agent
he would seek to use against me.
I challenge every spirit of darkness and of oppression,
and command him to depart right now away from me,
and go to the feet of Jesus,
to be bound, and not to return.
Lord Jesus, cover me with Your precious blood
and let me experience the fullness of redemption.
Amen.

## A POWERFUL HEALING PRAYER

Heavenly Father,
I call on You right now in a special way.
It is through Your Power that I was created.
Every breath I take, every morning I wake up,

and every moment of every hour,
I live under Your power.
Father, I ask You now to touch me
with that same power,
for, as You created me from nothing,
You can certainly recreate me.
Fill me with the healing power of Your Spirit.
Cast out anything that should not be in me.
Mend what is broken
and root out any unproductive cells.
Open the blocked arteries or veins
and rebuild all damaged areas.
Remove all inflammation and heal any infection.
Let the warmth of Your healing love
pass through my body
to make new the unhealthy areas,
so that my body will function
the way You created it to function.
Father, restore me to full health in mind and body,
so that I may serve You the rest of my life.
Amen.

## SERENITY PRAYER

God grant me the serenity
to accept the things I cannot change;
courage to change the things I can;
and wisdom to know the difference.
Living one day at a time;
enjoying one moment at a time;
accepting hardships as the pathway to peace;
taking, as He did, this sinful world
as it is, not as I would have it;
trusting that He will make all things right
if I surrender to His Will;
that I may be reasonably happy in this life
and supremely happy with Him
forever in the next.
Amen.